Arthur Horner:
A Political Biography

Volume I
1894 to 1944

Arthur Horner:
A Political Biography

Volume I
1894 to 1944:
South Wales Miners' Federation;
fighting fascism

Nina Fishman

Lawrence and Wishart Limited
99a Wallis Road
London
E9 5LN
www.lwbooks.co.uk

First published 2010

British Library Cataloguing in Publication Data.
A catalogue record for this book is available from the British Library

Volume 1:
Hardback ISBN 9781 907103 056
Paperback ISBN 9781 907103 070

Boxed set:
ISBN 9781 907103 087 094

Text setting Bernard Knight
Printed in Great Britain by the MPG Books Group,
Bodmin and King's Lynn

Contents

List of illustrations

Illustrations are between pages 250 and 251

All photographs are courtesy the Arthur Horner Collection, South Wales Coalfield Archive, unless otherwise stated.

Acknowledgements

This biography has been so long in the making that I have incurred many debts to colleagues, friends, and archivists. Friendly historians of the communist party have given freely of their time and knowledge. They have also been generous in the primary source material which they have provided. In that sense, its writing has been a collective effort; although I do not expect them to agree with my interpretations! So, thanks to Kevin Morgan above all, and also to Andrew Thorpe, Gidon Cohen, Matthew Worley and Andrew Flinn. Chris Williams has been unstinting in his support and in sharing his profound knowledge of the Rhondda and the South Wales labour movement. He has also tried to tutor me in South Walian geography. I owe him special thanks for shouldering the task of finalising revisions and copy editing of Volume II. This is true friendship. Others who have helped me with South Wales are Kenneth O Morgan, Alun Burge and Leighton James. Peter Ackers and Michael Casey were invaluable guides to the Churches of Christ.

I have received generous assistance from archivists and librarians. Grateful thanks to Christine Woodland and Helen Ford at the Modern Records Centre, Warwick University; Wayne Thomas, President, South Wales Area NUM; Carolyn Jacob at the Borough of Merthyr Tydfil Archive; Elisabeth Bennett at the South Wales Coalfield Archive, Swansea University; John Callow at Marx Memorial Library; Sian Williams at the South Wales Miners' Library; Stephen Bird and Nick Mansfield at the CPGB Archive, Peoples' History Museum, Manchester; and last but hardly least, Chris Coates at the TUC Library Collections, London Metropolitan University.

Two witnesses to Arthur Horner's life have been invaluable to me. Ronnie Frankenberg was generous in recounting his Arthur stories as well as providing assessments of the other dramatis personae. And his notes were a veritable treasure. Geoffrey Goodman has been a mentor. Without his constant encouragement I should not have finished. He has read the book in various stages of gestation and provided shrewd insights into its shortcomings, which I hope I have corrected. I have been able to mine his memory of Horner and the others on the NUM Executive to deepen my own understanding. Other colleagues who have read chapters and provided advice are Chris Williams, Andrew Thorpe and Andrew Flinn. Despite all this help, there will be errors and mistakes in the book, for which I alone am responsible.

I am grateful to the history department of Reading University for inviting me to give a seminar on Horner in February 2008. It clarified my thoughts and enabled me to see more of the wood for the trees. I am equally grateful to the Modern British History seminar at Oxford University for inviting me to speak about Horner in February 2009. This time, I realised that I was not going to think any new thoughts about Arthur and that the book was really ready to make its way in the world.

I owe profound thanks to David Marquand for his constant friendship and moral support, and also for reading the book in an early draft. His optimism and interest have greatly sustained me. Thanks to others who have spurred me to finish: Donald Sassoon, Steve Smith, and, of course Eric Hobsbawm. It is to Eric that I owe my foray into spies. His objectivity enabled me to overcome my prejudice. Last, but certainly not least, is Hywel Francis. His commitment to history and determination that I should finish has underpinned my effort. Sally Davison at Lawrence & Wishart has had the patience of Job, and I thank her for it. Bernard Knight has done a heroic job coping with footnotes, formatting and more footnotes.

I would not have been able to finish the book without the encouragement of Phil McManus. Thanks to him for believing that could do it! There are friends who merit special mention for their unwavering support and willingness to live with me and Arthur Horner. Ros Mitchell and Christopher Brumfit ferried me about a windy Bournemouth to interview Horner's eldest daughter. Sybil Crouch and David Phillips gave me a bed and fed me during my many research trips to Swansea. Since Phil McManus and I have moved to Swansea, they have borne my writing with fortitude and encouragement. Terry Harrison provided constant insights into coalmining, the NUM, and the CPGB at Betteshanger in the 1950s. Phyllis Harrison was generous in her memories of her father, a leading member of the Betteshanger branch of the CPGB and the NUM branch committee during the Hungarian events of 1956. I have greatly benefited from talking to Jane Bernal about her memories of her mother, Margot Heinemann, who played an important part in Horner's life in the 1940s.

The Barry Amiel and Norman Melburn Trust provided important financial assistance to myself and Hwyel Francis to pursue the initial research in 1995–6, and then in 1998 to myself to enable me to begin the writing.

Finally, my thanks and admiration to Nick James for compiling a comprehensive *and* intelligent index. Good indices are – these days – few and far between. I was fortunate indeed to find Nick.

Abbreviations

AACP	Anglo-American Council on Productivity
AAS	Anglo-American Secretariat of the Communist International
AEU	Amalgamated Engineering Union
AFL	American Federation of Labour
ARP	Air Raid Precautions
ASLEF	Amalgamated Society of Locomotive Engineers and Firemen
ASSET	Association of Supervisory Staffs and Engineering Technicians
BSP	British Socialist Party
CGIL	Confederazione Generale Italiana del Lavoro
CGT	Confederation Generale du Travail
CIO	Congress of Industrial Organisations
CINA	Coal Industry Nationalisation Act 1946
CINB	Coal Industry Nationalisation Bill
COSA	Colliery Officials and Staffs Area of the NUM
CPA	Communist Political Association (USA)
CPC	Coal Production Council
CPGB	Communist Party of Great Britain
CPUSA	Communist Party of the United States of America
CSC	Central Strike Committee for the putative South Wales unofficial strike in January 1931
CTAL	Confederation of Latin American Workers
DMA	Durham Miners' Association
DPC	District Party Committee of the Communist Party of Great Britain
Donbas	Donets coalfield in the Ukraine, USSR.
ECCI	Executive Committee of the Communist International
ERP	European Recovery Programme

ETU	Electrical Trades Union
EWO	Essential Works Order
Federation	South Wales Miner's Federation (see also SWMF)
FO	Force Ouvriere
ICA	International Co-operation Agency
ICWPA	International Class War Prisoners' Aid
ILP	Independent Labour Party
Inprecorr	International Press Correspondence
ITGWU	Irish Transport and General Workers' Union
IWW	Industrial Workers of the World
JNNC	Joint National Negotiating Committee
JSCC	Joint Standing Consultative Committee of MAGB and MFGB
JUC	South Wales Joint Unemployment Council
King Street	CPGB head office, used in context to designate the CPGB leadership
KMA	Kent Miners' Association
KPD	Communist Party of Germany
LSE	London School of Economics and Political Science
LRD	Labour Research Department
MAGB	Mining Association of Great Britain (coalowners' association)
MFGB	Miners' Federation of Great Britain (after 1936, Mineworkers' Federation of Great Britain)
MIC	Miners' International Committee of RILU
MIF	Mineworkers' International Federation
MIU	Miners' Industrial Union (non-political)
MMM	Miners' Minority Movement
MSS	Mardy Socialist Society
NAFTA	National Amalgamated Furnishing Trades' Association
NCB	National Coal Board
NCL	National Council of Labour (representatives from TUC General Council, Executive Committee of PLP and Labour Party NEC)
NEC	National Executive Committee of the Labour Party
NEP	New Economic Policy
NHS	National Health Service

NKVD	Secret Service of the USSR (People's Commissariat of Internal Affairs)
NMA	Nottinghamshire Miners' Association
NMIU	Nottinghamshire Miners' Industrial Union
NMM	National Minority Movement
non	non-unionist
non-pol	non-political trade union
NRT	National Reference Tribunal for the coal industry
NUDAW	National Union of Distributive and Allied Workers
NUGMW	National Union of General and Municipal Workers
NUM	National Union of Mineworkers
NUR	National Union of Railwaymen
NUSMW	National Union of Scottish Mine Workers
NUWM	National Unemployed Workers' Movement
NUWCM	National Unemployed Workers' Committee Movement
NWQU	North Wales Quarrymen's Union
OEEC	Organisation for European Economic Co-operation
OMS	Output per Man Shift
OPEC	Organisation of Petroleum Exporting Countries
PAC	Public Assistance Committee (local government body to administer state unemployment assistance)
PCE	Spanish Communist Party
PCF	French Communist Party
PCI	Italian Communist Party
PLA	People's Liberation Army, China
PLP	Parliamentary Labour Party
Politburo	Political Bureau of a national communist party (functioning as a de facto inner cabinet above the Executive, working in tandem with the Secretariat)
POUM	Partido Obrero de Unificacion Marxista (Marxist Workers' Unity Party)
Presidium	Executive Committee of the Comintern and also of RILU
Profintern	Red International of Labour Unions, also RILU

ABBREVIATIONS

RILU	Red International of Labour Unions, also Profintern
RIRO	Regional Industrial Relations Officer of the Ministry of Labour
RSS	Rhondda Socialist Society
RTUO	Revolutionary Trade Union Organisation
SARA	Special Areas Reconstruction Association
SDF	Social Democratic Federation
SLP	Socialist Labour Party
Soviet Union	Union of Soviet Socialist Republics, also USSR
SPD	German Social Democratic Party
SSWCM	Shop Stewards' and Workers' Committee Movement
SWCA	South Wales Council of Action
SWCC	South Wales Communist Council
SWMCA	South Wales Miners' Council of Action
SWMF	South Wales Miners' Federation; see also Federation
SWMIU	South Wales Miners' Industrial Union
SWML(SU)	South Wales Miners' Library, Swansea University
SWSS	South Wales Socialist Society
TGWU	Transport and General Workers' Union
Transport House	headquarters of TGWU, TUC and Labour Party; used in context to designate the three leaderships either collectively or variously.
TSSA	Transport Salaried Staffs Association
TUC	Trades Union Congress
UAB	Unemployment Assistance Board
UDC	Urban District Council
UMGB	United Mineworkers of Great Britain
UMS	United Mineworkers of Scotland
URC	Unofficial Reform Committee
USDAW	Union of Shop, Distributive and Allied Workers
USSR	Union of Soviet Socialist Republics, also Soviet Union
WBTU	Watermen, Tugmen and Bargemen's Union
WEB	Western European Bureau of the Comintern
WIR	Workers' International Relief

7

| WSF | Workers' Socialist Federation |
| YMA | Yorkshire Miners' Association |

Foreword

Eric Hobsbawm

In this book Nina Fishman, building on earlier attempts, has done justice to the life and achievement of Arthur Horner who, with Ernest Bevin, was the British trade union leader with the greatest impact on the history of the United Kingdom in the first half of the twentieth century. Both became national figures as leaders of labour organisations in a Britain whose labour-intensive nineteenth-century industrial economy was beginning to totter, but which remained essentially the only country in which most citizens (or rather 'subjects of the king') were or defined themselves as 'working-class'. Both operated essentially in, and made their career through, class-conscious trade union action; in Bevin's case this eventually led to the Foreign Office, while in Horner's case it probably ruled him out of a leading political role in the Communist Party. Though both had very sharp minds, neither was much of an intellectual by nature. Both, in Nina Fishman's quote from the *Manchester Guardian*, 'shared an almost mesmeric power to persuade others to follow them, and both shared an absolute mastery of administrative detail. Both earned immense respect from the employers against whom they fought'.

In hardly any other respect are they comparable as men, in their style of action or in their achievement, though it happens that both were of English origin and had begun their careers by moving from nonconformist protestant preaching into fulltime labour organisation. To take the most obvious difference, Bevin, ten years the older, was physically a huge man, who expected to be treated as such. Horner was a notably small man, who compensated for his lack of weight and inches by systematic body-building exercise and sports. Football and boxing, at the very light weights so characteristic of the famous South Wales pugilists of the time ('The ghost with a hammer in his hand' was the journalists' phrase for the champion of the valleys Jimmy Wilde), both made him strong enough to hold his own in the very macho culture of the mines, and gave him an impressive degree of physical fitness that was to serve him well almost until the end in the hard-drinking ambience of national union politics.

Moreover, their careers as trade union leaders were notably different, as indeed were their curiously inverse political careers. Both admittedly began on the extreme left of the labour movement, Bevin in a body affiliated to the Marxist Social Democratic Federation, Horner in the militant crucible of the South Wales left. In the 1920s Bevin was primarily a trade union chieftain, though after the catastrophe of 1931 he increasingly became a king-maker in the Labour Party, and from 1940 was a pillar of governments. On the other hand, in the 1920s Horner was chiefly prominent and controversial as a leading Communist, nationally and even internationally, but while he maintained his party membership throughout his life, sometimes not without serious hesitation, from the early 1930s on he became almost totally involved in his trade union work.

This is illustrated by their career curves. By the age of thirty Bevin was a fully-paid union organiser for a national union, and by the age of forty he was an acknowledged national figure in the union movement and about to establish and lead the great and all-comprehensive Transport and General Workers' Union. In some ways Arthur Horner had an earlier start, being elected as checkweighman at Mardy colliery by the age of 25, but for a long time afterwards he essentially remained a rank-and-file communist militant, though an impressive reputation as a hero of the miners' struggle in 1926 to 1927 gave him a short-lived spell on the Executive of the Mineworkers' Federation. Blacklisted, victimised and in a coalfield fighting both unemployment and union defeat, for much of the time he had little to live on other than his modest wage as a party functionary. He was not elected to his first full-time paid trade union post as the South Wales Miners' Federation Agent in the Anthracite District until 1933 at the age of 39, but after this his advance was quick. President of the South Wales Miners' Federation since 1936, he was fifty-two when he achieved his lifetime ambition, the creation of a National Mineworkers Union in a nationalised coal industry.

The two men differed even in their constituencies. Bevin made his name in a union that had never confined his interests to any single industry, though he first became nationally known as the spokesman for one of its components, the dockers. Nor, from the moment he took command at the TGWU, was he ever seriously challenged by rivals or rebels. Horner, architect of the National Union of Mineworkers, belonged to one industry only. Indeed, for most of his early career he was rooted in one specific area within one specific coalfield: the Rhondda. And he made his way and remained at the top under constant challenge, not least from within the CP nationally and locally, in the ever-changing electoral jungle of the notably democratic mining politics of South Wales. Finally, Bevin's profound commitment to the working class can never be disentangled from his pursuit of success and recognition in a society of class rule, as a man of working-class background who was conscious of his own very remarkable talents. Perhaps this is what helped to make him a greater figure in twentieth-century British labour history than Horner, whose political commitment had no comparable element of personal ambition. Bevin was an intelligent bull-dozer, Horner an inspirer and persuader.

Britain, to adapt a phrase of Aneurin Bevan, was an island built on coal and surrounded by the sea. When Arthur Horner first began work in the Rhondda, something like a million men were working in the mines of Great Britain to produce the coal that was still the industrial world's major source of energy. At their peak (1913), almost a quarter of them worked in the area that was the base of Horner's influence, South Wales. Today only a few thousands are left. For readers born since Mrs Thatcher's government came to power and set about destroying their union in 1984 to 1985, the miners and their role in the labour movement belong to a distant and dead past. Were they really the Brigade of Guards of labour's army, whose battles were central to Labour's political fortunes? Were they really the irreducible bedrock of Labour Party strength – a union almost 80 per cent of whose members affiliated to the Labour Party in 1946 to 1947, more than any other large union, and which provided almost half the Labour MPs after the disastrous 1931 election? They were, and they were known to be so. Past generations took for granted the rock-solid commitment of the coalfields to parties identified with a nationwide class consciousness. Actually, they came into national labour politics relatively late. Still, between 1918 and the effective end of the union it was true enough.

The industrial world in which the miners played so eminent and decisive a part will be as remote to most readers today as the world of the eighteenth-century cattle-drovers, and as unknown as the medieval manorial economy. In effect, what was classified as a national industry consisted of largely self-contained and iso-lated villages round the several thousand pits of varying depth (opencast mining was not of major importance) that employed almost the totality of their male inhabitants. The lives of the miners were almost unbelievably localised. The puzzle is not that a man like WP Richardson (1873 to 1930) was born and lived all his life in Unsworth, County Durham, that he worked for thirty years in Unsworth Colliery, married a miner's daugh-ter, directed the Unsworth Colliery Primitive Methodist chapel choir, and wrote a column on poultry for the local paper. It is that while remaining in Unsworth he helped to found the local branch of the Independent Labour Party, joined the board of the *Daily Herald*, championed the nationalisation of mines and became national treasurer of the Miners' Federation of Great Britain. In fact, the history of miners' trade unionism was a con-stant tension between the need for legal protection, which gave their struggle a national dimension, and the continued, visceral, almost ineradicable specificity of each coalfield – one might even say of each pit – which worked in the opposite direction. Each field had its own traditions, its own methods and customs, not all of them determined by geological and geographical structure, nor even by the basic division between coalfields specialised in exports, such as South Wales, and those relying on the less storm-tossed home market such as the Northeast. I remember being told by an official of the Board of Trade during world war two that it was impossible to allocate textiles for standard national working clothes for miners, since the men in every field insisted on their own wear, often made from specific materials.

Paradoxically, the sheer specialisation and local rootedness of mining was what gave its workers considerable strength. They were the most unionised, except for the years following the great defeat of 1926 to 1927, when mining temporarily dropped a good way down the ranking order. Coal-mines were by far the most combative industry in the country – indeed, in most years between the 1890s and nationalisation they provided the largest number of disputes. They were ready for battle because for them pit problems came before all others, including national ones, to an extent difficult to recall. At the height of world war two, even as the Communist Party urged workers to give absolute priority to production, in the mines 'there were many stoppages of a trivial kind ... [and] the lack of confidence which the men showed in their own leaders and the frequent disregard of the advice of trade union officials by their members'. Three months before D-Day, as war factories worked all out to produce supplies for the invasion of Europe, over 120,000 miners were involved in unofficial strikes.

Mine-owners could defeat miners, but while coal was king they had to live with and were vulnerable to the mining village's amalgam of class consciousness and workplace, community, neighbourhood and gender solidarities, which rejected scabs but assimilated incomers. In the great boom years of coal the population of Glamorgan and Monmouth had multiplied by two and a half, a mass immigration – in this case mainly from England – comparable proportionately to that into the USA. Overwhelmingly it went into the pits. Yet this did not make the valleys any less militant or consciously Welsh, though the language of the lodges was anglicised.

To form this agglomeration of local autonomies, often with diverging interests, into a single national Miners' Federation of Great Britain was itself a massive step forward, but even this decentralised coalition, with the major exception of the old Northeast, was itself largely an aggregate of autonomous sub-federations – not least Horner's own 'Fed', the South Wales Miners' Federation. At the time of the General Strike in 1926 it had nineteen districts and several hundred lodges, ranging from the four of Dowlais district to the seventy-one of the Anthracite District. Only if we grasp the extraordinary localisation and complexity of coal-mining can we appreciate the sheer scale of Horner's achievement in realising the dream of leading its workers into a single national union. The disastrous defeats of 1926 to 1927, which had reduced the strength of unions in

13

the coalmines to little more than half the workforce (1933), and allowed the employer-friendly Nottingham-based 'Spencer Union' to emerge as a potential rival to the Federation in some regions, made it look even more difficult.

Fortunately, unification had two important potential assets. The first was the growing sense among rank-and-file pitmen that the gigantic national battles in which they were involved called for an all-out national answer to the miners' problems. 'It is quite probable that a majority always favoured unification [after 1926] ... the officials of the district associations were as rule less enthusiastic about a change in the organisational structure than the rank-and-file of the union membership' (N Barou, *British Trade Unions*, London 1947, p. 238). Horner and the new generation of socialist activists in other coalfields set sail for a single union with the wind in their favour. The second asset was the inability of twentieth-century Britain to do without coal, a fact of which the British government, unlike the employers, could never lose sight. Even before Ernest Bevin joined the war cabinet, Downing Street and Whitehall could in some respects be as unhappy about the structure and labour relations of the mining industry as the militants were, for very different reasons: Parliament passed six Coal Mines Acts between 1908 and 1931.

Nothing demonstrated the country's dependence on an unbroken supply of coal more dramatically than war. As in 1914–18 so in 1939–45 war in practice gave the miners' demands an irresistible force. This dramatic rise in the miners' strength in the first world war led nowhere. Neither nationalisation nor the single national miners' union were achieved. Both were achieved in and after world war two under Arthur Horner's leadership of the MFGB, politically handicapped though he was in union and official dealings by his well-known membership of the Communist Party. Even though this was obviously not a one-man victory, it should be seen as a measure of Horner's leadership, and his practical realism and strategic and diplomatic skills. But – more than this – he came to be recognised as the key man in setting up and supporting the new National Coal Board – in the words of the *Economist* quoted by Nina Fishman, he was 'almost an unofficial Minister of Fuel and Power [in the 1945 Labour government] [who] ... often produces the impression that but for

14

his party attachment a way would be found to make that position official, to the noticeable improvement of the Cabinet'. But,
though tempted, he did not join the establishment, or leave the
Communist Party. He remained Arthur Horner. He deserved
well of his class, his party and his country.

Next to his contribution to twentieth-century British history
as a trade union leader, Horner's role in the history of the world
communist movement, and of the Communist Party of Great
Britain, is small. Nevertheless it is vital to an understanding of
the man, as well as to the much-controverted history of Moscow
and its relations with the parties of the Communist International.
Horner belonged to the minority of revolutionaries who joined
the new CP from outside the British Socialist Party, which formed
the main body of the new organisation; instead he came from
the intransigent ultra-left, which dominated the notoriously
militant South Wales valleys, and against which Lenin launched
his famous ideological missile on *Radicalism, the infantile disease
of Communism*. Horner's gifts as an agitator and a leader made
him stand out from the rest of the modest number of South
Wales communists. As the chairman of the founding conference
of the South Wales Miners Minority Movement (1923), he soon
became prominent in the militant National Minority Movement
within the unions, the CP's major success in the 1920s; and the
sheer centrality of mining in Britain, and in the industrial conflicts of the 1920s, gave leading communists in this industry
an important position in the movement, which was to serve
Horner well in the time of his troubles. By the end of 1923 he
was a prominent figure in the Comintern's Red International of
Labour Unions (RILU), and a part-time member of the CPGB's
Politburo and Executive.

As the closest associate of the great tribune of miners' militancy, AJ Cook, Horner won a substantial reputation in the
General Strike, nationally and in the international movement –
he was on the presidium of the RILU, and was endorsed as a candidate member of the ECCI, the highest body in the Comintern,
whose Sixth Congress he attended in 1928. He was clearly a
coming man. Even in 1947 the French CP leader described him
to Stalin as 'a remarkable comrade, hard, stubborn, dedicated
and loyal who has great authority among the miners'. Yet, while
he shared the general leftward shift of the CPGB after the disas-

ters of the General Strike and Miners' Lock-Out of 1926 to 1927, he resisted the new 'class against class' strategy announced by ECCI in 1928, which amounted to the secession of new 'revolutionary' organisations from the irredeemably reformist British trade unions. It made – it could make – no sense to a communist whose entire career had proved how effective the leadership of a tiny handful of revolutionaries could be in moving vast masses of non-revolutionary workers in non-revolutionary unions, whose political loyalty was solidly with a reformist Labour Party.

Horner was not the only British Communist leader to disapprove the increasingly strident 'class against class' line imposed on the parties of the Comintern, not least because it meant abandoning and antagonising the existing trade unions that were the effective field of action of British communists. However, he was the only one who never ceased to be publicly critical of it, from the moment he first expressed his disagreement at the 1928 RILU Congress in Moscow. According to the conventional version of Comintern history, he should not have survived this. He was branded a dissident, accused of 'Hornerism' – a special 'deviation' from orthodoxy – and indeed was officially expelled from the CP by a Politburo dominated by young Moscow-loyal ultras. He was summoned to Moscow to explain himself to an Appeals panel of the ECCI. And after all this 'he returned with the Comintern's approval to resume his place as a leading British comrade'. Well, perhaps not quite. Formally Horner returned to the Executive of the CP, but henceforth he took very little part in its political operations, let alone the international communist movement. But this may also be due in part to Horner's choice. Having fought off the revolutionary intransigents in the Welsh Communist Party, he was free to concentrate on his enormous tasks as a union leader.

The way in which Horner managed to survive his troubles in the communist movement throws light on the much-debated question of autonomy and independent policy formation in the parties that accepted the unquestioned command of the Moscow 'centre'. It also throws light on the much less debated question of the command structure of that centre in the 1920s and even the early 1930s. In part Horner was helped by the British CP leadership's reluctance to solve political disagreements by excommunicating its old comrades; this was seen as an insufficiently bolshevik weakness by some in the Comintern, but never stamped out. As under the analogous command system of the Catholic Church, national communist parties could remain recognisably national in style, even as they did what they were ordered to do from headquarters. But mainly his survival was due to the divisions within both the Comintern and the local parties, neither at this stage the solid monoliths of conventional Comintern mythology.

As we know, between 1928 and 1932 the 'class against class' line caused Communist Party strength and influence in most of Europe to haemorrhage to the point of pernicious anaemia – in Germany, where it did not, it helped to bring Hitler to power. That it might do so was immediately obvious to experienced local leaders, though not to the confident shock-troops from the Communist Youth whom Moscow mobilised to take over from them. They could not oppose 'the line' once it had been promulgated from on high, though there was still scope for diplomatically formulated argument, for using influence in Moscow, and for actions to keep the party protected and prepared for a change for the better. Unquestionably Horner was protected by Pollitt and others against Moscow's Young Turks, and also (especially in his own turbulent Wales) against the ultra-radicals for whom there is always a body of support in parties whose objective is revolution. ECCI, though bedevilled by the additional complications of Stalin's take-over of total power, was also divided between genuine ultras and closet realists who feared – and as time went on could increasingly see – the disastrous consequences of 'class against class'. That the Comintern reversed Horner's expulsion demonstrates that there were genuine differences of opinion, as did the fact that the Seventh Congress, which was to inaugurate the new antifascist policy, had to be postponed for almost a year from its planned date in September 1934 because of continued opposition within ECCI.

Horner's survival was probably due, not least, to his persistent public refusal to toe the line, apart from the very qualified 'self-criticism' eventually required for official rehabilitation. This forced the International, which knew well that 'the mining question [was] the most important question now before the Party', to face the possible consequences of losing an irreplaceable leader with a firm and lasting personal and political base

17

in the most rebellious of coalfields. It seems clear that ECCI, and certainly RILU, were always aware of this, but Horner's continued intransigence allowed the bureaucratic mills of the International the time to grind slowly enough to give its cautious realists a chance.

But let us not forget that for Horner himself more was at stake in the years of his troubles than a set of calculations about party and Comintern strategy and tactics. Comrades sent by the CP to South Wales from other areas were shocked at the sheer poverty in which he lived, which was shared with the rest of the battered and defeated miners of the valleys. During the time when even his party wage was withdrawn, the Horners lived as an unemployed couple on 30 shillings a week (£1.50) outdoor relief. Among disaffiliated lodges in the debris of defeat, under the constant threat of being abandoned by the Party, he never ceased to fight for what he knew to be the right way for Communists in the British labour movement. He considered submitting to the Party and leaving it, but in the end he fought, remained and won. Loyal but independent in mind and increasingly critical, he resisted all the temptations of power and official status and remained in the Communist Party for the rest of his life. The establishment withheld its rewards, but so did the Communist Party.

Nina Fishman's book is, at last, a worthy record of the significant contributions to the working class and the history of twentieth-century Britain by a very remarkable man.

London, October 2009

Chapter 1

Introduction

Arthur Horner was the British communist who exerted the greatest influence on the course of British history. As Vice-Chairman of the Mardy Lodge and member of the South Wales Miner's Federation Executive, he achieved fame across the British coalfields during the eight months long Miners' Lock-Out in 1926. Elected President of the SWMF in 1936, from then on he took a leading role nationally in the Miners' Federation of Great Britain. After playing an outstanding role during the second world war in ensuring the maintenance of coal supplies while at the same time defending miners' working conditions and pay, in 1946 Horner was elected general secretary of the National Union of Mineworkers, the successor organisation to the MFGB. After the coal industry was nationalised in 1947, Horner took the lead in ensuring that the new National Coal Board was a success: his sense of social democratic responsibility meant the he was always concerned about producing enough coal for the nation as well as the interests of union members.

Coal was the primary source of energy for industrialised economies for most of Horner's life. Industrialised countries, including Britain, depended on coal to generate electricity, and to produce the town gas used for domestic appliances, domestic gas fires, and, until the 1930s, gas lighting. Coal was used to stoke the boilers of many industrial undertakings, railway locomotives and steamships. It was delivered to the majority of British households for use in open grates for heating and in large copper boilers to produce hot water for baths and washing clothes. In 1915, the year Horner was first employed in coalmining, on the surface at the Standard colliery, Ynyshir, there were 953,600 mineworkers employed in Britain. In 1947, when the National Coal Board took over coal production 'for and on behalf of the people' on 1 January, there were 703,900 mineworkers employed in 958 collieries, from Somerset and Kent in southern England to Fife in central Scotland. In 1959, the year Horner retired, there were still 737 collieries and 658,200 mineworkers.[1]

There was a chronic shortage of coal in Britain from 1942 to 1955. In his role as a spokesman for the MFGB and then the NUM, Horner's passionate commitment played a vital role in reassuring the public that British miners would give their all to maximise coal production, provided they were working in modern conditions and earning a fair day's wage. After nationalisation, the NCB came to rely on his charisma and good humour to ensure that the industry and its employees maintained a positive public image. In 1958, the *Daily Herald* industrial correspondent recalled that Horner was 'once described as the most powerful man in Britain – because he could have stopped all coal production'.[2] Not surprisingly, his activities were well reported in the media. He was in great demand as a public speaker. He broadcast on the BBC, and addressed groups of businessmen, undergraduates, Labour Clubs, Fabian Societies, Liberal Societies and youth clubs.

Although Horner was a familiar public figure in the 1940s and 1950s, he had disappeared from the public stage and gaze by the time of his death in 1968. He was not forgotten, however, by the thousands of people who had worked alongside him, socialised with him or heard him speak. His diminutive stature – five feet three inches or 1.6 metres – thick spectacles and blue eyes gave him a distinctive appearance, which combined with an impish smile to make him truly memorable. A keen athlete in his youth, his physical demeanour remained vigorous and alert on public occasions. In large meetings and at close quarters, he radiated warmth, good humour and enthusiasm, and inspired affection, loyalty and respect.[3]

Horner's autobiography, *Incorrigible Rebel*, was published in 1960. In a review, the *Manchester Guardian*'s industrial editor observed that Horner had been 'largely responsible for the fact that [coal] nationalisation has worked, and that the shortage of coal throughout the 1950s was less serious than it might have been.' Moreover, he was 'the only British trade union leader in the past thirty years who can fairly be mentioned in the same breath as Ernest Bevin'.[4] The comparison was regularly made in the 1940s, even though Horner was a foundation member of the British communist party and Bevin had become a notable anti-communist.

Horner was born in 1894 in the County Borough of Merthyr Tydfil; Bevin was born in 1881 in a village on the edge of Exmoor. They both became union activists in young adulthood, leading members of a self-confident working class who believed that well-organised unions were the main agency by which ordinary people could gain better conditions of life. In addition to the 'new unionism' which had emerged in the 1890s, Bevin and Horner also embraced the new political doctrine of socialism. Bevin joined the Marxist Social Democratic Federation around 1904. Horner joined the Independent Labour Party after encountering local activists and its general secretary, Keir Hardie was re-elected MP for Merthyr in 1906 having been first elected in 1900 (as is explained in the following chapter).

The cohort of British workers who reached political maturity before 1914 had ample cause to fight for concessions from employers, and campaign for social reforms from the government. High rates of infant mortality were typical. Horner was one of a family of seventeen, of whom only six survived through infancy. Although many, if not most, manual workers had experienced rising living standards in the 1870s and 1880s, they were still likely to experience periods of protracted unemployment in the 1890s and 1900s. Their dependants still regularly lived with poverty, malnourishment, inferior housing and the fear of ending their days in the workhouse. The onset of physical decline from hard manual labour came comparatively early to men and women in their late forties and early fifties.

Like most of their trade union contemporaries, Bevin and Horner welcomed the revolutions in Russia and Germany in 1917 and 1918. Bevin played a leading role in the Hands Off Russia movement in 1920, when the Labour Party and trade unions threatened to organise a general strike to stop the British government sending troops to assist in overthrowing the communist government. He was the prime mover in the foundation of the Transport and General Workers' Union in 1922 and became its first general secretary. He also played a leading role on the General Council of the Trades Union Congress during the 1926 General Strike. Although Bevin continued to support the USSR's right to undertake its own experiment in socialism unhindered by invasion from other countries, he was conspicuously loyal to the Labour Party, and suspicious of the motives and intentions of British communists.

Horner was the most prominent communist in the 1926 General Strike and Lock-Out. He earned a reputation for the energy and ingenuity with which he put the communist case for maximum militancy during the protracted dispute. He also maintained his revolutionary optimism after the miners had been forced back to work at the end of the year, and began preparing the ground for the amalgamation of the twenty-three district coalfield unions into One Big Miners' Union, which, like Bevin's TGWU, would gain strength through unity.

Bevin was Minister of Labour in the wartime coalition government of 1940 to 45. He and Horner met regularly in 1941 to 1944 on opposite sides of the negotiating table, when the MFGB was manoeuvring to win increased wages and improved conditions for mineworkers during the wartime emergency. Nevertheless, both men's aims were the same: to win the war and reshape labour relations in the coal industry. In July 1945, Clement Attlee appointed Bevin Foreign Secretary in the Labour government. Bevin, nevertheless, maintained a close interest in industrial relations, and regularly advised the cabinet on trade union matters. He recognised that Horner's performance as NUM general secretary was crucial to the success of the newly nationalised coal industry, and praised his outstanding role in settling complex industrial disputes and pre-empting others, which had the potential to seriously damage the Labour government.

Horner could also have played a positive and decisive role in shaping the relationship between the Labour government and the trade union movement. He had been keen to join the TUC General Council since 1936, because he aspired to play a leading role in guiding the whole of the trade union movement. But in 1938, Bevin and Walter Citrine, TUC general secretary, had manoeuvred to block the MFGB's nomination of Horner to fill the General Council vacancy created by the departure of the MFGB President Joseph Jones. By 1946, Bevin and Citrine, who had dominated the interwar General Council, were no longer trade union office holders. Their departure left a palpable dearth of men and women capable of dealing with the novel and formidable problems of supporting a socialist administration through a period of austerity, international uncertainty and labour shortage.[5] Despite Horner's outstanding abilities, however Vincent Tewson, Citrine's successor, and Arthur Deakin, Bevin's successor, continued to block Horner's election to the TUC General Council.

Horner remained a communist during his tenure as NUM General Secretary. Since the NUM was a major trade union affiliated to the Labour Party, there was an evident contradiction between these two roles, which many observers predicted would result in grief as the cold war gathered momentum. In the autumn of 1948 a bitter conflict developed inside the NUM Executive about Horner's future. It seemed likely that he would either resign or be compelled to resign by the Executive. But against all the odds, he served his full term as NUM general secretary. The key players in this battle were Sam Watson, general secretary of the Durham Area, NUM President Will Lawther, and Vice-President Jim Bowman. Lawther had been influenced by Tewson and Sam Berger, American Embassy Labour Attaché, to arrange Horner's ejection from office on a pretext. However, Watson intervened, with Bowman's support, because they judged that Horner's continuation in office was critical to the success of the National Coal Board. Horner remained in office until his retirement in April 1959.

Given Horner's prominence, it is not surprising that there were three previous attempts to write his biography. In 1947 when he was at the height of his celebrity status, and the cold war had not yet overtly affected NUM politics, Giles Romilly wrote 'Gentle Revolutionary: A Portrait of Arthur Horner' for a collection of progressive essays. The editors' introduction commented: 'Little is known about Arthur Horner, Communist miners' leader and one of Britain's most controversial public figures.' It also explained that Romilly was 'working on a full-length biography of Horner'.[6] The biography never appeared, perhaps overtaken by the dramatic events of 1948.

In 1957, Dr Ronnie Frankenberg, a young communist sociologist, who had become education officer of the NUM South

23

Wales Area in September 1956, conceived a project to write Horner's biography. He consulted the veteran communist, Dai Dan Evans, NUM South Wales Area Vice President, about his idea, and Evans was supportive. Frankenberg had read Vic Allen's recently published book about Arthur Deakin, and was keen to show that Deakin's achievements were insubstantial by comparison to Horner's. Deakin was born in 1890, and had lived in Dowlais, near Merthyr, from 1901 to 1910, when he and Horner met and became friendly through a shared family connection. Evans took Frankenberg's proposal to the South Wales Area Executive, and it was agreed that he be granted paid leave of absence to research Horner's life. [7]

Frankenberg spent a fortnight in London with Horner in early 1958. A meticulous participant observer, he watched Horner's work patterns at the NUM Head Office in Westminster Bridge Road and socialised with him in the evenings. He interviewed Horner on five successive occasions, and made copious notes. Horner was surprisingly candid, probably in response to the sympathy he could feel flowing so strongly from the younger man. He told Frankenberg about growing up in Merthyr, and progressed through the 1920s and 1930s up to his first few years as NUM general secretary. Although Frankenberg stopped work on the biography project later in the year, he preserved his notes and the substantial amount of primary evidence he had collected. He passed them on to Hywel Francis in 1982, when Francis approached him for assistance.

Francis had signed a contract with Lawrence & Wishart to write Horner's life, and knew about Frankenberg's attempt through his family networks. His father, Dai Francis, had been a communist and SWMF activist in the 1930s. He had become a full-time official in the NUM South Wales Area, and served as General Secretary between 1963 to 1976. By 1982 Hywel Francis was a recognised expert in South Wales coalmining history. He and Dai Smith had written the official history, *The Fed, A History of the South Wales Miners in the Twentieth Century*, published in 1980 by Lawrence & Wishart. The book had drawn extensively on Smith's 1976 doctoral thesis, 'The Re-building of the South Wales Miners' Federation 1926–39'; Francis' 1977 doctoral thesis 'The South Wales Miners and the Spanish Civil War: A Study in Internationalism'; and the impressive number of interviews conducted by the Coalfield History Project in 1971 to 1974. Francis had been centrally involved in this innovative research; the transcripts of the interviews had been deposited in the South Wales Miners' Library in Swansea.

In addition to Frankenberg's material, Francis collected letters, memorabilia, photographs and other valuable material from Robin Page Arnot, and Horner's eldest daughter, Vol Tofts. He received a grant from the British Academy, which enabled him to undertake research in the archives of the Communist International in Moscow in July 1984 about the Hornerism controversy of 1930 to 1931, when the CPGB leadership had tried to expel Horner for having committed a serious ideological error. He also searched the Soviet Miners' Union files in the Ukrainian coalfield, for evidence of Horner's visits in the 1920s. Noreen Branson, who had succeeded James Klugmann as the official historian of the CPGB, passed on the extensive notes made by Klugmann from the Comintern archives of CPGB Politburo and Central Committee meetings in 1930 to 1931. She also provided an introduction to the chief Comintern archivist.

In 1985 Francis set the Horner biography to one side, without formally abandoning it. In early 1987 he presented a paper on the 1930 to 1931 Hornerism controversy to the Communist Party History Group. His notes of the meeting reveal a lively, wide-ranging discussion during which Jim Fyrth recalled listening to Robin Page Arnot speak about his own role in the Comintern hearings. The centenary of Horner's birth in 1994 was marked by a radio documentary, commissioned by Dai Smith, then head of the BBC in Wales. It was produced and presented by Joanne Cayford, herself a labour historian. Early in her preparation for the documentary, Cayford consulted Francis. Mindful of the centenary, he had written a paper which compared the leadership qualities of the 'three Arthurs', AJ Cook, Horner and Scargill.

Francis suggested to Cayford that she should interview me about Horner's struggle for survival as NUM general secretary in 1948. Since 1993 I had been researching the impact of the cold war on trade union politics. Since the NUM was one of the main battlegrounds in the conflict between communists and social democrats, I had accumulated substantial evidence about Horner. (In 1994, a British Academy small research grant enabled me to extend the range of my research to use the NUM

Executive minutes in Sheffield, the Scottish Area minutes in Edinburgh and the South Wales Area minutes in Pontypridd.) I subsequently suggested to Hywel Francis that we should work together to revive the Horner biography. Hywel would be primarily responsible for Horner's life up to 1939, and I would assume the principal responsibility for his life from 1939 to 1968. After a suitable pause for reflection, we decided to collaborate and signed a new contract with Lawrence & Wishart in December 1995. We were fortunate received a generous grant from the Barry Amiel and Norman Melburn Trust in July 1996.

In practice, our agreed division of labour was flexible. We joined forces to interview people who had known Horner in South Wales and London. We interviewed Lord Callaghan, whose acquaintance with Horner dated from July 1945. Having been elected MP for Cardiff South in the general election, Callaghan, aged thirty-three, had joined the group of Labour MPs and Arthur Horner who travelled from London to South Wales on Thursday evening, and who regularly shared the same railway compartment. He remembered the warm conviviality, laced with political gossip, humour and high hopes for the Labour government. He had liked Horner and been deeply impressed by his energy and sense of mission for the coal industry.

Hywel and I walked through Merthyr Tydfil and met one of Horner's nieces-in-law who lived in one of the houses built by his father in the early twentieth century. We also visited Ronnie Frankenberg in Newcastle-under-Lyme to collect additional material, which he had recently found in his files, and interview him about his biography project. Personal contacts facilitated us in making contact with people who had worked with Horner at the SWMF office in Cardiff and the NUM Head Office in London. We interviewed Sybil Griffiths, who had been a telephonist-receptionist in Cardiff from 1942. I interviewed Irene Blakeway, who had been Horner's secretary in London from 1946 and David Branton, who had been a junior clerk in London since 1945.[8]

It was Lord Callaghan who first alerted us to the role played by Sam Berger, the American Labour Attaché, in British trade union politics, and particularly in the NUM Executive's conflict about whether to sack Horner in 1948. Research in archives and memoirs revealed further evidence. Geoffrey Goodman fleshed out the picture with his memories of the activities of Berger's successor, Joe Godson. Goodman had reported on Horner from the late 1940s until his retirement as industrial correspondent and industrial editor for national daily newspapers. He was unfailingly generous in recalling Horner and his milieu, and sharing his analysis of the events in which he was an interested party by virtue of his status as a participant observer. As he has written, 'the industrial/labour correspondent ... was one of the key posts in the national press, on television and radio ... [In the 1950s] the role of the national newspapers' industrial journalists was crucial and, without exaggeration, of real national importance.'[9] Discussions about the relations between Horner and Trevor Evans of the *Daily Express* and Hugh Chevins of the *Daily Telegraph*, key players in 1946 to 1959, were especially helpful.

We were fortunate in being able to draw on published work and others' archival research to add flesh to our own, and Frankenberg's, research. In the course of investigating some sketchy facts about Horner's early life, I discovered, more or less simultaneously with Peter Ackers and the late Michael Casey, that Horner had not attended a Baptist theological college, as he had stated in *Incorrigible Rebel* and countless interviews. With the help of the Birmingham Reference Library, I traced the site of his studies to the Reverend Lancelot Oliver, who ministered with the Churches of Christ in Birmingham. I had insufficient time to do much primary research about this fascinating nonconformist sect. But Hywel and I both derived enormous benefit from reading Ackers' and Casey's work. When Michael visited Britain, we had a long afternoon's discussion with them about the sect's history and culture, and how Horner's religious beliefs and theological training had influenced his subsequent intellectual development, political beliefs and union career.

In the spring of 2000 Hywel Francis was selected as the Labour Party's prospective parliamentary candidate for Aberavon, one of the safest Labour seats in Britain. Although I had written a first draft of the post-1939 period, Hywel had been unable to make progress with the pre-1939 section. After his selection, it was clear that he would be unable to continue with the biography. But a practical solution soon emerged. Our authorial partnership was amicably dissolved and I assumed sole responsibility for the biography. Hywel loaded the boot of his estate wagon

27

full of the cardboard file boxes containing his and Frankenberg's notes, and drove them from Neath to North London. I mined their riches when writing the South Wales portions of the biography in the summer of that millennium year.

I had finished writing the first draft when Eric Hobsbawm urged me to request sight of Horner's MI5 records. Fortuitously, the MI5 archivist had been preparing Horner's five files for deposit at the National Archive. I am grateful to him for allowing me to see the material in February 2004, prior to their release to the public in May. Although much of the Horner files had been destroyed by Luftwaffe bombs in 1941, what remained and what followed, were invaluable. After nearly ten years of researching and thinking about Horner's life, I had clear views about pivotal episodes, relationships and turning points. The MI5 files provided valuable evidence to substantiate my suppositions, presumptions and conclusions. They furnished new insights into the relationship between Horner and the CPGB general secretary Harry Pollitt, as well as important detail about how the political conflict inside the NUM had affected Horner.

This book is subtitled a political biography to alert potential readers to the book's contents. Horner had other abiding interests besides socialism, communism, and the British labour movement. Space and coherence prevented me from including detail about his football, running and boxing exploits as a young man, nor his abiding passion for watching all sporting fixtures.[10] Nor could I discuss the cultural implications of his abiding passion for cowboy novels and short stories. As a union official Horner built up a formidable expertise in the occupational injuries and diseases to which coalminers were prone. He maintained a keen interest in medical and occupational health research that might result in making coalmining a safer and healthier occupation. But space and time have not allowed me to delve into this area of his life. I can only flag it up for future historians to investigate. I have provided a short description of the everyday life which Horner shared with friends, neighbours, and colleagues for twenty-first century readers. It is pleasing to note that there are a growing number of publications about twentieth century British social, cultural and local history which will enable the curious reader to deepen their knowledge about pre-1939 South Wales and post-1945 suburban northwest London.

I have not followed the current convention that biographies should contain intimate details their subjects' personal lives. If I had been writing the biography of Don Juan, Casanova or Frank Harris, I would certainly have investigated and written about sexual encounters, manners and erotic adventures. But I found no evidence that Horner's sexuality affected his political conduct or his career as a coalmining union official. On the other hand, Horner's companionate marriage to Ethel Mary Merrick, and his close relationship to their eldest daughter, Vol, significantly influenced his decisions about whether to remain in the communist party. I have accordingly examined these, as well as his emotional attachment to Pollitt.

I have concentrated on analysing Horner's historical significance for British politics and trade unions. I have tried to provide sufficient background and context to enable readers to make their own judgements about the significance of his life and the difficult decisions which confronted him. Those who persevere will, I hope, find their patience rewarded by a greater understanding of the important areas of Horner's life: industrial conflict, communism, coalmining, and the politics and the personalities of leadership of the British trade union movement. The bibliography and notes should enable the inquisitive and/or doubting reader to investigate for themselves the sources upon which I have relied.

Horner's political trajectory was unusual, not only in Britain but also in western Europe. His decision to remain a communist whilst simultaneously acting as one of the principal proponents of social democratic responsibility inside the nationalised coal industry is still contentious, nearly a generation after the fall of the Berlin Wall marked the end of the cold war in Europe. Sam Watson wrote to Horner after reading *Incorrigible Rebel*. 'That you made a big contribution, and in mental equipment were abreast of many who received greater recognition are proud laurels you and your services will always wear, long after you are gone ... By any criteria you were a "big" man.'[11] The complex story of how Horner, a communist, provided the creative inspiration and continuing commitment to sustain the National Coal Board will be unwelcome for the new generation of cold warriors, busily wielding the airbrush to eradicate all evidence that communists and socialists were not only able but willing to work together. I hope this biography will kindle readers' interest in moving beyond their glib myths, to find out what really happened in the fateful years of the first Labour government. Horner stands as a *non pareil* amongst the cohort of pioneers who made the 1945 to 1951 British social democratic commonwealth.

Chapter 2

Growing Up

Arthur Lewis Horner spent his first sixteen years in Merthyr
Tydfil, the largest inland conurbation in South Wales. He was
born at his paternal grandparents' home at No. 4 Bridge Street
in Georgetown, 'the toughest part of town' on 5 April 1894.[12] His
father, James Jobson Horner, was English. Born in Nottingham
in 1868, James was taken to South Wales in the 1870s by his
parents, William and Mary Jane, at the beginning of a decade-
long slump, which had spread to the rest of western Europe
from Germany. The Horners were living in Merthyr when they
were enumerated in the 1881 Census.[13] Merthyr had become
a boom town in the mid-eighteenth century, when ironmasters
from England had located in the upper Taff river valley in East
Glamorgan, to establish iron mines and iron smelting ventures,
often in partnership with Welsh entrepreneurs. The building
of canals and then railways to transport the smelted pig iron to
Cardiff for trans-shipment had established the conurbation as
one of the centres of the British industrial revolution.

In the second half of the nineteenth century, capitalists who
had pioneered the smelting of iron and then steel began to move
their blast furnaces and rolling mills down the Taff Valley to
towns along the Severn Estuary, where supplies of iron ore from
Spain could be more efficiently utilised. (The indigenous ore was
unsuitable for making steel by means of the new Bessemer process.) Though some iron works in the Merthyr hinterland were
adapted to produce steel, as in Dowlais in 1866, many others
closed. Nevertheless, alternative employment appeared almost
simultaneously. The rich coal seams, hitherto mined mainly
for use in iron smelting, had become profitable in their own
right. The worldwide demand for coal at this time was expanding dramatically. The coal produced from the Glamorgan seams
was particularly suitable for the steam boilers used in locomo-

31

tives, steamships and factory boilers. It was exported from the expanding ports of Cardiff, Barry, Newport and Swansea as far afield as South America.

Merthyr was a lively place at the turn of the nineteenth century. It was sufficiently large and prosperous to support a rich mix of culture, including music hall, variety theatre, rugby, soccer and boxing – both amateur and professional. There was also a multitude of chapels, a central feature of Welsh and English working class and middle class life at this time. Participation in the myriad different kinds of activity associated with non-conformist chapels was an important form of self-expression and personal development for chapel members. Merthyr also had thriving Catholic chapels (as they were known in Britain at the time), for its Irish and Spanish inhabitants, a Jewish synagogue and parish churches of the Anglican Church.

South Wales produced the best world-class steam coal, used by high performance steamships including battleships. The two Rhondda valleys, 'by the turn of the century numbered fifty-eight large concerns which employed some 41,000 coal miners. Their population had increased nearly fourfold in the 1870s, and by 1890 it had more than doubled again'.[14] There were insufficient young people in the central belt of Wales to meet the demand for labour, and coalowners were compelled to bid up the wages and offer better conditions of work to attract labour. Not surprisingly, increasing numbers of men and women migrated from the adjacent rural counties in England, Gloucestershire, Somerset and Shropshire to find work. Typical emigrants were from agricultural stock, like the future SWMF leaders Arthur Cook and Frank Hodges. They came to South Wales from Somerset and Gloucestershire respectively in the early 1900s. Hodges settled in Abertillery in Monmouthshire; Cook found work in the Rhondda Fach river valley in east Glamorgan.

Merthyr and its hinterland possessed a sufficient social and economic infrastructure to enable entrepreneurs to reap a speedy return on their investments. Men and boys worked in the wide range of trades and businesses, typical of a prosperous Victorian town. Arthur's grandfather, William Horner, was enumerated in the 1891 Census as the head of household and an assistant brewer. The six lodgers in his house included woollen weavers and dyers, a boilermakers' labourer and a hay haulier.[15]

James Horner's future wife, Emily Lewis, lived at No. 30 Bridge Street. She had been born in Penybont in Radnorshire in 1870, and evidently arrived in Merthyr with her family soon afterwards. Her father, John Lewis, was recorded in the 1891 Census as being a general labourer.

When James Horner and Emily Lewis were married on 14 January 1889, aged twenty-one and nineteen, James' occupation was listed as mason's labourer and his father's as brewer. Though Emily was a spirited, bright woman, James evidently had no desire to learn her mother-tongue, and Welsh was not used in their household. This may have been because he was ambitious, and could see no benefit to be derived from his children growing up bilingual. James' Conservative political allegiance may have been another way of expressing his English identity.

Eighteen months after their marriage, Lily was born, followed in 1892 by another daughter, Annie. Two years later to the day, on 5 April 1894, Arthur Lewis arrived. He remained attached to his second name, which was his mother's maiden name, and continued to use it or its initial in his signature and in official union documents. James Horner's occupation was listed as storekeeper at public railway station on Arthur's birth certificate. He had found permanent employment as a porter at the Taff Vale Railway Company railway freight station, one of the busiest freight depots in Britain, and within easy walking distance of Bridge Street. Evidently competent, he had been promoted to foreman by the time of Arthur's adolescence. This was a responsible position which called for quick thinking and taking urgent decisions on the spot. Although his wages were lower than skilled manual workers, for example iron and steel puddlers, blastfurnacemen and colliers, being a foreman gave him status, comparative job security and a small company pension on retirement. Along with most other Taff Vale Railway employees, he joined the thriving railway trade union, but remained a passive member.

Arthur remembered that his father had worked a twelve-hour day, as well as doing frequent compulsory overtime. Nevertheless, James found time to be active in the Ancient Order of Rechabites, a temperance friendly society, and also became the first Chairman of the Dowlais Co-operative Society. He cultivated a large garden, and sent young Arthur around

Merthyr hawking its produce. Using his savings and perhaps with the help of a loan from the Dowlais Co-operative Society, he bought a plot of land in Clare Street, on which he had three substantial houses built. He rented two of them out to tenants, and moved his family into the third, the most spacious corner house. Arthur recalled that the first branch of the co-op in Merthyr had then been opened in their front room, 'rather like the Toad Lane Store of the Rochdale Pioneers. My mother looked after the shop, as well as the family. My father kept the books after he had finished work.'[16] Though not far from Bridge Street, Clare Street was in a better neighbourhood, where James was evidently confident that his investment would prosper. He was part of the rising class of small property speculators in an increasingly integrated European economy, whose continuing expansion was unquestioned by large and small capitalists from Budapest to Birmingham.

James also progressed in the Rechabites, becoming secretary of the Merthyr Tent (branch), a responsible position with status. Because the Rechabites had been expanding in South Wales since the 1880s, James was part of a successful institution, socialising with men of like mind, from a genuine occupational cross section. Though the Rechabites operated as a savings bank and friendly society, their principal object was to promote abstinence from alcohol. They sponsored temperance social activities for adults, and educational ventures for children and young adults, including Junior Tents. Although there is no record of the Horner children becoming junior Rechabites, they were socialised into strict abstinence. When Arthur began boxing training in a gym above a pub, James strongly objected on the grounds that his attendance compromised his own position as Secretary of the Rechabites Merthyr District. Horner recalled a meeting during the 1921 MFGB Lock-Out as being 'the only time I went into a pub in Mardy, because my father was so fanatically opposed to drinking'.[17]

Like so many Victorian working-class families, the Horners had a very large family, seventeen children, of whom only six survived infancy. Lily died in childhood, leaving Annie as the eldest child. Arthur was the eldest son. The other four who survived were Millie, born in 1896, Charles Albert (always known as Albert) born in 1901, Mabel born in 1904 and Frank. The six siblings remained in regular contact throughout their lives. Annie and Arthur had a particularly close relationship. The fact that Arthur remained James' favourite probably contributed to Millie's abiding jealousy of her elder brother. Family stories depicted Arthur as high-spirited, and exhibiting a headstrong, emotional turn. Annie's children remembered her stories about Arthur threatening to leave home if Emily had carried out her threat to banish a young dog whom he had adopted, and also refusing to clean his boots. He apparently also developed his winning manner in early life, since the stories did not finish with his being punished for these transgressions. He enjoyed an affectionate rapport with parents and extended family of maternal grandparents and maternal uncles.

The difference in age between the three eldest and the three youngest children created an emotional distance, from which Albert, Mabel and Frank worshipped Arthur. In adult life, he was their constant protector. Frank and Albert found secure jobs in the 1930s due to his intervention as part of the CPGB's informal job network. Mabel made an unhappy marriage and came to live in London before the war. When Arthur and his wife, Ethel, moved to London in 1947, Mabel probably depended on them for emotional support and financial help.[18]

In 1902, aged eight, Arthur started working after school and at weekends, first as a lather boy in a barber's shop and then delivering for a grocer's shop. In *Incorrigible Rebel* he remembered being 'able to lift a hundredweight sack off the ground on to my shoulder' at age nine, and carrying 'a sack of flour weighing 280 lb', it is evident that he had an early ambition to build up his physical prowess. He recalled swallowing raw eggs from the grocer's warehouse to build up his stamina. His onerous work experience was typical for a boy of his class, though Merthyr probably afforded more varied opportunities for child labour than many English conurbations. In 1908, aged fourteen, having passed the prescribed examination, he became eligible to leave full-time education. However, James was evidently ambitious for him, and enrolled Arthur at the Higher Grade School. After a few months, James, compelled by economic necessity or frustrated by Arthur's indifference to formal study, found him a full-time job at the Goods Yard, looking after the telephone and telegraph.

35

Although his autobiography records no regret at leaving school, he showed little enthusiasm for his new clerical duties. He probably remained absorbed in boxing and soccer, and evidently found it difficult to accept the discipline of being a very junior employee in a highly regulated company. His head-strong, self-willed personality soon collided with its rigid hierarchy. 'One day someone on the telephone line from the General Office in Cardiff ordered me to stand aside. I said, "I'm not going to stand aside." I was reported for insolence, and I had to go to Cardiff to be interviewed by the Goods Manager and the Superintendent of the line ... '. James stood by Arthur, buying him a new suit and accompanying him to Cardiff, where his own exemplary record and competence were undoubtedly the contributory factors in persuading the managers to reprieve his son. Nevertheless, Arthur left the Goods Yard job soon afterwards.

He showed no inclination to embark on training for skilled manual work, which would have yielded significant economic rewards. He may have imbibed some of his father's preference for white-collar work. He was probably discouraged from starting in coalmining by both James and Emily. His maternal grandfather had moved from general labouring into coalmining, and was working a fourteen-hour day. 'Then one Sunday, somebody left a ventilator door open in the Glynmeal Level, and my grandfather, going in at evening to examine the pit, was blown to pieces by an explosion. They collected his remains with a rake, and brought them home in a sack ... My uncle worked in the mines until his back was broken by a fall of roof. Another uncle went nearly blind with nystagmus. I learned very early that there was blood on the coal.'[19]

Like the young Bevin, Arthur moved into the commercial sector, where he found jobs easy to come by before 1914, owing to the dense population of the coalmining and iron and steel communities in East Glamorgan and nearby Western Monmouthshire. He worked as an assistant to Mr John Thomas, a margarine merchant, for a year, and then was employed for a year as a traveller for another margarine merchant, Howells & Co. Between 1911 and 1912, he worked as an assistant for Messrs. Jones & Co., Grocers, in Rhymney.[20] The jobs offered a varied work routine, and social contact with customers. As a salesperson, Arthur had scope to develop his interpersonal skills. He continued, however, to concentrate his attention on leisure activities. Politics and religion were now competing with sport for his spare time, and Merthyr provided exciting opportunities in all three.

There was a professional boxing booth on Plymouth Street, where Arthur was probably a regular attender on Friday and Saturday evenings. Despite his father's objections, he began to work out at the gym above a pub, where he trained with professionals, 'which I wasn't supposed to do strictly according to amateur rules, but I was a punch-bag for some first-class boxers in Merthyr – fellows who were of national standard like Eddie Morgan – fellows who used to come to London to fight, in the National Sporting Club'.[21] He also played in an amateur soccer team, keenly enjoying a full season of fixtures. The high proportion of English immigrants, settled in Merthyr since the eighteenth century, had tilted the leisure pursuits of its boyhood population towards the English game. In common with other dedicated boys, he took training seriously, doing regular work-outs and running.

Horner's youth coincided with an upsurge of interest in politics in Merthyr. In 1905, as part of the general reform of local government, Merthyr was granted a Royal Charter and achieved formal status as a town, with attendant rights to elect a town council. The local capitalists were suitably gratified. Public festivities were organised to celebrate and inaugurate a fountain in the town centre, which Lord Merthyr had commissioned to commemorate the town's elevation. The first elections to Merthyr council were contested by the Conservatives, the Liberals, and the Independent Labour Party, which had put down roots in 1895. The world-wide economic slump, which began in 1893, produced protracted economic distress in South Wales. ILP activists contrasted the starvation conditions of unemployed miners and their families with Socialism, when poverty and hardship would be banished from the earth. By 1898 there were 278 members in the Merthyr branch, and other branches in nearby Aberdare, Merthyr Vale, Penydarren and Troedyrhiw.[22]

The charismatic ILP leader, James Keir Hardie, came to South Wales during the coal dispute in 1898, and held meetings at Penydarren and Troedyrhiw, preaching socialism, 'My cause is Labour's cause – the cause of Humanity – the cause of God ... I first learnt my Socialism in the New Testament where I still find my chief inspiration.'[23] Hardie had been a miner in Ayrshire, where he had played a leading role in establishing mining trade unionism. When a general election was called for October 1900, the trade unionists and ILP activists who comprised the Merthyr Labour Representation Committee decided to nominate him as the Labour candidate for one of the seats in the double constituency of Merthyr boroughs. There were competing claims from two rival local coalmining union leaders and the charismatic engineer, Tom Mann, who had risen to fame during his leadership of the 1889 London Dock Strike. Hardie was eventually selected as the compromise candidate for the Labour cause. He gained a comfortable victory over the second Liberal candidate and served in tandem with the Liberal coalowner, DA Thomas. He remained MP for Merthyr seat in the three following general elections – January 1906, January and December 1910 – until his death in 1915. His success helped ILP candidates contesting local elections in the double constituency. 'Most remarkable of all was the success of all twelve Labour candidates (nearly all miners) in the 1905 municipal elections, and Enoch Morrell, a Welsh-speaking checkweighman ... was elected the first Labour mayor of Merthyr.'[24]

Horner remembered attending Hardie's open-air meetings at Lord Merthyr's fountain, probably during the 1910 campaigns. 'I used to watch him with real hero worship and I would fight any boy who dared to interrupt.' There was high entertainment value in the public appearances of Hardie, Mann and the other orators who made regular lecture tours of South Wales. The collective emotion they generated was comparable to pop concerts today, as indeed were the sermons preached by itinerant evangelists. The intense political atmosphere of two general election campaigns during 1910 may have prompted the sixteen year old Horner to read ILP literature and begin attending their meetings. Welcomed and encouraged by the adult activists, he wrote articles for the weekly paper which Hardie founded, the *Merthyr Pioneer*. '[W]e had a discussion group and I was the youngest member.'[25]

He had also found religion, a mass pursuit in Britain at the time. South Wales had witnessed a spectacular upsurge in 1904 to 1905, when Evan Roberts, the young Welsh evangelist lit up the population with 'a sense of a new social apocalypse, a belief in overwhelming, almost total change'.[26] Literally a thousand flowers bloomed in the form of new chapels founded by the many different nonconformist churches already in the coalfield. Although neither James nor Emily Horner were observant Christians, they did not restrain Millie from becoming a committed member of the Churches of Christ Sunday School at its Plymouth Street chapel, when it opened in 1904. She was joined by Arthur, perhaps soon after leaving school in 1908, apparently curious to find out more about a part of life to which he had hitherto paid little attention.

The Churches of Christ was a small Protestant sect, imported from America, which had arrived in South Wales in 1870. Its most famous British member was David Lloyd George. One of its distinctive features was a reading of the New Testament which involved adult, full immersion baptism out of doors to mark the believer's acceptance into the Churches' communion. It is probably why Horner habitually described himself as having been a Baptist, although the Churches' strict interpretation of the biblical injunction was stricter than most British Baptists who practised adult baptism.[27] The Churches had no professional ministers, viewing evangelising as a collective responsibility. It relied on laymen who were specially trained to preach and carry the message forward. Though placing greater emphasis on Bible reading than the Unitarians or Quakers, the Churches of Christ shared their compassionate approach and focus on inner reflection and spirituality, underpinned by reason.

The most prominent Churches of Christ laymen in Merthyr were the brothers John and Urbane Nicholls, who had a grocery business. They had grown dissatisfied with Congregationalism, and founded their own sect, the Immanuel Mission, before encountering William Webley in 1898. He had been sent back to his native Wales on mission by the Churches of Christ in 1894, and was living in nearby Treharris. It was a true meeting of souls, and the Immanuel Mission congregation was received into the Churches after full immersion baptism in the Taff at Quakers Yard, nine miles from the town centre. '[T]he surrounding woodland re-echoed with hallelujah songs as each candidate rose from the water to begin a new life.' The Churches' history described, 'the courage of the [Merthyr] brethren (*sic*) in going into the open air to proclaim the Gospel of Christ, and marching through the streets singing the songs of Zion'.[28] The consecration of the new Plymouth Street chapel was firm evidence of their evangelising success.

Arthur and Millie were old enough to have been baptised and received into the Churches in 1908 or 1909. They participated in the religious and social life of the Plymouth Street Chapel, although Arthur also made time for his other two avocations. He evidently showed promise as a speaker. His precocious skills may have prompted the Nicholls brothers to propose that the Churches' Training Committee should sponsor him to study with the Reverend Lancelot Oliver in Birmingham. (The Nicholls brothers had employed Arthur before he left school as a delivery boy in their shop in Brecon Road. They may have subsequently taken him back after he left the Railway Goods Yard.) Their influential support secured his place. The Churches' journal, *Bible Advocate*, edited by Oliver, reported that Horner had made a 'stirring speech' at the Churches' South Wales conference, along with William Webley, on 11 October 1912. He departed for Birmingham soon after. The Churches' *Yearbook* for 1913 reported: '[D]uring the year Bro. Oliver has had under his care for personal training four brethren from different parts of the kingdom, viz. Brethren Horner, Lister, McKerlie and Wilson. They all came strongly recommended and stayed about six months each. Differing in temperament and in previous experience, they all made good progress, and should be heard of as giving valuable service.'[29]

Horner is likely to have found it exhilarating to live in Birmingham, Britain's second most populous city. He was intellectually capable, but not committed to being a one hundred per cent dedicated student. He proceeded to explore the conurbation, which provided an abundance of new experiences. There were large-scale engineering factories, and a warren of small workshops, making metal goods of all kinds, as well as a thriving gold-working and jewellery quarter. In November and December 1912, there was a strike at the scalemakers, Avery's, in which the Workers' Union, led by Tom Mann, played a prominent part. Birmingham was also a centre of suffragist activity. Arthur could attend public meetings of all sorts, and sample a variety of rhetorical styles and flourishes, storing the best up for his own future use. He even went to the Town Hall to hear the flamboyant jingo orator, Horatio Bottomley, speaking for the National League.[30]

Trainee evangelists usually studied with the Rev. Oliver for a three months stint, which was extended for a further three months if their progress was satisfactory. Horner duly completed his six months, during which he remembered being taught Greek, theology and public speaking. 'I learned that you should always know how to begin a speech and you should always know how to sit down and close your speech, and in later life ... I have always carried out that lesson'.[31] He returned to Merthyr in March 1913. His performance in Birmingham evidently determined the Churches' deacons to send him further afield to a more testing location, where the Churches were weak and could benefit from his ministering. He went to assist the brethren at the small Ynyshir chapel, founded in 1910, in the Lower Rhondda Fach valley. To support himself, he found work a few miles away, as a haulier for the grocer's shop owned by JD Jones in Ivor Hael, Llwynypia, a substantial pit village in the Lower Rhondda Fawr valley, a mile north of Tonypandy. (The confluence of the Rhondda Fawr (greater Rhondda) and Rhondda Fach (lesser Rhondda) rivers is at Porth, south of Ynyshir. Ten miles further south at Pontypridd, the Rhondda flows into the Taff river.)

At first, Horner continued to live in Merthyr whilst working at Llynypia and ministering at Ynyshir. In 1913 he could have accomplished the eight mile journey between Merthyr and Llwynypia either by walking over two small, but steep, mountain ranges, each rising to over 350 metres, or taking the train along the Taff valley to Pontypridd and changing to the line which ran down the Rhondda valley. (Railways mostly ran north-south, from the coalfields to the coal ports and towns on the Severn Estuary.) Neither option was an easy commute, although energetic young people often walked in the mountains for pleasure and the joys of courtship. In November 1910, during the Cambrian Combine dispute, perhaps accompanied by other ILP members, Horner had walked over the mountains from Merthyr to Tonypandy by night, determined to watch the anticipated confrontation between striking miners and the troops sent in by Winston Churchill on the previous day.[32]

The daily journeys soon induced Arthur to leave home. He probably found lodgings in Ynyshir, a village where most men and boys worked in the adjoining Standard collieries. He never lived in Merthyr again. But he maintained close relations with his parents, making time to go back to Merthyr to see them and also engage in various sporting pursuits. The Churches of Christ chapel in Ynyshir had begun with six foundation members. The chapel secretary wrote to the *Bible Advocate* in October 1913, complimenting the Training Committee on their Birmingham student. He reported that Horner 'is doing good work here, and willing to do his best at all times'.[33] For the next twenty years, until 1933, Horner's life revolved around the steam coalfield of the two Rhondda river valleys.

The Churches of Christ did not demand single-minded devotion from those called to serve it, and Arthur continued to pursue his other two passions with energy and gusto. Although amateur boxing was probably pursued impromptu in the open air by miners, he may have refrained from participating, since the contests involved keen betting, which the Churches deplored. He probably concentrated on soccer, and enjoyed the comradeship of miners in the scratch amateur teams which assembled on a Saturday afternoon. Ynyshir was actually much better provided for in politics than in sport. The Standard collieries had a large, militant lodge of the SWMF, whose more active members regularly convened meetings for the socialist, suffragist and trade union stars touring on the South Wales circuit. Horner may have first met Noah Ablett at a meeting at the Ynyshir Workmen's Hall, at which Ablett would have been the main attraction.

Ablett had grown up in Ynyshir, and had commenced working at the Standard in 1895, aged twelve, with his father and elder brothers. He became a boy preacher, but also joined the ILP in Porth. In 1907, he won an SWMF scholarship to attend a diploma course at Ruskin College in Oxford. The college had been founded in 1899 by American philanthropists in association with leading British trade unionists and co-operators to give working men and women a chance to pursue higher education. The intention was that they would use the knowledge gained to enrich their communities.

Ablett was an outstanding student. On his return from Ruskin in 1909, he was elected checkweighman for one of the two Mardy

collieries, five miles up the Rhondda Fach valley. But he kept his
close union and family ties in Ynyshir. He was a popular speaker
combining a 'sparkling intellect ... [with] impish and acerbic
wit. He liked nothing better than crossing swords with academic
commentators and philosophers'.[34] He continued to be active in
the ILP until 1910, when the Cambrian Combine dispute caused
him to re-think his ideas about the relative importance of parliamentary and party politics compared to union power.

Ablett's intellect and his base in Mardy made him a formidable force inside the SWMF during the Cambrian Combine
dispute. His official position was underpinned by his prominent
role in the Unofficial Reform Committee, a loose grouping of
leading militants who had coalesced in 1910 to ensure that the
SWMF Executive kept to a militant course. (The SWMF had
been founded in 1898, with young militants in the lead. They
adhered to the strategy of new unionism, which aimed to organise all classes of workers, irrespective of skill or seniority.)[35] The
URC's rationale has been frequently described as syndicalist.
Its practical tactics were a development of new unionism. Since
1889 progressive trade unionists in Britain had founded general
and industrial unions, as well as ginger groups inside existing
craft unions to promote mergers and industrial unions. Rather
than rejecting parliament and political parties for principled
and dogmatic reasons, they merely viewed them as an ineffective
means for gaining working-class emancipation.

Ablett became the URC's principal strategist and most influential leader, by virtue of his base in the Rhondda and also his
place on the Federation Executive, to which he was elected just
prior to the Cambrian Combine dispute. His address, 'Is Political
Action Really Necessary' given at the Ynyshir Workmen's Hall in
November 1917, is typical of his argument.

> In politics things were done for the workers; in industrial
> matters they were, from the bottom up, beginning to do
> things for themselves. The weapon of political action
> was a speech, its end hot-air in a gas-house on the way
> to become a dung-heap ... The industrial union did not
> need the backing of a political organisation, therefore
> it was foolish to swim the river to fill the bucket on the
> other side ... .[36]

The URC had lain dormant, however, from 1912. Its leading founders had been elected to full-time union office, and become preoccupied with the day-to-day business of administering a healthy, growing union. The SWMF President and Secretary, William Brace and Tom Richards, were promoting progressive, forward-looking policies inside the Miners' Federation of Great Britain, and there was no enthusiasm in South Walian lodges for continuing to support the URC.

Arthur began travelling to Tonypandy on Sunday afternoons to the Plebs Club and Institute. He heard speakers on a wide variety of topics, feminism and votes for women being amongst the most popular. Prominent supporters of suffragism from outside South Wales who spoke included Minnie Pallister, Tom Mann, Jack Tanner, and Sylvia Pankhurst. But the staple weekly fare consisted of classes, organised more or less formally by the Plebs League, a loose association of socialists committed to education and propagating the socialist word. Ablett came down from Mardy to take his turn in leading them, along with other South Walian luminaries and Ruskin graduates, WF Hay, Noah Rees, George Dolling and Ted Williams. After the formal meetings, participants adjourned to the nearby Aberystwyth restaurant for physical sustenance, socialising and further intellectual refreshment.

Tonypandy had become the common meeting point for socialist and Federation activists from the East Glamorgan and West Monmouthshire valleys in the early 1900s, after the Rhondda Urban District Council had commenced the operation of an electrified tram service serving both Rhondda Fach and Fawr valleys. Activists from towns in adjoining valleys in western Monmouthshire and eastern Glamorgan – Merthyr, Tredegar, Aberfan, for example – making their way to Tonypandy would take the train from their local station either to Porth, the town situated at the convergence of the two Rhondda valleys, or to Pontypridd, a major railway junction some four miles further south. From either town they could catch the municipal tram to Tonypandy. Though the journey required two stages, both train and tram were speedy, reliable in most weathers, and affordable for those in work. Public transport thus facilitated public politics and trade unionism.[37]

Horner had moved away from the Rhondda valleys in 1914, probably because the Churches of Christ elders were worried that his allegiance was waning. He started work as an assistant and traveller at Evan Evans, Grocer, Aberfan, a pit village in the Taff river valley, some five miles south of Merthyr. The Aberfan chapel membership was larger than Ynyshir's, and could provide a stronger anchor for a talented young preacher perceived to be in danger of straying into worldly pursuits. Millie Horner had moved to Aberfan in 1913 to help in the Churches, and Arthur may have found lodgings along with her.[38] But the move failed to curb his secular proclivities. He was increasingly drawn, not only to politics, but also to Ablett and his gospel of industrial unionism.

The outbreak of the war provided an incentive for Ablett and others to resuscitate the URC. Impressed by the upsurge of militancy in the coalfield in July 1915, they were hopeful that its organisational shell could provide the means to push the SWMF Executive further to the left. From the autumn of 1915, URC meetings were convened in an upper room of the Aberystwyth restaurant on Sunday evenings after the Plebs classes had finished. The Rhondda Socialist Society re-appeared at the same time, on the occasion of a conference of the Rhondda ILP chaired by William Phippen. The intense political controversy surrounding the war evidently produced a renewed interest in politics on the part of many activists who had been putting all their energies into trade union activity. Originally founded in August 1912, the RSS resumed regular meetings in the Plebs Club and Institute. It was a catholic institution, encompassing socialists of all sorts, ILP members, SDF members, adherents of the SLP, industrial unionists, and also anarchists.[39]

These developments may have prompted Horner's decision to leave Aberfan in the autumn of 1915 and return to Ynyshir. He started work as a surface worker at the Standard collieries, probably taking up a job vacancy created by the rush of South Wales mineworkers to volunteer for the armed forces at the outbreak of World War I. He kept his wage packets, perhaps as a memento of his first formal association with coalmining. On them his job was listed variously as Tipper, Night Tipper and Night Emptier, all of which involved manhandling the wagons of coal. The principal requirement for this work was physical stamina and strength. His new job made him eligible to join the SWMF, and he began attending meetings of the SWMF Standard lodge. He resumed preaching at the Ynyshir Churches of Christ chapel, but was increasingly drawn into trade union and political activity.

As Horner's contacts with Ablett became more frequent, a strong rapport developed between them. Ablett began to regard Horner, half a generation younger than himself, as his protégé. He had cultivated an habitual interest in the younger generation, being keen to propagate the URC's industrial unionism. Horner was already acquiring a reputation for militancy in the colliery. Probably as a result of Ablett's patronage, the Standard Lodge appointed him as their delegate to the URC meetings on Sunday evenings in Tonypandy. Horner remembered that about forty delegates had regularly attended, including well-known activists WH Mainwaring and Mark Harcombe, and David Phillips from Ferndale.[40] Arthur reported back to the Lodge Committee, and may even have been co-opted as a committee member. Lodge Committee members became his principal companions in Ynyshir, although he continued to travel back to Merthyr to play football and also considered himself a Churches of Christ minister, despite doing little preaching.

With hindsight, the most important event in Horner's brief sojourn in Aberfan was meeting his future wife, Ethel Mary Merrick. Born in Aberfan on 20 September 1895, she was eighteen months younger than Arthur and two or three inches taller. Her parents, Joseph and Martha Merrick, had come to South Wales soon after their marriage in late 1894 from Banwell, a village in Somerset on the edge of the Mendip Hills. When Ethel and Arthur met, her father was working as a mechanic at the nearby Merthyr Vale Colliery. She became a regular customer at the grocer's shop in which he served – perhaps because she was attracted to him. He was evidently inexperienced in chatting up young women. He recalled that when Ethel had made the first move in the grocer's shop, 'I blushed to the roots of my hair'. It was a casual relationship. They merely 'kept company for a time', probably no more than five or six months, with Arthur inviting Ethel to hear him deliver sermons.

Arthur had moved to Ynyshir before they had progressed to the more formal and serious stage of courting. But before he left

Aberfan, he and Ethel had probably progressed from her listening to him preach to their travelling together to Tonypandy to
attend the Plebs Club and Institute. Joseph Merrick died around
the time of Arthur's move, and she was preoccupied with helping with her mother to cope with the bereavement and looking
after her two younger sisters. After her mother re-married, the
family moved to Newport with Martha's new husband, George
Dane, Ethel followed and found work in a shop. Evidently, neither Ethel nor Arthur took the relationship seriously enough to
keep in formal contact with one another. Ethel was an attractive,
magnetic young woman, and may have found Arthur too serious for her taste. Nevertheless, they met again, probably in late
1915, 'quite by accident ... in the street in Tonypandy'.[41]

That Arthur and Ethel would chance to meet one another in
Tonypandy, probably on a Sunday afternoon when they were
each on their ways to the same class or lecture, was entirely predictable. When she found time to resume Sunday afternoon pursuits in Tonypandy, it would have been in the knowledge that she
was likely to encounter Arthur. But Ethel was her own woman.
She had been inspired by the suffragist speakers, and did not
return to Tonypandy merely because she might meet Arthur.

It would have been difficult for Arthur to patronise Ethel,
even if he had been temperamentally inclined to do so. She had
her own clearly-formed interest in the wider world. Her father
had enlisted in the Royal Navy in 1876 at the age of sixteen,
and served as a stoker until his retirement on a Shore Pension
in 1898. She evidently absorbed aspects of his cosmopolitan outlook as a child and adolescent.

Ethel probably also assimilated a visceral contempt for
authority, as a result of her father's experiences on the battle-
ship HMS *Camperdown* in 1893. During naval manoeuvres in the
Mediterranean in June, the responsible officer, Rear Admiral
Markham, had obeyed an order which he knew to be erroneous,
given by the Commander-in-Chief of the Mediterranean Fleet,
Sir George Tryon. Although Markham had queried Tryon's
order, he had carried it out after Tryon had confirmed it. As a
result, the *Camperdown* collided with the HMS *Victoria*, which was
fatally hit and sank almost immediately. Almost every man on
board, including Tryon, drowned; a total of 357 men and boys
were lost. When Merrick left the Navy, he was unlikely to have

retained any residue of deferential respect for authority. It is likely that his experience in the collision radicalised him. Each time he re-told the story to his family, their contempt for the officer class was probably reinforced.[42]

From the outset, Arthur and Ethel regarded one another as equals. He evidently found her emancipated outlook immensely attractive. After meeting again, they quickly progressed to formal courtship. He became emotionally dependent on her, and they began a passionate, companionate relationship. Ethel was apparently as indifferent to the Churches of Christ, as she was enthusiastic about socialism and feminism. Nevertheless, she acquiesced in his ultimatum, 'Ethel, it's finished unless you get baptized [by full immersion]'. As a result of shrewd observation, she may have anticipated that his commitment to the Churches was waning. He recalled: 'She remembers thinking how daft she was to agree ... Ethel fixed up to be baptized at a week-day service, and I found the date coincided with a football match I had promised to play at Merthyr. I went to the match, while she was baptized.' Arthur and Ethel were married by E Roderick Jones, a Calvinistic Methodist minister, in Pontypridd on 8 June 1916.[43] She then joined Arthur at his lodgings at 2 Cross Street, Ynyshir. It was typical of Ethel's warm sociability that their landlady became a good friend, to whom they were able to turn to in 1940, after being bombed out in Cardiff.

Ablett had persuaded Horner to apply in the winter of 1915 for one of the scholarship places provided by the SWMF for the Central Labour College in London. Arthur Cook, an exact contemporary of Ablett, working at the small Coedcae pit in the Lewis-Merthyr collieries not far from Ynyshir, had won the first scholarship to the CLC given by the SWMF Pontypridd and Rhondda District in October 1911, probably with Ablett's support. From the CLC's foundation in 1909, he had kept a weather eye open for Rhondda miners who could fill the scholarship places. (He had been in the forefront of the successful drive to persuade the SWMF to support the establishment of a more class-conscious, political rival to Ruskin. He had 'toured the coalfield ... to persuade SWMF districts to subscribe to the CLC with great success.'[44])

Ablett recognised Horner's quick intelligence, and presumed that he would develop into an industrious student, eager to acquire greater knowledge of history, politics and economics. He stressed the CLC's comparative merits in providing a rigorous materialist training, in contrast to Ruskin, and evidently expected great things from Horner's return. Horner duly secured the scholarship, and plans were made for him to enrol at the CLC in September 1916. Nevertheless, Horner reneged at the last minute, using his marriage as justification. Ablett regarded Horner's change of mind as a betrayal,[45] though friendly relations between the two men were re-established sometime in 1917.

Ethel could certainly have accompanied Arthur. Though the CLC and Ruskin were both residential, married students frequently arranged for their wives to take lodgings near them. The wives usually found work to support themselves and provide a supplement for their husbands' stipends. Although there is no record of Ethel's views, it is likely that this plucky young woman would have been willing to live in London and see the wider world at first-hand. Horner never expressed any regret about not taking up his CLC scholarship. Despite his mental agility and evident ability, he remained indifferent to the attractions of pure knowledge, and only undertook sustained intellectual effort during periods of physical confinement in gaol.

His indifference was a stark contrast to the attitude of his contemporary SWMF activists, who attached great significance to having completed a rigorous course of higher education. (They included Bryn Roberts, Frank Hodges, WH Mainwaring, SO Davies, Arthur Jenkins, Jim Griffiths, George Daggar, WJ Saddler, Oliver Harris, Ness Edwards and Aneurin Bevan.) But Horner's decision not to pursue full-time higher education is likely to have had two sources.

Firstly, the Churches of Christ deacons would have regarded his attendance at the CLC as a betrayal of his religious commitment, and he was not yet prepared to make an irrevocable break with his Christian calling and embrace materialism, the alternative that the CLC were offering. He had continued to hold responsible positions inside the Churches, acting as Recording Secretary to their plenary South Wales Conference, and chairing the meeting held in October 1915. He was still preaching regularly, and played an active part on the pacifist side in the debate going on inside the Churches about whether its members, along with other Christians, should oppose the war and

49

conscription. In September 1915, he contributed two articles to the *Merthyr Pioneer* entitled 'Christianity and Socialism'. They were scrupulously even-handed, and it would have been difficult to conclude from the texts whether Horner was any longer an observant Christian.[46] He eventually drifted out of his ministry, however, in the year after his marriage. The last evidence of his formal involvement was in Easter 1916, when he again chaired the meeting of the Churches Plenary South Wales Conference. He also joined four other members of the Ynyshir Chapel in signing a resolution against compulsory conscription that was sent to the conference.[47] Although he took no further part in the Churches' institutional activity, neither he nor Ethel showed any hostility towards Christianity.[48] His rhetoric and cultural references continued to be redolent of religiosity until 1928 to 1929.

Secondly, Horner had discovered during his six months in Birmingham that he was no swot. Though capable of mastering any of the intellectual disciplines to which Lancelot Oliver exposed him, he gained neither pleasure nor fulfilment from sustained study. At Plebs League classes he listened to lectures about Marx and Engels, and digested the simple catechisms which explained *Das Kapital* and Dietzgen (the prolific German socialist auto-didact whose exposition of vulgar materialism attracted British working-class intellectuals, who regarded Protestant spirituality as the principal ideological enemy). Horner, however, was more interested in reading about current politics and political argument – such as HN Brailsford's compelling denunciation of national capitalist rivalries, *The War of Steel and Gold*, published in May 1914.[49] Unlike some of his working-class contemporaries, notably Aneurin Bevan, Arthur Jenkins, and Johnnie Campbell, Horner did not aspire to become an intellectual. He viewed himself as a man of action, for whom knowledge and intellectual training were a pragmatic acquisition, to enable him to analyse his experience and act as a guide to his future conduct.

Chapter 3

The Young Man

Arthur and Ethel Horner began their married life as the pace of political life in the Rhondda was quickening. Miners and union officials in the South Wales coalfield had divided views about World War I, and the divisions polarised as the conflict settled into a war of attrition. In the early months of the war, large numbers of enthusiastic South Wales miners had volunteered, and prominent officials had resigned their union jobs to devote themselves to military recruiting.[50]

Other miners opposed the war, and this led to bitter disagreements within the union. In these difficult circumstances, the remaining officials and the Executive strove manfully to avoid a fatal fracture inside the Federation. The union had to contend with pressures on production levels, as well as differing attitudes to the war. Thus there was an official, but illegal, coalfield strike in July 1915, which eventually yielded significant advances in wages and conditions, to counter continuing inflation. This success reflected the union's skilful handling of the dispute. Under duress, South Wales coalowners had conceded an attendance bonus of an additional shift payment for daywagemen working on afternoons and night shift when they worked five consecutive days. The bonus, known as 'six for five', was viewed as essential to counter the impact of the labour shortage caused by the high numbers of South Wales coalminers volunteering for the armed forces, and the Royal Navy's insatiable demand for South Wales steam coal.

Although Ablett was the only member of the SWMF Executive who took a consistent anti-war position, it was not merely left-wing socialists who opposed the war. A vigorous pacifist tradition existed in nonconformist churches throughout Britain; in Wales, its expression was well-organised and articulate.

The introduction of conscription had been widely anticipated since the autumn of 1915. Prime Minister Asquith was reluctant to grasp the nettle, however, and conscription was not finally introduced until January 1916 for single men, and May 1916 for married men. Because the war effort required British coal, miners were exempted until January 1917, when the army's demand for men had further intensified. But the first 20,000 miners conscripted were not South Walians. The government's acute nervousness about the SWMF's potential militancy, and the Navy's demand for steam coal, combined to postpone the decision to implement the call-up there.[51] Nevertheless, both pacifist and political wings of the anti-war movement remained vigilant. The URC organised a series of public meetings, attended by huge crowds.

Arthur Cook and George Dolling took leading roles in the Rhondda in this period. Cook lived in Trehafod, and was a frequent speaker at Ynyshir public meetings. He had left Coedcae and started in the larger Hafod pit, also part of the Lewis-Merthyr company's collieries, and with a labour catchment area bordering on the Standard colliery, where Dolling and Horner worked. In early 1917 there was further reason for debate and excitement. The unexpected collapse of the Tsarist state in Russia in February 1917, followed by the installation of a provisional government committed to constitutional democracy, caused great elation amongst European liberals and socialists. Pro-war liberals and socialists were convinced that a reinvigorated Russia would tip the balance decisively against the Germans, while anti-war socialists pointed to the opposition to the war inside the soviets, the Russian name for the new representative institutions, workers' and soldiers' councils, which had provided the motor force of the revolution.

It was during this period of heightened emotion and expectation that Horner's and Cook's acquaintance ripened into close friendship. Though Arthur James Cook was eleven years older than Arthur Lewis Horner, and had attended the CLC, he never treated the younger man as either protégé or pupil. They were best friends and fellow men of action. Horner later described Cook as 'probably the best agitator I ever knew', and 'a man with a sense of adventure'. Cook had been socialised into Baptism in Somerset by his devout mother. Cook had continued the association on migrating to South Wales, becoming a lay preacher and Sunday School teacher. But when challenged by Baptist elders around 1907 to choose between the chapel and his union and ILP activities, he had abandoned his institutional connection with Christianity. Cook's memories of his break with Baptism may have influenced Horner eleven years later, when he was agonising about his own link with the Churches of Christ. He had begun to choose anti-war subjects for his sermons. Ynyshir deacons who had sons in the armed forces organised counter-meetings to refute his arguments. Horner refused their demand to vet his sermons, 'and that led to quite a difference'.[52] However the fact that Cook had remained an observant teetotal[53] made it easier for Horner to keep faith with his father and continue his own abstention from alcohol.

As the two men spent increasing amounts of time together, Cook became passionately fond of Ethel. He was a deeply emotional man, but his wife, Annie, had never shared his interest in politics or union matters. Ethel's interest in both, and her open-hearted affectionate manner, were welcome solace for Cook as his relationship with Annie came under increasing strain.[54]

Cook enlisted Horner's help when he decided to take a leading role in reviving the Rhondda Socialist Society. They both recognised that the RSS provided an excellent platform from which to develop opposition to conscription and the war. Horner became the Society's Secretary; he arranged meetings and invited speakers with exemplary efficiency. And he also became more active in union activity. In December 1916 he was arraigned before the Porth Police Court for assaulting another miner at the pit head and knocking out several of his teeth. He escaped comparatively lightly, paying costs and being bound over for 12 months, perhaps because the stipendiary magistrate was concerned not to exacerbate an already tense atmosphere at the colliery.[55]

As a novice at the colliery, Horner was at the end of a seniority queue for the best-paid mining job, working as a hewer or collier at the coalface. British colliers were paid by the weight of the coal they hewed or dug out from the coal seams. In South Wales during the war, if they were competent, strong, and working good seams, their earnings were very high. Horner's job as a coaltipper involved hard physical labour, but was not well-paid. Nevertheless, he occupied a strategic position as far as the Lodge committee was concerned. '[I]f I stopped tipping the coal, within a very short time nobody could work at all. If the men wanted to strike, they had only to tell me to stop working and the strike became effective almost at once.' But having observed his willingness to stop the pit at times of industrial conflict, management resolved to rid themselves of this young agitator. They laid off the entire nightshift in order to accomplish his removal, so as not to lay themselves open to a charge of having victimised him.

Horner was now not only out of work; he also found himself on a coalfield blacklist. Using a false name, Arthur Hornet, he was taken on at the Bertie pit, a Lewis-Merthyr colliery, but a manager who knew him by sight flushed him out. Cook, who had become chairman of the Lewis-Merthyr Lodges Joint Committee, then called a strike which succeeded in winning his re-employment. Nevertheless, he recalled that: '[The owners] had their own back by forcing him to work in the intake airway on the main and forbidding him to go beyond the point where the airway split. He was thus unable to contact the rest of the men "to spread subversion" and also perishing cold and on afternoons permanently.'[56]

Political events compensated for Horner's frustration as a workplace militant. Over the summer a conflict unfolded in the Russian capital between the two centres of power, the official provisional government, now led by right-wing social democrats, and the de facto national network of soviets led by both groupuscules of the left-wing social democrats, the Mensheviks and Bolsheviks. Events in Petrograd were watched with great excitement by all European socialists. A national conference was held in Leeds on 3 June 1917 to discuss the prospect of British workers' councils. Chaired by the MFGB President, Robert Smillie, and attended by 1150 delegates, including most leading lights of the labour movement, the conference endorsed the demand for councils in Britain, viewing them as the embodiment of workplace democracy.

Although Leeds delegates had agreed to organise regional conferences, the South Walian conference, convened in the Elysium Hall, Swansea, on 29 July 1917, was one of the few which actually took place. This was because there was little or no sense of grievance amongst British workers about autocratic bosses in comparison with either Russia or Germany. In practice, works committees in engineering factories had greatly increased their power during the war, because the government had compelled engineering employers to negotiate about piece-work prices, and about working conditions, with the trade union shop stewards serving on them. In coalmining, piece-work bargaining had been well developed before 1914, usually undertaken on faceworkers' behalf by the colliery checkweighman. After the government had assumed control of coalmining in December 1916, colliery absenteeism committees were formed, on which lodge representatives sat alongside employers. This experiment in joint control proved problematic for the union men, however, most of whom were reluctant to exercise discipline over fellow workers.[57]

The fact that South Walian socialists found the time and energy to organise a conference was evidence of their continuing interest in new, revolutionary ideas. As RSS secretary, Horner had arranged warm-up meetings for the conference earlier in July in Ynyshir and Porth. And Cook and Ablett spoke with Tom Mann, Sylvia Pankhurst and Minnie Pallister, who had travelled down from London to fan the embers of anti-conscription agitation, which they hoped might kindle a British-wide resistance to the war. But although they succeeded in encouraging anti-war activists, the meetings produced a stronger response from the more numerous pro-war side.

The Swansea conference was the scene of a full-scale set-piece battle. The Glamorgan Chief Constable, Lionel Lindsay, allowed 500 pro-war activists to force their way into the hall, with 'sticks, flag-poles and a motley assortment of other weapons'. Many of the 200 anti-war conference delegates gave a good account of themselves, leaving the conference floor and seizing stair railings on their way up to the gallery to confront the pro-war party. Horner took the offensive, armed only with his fists. Dolling, a former army sergeant physical training instructor, saved him from serious injury by interposing himself between Horner and his attackers. Horner was nimble enough to vault down from the gallery onto the conference floor. Newspaper reports stated that he ' ... had his teeth punched out of his head and his eye and upper face badly bruised ... '[58]

The fracas became notorious throughout the coalfield. The conference failed to produce any concrete result, but anti-war activists were bucked up by their battle with the jingoes. The pro-war invaders may have disrupted the conference, but they had signally failed to subdue anti-war delegates' spirits. Dolling and Horner became local heroes inside the RSS. Unbowed, Horner organised another round of well-attended anti-war meetings in August. At the Ynyshir Workmen's Hall, 1000 people listened to the speakers and unanimously adopted a resolution calling for the immediate cessation of hostilities, with no annexations or indemnities. The *Merthyr Pioneer* reporter noted, '[T]hree cheers for Russia were given with such force and volume, as I believe have never been heard in this town before.'[59]

During 1916, when Tom Mann had spoken at Ynyshir Working Men's Hall, Horner had taken the opportunity to initiate a friendship with him. He admired Mann, the quintessential man of action whose courage and audacity in leading industrial conflict had made British trade unions more powerful and democratic. Mann was evidently touched, and responded by accepting an invitation to speak in August 1917, at the Ferndale Hall and the skating rink in Porth, on the Eight Hour Day and problems of demobilisation and peace by negotiation.[60] Nevertheless, the South Wales coalfield remained quiescent throughout the autumn.

In Russia, the Provisional Government lost its hold over Petrograd and Moscow in October. The Bolshevik wing of the social democrats led a successful bid to seize state power on behalf of the Workers' and Soldiers' Soviets. They met surprisingly little resistance, and proclaimed the events a genuine, proletarian revolution.

The British war cabinet was determined to deal summarily with any attempts to emulate the Bolsheviks. In South Wales, the local forces of law and order responded by seeking exemplary convictions under the Defence of the Realm Act. The police began attending URC and RSS meetings and conferences, making notes of the speakers and taking the names and addresses of those present. In December 1917, Chief Constable Lindsay 'urged the military authorities in Cardiff to sanction the prosecution of Cook, George Dolling and Arthur Horner from Ynyshir'.[61] In January 1918, when the Home Office conscripted a fresh draft of 50,000 more miners, men from the South Wales coalfield were finally included. The URC responded by a demand for a coalfield strike against conscription. The SWMF General Secretary, Tom Richards, exerted himself to minimise the effect of the URC offensive. He issued a 'Letter of Warning' to Federation members, explaining that there was no longer any reason for the URC's existence since the SWMF was now run along thoroughly democratic lines.[62] The Federation Executive called a coalfield ballot on the question of a coalfield strike, which produced a decisive vote – 98,948 to 28,903 – against industrial action. Conscription proceeded without major incident.[63]

Cook and Dolling were arrested in March 1918, and tried for making statements likely to cause disaffection. Cook was convicted. But the case against Dolling collapsed. He had chosen his words very carefully at public meetings, and made no explicit incitement to resist conscription.

By the time Horner's call-up papers were delivered to his lodgings in Ynyshir, he had disappeared. RSS and ILP comrades had prepared a new identity for him in Mardy, a large pit village ten miles further up the Rhondda Fach valley. Mardy was socially, economically and physically discreet from the dense lower Rhondda Fach cluster of coalfield villages and collieries, including Ynyshir.[64] Its comparative isolation enabled Horner to use someone else's National Registration Card, exempting him from conscription by virtue of his occupation as a coalminer, and pass himself as Arthur Jones from Llangyfelach. (Mrs Tommy Knight from Barry, whose husband was a witness at the Horners' wedding, prepared the necessary alterations on the card.)

Arthur Horner, alias Arthur Jones, was taken on the night-shift as a coal tipper at one of the pits. Although lodge activists were drawn into the secret of his identity, they kept it secure. He lodged in James Street, across the road from the SWMF Mardy Lodge Committee members, Charlie Jones and Ted Williams. He participated in lodge activities, attending meetings and casting his vote for Ted Williams in the ballot for checkweighman for Nos. 3 and 4 pits, when Noah Ablett left to become Federation Agent in the Merthyr District.

Horner could probably have remained safe in Mardy until the Armistice was declared in November 1918. But he chafed at the concealment required. There was no prospect of participating in public politics, and he was even afraid to do his own shopping. He was pining for Ethel, who dared not travel to Mardy in case the police Special Branch followed her. The couple met clandestinely on the mountains above Tylorstown, halfway between Mardy and Ynyshir. Although they appreciated the spectacular view, it was a very cold winter, and serious physical contact had its discomforts.

Charlie Jones remembered: 'One night he [Arthur] announced he wasn't going to work but going down to Ynyshir to see Mrs. Horner and would then give himself up.'[65] But he did not plan to go peacefully. J Walton Newbold, the ILP leader, was booked to speak at Ynyshir about the Irish nationalist cause, probably on a Sunday afternoon in mid-March 1917, to commemorate the impending first anniversary of the Dublin Easter Rising and the death of James Connolly, the only martyred leader who had been a socialist as well as an Irish nationalist. Horner chaired the meeting, and expected to be apprehended by the police Special Branch men attending it. He hoped to precipitate a political confrontation, if not a physical riot. The meeting finished without incident, however; the police present may have been unwilling to act without orders. So Horner went home with Ethel, and later that night decided to flee to Ireland. (Bill Mainwaring, the anarchist not the URC leader, had evidently been in the audience, and spontaneously offered to arrange Horner's sea passage to Dublin.) The next morning Horner accompanied Newbold to the ILP and Federation activist Sam Fisher's house in Wattsville, western Monmouthshire, where Newbold had been staying. About a week later, Sam 'walked down the canal bank with Arthur to Newport ... they went to Bristol after and he got on a boat to Ireland'.[66]

Horner's flight from conscription was hardly unique. By early 1918 it was evident that being drafted for active service meant terrible hardship and suffering at the very least. High casualty rates had produced pervasive, collective war weariness. Pacifism and anti-war feeling was particularly strong in South Wales. The war cabinet had bowed to expediency with regard to Ireland and decided not to introduce conscription there. Consequently, ad hoc clandestine networks, mainly operated by the No Conscription Fellowship, assisted young British men to flee to Ireland, where they were provided with false papers giving them an Irish identity. They could then go back to Britain, and find work, typically in a London war factory where anonymity was easy to preserve. Geography made it comparatively easy for Welsh refuseniks to get to Ireland.

But having arrived safely in Ireland, Horner decided not to come back to Britain. He joined the Irish Citizens' Army instead. He was not the only draft dodger who enlisted in this workers' militia, which had been organised in November 1913 by Connolly and James Larkin to augment the Irish Transport and General Workers' Union forces during the protracted strikes and lock-outs that had been shaking Dublin since August. The example of the Ulster Protestant Volunteers, who had recently armed themselves to resist Home Rule, was very much in their minds. When Jack White, an Ulster Protestant and professional soldier, offered his services, they accepted, recognising that militarisation of their forces would be a powerful propaganda weapon, as well as acting as a deterrent against physical attack from the Royal Irish Constabulary. Sean O'Casey, a young ITGWU militant, became its secretary. When Britain declared war on Germany and Austria-Hungary in July 1914, Connolly had seized the opportunity to harass the Empire from the rear, concluding an alliance with radical nationalist political leaders in Sinn Fein to demand Irish independence. Although he merged the Citizens' Army into the nascent Irish Republican Army, he understood its importance as a trade union institution, and retained its separate identity and formal connection to the ITGWU. The association with Sinn Fein re-established the Citizens' Army as a serious force; 211 of its members took part in the Easter rising, eleven of whom were killed.[67]

South Walian socialists knew about the Army because Jack White had addressed meetings in South Wales soon after the Easter Rising in March 1916. Evidently impressed by the illegal SWMF strike in July 1915, he had called on South Wales miners to strike again to demand clemency for Connolly and set an example for other British workers to follow. (Horner may even have booked him to speak for the RSS.) White's immediate reward had been arrest, trial and three months in Swansea gaol. But his description of the Citizens' Army had impressed militant listeners.

Horner was accepted by the Citizens' Army, and given another new identity. He took on the identity of Jack O'Brien, a recently deceased young man from County Longford in the Midlands, whose family had donated their son's papers for the nationalist cause. Arthur explained his foreign accent by inventing a period of work in America. But even though he was ready and willing to fight British imperialism, his six months in Dublin were mostly peaceful. The insurrection which Connolly had hoped the Easter Rising would unleash had not occurred, and life had returned to comparative normality with surprising rapidity. The British government felt sufficiently secure by Christmas 1916 to return the Sinn Fein/Citizens' Army leaders, who had been interned in North Wales to Ireland, where they were allowed to remain, with no restrictions being placed on their civil liberty.

By the summer of 1918, most of the Irish Catholic population were preoccupied by the possibility that conscription might be extended to Ireland; they were not interested in opposition to the war or support for national independence. After the South Wales coalfield, Ireland was the last remaining pool of available young men. Although the government were hoping to avoid the potential incendiary of conscription in Ireland, they used the Defence of the Realm Act, just as they were doing in South Wales and on the Clyde, to effect exemplary arrests and convictions of men and women whom they believed to be fomenting disaffection.

The Citizens' Army helped Horner to find accommodation and work. He obtained and left two jobs in quick succession, as a gardener and a window cleaner. He finally settled as a packer for wholesale chemists in the city centre. In *Incorrigible Rebel*, he recalled having recruited fellow workers into the ITGWU, whilst remaining notably vague about his military activities. Nevertheless, he hinted to Frankenberg in strictest confidence that he had been engaged in serious covert military actions.[68] It is unlikely that the Citizens' Army was drilling openly during this time, but Horner is likely to have been involved in night exercises and manoeuvres. During his leisure time, he probably participated in discussions after public meetings with union activists and Sinn Fein members.

Although he was an avid observer of his new surroundings, his 'thoughts in Dublin were much more in Ynyshir with Ethel', who had been four months pregnant when he absconded. When she gave birth to their daughter on 28 June 1918, his home-sickness became overwhelming. The couple had been com-municating by letters, enclosed in other letters which they had sent to third parties, including the Fishers in Wattsville. Arthur learned of Ethel's safe delivery via this circuitous method. He wrote back asking her to name the girl Voltairine, at the sug-gestion of one of his Army comrades. Voltairine de Cleyre, the American anarchist and feminist, had been named in honour of Voltaire by her French socialist father. She had died in 1912. Ethel evidently agreed that their daughter should bear the unu-sual name. (Arthur and Ethel may have known about de Cleyre by repute, through talking to older socialists who had heard her speak on one of her two European lecture tours. Her topics were American anarchism, the woman question, and anarchism and the labour question.) [69]

Arthur now determined to take the risk of being apprehended and made plans to slip back to Wales to see mother and child. The Citizens' Army released him. Having no urgent need of men, their acceptance and sponsorship of political refugees from Britain was an act of solidarity, without immediate practi-cal benefit to the Irish cause.

Horner boarded the ferry at Dun Laoghaire harbour with a case full of anti-war leaflets. His lack of circumspection was fool-hardy: by this point in the war, police surveillance had become proficient. He was arrested when the ferry docked at Holyhead in North Wales, along with two other South Walian miners, Frank and George Phippen, brothers from 'an ILP family in Pentre, Rhondda. The brothers had fled to Ireland with two friends and made contact with the No Conscription Fellowship. Having been furnished with false papers, they were making the first leg of the journey back to Britain to take up jobs at a war factory in Bermondsey, South London.[70]

The three men were taken to the nearest army base, the Wrexham barracks of the Royal Welch Fusiliers, and court-mar-tialled for evading conscription. Sentenced to six-months' hard labour, they served their sentences at Wormwood Scrubs Gaol in West London. On 10 August 1918, the *Merthyr Pioneer* car-ried Horner's speech at the trial under the headline, 'Arthur Lewis Horner, Well-Known Rhondda Socialist Court-martialled for Refusing to Obey Military Orders'. The text had been smuggled out of the Wrexham barracks, probably through the good offices of the North Wales mining union activists who had taken the three prisoners books and food parcels. Its rhetoric reflected Horner's Churches of Christ training, being logically and concisely developed, with a strong moral thread running through its main argument.

> I have no intention either now or in the future, of becoming a soldier in any army whose sole object is to carry out the behests of a privileged and exploiting class. I have taken up this attitude not out of any spirit of bravado, or because I seek martyrdom, but because I know the army in every country to be the means used to crush the rightful aspirations of the class to which I belong ... This War is the rational climax to the trade war which has been so bitterly waged between the capitalists of all highly developed industrial countries for years past, and especially between England and Germany ... .
>
> I live alone to destroy the system, the cause of so much sorrow and misery to my class, and wait for the awakening of the workers of the world to a true understanding of their interests ... Therefore gentlemen it should be clear to you that my conscience of these things has erected an insuperable barrier to the exclusion of any plans which have for its aim the transforming of me into a soldier, in any capitalistic army.

Wormwood Scrubs was full of other refuseniks. Horner knew some of them from South Wales, and quickly made friends with others. Although the prison regime was harsh, Horner's physical condition was excellent, and he continued to look after his body with the meticulous care of a keen amateur athlete. WJ Davies, an ILP member from Aberdare who met him in the Scrubs, recalled that Arthur and Tom Thomas, from Hirwaun, had volunteered for labouring duties in the prison garden, from whence they ate carrots to supplement the meagre prison diet. Horner's mental state was less robust. In early September, he received news of his maternal grandmother's death. His grief was evidently compounded by the physical distance separating him from his family, and the fact that being a draft dodger had prevented him from seeing his grandmother during her last, protracted illness. Allowed to write a special letter to his parents, he confided that during the last few weeks he had thought often about 'dear generous Granny'. He had resolved 'to do much more for her in the future, than was done for her in the past ... I am sorry as I think of my childhood days when always she was glad to see me and shield me from the consequences of my ...' The end of the letter is torn, but evidently refers to his boyhood hot-headed, self-willed behaviour. He may have been reflecting on the folly of his adult decision, taken in hot blood, to return to Britain. He was still pining for Ethel and a sight of Voltairine.[71]

But Horner was determined to remain true to his conscience above all else. On 11 November 1918, when the Armistice came into effect, the Conscription Act ceased to operate. The Home Office freed all draft dodging prisoners in a pragmatic attempt to defuse a potentially explosive situation. They were then immediately sent before another military tribunal, from whence, providing they apologised for evading military service, they were discharged unconditionally from further military obligations. WJ Davies remembered asking Arthur what he should do at the Tribunal when they met each other in the Exercise Yard. Davies was not sorry to have evaded the draft, and was agonising about whether he should perjure himself. Horner advised him to say he was sorry, because he could do more for the cause outside than in gaol.[72] Horner himself was not given the opportunity to perform this de facto contrition. Probably because of the publicity which his trial speech had received, when he walked out of Wormwood Scrubs a sergeant in the military police was waiting to re-apprehend him. Horner received the news that he had been transferred from the Royal Welch Fusiliers to the Fourth Battalion of the Welsh Regiment, and the sergeant was there to transport him to that regiment's barracks at Llanon, ten miles south of Aberystwyth.

Arthur's father was also waiting outside Wormwood Scrubs on the morning of his son's release. Having watched him being re-arrested, James Horner exercised his ingenuity, organisational skills and knowledge of train timetables to mitigate Arthur's sorry plight. He arranged an illegal meeting between Arthur and Ethel at Cardiff station, where he knew Arthur and the ser-

ARTHUR HORNER: A POLITICAL BIOGRAPHY

geant would have to change trains. Ethel's response on receiving her father-in-law's telegram about Arthur's stop-over in Cardiff was to organise a political demonstration. Her determination to transform her meeting with Arthur into a public, political occasion was strong evidence of her political commitment and creative energy. Probably leaving Voltairine with their landlady in Ynyshir, she travelled down to Cardiff station with fifty or sixty miners, 'some of them with black faces and working clothes because they did not have time to bath or change'. On receipt of a pound from James, and Arthur's pledge not to abscond, the sergeant disappeared. After his exit, the group proceeded on a scratch march through the streets singing the *Red Flag*. They stayed with Arthur until they had to catch the last train back to Ynyshir.

Having arrived at Llanon Barracks without further incident, Arthur spent time talking to the serving soldiers whom he encountered during his detention about the likelihood of their having to fight in a war of intervention against Soviet Russia. His subversive agitation must have contributed to the heavy sentence of two years imprisonment he received when court-martialled for continuing to refuse to do military service. He was sent to Carmarthen Gaol, where his fellow prisoners were 'mainly conscientious objectors or soldiers and sailors who had been convicted for being absent without leave or some other crime against military law'. In March 1919 Ethel and his mother visited. They brought the nine months old Voltairine, already being called by her lifelong diminutive, Vol, to finally meet her father. Though he disagreed with Arthur's reasons, James Horner strongly supported his son's right to opt out of military service. He provided not only psychologically important emotional support, but probably also financial help for Ethel.[73]

Meanwhile, socialists and Federation militants in the Rhondda orchestrated a groundswell of support for Horner. In Mardy, a stratagem emerged to secure his early release. Having won the election to replace Frank Hodges as SWMF agent for the neighbouring Garw valley, Ted Williams had left his job as checkweighman for the No. 3 and 4 pits at Mardy colliery. (Hodges had been elected the first full-time secretary of the MFGB, and was establishing the union's office in London.) Charlie Jones and three other lodge activists, Tom Thomas, Bob Thomas, and

Dan Williams, nominated Horner to fill the resulting vacancy, and organised a campaign to get him elected.

Being a checkweighman was a highly desirable position for a young militant with a growing family. A checkweighman's job was to oversee the weighing and sorting of the tubs of coal sent to the surface by the hewers, to prevent the colliery management falsifying either the weight of the coal or the amount which was saleable (being the right size and not dross or stone). Wages and working conditions were good, and employment reasonably secure.[74] Horner's Mardy campaign committee successfully lobbied Tom Richards, who used his influence as Privy Councillor with the Home Secretary. Richards interceded on Horner's behalf, and not only to avoid conflict between Federation officials and the Mardy Lodge. He recognised Horner's potential as a future leader, and was keen to encourage such a promising young man. The Home Secretary responded to this pressure, anxious to avoid unnecessary friction in the troublesome coalfield. Horner was allowed to compose and send off his application for the vacancy.

Horner's backers staged a high profile campaign. They secured other supporters, including Alderman Theo Griffiths and Dai Lloyd Davies, who was checkweighman for the No. 1 and No. 2 pits and Chairman of the Mardy Lodge. Dai Lloyd had worked at Mardy since his youth, and was well respected amongst all shades of political opinion in the lodge. A native Welsh speaker, he had abandoned his youthful vocation as a lay preacher for left-wing socialism. He was an influential voice in the contest, in which Horner's status as a political prisoner was not necessarily an asset. The vacancy had attracted a strong field of candidates, and none of the other militants offered to retire from the contest in Horner's favour. Horner recalled that his other left-wing opponents included WJ Hewlett from Abertillery, Charlie Gibbons and WF Hay. Horner's time in Mardy had been fleeting and furtive; and as Arthur Jones, he had not had the opportunity to establish himself as a strong union man who could be relied upon to fight the collier's corner. But another important boost was Ablett's deputising for Horner at the meeting where the candidates presented themselves.[75]

The Federation used the alternative vote system, because it was more democratic than the first-past-the-post system in the typically large fields of men contesting for union positions. Candidates receiving the fewest votes were eliminated in successive ballots, until someone emerged winning a clear majority of the votes. Horner's left-wing opponents were eliminated in the early ballots, evidence of the effective campaign conducted by Ablett and his Mardy supporters. He was contesting against pro-war candidates in the final ballot. To his surprise, he was told that it was the vote of the returned servicemen which decided the result. Soldiers' visceral reaction against the war, which had precipitated revolution in Russia and Germany and mutiny in France, also determined Horner's election in Mardy.

The Mardy Lodge Committee met on 29 April 1919 to receive the ballot result, and duly declared Horner elected. Charlie Jones sent three telegrams announcing his victory, to Ethel, Tom Richards and Horner himself in Carmarthen Gaol. The Lodge General Meeting endorsed Horner on 1 May, and sent their chairman and secretary to notify the colliery general manager of the new checkweighman's identity.[76] The meeting also received a deputation, probably consisting of Ted Williams and Ablett, and accepted their proposition that the Lodge should pledge to take action to gain Horner's release from gaol. The action suggested was calculated to pressurise Richards and Brace to apply more pressure on the Home Office.

Charlie Jones' telegram, saying 'Come – the job is yours', was brought to Horner along with his supper. He had already prepared his own plan of action. Emulating the militant pre-war suffragettes, he immediately embarked on a hunger and thirst strike. This drastic step meant that it would only be a few days before he died of dehydration, and the Home Office would therefore have to move quickly in deciding whether to release him or let him die and create a martyr. He may have told other draft resisters in the prison with him about his intentions. Six of them, including Iorrie Thomas, who was elected MP for Rhondda West in 1950, joined him in refusing food and water to gain their own release. They soon weakened, but Horner's will power was stronger. He concentrated on dramatising his condition in order to impress the prison doctor. On the sixth day, the doctor concluded that he was going mad. Horner remembered, 'I was in a sort of coma, but with my mind remarkably clear.' Charlie Jones remembered that funeral arrangements were being made for him, and that the prison governor had sent for his parents and Ethel.

The combined lobbying of Richards and Brace, and the probability that Horner would achieve his own martyrdom, proved effective. He was offered the prospect of release if he ate and drank. Horner had prepared tactics for this eventuality. Having taken some bread and milk, he told his warders that he would resume fasting the following morning unless he was sent home immediately. He was released the next day, a Friday. He gave Ethel a profound shock when he appeared unannounced at Cross Street, Ynyshir, presumably escorted by police because of his weak condition. Six weeks later, he received an official discharge from the Welsh Regiment for incorrigible misconduct.[77]

A fortnight after his release, Horner was fit enough to start work. Mardy Lodge minutes record Horner's attendance at a General Meeting on 14 May. He thanked the colliers for electing him and made a long speech outlining 'his future activities and dealt with grievance [*sic*] which exist at present ... and which he hoped to be able to remedy to a great extent'. He also 'repudiated rumours of not being willing to fight, and stated that he was willing to shoulder a rifle to fight for the working classes, but not for the enemy of the workers (the capitalists)'. Mindful of the large vote he had received from ex-soldiers, he was evidently keen to dispel rumours that he had been a draft resister because he was a pacifist.

Horner moved his family into lodgings at Mardy and commenced his duties. The Report to the Assizes stated that Horner worked underground at Mardy for six weeks in 1919. It is likely that the management agreed that he should familiarise himself with the jobs underground. His first eighteen months as checkweighman were comparatively peaceful. Two small speculative capitalists from Brecon had sunk Mardy Nos. 1 and 2 pits in the mid 1870s. They hit good coal-bearing seams, and following the dramatic growth in the export market for steam coal, leased their pits to Lockett's Merthyr Collieries (1894) Ltd. Company. Lockett's Merthyr sunk Mardy Nos. 3 and 4 pits, just over a mile up the valley, in 1893 and 1914. By then around 2800 men were employed, a typical number for large collieries in the Rhondda. The SWMF Mardy Lodge included miners working at all four pits. The village of Mardy had expanded in tandem with the colliery, and by 1909 there were approaching 7000 people, housed there in 880 dwellings. Its housing and infrastructure were more recent than those of other Rhondda pit communities such as Llwynypia, Ynyshir and Wattstown which had grown along with their surrounding collieries twenty to thirty years previously. In 1905, the Mardy Coffee Tavern, with attached Reading Room and Library, had become 'the Workmen's Institute, the largest and most central building in the community ... a large hall, with a balcony, that could hold 1,200 people, a billiard room and gymnasium, and two reading rooms, one especially for ladies.'[78]

Horner took his new job in favourable circumstances. Under pressure from a self-confident, opportunist lodge committee over a protracted period, management had conceded excellent wages and working conditions. (Ablett's predecessor had been an astute negotiator, TI Mardy Jones, later MP for Pontypridd.) The Lodge's left-wing reputation did not develop until the 1920s. Mid-Rhondda, location of the Cambrian Combine pits, and the Aberdare Valley, had been the previous storm-centre of militancy and the Unofficial Reform Committee. Rhondda coal continued to be in strong demand, and sold at high prices. It was not until the end of 1920, eighteen months after Horner started, that coal export prices fell drastically, precipitating a collapse in the market. Horner discharged his duties with characteristic energy and even zeal; it was at this period that he laid the foundations of his legendary knowledge of the industry, mastering the jungle of detail contained in statutory requirements and collective agreements about safety, work organisation and methods of payment. He experienced a pervasive euphoria over the remarkable turnaround in his fortunes, which reinforced his determination to prove his worth to the colliers who had elected him. He not only attacked the mundane tasks involved in his new job with vigour, but also found time to attend the Labour College evening classes held at the Workmen's Institute. 'The lecturer was [Alderman] Theodore Griffiths and we paid two pence a lecture. I used to start for the pit at 5 a.m., rush home [after the shift] to take a bath and then get to the lecture. I often fell asleep before the end, but to this day I marvel at how much education in economics, sociology and other subjects I was able to absorb.'[79]

Horner's combativeness on his members' behalf soon pre-cipitated a challenge from the colliery management. In early 1920, management applied for an injunction to prevent him from entering the pits on the grounds that he had exceeded his checkweighman's statutory duties. Their bid to victimise him was not unusual. Because of their pivotal position, many – if not most – checkweighmen regularly crossed the boundary between their statutory duties and collective bargaining. Most managements tolerated this technical transgression, and were keen to solve a conflict with their colliers quickly in order to maintain production. But when they considered that the check-weigher had transgressed the unwritten rules of common sense and compromise, management retaliated, either by applying for an injunction or by simply refusing the checkweighman entry into the colliery yard. Arthur Cook had recently been elected as the second agent for the SWMF Rhondda No.1 District, which included Mardy. (His own pit was in the adjoining Pontypridd and Rhondda District. Horner had probably canvassed support for him in Mardy, even though Dai Lloyd Davies was also stand-ing for the post.) As agent, Cook responded to Horner's victimi-sation by organising a district-wide strike. After two days, the other colliery companies compelled Locket's Merthyr to con-cede Horner's reinstatement.[80]

The Horners were sufficiently confident of their new-found security in the postwar boom to buy a house in Mardy, at 37 Edward Street. Arthur apparently borrowed the money from his father, instead of obtaining a building society mortgage. Their new status as owner-occupiers was not unusual in the South Wales coalfield. A significant proportion of the housing stock was either owner-occupied or rented from private landlords, in con-trast to other coalfields where company housing predominated. The terraced houses in Edward Street were a typical miners' row, with small rooms and low ceilings. Arthur and Ethel, who had spent their previous married life in lodgings, found it comfort-ably spacious. Their second child, Rosa, was born here on 24 June 1920. They named her after Rosa Luxemburg, the left-wing Polish/German/Jewish socialist. Luxemburg and another left-wing German social democrat, Karl Liebknecht, had been brutally murdered in January 1919 in Berlin.[81] They had led the left-wing opposition to the infant German Republic's Provisional

Government, which was dominated by the Social Democratic Party. They had also opposed the SPD's decision to take a leading role in founding a democratic republic.

Luxemburg's and Liebknecht's martyrdom had taken place in horrific circumstances. Although the Provisional Government denied complicity, the consensus was that the SPD had blood on their hands. This tragedy persuaded many socialists, previously wary of the Bolsheviks' claim that the Soviets' seizure of state power in Russia was a genuine socialist revolution, to support the Russian Communist Party, the name which the Bolsheviks had adopted in the autumn of 1918 to mark their formal break with past social democratic tradition. Communists and social democrats agreed that the central difference between them was Lenin's insistence that a dictatorship of the proletariat, embodied in a one-party state, was an essential prerequisite for a successful socialist revolution. By naming their daughter Rosa, Arthur and Ethel showed that they had decided that the German social democrats were wrong and the Russian communists right.

Along with other South Walian socialists, the Horners had associated themselves with the new Soviet Russia and the communist party leading it. In February 1919, whilst Arthur was in Carmarthen Gaol, the URC had convened a conference in Cardiff. A heated debate about the way forward occupied the whole day. Although there was an obvious parallel between Russian soviets and the URC itself, few delegates were prepared to follow this similarity through to its logical conclusion and reject the Labour Party and SWMF in favour of the URC and a new communist party.

Cook proposed that the RSS be re-formed as the South Wales Socialist Society, which would be 'open to all who accepted the class war theory ... [T]he Society was to be composed of groups of trades which would consider their own problems and receive the co-operation of the whole in bringing about reforms in their own industries.' Aneurin Bevan disagreed, and argued against 'the real aim of the URC [which] appeared to be the removal of political organisations as obstructions.' Although the conflict over whether industrial or political organisation was more appropriate was not resolved, delegates agreed to found the South Wales Socialist Society as an umbrella organisation for socialists of all persuasions. Adopting the existing constitution of the RSS, they elected DA Davies from Porth Secretary and WF Hay President.[82]

In March 1919, the founding congress of the Communist International, or Comintern, was held in Moscow. (The Comintern was frequently described as Third International, to stress its claim to be the legitimate successor to the Second Socialist International, which had betrayed its Marxist roots by acquiescing in World War I.) There were no British delegates, but their absence was not particularly significant, since the congress had been an ad hoc affair. But afterwards, left-wing socialists all over Europe scrambled to join Lenin's International. Various socialist organisations in Britain participated in protracted negotiations between May 1919 and April 1920 in the expectation of forging a united institution which the Comintern would accept as a legitimate affiliate. At some of them the SWSS was represented by George and Frank Phippen and Ness Edwards.[83] However, in April 1920, political divisions fractured the SWSS, and individual branches went their own ways. Hay and Davies resigned their offices in June 1920. They were formally replaced by Horner and Charlie Gibbons, now checkweighman at Ferndale, but the SWSS effectively ceased to exist. The existing RSS branches, including Mardy, continued to meet, however. The RSS remained a loose network of socialists who enjoyed hearing speakers, debate and discussion on an irregular basis. The frequency of local meetings depended on the sense of urgency felt about the issues of the day and local priorities.

Horner's energies remained focused on his checkweighman's job and being an active member of the Federation Mardy Lodge Committee. Because he took pride in doing his job thoroughly and successfully, he was able to record small daily victories, which had a significant cumulative impact on miners' lives. It is unlikely that either Ablett or Ted Williams had been able to win so many concessions from the management, since they lacked Horner's meticulous attention to practical detail.[84] He was by now being appointed lodge delegate to various union conferences, including national conferences of the MFGB, where he was meeting and becoming friendly with other young delegates, notably Aneurin Bevan from Tredegar. Many of them, like himself, considered themselves industrial unionists. Against the

71

background of the SWMF's epic victories in militant conflicts from 1910 to 1915, few Federation activists questioned the validity of a perspective which put union power first and political representation second. Nevertheless, most of them, including Horner, were also pragmatic with regard to parliamentary activity. Although inclined to dismiss parliament's importance for achieving the socialist revolution, they readily participated in local Labour Party activity on behalf of their lodges, and regularly stood as candidates in local government elections.

In December 1920, Horner was elected Vice-Chairman at the Annual Meeting of the SWMF Mardy Lodge. This was a strong, positive affirmation of Horner's fitness for leadership. Although checkweighmen frequently also occupied leading union positions, Horner was a comparative newcomer in Mardy, and was also very young to assume such a prominent position. In January 1921 he was appointed the Lodge Delegate to the Rhondda No. 1 District Executive. He was an assiduous attender, and subsequently gave full and detailed reports from its meetings at lodge meetings. In March, he topped the poll at a lodge meeting in the election to appoint a delegate to attend the Federation coalfield conference in Cardiff to discuss the owners' wages offer.

South Walian socialists remained intensely interested in communism and the Third International. By the time its second Congress convened in Moscow in July 1920, there was a much higher attendance, and Russian communist leaders had produced a model organisation, appropriate for parties with truly revolutionary intentions. Congress delegates approved Lenin's Twenty-One Conditions as conditions to which socialist parties must agree before their application to join would be accepted. Central to Lenin's conditions was the necessity, after a revolution, for the new socialist state to implement a dictatorship of the proletariat in order to pre-empt bourgeois counter-revolution. Before the revolution, affiliating parties had to establish a network of soviets in factories and mines, expected to provide an indispensable means of seizing state power. (The network of Russian soviets had played a critical role in enabling the Bolsheviks to organise the seizure of power from the provisional government.)

Lenin had taken great care when formulating the theses to guard against left-wing purity, which he had memorably described as 'an infantile disorder' when delivering a stern rebuke to Dutch revolutionaries against their 'sectarian tendencies'. Even though parliaments were instruments of the bourgeois state, he warned that communist parties had to take them seriously and energetically contest elections. In Britain, where the Labour Party was made up of affiliated trade unions and socialist groups, including the ILP and the British Socialist Party, the communist party must also affiliate, and apply pressure on the Labour Party to adopt genuine socialist policies.

Despite strenuous attempts, insufficient progress had been made by British left-wing socialist leaders to form a bona fide British communist party in time for the second Comintern Congress in July 1920. Ideological differences continued to dominate the Joint Provisional Committee, which included representatives from almost every socialist organisation in Britain.

Whilst Lenin's strictures were acceptable to the majority of potential members of the British communist party in the BSP and ILP, a vocal, committed minority adopted a principled abstentionist position against having anything to do with the bourgeois state. They argued for the overwhelming importance of organised industrial power. The principal exponents of this position were the syndicalist Socialist Labour Party, whose base was in Scotland; the South Wales industrial unionists grouped around the URC and RSS; Sylvia Pankhurst's Workers' Socialist Federation, based in East London; and activists from the pockets of industrial unionism remaining inside individual unions, for example the Electrical Trades Union and the all-trades union shop stewards movement in West London under Jack Tanner's leadership.

Finally, at the end of July 1920, the Joint Provisional Committee convened a Communist Unity Convention in London to establish the British communist party. No delegates from the SWSS attended. WJ Hewlett, an SLP member from Abertillery, had participated on the Committee as the representative of a new organisation, the South Wales Communist Council, and he attended the Convention in this capacity.[85] Hewlett had persuaded other SLP members and other socialists to coalesce in the SWCC, because he was afraid that the industrial unionists in

73

the SWSS and URC would claim to be the legitimate representatives from South Wales. In early July, the SLP journal reported that there were eight local groups in the SWCC. Nevertheless, the Council's actual existence was as tenuous as its shadowy rival, the SWSS.

Charlie Gibbons attended the Unity Convention on behalf of the Ferndale Socialist Society, part of the RSS loose network. He argued vigorously against the Leninist position. 'We needed every man, every penny, every ounce of enthusiasm, and every moment of time in the vital work of the educational and industrial field.'[86] Gibbons was also the only delegate who supported Sylvia Pankhurst in her audacious bid to outflank the Joint Provisional Committee by creating her own Communist Party (British Section of the Third International). The Unity Convention culminated in the formation of a British communist party, and Hewlett became a member of its Provisional Executive Committee. Pankhurst, however, continued with her rival party. Because of her political prestige as a socialist feminist and manoeuvring skills, the Comintern was reluctant to repudiate her political child. They urged the two competing communist parties to come to a comradely agreement instead.

Arthur and Ethel routinely described themselves as foundation members of the communist party. Along with Charlie Jones and his wife Hannah, and Dai Lloyd Davies, they were leading lights in the Mardy Socialist Society, whose participants were a catholic cross-section of different socialist varieties, ranging from ILP members to anarcho-syndicalists. (The Mardy ILP branch had been the first one founded in the Rhondda.) Arthur had already told Arthur MacManus at the Portsmouth TUC in early September 1920 that he was willing to join the British communist party formed in July.[87]

J Walton Newbold attended a special meeting of the RSS in mid-September 1920, to put the Provisional Executive Committee's case in favour of the formation of one British communist party, committed to all Twenty-One Conditions. Charlie Jones remembered attending the meeting, along with Horner, Cook, Mainwaring and Jack Williams of Llwynypia. Other prominent local left-wingers probably included Gwen Ray Evans, the local primary school headmistress at Porth, and her husband, David Evans, manager of the large Porth Co-operative Society store. The audience agreed that the RSS should join the new party collectively, or *holus bolus*, as Charlie Jones described it to Frankenberg, after Newbold had assured them that parliamentary activity would be merely an agitational tool. Since most pragmatic industrial unionists and syndicalists were already engaged in some form of party electoral activity, Newbold's answer was evidently sufficient to tip the scales in Lenin's favour.[88]

However, the problem of the two rival communist parties was not finally resolved until the end of January 1921, when a second Unity Convention held in Leeds produced the Communist Party of Great Britain. During the winter of 1920 to 1921, socialist groups up and down Britain had been hotly debating which of the two rivals they should support and whether Lenin's conditions were acceptable. Cook and Dolling formed the Communist Party of South Wales and the West of England, which affiliated to Pankhurst's communist party. Horner evidently remained indifferent. Perhaps in response to an appeal from Cook, he attended a 'unity conference' convened in Cardiff on 4 to 5 December 1920 by Pankhurst's party as a delegate from the Mardy Socialist Society. He made only a minor contribution in Cardiff, however, speaking about the need to retain local autonomy of action. It seems likely that Horner did not feel very strongly about the question of whether or not a communist party should be involved in parliamentary politics. Although his principal arena of activity remained the SWMF, he was involved in Labour Party activity via the Mardy Lodge.

The Cardiff conference proved to be the last public appearance of Pankhurst's party. She and her supporters realised that a merger was inevitable, since the Comintern insisted that neither competitor would be accepted on its own. The conference was apparently designed to maximise the influence of the Pankhurst party and its supporters on the Leeds Unity Convention scheduled for the following month. When they formally merged with the other communist party, Pankhurst's party formally renounced their industrial unionist/syndicalist perspective. In South Wales Cook, Dolling and their allies duly joined the CPGB, which proceeded to apply for affiliation to the Labour Party. A few other principled industrial unionists, notably Jack Tanner, resigned from the newly unified party. But Tom Mann enthusiastically adhered to Lenin's International.[89]

Though smaller and more loosely organised than the former BSP branches in London and Manchester, the Rhondda groups which merged into the CPGB were a significant local presence. Local Labour Party organisation was effectively an extension of the SWMF Lodge. Consequently, the SWMF lodge officials in the Rhondda who were communists continued to play leading roles inside the South Wales Labour Party. Horner continued to attend Rhondda East Constituency Labour Party meetings as a Mardy delegate. He recalled that Ferndale, Tylorstown and Llwynypia SWMF lodges had been similarly willing to delegate communist lay officials to attend Labour Party meetings.[90] In 1921, however, Labour Party activity was not high on the Mardy Lodge's list of priorities. The Coal Wars were about to commence, and the energies of the lodge were concentrated on preparing for the first skirmish.

Chapter 4

The Coal Wars:
Skirmishes and Manoeuvres

When the Sankey Commission was appointed in the spring of 1919, the most efficient coalowners and many Tory MPs, including members of the government, were convinced that the government would have to broker some basic changes in the industry's organisation if it was to be able to compete in the new circumstances of the postwar world.[91] It was clear to all informed observers that the British coalmining industry was ripe for re-organisation. Its ownership structure was chaotic and large swathes were under-capitalised.

When the Sankey Report came out, MFGB President Robert Smillie brought pressure to bear on the government in support of its far-reaching recommendations about re-organising the industry, because he recognised that it would only be a matter of time before the government ended the state control of the industry that had been in place since February 1917. This would mean a return to the chaos of the prewar period. Along with other progressive leaders in the MFGB, he was committed to miners in the different coalfields being paid equal wages for equal work. They wanted to ensure the continuation of wartime control arrangements such as the pooling of profits amongst all the coalowners, and the provision that profits from coal production would be equably distributed between labour and capital.

In 1919 to 1920 these goals were ambitious, but not unrealistic. The highly fluid political situation was being utilised by leaders of other unions to achieve practical advances. In February 1920 Bevin had been able to win significant advances in dockers' wages and conditions as a result of his appearance before the Court of Enquiry chaired by Lord Shaw. However, when the MFGB was at the peak of its national strength, in October 1920,

Smillie had to respond to pressure to lead the nineteen affiliated district unions into a national strike over wages, though he himself considered the issue of nationalisation as being far more important, and viewed the strike as a perverse waste of the miners' bargaining power. Prime Minister Lloyd George recognised this tactical weakness, and settled the strike after a fortnight by granting a sizeable wage increase, while flatly refusing to make any promises about the contentious issue of nationalisation or reform of the industry.

For a while after the strike Smillie and the MFGB general secretary, Frank Hodges, doggedly pressed their case; there was an almost daily exchange of letters between Smillie and Lloyd George during December. Then, on 24 February 1921, the government announced that state control of the coal industry would be ended five months earlier than planned, on 31 March. Smillie resigned in the first week of March 1921, leaving Hodges and the Vice-President, Herbert Smith of Yorkshire, who now became Acting President, to deal with the rapidly deteriorating situation. An international economic slump had driven coal prices down on the world market. And the officers of the Mineowners' Association of Great Britain were increasingly confident that, once government control ceased, they could return the industry to its pre-war basics. The revised contracts of employment they offered the MFGB not only included lower wages and worsened terms and conditions, but also marked a return to wages being determined on a district basis alone, without any national element. (During the course of the war, government control had super-imposed a national, flat-rate war bonus on top of the district rates. The war bonus had increased to compensate for inflation, until by November 1918 it was a significant part of every miner's wage packet.)[92]

On 17 March Hodges proposed to the MFGB Executive that they cut their losses and accept the principle of a return to district negotiations. 'Why is it these districts have to have such a big reduction? Because their productivity per person employed has gone down and down and down ... If we strike, what are we striking for? We are striking for a subsidy ... Do you think you can get a subsidy out of the Government by means of a strike? ... You know you cannot.' He was opposed by South Wales delegates, including Ablett, who argued, 'We are the biggest union in this

78

country – perhaps in the world – today, and the only one capable of fighting ... [W]e say that every man with the spirit of Trade Unionism in him will attempt to resist.' Though the Executive supported Hodges by a two to one majority, their decision was rejected by a majority of the delegate conferences of the affiliated coalfield unions.[93]

The result of the MFGB's rejection of the MAGB's terms was a National Lock-Out, commencing on 31 March. The coalowners were well-prepared for a protracted conflict. Winter was over, and the international slump meant that coal stocks had accumulated in the exporting coalfields, which could be sold on the domestic market if a scarcity developed. But on 30 March the MFGB Executive took steps to inflict severe economic injury on the coalowners. They voted by 10 to 8 to order colliery safety and maintenance men to stop work. (Management had not locked-out them out, since their presence was essential to maintain the steam boilers which powered the pumps keeping pits from flooding. They also regularly inspected the timbering to minimise falls of rock.) This move was tantamount to a declaration of total war, particularly since the Executive's sanction enabled official picketing to be organised in order to stop any safety and maintenance men from going in to work.

The MFGB Executive also tried to apply general political pressure on the MAGB and the government by invoking the Triple Alliance, a pact for mutual assistance in case of a national dispute, agreed in 1914 between the miners, railway and road transport unions. On 5 April a conference of transport unions agreed to give the MFGB 'all the assistance in our power'. On 8 April, an NUR delegate conference voted unanimously to go on strike, if the other transport unions 'struck "jointly and simultaneously" with them'.[94] A fortnight of tactical manoeuvring followed. The MFGB Executive agreed, under pressure from the transport unions, to withdraw their instructions to safety and maintenance men. When this gesture of good faith, however, produced no equivalent concession from either the government or the coalowners, a strike by the Triple Alliance, called for 10 pm on Friday 15 April, appeared inevitable. 'Enthusiasm ran high ... a joint meeting of the [TUC] Parliamentary Committee, the [Labour] party executive, and the parliamentary [Labour] party pledged support.' When the transport unions called off the strike at the last moment, Walter Citrine, assistant general secretary of the Electrical Trades Union which had pledged its own assistance, recalled the 'tremendous indignation' throughout the movement.[95] The stillborn strike was soon dubbed Black Friday.

The MFGB's resistance continued for nearly three months in total; exceptionally fine summer weather stiffened the miners' and their families' will to stay out. But on 28 June 1921, the Executive agreed provisional terms with the coalowners. Although the government sweetened the bitter pill with a three months government subsidy, to cushion the speed with which miners' wages were reduced, the MFGB's acceptance of the new contracts marked the first occasion on which the coalowners had won a national industrial conflict. They responded by pressing home their advantage and refusing to play their part in the consultative committees included in the 1920 Mining Industry Act.[96]

During the Lock-Out the CPGB had been too young and disorganised to play any significant role. Different coalfield district unions conducted the conflict with varying degrees of intensity and enthusiasm, and the several hundred Lodge Committees within them had exhibited varying degrees of commitment and resourcefulness. Mardy Lodge exhibited an exemplary discipline and élan throughout. Dai Lloyd Davies had been an SWMF delegate at the MFGB conference on 17 March. His report back to the Mardy lodge meeting on 3 April was received by members who were already preoccupied with arranging the vital details of daily life during the Lock-Out – dispute pay, communal feeding, picket duty, publicity and social activity.[97]

On 6 April, with Dai Lloyd Davies in the chair at a Mardy Lodge meeting, Horner and other committee members, including Sam Davies the lodge secretary (who was also a deacon of the Congregationalist Siloam Chapel), argued in favour of the Lodge preventing the safety and maintenance men from working. This was a highly contentious case, since the MFGB Executive had by then already countermanded its initial instructions and informed lodges that safety work should be allowed to continue. The Lodge accepted the Committee's recommendation, however, and members followed their committee men in 'a procession of 800 to 1000 persons under cover of darkness, and compelled the stokers to withdraw fires, thereby flooding the pits'. Horner seized the opportunity of having massed forces at his disposal. He used them to commandeer fifty laden railway wagons of coal, which they found standing at the colliery sidings.

Horner's decision to appropriate the wagons was taken in the heat of the moment; his quick thinking, decisive action and ability to lead men under pressure showed audacious courage and real flair. His justification was that the miners were simply taking what was their normal allowance of housecoal from the colliery, with which the lodge committee contended the colliery company was in serious arrears. Having secured their supplies, a deputation 'headed by Horner, [Charlie] Jones and others called at the house of Mr. H.E. Maltby, Agent, and stated that no coal would be allowed to leave the sidings ... [T]hey also stipulated that no proceedings would be instituted [by the colliery management] for coal stealing up to that day.' Faced with half his collieries' workforce, Maltby sensibly agreed their terms.[98] It was a signal victory, and the Mardy men's militant reputation grew as a result. The lodge's booty provided a welcome means of subsistence through the Lock-Out. Miners could sell lots of coal outwards in the informal market of the valleys, and gain valuable cash for buying other necessities.

The police waited their moment to move. On 20 May, when the MFGB were clearly on the defensive nationally, proceedings were instituted against thirteen members of the lodge, including Horner, at the Pontypridd Police Court, for unlawful assembly and intimidation. The case was postponed, however, out of compassion for one of the accused, whose wife had terminal cancer. They were not finally tried until a month after the Lock-Out, presumably to avoid any possible flare-up of collective sympathy in the South Wales coalfield, where the Lodge's deeds of derring-do had caused great excitement. Immediately after the Lock-Out, management victimised the two checkweighmen, Horner and Dai Lloyd Davies. They were only taken back after a protracted dispute, in which Cook, who had joined Ablett as one of the SWMF's four representatives on the MFGB Executive, took the lead.

The Mardy men appeared at the Glamorgan Assizes in Swansea on 28 July, along with Cook, Dolling and some thirty others, who

81

were arraigned on similar charges. 'That morning, special buses set out from Mardy with wives, sweethearts and other supporters singing The Red Flag, The International, and other working class songs.' Horner, Dai Lloyd Davies and Charlie Jones were anxious to protect Sam Davies from possible dismissal from his position as a deacon of the Siloam Chapel. Accordingly, they manipulated their testimony to portray his role as strictly non-combative. The SWMF solicitors had engaged in plea bargaining with the judge, who was anxious to finish the case and travel to Scotland for the start of the grouse shooting season. All the SWMF accused pleaded guilty, but received comparatively light sentences. Sam Davies was fined £20, Charlie Jones only £10 (presumably because he was not a lodge official). Dai Lloyd Davies and Horner each received one month's hard labour, of which they only had to serve one week, in Cardiff gaol. Dolling and Cook were given more exemplary sentences, four months and two months hard labour respectively.[99]

As soon as they were freed, the two checkweighmen led the Mardy Lodge Committee's opposition to the demand from the Pontypridd Board of Guardians that miners pay back the outdoor relief which they had received from them during the Lock-Out.[100] Miners throughout the British coalfields had received outdoor relief from their local Board of Guardians. In Durham, where the DMA had a strong presence on the County Council and in local government, there were no demands for repayment. But strong pressure was being applied by the non-Labour political establishment in South Wales to ensure that local Boards recovered the relief they had granted.

Horner flatly refused to pay back the substantial sum he had received. He took this principled stand rather than pleading the acceptable mitigating circumstance that he did not have the money, as so many others were doing. 'I had drawn £3 17s. 0d. and the local authorities decided to use me as a test case. The Chairman of the Board of Guardians [Noah Tromans] ... a Labour man, offered to pay the money. I refused because I knew that if I refunded the money it would be a signal for an avalanche of summonses ... '

The Guardians had little choice but to stand their ground in the face of his implacable refusal to bend. Having secured a court order for bailiffs to seize the Horner family furniture to discharge the debt, they encountered further resistance. 'I studied the Law ... and discovered that they had no right to force the doors or windows, nor could they come to the house after sunset, or on Sundays, or on bank holidays. If I could keep them out during the hours of daylight on weekdays they would never collect. We were in a state of siege for weeks. The whole street backed us, signalling to Ethel, when I was at work, whenever a bailiff was lurking near by.' The bailiffs eventually gained entrance three days before Christmas, when Arthur had gone 'out back [probably to the outside toilet] and forgot to bolt the door when I came in and sat down to breakfast'. The furniture was sent for sale at auction. But Lodge allies arranged for Horner sympathisers to attend and rig the bidding, so that the auctioneer had to accept greatly reduced prices for the Horner family's belongings.[101]

The Mardy Lodge faced a bleak prospect in the New Year. In common with the rest of the SWMF, the Rhondda No. 1 District had lost a significant proportion of its members during the Lock-Out. Unemployment continued, and union membership remained not only low but also apathetic. Horner recalled that he and his colleagues concentrated on reviving the URC. 'The Communist Party began to make progress throughout South Wales and we built up a local section of the National Unemployed Workers Committee Movement [NUWM] ...'[102]

In late 1922 international economic conditions began to improve. As a result of a 16-week coal strike in the USA and the French occupation of the Ruhr, coal was in short supply on the world market. British exporting coalfields expanded their production accordingly. Although thousands of Rhondda miners were now able to find employment, most of them did not re-join the union, having been disillusioned perhaps by the MFGB's failure to win anything from the Lock-Out. In January 1923, Cook's monthly report as agent in the *Colliery Workers' Magazine*, the Federation monthly journal, noted that:

> like every other District of the Federation, [Rhondda No.1] has had enormous trouble since the resumption of work after the last stoppage ... Depression of trade was felt severely, especially at Mardy, Fernhill, Coedely and Penygraig, where, in addition to having pits closed down,

the remainder were working short time ... We have just
finished a successful campaign to rouse the men to re-
join the Federation, with Mr. Ben Wilson, of California,
as chief speaker. The special feature of these meetings
was the new spirit of enthusiasm created and the large
attendance, especially of women. Comrade Wilson is an
orator with a message ... .

Cook led a district-wide strike in April 1923 after which a satisfactory increase in membership, from 18,000 to 40,000, was finally
recorded. (The strike was intended to put pressure not only
on the non-union members, but also on managers to enforce
Federation membership as a condition of further employment
in the pit.) Though the economic situation made a revival of
lodge militancy viable, Horner later recalled that the membership in the Rhondda had become notably more cautious about
taking industrial action.[103]

The CPGB national leadership hoped to take advantage of the
more favourable economic conditions to rebuild and remould
mass workplace organisation. Since its foundation, the British
party had signally failed to make any progress in implementing
the Comintern Condition enjoining affiliated parties to establish soviets, i.e. factory councils which established control over
the workplace on the workers' behalf. This was not for lack of
trying. In December 1920 the Provisional Executive Committee
of the putative, unified British communist party had encouraged
engineering union activists, including Tanner, Willie Gallacher
and Jack Murphy to formally re-establish the wartime shop stewards movement, the Shop Stewards' and Workers' Committee
Movement, installing Mann as chairman. The SSWCM affiliated
to the provisional committee of the Comintern's trade union
equivalent, the Red International of Labour Unions, often
described as the Profintern. Fortified by money from Moscow,
RILU opened an office in Manchester, which, however, did very
little.[104]

The actual centre of shop steward activism was London. From
January 1921, the SSWCM London branch secretary was Harry
Pollitt, a talented boilermaker from Manchester, whose wartime
base had been the Thames Estuary. He became a highly effective agitator in the docks and ship repair yards of the Port of

London. Just turned thirty, raised by a strong, observant BSP mother, he was an inspiring speaker with palpable political ambition. Inside the SSWCM he developed good working relations with Tanner, and other engineering union militants based in West London, including Joe Scott, Claude Berridge and Wal Hannington. Both the SSWCM and the CPGB leadership were anxious to bring coalmining activists under the SSWCM umbrella. Pollitt enlisted Nat Watkins, a Maesteg communist miner living in London, to do the job. At the end of January 1921 Watkins organised a meeting that was attended by miners from South Wales, Yorkshire, Durham, Northumberland and Fife, including Horner in his capacity as URC secretary. (The meeting was arranged to coincide with an MFGB delegate conference in order to maximise numbers.)

Horner and Dai Lloyd Davies also attended the national SSWCM conference in Sheffield at the end of March 1921, probably the first time they had visited Yorkshire. Although there is no record of delegates' names, mining participants may have included Will Lawther from Durham, Willie Allan and Davey Proudfoot from Scotland, and Tommy Degnan from Yorkshire, and Cook and SO Davies from South Wales. Delegates made no attempt to confront the unpalatable reality of the SSWCM's inactivity. They drew comfort from the impending wages dispute in coalmining, and the possibility that existed for sympathetic strikes in transport, and reiterated the need for a national unofficial trade union movement. Mining delegates had agreed to form a Mining Section of the SSWCM.[105] But before the Mining Section could be formally inaugurated, the shell of the SSWCM had been abandoned by the engineers with clear approval from the CPGB Executive.

Because mining and engineering activists were preoccupied by major official industrial conflicts at the national level in 1921 to 1922, it was not until 1923 that a CPGB sponsored unofficial movement emerged. At that time Pollitt, Tanner and other engineering militants launched a national unofficial movement, eventually named the Minority Movement.

Unlike the lifeless SSWCM, pre-war and wartime unofficial movements were still operating in coalmining, in South Wales and Fife. Nevertheless, the founding conference of the South Wales Miners' Minority Movement was convened in Cardiff on 27 October 1923. Horner presided in his capacity as URC chairman. The MMM gained credibility and indeed remained synonymous with the still vigorous URC. But the new MMM also appealed to Federation militants, who were enthused at the prospect of joining with workers from other coalfields and industries in a national movement. 'The Chief Constable of Cardiff informed the Special Branch that Cook was one of the convenors of the [27 October] conference, and that he claimed the Minority Movement has a legitimate role as "advance guard in the SWMF"'. (The Chief Constable also reported Cook's claim that half the SWMF Executive supported the new movement.) On 30 October, the Mardy Lodge meeting heard a report of the conference and agreed to affiliate to the MMM, making a £5 donation.

After conferences in other coalfields, the national MMM was launched at Sheffield on 26 January 1924. Horner, Will Pearson from Durham and George Allison from Fife were amongst the delegates. The incoming MMM Executive appointed Nat Watkins, who was now working for the British Bureau of RILU, as national organiser. MMM district committees appeared in South Wales, Durham, Lancashire and Cheshire, Yorkshire, Nottinghamshire and Scotland. A journal, *The Mineworker*, was published on 16 February.[106]

Though the miners were the furthest advanced in forming an industrial Minority Movement, workers in engineering, railways, furniture and electricity were better represented both in terms of numbers and geographic coverage at the founding conference of the National Minority Movement held in London in the last week of August 1924. (The date ensured that the NMM's resolutions and debates could exert maximum influence on the Trades Union Congress, which convened the following week. To emphasise its good intentions towards official trade union institutions, the NMM conference issued a Manifesto conveying its fraternal greetings to the TUC meeting in Hull.) Horner moved a resolution urging the concentration of union power in the TUC General Council. He also seconded Pollitt's resolution about the NMM's structure and aims.[107]

Horner played a leading role in the new movement. Its historian observed that Pollitt was 'the lynch-pin ... with Nat Watkins and Wal Hannington as his most consistent and active

aides ... They relied for advice about local conditions upon a
number of able younger men, like Arthur Horner, Jack Tanner
and WC Loeber, who remained primarily concerned with their
own unions'. The first NMM Executive included Hannington,
George Hardy, Mann, and three miners, Watkins, Horner and
Herbert Booth, from Nottinghamshire.[108] Horner was able to
attend its meetings regularly. It is likely that he and Dai Lloyd
Davies had a standing contingency arrangement, so that when
one of them was away from the colliery on political or union
business the other would cover his checkweighman's duties.

At the Hull TUC Pollitt was a Boilermakers' delegate; the
CPGB member and NMM supporter, Hugh Hinshelwood
from the AEU, was also a delegate. In the SWMF delegation,
it was evident that Cook and SO Davies were putting forward
MMM arguments. Their presence helped maximise the NMM's
impact, despite the small number of delegates who supported
it. The MFGB delegation was one of the largest attending the
TUC, and within it, delegates from the SWMF regularly predominated. In 1924, there were thirty-one delegates from the
SWMF, including not only Cook and SO Davies, but also Ablett.
Cook seconded the resolution which welcomed the granting
of wider powers to the General Council to intervene in industrial disputes, 'acknowledg[ing] ... that "even the miners, with
their big forces in this Congress, have realised that the time has
passed when they can fight alone".' Mikhail Tomsky, attending
Congress as a fraternal delegate from Russian trade unions, was
enthusiastically received.[109]

The cordial welcome for Tomsky reinforced the case which
communists and other militants were making for British unions
to affiliate to RILU. The CPGB leadership had initially intended
that the NMM should not have a formal relationship to RILU,
whose affiliates were meant to be official union institutions.
Although French and Italian unions had joined, there had been
few links established with British unions. During 1922, the
Comintern had despatched Michael Borodin, a fluent English-
speaker, to Britain, and amongst other tasks, he had agitated
on behalf of RILU, with South Wales becoming an important
focus of his work. In April the SWMF annual conference passed
a motion proposing that the MFGB affiliate to RILU. Cook and
SO Davies duly proposed it at the MFGB Annual Conference in

July, but it was decisively defeated by 118,000 to 883,000. Cook's long speech had stressed the need for 'an effective international trade union organisation which could be of assistance to the MFGB during a dispute ...'[110]

Not surprisingly, South Wales militants concentrated their energies on building the Minority Movement, although intermittent pro-RILU activity continued. On 6 September 1922 a Mardy Lodge General Meeting deputed Horner to attend a RILU Conference in Cardiff on 16 September. But Mardy Lodge did not discuss RILU again until June 1923, the week after Horner had decided to accept an invitation to attend the second RILU Congress in Moscow. He was evidently a belated choice. 'I was sitting in the tub, naked, after coming home from the pit, when Nat Watkins burst in to ask me if I could go to Russia the following week ...' He left for Moscow in haste, before the Mardy Lodge meeting on 13 June which duly granted him three months leave of absence from his checkweighman's duties. Their support confirmed his status as an official SWMF delegate at the Congress.[111]

Because the Third Enlarged Plenum of the Comintern Executive was taking place at virtually the same time as the RILU Congress, between 12 and 23 June, a sizeable contingent of British trade unionists and CPGB members travelled to Moscow.[112] Horner, Watkins, Frank Smith and Johnnie Campbell did double duty. In addition to the RILU Congress, they were deputed to attend meetings of the Plenum's British Commission, which was considering how to put more active trade unionists into party leadership positions in the light of the Comintern's bolshevisation drive. After the Commission had reported, Pollitt became a full-time member of the CPGB Political Bureau, or Politburo. (In emulation of the Russian communist party, this was the name given to the small, policy-making body which sat above the Executive in all Comintern affiliated parties.) Horner and Wal Hannington, who was also attending the RILU conference, became part-time Politburo members, and Campbell a substitute member. As a result of their Politburo positions, they became co-opted members of the Party Executive Committee.[113]

There is no evidence that Horner viewed his party leadership position as being more important than his activity inside the SWMF Mardy Lodge and the MMM. He could plausibly claim that the SWMF Rhondda No. 1 District was the centre of revolutionary activity in Britain. But as a committed party member, he was evidently prepared to accept his new responsibilities. He had ample opportunity in Moscow to talk to Pollitt, who was clearly determined to make his mark inside the new party. Horner agreed with his ambition to transform the CPGB into a fighting instrument, and probably thought that his own membership of the Politburo and Executive could provide useful backing for Pollitt.

Horner teamed up with Hannington to get out and about in Moscow. The two men's enduring friendship dated from this time. As minor delegates with few responsibilities, they could socialise with other delegates and make contact with Moscow night life. Hannington, two years younger than Horner, was also a keen amateur boxer. He had joined the BSP as a young toolmaker in Kentish Town, North London, and become prominent in the wartime shop stewards' movement and SSWCM. He had proved his organisational flair by shaping the unemployed workers' movement, leading the first British hunger march in 1921.

Amongst Moscow's political inhabitants and transient residents, there were many who had had become conversant with English, whether through exile, itinerant work or intellectual curiosity. Arthur and Wal were apparently not intimidated by their lack of Russian, and are likely to have enjoyed sitting in cafés in Moscow and talking to men and women who were attracted by their English conversation. They also became friendly with American and Canadian comrades, including Big Bill Haywood, WZ Foster and Earl Browder.[114] They were also enthusiastic participants in the tours organised for them on their rest days from the conference.

Hannington recalled their visit to a Red Army airfield, along with Frank Smith and Fred Jackson, 'a printing worker from Hull, who since 1920 had been working in a Moscow printing works on English translations'. They accepted an invitation to go up in one of the 'very incongruous and ramshackle' airplanes. None of them had flown before, and the trip in 'an old German bomber ... which the Red Army had captured' was an exciting prospect. Having climbed through 'an opening about 4 feet square under the belly of the fuselage into a small space ... originally ... the bomb-bay', they sat on narrow forms parallel to the four sides of the hold, 'so that ... our feet were quite near the edges of this opening'. The hole remained open after take-off, and 'we realised our precarious position as the plane rose higher and higher. If the plane lurched we might slide off our narrow seats and plunge through that hole ... ' The four looked out by 'grip[ping] the edges of our seats with both hands and star[ing] ... through that hole at the numerous golden church domes as we circled slowly over the city of Moscow – indeed, a wonderful, but terrifying sight.' On landing, Horner, 'instead of walking away from the side of the plane, walked forward with his head down towards the single nose propeller which was still revolving ... Fortunately, he was saved by the alertness of a Soviet airman who dragged him back just in the nick of time.'[115]

Besides sightseeing, Horner and Hannington were keen to observe the impact of the New Economic Policy (NEP), the controversial retreat towards a market economy, undertaken by the Russian Communist Party in March 1921. Lenin had used all his persuasive powers to convince the Tenth Party Congress to adopt it, overcoming stiff resistance from many veteran Bolsheviks who viewed it as a fatal compromise with capitalism. But NEP's success had stopped the decline of Russian society into poverty, disease and famine. Under Lenin's determined leadership, the Soviet state enlisted the co-operation of Mensheviks and other former socialist opponents who were economic experts. They speedily implemented the main lines of the new policy, mobilising the technical and managerial expertise of former owners and managers. Russia's industrial enterprises re-emerged in an unexpectedly robust condition, with production levels soon returning to pre-war levels.

By June 1923, Russian society had regained an apparently stable equilibrium for the first time since World War I. Renewed prosperity and security, however, nurtured disputatiousness amongst political activists. Many men and women who had been activists in the other socialist parties were enthused by the eventual prospect of a socialist soviet Russia, and applied to join the communist party, now the only legal party. They were accepted into membership, and participated in a lively discourse about the essentials of socialism, and about how quickly the young Soviet state could move forward, away from NEP with its compromises with capitalism, towards real socialism, when all market mechanisms could be abolished.

Hannington left Moscow at the end of June. Along with other European delegates Horner embarked on a tour lasting several weeks of the Soviet Union's principal coalfield, the Donbas. The pits in this region had been extensively damaged in the Civil War, and the workforce decimated. Coalmining trade unionists, along with other industrial workers, had been the shock troops in Trotsky's Red Army, and had suffered heavy casualties. Tour members met the new cohort of activists, mainly emigrants from the nearby rural Ukraine. Their Russian hosts expected them to offer advice about the tasks confronting the newly arrived peasants: re-establishing trade unionism and electing workers' councils under NEP, and also about taking the lead in improving miners' productivity and efficiency. Horner closely observed physical and social conditions. He was excited to find 'traces of some three hundred people who had originated from Welsh immigrants, who came to man the mines and steelworks about 1870. Most had disappeared during the civil war but I met one chemist who spoke English with a rich Welsh accent.' He recalled that he had assisted in the election of pit committees which was causing some difficulty at the time. [116]

The tour proceeded through the Caucasus, but was cut short when German communists went back to participate in the intensifying civil and political conflict from which the KPD was confident that a revolutionary situation would materialise. [117] Horner stopped in Berlin on his way back in late July, in company with Palme Dutt and Horace Young, National Organiser of the Young Communist League (YCL). Arthur was walking down *Unter Den Linden*, the Berlin equivalent of Whitehall, when he encountered Hannington, stranded and without a passport, money or change of clothing, or any means to convince German communists of his bona fides. Hannington remembered that Arthur 'immediately helped me financially to buy food and clothing.' They proceeded to the KPD offices, where Horner was able to vouch for Hannington. He was given the address of friends in Hamburg who would protect him until he got away, and ten American dollars, sufficient to tide him over until he could jump a ship. Wal probably stayed in Arthur's hotel room that night. They remained together until Arthur left on 'the evening of the following day ... on the boat train for England via the Hook of Holland.'[118]

Horner returned fortified by a strong sense of mission. 'I gave reports of visit all over South Wales describing conditions ... [and t]he meaning of NEP, which Lenin had launched which reactionary elements were describing as return to capitalism.' Personal observation had persuaded Horner that Lenin was right. He energetically rebutted well-informed comments and criticisms from Ruskin/CLC graduates and Plebs League lecturers who were disillusioned with Soviet Russia's return to market capitalism. He had assimilated sufficient knowledge during his trip – about actual conditions and the ideological debate about NEP – to give a good account of himself in verbal duels with sceptics WH Hay and Noah Ablett.[119] He was supported by Cook, who was becoming increasingly prominent inside the SWMF and on the MFGB Executive.

Cook, like many other British union leaders, was impressed by NEP's results. Successful Soviet Russia presented a sharp contrast to the beleaguered German republic, where the situation continued to deteriorate. At the end of 1924, the TUC General Council delegation, including Herbert Smith, returned with a 'warmly favourable report on the Soviet system ... and proposed that the General Council should seek power to "act jointly with the Russians for [trade union] unity".' The Anglo-Russian Joint Advisory Council was established in April 1925. When Congress met in September, a resolution urging the General Council to 'do everything in their power towards securing world-wide unity of the Trade Union Movement' was passed without dissent. (Horner had moved a similar resolution at the Second Annual NMM Conference the previous week.)[120]

Although Horner continued to be active in the Mardy Lodge and Lodge Committee, he began to concentrate on the strategic aim of building the Miners' Minority Movement and the NMM. Since national NMM and MMM meetings were held in London, and were usually scheduled to coincide with party meetings, he also attended meetings of the CPGB Executive. His article, 'Why a Minority Movement?', appeared in October 1924 in the *Colliery Workers' Magazine*, and answered criticisms from other activists, who were evidently concerned that the new movement would supersede official trade unionism. He justified the NMM by associating it with other past unofficial movements and the goal of industrial unionism. His style was permeated with the new discourse of Soviet Russia, its certainties of scientific reason and a modern outlook.

The birth of movements within the Unions, bearing various titles, but which can now be known as sections of the 'National Minority Movement' has caused grave misgivings ... This symptom of modern Trade Unionism has been dismissed summarily, by many superficial leaders ... with the statement that it is merely the clamour of disappointed aspirants for jobs ...

A Minority Movement gathering is almost invariably made up of men, engaged in spare time Union work in the localities, they are of the type which I regard as the 'Back Bone' of every workers' organisation. They are in direct contact with the men, attend to all the sordid detail work, are depended upon to ... be the persons who are expected to operate the policy of the organization on the spot ... They are always progressive and prepared to bear the burden of the battle into which they may be thrown by the urge of events ...

The conditions governing the leading Official Organisation, within a modern Trade Union, determines an ever increasing distance between the elements making up the E.C. and the rank and file. This is not the consequence of any act of will ... but is determined by the development of working class organisation itself ... This logical and scientific process possesses the dangers of Bureaucratic Control from above in a greater degree than otherwise would exist ...

The path towards Organisation by Industry, is one which we must take whatever the consequences, but this involves us in the task of examination of its weaknesses, and should determine us to find checks for the elimination of the bad effects. Our solution is the Minority Movement ... [which] can secure close contact and mutual support for workers in different industries, and can have regard to the class character of the workers' struggles, without too great a regard for Trade Union etiquette.

With the formation of the minority Labour government after the December 1923 general election, 'the struggle for the workers has been thrown overboard, for the platform of community representation on the mistaken assumption that it is possible to represent fairly the robber and the robbed simultaneously ... ' In conclusion Horner stated, 'The effective counter ... is the Minority Movement, which opposes Sectionalism, and pursues a progressive policy on every issue and question, of tactics, organisation, or the politics of a situation.'[121]

Horner and Cook viewed the MMM and the MFGB as mutually reinforcing, a view shared by most militants. In the autumn of 1923, they began to build a national network of militant activists – full-time officials, checkweighmen and lodge committee members. Amongst them were Henry Hicken and Sammy Sales in Derbyshire, George Jones in Warwickshire, Jim Hammond and John McGurk in Lancashire, and Tommy Degnan, Joe Hall and Alwyn Machen in Yorkshire. In Durham, the MMM's first supporters were probably veterans of the strong pre-war reform movement there; Will Lawther and his three younger brothers, Steve, Eddie and Cliff, provided welcome, comparatively young recruits. Lawther was five years older than Horner, and had been elected checkweighman at Victoria Garesfield colliery, a small pit southeast of his home village, Chopwell, in northwest Durham, in 1919. Unlike the SWMF, the Durham Miners' Association was a conservative organisation, proud of its unchanging traditions and rules. Veteran officials gave ground grudgingly to younger blood. Will Lawther had stood unsuccessfully for agent's vacancies inside the DMA. His chequered left-wing politics, ranging from Kropotkin through to the ILP and Marxism made him an unwelcome interloper. His wife, Lotte, too, was an important part of his political life. She was a feminist and Labour activist, and took an keen interest in birth control and child welfare issues, as well as helping to organise support for miners' families during the 1921 Lock-Out.

Horner and the MMM networks provided critical support for Cook in the 1924 election for MFGB general secretary. Hodges had been compelled by rule to resign from office when he was elected to parliament in the December 1923 general election. On 5 February 1924 the MFGB Executive called for nominations for his successor from affiliated district unions. The SWMF Executive convened a coalfield conference for 8 March, when delegates would cast their lodge votes to decide which of the six candidates whom lodges had nominated would go forward as the SWMF's nomination.

It would be a hotly contested election. Federation activists calculated that the SWMF nominee was likely to win the national election. MFGB rules provided for each candidate's votes to be aggregated on a national basis, and the transferable voting system, adopted in 1919, ensured that every vote would count in deciding the final result.[122] They expected that the SWMF candidate would win the vast majority of the South Wales miners' first preference votes, just as Hodges had done. The main opposition was likely to come from Joseph Jones, the moderate general secretary of the Yorkshire Miners' Association. But since the MFGB President, Herbert Smith, was also a Yorkshireman, miners in other coalfields were likely to be reluctant to allow Yorkshire men to occupy both national union offices. Rivalry between Yorkshire and the Northeastern districts would reinforce the chances of a South Walian candidate. Moderate activists from outside Yorkshire were likely to give their first preference to another moderate candidate than Jones, and then might give the SWMF candidate their second preference votes.

In 1919, Hodges, then an ebullient, self-confessed left-winger, had defeated four other candidates to win the SWMF nomination for MFGB general secretary. (The URC had not been sufficiently active then to formally endorse a candidate.)[123] In 1924, lodges nominated seven candidates, five of whom were left-wing, Cook, Mainwaring, Ted Williams, SO Davies and Ablett. Horner was apparently determined to ensure a more disciplined approach. He convened a URC conference and made arrangements for an unofficial lodge ballot to be held prior to 8 March which would produce a legitimate collective decision about whom to endorse.

Active Lodge Committees, including Mardy, would have thoroughly discussed the merits of each candidate. Williams and Davies were comparatively inexperienced; they probably stood with no real expectation of winning, in order to raise their profiles in order to compete successfully in future for full-time office or a parliamentary nomination. Cook had a reputation as a fear-

95

less fighter and charismatic speaker. Observant activists could see that Mainwaring and Ablett were his intellectual superiors, but they lacked the charisma to lead the national battle with the coalowners which mining militants now considered inevitable. Mainwaring was notoriously dour, to the point of misanthropy, and an indifferent speaker. Although Ablett once matched Cook's magnetism, his alcoholism had rendered him only inter-mittently effective. Nevertheless, as the veteran leader of the Cambrian Combine dispute and reputedly main author of *The Miners' Next Step*, he commanded loyalty and admiration. In the 1921 Lock-Out, Cook had countenanced retreat without guilt or hesitation. Ablett had been unwilling to support a compromise settlement, even when its purpose was to postpone the fight to another more favourable occasion.

Horner and his close confidants on the Lodge Committee evidently plumped for Cook, and convinced the general meet-ing to back him. At the URC conference, Mainwaring, Williams and Davies were eliminated in the early stages. Lodges loosely affiliated to the URC since its inception appointed delegates. Lodges which had been newly energised by MMM activity were also represented. The result of the final ballot between Cook and Ablett was a dead heat. When this was reported to Horner as chairman, he used his casting vote for Cook. *Incorrigible Rebel* recalled his intense personal angst at having to choose between the two men. At the time, he had probably not hesitated before making the choice, knowing that his closest allies in Mardy sup-ported Cook.

At the SWMF conference, Mainwaring emerged as the lead-ing contender. At SWMF conferences, important decisions were routinely decided by a 'financial vote', in which each lodge del-egation cast a vote reflecting their number of paid-up members. (Other district unions used the same system, as did the MFGB at national conferences, with affiliated district unions casting their financial or card votes according to the size of their member-ship.) On 8 March, Mainwaring received marginally more first preferences than Cook, followed closely by Ablett, with Williams and Davies much further back. He remained the favourite until the sixth count, when the transfer of Ablett's 29,286 votes brought Cook to the top by a narrow margin.'[124]

The URC endorsement of Cook had probably been decisive in determining the result. Although Mainwaring was formally enrolled in the communist party, he was apparently the preferred choice of moderates, including Richards and Morrell. He evidently remained a largely silent communist, and had taken no part in either the revived URC or the MMM. At lodge meetings convened to mandate delegates, the close result of the URC contest between Cook and Ablett would have been widely discussed. News of the conference and Horner's casting vote would have been reported not only to lodges represented there, but also by word of mouth at social, political and union gatherings to a much wider circle. Many lodges probably decided for Cook and Ablett, as first and second choices or vice versa, depending on their own parochial views.

Page Arnot observed that Horner was called to account by the CPGB leadership for his endorsement of Cook, who was not a communist, in preference to Mainwaring, who was: 'Had Horner and other Communists gone against instructions? The matter was considered to be of national importance: and was discussed at Communist Party headquarters where, after a sharp tussle, a majority gave approval to the choice [of Cook].' Arnot's source is unattributed, but presumably was his own memory, since he was close to the central party leadership and, as Secretary of the Labour Research Department, well informed on MFGB affairs.[125] Horner was certainly culpable. He had flouted party discipline by taking a critical decision without reference to the party *apparat*. Nevertheless, he escaped punitive retribution. The Politburo were evidently persuaded by his, and probably Pollitt's, post hoc arguments in Cook's favour.

Having been defeated for national office, Mainwaring won the election to succeed Cook as SWMF agent for the Rhondda No. 1 District. The *Mineworker* reported on 10 May that Horner had turned down the Rhondda Minority Movement's request that he should stand, because he considered it more important to campaign for the MMM. Had he been a candidate, he probably would have received Cook's endorsement and won the contest. Horner's role as a leading coalmining activist was recognised by the CPGB leadership when he was elected to the Party's Executive as a full-time member at the Sixth Party Congress in

May 1924. Immediately prior to the Congress, Pollitt had been given greater responsibility for industrial work.[126]

Eight candidates stood in the national election for MFGB general secretary. Cook's main opponent was Joseph Jones. Cook and Henry Hicken were the only left-wing candidates. Arnot observed that Cook 'was the favourite candidate ... in many other Districts [besides South Wales] ... especially amongst the younger miners and those who belonged to the recently formed Miners' Minority Movement'. On the first count, Cook's lead over Jones was 40,000 votes; on the final count it was 15,000. Cook's victory was viewed as a spectacular affirmation of the MFGB's militant intentions. *The Mineworker* printed the news in large letters, claiming 'a victory for the MMM'. *The Times* announced starkly: 'Miners' Secretary – A South Wales Extremist.'[127] Nevertheless, the narrow majority reflected an increasing polarisation inside the MFGB. Most miners voting for Hicken probably gave their second preferences to Cook. But many Northeastern and Lancastrian miners had evidently subordinated their provincial animus towards having two Yorkshire national officers.

Soon after his election, Cook, accompanied by Horner, began to make extensive weekend tours, speaking at MMM conferences in Lancashire, Cheshire and Nottingham. Their campaign had a dual aim – to build support for the Minority Movement and strengthen the militant voice inside the MFGB. Cook was the main attraction. 'His speeches were not so much pragmatic as revivalist ... He came to be a mirror of the coal-fields ... The effect was that soon a greater trust was reposed in him than had ever before been confided in any miners' leader.' Horner acted as Cook's warm-up speaker. A Northumberland MMM was established, and the Yorkshire MMM arranged a tour for Cook. During 1925, Horner conducted a fortnight's tour of the Durham coalfield on his own, after which nine MMM groups emerged with a membership of 250.[128] Horner made no attempt to replicate Cook's style. He had already evolved his own, developing tight, logical arguments, liberally illustrated by practical detail. Though he lacked Cook's messianic qualities, he was nonetheless effective, finding his own rapport with coalfield audiences, and building his reputation as a compelling speaker.

Moderates on the MFGB Executive were evidently reluctant to question Cook's promotion of the Minority Movement.

As MFGB general secretary, he could not have spoken in any coalfield under MFGB auspices unless he had received an official formal invitation from the affiliated coalfield union. Such official invitations were infrequent, due to complex internal political rivalries and their officials' habitual desire to preserve their parochial prerogative. MMM activists were typically lodge officials, and they could mobilise their membership unofficially, but effectively, to listen to the MFGB general secretary speaking on an MMM platform. By the beginning of 1926, the MMM had constructed a loose national organisation in parallel to the MFGB's, an impressive result achieved largely by Cook's charisma combined with Horner's energy and will. The MMM letterhead listed Horner as President, followed by nine district secretaries: Northumberland, South Wales, Yorkshire, Durham, Nottinghamshire, Forest of Dean, Lancashire, the Lothians and Lanarkshire.[129]

Cook and Horner refrained from campaigning in Scotland. Scottish activists remained preoccupied with their own internal union problems. In January 1923, a separate union, the Fife, Kinross and Clackmannan Miners' Reform Union had been established by the veterans of the pre-war reform movement. Though Fife remained its principal terrain, its officials actively recruited members from other parts of the Scottish coalfield.[130] But the Reform Union failed to displace its rival, which remained affiliated to the official Scottish coalfield federation, the NUSMW, and through it to the MFGB. Visits from the MFGB general secretary to a breakaway union would have been highly problematic, and Cook was evidently keen to avoid any charges that he was promoting a breakaway union.

Horner's regular weekend absences on campaigns do not seem to have been a problem for Ethel. She was well integrated into the social life of Mardy communist families, and evidently self-sufficient emotionally. She was caring for two young daughters in reasonable domestic conditions, and money was not an immediate worry. Horner's checkweighman's wages were secure, and his travel expenses to London and on MMM campaigns were probably being met through a combination of CPGB and union sources. On 25 April 1924, the Mardy Lodge minutes noted that Mrs Horner was the Rhondda District No. 1 Woman Delegate to an unspecified London Conference. She and Arthur probably

99

enjoyed a weekend in London amongst communist friends, perhaps including Albert Inkpin and his wife, Wal Hannington and Harry Pollitt and his future wife Marjorie. Other weekends away together probably occurred regularly, since Vol and Rosa would have been able to stay with Charlie and Hannah Jones' family or Dai Lloyd Davies' family.

As general secretary, Cook was bound by MFGB rule to live in London. A house was purchased for him in the MFGB's name with MFGB funds, for which he paid a rent well below market value. Horner may have stayed with him when he was in London for MFGB delegate conferences. He probably also spent increasing amounts of time at the MFGB offices which Hodges had established at 55 Russell Square. Horner recalled that Cook had treated him as 'probably his closest confidant' in this period.[131] Horner's other regular ports of call were convenient to Russell Square. The NMM offices were two or three minutes' walk away in Great Ormond Street. The CPGB headquarters in Covent Garden were ten minutes' brisk walk for a young man in peak physical condition. The LRD offices were a pleasant stroll through St James's Park, in Buckingham Palace Road.

Cook inherited an outstanding chief clerk, Joe Elliott, from Hodges. Because coalmining was a highly regulated industry, there was frequent liaison between the MFGB and the Department of Mines. The Russell Square office also had to progress complaints and problematic compensation cases from affiliated unions. Elliott evidently shouldered much of this routine business. But many of these apparently mundane tasks also involved taking decisions with political repercussions. By leaving them to Elliott, Cook lost the opportunity to intervene and obtain the best results for district unions. Horner was well aware of Cook's bureaucratic shortcomings. Much of the MFGB's day-to-day business concerned preparations and aftermath of the monthly Executive meetings. Minutes had to be written and circulated, agendas compiled and relevant paperwork prepared. When he was at Russell Square, he may have helped Cook compose circulars to the district unions, answer correspondence and prepare agendas. His presence helped to keep Cook's attention concentrated on union matters.[132]

100

Despite his leadership of the MMM, Horner did not neglect activity inside the Labour Party. He attended the national Labour Party conference in 1924 as a delegate from Rhondda East constituency party. At the 1925 Labour conference, communists were banned from becoming individual Labour Party members and therefore were disqualified from attending as constituency delegates. Horner, however, attended Labour Conference as part of the SWMF delegation for three years, 1926 to 1928. The SWMF remained emphatically committed to an all-in Labour Party. Most Federation activists agreed with Oliver Harris, editor of *Colliery Workers' Magazine*, writing in his 'Notes and Comments' column in December 1924:

> The strength of the Labour Party lies in the Trade Unions affiliated to it ... We expect every workman employed at a Colliery to become a member of the Miners' Federation ... We could only exclude him from the Labour Party by excluding him from the industrial organisation, which is, of course, an impossible proposal ... [W]e know that the resolution against the Communists was carried only by small majorities in several large unions ... The Communists are among the most active Trade Unionists in every industrial organisations (*sic*); there are, of course, plenty of others, but the Labour Party platform should be broad enough to include all who are prepared to join in the attack on the existing order.[133]

Harris knew that Tom Richards, SWMF general secretary, was also sympathetic to an all-in Labour Party. Richards had been Labour MP for West Monmouth from 1904 to 1920, resigning when the constituency was redrawn and the SWMF's rules were changed to make the post of general secretary full-time and barring occupants from being MPs. A champion of new unionism in the 1900s, Richards was keen to promote high calibre future leaders, and reluctant to lose them to the extreme left. He recognised Horner's talent and encouraged him.[134]

Soon after Cook took office, the MFGB Executive concluded a settlement with the coalowners that contained few concessions. Subsequently rejected by a narrow majority in a district

101

vote, most of the Executive, including Cook, nevertheless recognised that the union was in no position to mount a national
strike against its terms. International economic conditions were
moving against the miners. Coal export prices had fallen by
12 per cent during 1924. And when the Conservative government returned sterling to the Gold Standard at pre-war parity
in the spring of 1925, the terms of trade for Britain's staple
exports, notably coal and cotton textiles, dramatically worsened.
'Coal, Keynes argued, would be "above all others a victim of
our monetary policy" and the miners "the victims of the economic juggernaut".' Continental coal producers were modernising and rationalising their undertakings to a far greater extent
than their British counterparts.[135] The MAGB did not view the
future with optimism, although there were notable exceptions:
large coal companies with sufficient capital were investing in
mechanisation and acquiring smaller, weaker companies. For
these reasons, coalowners were looking to make cost savings,
while the miners were in a weak position in negotiations.

The MAGB were determined to dismantle the framework of
national wage bargaining, and to lengthen the statutory working
day. Cook was determined to continue the miners' strategy of
bringing the maximum forces to bear on the coalowners and the
government to win a fair national minimum wage and retain the
statutory eight hour working day. He took the initiative in meeting the TGWU and other unions to revive the Triple Alliance on
a more formal basis. He also cultivated closer relations with the
TUC General Council, a new institution established in 1921.
His strategy was supported by the SWMF Executive, and therefore by the SWMF delegates on the MFGB Executive, Ablett, SO
Davies and Enoch Morrell.

From his vantage-point at the LRD, Arnot would have received
regular news about MFGB Executive discussions. He observed
that Ablett and Davies 'together made a pair of keen and quick-
witted debaters ... that could not be matched from Yorkshire,
Durham, Midlands or Scotland'.[136] Herbert Smith took little
part in Cook's moves. He had ignored the MFGB rule requiring
national officers to live in London, and avoided many meetings
he should have attended. When he chose to step down from
the General Council in 1924 after only two years membership,

his place was taken by Tom Richards, newly elected MFGB Vice President.

Union leaders and GDH Cole, who were the General Council's principal architects, envisioned it as a permanent general staff, serviced by a permanent full-time general secretary, which would maintain and strengthen the central role which unions had played in the economy during World War I. The NMM and CPGB leadership viewed the Council optimistically as a potential centre of working-class power in a revolutionary situation. It consisted of thirty-five members representing eighteen industrial groups, elected at the annual Trades Union Congress. The MFGB dominated Group No. 1, Mining and Quarrying, which contained only two other very small unions, for quarry workers and colliery managers.[137] The Council met quarterly; its various subcommittees met monthly, more often when they had urgent business.

Cook himself did not serve on the Council until 1927, when Robert Smillie vacated a Group No.1 place. Smillie may have remained on the Council after his resignation as MFGB President in response to concern from the older generation of union leaders and the TUC's general secretary, Fred Bramley, about Cook's suitability for high office. His extreme left-wing views were well-known, and his judgement was generally considered flawed, to the point of recklessness. Prejudice against Cook subsequently abated under pressure of events and evidence of his persistence, transparent honesty and ability to put an argument forcefully. Although many veterans still harboured strong misgivings about his reliability, he was generally accepted as a legitimate union leader.

Discussions about a revamped Triple Alliance were protracted until Bevin was drawn into them. He was enthused by the prospect of a strong, all-in union front, and wrote a constitution for a new Industrial Alliance, which was approved by the TGWU's first biennial conference in mid-July 1925. Bevin and Cook were both aware, however, that the TUC General Council had far greater potential. The TUC's authority had increased as a result of a decision taken at the 1924 Congress whereby the General Council was empowered to take the initiative in serious industrial conflicts. Thus when negotiations between the MFGB and the coalowners broke down on 13 July 1925, the MFGB took their case to the General Council. Moved by Cook's and Smith's advocacy and buoyed up by Bevin's enthusiasm for the Industrial Alliance, the General Council committed the TUC to organising an embargo on the movement of coal. Bevin and the leaders of the three railway unions were appointed to a Special Industrial Committee to draft detailed plans.

The Committee's instructions for a total embargo on handling coal were issued on 30 July, the day before the coalowners' planned reduction in miners' wages and increase in working hours was due to take effect. Their action was endorsed later the same day by a special conference of trade union executives 'with unanimous and enthusiastic approval'. The prospect of this united industrial action was sufficient to intimidate the Conservative government. The Cabinet had previously been divided between hawks who favoured standing back to let the inevitable conflict between the two sides proceed, and doves, including the Prime Minister Baldwin, whose priority was keeping industrial peace. They had already offered to establish a further inquiry into the industry 'to try to get to the bottom of the economic difficulties of the industry'. Under pressure, they also offered to provide a subsidy to the coalowners, sufficient to maintain the miners' wages and working hours at their existing levels for a further nine months, until May 1926.

On Friday 31 July 1925, the MFGB agreed to co-operate with the government enquiry, and the TUC withdrew its threat of an embargo on coal, leaving the Chancellor, Winston Churchill, to find an estimated £10 million for the subsidy to the coalowners. Delegates to the TUC at Scarborough in the first week of September were full of self-congratulation about the satisfactory conclusion to 'Red Friday', as it had been immediately described. This dramatic assertion of union power persuaded delegates to approve expansive resolutions. One bound the General Council to the pursuit of world-wide trade union unity; another declared the overthrow of capitalism to be a union objective and pledged Congress to promoting workshop organisation.[138]

Throughout this exciting time, Horner was indefatigable. In addition to his CPGB and MMM activities, he played a full part in the meetings and conferences of the SWMF. He was now established as a leading coalfield activist. Other militants in his age cohort, like Aneurin Bevan, were less well known. In May

1924, Horner moved a resolution, seconded by Jack Jones of Garw Lodge, to end the national agreement with the coalowners at a special SWMF delegate conference, which was narrowly carried on a card vote against the Executive's recommendation. After the MFGB Executive had accepted the national agreement, Horner and Jones moved the same motion successfully at another SWMF conference in February 1925. Because neither were members of the SWMF Executive, they were not bound by collective responsibility to support its moderate position.[139]

Horner took an active part in the monthly meetings of the Rhondda No. 1 District Committee, held on the first Monday of each month at the SWMF Porth Offices. As a Mardy Lodge delegate he met delegates from the other 35 lodges, the No. 1 Agent, Mainwaring, and the SWMF Executive member for the District. The sponsored Labour MPs for the two Rhondda constituencies, William John and Dai Watts Morgan, also regularly attended. On 2 February 1925, Horner spoke in support of a Mardy motion:

> That this District Meeting registered its strong disapproval of those members of the SWMF in Rhondda No. 1 District who, notwithstanding the definite mandated decision of the District instructing its members not to repay [indoor] relief, have in their capacity as members of the Pontypridd Board of Guardians, wherein they are chiefly financed by this Federation, defied the District by advocating and enforcing repayment even to the extent of distraining upon goods, thus ... breaking up the homes of those members who have attempted loyally to abide by the District decision.

He concluded that, 'the Labour Guardians were acting contrary to the interest of the working class and deserved to be severely censured'. Having heard the reply from the Labour Guardians Noah Tromans, J Treharne, WH Jones and David Evans, the meeting rejected the Mardy motion by 15 to 7.

At the District Committee on 2 March, Horner and Mainwaring reported on a Special MFGB conference they had attended in Blackpool.[140] At the September District Committee, they jointly applied pressure on the Advisory Committee of the Pontypridd Board of Guardians, who had attended to discuss 'the distress prevailing generally throughout the area': 'Mr. Mainwaring ... emphasised the suffering arising from the exceeding short time now worked at the Collieries throughout the District ... Mr. A. Horner spoke on behalf of the district and pointed out that there was one particular at least where the Board failed to operate even their own agreed scale [of outdoor relief], and went on to point out how in other respects the present position dealt very harshly with people unfortunately compelled to depend upon relief for the means of life.'[141]

The long-term prospects for the MFGB being able to defend national wage bargaining and a statutory eight-hour day were not good at this time. As Harris observed in the November *Colliery Workers' Magazine*:

> There is a great deal of truth in the statement of Mr. Gowers of the Mines Department, in his evidence before the Coal Commission [the Samuel Commission], that were it not for the accidental circumstances of the Ruhr Coalfield stoppage and the strikes in the United States, the British coal industry would have reached its present state of depression two or three years ago ... The view has been expressed in these columns during the last two or three years that the heyday of British coal production is over ... The development of oil fuel, hydro-electric power, and the declining use of raw coal for various purposes, together with the development of coal production in other countries, has created a situation that must be faced, and the sooner it is dealt with on right lines the better.

Nevertheless, the MFGB managed to win its unexpected victory in 1925, the result largely of Cook's dogged persistence, the MMM's militant optimism and Bevin's radical opportunism. But, in spite of the government's expeditious retreat on Red Friday, the MFGB Executive now faced the question of how to prepare their forces for the conflict which most observers expected to start when the government's subsidy to the industry expired on 30 April 1926. Harris described the situation in the January 1926 *Colliery Workers' Magazine*:

During the last few months the coalowners have simply allowed things to slide, each Company grabbing as much of the trade as possible and underselling each other to an extent that has made it impossible for the industry to support itself ... [I]t should be apparent to everyone, including the Government, that some outside authority will have to step in and place the industry on a sounder basis.

... [I]f a conflict is forced upon us by the coalowners, supported by the Government, we will be able to rely on the staunch support of all other sections of workmen ... [I]f a struggle comes organised labour will take up the challenge, and ... we are satisfied that if the destinies of the nation were controlled by organised labour, as it will be, sooner or later, it would not result in the welter of blood shedding, misery, suffering and destitution, which mankind has experienced during last centuries when its destinies were controlled by the so-called 'educated' classes.

The government had been making its own preparations for some months. On 13 October 1925, detectives had raided the national and London offices of the CPGB, the YCL and the NMM, arresting eight people, including Pollitt, Campbell, Willie Gallacher, Albert Inkpin and Bill Rust, secretary of the YCL. Four others, including Arnot and Hannington, were arrested some days later. They were tried and found guilty in mid-November for various offences of conspiracy with the intent of encouraging sedition and mutiny amongst persons in HM forces. The five with previous convictions, including Pollitt and Hannington, were sentenced to twelve months; the remaining seven to six months. There was an angry reaction to the convictions in the labour movement. The MFGB Executive called for their instant release, along with the London Trades Council and around 70 Labour MPs. MacDonald moved a motion on 1 December in parliament, condemning the verdict as a violation of the traditional British right of free speech and publication of opinion.

The CPGB leadership was faced with a serious gap in its leadership by the imprisonment of eight out of ten members of the Politburo. Pollitt's absence was critical. As the dynamic, proactive secretary of the NMM and the CPGB's Industrial Organiser, he had been busy building the Minority Movement network of activists in readiness for the expected battle. He had, however, been able to arrange his stopgap successors before the trial, when all twelve accused had been at liberty on bail – surety having been provided by a variety of labour movement celebrities, including Bernard Shaw, Cook, HN Brailsford, and Colonel Josiah Wedgwood MP. George Hardy, the NMM's organising secretary, became temporary general secretary, and Horner was made CPGB Industrial Organiser.

Horner obtained leave from his checkweigher's post for the six months Pollitt was in gaol, until 10 April 1926.[142] Horner probably worked two or three days a week in London, and divided the rest of his time between Mardy and campaigning with Cook in other coalfields. He and Hardy were effectively job-sharing. The dividing line between Pollitt's work as party Industrial Organiser and NMM General Secretary had been practically seamless. It is likely that during Horner's absences from London Hardy discharged both jobs simultaneously, as Pollitt had done.[143]

Some weeks after the Communist Twelve started their sentences, fifty South Wales miners were tried and convicted for their part in a hard-fought strike in the Anthracite District in West Wales in July and August. Their sentences ranged from fourteen days to twelve months. A support campaign for both lots of 'political prisoners' quickly materialised, equipped with a Free Speech and Maintenance Fund. The sponsoring committee included Cook, General Council members, and George Lansbury as treasurer.[144] Harris commented in the December *Colliery Workers' Magazine*:

> There is every indication that the employers, supported by the Tory Government, are preparing for a frontal attack on the workers of this country during next year ... A further indication of what is contemplated is the action of the Tory Government in forming a black-legging and strike-breaking organisation [the Organisation for the Maintenance of Supplies], with local dictators in the various areas ... The prosecution of the Communists was only in keeping with the general policy of the Tories, and is part of the general attack on the Labour forces.

108

Labour leaders may well ask, Whose turn next? ... The scales of Justice are heavily weighted against the workers every time, and the conviction is growing that the only argument our enemies understand and appreciate is the argument of force. That a great storm is brewing in this country is becoming increasingly apparent, and it is up to the Labour forces, both industrial and political, to meet it, and conquer when it breaks upon them.

Chapter 5

The Coal Wars:
Battle, Siege, Rout, Retreat

At the end of 1925, the Rhondda No.1 District selected Horner as one of its rank-and-file members of the SWMF Executive. He replaced the incumbent, Noah Tromans, who was also Labour member for Ferndale/Mardy on the Pontypridd Board of Guardians. Jack Hughes was confirmed in office as the second rank-and-file member. (As agent, Mainwaring held a third ex officio place.) Because of its loss of membership due to unemployment, the District's representation should have been reduced. But when the Executive proposed that Horner, as the non-incumbent nominee, should lose his place, the District Council put a counter-proposal that Horner should occupy his seat until May 1926 – a clear reference to the impending national battle. The Executive agreed to consider the number of Rhondda No. 1 District's representation after the MFGB Annual Conference in June 1926, and confirmed Horner as an Executive member in the meantime. He attended the next SWMF Executive meeting on 27 February 1926, and most meetings thereafter. He remained on the SWMF Executive throughout the Lock-Out, because the MFGB Annual Conference in June was postponed.[145]

Horner used his place on the SWMF Executive to good advantage. Although he had been attending MFGB conferences as an ordinary SWMF delegate, his new status gave his contributions greater weight in debates. He was also routinely included in the SWMF delegations to the TUC and Labour Party Conference. Since he was not a member of the MFGB Executive, he was not bound by collective responsibility for its decisions, and could oppose its recommendations. He was routinely perceived as speaking not only on behalf of the South Wales rank-and-file but also the MMM.

The relationship between the Federation and the Minority Movement had been finessed with some determination by Richards, Morrell and Harris. Although they were not prepared to countenance official support for the Minority Movement, they were also unwilling to agree to the demands from the centre-right that the Executive should prevent lodges from supporting the MMM financially or sending delegates to Minority Movement conferences. With a national conflict imminent, they were anxious to maintain a solid, united front.[146] The scale of Minority Movement activity increased in the early months of 1926, in preparation for the anticipated conflagration. On 5 March, the Mardy Lodge committee discussed a request from Cook sent to all Rhondda Fach lodges under the MMM imprimatur. He asked them to organise a meeting for him on Sunday 14 March at 11 am The Mardy committee agreed, and approved Ferndale as the venue.

On 12 March, an MFGB Special Delegate Conference was convened to consider the Samuel Commission Report, published the previous day. Horner moved a motion rejecting the MFGB Executive recommendation that the report be noted, pending developments from the governments and coalowners:

> They have put it before us that the best policy ... is to fold our arms and stand to, and just wait and see what happens. It seems to me that there is an assumption right away through that argument to give time to the coalowners and the Government to make up their minds as separate units ...
>
> The Government are preparing. You can see what they are doing. They are not preparing for any wait and see policy. The O.M.S. was organised to defeat the miners by strength ... We ought to frame a policy for ourselves ... [W]e have seven weeks to prepare for a struggle in the most effective fashion we can and counter these attempts which are now before us.

Herbert Smith was provoked by this speech into responding from the chair. 'It is a deliberate attempt to infer that the Executive are going home to do nothing. I want to say that we have all got to do something. Your Executive has been trying to

111

prepare ... We may have got nystagmus, but we are not blind. We know what the Government is up to equally as well as you ... ' Horner's frontal challenge to the Executive position polarised the debate. James Robson, Secretary of the DMA, observed, 'I listened to Mr. Horner, and I want to pay this compliment, that while I disagree with him, I am bound to admit he has capably analysed the position which he takes up ... [B]ut I think Mr. Horner and his friends ... will be well advised to accept the resolution I have moved [on behalf of the Executive].'

Robson's reference to Horner's friends could be taken to mean the other South Walian delegates, the Minority Movement, or both. Ted Williams' rejoinder presumed he had meant the SWMF: '[N]ot questioning the honesty and sincerity of the Executive, but ... their wisdom and their prudence ... We [in South Wales] know so far as we are concerned they will want to take off the bonus turn and the other customs which we are being paid now. We know these will be attacked, and knowing that we ought not to wait.'[147]

South Wales delegates could and often did dominate MFGB conferences. The SWMF usually sent 40 to 49 delegates to MFGB conferences. Durham and Yorkshire, district unions of comparable size, sent less than half that number. Representation at the 12 March conference was typical, with the SWMF having 40 delegates, Durham 11, and Yorkshire 7.[148] Though the other district union delegations could always defeat SWMF motions in a card vote, the South Walian delegates' numerical superiority gave them a clear psychological advantage. Herbert Smith tried to redress the imbalance by routinely discriminating against Federation delegates and allowing other delegates to speak more than once.[149] On 12 March, he took the vote on the Executive recommendation after calling three more SWMF delegates, Vernon Hartshorn MP, Ablett and an unnamed delegate, followed by Peter Lee from Durham and John Doonan from Scotland. Doonan concluded the debate: 'I just want to say a word or two at least, to have some districts voicing an opinion apart from South Wales, because I think the greater part of the discussion this morning has been monopolised by our friends from South Wales ... There is sufficient ammunition in this to keep a propagandist meeting going for a long time ... '. Though Horner's motion was defeated, by 133 to 16,

the South Walian militants had clearly asserted their position.[150]
As a result, the MFGB Executive had less room to manoeuvre
and compromise.

The MMM meeting at Ferndale on 14 March would have
heard reports from Cook and Horner on the MFGB Blackpool
conference. They would also have discussed items on the agenda
of the Special NMM London conference to be held the following Sunday. Nat Watkins' letter inviting mining delegates to the
Special London Conference used sober language, designed not
to cause offence to centre-right union leaders: 'In view of the
threatening clouds overhanging several of the important industries at the moment, particularly the Mining and Engineering,
and the abstinate (*sic*) attitude adopted by the employers to
the reasonable demands of the workers to increased wages and
improved conditions of labour, the National Minority Movement
feels there is not a moment to be lost in the task of preparing
our plans for resisting the employers' attacks and formulating
our demands to improve the workers' status.'[151] The effect of
the inconclusive MFGB special conference was partially negated
by the uncompromising tone and impressive attendance at the
NMM Special Conference on 21 March. The main resolution,
'On the Capitalist Offensive', was moved by Horner, whose affiliation was described as SWMF, and seconded by Peter Kerrigan,
representing the Glasgow NMM District Committee. It called
on the TUC General Council to take the lead, as it had for Red
Friday: 'it is imperative that all forces of the working class movement should be mobilised under one central leadership to repel
the attack and to secure the demands of every section of the
workers.' Its practical clauses were straightforward:

> 1. Each Trades Council to constitute itself a Council
> of Action to mobilise all forces of working class move-
> ment ... by establishing as far as means permit a com-
> missariat department in conjunction with the local
> co-operatives ...
> 2. The General Council to immediately convene a
> National Congress of Action at which plans shall be pre-
> pared for: ... [T]he complete scientific utilisation of the
> whole Trade Union Movement in the struggle ... Active
> participation of Parliamentary and National Labour

Parties in organising of struggle to place them at the
disposal of the General Council; ... [152]

Throughout this period Horner continued to play a full part in
the SWMF. Mardy Lodge Minutes record him regularly taking
the chair at Lodge meetings and undertaking delegate's duties
on the Lodge's behalf during the six months he acted as CPGB
Industrial Organiser. The Lodge Committee remained his indispensable base; its members provided each other with emotional
succour, companionship and argument. Horner used the committee as a sounding board for his ideas; he made his mind
up about developments in the coal wars after participating in
the committee's intense debate and then testing their collective
decision in the general lodge meeting. On 13 April 1926, the
Mardy Lodge meeting decided on nominations for the MFGB
Executive and SWMF offices in advance of the SWMF and
MFGB annual conferences. Horner came top of their list for the
Executive, followed by John Hughes, agent for Llwynypia, and
SO Davies. He also received the lodge nomination for SWMF
President. [153]

Horner resumed full-time checkweighman's duties when seven
of the twelve communists, including Campbell, were released
from gaol on 10 April 1926, even though Pollitt was still inside.
He took the chair for most Lodge meetings from May until the
end of 1926, and made the public statements on behalf of the
Lodge. The party leadership evidently felt that with the 1 May
deadline fast approaching when the government subsidy to the
coal industry would end, he should remain in South Wales and
concentrate his energies on the SWMF and impending confrontation. Horner had drawn very negative conclusions from his
brief experience of deputising for Pollitt. He recalled that he was
'very glad when communists came out of prison as he [thought]
the life of a professional revolutionary awful. No security, nothing to live on, sentiment counts for nothing. If you make a mistake you are out.' He evidently felt neither intellectual interest
nor emotional involvement in the quasi-theological discussions
and personal tensions which preoccupied so many comrades at
the Party Centre. He was also his father's son, concerned to earn
a steady income sufficient to provide for his growing family. His
third daughter was born on 15 March 1926, evidence of Arthur's

and Ethel's revolutionary optimism and Ethel's determination to have another go at giving Arthur a son. They named her Joan, in honour of Shaw's *Saint Joan*, the new play that Mabel Horner had told them about seeing in 1924 with Sybil Thorndike playing the heroine.[154]

Campbell's formidable intellectual ability and evident flair for politics made him an important force in the party leadership. His release restored a basic equilibrium in the party offices, enabling the Politburo to analyse and respond to events quickly. Horner may have appreciated Campbell's presence when he came to London for Executive meetings. Campbell's influence was evident in the CPGB Executive's Open Letter to the National Conference of Trade Union Executives on 29 April. It was practical, taking a similar position to the NMM, and also couched in language easy to understand and relate to: 'We call upon the conference ... to issue a call to every worker in Britain to stand solidly behind the miners in the struggle, and to issue a similar appeal to the workers of the world ... Declare for a United Front, and we are confident that every section of the working class ... will give you whole-hearted and willing support ... '[155]

Until 12 May 1926, the practical difference between trade union militants, the CPGB leadership and Bevin, the guiding force on the General Council, was one of degree, not principle. They all concentrated on organising a disciplined show of force behind the MFGB. The CPGB's pamphlet, *The Reds and the General Strike by C.B. The Lessons of the first General Strike of the British Working Class* acknowledged that Bevin's 'plans for conducting the strike [were] ... marred by several weaknesses, but ... much in advance of anything which had ever been previously suggested in the British Labour Movement'.[156]

The Mardy Lodge Committee had made thorough preparations to enable the community to survive a protracted conflict, building on their experience of 1921. On 28 April, arrangements were finalised for a May Day celebration for the children. Events moved swiftly. The conference of union executives, convened by the General Council on 29 April, had agreed the plans made by an ad hoc committee. Instead of an embargo on the movement of coal, the plan provided for a 'national strike', as the TUC described it. Printing, iron and steel, heavy chemicals, parts of the construction industry and transport were in the

115

first wave. If necessary, there would be a second wave consisting mainly of engineering and shipbuilding. When the miners were locked-out on 1 May, the General Council requested authority from the MFGB Executive to conduct the dispute on their behalf. Herbert Smith replied that 'they understood the position was that all negotiations would now be carried on through the General Council, but that they, the Miners' Federation, would be consulted'. The MFGB Executive adjourned, and members went back to their own coalfield. The General Council circulated its national strike plan to union offices for onward transmission to trades councils and district and local union officials. On Sunday 2 May, Horner gave a 'full report on coal crisis' to a Mardy Lodge meeting.[157]

Also on 2 May three General Council members (Arthur Pugh, Alonso Swales and Jimmy Thomas) and Walter Citrine, acting TUC general secretary, continued negotiations with Baldwin and two Cabinet members, FE Smith, the Minister of Labour, Arthur Steel-Maitland and the Ministry's permanent secretary, Horace Wilson. At 11.15 pm, negotiations were temporarily suspended to enable both sides to report back to their respective institutions. Baldwin found the rest of the Cabinet deeply unhappy at the prospect of making any concessions to the MFGB. The TUC side, reporting to MFGB officers and the General Council assembled in Downing Street, met with equal disquiet. Bevin proposed a national board, nominated from the MFGB, MAGB and independent experts, with power not only to decide wages questions but also to carry through a re-organisation of the industry. At midnight the union side received the news that members of the Operative Printers and Assistants union had refused to print the *Daily Mail* because they considered its leader about the dispute to be provocative. At 1.15 am on 3 May they were informed that the Cabinet regarded the printers' action as a casus belli, and Baldwin broke off negotiations. The General Council failed to persuade him to re-open negotiations on the basis of Bevin's proposal for a tripartite national board.[158]

The General Council's hastily produced plans for the 'national strike' proved to have been well laid. 'By general agreement, the response to the strike on Tuesday, 4 May, was excellent.' Mardy Lodge convened a public meeting on 5 May to discuss feeding arrangements. The Lodge Committee interviewed grocers and discussed their plans should rationing prove necessary. They agreed the amount of food to be allocated to families and single people. A subcommittee of twelve was appointed to oversee the arrangements: six grocers, three lodge officials and three others. Horner told Frankenberg, 'Mardy was headquarters of the Rhondda strikers. From here a daily news bulletin was printed on an old roneo and distributed ... edited by Arthur who had the latest news at 11 a.m. every day by telephone from Bob Stewart in London. The police seemed very simple about it. They had the entry into Mardy covered on the Rhondda side and the exit on the Aberdare side. The papers were taken over the mountain [to the west of Mardy, probably to Abergorky] on foot'. From there the bulletins were taken by motorbike riders waiting to courier them across the valleys. Horner owned a motorbike at the time, and may have had the excitement of acting as courier for some of the consignments.[159]

On 12 May, after having despatched the orders to the unions involved in the second wave to bring their members out on strike, the TUC General Council announced the end of the General Strike. They were evidently concerned about information from their Intelligence Committee that strikers in the first wave were drifting back to work. They were also worried that conduct of the strike was 'passing out of the hands of responsible [union] Executives into the hands of men who had no authority, no control, no responsibility'. But the General Council also believed they had won genuine concessions for the miners. They presented the MFGB Executive with terms they had agreed with Sir Herbert Samuel (who had not been authorised by the government to meet them). The MFGB Executive peremptorily rejected the Samuel-General Council compromise, but the national strike was over, and the miners now faced the prospect of fighting the Lock-Out alone. Baldwin tried on 14 May to bring the MFGB and the coalowners back to the negotiating table, but his attempt was dismissed by both sides.[160]

Observers reckoned that mining communities' willingness to stay out was reinforced by the exceptionally good weather which prevailed in the summer, and lasted well into the autumn. (Almost without exception, protracted miners' strikes in Northern Europe have occurred during good weather in summer months.) Three other factors underpinned the miners'

117

determination. Firstly, there was the recent experience of the 1921 Lock-Out when lodges had coped with marshalling collective resources through communal feeding, rationing, etc. Mardy Lodge was probably not unusual in having the same committee members who had negotiated the 1921 arrangements with local shopkeepers and co-operative societies. Secondly, mining families were skilled in being able to forage, scavenge and steal to provide many daily necessities. Thrifty families also depleted their Post Office savings accounts and/or dividends lodged at the local co-operative store. Finally, there was the support given to miners' families under Poor Law provisions. During the 1926 Lock-Out, there was an increase of 1.2 million persons in receipt of relief, many of whom were single men, in contravention of a 1921 court judgement. The Ministry of Health Annual Report for 1926 to 1927 noted that school meals had been utilised by local authorities and commented: 'There is abundant evidence that the health of the children actually improved in many areas during the dispute.'[161]

In early July 1926, faced with the complete break-down of collective bargaining between the MFGB and MAGB, the government legislated on future working hours by fiat. Parliament agreed a new Coal Mines Bill, restoring the statutory working day to eight hours. (The miners had won a statutory reduction in hours from eight to seven in 1919.) The government claimed that this alteration met with the MFGB's approval. This was patently untrue, and there was a general reaction in the wider British public against the government's apparently high-handed behaviour. The bill's passage re-united the General Council and the MFGB Executive for the first time since the General Strike. It also precipitated serious attempts from the great and good to effect a compromise. The most important initiative was taken by a group of Anglican and nonconformist church leaders, including the Archbishop of Canterbury. Their proposals, universally described as the Bishops' Memorandum, involved the government's willingness to subsidise the industry whilst the full recommendations of the Samuel Report were implemented.[162]

Cook, Smith and Richards had already concluded that the MFGB needed some line of retreat, and pressed the MFGB Executive to take the Bishops' Memorandum seriously. The Executive provisionally approved the proposals and agreed that the bishops should present them to the government to secure their agreement to finance the subsidy. When the district unions considered the Bishops' proposals, however, both South Wales and Durham registered strong opposition. South Wales' negative was predictable. Durham's unexpected militancy was the fruit of intense CPGB and MMM activity in the coalfield, in which Horner had played a prominent part. On 17 July the SWMF Executive formally requested the MFGB Executive to withdraw their approval for the churchmen to act as mediators and to convene a Delegate Conference to discuss their proposals. The DMA Executive followed similarly on 21 July. The MFGB Executive duly convened a conference on 30 July. It was the first time delegates from the different coalfields had met since 20 May and they agreed to put the Bishops' Memorandum to a national ballot. Votes were taken at specially convened lodge meetings, normally by a show of hands. The method was probably critical in determining the result, a small majority against the proposals, 367,650 to 333,036. The two largest district unions, South Wales and Yorkshire, were joined by Cumberland, Lancashire and Cheshire, and the Forest of Dean in voting against. Scotland and Cleveland failed to hold a ballot. All other affiliated districts voted in favour. (If the NUSMW had voted in favour, it had sufficient members to have affected the overall result, which would then have been a small majority in favour.)[163]

The miners' rejection of the Memorandum surprised the political establishment and trade union leaders. Most observers agreed that the MMM and communist party activists were responsible. Many miners had agreed with their tireless arguments that the MAGB would have been compelled to back down in the 1921 Lock-Out if the MFGB Executive had not capitulated in late July. Militants had put the arguments for fighting on at MMM meetings; they also spoke at Lodge meetings in the debate preceding the vote on the Bishops' proposals.[164] Although Cook remained an unrepentant advocate of the Bishops' Memorandum, his close relationship with Horner endured. Their intimacy had survived sharp disagreements before, and they were evidently able to subordinate political differences.

The ballot result created a serious problem of how to preserve national unity for the MFGB Executive. Before the Lock-Out coalowners in Nottinghamshire, Derbyshire, the Midlands

Federation (the Warwickshire, Leicestershire and Staffordshire coalfields), Somerset and Bristol had been able to sell coal profitably on the domestic market, and they were not proposing to make any wage reductions in their district agreements. Not surprisingly, miners in these districts were reluctant to continue to stay away from work, when the national chances of success now appeared so tenuous. They could have gone back to work at any point on their pre-1 May wages and conditions.[165] The Nottinghamshire Miners Association was the largest and most outspoken of the district unions affected.

The ballot result was discussed at a national delegate conference on 15 to 16 August. There was a well-known precedent for the conference to set the result aside and instead plump to accept the Executive's recommendation in favour of the proposals. In the 1912 national dispute on minimum wage rates Robert Smillie had persuaded both the MFGB Executive and a delegate conference to set aside a similarly narrow ballot result that had supported fighting on, and accept a compromise settlement.[166] Horner had evidently been chosen by the SWMF delegates to speak on their behalf. Because of the Federation's importance, his was the main speech against the Bishops' Memorandum. He made it clear that neither he nor South Wales were ruling out a compromise settlement. This was simply the wrong time and the wrong terms on which to settle. If the MFGB was promoting a compromise settlement now, their negotiating position would be significantly weakened. He then presented a coherent alternative to the Executive's position:

> ... Nobody attempted to justify the Bishops' proposals on their merits. Our General Secretary's statement ... was attempting to prove that our men were too weak to achieve any more ... They are as the Chairman said yesterday, a compromise ... justified on the ground that the men were too weak to struggle for the original objective ... We said, in effect, let us ask the men whether they are strong enough, and if they are strong enough, then we must fight on. If they declare they are too weak, then you must develop a new line of tactics. The answer has come, demonstrating something which ought not to inculcate fear in us, it is such as should hearten us, that

after 16 weeks of struggling the people have not broken away at all, they have voted and told us in no uncertain sound that there is no justification in being afraid for them ...

... [E]verybody is living and talking in an atmosphere of defeatism. Do you suggest that our enemies don't know ... If the Government know, the coalowners know that we are going to meet them because we cannot fight them any longer ... I say it is unfair to send any men into negotiations with the enemy whilst recognising that these men are going in with a pistol at their heads ...

... [W]hat we have been endeavouring to do since the beginning is to starve the enemy of coal. The enemy has been endeavouring to starve us of food. These have been the two lines ... Now ... before there can be any hope of a fight for the status quo, there must be a giving up of this position of opening our mouths to see what God will send us ...

Horner concluded by describing the positive steps taken to strengthen the miners' front. Whilst he omitted any mention of the MMM and CPGB by name, delegates would have been well aware of their activism. He obliquely criticised MFGB leaders for their failure to carry on the fighting with sufficient vigour:

I remember ... suggesting to this Conference that the ... Secretary should make a plan of all districts with a view to concentrating on the weaker areas ... I was told if I desired a plan, I had better make it myself. I would point out you have had results, that the last time we met here, [the numbers working in] Warwickshire had been reduced to 1,500 from round about 4,000 or 5,000, and having reduced it we left Warwickshire. Mainwaring, Cook, and others came away, a lot of other people stopped away and went protecting men where they were preaching a defeatism policy. I suggest as a definite concrete proposal that the secretary shall concentrate all the speaking ability ... on the weakened areas. Having cured the broken places ... we must then approach those workers in our industry who are importing foreign coal ... We must get down to ways and means ...

Ebby Edwards, from Northumberland, spoke next, replying on behalf of the Executive:

> I am sure that the whole of the delegates have listened to the speech which has just been delivered with the greatest amount of interest. I think we can congratulate Mr. Horner ... in placing the case no one can complain, because I believe he has put it from his point of view in a clear and impartial way, without personalities, as far as it is possible to be. [H]ad there been no Bishops' proposals it would have been necessary for the conference to review the general situation. You cannot afford to be in a great conflict with 1,000,000 men and not review from time to time the general situation ... therefore we can conduct this conference apart from the Bishops' proposals ... What is the alternative to negotiating some sort of settlement ... That is the position this conference is bound to face, and while ... we have ... [a] right to object to the extreme left going outside the organisation in direct contradiction to our own policies ... I am going to suggest, and I think I will be able to show through the official organ of friend Horner, a fundamental difference of opinion. We are first told we have to intensify the struggle by the whole working-class movement ... [D]o you expect that every section of the working-classes are coming out? I put it, it only needs to be put to be exploded ... I believe if, as Horner says, the organisation is strong now and we agree this is the time, then we should use the power of the organisation to negotiate a settlement in the interests of our men. [W]e say negotiate with the forces of the organisation now ...

Edwards was followed by Aneurin Bevan:

> I did not propose this morning to add to the number of South Wales delegates who have spoken ... were it not for the manner in which Mr. Edwards concluded his

speech ... [with] the exposition of what he considered to be the fundamental falsity of the attitude taken up by Mr. Horner.

Whenever we arrive at a stage like this, when a leader rises to his feet he begins to talk about the responsibilities of leadership and the rank and file ... Leaders become conscious of a sense of responsibility when it becomes necessary to negotiate reductions. I thought there was another form of responsibility, the responsibility of so far as possible mobilising our available forces so that if we cannot secure complete, ultimate victory, to secure as favourable a settlement as possible ... [T]he organisation has maintained the struggle for 16 weeks because of our power to mobilise the spirit of the rank and file.

... We have had a long stoppage, in which Mr. Herbert Smith ... and Mr. Cook ... have had a more loyal following than any other leaders have ever had in this Federation, and yet at the limit of their material exhaustion, as pointed out by Mr. Horner, there is sufficient spirit in the rank and file to reject the advice of the leaders and conduct a policy in advance of what has been seen here ...

... I say that we ought to have a more experimental spirit, and we ought to develop a sense, shall I say of recklessness, and use our machinery, looked at from the point of view of ultimate victory to the working-classes, and Mr. Edwards would not have an opportunity of philosophising at this point of view ... Mr. Spencer [NMA general secretary] suggests sending Cook and Smith with a white flag. I think it is utterly absurd ... I suggest that if there is nothing else left a good deal of bluff can be put up yet. There are still possibilities of bluff, and not negotiations which are conducted in the spirit of a funeral march to the cemetery.[167]

Delegates from Kent and Bristol rose to oppose Bevan, conflating his views with Horner's and South Wales generally. They stressed that they were not being defeatist, but merely realistic. Two Yorkshire delegates followed; one supported negotiations, the other wanted to carry on fighting. George Jones of Warwickshire spoke in favour of negotiations:

> If this is only an incident in the class war, then we should regard this as an incident, and we ought to think about the army and how effective we can get it in order to carry on that fight ... I quite frankly admit I want to fight, but the question is this: Can we really as our friend Horner suggests and others suggest in the Midlands, can we get the blacklegs out of the pits? I don't think any intensive propaganda at this stage is going to achieve this end ... I want to say unless the Executive does begin to negotiate ... the facts are there, you may have eventually them negotiating with the Midlands blacklegging. That is the position ... It is not true to say as friend Horner says, that we have reached a stage in advance of May 30th ... [168]

From the chair, Smith urged delegates to accept collective responsibility and give the Executive authority to open negotiations with the MAGB on the basis of the Bishops' proposals. Horner immediately rose to his feet, unwilling to let Smith have the last word. Conceding that the mood of the conference had swung behind immediate negotiations, he trimmed and stressed the importance of building up a position of strength before meeting the MAGB: 'We hope you will win [in the negotiations] ... I think there should be central direction of propaganda to assist those districts where they are weakest. I suggest the Executive take certain steps with a view to taking responsibility for action in these districts, the propaganda being directed from the centre ... '

George Jones supported Horner's point; Smith also agreed. But Cook did not, saying: 'It would get into the Press and would be taken as a sign of weakness ... if headquarters sent someone down [to the laggard districts].' A string of speakers recounted their own experiences of meetings and police behaviour, as well as the pros and cons of sending volunteers to staunch the drift back to work in the Midlands. Mainwaring declared, 'I consider as a Welshman, if I can assist, it ought to be the duty of every member of this organisation.' Smith responded, 'I want to say that anyone who wants to volunteer their services, I don't want to stop anyone. I would speed you on with it but what I say is that we cannot take any more responsibility financially [for subsidising volunteers], that is my difficulty.'

The delegate conference decision on 16 August to open negotiations, but simultaneously to build up a position of strength, was the climacteric of the Lock-Out. Horner's trimming tactics had enabled the militant left to unite behind the Executive and prevented a breach which was threatening to open between the South Walian militants and Smith and Richards. George Jones' acknowledgement of the Midlands' weakness made it easier for the MFGB to discipline the moderate right Nottinghamshire officials, George Spencer MP and Frank Varley MP, who had been pushing for immediate retreat and compromise. At the close, delegates recorded thanks to the Soviet unions for their financial help and to the American Miners who had assisted WP Richardson, DMA President and MFGB Treasurer, in arranging a campaign of meetings in the USA. A 'hearty vote of thanks' to Herbert Smith was recorded; the audience apparently appreciated the difficulty with which Smith had kept the conference from disintegrating.

When the MFGB Executive met the MAGB on 19 August, the district coalowners' associations had already withdrawn the authority previously ceded to the national association. District wage agreements were the only option on offer. It became even more problematic for district union leaders in Nottinghamshire and the Midlands to hold the MFGB line and fight on. Nevertheless, following the delegate conference decision of 16 August, activists from other coalfields and communists from everywhere were pouring into the Midlands. They scored brilliant, temporary victories. Pollitt had been released from prison on 10 September. He recalled that after a short holiday: 'I was ... sent to the Leicestershire coalfields [by the CPGB] to try to stop the rot. I had to change at Leicester for Coalville, and met ... Herbert Smith on the platform. We had a very friendly talk and he scribbled me a note of introduction to the miners, which served me in very good stead during some very difficult times which lay ahead.'[169]

Probably caught up in efforts to re-start negotiations with the MAGB, Cook and Smith were absent for most of the TUC in the first week of September. Cook evidently made arrangements for Horner to attend Congress as a delegate from the

MFGB Head Office. (The SWMF Executive had decided at its meeting on 27 August not to send a delegation, presumably to divert the money for use in relieving distress in the coalfield.)[170] Throughout the week, Horner's presence was manifest. He intervened eleven times, in contrast to Cook's three. Some of his contributions were designed to harry the right-wing Chairman, Arthur Pugh, of the Iron and Steel Workers. A protracted, ill-tempered exchange occurred between them about the General Council's conduct before the General Strike. But Horner also questioned the General Council's rationale for abandoning the General Strike, and their current failure to marshal support for the MFGB. When he complained about a paragraph in the General Council's report, Pugh made no attempt to stop him, although his intervention, commenting on the paragraph rather than moving its reference back, was certainly out of order. Horner's criticism was supported by Ellen Wilkinson MP – who was even more aggressive towards Pugh – Sam Elsbury of the Tailors and Garment Workers, and Jack Tanner. Pugh's chairing tactics were evidently considered, and were a calculated effort to preserve unity by allowing the maximum ventilation of views throughout the week.[171]

Horner's most substantive intervention was to move an emergency resolution on the MFGB's behalf on the Chinese situation, where a local warlord had seized ships belonging to the Chinese Eastern Railway, owned by Soviet Russia. His speech was exemplary communist rhetoric, and had probably been fashioned after he spoke to the party experts, Johnnie Campbell and George Hardy:

> He said that all who had read the *Daily Herald* would have seen that there was an immediate and definite possibility of a war against an Eastern people which would be bound eventually to culminate in a war against the Soviets of Russia, which was the main objective of world capitalism. The Miners' Federation were naturally very anxious that the Russian people should not be repaid for their generosity to them by a war waged against them ... [H]ad it not been for their Russian comrades the miners' wives and children in this struggle would long since have starved.' Pugh intervened at this point,

asking Horner to confine himself to the resolution. After having been seconded by another MFGB delegate, the motion was passed with only cursory debate, probably reflecting the General Council's determination to avoid political division.[172]

When parliament re-assembled at the end of September, Baldwin and Churchill signalled their determination to abstain from serious engagement with the coal problem. However, their earlier proposal for settling the dispute remained on the table. It left district wage bargaining intact, whilst 'offering ... to secure by legislation that the main principles that a National Agreement would be designed to secure should be applied by a National Appeal Tribunal'.[173] On 29 September the MFGB Executive told a delegate conference that 80,000 miners – about 6 per cent of the labour force – had returned to work.[174] The Executive resolution before delegates proposed that the Government's proposal be referred to districts without any recommendation, and that conference re-convene the following week to consider their responses. Evidently, neither Cook, Smith or Richards felt able to give the EC a lead in favour of compromise.

Unusually, Smillie was moved to intervene. He had taken little part in previous conferences, but evidently felt compelled to step forward as the person who had led the 1912 national dispute. His speech was designed to ease the Executive's difficult task of leading a retreat. He argued that delegates should feel collectively bound to recommend the government's proposals to their districts, because they preserved the principle of national wage determination:

> I think the time has come when we must divide the responsibility a bit, and not put it all on one. The [Executive] Committee during these terrible 21 weeks have borne practically the whole responsibility of the national movement ...
>
> You will find ... the finger of the mineowners of this country [in the proposals] ... [T]hey make the chief aim ... to divide this great Federation of ours into sections. To make it impossible for all time that we will ever take joint action again ... I agree with my friend Mr.

Richards, that the time has come when each and all of us representing the men shall take our share of the responsibility with the Executive ... The mineowners, for weeks and weeks, have said [to the government] just keep away, let us finish this fight with the miners ourselves, knowing full well that privation and starvation would do its work. Our men and women have done magnificently. Never in the history of our country or the world has there been such a splendid army of men behind the leaders as in this struggle, but this cannot last for ever. There is no hunger in the homes of the coal masters. None of their bairns are crying for food ... I think it is far better to look this situation in the face and try to save something from the ruin.[175]

Smillie's unexpected intervention carried great weight because of his experience and successful record as MFGB president. His cogent argument transformed the mood on the floor, and persuaded delegates to seriously contemplate retreat. Smith was poised to take the vote, when Horner caught his eye, probably by planting himself squarely in the aisle, making it impossible for Smith to ignore him. He wanted to move an amendment to the resolution 'if it were possible':

> After all there is an assumption ... that only those who are anxious to bring this dispute to a termination at any price are the people at all concerned for the welfare of the people in their districts. If that is the argument to get back to work under any conditions which is to have weight in this Conference, then it is a pity we ever started on this fight at all.

Horners's provocation elicited the following response:

> The Chairman: Is that a fair assumption?
> Mr. Horner: I am making that.
> The Chairman: Don't put it on me.
> Mr. Richards: Nor me.

Horner's speech was filled with bluster and lacked his usual coherent arguments, probably because he had not had time to think about what he would say. He had acted spontaneously, to counter the strong effect of Smillie's speech. His amendment was actually a counter-motion. It rejected the government terms, instructed delegates to recommend rejection to their districts, and instructed the Executive Committee to withdraw its offer to negotiate. It should instead 'prepare a plan for intensifying the struggle by every means in our power'. His purpose was to deflect the conference from taking a collective decision binding themselves to compromise and retreat. Although the amendment was seconded by an unnamed delegate, Enoch Morrell protested that the amendment had not been endorsed by the SWMF delegation, an oblique invitation to Smith to rule it out of order. Smith, however, evidently felt that Horner had significant support from the floor. After a cursory discussion, he merely proposed to conclude the day's proceedings without taking a vote, whilst asking Horner to withdraw his amendment.

Before Horner could reply, Bevan rose to object. Although the conference was due to re-convene on the following day, delegates knew that Smith and Cook would be in Ostend, where they were scheduled to meet the Miners' International Federation about imposing an effective embargo of coal exports to Britain. Bevan pointed out that if Horner agreed to withdraw his amendment, the conference would have little option but to accept the Executive recommendation. 'I want the Executive to meet to-night and draw up a recommendation for the Conference tomorrow, upon which we might vote to-morrow morning.'

Smith ignored Bevan's suggestion and appealed again to Horner to withdraw the amendment. When he refused, Smith tried to take a vote on the question 'whether the Government proposals be referred to the districts or not', effectively disallowing Horner's amendment. Mainwaring and Jack Williams (General Secretary of the Forest of Dean miners) rose to press for an adjournment, apparently hoping to keep Horner's amendment on the table. Smith resisted. 'If you are not prepared to take my ruling you had better go out.' Williams rejoined, 'I can go out, but I am only demanding elementary rights.' When James Robson of the DMA supported Mainwaring and Williams, Smith finally allowed a vote on the adjournment, which was carried. Horner's amendment remained in play.

The next day, besides Smith and Cook, Horner was the other notable absentee. The Executive had not met, and there was no indication about how the conflict between Horner's amendment and the Executive recommendation would be resolved. Tom Richards, presiding in Smith's absence, sought guidance from Jack Williams and Robson, on the grounds that they had moved the adjournment. Robson declined to answer. Williams said only that 'the adjournment was to enable districts to have before them the resolutions [the Executive's and Horner's amendment] which were before the meeting yesterday so that they might discuss them.'

Richards then proposed to treat Horner's amendment as a counter-motion to the Executive's motion and have delegates vote on both. Morrell offered a compromise. He pledged that the whole South Wales delegation, including Horner, would accept the Executive resolution, 'subject to you giving an undertaking on behalf of the Executive that they will make every possible effort to hold the present position in the Midlands intact in the sense that it may not get any worse, pending our further meeting ... The one object which underlines Mr. Horner's amendment is an honest endeavour to hold the position ... '

Richards was reluctant to give ground. '[I]n order to placate Mr. Horner I suppose the desire is that an undertaking shall be given that the [Executive] Committee shall adopt plans for intensifying the resistance we are offering ... I must say, however, I do not think that the Committee, despite everything which was said by Mr. Horner yesterday – could do any more gingering up, because so far as members of the Committee are concerned they have given their services and have done whatever they could quite freely ... '

Apparently unaware of his absence, Richards addressed Horner from the chair. After being told of his absence, Richards responded, 'He ought to be here. However, in his absence I won't say anything about it. There is nothing for it but that there is a strong feeling in the country, strong in opinion, who believe that the time has come for an intensification of this struggle. [But] I don't think that is intended at this Conference.'

Morrell's ill-tempered reply highlighted the tensions inside the SWMF. He applied more pressure on Richards to give way, and abort the Executive's attempt to start a retreat. 'Pardon me if I say I don't think it is quite fair to the South Wales delegation taken collectively. I think [the request for an Executive undertaking] ... was an honest endeavour to arrive at a greater measure of unanimity ... I don't care whether Horner is here or not ... He is not the only delegate and what we desire is to give the strongest possible support to the officials in the several districts.'

Ted Williams put a direct question to the Nottinghamshire delegates. 'It is rumoured that in all probability Notts will make a district settlement sometime this week. Can they tell us whether there is any truth in that at all? We have heard it from various sources.' Spencer replied frankly that it would depend on the NMA Executive meeting the next day. 'If we can do anything to stem the tide, or anybody else can, we shall be very thankful for it ... but we cannot tolerate men coming into the district [from other coalfields to staunch the return to work] ... Some of the men have gone to work as a result of the speeches which have been made ... [I]f the circumstances are anything like favourable ... we shall remain loyal, but if there are many more thousands gone to work in Notts by next Thursday we shall have them all back at work.'

Varley agreed. 'We have worked unremittingly, and although I do not agree with Horner's policy, I must say he has worked like a Trojan in our district ... Whatever we have lacked it has not been oratory. They have been at it from early morning to dewy eve, and right into the hours of darkness ... We welcome anyone, but I am afraid that we have had too many of one sort ... If we could have had the official element better represented it may have had some influence, although I am not going to say it would. You find there a different mentality to what you find anywhere else.'

Joseph Jones reassured delegates that the Executive were already intensifying their efforts to ensure that Nottinghamshire and the Midlands held firm. 'No one wants to shout the odds on Spencer and Varley. That will not help the present situation we have got to face.' Richards ended the conference on this united note. Morrell's intervention and Horner's absence had enabled a compromise to be found without loss of face on either side.

131

Cook may have persuaded Horner to absent himself on 'official' business in Ostend in order to avoid a confrontation at the conference. (The MIF general secretary, Frank Hodges, was known to be resisting any export embargo.) Horner could see that the MFGB was close to disintegration, and like Smillie he was anxious to preserve the increasingly precarious unity.

During the following week, the line began to break in every coalfield. Although Nottinghamshire and Derbyshire remained officially out, Spencer assisted NMA lodge officials in negotiating a return to work in one colliery. In the face of this desperate news, the SWMF delegation brought a resolution to the re-convened delegate conference on 7 October, which went even further than Horner's amendment the previous week. It rejected all compromise and called for a strategy of total war against the coalowners. In proposing the resolution, Morrell emphasised that it represented the Federation's collective commitment. 'In my experience of perhaps nearly 30 years I never saw a stronger one [delegate conference] than the one in Cardiff on Tuesday last ... [T]here was tremendous unanimity.'

Horner's seconding speech used biblical metaphors to make its unremittingly optimistic point.

> I believe if we had had national conduct of this struggle right from its beginning and simply persisted in the policy that is always persisted in war ... If we had sent reserves to the weak spots there would have been official backing to the local officials ... [t]hen I believe we could have held this position ... Our proposals mean this. Let us drop making our men's hearts sick by continually arousing hope in them that must be deferred to the following week until the new move comes ... Take back our proposals ... and let it [the struggle] go forth ... Let us start a new campaign with a new spirit, a new faith, with a belief in our strength to carry on ...

The resolution committed the MFGB to a significant escalation of the conflict and a less flexible negotiating position. But Smith and Richards felt too exposed to oppose it. Smith 'was determined to wait ... [He] had no intention of allowing the Minority Movement to create another myth of betrayal by their leaders of a loyal rank and file who had victory in their grasp.'[176] Richards needed to keep the confidence of the SWMF. If he had distanced himself from the Federation resolution, his own position as SWMF general secretary would become precarious. However, Cook, as a national officer without a district constituency, could oppose the resolution root and branch. He made a compelling plea to delegates. Horner from South Wales says:

> I ask will not the last stage be worse than the first? It is known to us. I have said it before. Better to starve in fresh sunlight or we had better not starve at all ... You have to consider whether we can come to a stage of negotiating peace, negotiating terms, or whether you are going to allow the employers or the Government to impose terms ... I thought it was wise for somebody to speak, as we might be charged with being cowards ... If you adopt the resolution from South Wales ... you would have the soldiers protecting the men at work, and you would have a repetition of 1921, which I hope never to see again.

The SWMF delegation remained adamant, and rebuffed all attempts by other delegates to modify the terms of the resolution. Bevan spoke soon after Cook, in an emotion-laden speech:

> I admit with the Chairman that the outlook is by no means bright ... We admit the obduracy and cynical disregard of other unions. There has not been much *camaraderie* with the other leaders ... This is the most silent funeral I have ever witnessed. If we are going down, at least, in going down let us inflict the maximum damage on the enemy inside as well as outside ... The rank and file will feel the hardest blow when this is over. We are accepting all the responsibility involved in this proposal ... that there shall be a drive throughout the country with the help of the political leaders of the movement and the industrial leaders in the coalfield, which, I am satisfied will persuade and convince the owners and the Government that the price they have to pay for bringing

133

out the Miners' Federation is too heavy and in the end
they will be forced to give us more reasonable terms.

Then Ted Williams and SO Davies, one of the Federation representatives on the MFGB Executive, also spoke in support of the
resolution's uncompromising stance.

There was no serious alternative put to the SWMF resolution.
It was passed by a decisive majority, supported by Yorkshire,
Lancashire, Durham and Northumberland, with only Scotland,
Derbyshire, Nottinghamshire, the Midlands and the smaller districts voting against. Smith ruled that the resolution should be
submitted to a district vote in the following week. Conference
dispersed after voting to order Spencer out of its proceedings,
and referring the question of his expulsion from the NMA and
suspension as a sponsored miners' MP to the NMA Council.[177]

The Labour Party Conference took place in the same week as
the district ballot was being held. The Conference Chairman,
Robert Williams, faced a difficult situation. Not only had the
Lock-Out reached a desperate state, there was also the contentious issue of the Labour Party's refusal to allow the CPGB's
affiliation. Williams was a foundation member of the communist
party, but had been expelled in May 1921 for his failure, as secretary of the National Transport Workers Federation, to support
the embargo on moving coal. As a born-again social democrat,
his chairmanship was bound to come under strong fire from the
left. Horner spoke at the conference as an MFGB delegate.[178]
Everyone, including Williams, made little attempt to disguise
their feelings about the miners' conflict. A newspaper report
described the first day in lurid tones:

> Bedlam broke loose again and lasted several minutes
> when the chairman announced that the resolution to re-
> open the question of affiliation of the Communist Party
> to the Labour Party was carried on a show of hands, but
> after a heated scene the resolution was defeated on a card
> vote by 2.276 million to 349,000. Loud and prolonged
> cheering greeted Mr. Williams' remark, 'the Communist
> Party and the Minority Movement still believe in the
> General Strike'. The applause was even greater, how-
> ever, at his next remark, 'the Labour Party looks with

134

confidence to the next general election'. [After Williams called for the Standing Orders Committee report, Pollitt, attending as a Boilermakers' delegate, had risen.] 'In view of the insolent attack made from the chair on the policy decided by the miners [the South Wales resolution] I move that this conference take the miners' crisis as its next business.' When Williams refused, Mr. Horner, the South Wales miners, and a thorn in the side of the Bournemouth [TUC] conference, also jumped up and shouted something about Buckingham Palace. The matter, however, was not pressed.[179]

Tempers had cooled by the following day, when Pollitt moved the reference back of the paragraph in the Executive Committee's report dealing with communist affiliation. He was seconded by a delegate from the Workers' Union. Herbert Morrison spoke on the Executive's behalf, and made a straightforward political case based on the CPGB's connection to the Russian communist party and the Comintern, and its support for the dictatorship of the proletariat. The Executive's resolution on 'The Mining Crisis' offered unconditional support to the MFGB whilst stressing that the only real solution to the industry's problems was nationalisation. There was no mention, however, of offering any practical assistance to the locked-out miners. Debate on the third day was punctuated by attempts to move the reference back of 'The Mining Crisis', from David Kirkwood MP, on behalf of the ILP and Pollitt. They were supported by Oswald Mosley, WJ Brown, of the Civil Service Clerical Association, and Horner.

Horner condemned the Labour Party and the TUC for failing to afford the miners any material aid. 'If the Miners won, they would win a victory not only for themselves but for the whole Working-class Movement. If they lost in this because of the cowardice of the Working-class Movement, then God help the Miners and God help the other workers afterwards.' The reference back was lost on a card vote by a substantial majority, 2.159 to 1.368 million. In the debate on the resolution itself, WP Richardson and Horner made the only substantial speeches from the MFGB delegation, which had evidently agreed that the two men should be their principal spokesmen. But Williams concluded the debate with difficulty, because so many non-mining delegates wanted to speak. The resolution was not carried unanimously as he had requested; the 210,000 votes against it were probably cast by the Boilermakers.[180]

The MFGB Executive met to consider the district vote on Friday 15 October, the last day of the Labour Conference. The South Wales resolution scored an impressive victory, 460,150 to 284,336. Durham and Derbyshire had voted in favour; the principal opposing districts were Northumberland, the Midlands and Yorkshire. The Executive took immediate steps to be seen to be implementing the resolution, transforming itself into a '"Central Council of War", with moveable headquarters. First meeting at Basford Notts.' Executive members met on Tuesday 19 October, and heard evidence of intense activity the previous weekend, which had succeeded in turning back the tide of men returning to work. On 18 October, the Ministry of Mines had reported that only 20,351 miners had reported for work.[181]

The Executive arranged a campaign of meetings in Nottinghamshire, and the CPGB did the same, throwing all its available people and resources into the effort.[182] Nevertheless, the numbers of miners back at work increased at an even faster rate. Spencer spoke in parliament about the MFGB Executive as 'the council of action which dragged the men out again', they would be victimised by owners and would be unable to find work in future.[183]

The South Wales resolution also required the MFGB Executive to meet the General Council to enlist its help in intensifying the coal embargo. On 22 October the General Council responded positively, evidently anxious to use the opportunity of the meeting for other ends. Despite the MFGB's declared intention of fighting to the bitter end, General Council members could see clearly enough that if an exit strategy presented itself, the MFGB Executive were likely to take it. After the meeting four senior members and Citrine, who had been confirmed as TUC General Secretary in September, met Baldwin, Churchill and the Secretary for Mines. The General Council's calculation proved correct; their intervention gave the MFGB Executive the pretext it required to begin a retreat. On 4 November, the Executive met the TUC intermediaries and the government, and negotiations continued throughout the following week. On 10 November, an interim report was given to an MFGB delegate conference, which remained in session over the four days when negotiations were proceeding.

On 13 November, the conference recommended that districts accept the terms agreed between the three MFGB officers and the government. Horner recognised the overwhelming feeling in favour of settling. But his own mood remained indomitable.

I don't think that this Conference is entitled to take its cue from what appears to be necessary in the districts which have been weakest in this struggle ... It seems to me to be a choice as to whether we shall allow our policy to be determined by a fear of the weak people or by loyalty to the desires who have remained strong. I frankly am in the position that I desire to express the policy desired by those who have remained with us from the first day until now, even if they were the minority instead of the majority ... [A]ccepting the eight hour day means that thousands of men will be rendered permanently redundant ... It means that these men have to continue an existence with the full consciousness that their means of getting bread will be cut off, who will have stomach requirements just the same as we ... [W]e will have a storm of locusts over the whole coalfield, and no position will be safe ...

Horner was followed by Joseph Jones, keen to be seen to be supporting the Yorkshire miners' declared intention to fight on.

Strange as it may seem, I find myself substantially in agreement with Mr. Horner ... What we want is satisfaction on the question of the [National Appeal] Tribunal ... I think it would come with very ill grace from the weaker districts to say to Yorkshire after having fought for six months for the less favourable districts that we should blindly accept these terms now ... [I]f we are face to face with a compromise let us do it on well ordered lines. What we are faced with now is capitulation ...

If there were a case on economic grounds for an extension of the working day, it has already gone, because the public have been prepared to pay money for coal to provide bonuses and bribes for the blacklegs, and if they can do that they can pay for the coal in order to give the men a decent wage and avoid longer hours ... because no one on the platform nor any Executive member will say any other than that they could feel there was a frantic desire on the part of the Cabinet to settle this matter. In view of this anxiety on that part of the Cabinet, I think it is up to us to extract all we can from this atmosphere.[184]

Other delegates were less sanguine. Bevan and WH Mainwaring both distanced themselves from Horner's reluctance to countenance retreat, although Bevan was clear that the proposed terms were unacceptable. At the conclusion of the debate, there was a narrow majority on a card vote for recommending the agreed terms. South Wales and Yorkshire were the largest opposing districts. Conference stood adjourned whilst a district vote was taken on them.

Richards had predicted on the first day of the conference that, because the Executive had been upholding an unqualified No Surrender position since May, the rank and file would reject the abrupt volte-face which they were now being asked to perform. Members would feel that it was perverse for the Executive to suddenly recommend a retreat when they had been consistently promising that standing fast and not accepting less would produce concessions. Richards' prediction proved accurate. The Minority Movement had remained active throughout the vote, issuing a circular under Nat Watkins' name which attacked the criminal folly of surrendering when victory was well within reach. On 19 November, the re-convened conference heard that the terms had been rejected in a district vote by 460,806 to 313,200.[185]

But at this juncture, the MFGB Executive had little room for manoeuvre. On 10 November, the conference heard from districts that well over a quarter of miners were now back at work. On 19 November, the Department of Mines figures showed that nearly a third were back at work. In Lancashire, nearly 50 per cent were working; in Yorkshire nearly 25 per cent; and in Scotland a third. In South Wales, the *Western Mail* reported that there were 20,000 men back at work, the majority in Monmouthshire, about 15 per cent of the workforce. In the Midlands, fully three quarters of the workforce had returned.[186] It was evident that if the Executive did not order an organised return, the MFGB would lose all credibility with the men and the coalowners.

On 19 November, the MFGB Delegate Conference met again and advised Districts to negotiate District settlements, the expedient which Bevan had proposed on 12 November. On 26 November, the MFGB Delegate Conference re-convened to consider what terms districts had obtained. The owners had refused to meet the district unions in four districts. The Nottinghamshire owners had de-recognised the NMA and instead granted recognition to the union formed by Spencer, the Nottinghamshire and District Miners' Industrial Union. Breakaway unions in other coalfields had been formed by the men who had gone back to work.

South Wales, Yorkshire and Durham were the last districts to go back to work. The SWMF agreed terms with the South Wales coalowners on 30 November, and the coalfield returned on 1 December.[187] But some union officials had broken ranks before then to represent men who were returning to work. Their justification was similar to Spencer's: the returning miners needed collective representation. On 13 November, Ablett had finalised arrangements for an organised return to work and completed the negotiation of terms and conditions for miners at Hills' Plymouth collieries, part of his patch as agent for the SWMF Merthyr District. The Federation Executive decided that he had been complicit in the return to work, and suspended him.[188]

Looking back at the course of the Lock-Out, it is apparent that Horner was the most consistent and effective of the principal players inside the MFGB. He had a well conceived strategy which he pursued single-mindedly, with great tactical finesse, throughout the seven months. Smith had no plan for pursuing the MFGB's goals. He certainly desired a settlement, but his inability to negotiate strategically was a continuing obstacle to achieving it. The view that he lacked intelligence would explain his dogmatism and lack of flexibility. Cook was more pragmatic, and from July had consistently pursued a course of damage limitation and compromise. He had, however, made no attempt to form alliances with Executive members who were also supporting compromise, for example George Jones, Ebby Edwards and Richardson. Each time Cook's compromise manoeuvres were deflected, he returned to the fold and made peace with his emotional anchor in the MMM. Instead of breaking with the SWMF militants and Minority Movement forces and forming a coherent, pragmatic bloc strong enough to challenge them, he kept faith with his friends. Not surprisingly, they remained tolerant of his passionate arguments for retreat in the expectation that when he had been defeated, he would rally round the campaign for intensifying the struggle.

Horner had become the main spokesman inside the MFGB for the strategy of total war. He had evidently participated in its formation inside the CPGB and MMM. The communist party leadership had supported the MFGB's No Surrender position in the Lock-Out, and had not directed their activists to call for the seizure of state power or the repudiation of the TUC General Council. Bell had attended the ECCI Presidium in mid-June 1926:

> First, he warned against any tendency to overestimate the decline of British capitalism or underestimate the resilience of, and resources available to, the British bourgeoisie. Second he stressed that it might take longer than the CI [Comintern] imagined to dislodge the right-wing leaders of the British Labour movement. Third ... the 'left' ... had not ... formed a majority on the GC [TUC General Council]; and, in any case the CP had never overestimated their potential. Finally, he issued a strong warning against any precipitate moves to the left, invoking Lenin's advocacy of the united front ... [189]

The MAGB and the government had, of course, contributed significantly to the protracted, bitter course of the Lock-Out. Evan Williams, who was also President of the South Wales coalowners, followed a consistent strategy of No Compromise with the greatest determination. His goal was to dismantle the system of national collective bargaining put in place during World War I and exclude the government from any part in regulating the industry. Baldwin may have appreciated the force of civil servants' and Churchill's arguments for government intervention. But in 1926, he was more concerned to keep the right-wing forces in his own party under firm control, and evidently considered that this would be accomplished most effectively by concurring with the coalowners. He was unwilling to incur the vindictive reaction from his own party and parts of Middle England if he was seen to be party to challenging the coalowners' case for recovering their freedom and prerogative.

The immediate aftermath of the Lock-Out was difficult in all coalfields. Because so many men had already returned to work, most miners and their families had to deal with the problem of how to relate to their neighbours and work-mates who had acted differently from themselves. In many pits and pit villages, the majority of men had drifted back, or even been led back by lodge committee members and district officials. In many others, the majority had stayed out, and kept faith with their union. Management victimised men perceived as dangerous militants, and many of them were forced to take their families to other coalfields to find work or look for employment in another industry. Though the coalfields which supplied the domestic market re-started production at full stretch, the export coalfields had to compete against the German and Polish coal which had supplied European markets during the seven months of the dispute.

Nevertheless, the mood of district union lodge officials and agents remained unrepentant, if not upbeat. They were proud that most of their members had acquitted themselves courageously and steadfastly. MFGB loyalists felt justified in accepting the Executive's order to return to work. The miners' dogged refusal to concede their point of principle and the fact that the MFGB had conducted the conflict without violence had been admired by most of the British public. Even the *Daily Mail* had organised a subscription scheme to help miners' children during the winter. Public opinion had also applauded the MFGB's decision to go back as having been taken for the children's sake, not out of cowardice or defeatism. The miners were admired inside the labour movement for their fearless resistance to the coalowners. The TUC and Labour Party agreed it was the government which bore the principal blame, for not pressurising the coalowners into conceding minimum standards in wages and hours that would enable miners working in the less profitable coalfields to rise above poverty levels.

The changes in wages and conditions forced upon miners were not initially catastrophic. The proposals agreed with

Baldwin provided for the temporary retention of 1925 wage rates. Moreover, the re-appearance of district wage bargaining was not accompanied by harsh reductions. As Joseph Jones had observed in November 1926, the general shortage of coal produced by the Lock-Out had resulted in significant increases in the price of coal. Earnings for the first quarter of 1927 were just over the average for the whole of 1925.

By the end of 1927, however, wage levels were only just above those set in 1921, with the exception of Nottinghamshire, Derbyshire and the Midlands. Miners in Durham, Scotland, Lancashire and South Wales experienced the worst reductions. Coalowners rebuilt their profit margins largely through the increase in working hours. But there was not a uniform increase to eight hours' working. District unions in Yorkshire, Nottinghamshire and Derbyshire had won seven and a half hours for all miners; the DMA and Northumberland Miners' Association had also won seven and a half hours for faceworkers. Many owners took the opportunity to close uneconomic pits and increase the amount of mechanisation. Although productivity rose, demand for domestic coal remained stable and prices fell. By 1928 unemployment in coalmining was over 20 per cent, much higher than the national average for all industries.[190]

As comparative normality returned, the atmosphere of total war and the bunker mentality which had sustained coalfield communities dissipated. Nevertheless, the spectre of the large numbers of men who had defied the union and broken ranks continued to haunt particular union lodges and their immediate hinterlands. Spencer's NMIU was not only prospering, he was also encouraging the breakaway unions which had formed in other coalfields. Along with WJ Brown, whose civil service union provided much of the funds, Spencer launched a national Industrial Union Movement to support the other coalfield breakaway unions and also the unions being formed in other industries in reaction to the MMM. They described their union as non-political. They argued that spineless moderate union leaders had allowed militant left-wing leaders to put political considerations before their members' real concerns. They also claimed that the MFGB had been manipulated by the Minority Movement and the communist party into prolonging the Lock-Out unnecessarily.

An experienced union official with a flair for self-publicity, Spencer provided a reasonable, apparently respectable platform from which sceptics and doubters could challenge the MFGB leadership. The problem which district union officials faced in refuting him was that prima facie evidence favoured his case. Had the CPGB and Minority Movement not been so energetic, persuasive and effectively led, the MFGB Executive would probably have accepted some form of district negotiations as a temporary compromise with the coalowners in July 1926.

The party leadership had not opposed the MFGB Executive's decision to lead an orderly retreat at the end of November. Indeed, they had recognised that this was the most likely outcome in early November, when negotiations with the coalowners and the government had resumed. On 10 November 1926, the CPGB Executive 'decided ... to issue the watchword of "One Miners' Union" as proposed by the comrades engaged in the mining industry ... From the outset the campaign was coupled with that of "a new fighting leadership".' During 1927, with Johnnie Campbell increasingly dominating the day-to-day conduct of party politics, the CPGB's perspective continued to be realistic. The Ninth CPGB Congress Report noted: 'Two pamphlets which were subsequently published – one by Arthur Horner, entitled *Coal: the Next Round,* under the auspices of Workers' Publications Limited, and the other, issued by the National Minority Movement, embodying a provisional constitution for a National Mineworkers' Union [British Mineworkers' Union] – had a big sale, and did a great deal to popularise the policy ... The policy of One Miners' Union was thereafter constantly advocated, through Party fractions, pit papers, the Party press, etc ... '[191] In the dark days that followed in 1928, reflective district union leaders, including Joseph Jones, agreed with the goal of a unified miners' union. Horner's advocacy of the British Mineworkers' Union reinforced his position as the leading left-wing leader inside the MFGB.

Chapter 6

Regrouping

Locket's Merthyr rationalized its operations in Mardy after the 1926 Lock-Out. The two older pits closed in 1928, while Nos. 3 and 4 produced coal intermittently, when the company had definite contracts. Management abrogated established custom by inviting married men with large families to work in other men's places, instead of re-employing the hewers who had previously worked the seams. As in many other pits in South Wales and elsewhere, this force majeure was intended to re-assert managerial prerogative.

In Mardy the change was resisted. The *Mineworker* reported on 7 January 1927 that when the married men had refused to take other men's places, the Board of Guardians had refused them unemployment benefit. Eighty police were stationed in Mardy in anticipation of trouble. The situation resembled '(in a smaller degree) that which prevailed during the ten days that shook the world [a reference to John Reed's classic account of the Russian Revolution]. The Lodge Committee is almost in perpetual conference receiving reports by men who have been called in to wrong places, but have refused, and from those who have been sent for to work in their own places.'

Management responded by curtailing production further. When the married men were locked-out, Horner, as Lodge Chairman, and Mainwaring, in his capacity as Agent for the District, fought their case for unemployment benefit. They finally won their point in March 1927 at an interview with a parliamentary secretary at the Ministry of Labour Unemployment Benefits Headquarters in Kew.[192] During 1927, the Lodge recorded 377 employed and 1366 unemployed members.[193] The situation was succinctly described on Horner's MI5 file. Mardy had been 'a prosperous industrial mining village, the Collieries employing 2,500 men, a large majority earning £9 per week, but there are now only about 650 men employed, the Company has gone into liquidation, the place is practically derelict, and respectable Colliers have been compelled to dispose of their houses, which cost £250 to £300 to build for a paltry £50.'[194]

Horner himself had been unemployed since 1927, whilst Dai Lloyd Davies had discharged the checkweighing duties at the two pits which remained open. His MI5 file noted that he had been paid 'sometimes £3.10.0., sometimes £4. a week' by either the communist party or the Minority Movement. This was a basic income, comparable to the average cash earnings of a South Wales miner in work, but higher than unemployment benefit or outdoor relief paid by the Board of Guardians. Later, when he became NMM General Secretary, after paying his rail fares and living expenses in London, Horner would have had very little surplus to spare for buying clothes and shoes for his growing daughters or paying back his father's substantial loan. Vol's recollection of their standard of living was that the Horners were not living any better than their unemployed neighbours.[195]

Mardy was an extreme example of the situation prevailing in other Glamorgan pits. Most miners were unemployed, with their families facing destitution. Frankenberg described Horner's account of how the Mardy Lodge Committee had tried to keep the employed men inside the Federation.

The Mardy men understood that impoverishment had driven their comrades to take this course [dropping out of the SWMF and leaving arrears], because of this no attempts at violence were ever applied. Main form of activity was propaganda, by leaflet and speeches ... [D]irectly opposite the pay office was a small park and it was possible to remain with one's toes an inch inside the park and address the men without police being able to interfere. There was also the fact that the road approaching office was Council property and the Lodge claimed that the Company had not the right to interfere with users of this road. The road was the scene of many struggles and Arthur was dragged along it and fixed himself to the railings to prevent his being dragged away.[196]

The dramatic worsening of living conditions precipitated a state of collective shock in the coalfield, which was reflected in a further leftwards shift inside the SWMF. Horner defeated Enoch Morrell, the SWMF President, in the summer of 1927, to become one of the three SWMF representatives on the MFGB Executive. There were two incumbents, Tom Richards and SO Davies, because Ablett, who previously occupied the third place, had been disbarred after his suspension from the SWMF Executive in November 1926. Although the suspension had been lifted on 31 December, Ablett made no attempt to resume his MFGB seat until February 1927, evidently because Cook was manoeuvring against him. The MFGB Executive had subsequently continued to obstruct his re-entry.[197]

When SWMF nominations for the three places opened in March, sixteen were received. The membership ballot required by rule was conducted according to the Alternative Vote system. After a long discussion the Executive agreed that only financial members, i.e. working miners who were up-to-date with their dues, and the bona fide unemployed, would be eligible to vote. Richards and SO Davies were elected on first preferences, whilst the third place was closely contested between Horner and Morrell. Horner eventually emerged victorious, and took his seat with ambivalent feelings. He told Frankenberg he had great personal respect for Morrell. 'Pride at being elected into the position which Enoch had previously occupied [in 1921 and 1924] was mixed with deep sympathy with him made more intense by the fact that they were both born in the borough of Merthyr within a couple of miles of each other.'

The CPGB leadership remained sanguine that the party had turned a decisive corner. During the General Strike and Lock-Out they had gained 5000 full members and 1500 YCL members, primarily in the coalfields. *Workers' Weekly* circulation had increased; over three quarters of a million leaflets were issued and 100,000 pamphlets sold. In October 1926, the CPGB Executive had been confident that the party would succeed to its legitimate place at the head of the labour movement's left-wing. 'The essentially new feature contributed by the General Strike ... was the utter discrediting of the former "Left-wing" on the General Council. They were revealed as a set of phrase-mongers ... At the third Annual Conference of the Minority

Movement [in September] the issue of changing the leadership of the trade unions ... [was] brought up sharply by our Party fractions in the light of recent experience.'[198]

Not surprisingly, the TUC General Council, prompted by Citrine, launched a *démarche*, proscribing trades councils which were associated with the Minority Movement, on the grounds that the Minority Movement was no mere ginger group, interested in influencing union policy, but rather an alternative leadership intent on using the official movement for its own ends. Left-wing General Council members and other union leaders previously friendly towards the Minority Movement acquiesced. Once the General Council's move had been affirmed by the 1927 Congress, centre-right leaders in affiliated unions pressed ahead with their own campaigns. The Labour Party leadership, which had refrained from acting before the TUC, now moved against the CPGB. Labour constituency organisations were systematically scrutinised for communist elements, and mechanisms put in place to expel those which were recalcitrant or unrepentant about their communist connections.[199]

Horner's presence on the MFGB Executive, which met monthly in London, acted as a strong tonic for Arthur Cook's morale. The two men had regular opportunities to socialise and talk politics. Cook was evidently determined to maintain his involvement in the South Wales coalfield. Since Richards and Morrell had no intention of affording him the opportunity, he accepted the *entré* which Horner and the MMM provided. In the second week of September the *Mineworker* reported that the South Wales MMM was launching an 'intense campaign' at a Special Delegate Conference, on Saturday 17 September at the Ynyshir Workmen's Hall, chaired by Horner. Speakers were Wal Hannington and Tom Thomas of Treherbert, MMM South Wales secretary and close friend of Horner and Cook. The agenda included the situation in British capitalism, trade union reorganisation and unemployment. The story announced 'a huge demonstration' on Panteg's Mountain on Sunday at 3 pm. Cook was advertised as the main speaker, followed by Horner, Hannington, Mainwaring and David Lewis (SWMF Rhondda No. 1 District Chairman). Another conference was scheduled for the following Saturday in the Anthracite coalfield in West Wales. Both were 'open to Trade Union branches, lodges, trades councils, unemployed committees, etc., and a large attendance [is] anticipated'. According to the *Mineworker* on 23 September, 10,000 people, with bands and banners from all parts of the coalfield, had assembled at Panteg's. The report noted that Cook had spoken about holding a hunger march. 'Something out of the ordinary must be done to draw national public attention to the terrible plight of the miner today ... [T]he seat of the trouble was in London.'

The South Wales MMM were determined to apply pressure on the government to provide adequate unemployment benefit, and hit on the expedient of a march. In 1922 Hannington had organised a national unemployed march to London, with Mainwaring leading the South Wales contingent.[200] In the intervening five years communists had concentrated on building the Minority Movement and fighting the coal wars. In 1927, however, the grim conditions made another unemployed march an attractive prospect for South Wales MMM leaders. Having canvassed all the difficulties, problems and potential gains, they decided to go ahead. Despite the organisers' subsequent protestations, Cook's suggestion could hardly have been spontaneous. Horner had probably commenced serious discussions with Hannington about a South Walian march in August. The CPGB and NMM leadership, notably Pollitt and Campbell, were more easily convinced of the march's feasibility when they knew that Horner had enlisted Hannington's formidable organisational talents. They appreciated his proven record in maintaining discipline and order in the potentially explosive situations which they knew the marchers would encounter.

Hopes were high at the outset that, unlike its 1922 predecessor, the 1927 march would be a genuine united front. Cook, Horner and SO Davies intended to persuade the SWMF and the MFGB to support the march, ensuring an official reception from local Labour Parties and Trades Councils along its route. It was planned on a grand scale, with 500 to1000 participants, who would set out on the first day of the new parliamentary session, and be welcomed in London by a monster All-London Trade Union and Labour demonstration.

The Home Office file on inter-war Hunger Marches contains a duplicated report, dated 6 October 1927, listing the Rhondda District organising committee for the 1927 march. They were men who either held Rhondda District SWMF positions or were NUWM officers. Horner headed the list, which included Tom Thomas, described as Organising Secretary of the Rhondda Trade Union Defence Committee (presumably an all-in ad hoc body organised to oppose Baldwin's Trades Union and Trades Disputes Bill), R Williams, Secretary of the SWMF Tylorstown Lodge, Jack Thomas, SWMF Rhondda District Council, Cllr DL Davies, checkweigher Mardy, and Charlie Jones, South Wales Area Secretary of the NUWM. (An appended note observed that several were active communists.) An appended leaflet listed a London Reception Committee of four: William Paul, editor of the *Sunday Worker*, Alex Gossip, NAFTA general secretary, Joe Vaughan, the Communist mayor of Bethnal Green, and Cook.[201]

The prospect of the march buoyed up morale. Cook wrote Horner, '*en route* to Berlin' on 10 October where he was attending an MIF meeting.

> Saw report of your speech you can look out the old school will be after your blood and mine. Fight we must and fight now ... Hope Dai Lloyd [Davies] and wife are getting on alright give them my best wishes also all the real heroes in little Moscow [Mardy]. Spoke to Mrs. Andrews [South Wales Labour Party women's organiser] re. methods of getting non-pols in Mardy. Going by plane because could not let down meeting Norwich four thousand welcomed me ... Now drop a line and keep going for victory will surely come to us. The Traitors will soon be found out. Yours in the Fight. Love to Ethel ... Arthur.[202]

Cook's reference was to the keynote speech which Horner had given to open the Ninth CPGB Congress on 8 October. The report in the *Sunday Worker* reported it under the headline, 'New Industrial Conflict Coming – Communist Warning'.

> The new industrial crisis was looming ... and the bosses had mistaken the leaders' cry for peace for a weakening on the part of the workers. The leaders at Blackpool [Labour Party Conference] had paved the way for liberalism in the Labour Party and while they shouted for

peace the bosses prepared war. The Communists' insistence on the united front meant unity among the workers and not with cowardly leaders, and the workers were
looking to the Communist Party and the dictatorship of
the Working Class.[203]

Cook's prophecy proved accurate. Citrine acted before official
support for the march had materialised, issuing a circular to
all affiliated unions and trades councils which advised that the
planned march was strictly unofficial, and suggested that trades
councils should refrain from offering marchers accommodation
or arranging to feed them. On 15 October, when the SWMF
Executive considered a motion to support the march, Richards
and Morrell cited the TUC circular, and the Executive duly withheld support. The Glamorgan Chief Constable, Lionel Lindsay,
sent a private note informing the Home Office of this result.
'The opinion now is that it [the march] will fizzle out, but we will
certainly keep an eye on developments and let you know what
is going on.' Richards and Morrell prudently refrained from
enforcing the Executive decision on the union's Rhondda No.
1 District, which provided the only official union support. Nor
did the MFGB Executive act to stop Cook's public involvement.
He became the march's official treasurer; the address given on
leaflets to which financial contributions should be sent was the
MFGB head office at 55 Russell Square.[204]

On 23 October the *Sunday Worker* published an appeal for
funds and support for the proposed march, signed by eleven
notable Labour figures, including TI Mardy Jones, MP for
Pontypridd, David Kirkwood MP, Ellen Wilkinson, Jack Williams,
Secretary of the Forest of Dean miners' union, and John
Strachey, still editing the MFGB journal, the *Miner*. The South
Wales organising committee were apparently chary of announcing that the march would definitely take place. Charlie Jones
and Tom Thomas were listed as joint secretaries of the march
organising council. Nevertheless, a note on the Home Office
file reported on 3 November: 'During the last few days, Tom
Thomas ... and ... Dai Lloyd Davies, have visited towns ... including Bristol, Bath and Swindon. They report a complete lack
of enthusiasm for the march on the part of all official Labour
bodies with whom they have come into contact.'

Hannington, Horner and Cook decided to go ahead with the march, apparently calculating that once the marchers were under way, trades councils, ILP and Labour Party branches would be aroused and moved, and unable to harden their hearts against South Wales miners in the flesh. In London, moreover, Hannington, Pollitt, the London NMM office and union activists had worked hard to secure promises of help. On 4 November, the London Reception Committee convened a meeting chaired by Sam Elsbury with 123 delegates, including two from AEU District Committees, 20 from eleven Labour Party branches, fourteen delegates from eight Labour and Trades Councils, 31 from sixteen CPGB branches and 27 from 13 NUWCM branches. The meeting was attended by a police sergeant, whose report is on the Home Office file. Delegates had asked many detailed questions to the chief speaker, Tom Thomas, who had explained that 300 selected men would take part, of whom one third were ex-servicemen. All would be medically examined before departing. 'All would give an undertaking to obey the orders of their leaders, and would be divided into detachments with a leader for each. All would be trade unionists.'

Thomas emphasised that there was 'no foundation for the allegations made against the Reception Committee as regards the march being organised by Communists'. 'The march had been organised with the idea of bringing home to the parties responsible and the population of the country the awful conditions in South Wales. No alternative to the march could be suggested. They were determined to conduct the march in a constitutional and legitimate manner. The marchers were determined to avoid any unpleasantness on the march or after they arrived in London.' Tom Mann spoke 'on the wretched conditions of the miners, and stamped up and down the platform during his tirade'. The meeting had concluded with a resolution supporting the march moved by Mann and seconded by Berridge, representing the AEU London District Committee. The sergeant summarised a conversation he had had with Hannington and Bill Holt, the Reception Committee Secretary. (Holt was an AEU shop steward and foundation CPGB member, a close friend of Hannington and Pollitt.) He concluded, 'I believe the demonstrations will be conducted in a most constitutional manner.'[205]

151

Although the marchers were fewer than the organisers had hoped, they embarked in high spirits on the morning of Wednesday 9 November. Hannington led 260 men, all bona fide paid-up SWMF members, from the centre of Newport. The Home Office file noted that the majority were between seventeen and twenty; about sixty were older men. The same day, a Home Office meeting, 'Hunger march to London', was convened to discuss the prospects. The minutes were phlegmatic. 'It ... appears from ... reports that the organisers of the march have made better arrangements for the marchers' reception en route than seemed likely at one time.'[206] The *Daily Mail* was unable to find much sensational to report about its organisers. A story on 10 November noted that Cook was an honorary member of the Moscow Soviet. Apparently unaware of their communist allegiance, the reporter noted that Tom Thomas was closely associated with the Minority Movement and that Mr DL Davies and Mr Charles Jones were extreme socialists.

The Mineworker reported on 11 November that MFGB Executive members SO Davies and Horner had met the marchers on the first stage, and accompanied them to Bristol, on the train under the Severn estuary, the only part of the journey not undertaken by foot. Hannington displayed military precision in dealing with the myriad logistical problems, feeding, boot repairing, accommodation, etc. Accompanied by Horner for most of the way, the marchers took ten days to complete the 120 mile journey from Bristol to London. (Other leaders who marched were Tom Thomas, Dai Lloyd Davies, Emrys Llewellyn, Jack Jones from Clydach Vale and Jack Thomas.) They remained in London for a week, all staying in the Bethnal Green Town Hall thanks to the hospitality of Mayor Vaughan and the Labour borough council. The Royal Arsenal Co-operative Society provided their food.

With the Lock-Out still fresh in the public's collective memory, there were large numbers lining the road in Chippenham, Swindon, Hungerford, Reading and Maidenhead, to watch the South Wales miners give an impressive display of marching. On 14 November *The Times* reported that Cook and his wife had met the march at Swindon and that Cook would stay and march to Reading with them. Strachey had marched with the miners on the last stretch into Swindon, and he and Cook both stayed the night in their billet. Cook marched to the end, 'sharing the rather basic accommodation and the comradeship, occasionally slipping back to Russell Square ... [H]e renewed acquaintances ... and ... seems to have been in fine spirits in their company.' The *Mineworker* reported that Tom Mann met the march on the last stretch of their seventeen mile stint to Reading. 'It was nearly 6 o-clock when the men came round the bend with a good swinging stride, with their lighted pit lamps, and actually singing the "International" ... [Having picked up Mann], they swung off after the "International", to chorus after chorus that was surprising after having done sixteen miles during the day.'[207]

Still only thirty-three and in excellent physical shape, Horner probably found little difficulty in staying the distance. Horner and Hannington excelled in keeping up the men's esprit de corps, through a mixture of exhortation, humour, banter and discipline. Both relished the adventure and carried memories of the march into old age. Horner later told Frankenberg about his first experience of fascists. 'The boys were resting in the workhouse and Cook and Horner were on their own addressing a meeting in Maidenhead park. A number of persons calling themselves fascists heckled, interjected and threatened to attack. Maddening to think that only 200 yards away were 260 tough Welsh miners who could have put them in the Thames in very short order.' (His absences were probably linked with Cook's trips to London, on one of which he may have provided an introduction to Will John, MP for Rhondda West since 1920. John had spent eight months in gaol in 1911 to 1912 for his alleged involvement in the Tonypandy riots during the Cambrian Combine dispute, and whilst imprisoned had been elected SWMF Agent for the Rhondda No.1 District. Horner and Cook may have hoped that John could organise the other ten SWMF-sponsored MPs to put pressure on the government to meet the marchers.) With typical impatience, on one occasion Horner tried to cure his own blisters by lancing them with scissors and then pouring iodine on the wound. The consequence was septic feet, a serious condition before antibiotics. He suffered 'as a result of this for many years'. But he was not a quitter, and apparently sustained himself on sheer exuberance as well as determination.[208]

The march arrived in Chiswick, the outskirts of West London, on Saturday 19 November. Cook welcomed them and paid tribute to the Police 'for the way in which they acted all along the route'. The Special Branch short-hand writer noted his peroration: 'He stood now and all the time for social revolution, the wiping out of poverty and the education of the working class towards this end.' The miners marched eight miles from Chiswick to Trafalgar Square on Sunday for the finale. The *Daily Herald* noted that many of the marchers 'had medals on their breasts some of them Mons medals'. At the welcoming meeting, George Lansbury MP had taken the chair; and Josiah Wedgwood MP was one of the speakers. Lansbury explained that he had changed his mind about the marchers. He had told the organisers that he would wait to see how London workers received them before deciding to support them. Because they had taken the miners to their heart, he was doing all he could 'by voluntary effort to help them carry through the task they have come to perform'.[209]

Cook was in inspirational mode; the short-hand writer captured his rousing emotion verbatim.

> [D]o not let this be like other demonstrations – protest and it is finished. Get back to your districts. London has got to be aroused this week. We will march through Whitehall. We shall sweep Baldwinism out. It is not Bolshevism you are suffering from, it is Baldwinism. Say it after me, 'Baldwin you must go.' 'Baldwin you must go.' (This was repeated with great gusto by the crowd.) He won't go if you tell him to go, but he will go if you organise well together to clear him out ... I am proud that Wal Hannington organised the march, and marched every inch of the way, with two others of my comrades – little Arthur Horner and Councillor Davies. Don't be afraid that you won't have leaders. If you stand true, you will make leaders.[210]

On Monday 21 November, led by Hannington, Horner and Cook, the miners marched to a meeting in a Westminster Hall committee room, which adjoined the House of Commons, probably booked by Will John. Six SWMF sponsored MPs attended and talked to the men, who would have been their constituents.

The MPs agreed to formally approach Baldwin with regard to meeting the marchers. It was a reasonable request. Contrary to sensational predictions from excitable quarters, including the *Daily Mail* and Winston Churchill, the marchers were not causing mayhem. Nor was there any evidence that they intended to seize state power. As the police sergeant had anticipated, they were behaving 'constitutionally', acting from a political repertoire thoroughly familiar to the British public. Their good order and patent pacifism were embarrassing for Citrine and the Parliamentary Labour Party. Moreover, the interest and publicity which the Hunger March had generated were in stark contrast to MacDonald's failure to impress the government with the need for action to relieve the serious distress in the exporting coalfields. (On 16 November, whilst the marchers were en route, the Labour Opposition had moved a vote of censure on the government for its negligence in dealing with the mining industrial situation. When the minister responsible for mining rose to speak, he was shouted down by the Labour backbenches, and the Speaker adjourned the House.)

Baldwin refused the Welsh MPs' request, using the TUC circular in justification. The *Daily Herald* faithfully reported No.10's spin: 'if the Prime Minister were to do so [see the marchers], it would be interpreted as "a stab in the back" for the official Labour Movement'. The prime minister's manoeuvre caused Citrine and Ben Turner, the Chairman of the General Council for 1927, to execute an immediate volte-face. Having been determined not to allow 'the communists' any quarter, they now received a deputation from the marchers. In a press statement afterwards 'they [Citrine and Turner] desired to make it clear that although the General Council had not been able to give official recognition to the march, the statement attributed to the Prime Minister had no justification so far as the General Council was concerned.' Probably at Citrine's instigation, the Minister of Labour agreed to receive twelve of the marchers, accompanied by the six Welsh MPs, on Friday 25 November. Later that day, they reported back to a marchers' meeting in the Memorial Hall, Farringdon. On Saturday, the miners marched from Bethnal Green Town Hall to Trafalgar Square for a farewell meeting before taking the train back to South Wales. An audience of 3000 listened to Dai Lloyd Davies, Hannington, and

Shapjuri Saklatvala MP; 'and a great deal of money was realised by collections and by the sale of miners' lamps and other
souvenirs'.[211]

The *Mineworker* adopted a conciliatory, magnanimous tone.
Its leader, 'The End Attained', observed that Citrine and the
new Labour Party secretary, Morgan Phillips, 'do not, of course,
admit that the march gave rise to their new-found zeal'. However:
'We care little how the end is attained, so long as it is attained
somehow ... And as the Miners' March has helped ... to induce
the more far-sighted Labour members to a glimpse of *this truth*,
we acclaim it as a highly successful trial trip, and suggest its
repetition on a national scale.' Hannington concluded that the
government had also received the message. He remembered
that 'within a very short time we found that thousands of miners
who had been struck off Unemployment Insurance benefit had
it restored to them and there was also a more generous Poor
Law Relief'.[212]

Once the march was over, Horner renewed his efforts to
achieve a unified miners' union.[213] He had taken his seat on
MFGB Executive after the MFGB Annual Conference at the end
of July.[214] Conference debates confirmed the swing in opinion
towards a unified miners' union inside most district unions. The
MFGB 1927 Executive Report noted that, after receiving letters
from Durham and Nottinghamshire, a special subcommittee had
been established early in the year to consider re-organisation.
Though the MMM's projected rules for a unified union were the
most prominent, other variants were being canvassed and discussed. Probably the most contentious question was: how much
sovereignty district unions would be expected to surrender to
the MFGB. The conference debate was polarised between the
MMM British Miners' Union model, proposed by Jack Williams
from the Forest of Dean, and supported by Nottinghamshire
and Somerset, and a more conservative variant proposed by WP
Richardson for the DMA.[215]

Horner spoke at the conference on behalf of the Mardy Lodge
in the debate on a motion condemning the Trade Unions and
Trade Disputes Bill, introduced by Baldwin in the aftermath
of the General Strike. His speech, however, hardly addressed
either the motion or the bill. He concentrated instead on his
own, and the MMM's, agenda. He attacked the 'theory abroad

that the way to fight this Bill is to wait ... and rely on the return of a Labour Government ... for our salvation':

> [I]t means, so far as the Miners' Federation of Great Britain is concerned, that we are making a declaration of impotence and inability to defend our men for the next two years ... We cannot afford to wait two years for action ... [I]f we have to wait for a Labour Government to come, what guarantee have we that the next Labour Government is going to act any differently from what the last [1923 to 1924] one did. I remember at Liverpool [1924 Labour Party Conference] hearing Ernest Bevan (*sic*) tell Mr. MacDonald – hearing Ben Turner say the same – that when they were in a struggle, during the period of office of the Labour Government, they received the harshest treatment they ever received from any Government ...

When a Lancashire miners' MP complained that Horner was not speaking to the motion, Smith rejoined, 'I cannot rule him out. That is the way he is built. I have to face him.' Horner proceeded to rebut the MP's challenge, without Smith calling him to order. 'The point I am seeking to make is, that the destiny of the miners, the salvation of the miners will depend in the last analysis, not so much on a Labour Government or any other Government, as it does on this Federation ... The only thing which counts, the only power we have which counts against the Government is the massed might of the workers in every industry in this country.' But he concluded by promising, presumably on the MMM's behalf, that all assistance would be rendered to ensure that every MFGB member contracted into the political levy, 'because we believe that the Labour Party if it has a position of any tenancy belongs to the working-classes ... It is no use saying it [the Bill] is rotten because everybody knows it. We have to say something else. We have to say to the General Council, they must call an immediate conference of the executives, and ... undertake action, the only action that they [the government] fear is the massed working class action, by means of a general strike in this country.'

157

Smith finally asked Horner whether he was supporting the motion. He replied, 'Oh yes. But I would like to move an addendum to that ... '. Smith refused: '[Y]ou have to leave it now. It is not dictatorship. It [the motion] was submitted to districts ... and an amendment could have been tabled to it this morning.' Nevertheless, Horner had successfully diverted the debate. Speakers following him, including four MPs, did not speak to the motion, but answered Horner's argument that the unions must re-group and prepare for total industrial war.[216]

The CPGB leadership had high expectations of what Horner could achieve on the MFGB Executive. The CPGB Executive's Report to the Ninth Party Congress had noted:

> So far as changing the [miners'] leadership is concerned, the most outstanding successes so far have been won in Lanarkshire, Fifeshire and Nottinghamshire, with lesser successes in Yorkshire. In addition, we must mention the election of Arthur Horner to the MFGB Executive ... The Party has had to learn that widespread sympathy among the workers for its policy, and even a relatively large membership, cannot take the place of a strong Party organisation in the sense of regular trade union work and reporting: this has been shown particularly in the cases of Durham and Lancashire.[217]

However, precisely because he was now a member of the MFGB Executive, Horner was constrained by collective responsibility, and felt unable to speak on behalf of the MMM or argue the communist party case. He did not speak at the 1927 TUC, and so was unable to challenge George Hicks, Congress president, who developed the TUC's case for co-operation between employers and unions. Horner attended the 1927 Labour Party conference in October as part of the SWMF delegation. In contrast to 1926, he made only three interventions; and though high-spirited, they failed to ignite the conference as he had done the previous year.[218]

The political problem which all left-wingers were facing was the apparent success of the General Council's new strategy, adopted in the light of their experience during the General Strike. Led by Bevin and Citrine, the Council capitalised on the profound impression made on leading employers and the political establishment by the unity of purpose and cohesion of the trade union movement during the General Strike. Encouraged by Citrine, Alfred Mond of ICI assembled a group of prominent industrialists who agreed that it was not only possible but necessary to seek accommodation with pragmatic union leaders. They argued that instead of accepting industrial conflict as inevitable, employers and unions should pre-empt it by seeking agreement and being willing to compromise. When meetings between the industrialists and the TUC General Council commenced in October 1927, Cook, who had finally succeeded to one of the MFGB's 'reserved' seats in September, was the only member of the General Council who opposed them. They were conventionally described as the Mond-Turner Talks, because Ben Turner, President of the National Union of Textile Workers, was Chairman of the General Council at their outset.

The talks received a hostile reception from many labour movement activists. Scottish ILP MPs Maxton, John Wheatley and Kirkwood led the political reaction against them. In May 1928, the CPGB Politburo deputed Campbell, Horner and Gallacher to arrange a meeting with Cook and the three ILP MPs to agree a common platform against them. The result, in early June, was the Cook-Maxton Manifesto, attacking the General Council and Labour leaders for abandoning the first principles of the labour movement pioneers. Cook had already produced a best-selling pamphlet, *Mond Moonshine*, in March. It was followed by *Mond's Manacles, The destruction of Trade Unionism*, in July 1928. His primitive prose style was enhanced and polished, probably by Strachey and Horner, and perhaps even Campbell. The notice for *Mond's Manacles* in *The Worker* advertised the pamphlet as having a new photograph of Cook and a Foreword by Horner.[219]

Cook's case was that the unions would have won the General Strike if the General Council had not betrayed the miners. First advanced in hot blood during 1926 by most MFGB activists, this was initially accepted by many trade unionists who had been puzzled by the Council's abrupt, ineptly executed retreat. In 1928, however, when the same argument was rehearsed in cold blood, it failed to resonate with a substantial section of union activists. The Trade Disputes and Trade Unions Act, passed in 1927, had not been nearly as onerous as many Tory backbenchers, seeking retribution for the 'transgression' of the General Strike, had demanded. Nor had many employers affected by the General Strike embarked on wholesale victimisation of union members, although they had taken the opportunity to sack 'ringleaders'. Many trade unionists could also appreciate the argument that parliamentary power would be more effective than industrial conflict in enabling the trade union movement to achieve its goals. The certainty that Baldwin would have to call a general election by 1929 gave this argument additional appeal. A logical corollary was the importance of maximising areas of agreement between unions and employers, whilst concentrating the movement's resources in an all-out campaign to elect a Labour government.

The debate on Mond-Turner at the 1928 TUC was hard-fought and acrimonious. Bevin and Citrine carried the day, arguing that they had not surrendered first principles, but applied them pragmatically from a position of strength to achieve tangible gains for their members.[220] The conflict between left and right inside the trade union movement continued, and even escalated in some unions, including the SWMF. Horner probably gathered detailed intelligence from Cook about the General Council's deliberations, which he then discussed with Pollitt and Hannington. Like most CPGB and NMM activists, Pollitt and Horner had moved leftwards during the Lock-Out. They remained committed, however, to modernising the existing trade union movement into an efficient instrument for waging industrial war. Nor were they demoralised by their defeat at the 1928 Congress. They regarded Citrine's continuing offensive against the Minority Movement as no more than an annoying distraction from the more important task of fighting employers.

The Comintern had been applying consistent pressure on the British party to move left since November 1926, when Bukharin had announced to the ECCI's Seventh Plenum that a new phase of capitalism had arrived. Qualitatively different, its emergence marked a 'third period' since the Russian Revolution. (The first was the revolutionary period of 1919 to 1920, which had then been succeeded by a second period of comparative stabilisation.) '[T]he process of the stabilisation of capitalism brings forward its contradictions in ever sharper form ... The leftward trend within the working class is an eloquent expression of this process.' The new approach, often described by communists as 'class against class', was not formally enunciated until February 1928 at the ECCI's 9th Plenum, when 'both the French and the British communist parties were instructed to come out in direct opposition to their respective Socialist and Labour parties.'[221]

Horner and Pollitt had initially welcomed the Comintern's move leftwards as being wholly consistent with their own experience and reflections. At this juncture, moreover, some militant trade unionists, inside and outside the communist party, concluded that union leaders' conduct in the General Strike and the Lock-Out proved that British unions were irredeemably reformist. Consequently, they argued that constructing revolutionary unions was the correct policy. This prognosis received enthusiastic support from the RILU general secretary, Alexander Lozovsky, at the Fourth RILU Congress held in Moscow in March 1928. And this more polarised approach to class conflict was accepted by the RILU Presidium and subsequently approved by the Fourth Congress. However, along with most NMM leaders Pollitt and Horner resisted this creative application of the Comintern's line, and opposed the formation of new, revolutionary unions.

Horner attended the Fourth RILU Congress. As a communist hero of the British General Strike and Lock-Out, he had a high profile amongst delegates. He also had the temerity to use his reputation to criticise the platform. On 13 April, *The Worker* reported 'Arthur Horner's striking criticism of some parts of the Report and Theses on the tasks of trade unionism'. Horner explained that the British delegation 'feel that there is in the report an underestimation of the strength of Amsterdam [the socialist rival International Federation of Trade Unions] and an exaggeration of the strength of the RILU'. His speech was fully reported, presumably because the NMM leadership were keen to show NMM supporters that their delegates had opposed Lozovsky's secessionist strategy.

Horner complained that Lozovsky had ignored the NMM slogan 'Change the Leadership'.

We are not convinced at the moment that this omission is accidental, because throughout the theses there is to be observed the tendency to generalise too much in the treatment of our attitude towards the reformist unions. There is ... the tendency to give up in every country the reformist unions into the hands of the reformist traitors ... [I]n practice these [reformist] unions are not all instruments in the hands of capitalism and part of the productive forces ... [I]t is not true to say that the mass of the workers themselves, or the unions up to now, have been committed to the role of the productive unions of the capitalists ... If the workers of Britain are forced by the reformists to occupy, inside the reformist unions, the role of units of capitalist production, they will resist, and in that resistance they must be led by revolutionary fighters of the working class, organised inside RILU.

He defended reformist unions which united workers regardless of politics or religion as capable of being won 'by the revolutionary fighters if we know how and when to fight – to realise our objective. We must see to it that they [the reformists] are the splitters, "the force cut off" and not us – the revolutionary fighters of the unions'. The main task in Britain was to build strong Minority Groups which would fight to win the leadership of reformist unions.

Not only were Horner and Alex Gossip re-elected onto the RILU Presidium; the platform failed to launch any counter-attack to Horner's outspoken criticism of Lozovsky's strategy. Evidently the RILU leadership were chary of challenging British trade union leaders, whose reputation for solidarity and militancy had impressed Marx, Engels and Lenin himself. It is likely that Horner and the British delegates attracted support from many other delegates who had come to similar conclusions themselves.[222]

Horner stayed in Moscow after the Congress to attend the Russian Miners' Union Conference. But he was back in Britain to speak at a One Day Discussion School at Bethnal Green Public Library on 22 April, on 'The Decisions of the 4th World Congress of the RILU'.[223] He duly repeated the British delegation's criticism of the RILU Congress decisions at the CPGB

Executive, observing that Lozovsky had shown 'a tendency to treat all reformist unions as having actually become units of capitalist production'. He concluded: 'We had to fight against a tendency to drive us into setting up independent unions.'[224] The Executive endorsed his position, and the NMM continued to carry on the fight against the reformist leadership from inside reformist unions.

In-between all these activities Horner was making strenuous efforts to maximise his time at home. He and Ethel were both enjoying their baby daughter. He also applied himself with habitual energy and determination to the problems of maintaining the Federation lodge, with its majority of unemployed members. As vice-chairman and disputes secretary, he continued to intervene at the pit on working members' behalf. But Horner's prominence made him a logical selection when the CPGB Executive had to choose a representative to replace Gallacher on the ECCI in early July. Although they appointed the veteran Tom Bell, they expected Horner to replace him after a few months, presumably after he had made the appropriate domestic and union arrangements. (ECCI membership entailed extended periods of residence in Moscow.) The ECCI endorsed Horner's appointment as a candidate member at the Sixth Comintern Congress in late July and also added Pollitt to the list. (Neither Horner nor Pollitt were in attendance.)[225] Horner's absence was due to his attending the MFGB Annual Congress taking place at the same time in Llandudno.

Horner would have held membership of both the ECCI and the RILU Presidium if he had actually removed to Moscow in 1928. As the leading communist in the 1926 Lock-Out, his revolutionary reputation was high, and he could have wielded considerable influence inside both institutions. Horner later told Frankenberg about his ECCI appointment, accurately recalling its date and his formal title. At the time he and Ethel probably viewed his appointments as evidence of his rising star inside the international communist movement. They would have been keen to experience life in the Soviet Union at first hand. Life in Mardy was increasingly grim. Arthur's frequent absences meant that Ethel was more exposed to the grinding daily round of life and its debilitating effect on everyone, including herself. Many younger families with children, including some of the Horners' close friends, had already left Mardy to find work in the Midlands or around London. There were also the South Walian comrades who had gone to the Lenin School whom they both knew.[226]

But Arthur and Ethel stayed in Mardy until late 1929, perhaps influenced by practical considerations. If he had left Britain earlier, Arthur would have had to vacate his position on the MFGB Executive. His term ran until July 1929, and he may even have been optimistic about retaining his position. Then there was the imminent general election, which Baldwin would be obliged to hold by the end of October 1929. In keeping with the adversarial attitude towards the Labour Party which the Comintern's 'Third Period' line entailed, the CPGB Executive had decided to put up candidates in twenty-five seats where they believed Labour was vulnerable. Horner was the obvious choice for his home constituency of Rhondda East. Pollitt and Campbell may also have calculated that Horner's continuing presence in Britain would strengthen the hand of other militant trade unionists who were opposing the formation of new, revolutionary unions. Arguments were escalating inside the Minority Movement about whether to lead secessions from 'reformist' unions in mining, engineering and passenger transport.[227]

The problem for the group of realists arguing against secession, led by Horner, Pollitt, Tanner and Scott, was that the Minority Movement no longer held the initiative inside the trade union movement. Militants inside the AEU and the MFGB were in retreat. Both the 1927 and 1928 TUC had been the occasions for emphatic condemnations of the NMM. In 1927 Citrine unleashed a storm of well-rehearsed, informed invective against various Minority Movement activities, citing chapter and verse from duplicated notices prepared for NMM supporters about which resolutions and candidates should be supported at union branch meetings.[227]

In South Wales, Richards had steered the SWMF towards a pragmatic centre position. With the help of Morrell and younger moderates like Arthur Jenkins and Jim Griffiths, he had assembled a reliable majority on the SWMF Executive and used it to isolate left-wing lodges and activists who continued to support the MMM. He did not try to enforce uniformity, however, and worked constructively with militants like Oliver Harris, Bevan and Mainwaring, who were trimming towards his centrism for their own pragmatic reasons. His supporters were located across the centre and left political spectrum, his position was more secure as a result. But Richards now moved relentlessly against Horner and Mardy Lodge, justifying his pursuit by the threat which the Minority Movement posed, not only to the Federation but to the broader labour movement's very existence. Although some left-wingers, notably SO Davies, continued to defend the Minority Movement, Richards' offensive received broad support from most lodge officials. Non-communist militants had already moved away from the MMM in many lodges. Horner and like-minded comrades kept the Rhondda Minority Movement operating as an all-in left-wing grouping through assiduous trimming and diplomatic tact. But deep rifts were opening in SWMF lodges elsewhere.

Following an SWMF Executive instruction, lodge committees were obliged from 30 June 1927 to take members who had not paid their subscriptions for two consecutive months off their books. (Unemployed members could remain provided their membership cards were properly initialled, i.e. if they continued to visit the lodge secretary to signal their intention of remaining Federation members.) The instruction was wholly justifiable from the point of view of the union's finances. But the sharp decline in lodge membership which resulted in Rhondda No. 1 District entailed the reduction of their three Executive places to one. Custom and practice determined that it was David Lewis, the District Secretary, who kept his seat. From July 1927, therefore, Horner only occupied an ex officio seat on the Federation Executive, by virtue of his seat on the MFGB Executive.[229]

Richards made no move to prevent Horner's re-nomination, for re-election to the MFGB Executive at the SWMF Annual Conference in June 1928, along with the other two incumbents, himself and SO Davies. He may have calculated that Horner stood little chance of re-election. The MFGB Annual Conference in July was likely to accept its Executive's recommendation to reduce the number of Executive places for South Wales, Durham and Yorkshire, because of their decline in membership. Nevertheless, Horner and his allies remained optimistic that he could retain his seat even in these straitened circumstances. At the conference, delegates duly approved the reductions in representation. Durham and Yorkshire, affiliated on 120,000 and 150,000 members respectively, were each reduced to two members. South Wales, affiliated on only 72,980, went down from three to one member. The twenty-three Federation delegates were consequently constrained to choose which two candidates to drop. They gave the Executive place to SO Davies, and dropped Horner and Richards, in the knowledge that Richards was unopposed in the election for MFGB Vice-President. When he was duly elected to that office, he would qualify an ex officio MFGB Executive seat. Durham and Yorkshire increased their Executive representation from two to three in the same way, by virtue of the re-election of WP Richardson and Herbert Smith as treasurer and president respectively.[230]

Horner's loss of the MFGB seat had serious implications for his leading role as a union activist. Although he had been deprived of the nomination by an adroit move which he himself would have been capable of deploying in order to achieve different political ends, he was evidently scarred by the experience. He blamed Richards for what he described as a sordid manoeuvre. Nevertheless, his disappearance from the Federation's nomination list was a comparatively minor event in the dramatic proceedings of the conference, which was held in the Winter Gardens Ballroom at the North Wales resort of Llandudno. Its highlights included the occasion when Herbert Smith left the chair, provoked by Willie Allan and Jimmie McKendrick, who were barracking him from the visitors' gallery. Conference delegates had earlier endorsed an MFGB Executive decision (taken by a vote of 11 to 8) to exclude Allan, McKendrick and two other delegates from the conference, even though they had all been elected by the Lanarkshire Miners as part of the NUSMW delegation. The four had subsequently gained admission to the balcony, probably through the connivance of the North Wales miners' stewards.

As Frankenberg retold the story: 'Smith marched up to the gallery and tried to throw them out, followed by S.O. Davies and Arthur, who as members of the executive were on the platform with him. Willie Allan could have made short work of Smith but instead he clung to a pillar from which, try as he would, Smith could not dislodge him. Meanwhile, Arthur, with his back to the scuffle, was standing at the top of the stairs talking to ... Nat Watkins. Suddenly Herbert Smith leapt on his back. Watkins

166

caught hold of the back of Smith's neck and had his fist raised to strike him, but Arthur called out to him to stop. They all let go of each other, went back to the platform and finished the conference.' The incident was widely reported in the press, including the *Worker*, whose reporter, 'A delegate', had watched Watkins pull Smith away from Horner, after which 'he [Smith] ejaculated (*sic*) "I'll get thee down yet" ... '![231] Had the row escalated to bare knuckle fisticuffs, further relations between the MMM leaders and Smith would have become virtually impossible. By avoiding a physical fight, Horner signalled his determination to carry on the political conflict. But it had been a close run thing. The incident became part of the canon of MFGB/NUM tradition, and was regularly invoked by veterans when reading the lesson of political unity to younger members.[232]

The close vote on the Executive about whether to admit the four Lanarkshire delegates reflected the complexity of the situation inside the MFGB. Since the Lock-Out, Minority Movement candidates had been winning union elections in Lanarkshire and Fife, apparently by legitimate means. However, whilst the MMM victors were less corrupt than most of the officials they replaced, their politics were not necessarily shared by the rank-and-file who voted for them. Smillie and the Fife Miners' secretary, Willie Adamson, both Labour MPs at the time, argued that the MMM activists were 'subverting' the Scottish miners' unions, steering them away from collective bargaining to permanent and futile battles against the coalowners. Nevertheless, many delegates found it difficult to ignore the fact that Allan and McKendrick had been duly elected. The *Worker* reported that in the private conference session held to consider the Executive recommendation, Ted Williams had joined Lancashire delegates in protesting against their exclusion.

The Llandudno conference reflected a more entrenched polarity. Both sides viewed the situation in stark either or terms. For Horner, Cook and other MMM activists, the choice was between either accepting the employers' terms, which would condemn their members and their families to starve in penury, or waging a 100 per cent total struggle against the employers from which victory would inevitably emerge. For Richards, Smith, Smillie and Joseph Jones, the choice was between either accepting a compromise, after having obtained the best deal for their members by applying industrial and political pressure, or fighting to the finish and inflicting potentially irreparable damage to the unions' credibility, solidarity and finances. The fact that conference debates did not escalate into overt civil war was testimony to the recognition by veteran delegates on both sides of the political divide that splitting would emasculate the union.

Between 1926 and 1927, it had been possible for many MFGB activists, including Smith and Cook, to tack between these two poles, because there had been significant fluidity in the industrial and political situation they had faced. But by 1928, the economics of the British coalmining industry and the coalowners' palpable determination to break the unions' power made the choices seem much more absolute. The Mond-Turner Talks had little apparent relevance for many MFGB activists working in the export coalfields. With Mond-Turner in mind, Jack Williams from the Forest of Dean moved a resolution at Llandudno on peace in industry. The *Worker* reported that he had placed 'special emphasis on the impossibility of attaining peace in industry under capitalism, and showing that such measures were incompatible with trade unionism'. Horner agreed, and attacked the 'reformists'. He said that the centrist conference delegates 'were wrong either yesterday or to-day, for yesterday, they declared in favour of nationalisation, and the same speakers to-day were ardently supporting its alternative (rationalisation). The Conference must decide whether it was going to use its power to support capitalism or to overthrow it ... '. Supported by SO Davies and Cook, the resolution was defeated on a card vote by 309 to 192, with Durham abstaining. After the conference Cook had a prominent article in the *Worker*, which attacked Joseph Jones and urged 'Let Us get that One National Union'.[233]

The MFGB Executive had lacked coherence and effectiveness during the sixteen months Horner had served on it. He had actually been a principal contributor to the national officials' continuing failure to obtain a consensus around meaningful positions. The disparate geographies, economic conditions and vagaries of the district agreements, customs and practices meant that a great deal of serious team-building was required before the British miners' caravanserai could move forward at more than a snail's pace. Smillie had moulded the district unions and their officers into a collective whole, cultivating their willingness to pool resources to gain practical goals. But neither Smith nor Cook could replicate his achievements. Smith transmitted a strong sense of commitment and discipline at delegate conferences. But in the closer, even intimate, confines of the Executive Council, where personal chemistry and tactical agility were vital, he was notably lacking. Cook seems never to have developed the basic skills of a committee person.

Horner had given Cook significant assistance in defending a militant, left-wing position on the MFGB Executive. He had helped him to withstand the increasingly determined offensives mounted against him by Joseph Jones and Richards. His early experience inside effective self-governing institutions in the Churches of Christ and the Unofficial Reform Committee had been further developed in the cut and thrust of Mardy Lodge, where personal friction was subsumed by humour and a general, avid interest in political issues. His skills had been honed at the Rhondda No. 1 District meetings. Delegates displayed debating skills, mastery of committee procedure and virtuosic rhetoric, sometimes with overweening pride. Unlike Cook, apparently, Horner had watched them and learned. He developed a formidable self-discipline, never speaking from vanity or self-indulgence, for the sake of scoring a point or making a flourish. He was calculating, and always knew where and how he wanted to carry the meeting forward. If he had remained on the MFGB Executive, he might have succeeded in leading procedural manoeuvres by which Cook could have retained some of his credibility.

But from the autumn of 1928, Cook increasingly lost heart, and quickly became the captive of his Executive, most of whose members had lost confidence in his abilities. To retain his job, he was constrained to say and do things with which he did not agree. Horner recalled in the second interview with Frankenberg that Cook had wanted to resign after the Llandudno conference. The MMM leadership had relied on Horner to dissuade him. They evidently felt that Cook's official trimming did not compromise either his political bona fides or his personal integrity. By virtue of his position at the top of the labour movement, Cook could still win worthwhile gains for the miners and the labour movement. Horner continued to see Cook regularly until his early death in November 1931, and they met on the same affectionate terms. Despite the well publicised political conflict between them in the run-up to the 1929 general election, the two Arthurs remained close personal friends.

The Minority Movement kept up both activities and appearances during the summer of 1928, despite their meagre, even counter-productive, results. The *Worker* reported on 17 August that 'three splendid conferences' had been held in the Anthracite the previous weekend, under the joint auspices of the Minority Movement and the Miners' March Committee. The committee was organising an unemployed miners' march to the TUC, which was meeting in Swansea on 3 to 8 September. Ianto Evans, Secretary of the Anthracite MMM, was reported to be confident that the march would be a huge success. Horner spoke at all three conferences: with Tom Thomas and George Maslin in Swansea on Saturday afternoon; with Bob Ellis (from Mardy MMM) and Maslin at Llanelli on Saturday evening and with Ellis and DJ Williams on Sunday in Ammanford. Delegates discussed rationalisation, trade union democracy and unemployment, and also appointed delegates to attend the Fifth Annual NMM Conference on 25 to 26 August in London.

At the NMM Conference, the main resolution was moved by Pollitt and seconded by Horner. Horner's head, sympathetically drawn by a cartoonist, appeared on page 3 alongside the conference report in the *Worker* on 31 August. The story noted that SO Davies, Lawther, Proudfoot, Cook and Maxton had all sent greetings. Although 844 delegates attended, compared to 718 in 1927 and 802 in 1926, they came mainly from NUWM branches and industrial sections of the Minority Movement itself, in contrast to previous years when union branches and district committees had been well represented. Leading NMM Executive members hoped that a core of loyal activists would fill the gap left by the falling-off of official union bodies until the political climate in the trade union movement changed. Their expedient was to enrol individual members and collect regular financial contributions from them. An article in the *Worker* of 17 August had explained: 'Many groups and comrades have long felt the need for placing the Minority Movement on a more secure organisational footing instead of continuing with the present amorphous structure.' At the conference Gossip moved the resolution on trade union democracy which emphasised 'the reason and the methods of autocracy in the trade unions'. Seconding, Johnny Mahon, a young party activist working at the NMM office, said that the resolution 'showed the need for a reorganised [Minority] movement and indicated clearly the lines on which it should be brought about'.

The mining portion of the conference was apparently a resounding success. Horner had presided on Sunday morning at the Mining Delegates' sectional meeting, and MMM committees from Scotland, Northumberland, Durham, Nottinghamshire, Derbyshire, Lancashire, Yorkshire, Kent, South Wales and Warwickshire were all represented. The resolution passed called 'upon all mineworkers to continue to work within the MFGB and to carry on the fight for full membership rights within the union ... ' Horner had an optimistic article in the *Mineworker* on 31 August about a dispute in Featherstone, West Yorkshire. He saw it as evidence of a revival of the national coalowners' association as 'an active, flaming and directing body for the coalowners as a whole. The MFGB, as the representative of the whole of the British miners, can, if it will, re-establish itself by calling a special Conference to decide upon immediate measures to provide support and assistance for our victimised comrades, and to renew the effort to secure a National Agreement ... '

The unemployed march to greet the TUC in Swansea on 3 September encountered formidable obstacles. The General Council refused to allow two marchers to address Congress, 'since they fail to see that any deputation can put before Congress any new phase of this subject ... [D]elegates of this Congress representing the Trade Union Movement of this country are fully alive to and are constantly making every effort to deal with this vital problem'. Horner was a delegate at Congress, and unsuccessfully moved the reference back of this portion of the General Council's report. (He had addressed a meeting of the marchers at a Swansea park earlier in the day.) Horner scored a memorable victory later in the week. The presiding TUC President, Ben Turner, allowed him to speak as an individual delegate, despite Richardson's and Herbert Smith's voluble objections that he would be speaking against MFGB policy which had already been decided. Turner explained: 'It seems to me quite fair that every person in this hall who is an admitted delegate is entitled to speak, but he cannot speak for his organisation if his organisation has taken another line. I think Mr. Horner is therefore entitled to speak as a delegate putting his own views and nobody else's.' Horner's speech was an appeal for unity, in opposition to a resolution on 'Dangers of Disruption'.

> Are you going to consider all persons who are not organ-
> ised inside the Labour Party as being disrupters inside
> the Trade Union Movement? If you are, Mr. Turner,
> good-bye to 50 per cent and more of the member-
> ship, for if political opinions are to determine rights
> and responsibilities inside the Trade Union Movement
> you are transferring the TUC from being an industrial
> organisation ... and you might as well liquidate it and
> merge it into the Labour Party ... [234]

Despite their apparent failure to reverse the movement's right-ward turn, Pollitt and his NMM allies remained committed to working within official union structures. After the TUC, Horner had laid his normal routine aside to concentrate on organising the MMM's Save-the-Union campaign, modelled on the Save-the-Union campaign in the AEU, which communist and left-wing engineering activists had launched after the union's defeat in the 1922 National Engineering Lock-Out. An MMM pamphlet, *Victimisation. An Analysis Showing its relation to Spencerism and Mondism*, explained that preparations had begun at the end of 1928, when district meetings and conferences met in Scotland, Durham, Nottinghamshire and Yorkshire to form local Save-the-Union Committees. Having made a token obeisance to the Comintern's New Line, the pamphlet concluded confidently.

> [S]o long as they [the old school of union leaders] per-
> sist in violating the will of the men the conflict in the
> industry and in the union will continue and out of both
> militancy will further develop and left wing forces grow.
> Assured thus of ultimate victory, winning ever more
> adherents to its side who recognise it as the only alter-
> native to the present febrile leadership, the Minority
> Movement pushes irresistibly on ... [E]very blow from
> the boss is additional justification for the policy of the
> Minority Movement ...

The campaign renewed the ties between most MMM activists and their 'reformist unions'. Horner was keenly welcomed in other coalfields, and renewed friendships and networks he had formed in 1925 to 1926. He played an important part in the Nottinghamshire campaign, where the General Council had been subsidising NMA collectors in order to reverse Spencer's dominance, and a de facto united front between the MMM and TUC against Spencer was evident. Spencer's NMIU had enrolled 18,000 members by the end of 1926, compared to the NMA's 10,000. By the end of 1929, the positions were reversed, with the NMA recording 14,000 members compared to the NMIU's 10,800.[235]

At the Tenth CPGB Congress, held in Bermondsey on 19 to 22 January 1929, Bell, in his capacity as ECCI representative, had stressed that the Save-the-Union committees must transform themselves into Miners' Councils of Action, welcoming non-union workers and pursuing revolutionary activities. Horner ignored his intervention, however. He continued the MMM's earlier strategy of reclaiming the district unions from the old school in order to transform them into fighting, revolutionary organs. When he moved the resolution on the mining situation at the Congress, he gave '[a] strong warning against the indiscriminate advocacy of new Unions. Splits were inevitable under certain circumstances, but the responsibility for splits must rest clearly on the shoulders on the bureaucracy as in Fife. To have set up a New Union in Lanarkshire would have meant the liquidation of the Party.'

Although a clear undercurrent of support for extreme interpretations of the New Line was evident, Horner received a sympathetic hearing at the Congress. The report in *Workers' Life*, the CPGB's weekly paper, stressed the strong support Horner had received from delegates, including Jim Ancrum and William Hall from Durham. A speech from Rust, who had travelled back from Moscow to be present, had been the only reported opposition. Rust had been initially been a protégé of NMM engineering union activists like Tanner and Scott, who continued to oppose the formation of new, revolutionary unions. But he was now the main British protagonist for Lozovsky's project. He worked in the youth international in Moscow, and knew which people to court and which arguments would persuade them. He had an engaging manner, and great facility in reciting Class Against Class catechisms.[236]

Horner met Rust's arguments head on, declaring that it was foolish to argue that militants could not win positions in the MFGB. He challenged anyone to say that the MFGB had expelled members for being communists. He described Rust's statement that Save-the-Union Committees were equivalent to Save-the-Bureaucrats as nonsense. The party's current situation 'was due to the lack of faith in the workers and discouragement at the difficulties they were facing'. Horner's New Year's message on the 'Miners' Page' of *Workers' Life* offered the same lesson. 'Away with defeatism and demoralisation; and let us be pledged not to rest in our labours for One Miners' Union.'[237] When the incoming Executive met in February, Horner was selected for the Politburo, along with Campbell and Pollitt.[238]

On Sunday evening, 20 January 1929, Horner, advertised as prospective parliamentary candidate for East Rhondda, was a featured speaker at Stratford Town Hall. On 25 January *Workers' Life* carried Communist candidates' profiles. Horner was described as being one of the youngest, and Dai Lloyd Davies was listed as his agent. The profile noted that his candidacy was supported by the recently disaffiliated Rhondda East constituency Labour Party, which had retained the support of three quarters of the Federation lodges and other union branches, as well as 100 active members of the women's section. The incumbent SWMF-sponsored Labour MP, Dai Watts Morgan, had offered to resign his parliamentary seat and run against Horner in a by-election, apparently presuming that the Tories and Liberals would decline to stand candidates, enabling a contest between Communist and Labour to decide the outcome. Horner had responded by calling for a miners' only ballot, excluding Liberal and Tory voters.[239]

Immediately after the Tenth Congress, Horner went to Berlin for the RILU Miners' International Committee annual conference of Revolutionary Miners. His conference report in *Workers' Life* on 8 February showed that he had maintained his pragmatic opposition to forming new unions, evidently without challenge. Back in Britain, however, the dispute inside the NMM and CPGB about interpretations of Class Against Class was escalating. Rust marshalled sympathetic confederates into a grouping which I

174

described as the Young Turks in my book about the CPGB and trade unions. They included another gifted YCL leader, Wally Tapsell, and John Mahon and George Renshaw, young party activists who were working at the NMM office in Great Ormond Street.[240]

The Young Turks were convinced that Britain was ripe for revolution, and conceived the youthful ambition to replace the old leadership inside the party and the Minority Movement. Pollitt, Campbell and Hannington recognised the necessity of fighting the Young Turks on their own ground and trimmed vigorously towards the New Line. Horner, by contrast, was unwilling to argue about the correct interpretation of the Comintern's New Line. Only ten years older than Rust and Tapsell, he had little sympathy for their political pyrotechnics. He may have been influenced in this by his experiences of theological disputation inside the Churches of Christ, with its moral imperative of 'speaking the truth'. But he was also impatient with their capacity to sit in the office and argue, apparently endlessly, instead of going out to do the hard agitation involved in serious 'mass work'.

Pollitt and Horner made common cause to pre-empt the formation of an independent miners' union in Scotland, even though the party Executive had sanctioned preparations for a new union in September 1928.[241] They were in a good tactical position at the NMM office to monitor moves being made on the ground towards independent unions, and to divert them into Back to the Union campaigns. Receiving support from Campbell and the non-communists in the NMM leadership, notably Tanner, they had succeeded in countering the Young Turks' arguments for New Unions. But they were unable to prevent the formation of the United Mineworkers of Scotland in April 1929. Left-wingers, such as Davey Proudfoot, Willie Allan and John MacArthur had been elected to full-time positions in the official Fife and Lanarkshire district unions. But they left the Old Unions in hot blood, faced, on the one hand, by mounting pressure from the Young Turks and Lozovsky for them to secede, and on the other, by a concerted campaign by officials in the NUSMW and MFGB against communist and MMM activists. Horner told Frankenberg that he had 'been sent' to Scotland to persuade the party activists to disband the UMS. Willie Adamson

175

MP had founded a new 'reformist' union in response to the left's advance inside the official Fife union. Pollitt and Horner were presumably sanguine that if the left closed down the UMS, opinion inside the MFGB would move against Adamson.

Horner's mission failed. Both Pollitt and Horner must have been profoundly discouraged by this, since neither was in the mood to concede any ground to the Young Turks. But even though some left-wingers had continued to doubt the wisdom of founding a new union, relations between the rival Scottish unions had by now descended into open civil war. The Young Turks had also gained sufficient ground inside the CPGB to influence many mining activists. An enduring result, however, of these protracted rearguard manoeuvres, was that Horner and Pollitt forged a close personal bond, which endured until Pollitt's death in 1960.[242]

Freed from the round of SWMF and MFGB meetings in Cardiff and London, Horner now concentrated on preparations for the expected general election, which Baldwin eventually called for 30 May. Serious electioneering in the Horner camp began in early April. He evidently relished the prospect of a hard-fought contest, and made painstaking preparations to beat his opponents, just as he had trained diligently for boxing and football matches. During the campaign, a much publicised and well-remembered exchange of open letters took place between Horner and Cook in *Worker's Life*, in which Horner vainly sought Cook's support. Although the episode is conventionally viewed as being the low point in the two men's friendship, it is unlikely that either took the encounter personally. They are more likely to have recognised it as a political duel which neither desired, but which political circumstances made inevitable.

The Mardy Lodge minutes record Horner's protracted absence from meetings, from 18 March to 26 September 1929. He may have decided on a diplomatic absence until after the general election, to pre-empt any attempts by the Federation Executive to discipline the Lodge for supporting him rather than Watts Morgan. On 22 April the Lodge again nominated Horner for the SWMF presidency. Their gesture was a token of defiance against the prevailing centre-right climate. At the Federation conference Horner predictably received only seventeen votes in contrast to Morrell's 112. He would have had a more realistic chance of winning the Vice-Presidency against the incumbent SO Davies. Davies had distanced himself from the MMM during 1928, in response to the NMM's increasingly shrill denunciations of all 'reformist' unions. As a result, the South Wales District Party Committee had pressed Horner to stand against him in 1928. Horner had refused, telling the Politburo that he wanted 'to keep on the best possible terms' with him.[243] They agreed, and over-ruled the South Wales party. In 1929, the DPC made no attempt to compel Horner to change tactics.

Horner's election manifesto, 'A Call to Action!' was issued on behalf of 'The Rhondda Borough Labour Party (Disaffiliated)'. Its peroration linked Horner to communism. 'Our Candidate is pledged to the complete programme of the Communist Party, i.e., to continue the struggle of (*sic*) the basis of Class Against Class. *We will not cease this fight until the working class has emerged victorious and triumphant from the struggle.*' It was signed by David Evans, Chairman, and JE Jones, Secretary on behalf of its Executive Committee. Evans added gravitas to Horner's camp by virtue of his job as Porth Co-operative Store Manager.

Horner's candidacy was publicly endorsed by three Federation lodges in the constituency, Mardy, Ferndale and Tylorstown. Their lodge committees are likely to have tabled the question of endorsement at lodge meetings, with a strong recommendation to opt for Horner, in the knowledge that their action would probably result in a challenge from the SWMF Executive. Their defence was that Horner had the support of the Rhondda Borough Labour Party (Disaffiliated), and that he was not standing as a communist candidate. (A candidate's party political affiliation was not printed after their name on ballot papers in British parliamentary elections until the late 1960s.) They may have hoped that Horner would win so many votes in the general election that the Executive would be unwilling to go against their members' clearly expressed preference.

The combined forces of the disaffiliated Labour Party, the MMM, the NUWM and the CPGB put up a strenuous fight. *Workers' Life* reported in the last weeks of the campaign that the Horner organisation was holding forty public meetings a week. Horner's passionate commitment to the fight had an important spin-off effect in restoring militants' morale. The communist

177

party gained new members, including Will Paynter, a militant miner, aged twenty-five, working at Cymmer colliery, near Porth. Watts Morgan had been unopposed at the general election in 1924, and there had been neither campaign nor poll. In 1929 there were four candidates: Watts Morgan, Horner, a Tory and a Liberal, Dr RD Chalke, headmaster of Porth Secondary School and a well-known local luminary. Horner retained clear memories of Chalke's candidacy, which he evidently believed had been critical in denying him anti-Labour votes. The Liberal national campaign was financed by Lloyd George's election chest, and designed to appeal to radical sentiments. The Liberal manifesto embraced Keynes's unorthodox remedies for alleviating unemployment, which coincided with solutions being contemplated by many union leaders. Although Chalke pushed him into third place, Horner still gained 5789 votes, 15.2 per cent, whilst the Tory lost his deposit. Of the twenty-five Communist candidates, only three others gained comparable results: Saklatvala in Battersea North, Alec Geddes in Greenock, and Gallacher in Fife West.[244]

After the general election, as a result of Comintern intervention, Pollitt was given a leading role in the CPGB *apparat*. The ECCI was making strenuous efforts in all its national affiliates to identify and promote capable, local cadres who could improve their parties' mass work. Pollitt's conspicuous success in organising the Minority Movement made him an obvious candidate for promotion inside the party. He joined the Secretariat in June 1929 on an equal footing with its incumbents, Campbell and Albert Inkpin. He continued as NMM General Secretary until the Sixth Annual NMM Conference at the end of August, when Gossip nominated Horner in his stead. When there were no other candidates, Horner was unanimously elected. He had already moved the main conference resolution, a role previously taken by Pollitt. Although Horner's succession had clearly been prearranged, he was also a genuinely popular choice. He was well-known to miners and other union activists, with whom he had liaised in planning and participating in national conferences, as well as co-ordinating support for the MFGB in the Lock-Out and for National Unemployed Marches and the Cook-Maxton Manifesto. The honorific post of Vice-Chairman was created for Pollitt, who joined Tom Mann, the Chairman, on the NMM letter-head.

Horner had spent most weekends away from South Wales in 1924 to 1925; he now had become a veritable itinerant in 1926. As NMM general secretary, he faced the prospect of leaving family and friends for long, continuous periods in a very different socio-economic climate. Unlike the earlier period, when their spirits had been high and rising, the miners and communists of Mardy needed lifting and sustaining. At the Mardy Lodge meeting on 26 September, Horner 'gave a personal explanation of why he had been away from Mardy and that he would be going again for a short period. He was appointed Secretary of the NMM but Mardy would always be his home and [he] would return again amongst them.' He probably also reported on the National Unemployed Workers' Movement conference in Sheffield earlier in September, which he had attended as a Mardy delegate. The Young Turks were lobbying the Politburo to bring the NUWM into line with Class Against Class by jettisoning the highly successful trade union model and turning it into a full-blooded red, revolutionary organ. Hannington had enlisted Horner's support in maintaining the status quo, calculating that his wide popularity would make it more difficult for Rust and Tapsell to attack. Horner had chaired the Sheffield conference and was elected NUWM Vice-President for the coming year.[245]

Horner had probably been deputising for Pollitt at the NMM office in Great Ormond Street since June 1929. He had gone to Moscow on 17 June to attend the RILU Executive Bureau, a duty which Pollitt would have previously performed. He had also been '"very busy" on the preliminary work' for the Tenth ECCI Plenum in July, although he was unable to attend it. His MI5 file noted that he 'remained in Russia until 17.7.29, when he hurried back to attend the Miners' Federation of Great Britain conference, which opened in Blackpool on 22.7.29.'[246]

The Tenth Plenum had ratcheted the Comintern's interpretation of the New Line further left. Social democrats were declared to be social fascists, and the importance of 'the struggle against the "right danger" inside the communist movement' was reaffirmed. Propelled leftwards by developments inside the Soviet communist party and state, the ECCI was precipitating sweeping changes in the leaderships of affiliated parties, in an effort to ensure that Class Against Class was fully implemented. Tempers had flared at the plenum during a protracted discussion on the CPGB. Manuilsky, the CPSU(B) representative, had subjected the British leadership to scathing criticism. Then, '[i]n what Pollitt described as a "prepared brief of all the shortcomings and deviations of our Party", Rust stressed the lack of self-criticism and called for a new leadership ... [naming] Horner, Campbell ... Inkpin and Rothstein as among those responsible for sabotaging Comintern policies.'[247]

Despite Manuilsky's premeditated outburst, the Tenth Plenum left the existing CPGB leadership intact. The ECCI evidently preferred to monitor developments amongst party members in Britain before taking any decisions. In this context, Pollitt's apparent insistence on Horner being confirmed as NMM General Secretary in late August is especially notable. His own personal standing remained high in Moscow, and he could plausibly have enhanced it further by joining with Rust, who along with Tapsell had moved swiftly to enlist the Moscow *apparat* on their side. Their confederates in Britain were gathering enthusiastic support from party members, many of whom were also young, particularly in the Northeast and the Midlands. Their appeal was voluntarist: a British revolution could be triggered by sufficient commitment, leadership and determination from communists.

Pollitt and Horner did not agree about all aspects of how the New Line should be applied in Britain. Pollitt was on the far left and Horner on the right about the CPGB's attitude to the Labour Party. At the end of June 1928, Horner had not only favoured the party's continuing to apply for affiliation to the Labour Party, he had also been 'prepared to do so on the basis that the party would obey Labour's constitution'.[248] Despite this difference, both men felt that the Young Turks constituted the principal threat, and continued to work closely together inside the NMM and on the Politburo. Inside the NMM they still had sufficient support to neutralise many of the Young Turks' initiatives. The NMM was enduring the withdrawal of affiliations and financial support from trades councils, union branches and district organisations. But the Sixth Annual Conference had a healthy attendance of 710 delegates. The majority now came

from engineering rather than mining, evidence of the demoralisation on the left inside the MFGB, and the centre-right's
success in isolating them.

Pollitt had taken his secretary with him from the NMM to
the party offices in King Street, Soho. Doris Allison, who had
been working for Albert Inkpin at King Street, went to work
for Horner at Great Ormond Street. Arthur knew her common
law husband George Allison from the MMM. He had apparently been victimised in the Fife coalfield in 1927, and met Doris
when he moved to London. He worked for the party centre, but
also kept up his MMM activity; for example, he was the main
advertised speaker for party meetings on Sunday 13 January
1929 in the Workers' Hall, Cwmparc in the afternoon and in the
cinema at Clydach Vale in the evening.[249] Doris and Arthur got
on famously, and their warm relations were probably a happy
antidote to what both regarded as the poisonous presence of
the Young Turks. Arthur spent most London evenings with the
Allisons, often in the company of Albert Inkpin, whom Arthur
knew from the party Executive and Politburo. Their friendships
ripened, and Arthur took up North London residence with
Inkpin and his wife at 41 Cecile Park, Crouch Hill.[250]

Perhaps encouraged by Pollitt and Hannington, who remained
active in the MMM, Horner renewed his connections with leading London AEU activists, Joe Scott, Claude Berridge and Jack
Tanner in the Metalworkers' Minority Movement. They had
continued to successfully evade the RILU's injunction to attack
their 'reformist' unions, and as a result had deterred engineering union officials from launching an anti-Minority Movement
offensive on the scale of those proceeding in the general and
mining unions. Whilst Horner was helping the MMM pragma-
tists, he also enjoyed their company. He had already earned
their respect through his forthright opposition to Red Unions.

Roderick Martin's history of the NMM depicts Horner as
an ineffectual general secretary, unable to operate policies and
organise activities which reflected his own and other pragma-
tists' opposition to the Young Turks' extreme interpretations of
Class Against Class. Primary evidence contradicts this conclusion. Mahon and Renshaw, two of Martin's principal sources,
were highly partisan participants in the internecine conflict
being waged at Great Ormond Street over whether the NMM

should encourage the foundation of revolutionary unions. When Martin interviewed Renshaw in the 1960s, he still harboured a grudge against Horner for frustrating their ambitions to form Red unions. Mahon's biography of Pollitt carefully damned Horner with faint praise at every opportunity.[251] Horner withstood intense assaults on his bona fides by Rust and Tapsell between June and November 1929. He rebutted their constant accusations head-on, offering robust defences of his own conduct and dismissing his critics as callow non-proletarians with a distaste for doing serious mass work out in the field. For example, at the first meeting of the CPGB Executive attended by those present at the Tenth Plenum, Horner described the division in the party as one between thinkers and doers. He added that Rust had never seen the working class except in pictures and from platforms.[252]

In September Horner faced fresh provocation when the Young Turks went public, taking their campaign against the 'rights' into the open. Manuilsky, apparently despairing of the entire party leadership *tout court* – Rust not excepted – arranged for the Tenth Plenum discussion about the CPGB to be published in *Inprecorr*, the Comintern's house journal, which appeared in all the main global languages. Noreen Branson commented: 'It was clearly Manuilsky's aim to stir up the rank and file against the leadership. He succeeded.' At an Executive meeting on 21 September, Horner complained 'that "much of the criticism taking place is of the most unscrupulous kind that has ever been practiced in the history of the Party." Saying that at the Scottish Conference Pollitt had been referred to as a right winger, "which was a libel", he ended by demanding that he, Horner, be relieved of all duties at the Party headquarters. A little later he insisted that his demand ... be put to the vote ... [It] was defeated by 16 votes to 3.'[253]

There was evident discontent amongst the rump of active party members. The party's political position appeared increasingly irrelevant against the background of the successful minority Labour government and a re-consolidated trade union movement, which was winning concessions, partly as a result of the conciliatory atmosphere accompanying the Mond-Turner talks. Faced with what was a depressing situation for revolutionaries, the Young Turks were keen to press their attack on the party's existing leadership and policies. Seizing the opportunity presented by the *Inprecorr* revelations, they found disaffected party members to be a receptive audience for their message about the need for apocalyptic change. Their supporters believed their promises of revolution tomorrow and began eagerly to spread the message.

Throughout the autumn, the balance of power inside the party continued to tilt towards the Young Turks. '[At CPGB] District conference after conference, calls were heard for further [leadership] changes ... One of the few regions where a desire to attack the Central Committee [Executive] failed to take root was the Rhondda in South Wales.'[254] Pollitt and Campbell, and Hannington tacked sharply leftwards, even supporting the formation of new, 'independent' unions. The prevailing winds from the Kremlin and the Young Turks' increased support inside the CPGB persuaded them that some accommodation was necessary to ensure their own survival in the leadership. Only Horner refused to trim.

At the end of November 1929, under pressure from Moscow and most party districts, the CPGB leadership convened another party congress. In the orthodox version of CPGB history, the Eleventh Party Congress in Leeds is remembered as the occasion when 'the rank-and-file' compelled a change in the party leadership and direction. It was actually a triumph for the Young Turks' ambitions, energetic planning and caucusing. The resolution passed by Congress on economic struggles was a faithful replica of Lozovsky's formula for new unions. Party members and the NMM were enjoined to stop recruiting unorganised workers into 'reformist' unions and instead 'develop an independent campaign to establish representative factory committees of both organised and unorganised, and expose the slogan of 100 per cent trade unionism ... ' Doubts were raised from the floor by Billy Stokes, a Coventry AEU activist, and Dai Lloyd Davies, who 'admitted bluntly: "When comrades speak of the radicalisation of the masses and the great wave of insurrection, I want to tell you that in my experience – which is not small – I have not seen a ripple of it."' The platform speakers responded with assurances that the Lozovsky formula would produce spectacular results if embraced with sufficient enthusiasm.

A procedural innovation was the Panels Commission, chaired by Rust, intended to ensure that only right-minded candidates for the Executive should be placed before delegates for their approval. Only twelve of the thirty incumbents were put forward for election to the Executive.

Although the Commission had kept Pollitt and Campbell on their list, Horner and Hannington were amongst the twelve dropped members. Angered at the insult, Hannington nominated himself for re-election, 'stating that he was "not standing on the penitents form because it happens to be fashionable, because I believe my line has been a left line all the time".' His leadership of the NUWM probably ensured his re-election, by 52 votes to 30. Horner had earlier told delegates that he did not want to be re-elected, 'I would rather do anything than stop there.' When he was nevertheless nominated by another delegate, he was only defeated by 25 to 56 votes, evidence of his standing as an NMM and miners' leader. Despite manoeuvres from the floor to prevent Tapsell's and Rust's election to the Executive, they were successful.[255]

The Young Turks had scored a signal victory at the Congress. They had seized the moral high ground as the true interpreters of the New Line and gained a decisive advantage inside the British party. Thorpe observes, 'The Secretariat elected at Leeds comprised – besides Pollitt – Rust, Tapsell, Gallacher and [Idris] Cox ... The five formed the core of the PB [Politburo] elected at Leeds ... other members, including Murphy, Arnot and Robson, were also on the left.'[256] Once the proletariat was freed from the bonds of bureaucratic reformist unions, they intended the Minority Movement to become the umbrella organisation for a panoply of new, Red unions. The Young Turks recognised that Horner presented the principal obstruction to their plans for the NMM's transformation. He had made incautious attacks at Leeds on the dangerous revolutionary zeal being exhibited by delegates. Campbell told the Executive in 1931 that in 1929 Horner 'never saw the fundamental justice of the change of leadership in this Party. He saw some people whom he considered good people being slighted and other people whom he considered not quite so good put in their place'.[257] After their triumph at the Eleventh Congress, the Young Turks could be confident of a compliant majority on the Executive, the Politburo and the

Secretariat. They had no intention of allowing Horner to continue in a position of political leadership or as NMM secretary.

Chapter 7

Trials of Will
and Conscience

Moscow, Essen, Berlin, Mardy

Despite his forthright opposition to Lozovsky's extreme position at the Fourth RILU Congress in March 1928, Horner had loyally accepted the New Line. In the last chapter we observed his participation in an informal group of veteran NMM activists who worked with Pollitt to mitigate its hyperbole and pre-empt erstwhile attempts to split unions from the left. But during 1929 Horner had become increasingly frustrated by the group's apparent helplessness in the face of Manuilsky's support for the Young Turks. Whilst Tanner, Scott and other AEU activists dismissed the New Line after meetings in the pub and took determined steps to insulate the Metalworkers MM from its worst effects, they were unwilling to expose themselves by challenging the Young Turks in their bid to gain formal control of the NMM *apparat*. Horner had experienced the Young Turks' reluctance to share the hard graft of organising, administrating and personal networking required to keep a mass movement like the MMM or NUWM afloat. He deeply resented the charges they levelled against him in the close personal combat which had become a normal feature of the party Executive. For example, in November 1929 'he was accused by one of the members of the Central Committee [Executive] of "alignment with Herbert SMITH and Joe JONES at the Blackpool conference [of the MFGB]."'[258]

After the humiliations and high drama at the Eleventh Party Congress, his emotions and thoughts became increasingly gloomy. Over the course of 1929, he had been compelled to acquiesce on the sidelines as the Young Turks disseminated NMM and CPGB propaganda which condemned 'reformist' unions as social fascist. This was particularly exasperating as he had had the opportunity to observe on visits to Berlin and Moscow in 1927 to 1929 that Lozovsky's extreme position about trade unions was not gaining significant ground either in the ECCI or the Miners' International Committee of RILU.[259] Leading trade unionists in the MIC had a positive vision and ebullient optimism about moulding European miners into a fighting unity. Their painful personal experience of the political, confessional and national divisions in mining trade unionism in the Ruhr, Silesia and Austria-Hungary before 1914 made them determined to work for all-in unity at the workplace and through existing unions. Their confidence in being able to do so was reinforced by their self-image as workers in an industry whose product was essential. They did not doubt that coalminers and their unions would continue to prosper and command an excellent bargaining position which they intended to exploit for their members' benefit.

Horner's profession of communist belief was genuinely sincere. From his personal observation of Soviet coalfields and close relations with Soviet coalmining union leaders, he believed that socialism in one country was a practical way forward. He knew, moreover, that there was strong support for this view from non-communist Labour and ILP activists. In January-February 1928, for example, John Strachey, still editor of the *Miner* and Cook's confidant, had undertaken an extensive tour of the USSR's coalfields, interviewing both union leaders and managers. He described his visit in a pamphlet published by the ILP, *Workers' Control in the Russian Mining Industry*, with a Foreword by Cook. He noted with approval the modernisation of the pits, the introduction of power-driven machinery to hew the coal and the opening of new seams. In the summer of 1930, after he was elected to parliament as Labour MP for Birmingham Aston, Strachey returned to the USSR with a group of other Labour MPs, including Bevan, George Strauss and Jennie Lee. The pamphlet they issued, *What We Saw in Russia*, published in 1931, was unmitigatedly optimistic. Bevan's private views were less sanguine.[260]

When Horner arrived in Moscow for the Fourth RILU Conference in December 1929, Stalin's extraordinary campaign to liquidate the kulaks, rich peasants, was at its height. Regional, district and local parties waged it with such enthusiasm and excess that Stalin was compelled to dispense an unmistakable order to moderate their behaviour, his 'Dizzy with Success' article which appeared in *Pravda* on 2 March 1930. He enjoined party organs to exercise caution. Village life was so disrupted that it was doubtful whether there would be sufficient labour and will to complete the spring sowing of grain. The enforced uprooting and banishment of hundreds of thousands of peasant families, during which millions had perished, had continuing, dire effects, including widespread famine in 1931 to 1932. It was not until 1934 that a viable equilibrium had been re-established in the countryside. Nevertheless, in 1930 Horner was certain that the Comintern and RILU provided a vital network of parties and unions which would enable workers of all countries (and colonies) to realise the promise of the Communist Manifesto. Along with other socialists, his belief in Soviet socialism had been reinforced by the October 1929 Wall Street crash, and the intensifying international slump. Non-communist left-wingers cited the success of the Soviet First Five Year Plan as evidence that revolutionary socialism was working, whilst in the German Republic, social democratic compromises with capitalism had failed to withstand the stress of the worldwide capitalist depression.

In the aftermath of the Eleventh Congress, with the Young Turks able to dominate the CPGB Executive, Horner faced the prospect of being compelled to admit his past errors and acknowledge that his opponents were right. After this confession, he would be expected to engage in self-criticism at party branch and fraction meetings, the process by which erring communists could rehabilitate themselves and become fit to re-enter the revolutionary struggle. At this juncture it is likely he considered leaving the party. His moral socialisation in the Churches of Christ had evidently inoculated him against all forms of repentance except private conscience-cleansing. Whilst accepting disputation, sermonising and witness-bearing as valuable aids in guiding personal reflection, he mistrusted ritual confessions.

Horner had proved himself capable of ending his allegiance to one confession, the Churches of Christ. Having experienced the wrenching self-doubt and soul-searching which accompany a decision to break strong ties, he recognised the personal trial which would be involved if he repeated the process. Ethel and the couple's close friends in the Rhondda were likely to have urged him to remain loyal to international communism. Pollitt and his closest London colleagues also viewed his voluntary exit from the party on conscientious grounds as unthinkable. Their combined arguments may have induced him to consider making some token obeisance towards self-criticism in order to conciliate the CPGB Executive.

Having resolved his doubts about remaining a communist, Horner had to deal with another, equally serious, personal conflict. He found himself wholly at odds with the Federation's officers and Executive. He believed that Richards and Morrell had connived with the police to ensure that he was unable to speak at a critical coalfield delegate conference. His relations with them had reached breaking point in September 1928, when an article by him appeared in the *Sunday Worker* attacking the high life styles of mining trade union bureaucrats, using the travel expenses which they claimed as an example of their corruption. The SWMF Executive had instituted libel proceedings against him, which had proceeded some way before they decided to drop them – probably as a result of successful conciliation between the two opposing parties by SO Davies.

Horner continued to behave as if the case for one miners' union was still practical politics. He argued that until the MFGB was transformed into One Miners' Union, able to enforce nationalisation, no advance in wages and conditions was possible. Because they declined to prioritise uniting the district mining unions, he condemned the mining union 'bureaucracy' as irredeemable, fit only for ejection in order to make way for the forces of a modernised, industrial union. Nevertheless, as Horner's pitiful vote in the election for SWMF President in 1929 showed, the great majority of Federation members remained loyal to the status quo. Though many may have regretted rejecting his bid for their votes, they could not agree that One Miners' Union was a realistic possibility.

In addition to his alienation from the Federation, Horner had to deal with the turn against him and towards the Young Turks inside the South Wales communist party. He had been a hero amongst them in 1926 to 1927, heading the forward momentum towards revolution. There had been a significant increase in South Wales party membership in 1926 to 1927, many of whom were women. At the Ninth Party Congress in October 1926, the South Wales district reported 2300 members and 43 factory or pit groups.[261] Funds channelled from the Comintern via King Street, though meagre, were able to finance office space in Cardiff and pay Area Organisers to lay down secure foundations for local party branches. These developments heightened the central party leadership's belief in South Wales' revolutionary potential. Many party veterans active in the SWMF continued to provide unconditional support for Horner's opposition to forming new, Red unions; however, an increasingly self-confident countervailing group of South Walian comrades emerged who supported Lozovsky's call for new, Red unions. They pointed to SWMF officials' determination to isolate and marginalise communist activists, Horner principal amongst them, as evidence. Paradoxically, the drama and comparative success of Horner's general election campaign reinforced their sense of grievance. Whilst Bevan had succeeded in getting the Labour incumbent at Ebbw Vale de-selected in favour of his own candidacy, SWMF officials had refused to ballot members in Rhondda East about whether the union should endorse Watts Morgan or Horner, a ballot which most communists believed Horner would have won.

From 1928 communist party membership had declined steeply throughout Britain. South Walian membership had contracted to 546 members in December 1929, had fallen further to 400 in May 1930, and reached a mere 264 in November 1930.[262] Nevertheless, revolutionary optimism was disseminated amongst the shrinking membership, by graduates of the Lenin School arriving back in South Wales eager to implement the New Line. They returned from Moscow with the latest versions of communist practice, including self-criticism. The new District Organiser, Len Jeffries, a recent arrival from the Lenin School himself, led his Area Organisers and keen unemployed party activists in a strenuous political programme. At District Party Committee meetings, comrades from the sub-districts in West

Wales, the Rhondda and Monmouthshire assembled to hammer out their political line. (The party offices opened in Porth for the 1929 general election were kept on.) They did their best to imbue the newly organised branches with a proper orthodox zeal for Class Against Class.[263]

Many veteran party members, including the Horners, found the new practices offensive. *We Live*, a novel by the Mid-Rhondda communist leader Lewis Jones, depicted the new self-criticism sessions in lurid detail. Horner is thinly disguised in the book as Fred Lewis.[264] Scepticism about this extreme variant of the New Line was shared by Andrew Rothstein, whom the Politburo had despatched to South Wales in August 1929. Rothstein had joined the CPGB Executive at the Eighth Congress in 1926, but had become increasingly outspoken about union and Labour Party issues. Instead of being re-educated in South Wales, however, Rothstein continued unregenerate, evidently drawing aid and comfort from the comrades supporting Horner. He was one of the incumbents who lost their Executive seats at the Eleventh Congress. On 8 December 1929 the Politburo recalled Rothstein to London. Rust, who had returned from Moscow to lead the Young Turks' offensive, was despatched instead. He arrived with an ambitious programme to transform the South Walian comrades, who, he was convinced, constituted the principal obstacle to South Wales becoming the cockpit of the imminent revolution in Britain.

On the eve of the Eleventh Party Congress, Horner had written to the RILU Executive Bureau in Moscow on NMM notepaper, in his capacity as General Secretary, to inform them of the composition of the British delegation to a meeting of the RILU Central Council in early January 1930. 'Tom Mann will not be well enough to travel, and ... Gossip will be unable to leave owing to pressure of work. Comrade Pollitt may be there at the time on Comintern business, in which case he will of course attend the [RILU] plenum. We have therefore decided that comrade Horner shall go, together with comrade J. Mahon in place of Tom Mann ... In the meantime we are placing comrade George Allison in political charge of the office here ... ' Horner left for Moscow on 8 December. The RILU plenum met between 16 and 24 December; Horner returned to Britain on 3 January 1930.

191

He may have hoped to canvass support at the RILU Plenum for his opposition to new, Red unions. But on 7 January, a duplicated letter signed by Horner as General Secretary was sent from Great Ormond Street convening a full meeting of the NMM Executive, and its agenda – which included a report from Moscow, the reconstruction of the Minority Movement, the preparation and conduct of strikes and the Special Industrial Campaign – was cast in full-blooded Lovozskian mode.[265] On his return from Moscow Horner was evidently determined to retire to Mardy and resume his existence as an unemployed miner and officer of Mardy SWMF Lodge, a rank-and-file party member on whom the party leadership had no particular lien.

During Horner's absence, the question of his political future had exercised the British party leadership. Having broken his diplomatic silence at the Eleventh Congress, he was highly vulnerable to party discipline, and the Young Turks were eager to mete out exemplary retribution. One option canvassed was making him Industrial Correspondent of the *Daily Worker*, the party's flagship daily paper whose first issue was scheduled to appear on 1 January. This was vetoed by Rust, whose ascendancy had secured him the paper's editorship. The option of returning Horner to industrial work – either in South Wales or at the NMM – was also rejected, despite Pollitt's argument that Horner should continue in a capacity where he had produced outstandingly successful results. The Politburo refused to let Horner remain in Britain, however.[266] The Young Turks apparently calculated that his presence in the Rhondda would merely encourage other comrades to emulate his rebellion.

Campbell later claimed responsibility for arranging Horner's secondment to the MIC in Moscow, in order to ensure that the party did not lose his outstanding abilities as a proletarian leader.[267] Campbell's acute political skills were critical in persuading the Executive that Horner's assignment to RILU, the option most attractive to Horner personally, was also the best option for the party. Having found himself unable to recant, it is likely that Horner contemplated exile with some cheerfulness, since it held out the prospect of his being able to return to some kind of political equilibrium. The CPGB Executive's approval was apparently obtained by mid-January 1930.

Before Horner departed, the situation inside the SWMF significantly deteriorated for communist activists. On 24 January, the SWMF Executive had de-recognised the Mardy Lodge. They had prima facie grounds: the MFGB rule that bound district unions to support Labour Party candidates in all elections. In early January SO Davies and Oliver Harris had addressed a mass meeting at Mardy Lodge on the Executive's behalf in an attempt to avoid an open breach, but they were unsuccessful. (Horner was still in Moscow for the RILU plenum at this juncture.) Had Horner been present, his emollient skills might have been deployed to good effect. A letter from the lodge sent to the Executive after the meeting had stated, 'the majority are convinced that the only revolutionary party prepared to fight ... is the Communist Party, which they intend as a Lodge to support, at every opportunity which offers, not because it is so named, but because it is prepared to fight against and not fraternise with our class exploiters'.[268] The Lodge had refused to repudiate its support for Horner's 1929 parliamentary candidacy and affiliate to the official Rhondda Labour Party. The Executive proceeded against only Mardy, even though the Tylorstown and Ferndale lodges had also endorsed Horner and refused to affiliate to the official Rhondda Labour Party. They may have calculated that the other two recalcitrant lodges would capitulate when they had witnessed Mardy's expulsion, and would then voluntarily affiliate to the official Labour Party.

News of the Executive's decision elicited widespread sympathy for Mardy inside the Federation; Rhondda No. 1 District passed a resolution of support for the lodge. Horner claimed to have been the lodge committee member who discovered the provision in the Federation rules which enabled Mardy to appeal to a Special Delegate Conference against the Executive's decision.[269] The Lodge duly exercised its right. Meanwhile, Arthur and Ethel were preparing to leave for Russia. They made arrangements which enabled their two eldest daughters to continue attending Ferndale Secondary School. Vol lodged with David and Gwen Ray Evans, in Porth; Rosa stayed in Mardy with Tom and Laura Jones. Joan, the youngest, was to accompany her parents.[270]

The Special Delegate Conference was scheduled for 20 February 1930. The 'Calling Notice to Lodges' for the conference included a 'Note' putting the Executive's case against

Mardy. The Executive had striven to avoid punitive action without success: 'During the [SWMF Executive] Council's negotiations, the Lodge Officials (admittedly Communists) avowed over and over again that the Lodge was not Communist, while now we have the declaration "that ... they intend AS A LODGE to support it.' Because the Executive 'were satisfied that there was a majority of the Mardy workmen who desired to be loyal to the Trade Union Movement and the Labour Party', expulsion remained the only option.

The Calling Notice was dated 11 February.[271] Horner had left from Harwich for Russia on 10 February, proceeding by train across northern Europe from the Hook. He later recalled: 'If I had had the telegram telling me of the decision [the conference date] I would have postponed my trip.'[272] Had he remained in South Wales, it is plausible that he would have led the Lodge Committee in an orderly retreat back into the Federation fold.

The last Mardy Lodge meeting Horner was recorded as attending was 29 January. He is unlikely to have revealed the Politburo's reasons for arranging his secondment to the MIC in Moscow to anyone in South Wales except Ethel, Dai Lloyd Davies and Charlie Jones. Nevertheless, most party members, and many SWMF activists interested in politics, would have had a shrewd idea that the intensifying differences between Horner and the new party leadership had provided the political motivation. Those who supported Horner probably kept their own counsel about this potentially explosive matter at party meetings. They either confined their contributions to pointing out the sheer impracticality of supplanting the SWMF, or, as Pollitt reminded the party Executive in April 1930, they left the party altogether.[273]

Those Federation activists who viewed themselves as standard-bearers for the union's militant traditions hoped that before the Special Conference Mardy Lodge would discreetly withdraw its support for the disaffiliated Rhondda Labour Party and affiliate to the official Rhondda Labour Party. They believed that in these circumstances Richards and Morrell would have been unlikely to insist on their pound of flesh, and the Executive would quietly take Mardy Lodge back into the Federation. They feared that the expulsion of a leading militant lodge would precipitate further secessions from the left, irreparably damaging the already

194

weakened union. After the Lock-Out, SWMF membership had plummeted. With the new non-political South Wales Miners Industrial Union canvassing and gaining new members, the spectacle of a loyal lodge being expelled was deeply disturbing. Federation loyalists lacked the means to exert moral pressure on miners who had fallen behind in their subscriptions to re-join the SWMF. The result was that non-union miners, or 'nons', were increasing faster than either unions' membership. With the CPGB and MMM both condemning the SWMF as social fascist, many unemployed communist miners dropped out of the SWMF. Many comrades still working stopped attending lodge meetings and volunteering for lay office.

After Richards' 'Calling Note' had been despatched, the Mardy Lodge Committee received an official MMM deputation, Willie Allan and Eddie Laughlin, to advise them about tactics. Allan and Laughlin were leading members of the UMS and enthusiastic advocates of Lozovsky's secessionism. Horner told Frankenberg that Dai Lloyd Davies, still Lodge Chairman, had capitulated to their pressure. Apparently, no one else at the meeting had spoken against them. Horner was probably the only committee member capable of facing down their ideological offensive. Committee members could and did think for themselves about SWMF and MFGB affairs. But they lacked familiarity with MMM discourse, and were not in the habit of disagreeing and arguing outside their own sphere of operations, the Lodge and the Rhondda No.1 District. The Lodge Committee decided its delegates would 'transform' the Special Conference into a demonstration of opposition to the SWMF and MFGB bureaucrats.

A *Daily Worker* report of the 'Calling Notice' and 'Note' appeared on Saturday 15 February. 'All the petty-bureaucrats will be at the special conference, and they will mechanically follow the lead of the [SWMF] Executive Council ... The special conference is but a passing phase.' The report announced that a more important conference was being organised by the MMM at the Jubilee Hall in Tylorstown 'to organise the forces behind the Mardy Lodge and to raise the real issue, the organisation of the pits and the fight for higher wages and shorter hours'. Although it stopped short of advocating secession, the article's substance and tone were calculated to intensify the antagonism between left-wing activists and the SWMF Executive.

The Mardy Lodge Committee could have taken two practical steps to ensure a positive outcome to their appeal. The first would have been to enlist SO Davies's support. It was common knowledge that, owing to Morrell's continuing ill-health, SO would be presiding at the Special Conference. Horner recalled that prior to the conference SO had taken a personal initiative. He had come to Mardy and called at Horner's house 'to persuade us to compromise'. 'He had planned to make a statement [at the outset of the Special Conference] which would give us a chance to withdraw with dignity.' But Horner had already left for Russia and the Lodge Committee refused to see him.[274] The second step would have been to argue the case at the MMM conference at Tylorstown for the Lodge drawing back from its collision course with the SWMF Executive. If a resolution in favour of compromise for the sake of unity had been agreed at the MMM conference, Mardy Lodge delegates would have felt justified in executing an expeditious retreat at the SWMF Special Conference.

Some delegates at Tylorstown may indeed have raised the possibility of a compromise solution; but their arguments for unity were evidently rebuffed. The *Daily Worker* report of the 15 February MMM Conference contained no reference to the question of Mardy Lodge's appeal even having been discussed. Allan's and Laughlin's advice to Mardy Lodge was calculated to ensure that the SWMF Special Conference would reject their appeal. Rust and the MMM leadership (Allison excepted) were keen that the Lodge should remain outside the official union pale. They believed that Mardy's expulsion would act as a catalyst for other militant lodges to secede from the Federation and concentrate their energies on the 'organisation of the pits' into new fighting institutions.

In these circumstances the outcome of the Special Conference was predictably negative. Delegates following the MMM line disrupted the Special Conference proceedings from the outset. George Maslin from Tylorstown challenged SO Davies in the chair; others tried to shout down Richards when he was putting the Executive's case. Davies lost patience and closed the debate after ten minutes of uproar. Mardy's appeal was lost by 150 to 9.

'Dai Lloyd Davies actually cried.' He apparently found the prospect of being outside the Federation unthinkable.[275] His tears were memorable evidence that no one on the Lodge Committee had faced up to the prospect of being banished beyond the Federation pale.

Mardy's expulsion and the spectacle that accompanied it severely damaged left-wing activists' morale and their credibility inside the Federation. When the Ferndale and Tylorstown lodge committees had seen that the SWMF Executive were serious in their intent to enforce the rules, they affiliated to the official Rhondda Labour Party forthwith. The SWMF Executive refrained from penalising them for the transgressions which they had now rectified.

With Horner in Russia, no one in Britain, either in the NMM or CPGB leadership, was willing to challenge the hegemony of Rust and other keen left-wingers. Mardy Lodge's expulsion from the SWMF gave them what they considered to be an outstanding casus belli. In March 1930 Rust, Cox and Gallacher proposed the fulfilment of Lozovsky's grand design for a new, Red union. Party miners should use the UMS and MMM to establish the United Mineworkers of Great Britain. But, although they carried the Politburo, the notion that the communists and their allies could successfully challenge and then break the MFGB lacked credibility. Allison, acting chairman of the NMM in Horner's absence, observed in April, 'if we cannot form a pit committee in South Wales, how can we form a union?' Encouraging secession from the MFGB was too radical even for many of Rust's allies. Strong opposition to the UMGB came not only from Pollitt, but also Tapsell, one of Rust's staunchest confederates, and other Class Against Class supporters, including Arnot and Murphy.[276]

When the UMGB project was tabled, Campbell was in Moscow, deputising for the recently elected incumbent, Alec Hermon. Campbell seized the opportunity which the Young Turks' revolutionary ambitions presented. The Comintern had begun to move centrewards in emulation of developments inside the CPSU(B). In February 1930, at an enlarged ECCI Presidium, Manuilsky had warned against overestimating the revolutionary situation, and of the problem of a left deviation rushing too far ahead inside affiliated parties. The Comintern began to stress

197

the necessity of striving to form 'united fronts from below' with socialist and social democratic workers, a pre-Class Against Class slogan which had been prudently retained from the old line.

To reinforce his arguments against the UMGB, Campbell arranged Horner's attendance at the Anglo-American Secretariat in early May 1930, when it met to consider the CPGB Politburo's proposal. Campbell:

> stressed the extreme weakness of the party in some of the major coalfields ... He attacked the RILU for sending out its letter [enjoining the formation of the UMGB] without seeking the approval of the AAS and the [ECCI] Political Secretariat ... What was needed, rather, was for Communists to exercise independent leadership within the reformist unions ... Horner broadly supported him, and although [Nat] Watkins – also working in RILU – supported Lozovsky, the big guns of the AAS all lined up behind Campbell.

When the ECCI Political Secretariat also supported Campbell, 'as Hermon reported to Pollitt, Lozovsky had "got it in the neck" for his failure to consult the CI [Comintern] before sending out his letter in the first place.'[277] Not surprisingly after this pronouncement from Moscow, neither the CPGB or NMM leadership deemed it expedient to challenge the Ferndale and Tylorstown lodges' retreat.

The stillborn UMGB proved to be the Young Turks' last foray into Red unions. Lozovsky, a seasoned veteran with a weather eye for the direction of political winds, refrained from any further intervention on British terrain. His retirement from the field left Gallacher and Cox very exposed. Pollitt, Allison and Joe Scott, who had been assiduously trimming towards Lozovsky, were now able to resume their previous positions and argue that Communists should exercise independent leadership within the reformist unions. Horner had spoken frankly and his judgement had been accepted, even deferred to, at the AAS. He probably appreciated the contrast between the Comintern operatives' realism in Moscow and the Young Turks' voluntarist revolutionism in London.

Ethel and Joan had followed Horner to Russia on 17 May on the Sovtorgflot freighter *Co-operatzia* from the London docks.[278] Like most seconded foreigners, they lived in the Hotel Lux. But Arthur was also given a half share in a dacha, (the Russian name for a second home in the country), along with the head of the Soviet Miners' Union, Semyonov. Arthur, Ethel and Joan were able to enjoy weekends in this semi-rural setting. The adults probably engaged in a crowded round of socialising with the Russian miners' union leaders and their families and the other MIC leaders, involving much alcohol, good food and conviviality. Neither Arthur nor Ethel mastered Russian, though Joan began to speak it with the daughter of a Russian couple with whom the Horners had become friendly. (When Ethel went on a sight-seeing holiday, she left Joan in the Russian couple's care.)[279]

Living and working in close proximity to Soviet party members, the Horners gained routine knowledge about events and party affairs. They had additional news from regular contact with Andrew Rothstein, whom the British Politburo had despatched to Moscow to work as a Comintern translator. (They had also unilaterally transferred Rothstein's CPGB membership to the CPSU(B), apparently believing that the Russians would be the best cure for his rightist tendencies.)

During 1930 all Soviet and international communist institutions in the USSR were undergoing the *chistka*, a rigorous cleansing process designed to root out hostile members and purge them before they could sabotage and wreak havoc. Cadres whose class origin was suspicious were particularly vulnerable; vigilance was required to ensure that kulaks or bourgeoisie did not conceal their identities. These vicissitudes preoccupied the men and women working in the RILU offices at the Soviet trade unions' Palace of Labour, where the MIC operated from room 457. (Arthur and the other MIC leaders probably lunched with Russian trade unionists in the Palace of Labour canteen and socialised with them after work.) Horner recalled that the MIC leaders were perfunctory about observing the *chistka*'s rigours. They had persuaded the party group in RILU to pass a resolution 'that, as far as the cleansing commission was concerned, social origin should only be brought into the picture if there was some supporting evidence to show that the person concerned was still addicted to the old ideas.'[280] The MIC were a close-knit, self confident group, reflecting the critical importance of coal and the distinctive mineworkers' culture. MIC leaders in Moscow were mining trade union veterans and the salt of the earth. Horner had been corresponding and meeting most of them regularly since 1923. His high good humour and sociability made him a popular leading participant in the committee's deliberations and administration. The MIC secretary, Grusha Slutsky, was from Donbas. He had joined the CPSU(B) in 1920 as part of a group of left Socialist Revolutionaries there. Horner's MI5 file recorded that he had arranged for Slutsky and another Russian miner, Ossipov, to visit Tilmanstone colliery in Kent in October 1929. Other leading MIC members were Gustav Sobotka, a miner from the large Polish community working in the Ruhr, and Vaclav Nosek, a miner from northern Bohemia.[281]

On the British front, in the face of further disastrous results for the Young Turks' campaign of revolutionary struggle, '[s]o far as Moscow was concerned ... the most pressing question in the summer of 1930 was why the party was still failing to expand, and that June it appointed a British commission to look into the matter more deeply ... ' Campbell ensured that Horner participated in the late July preparatory meetings of the AAS. Thorpe comments that the different positions taken up at the pre-meetings 'showed the extent to which heated argument continued in the CI's highest bodies even by 1930'. He speculated that Rothstein 'effectively gatecrashed' the AAS second pre-meeting as a result of information from Horner. When IG Mingoulin, a leading AAS member, attacked Horner and Rothstein from the chair, Horner 'admitted that he had not published a self-criticism, but only because such declarations were "worthless". But Mingoulin had demanded that both he and Rothstein should do so'. Horner also attended the Special Commission itself in August. Transcripts show both left and right interpretations of Class Against Class being put with clarity, intense conviction and passionate combativeness. Horner 'attacked the use of coercion against the "rights" [inside the CPGB], in particular; and this contribution – along with further shouted interruptions in defence of Hannington – clearly suggested to those present that he was an unrepentant rightist. They also showed the apparently repentant rightist, Campbell, in a very good light by contrast.'[282]

The ECCI Political Secretariat met the British comrades who had participated in the Special Commission to consider its report and the Secretariat's accompanying resolution, which stressed not only right errors but also left ones. Manuilsky, now the dominant figure in the Secretariat, declared that '[w]hile Communists should avoid trade union "legalism", they must try to work through the reformist unions'. It was evident that the Young Turks' hegemony and freedom to manoeuvre had been summarily curtailed. Another consequence was that Pollitt moved into close alliance with Campbell, possibly as a result of having worked so closely with him on the Special Commission to rout the Young Turks.

Despite this political victory, Horner could hardly avoid the conclusion that the ECCI Secretariat expected him to perform an act of self-criticism, not only for his outbursts in Britain on the CPGB Executive and at the Eleventh Party Congress in late 1929, but also for his recent positions during the Special Commission. It was probably Pollitt, whose arrival in Moscow had been delayed by illness, who persuaded Horner to concede. At the meeting between the Political Secretariat and the British comrades, Horner declared that his past behaviour had been wrong, 'albeit while repeating that he still believed some members of the current CEC [Executive] were "unfitted for national leadership"'. Evidently to test his sincerity, Manuilsky asked him whether he wanted to intervene in the British situation. Horner agreed to write an article for the *Daily Worker* backing the most recent interpretation of Class Against Class.[283] The act of contrition having been arranged, it was finally expedient for Horner to go home; the ECCI Secretariat agreed, with the proviso that Horner's position would be further reviewed at the end of 1930.[284]

The *Daily Worker* published Horner's article on 25 September, under the headline 'Arthur Horner writes on Coming Attack in South Wales. Mistake of Trusting "Left" Phrasemongers'. Whilst observing the terms of the Special Commission resolution, the article also reflected the MIC's ambitious plans and the Comintern's overriding concern to get practical results. Having rehearsed the worsening of conditions for South Wales miners since the imposition of the Eight Hour Day, Horner warned that coalowners in many countries were either engaged in or preparing to launch offensives against miners' wages and working conditions. In Germany, 340,000 Ruhr miners faced a demand for a 10 per cent wage reduction, as did miners in Upper Silesia. A wage reduction of 5 per cent had already been imposed on Belgian miners, and Czech miners were taking action to stop an increase in working time.

> ... [T]he gravest injury has been done by our past serious mistakes ... the failure to understand and expose the role of Cook, [SO] Davies and Co., led to the continual weakening of our position ... In this ruinous policy I took a leading part, a part which warrants the most definite condemnation. Only as this is clearly recognised and the necessary lessons drawn, can we hope to go forward on the basis of a new, clear understanding of our tasks.

Having noted that defeats inflicted on the miners had created a measure of pessimism and passivity, especially in Mardy, he concluded:

> An attempt is being made to screen this passivity behind the claim that I or others are being subjected to persecution or political victimisation. This is an absurd excuse for the failure to carry on the struggle ... The new leadership of the Communist Party [installed at the Eleventh Party Congress] acted quite correctly in the course taken ... Every active miner should be on the job of building up the Miners' Minority Movement, on the basis of pit organisation of action, relating them to the fight of the miners and to the general struggle of the working class against the Labour Government, embodied in the Workers' Charter.

Campbell may have suggested the form of words which Horner used in the paragraphs of self-criticism. He and Pollitt were anxious to ensure that Horner returned to Britain, and a clear prerequisite was that his self-criticism had to conform to the currently prevailing orthodoxy. In the meantime, Campbell had returned to Britain and reported to the Politburo on developments arising from the Special Commission. The CPGB

Politburo endorsed its decisions, including Horner's return, in mid-October. Pollitt noted that Horner would energise the campaign for the Miners' Charter, part of the Workers' Charter campaign which the Political Secretariat had charged Pollitt to organise to show that under his new leadership the CPGB could actually accomplish a mass mobilisation.[285]

In mid-November 1930, the Comintern agreed that Horner should return immediately to South Wales, 'in order to play a leading part in the forthcoming struggle'. (Pollitt complained that it had taken six weeks for the ECCI Political Secretariat to formally send their resolution to the CPGB.) The Horners finally returned to Britain after an absence of ten months for Arthur and six months for Ethel and Joan. Horner set out at the end of November, stopping in Berlin to attend an MIC meeting about the situation in Germany, France, Belgium and Britain. (Ethel and Joan may have travelled with him by train to Berlin.) Compared to many expatriates, they had settled easily into Moscow life, and apparently savoured its particular pleasures. Arthur told his friend and comrade Frank Williams that he had decided to leave Moscow because the winters were too cold. Although he had weathered other Moscow winters for shorter periods, Ethel and Joan may have found the temperatures a severe shock in 1930. They may also have been pining to see Vol, Rosa and friends and extended family. However, the principal reason for the Horners' return in December was probably Pollitt's and Campbell's determination that Arthur should resume activity inside the MMM. He himself was also keen. Having anguished over the saga of Mardy Lodge's de-recognition by the SWMF and his inability to reverse it, he was eager to resume a leading role in directing the MMM (including comrades in the disaffiliated Mardy Lodge) back into 'reformist union' activity.[286]

The MIC leaders expected a great deal from Horner's return. They had made ambitions to outflank the reformist Miners' International Federation, and make the MIC the dominant Miners' International. To this end, they had planned a European-wide miners' strike commencing in January 1931 over working hours, an issue which affected miners in all countries. In Britain the Labour government's Coal Mines Act was due to come into force on 1 January 1931, replacing the Eight Hours Act passed by the Conservatives during the Lock-Out. However, the government's intention, that the new law should secure a uniform reduction in hours to seven and a half, had been frustrated by an amendment during the bill's passage through the Lords. The Act now enabled coalowners to negotiate with miners' unions about how to achieve a more flexible working week, i.e. spread-over shifts, either an eleven day fortnight with alternate Saturday rest days, or a week of five eight hour shifts and one Saturday shift of five hours.[287] The MIC leaders believed that Horner's presence in Britain would ensure that the British strike would be sparked off from the militant crucible of South Wales, and would compel the government to pass fresh legislation further reducing working hours.

Horner arrived in London on 3 December 1930, armed with a long list of things to do in preparation for the European-wide strike planned for January.[288] He was charged with organis-ing an MMM all-in British coalfields conference by Sunday 14 December, from which delegates would be elected to attend an International Miners' conference in Essen, in the heart of the Ruhr coalfield, to be convened before Christmas. Horner went to the NMM offices on 4 December. To his horror, he was unable to commence organising activity. The only person he found was Johnny Mahon – everyone else was evidently recovering from the rigours of working for Pollitt in the Stepney by-election, held the day before. Mahon was one of the most zealous Young Turks and he also had a visceral personal dislike of Horner, perhaps because he resented Pollitt's evident affection for him. When Horner asked Mahon to help him, he replied, 'it [the miners' conference] is nothing to do with me ... you must ask someone else'. But no one else appeared at Great Ormond Street on the following two days. Horner finally went to King Street, where he 'found J.T. Murphy who helped'.[289]

Horner is likely to have seen Cook at the MFGB office ear-lier in December, and to have become concerned about Cook's deteriorating health. Cook had suffered regular bouts of fatigue, nervous exhaustion and hoarseness since 1926, but refusing to retire, he carried on as MFGB general secretary and played a full part in labour movement politics. At the end of 1930, an earlier leg wound which he had neglected was becoming increasingly serious.[290]

During the week Horner arrived back in Britain, Cook had been a signatory to a four page manifesto, 'A National Policy for National Emergency', described by the press as the Mosley Manifesto, after its principal progenitor, Oswald Mosley MP. Other signatories were sixteen Labour MPs, including Bevan and five other mining MPs, Strachey, and WJ Brown, the civil service clerical union leader who had been elected Labour MP for Wolverhampton in 1929. Influenced by the suggestions which Keynes had provided for Lloyd George in 1929, the Manifesto called on the Labour government to adopt radical, contra-cyclical economic policies, and argued for sweeping reforms to parliamentary procedure to enable governments to implement legislation speedily and comprehensively. Mosley's flair for self-publicity ensured that the Manifesto achieved immediate notoriety. Roundly condemned by centrist Labour opinion and warmly welcomed by maverick Tory radicals Robert Boothby, Leo Amery and Harold Macmillan, its reception at Westminster was gripping political theatre. The two Arthurs would have discussed its detailed politics, i.e. how it might affect the balance of forces in the Labour Cabinet and the Parliamentary Labour Party, as well as its bearing on the British coal industry's prospects for recovery. They had both come to know Mosley well in 1926, when he been unstinting in speaking for the MFGB during the Lock-Out. Strachey had moved closer to Mosley since his election to parliament in 1929; and it was he who probably made the first approach to Cook.

Horner would also have been keen to hear news of Cook's negotiations with the government over the operation of the Coal Mines Act. He needed reliable information about what was expected to happen on New Year's Day, when the spread-over shifts came into operation. Mutually acceptable agreements had been reached between the owners and the unions in coalfields where the normal working day had not previously exceeded 7 hours, for example in Northumberland and Durham, where there was three-shift round-the-clock working. In Scotland and South Wales, however, the coalowners had insisted on wage reductions in exchange for the reduction in hours which the Act entailed.

Horner told Cook about Moscow and his fear that the UMS was burning the bridges which might have provided a means of reconciliation with the official Scottish district unions. Cook confided in Horner about his difficulties with the MFGB Executive and the TUC General Council. Horner also wanted news of the MIF. Cook regularly travelled to Geneva to the International Labour Organisation (ILO) negotiations, through which the MIF hoped to achieve a European-wide reduction in the miners' working day. Horner had accompanied Cook in 1928 on one round of those negotiations,[291] and he would have been keen to utilise Cook's knowledge of their current state to help the MIC.

Horner may have found time to go to Mardy before the coalfields conference, which he and Murphy had arranged to be held in Sheffield. A *Daily Worker* article on 13 December carried a picture of Horner alongside the text. Its headline reflected the post-Special Commission line: 'Issues before the Miners' Unity Conference. Establish Unity on the Fighting Basis of "Class Against Class"'. It explained that all district unions in the MFGB had to resist the spread-over shift, even though coalowners in Yorkshire, Durham, Northumberland, Kent, Nottinghamshire and North Derbyshire did not intend to introduce it.

The *Daily Worker*'s post-conference report on 15 December judged it 'a splendid success', with thirty-five delegates from Scotland, Durham, Wales, Lancashire, Yorkshire, Staffordshire, Nottinghamshire and Derbyshire. Allison moved the main resolution, which Willie Allan seconded. Delegates decided to start an International Solidarity Fund immediately, and elected five delegates to the Essen International Conference. On 17 December, the *Daily Worker* reported the speech of the fraternal revolutionary delegate from the Ruhr who had been at the Sheffield conference. It had evidently been carefully crafted to include 'reformist union' activity. 'The important question is that of our positions inside the trade unions we have in our lands ... We have to use these positions to build around them a strong revolutionary miners' movement. By doing this we prepare together and fight side by side for victory.'

Horner travelled to Essen on 17 December to attend the conference on the weekend of 20 to 21 December. On 24 December the *Daily Worker* published a conference report by Willie Allan, and an article by Ianto Evans, both of whom had attended. There had been twenty-five mainly rank-and-file delegates, from Germany, Poland, Belgium, France, Czechoslovakia, the USSR and Britain. Saturday had been devoted to working commissions, on the British situation and the situation in western European coalfields. On Sunday the commissions' reports had 'stressed the developing crisis in each capitalist country, the nature of the attacks in all countries, the urgent necessity for the independent leadership of the miners against every attack and the need for real international unity of the miners'. Reports were given on the developing strike situation in the Ruhr and Upper Silesia. (Ruhr coalowners were imposing a 12.5 per cent wage reduction from 1 January.) Ianto Evans observed that the conference was a somewhat belated 'step in the right direction, and supplies the standing need, viz., the establishment of a real fighting miners' international'. The final session had been open, and was attended by delegates from Ruhr mines.

London, Mardy, Moscow

Horner arrived back in Britain on Christmas day,[292] and may have called on Arthur Cook at his home in Kenton, near Wembley in North West London, and Harry Pollitt who lived in the adjacent suburb of Colindale, literally down the road from Johnny Campbell. He had a great deal to discuss with them. In South Wales, a Federation Delegate Conference had voted on 23 December not to accept the coalowners' proposals for the spread-over shift, which included a sizeable wage reduction. Since MacDonald had failed to persuade the South Wales coalowners back to the negotiating table, a Lock-Out would commence on 1 January 1931. The odds were against the Federation; there were only 75,480 SWMF members in the coalfield work-force of 140,000. But, as Ness Edwards wrote in 1938, Federation activists responded to the owners 'high handed dictatorial attitude' with 'stern opposition' and 'critical hostility, made more bitter by a recognition of the weakness of the organization'.[293]

The SWMF was the only district union to take action against the new spread-over arrangements. The MMM optimistically anticipated that if South Wales stood firm in the Lock-Out, the MFGB would offer national support. The MIC believed that British miners' militancy would trigger strikes in the Ruhr, the Borinage in Belgium and the French Nord/Pas de Calais. But

the portents for strong resistance were not good. On returning home, Horner quickly observed that the South Wales MMM
had allowed the unofficial network of Federation militants to
atrophy. The new leadership whom the South Wales DPC had
imposed on the MMM were 'left' supporters of the Young Turks.
The DPC – with active encouragement from the Party Centre –
had discouraged party activists and the MMM from continuing
activity inside the union, directing them instead to concentrate
on establishing independent councils of action and party pit
cells. The practical result was that no mass activity had been
organised around the spread-over issue.

Horner was in no mood to surrender to the apathy and
demoralisation he encountered amongst communist miners.
The previous autumn in Moscow, he had sincerely believed it
possible to organise solid, militant action in South Wales. He
had probably occupied many rousing hours in the Palace of
Labour trading stories and anecdotes with Slutsky, Sobotka and
other MIC people about past industrial battles, from epic strikes
to small skirmishes. He regaled his audience with narratives not
only about the struggles of 1915, 1921 and 1926, but also the
Monmouthshire hauliers' strike of 1893 and the great Cambrian
Combine Stike in 1910, which he had heard in countless re-
tellings from veterans. The veterans in Room 457 considered
South Wales miners to be the epitome of united, militant organisation, and believed in Horner's sanguine expectations for the
struggle in 1931.

Horner's response to the apathy and demoralisation he
encountered in the MMM was to embark on a round of hyper-
activity, beginning in Mardy. In his absence, a new official lodge
had been established with the encouragement of the SWMF
Executive to represent working miners; the disaffiliated Lodge,
as its officers now styled it, had not met since 15 October 1930,
when there had been complaints about poor attendance at its
previous meetings. Horner's arrival precipitated a flurry of
organisation. The disaffiliated Mardy Lodge Committee held a
general meeting on 31 December, with Percy Jones in the chair,
to receive a report from Horner. A resolution was passed to resist
all wage cuts, and preparations were begun for the Lock-Out,
including convening an organising committee.

New Year's Day saw another disaffiliated Lodge general meeting, with Horner in the chair. In the space of twenty-four hours, pickets had been organised and an invitation issued to the official SWMF lodge to co-operate in the struggle. (Evidently the disaffiliated lodge committee had made no previous approaches to the official lodge to forge a united front from below.) Three picket-whiters, whose job was to chalk the pavements, were appointed. On 2 January, the disaffiliated lodge sponsored an all-in mass meeting for organised, unorganised, employed and unemployed miners. Sam Davies was the convenor, and Horner was appointed chairman. Twenty people were nominated from the meeting to form a joint committee with the official lodge.

On 1 January 1931, the response to the Lock-Out had been sufficiently solid throughout the coalfield for the coalowners to make no attempt to keep production going. The only exceptions were collieries where the SWMIU and the separate craftsmens' union were strong, notably Taff-Merthyr and the Parc and Dare collieries in Rhondda Fawr, and the Emlyn colliery in the Anthracite.[294] Having shored up a unified organisation in Mardy, Horner became an itinerant, moving from meeting to meeting of militants and friendly official lodges throughout the coalfield, hoping to re-vitalise his network of SWMF activists and re-connect them with the MMM. His version of the 'united front from below' was to encourage all-in committees, like the ones which Mardy Lodge had organised in 1921 and 1926. Unemployed miners who had dropped out of the SWMF could come in under this umbrella, together with SWMF lodge members, MMM activists, and now in Mardy, members of the disaffiliated SWMF lodge.

As a result of his acceptance of the Special Commission report, his putative goal should have been to organise independent all-in committees, as he had been compelled to do in Mardy because of the existence of an official and a disaffiliated lodge. He made little effort to follow this line, however. His first priority was practical: to re-vitalise militant organisation and morale inside Federation lodges and to mobilise them around the MMM. He considered himself to be acting in good faith to achieve practical results. To him, 'independent leadership' meant being critical of trade union bureaucrats and arguing for militant action inside official unions. He wanted to direct his own and other comrades' energies into mass work to persuade working 'nons', who had allowed their membership of the SWMF to lapse, to re-join the Federation, and also to persuade unemployed miners to pay the minimal unemployed subscription to maintain their SWMF membership.

When the disaffiliated Mardy Lodge Committee met on 5 January, David Williams reported from the chair that 60 miners were paying their subscriptions into the new, official lodge, and 50 miners were in the scab union, the SWMIU. The committee decided to approach County Councillor Alf Evans over the question of relief. The putative joint committee of the two lodges met later the same day, although it is unclear whether anyone from the official lodge committee participated. A general meeting for all workers followed, with Horner in the chair. Arrangements were made for picketing, lobbying of councillors, concerts and other entertainment. Further general meetings with Horner in the chair took place on 7 and 11 January. He told the meeting on 11 January that 'the German delegate' at the Cardiff MMM conference had been constrained to leave straight after the conference. The MI5 file recorded him as Gustav Sobotka. Horner had probably arranged for him to speak in Mardy.[295] George Maslin attended from Tylorstown and reported on the funding of relief by the Rhondda UDC. It was noted that there were 20 people picketing.

South Wales miners were sufficiently solid for the coalowners to make some concessions. '[A] provisional agreement was reached ... that was to last three years. The terms were the maintenance of the November 1930 rates of pay and a 7 hour day, but the minimum percentage and subsistence wage were to be considered immediately by a new Independent Chairman [of the District Conciliation Board, FPM Schiller KC], whose award would be operative from 31 March.' An SWMF delegate conference voted on 17 January to accept the Executive's recommendation by 169 to 72.[296] Horner chaired an all-in meeting of Mardy strikers and unemployed strike supporters the next day, which received a report of the 'reactionary' vote of the official Mardy Lodge delegate at the SWMF delegate conference, in favour of a return to work. Horner then chaired another meeting of men who had been working before the Lock-Out. They had been victimised when trying to return to work, and they had come to him rather than the official lodge committee, presumably because they felt his advice would be more efficacious.

Horner had criticised the SWMF Executive's lack of organisational preparation and will to fight. But he was unprepared for the size of the conference vote to accept the owners' concessions: more than 2 to 1. It was a moot point whether the struggle could be continued with independent, revolutionary leadership. Horner blamed the absence of militancy on the fact that so many party members had ceased to participate in their lodges. When the South Wales DPC met on 17 January after hearing the delegate conference decision, Horner told them that neither the party nor the MMM had sufficient resources or organisation to lead an unofficial strike. He also said that the principal reason SWMF militants had lost the conference vote was that they had received virtually no practical support from the party *apparat*. Only one of the conference delegates had been a party member.

The DPC accepted Horner's judgement that no attempt should be made to precipitate an unofficial strike under 'independent leadership', along with his recommendation that party members should resume activity inside the SWMF. Horner had been keeping in regular contact with the MIC by letter. On 21 January he sent a letter in English to Rothstein in Moscow, trusting him to translate it accurately, without revealing its contents to anyone but its intended recipients in Room 457 in the Palace of Labour. It contained a full recitation of the situation in South Wales and the passive mood of many militants. 'Am writing to you in this way, so that you may have a clear insight into what has happened here, having in mind your previous interest in and association with South Wales. You can use this letter, show it to those interested. Yours fraternally, Arthur'.[297]

Horner elaborated his conclusions in a lengthy report to the CPGB Secretariat, which now included both Pollitt and Campbell. He complained that the two full-time party workers in Cardiff assigned to coalfield activity, Garfield Williams, South Wales MMM organiser, and Charlie Stead, party district organiser, had:

> received not a farthing from HQ [Cardiff headquarters] of CP. Williams had to beg and borrow for 10-minute

train fare. Yet [also] had to find fare money for Strike Committee [members]. Asked for but did not get typist ... Don't believe Stead attended more than 1+ and Williams 3 meetings during 18 days of struggle. Kept on Typewriter or duplicator, doing inefficiently work that could be done better by a girl at £2 per week. HQ to blame. We had, apart from casual chats between W, S and self, no Party meeting called in South Wales centre, nor a single DPC, during whole of strike. 3 locals held 1 meeting.

Stead had replaced Len Jeffries as party district organiser in the summer of 1930 in the changes imposed by the Politburo as part of their drive to get better results in mass work.[298] The Secretariat discussed his report on 21 January, but did not table it at the Politburo meeting on 22 to 23 January. They apparently feared another eruption of internecine conflict. Although Horner's conclusions were practical, they veered too far towards the 'old line' of working inside 'reformist unions' for the current balance of power inside the CPGB leadership. His criticisms of the Party Centre's inaction and ineptitude were a direct challenge to the Young Turks' ability to organise mass activity.

But Horner was determined to be heard. He came to London and attended the Politburo meeting. The civil war duly reappeared. Rust, Murphy, Robson, Hermon and Gallacher launched a strenuous counter-attack. Pollitt and Campbell responded by distancing themselves from Horner. Pollitt replied to Rust's attack on Horner by reminding the Politburo, 'What do we want with Horner? We want him to work with the new cadres, to give them the benefit of his experience, to be a leader of MM. So bring Horner onto national work with weekends in S. Wales.'[299] As National Organiser, Cox had taken a particular interest in the SWMF strike, and he hotly disputed Horner's criticisms. Horner rejoined that 'he would rather leave the party leadership altogether rather than be made a "scapegoat" for the party's weaknesses'. The Politburo decided to send Cox to South Wales immediately to assume responsibility for organising a coalfield strike under independent leadership.[300] They evidently did not follow up Pollitt's suggestion of bringing Horner to London, perhaps fearing that he would take the opportunity to ignite a full-blown conflict in the party's large and potentially volatile London district.

Horner may have used his genuine desire to see Arthur Cook as a reason for travelling to London and gate-crashing the Politburo meeting. Cook had been admitted to Manor House Hospital on 9 January; his right leg was amputated just below the knee on 19 January. When Horner visited him, he was joined by Citrine, Mosley and Lansbury. He recalled:

> George would not speak to Mosley because they had quarrelled over the unemployment committee ... Citrine had no time for any of us. There we all sat, Cook talking away with hardly anybody else saying a word. Finally, Mosley went away, then George Lansbury followed, leaving Cook, Citrine and myself ... [We] had a long discussion on whether there could be any circumstances which would justify the trade union movement being dependent for its policy on a political party which could become the Government, and especially a party which might form a minority Government ... Citrine contended that it could mean that the trade union movement would become subservient to such a party ... He told us that he had had the same discussions in 1924 with Tomsky [head of the Soviet trade unions] ... but Tomsky had declared that it was possible for the Russian trade unions to be independent although attached to the Communist Government. Citrine certainly did not want to sever the links between the trade union movement and the Labour Party, but obviously he was thinking very seriously of this problem of their relationships. We sat there a couple of hours talking, with Cook doing most of the listening.[301]

In South Wales Horner continued to defend vigorously his views on what party members should be doing in the coalfield. He probably felt particularly vindicated, because Cox was making no headway in organising militant activity under 'independent leadership'. The Politburo responded by despatching Rust and Ben Francis to South Wales to combat Horner's 'errors'. A full-scale ideological battle inside the British party was clearly gaining momentum. On 5 February the Politburo agreed that unless Horner performed a full self-criticism acknowledging his incorrect conduct since his return to Britain in December 1930, he would be removed as Chairman of the MMM.[302] Rust was deputed to go to Berlin to discuss the affair with the Comintern Western European Bureau.

Pollitt, however, was determined not to let Rust take the initiative. Using his prerogative as general secretary, he replaced Rust and travelled to Berlin to engage in damage limitation manoeuvres. Horner should also have been in Berlin, attending the Annual Conference of the MIC.[303] But he remained in Mardy, evidently determined to maintain his political stand. Pollitt met MIC leaders in Berlin. As he probably anticipated, they were keen to keep Horner at the centre of the miners' struggle. They requested the RILU leadership to arrange Horner's return to Moscow. Having engineered an expeditious exit route for Horner, Pollitt returned to Britain and persuaded the Politburo to approve the secondment. His suggestion that Horner was bound be cured of his errors in Moscow was difficult for Rust and others to oppose.

But Horner refused to take the opportunity Pollitt had created for him. He would not go back to Moscow, and he continued to insist that he had not committed any political errors which necessitated further self-criticism. He maintained that the party *apparat* must bear the responsibility for the Lock-Out ending after only a fortnight without gaining significant concessions. The case against Horner made by Rust was that his advice to the South Wales DPC not to attempt to precipitate an unofficial strike constituted a prima facie error; he must either admit to this and engage in self-criticism or be expelled from the party. Pollitt and Campbell, along with other sympathetic colleagues in the party leadership, including Hannington, judged it impolitic to side with Horner and distanced themselves from his continuing refusal to acknowledge any transgression. Led by Rust, the Politburo expelled Horner on 26 February. Rust had not yet abandoned his ambitions to lead the British revolution, and apparently believed that he could use Horner's transgression to re-take a commanding position inside the British party.

Having received the news of Horner's expulsion by telegram, the ECCI Political Secretariat responded on 28 February by instructing the CPGB Politburo 'to desist from immediate expulsion on the grounds that any such action would have to be preceded by "a wide ideological campaign among the party membership and the working masses".' Given Horner's high public profile, the Comintern's directive was expeditious and prudent. The British press had shown great interest in the public details of the conflict, depicting Horner as the victim of a summary injustice. Rust, however, interpreted the direction as an endorsement. He had already arranged for the National Committee of the Miners' Minority Movement to remove Horner as Chairman on 22 February and install Eddie Laughlin in his stead. A *Daily Worker* report by Ben Francis on 28 February announced the new chairman. 'In order to combat all opportunist tendencies and strengthen the line of independent leadership ... the [MMM] Committee has decided to conduct an intense enlightenment campaign throughout the ranks ... in explanation of the role of the trade union bureaucracy, and in popularisation of the MM policy and its application in the immediate struggles of the miners against coal capitalism and its Labour and trade union allies.'

The *Daily Worker* published a series of articles elaborating Horner's errors, and also reported those party districts which had met and condemned 'Hornerism' – the term was first used on 6 March in a report of the Middlesbrough aggregate meeting (a membership meeting of all branches in the city). Reports of aggregates held in Bradford and Birmingham noted that comrades had recalled the events of the Leeds Congress, when Horner's 'deeply ingrained opposition to the line' had been revealed. However, support for Horner was sufficiently strong for Rust to publish some examples. On 19 March, the *Daily Worker* report of the Maesteg local aggregate noted that two prominent members, Jim Thomas and Jack Davies, had admitted their error in not trying to lead an unofficial strike. The report then quoted Mel Thomas' view that Idris Cox had been mainly responsible for party activists' failure to march to the pit and bring the men out.

Having lost his MMM post, Horner also lost his weekly wage. He had no prospects of finding work either. Many Rhondda families had sold their houses at a fraction of the prices they had paid for them. They had emigrated to Oxford, Birmingham,

Slough or London, where the men, and frequently the women, could expect to find work. Party members had gone, including Dai Lloyd Davies, who was now running a dairy from New North Road in Islington. But the Horners stopped in Mardy, remaining in the same straitened circumstances as their friends and neighbours. The Horners were at least secure in keeping their home. Although he received the standard 30 shillings per week outdoor relief to feed his family,[304] Arthur had no means to continue paying his father back for the loan he had made them in 1920. James Horner responded as he had done during Arthur's imprisonment for evading conscription, by giving unstinting support for his eldest son's conscientious refusal to do something in which he did not believe.

Arthur adopted the habits of most unemployed miners in Mardy, making the Workmen's Hall, still under the control of the disaffiliated lodge, his social club. He drew emotional sustenance from the men who were in the same apparently hopeless economic position as himself, and occupied his days playing billiards with them at the Hall. He approached the game with the same sporting earnest as he had devoted to boxing and football. Having lost most of the two middle fingers of his left hand, he knew he would never be a champion. But the boys in the Workmen's Hall always allowed him a handicap, and he expended copious physical and emotional energy in sporting conflicts of the billiards room.

Pollitt redoubled his efforts to persuade Horner to make another self-critical confession. He is likely to have found a pretext to visit Mardy, where he could also enjoy socialising with the boys and argue at leisure with Arthur. He probably emphasised that it was not necessary for Horner to abandon the fundamental principle of the importance of working inside reformist unions. Arthur had only to make a ritual obeisance to conclude a temporary truce with Rust and Cox and await the favourable developments inside the Comintern which he and Campbell confidently expected. Pollitt even arranged for Tom Mann to write him to 'get him working in a team spirit'.[305]

But at this juncture, Horner was not a member of any trade union team. He had forfeited his SWMF membership and was now officially a 'non' by virtue of remaining in the disaffiliated Mardy Lodge. Although he remained an MMM member, he was an anonymous rank-and-file footsoldier. On Saturday 21 February, an MMM conference met in Cardiff to prepare a campaign in anticipation of the award for South Wales miners' wages due from the District Conciliation Board Chairman, Schiller, in March. The *Daily Worker* report on 23 February made no mention of Horner, only reporting Garfield Williams' speech, 'We must not repeat the mistakes we made in January ... If we go direct to the miners and call them to action they will follow our lead'.

But Horner remained a leader in Mardy. When the Schiller Award was published on 6 March, Horner took the chair when the disaffiliated Mardy Lodge met on 8 March to discuss it. The minutes of the disaffiliated Lodge meeting recorded that Horner outlined the terms of the effects of the Award, describing SWMF officials as 'Bureaucratic leaders'. Those present passed a resolution condemning the settlement and pledging themselves to prepare for strike action in a united front [i.e. with SWMF members] against the mineowners, the Labour government and trade union bureaucracy under Independent Leadership.

The Award had grim implications. To compensate the owners for the men working seven and half hours rather than eight hours per shift, '[Schiller] reduced the minimum percentage payable on the 1915 standard base rate from 28 to 20 and he brought the subsistence wage down from 7s. 10d. a shift. For daywagemen this meant a reduction of anything from 8d. a shift ... '[306] Following the Award's announcement, there had been 'angry meetings' and even strikes at individual pits, none of which were led by MMM supporters. The SWMF delegate conference which met on 9 to 10 March to consider the Award was adjourned whilst Richards and Morrell sought further concessions, and was expected to re-convene on 21 March.

Strikes continued intermittently in individual pits; the MMM nevertheless failed to build a concerted strike movement under independent leadership.[307] On 19 March Horner wrote to the party secretariat, expressing his willingness to go to Moscow once he had dealt with domestic matters. He had 'practically decided' that the 'path of my revolutionary duty lies in the direction of submission to the Party'.[308] His evident willingness to undertake the requisite self-criticism was probably the result of two calculations. Firstly, the belief that once he was in Moscow he could speedily accomplish his rehabilitation. He expected the Comintern to take due account of the MMM's palpable failure to make any progress in South Wales under the Young Turks' leadership. Secondly, he wanted to effect his re-entry into the conflict between the SWMF and the coalowners. In a letter written on 20 March, Horner lamented: 'I have been completely cut off from the miners' struggle ... To participate in the miners' fight I must associate with the trade union officials or with the revolutionary forces or get out altogether. *I cannot find any common ground with the former.*'[309]

Horner chaired a meeting of the disaffiliated Mardy Lodge on 20 March, when preparations were made for a strike against the Schiller Award, which the MMM pledged would proceed whatever the outcome of the SWMF delegate conference the next day. The lodge was told that a meeting of the MMM's Central Strike Committee would take place simultaneously with the SWMF delegate conference, presumably to emphasise the MMM's genuine independence. Horner was deputed to be the Lodge Delegate to the CSC, a clear indication that the men of Mardy were keen to enter the lists against the Young Turks in Cardiff. The meeting concluded with a discussion about the difficulties of representing members' interests. It was decided that the Committee should meet 'to seriously consider the future of the lodge'. The implication was that the committee might consider disbanding the disaffiliated Lodge to enable its members to re-join the SWMF.

On 21 March, Morrell and Richards informed the SWMF delegate conference that they had been unable to win any improvements in the Award. Resolutions were proposed for a coalfield strike and the Executive's resignation, but they were both defeated. The subsequent card vote to accept the Award was won by a majority of 2000 of the 76,700 numerical votes cast.[310] The large number of lodges voting against the settlement was evidence of a strong will to resist amongst non-communist Federation activists. For Horner, the result was evidence that if the South Wales DPC and MMM had concentrated on official union activity, they could have gathered sufficient votes from other lodges to ensure an official strike.

Horner received a draft of the self-criticism which the CPGB Politburo required him to make at the end of March. On 1 April, he wrote to the party Secretariat, saying he could not admit his errors 'without all the "questions of fact" being thrashed out'. The Politburo's draft 'would damage the party by giving the impression that the Communists' failings in the South Wales strike had all been down to his own errors, when "much more important causes" had really been responsible.' It would help neither the party nor the NMM if he accepted responsibility for errors which their *apparats* had committed.[311]

When Horner's refusal to accept the Politburo's draft self-criticism became known in South Wales, party officials deemed it prudent to convene a full DPC meeting to confirm the party's opposition to Hornerism. An anti-Horner resolution was passed by 19 to 1, with Paynter the probable dissenter. (Paynter had attracted Horner's attention as a bright young comrade. With Horner's patronage, he had risen rapidly in the district party hierarchy and the SWMF.) An amendment omitting Horner's name from a recital of the mistakes made by the South Wales party gathered only two votes. Whilst Cox acknowledged that he had made mistakes at Maesteg in January, he stressed that he had been 'trying to carry out the line and [this] was totally different from actual opposition to the line as in the case of Cde Horner'.[312]

Pollitt and Rust were in Moscow on 1 April at the Eleventh ECCI Plenum. Pollitt and Campbell had been working patiently and in close co-operation to prepare the ground for the Comintern to sanction a change in the British party's tactics to enable its members to re-direct their mass work inside unions. Their efforts bore fruit at the Plenum. Manuilsky demanded the intensification of British communists' efforts inside reformist unions, and castigated the party for '"most unsuccessfully politicizing" the NMM'. Pyatnitsky attacked its slogans as 'abstract'. Whilst publicly criticising Horner, Pollitt also criticised the CPGB's continuing sectarianism. Privately he canvassed ECCI members to rescue Horner for the movement, and was assured that they did not desire his expulsion from the CPGB.[313] When he returned to London in mid-April, Pollitt felt on sufficiently firm ground to launch a fresh attempt from the Secretariat to bring Horner back to the fold.

Pollitt and Campbell spent much of May in South Wales. Pollitt had been released temporarily from his party duties to concentrate on the Workers' Charter campaign, and he spoke at meetings throughout South Wales. Campbell was campaigning in the Ogmore by-election, caused by Vernon Hartshorn's death. Campbell was the only opponent of the SWMF-sponsored Labour candidate, Ted Williams. The election took place on 19 May and Campbell gained a substantial 21.2 per cent of the votes in a low turn-out, 50.8 per cent. Harry and Johnnie apparently found time to see Arthur in Mardy. Ethel is likely to have given them every encouragement. Her own loyalty to the communist party was unwavering. She also believed Pollitt's optimistic prognosis about the Comintern's imminent endorsement of the importance of working inside reformist unions. Deeply disturbed at the prospect of Arthur's expulsion, she used her influence on him to reinforce their efforts.

The Comintern files include a letter from Pollitt to Horner written on 6 May. Its contents were evidently intended not only for Horner but also for official eyes in Moscow. Pollitt referred to his visit with Horner the previous weekend in Mardy, and explained:

> I got a Secretariat meeting first thing this morning, and reported on all our conversation. They unanimously endorsed the proposals I put to you ... We hope you will let us know immediately what you think, so that we can all get to work again ... I beg you to accept my proposals, they will absolutely settle the question, and if you are still hesitant and think that your last draft declaration [probably his letter of 19 March] still represents your final opinion, then send us that, and let us consider it again. I am worried to death about this business, and thought about our conversation all night in the train coming back ... I will go anywhere with you as I stated and show that the Party leadership really wants to work with you and between us do a damned good job as it can be done. No one wants to drive you out, and you know it Arthur, after this fight on fundamentals, you will find that the whole Party, and particularly yourself will be all the stronger in its future work, we shall avoid mistakes and go right ahead. You have had sufficient experience to know from all International work, that in the present

period, there can be no effective drive forward without
the Party ... Regards to Ethel and yourself, Excuse the
one finger exercise. Yours fraternally ... [314]

Despite these best efforts, Horner remained implacable and
unemployed in Mardy. His public persona continued to haunt
the London political stage. The minority Labour government
was experiencing a period of exceptional political turbulence,
caused by the British economy's poor performance amidst
continuing international economic uncertainty. At the end of
February 1931 Mosley had resigned from the Labour Party. But
he kept his parliamentary seat, and in March he and Strachey
announced the formation of the New Party. There was talk that
Bevan would join them. On 30 April the New Party candidate at
a by-election in the Lancashire mining constituency of Ashton-
under-Lyne gained 16 per cent of the votes in an 85.3 per cent
turn-out, enabling the Conservative to win the seat from Labour.
Strachey canvassed the MFGB leadership assiduously about the
New Party. He told Mosley in June that Cook had responded
favourably. Press reports had appeared 'that Arthur Horner ... was
also on the point of joining the New Party'.[315] Horner's defection
did not seem implausible to Fleet Street correspondents. The
well-known Merthyr miner-turned-writer, Jack Jones, had been
a communist in the early 1920s. He now gained further notoriety by joining Mosley to become a New Party neophyte.

When Pollitt wrote to Horner on 22 May inviting him to meet
the Secretariat the day before the Executive considered his expulsion, he added: 'Did you notice in the *Daily Herald* how the social
fascists are attempting to use our differences as the basis for
making innuendoes (*sic*) that you have joined the Mosley Party.
Everybody here entirely discredits this statement which only
appeared, as far as we can gather, in the Southern edition ... but
it is a serious thing that they should be able to utilise our differences in this way.' Pollitt's letter carried an additional punch. He
knew from his Moscow sources that the Comintern had decided
to assist Horner. Pollitt told him: 'I understand that you are
shortly to receive a letter from Comrade Arnot's Department
[the AAS], but so far, nothing has come to us. Perhaps it will be
sent to you direct.'[316]

On 26 May, Pollitt told the Politburo that he had received a telegram from Arnot, saying that the ECCI did not think it advisable to expel Horner and that the ECCI Political Secretariat was writing to Horner. The Politburo should refrain from taking any action against him, until he had received the letter and replied. The letter, sent under the imprimatur of the ECCI Political Commission, was dated 27 May and was delivered personally by Grusha Slutsky to Horner. Slutsky arrived in Britain on 4 June on the first leg of a previously arranged fact-finding visit for the MIC. He stopped in London to give Pollitt a copy before travelling to Mardy the next day to deliver Horner's copy.

In the nine days from 26 May to 4 June, Rust engaged in frantic attempts to retrieve the political high ground, which he realised he was in danger of losing to Pollitt and Campbell. On 31 May, the CPGB Executive duly convened, with Horner present, to consider his case. Pollitt told them about the ECCI letter in transit to Horner, and read a telegram from Manuilsky, instructing the Executive to enumerate the facts of their case against Horner in full. Although he agreed they had the power to expel him, Manuilsky advised against their taking that decision, when the Politburo opposed it. Because Manuilsky gave no indication whether he favoured the Executive's or the Politburo's assessment of Horner, Rust had room to manoeuvre.

Rust anticipated that Horner would hold his entrenched position. He contrived an Executive resolution which stopped just short of expelling Horner, instructing the Politburo 'to apply disciplinary action if necessary in conjunction with the [Communist] International'. As Rust had expected, Horner rebelled. He insisted that he would only accept it 'after the facts have been corrected, otherwise, if I accept the resolution with the facts, I am accepting responsibility in the eyes of the membership to admit myself guilty ... but I cannot do this. If these charges are admitted by me I should not consider myself to be a fit person to be a leading comrade.'

Pollitt and Campbell reserved their position by acquiescing in the resolution. Hannington came out strongly on Horner's side, moving an amendment to the resolution deleting all mention of Horner's opposition to Class Against Class and his pursuance of an opportunist line. Having cast the only vote in favour, he then abstained in the vote on the main resolution, which was otherwise unanimous. Pollitt then made the obvious move against Hannington before Rust could do so, insisting that the Executive should refer *his* position to the Politburo to examine whether he had slipped into Horner's erroneous ways.[317]

Slutsky's doubling as MIC investigator and Comintern courier was convenient, but also fortuitous. Horner recalled that it was Slutsky who 'persuaded me not to leave the Party, and reminded me that ... I still had the right of appeal to [the Comintern] ... When he arrived at our house in Mardy, I at first would not come from the pit to see him. I was so angry.'[318] It is more likely that Horner was at the Workmen's Institute playing billiards when Slutsky turned up. But his recollection of the emotional impact of Slutsky's arrival and the effect of his arguments on his mood was accurate. The letter, written by Arnot and Otto Kuusinen, was not merely friendly. Arnot's fastidious but florid prose style had an apocalyptic undertone which hit home. It presented a transparent opening, a chink through which Horner could wriggle with conscience neatly intact, were he so inclined. Loyola's *Spiritual Exercises* could hardly have done better in creating a mood of obedient repentance:

> Two things ... are not as yet clear to us. The first is whether you want to break with the Communist International. The second is whether in principle your present general position is compatible with the line of the Communist International. As an old member of the Central Committee [CPGB Executive] and candidate of the ECCI and as one who has been a capable and active comrade, we would wish to rescue you for the Communist International. Therefore we invite you to come to Moscow in order that we may have a thorough discussion with.[*sic*] We want to make this last attempt to find if we have still a common language and to see whether their [*sic*] exists any political basis for further work in common. Please let us know immediately whether you will come or not.[319]

On 11 June Pollitt told the Politburo that Horner regretted his inability to make an unconditional submission to the CPGB Executive. He had replied to the ECCI, declaring himself willing to go to Moscow to discuss the points raised in their letter. The matter was now in the ECCI Political Secretariat's hands. Rust, the principal protagonist wanting a pound of Horner's flesh, was too astute to encroach on their terrain.[320]

Horner chaired a general meeting of the disaffiliated Mardy Lodge on 19 June. Reports were received on the disaffiliated Lodge Committee's negotiations with the official Lodge Committee, Rhondda No. 1 District and SWMF officials. These would continue in an attempt to achieve unity. Horner then explained that he would probably be away on the Continent meeting the International Bureau on a personal matter. He sailed for Russia on 1 July. Before his departure Horner had the satisfaction of knowing that in mid-June, before returning to Moscow, Slutsky had told the Politburo that any calls for an immediate coalmining strike were misplaced. Instead, 'the party should campaign for shorter hours and a national minimum wage for miners ... [H]e stated that the CI's view was that "the mining question [was] the most important question now before the Party".'[321] Slutsky would have known from Sobotka about the shortcomings of MMM activity in South Wales in January 1930. He had also been talking to Horner.

The coalmining stakes were certainly high. Under a provision in the 1930 Coal Mines Act, pre-war legislation prescribing a 7 hour day was due to come back into force on 7 July. But economic conditions compelled MacDonald to recognise the coalowners' case for its continuing suspension. Nevertheless, as a result of vigorous lobbying by the TUC General Council and the MFGB, on 6 July, at the last moment, he piloted a further Coal Mines bill through its second reading in the House of Commons, which kept the miners' working day at 7 hours and guaranteed existing minimum wage rates for a further year. The MFGB Annual Conference had approved these terms the previous week by a vote of 346 to 186, with Yorkshire, South Wales, Cumberland and the Forest of Dean opposing.[322]

Horner returned to Moscow in the summer of 1931 in the expectation of being vindicated. Before leaving, he told Hannington 'that he expected to get away with it'. This snippet, evidence that Horner's habitual breezy optimism had returned, quickly became common King Street gossip. Rust heard it, and immediately wrote to Arnot, hoping he would use it as prima facie evidence against Horner.[323] But despite continuing ideological differences with Horner, Arnot was an astute politician. He had quickly acclimatised to ECCI politics, and knew which way the wind was blowing in the corridors of power. He had acquired detailed knowledge of mining trade unionism in 1926 to 1927, and he knew that expelling Horner would badly damage the CPGB's credibility amongst coalmining union loyalists. Miners viewed Horner as second only to Cook as a hero of 1926. Arnot told Jim Fyrth that he had been personally responsible for effecting the compromise between Horner and the Comintern.[324] Although this boast was probably exaggerated, it is apparent that Arnot wanted to keep Horner in the party and that he played an important emollient role in Moscow.

Despite the fact that the ECCI Political Secretariat had invited Horner to Moscow, the proceedings were formally described as Horner's appeal against the CPGB's decision to expel him. The Appeal was heard by five members of the Secretariat, including Arnot; Kuusinen chaired it. The process was apparently protracted, partly because of the serious nature of the British Politburo's charge that Horner had committed the ideological deviation of 'right legalism', against which Stalin had urged special vigilance. The Appeal panel evidently took great care to avoid any appearance of backsliding towards the old line of the united front from above. But Horner relished exercising his virtuosic forensic skills in front of a discerning audience, and made no attempt to shorten his disquisitions.[325]

The exigencies of British politics intervened to provide the Appeal panel with a practical reason to conclude the Horner case. During the parliamentary recess in July and August, another international financial crisis had developed, causing sterling to fall. The Chancellor, Snowden, proposed to staunch the run on the pound by imposing significant cuts to the rate of unemployment benefit and public employees' pay, which had been recommended by a committee of orthodox economic experts appointed by the government to advise them. Although MacDonald supported Snowden's proposals, he was unable to win the support of most of his government colleagues. The majority of the Cabinet agreed with the Labour Party NEC and TUC General Council, both of which opposed the cuts. MacDonald resigned as Labour prime minister on 24 August, but returned to Downing Street on the same day, having accepted the King's invitation to form a National Government. His new cabinet was composed mainly of Conservatives, including Baldwin, along with a few 'National Labour' members. Bruised by the internecine conflict, the Parliamentary Labour Party retired to the Opposition benches. There was a strong expectation that a general election would be called soon after parliament reconvened in October.

The AAS and the ECCI Political Secretariat regarded Horner's prominent public persona as an asset to be utilised in the impending election campaign. His case was concluded so that he could return to Britain and prepare to contest Rhondda East as a communist candidate. Arnot returned to London and met with the Politburo on 17 September to lay the foundations for Horner's smooth rehabilitation back into party life. He did not find it easy to effect a reconciliation. He explained that Horner:

> said he did not want to break with International but declined to agree that he had adopted an opportunist line or even a different line [in January 1931]. However, after detailed examination of whole position of the strike and his attitude and after many discussions in which members of A/A [Anglo-American] Secretariat participated, on last day of discussion Comrade Horner made a declaration in which he analysed his mistakes and showed how he had carried on an erroneous line since the Ninth Plenum [February 1928] to the present time, and stated that after all those tremendous discussions and after great deal of thought ... he had come to the conclusion that the Party had been correct and his line has been incorrect.

Nevertheless, Gallacher criticised Horner's presumably public statement, 'that he could not say he had not had a fair hearing in Moscow', as 'one of the worst bits of cheap opportunism he had ever heard of'. Cox doubted that there would be any change in Horner's behaviour.[326]

Horner had gone to Moscow to prove his bona fides; he returned with the Comintern's approval to resume his place as a leading British comrade. He had acknowledged that he had incorrectly followed Class Against Class; but he had not been required to withdraw his criticisms of the South Wales DPC's failure to prepare for the January 1931 Lock-Out. According to his MI5 file, he returned to Britain on 19 September, arriving in time to attend the second day of the party Executive meeting on 20 September, where he duly repeated the required self-criticism. 'This declaration must have the consequence of determination on my part to struggle for the [new] line and against deviations from the line. I hope this is the last time I will have the painful and unpleasant duty of coming before the Central Committee [Executive] to confess such gross mistakes and failures.' Evidently fearful that Cox and Horner would begin disputing the failures in the South Wales party's activities in January 1931, Pollitt curtailed discussion. A short resolution was passed stating the Executive's 'agreement with the Resolution of the Political Secretariat of the ECCI on the South Wales miners Strike [sic] and the line of Comrade Horner.'[327]

Back in Mardy, Horner's MI5 file recorded that his weekly wage from the party had resumed in August 1931. Evidently, when he had agreed in Moscow to account for his conduct, Slutsky arranged for him to resume being paid as part of the MIC leadership.[328] On 2 October he attended a meeting of the disaffiliated Mardy Lodge, which had failed to meet at all during his absence. The main recorded business of the meeting was to receive reports of the ongoing negotiations with the official lodge. Horner apparently made no report on his Moscow sojourn, perhaps on the grounds that the Appeals panel's deliberations were an internal communist matter. He was probably anxious to keep the disaffiliated lodge focused on union activity. The *Daily Worker* reported his self-criticism under the headline 'Comrade Horner Submits to the Party' on 8 October. The timing was fortuitous for Horner. Because MacDonald had dissolved parliament on 7 October in preparation for a general election on 27 October, the Young Turks were unable to reap any political advantage from Horner's repentance. Instead of magnifying and embellishing Horner's self-criticism during the following weeks, Rust was compelled to ensure that the *Daily Worker*'s reports and leaders praised Horner's suitability as the Communist candidate for Rhondda East.

Horner's election campaign benefited from his topical news value as a Moscow penitent. The three parties participating in the National Government (National Labour, Liberal and Conservative) declined to stand a National Government candidate in Rhondda East, evidently worried that Horner the communist, recently returned from appearing before the Comintern in Moscow, had a serious chance of defeating the Labour incumbent, Colonel Watts Morgan, who had raised a regiment of volunteers in World War I. Local newspapers' normal practice of printing candidates' election addresses was not observed by either the *Porth Gazette* or the *Rhondda Fach Gazette*, which only printed Watts Morgan's. The *Western Mail* deployed innuendo. On 27 October, reporting Horner's eve of poll procession through the constituency, it noted 'the large number of children and non-voters'.

Jack Davies was standing for the CPGB in Rhondda West – the first time a communist candidate had stood against the Labour incumbent Will John. It is likely that Horner and Davies teamed up to conduct a model all-in united front campaign. On 8 October, the *Daily Worker* reported a meeting of the Rhondda Council of Action at Ystrad Rhondda, attended by delegates from six NUWM branches, five women's guilds, two working men's clubs and various SWMF lodges including Ferndale. On 19 October, the *Daily Worker* reported that Horner and Davies had recruited over 500 election workers. The owners of the largest hall in Horner's constituency, Porth Empire Cinema, had refused to let him hire it, whilst making it available to Watts Morgan. On 24 October, the *Rhondda Fach Gazette* reported, 'Mr. Horner and his crowd are working very hard holding open-air meetings every day and no doubt making great headway with the unemployed ... and we believe Mr. Horner will greatly increase his vote this time.' The *Porth Gazette* agreed, noting his 'engaging and eloquent' speech-making. 'Mr. Horner will poll heavier this time because his type of candidature thrives on poverty and distress ... '

As in 1929, Horner and Davies mobilised the local voluntary unemployed infrastructure to find unemployed volunteers across the constituency.[329] The local NUWM had continued to encourage the all-in Miners' Distress Committees, formed during 1926 to encourage self-help and as a focus for organising money raising activities in the rest of Britain, for example the small choirs of unemployed miners who busked in large English cities. The Mardy Distress Committee was probably better organised than others, with a regular attendance by delegates from the Labour Party, the Women's Labour Section, the MMM, the Weslyan, Bethania, Sion, Siloam, Ebenezer and Carmel chapels, the Spiritualists, the Salvation Army and local teachers.[330] During the election campaign, the Mardy Distress Committee minutes recorded that its members organised a fund-raising concert for Horner, arranging canvassers and their red ribbons to wear as official badges.

Horner's result was a creditable performance. He received 10,359 votes, 4500 more than in 1929, and more than any of the other twenty-five communist candidates. His percentage, 31.9 per cent of the total, also compared well to the average of 7.5 per cent for all communist candidates.[331] Watts Morgan's vote increased by 3000 to 22,086. The constituency turn-out, 73.7 per cent, was significantly down on 1929. Large numbers of Tory and Liberal voters evidently abstained, despite Lloyd George's advice that Liberals should vote Labour where there was no Liberal candidate. Jack Davies's result was also creditable, given Will John's popularity as an SWMF leader. In a two-horse race, Davies won 4296 votes, or 15.7 per cent, on a 66.7 per cent turn-out, sufficient for him to save his deposit.[332] One of the few decent results for Mosley's New Party was in Merthyr, where their candidate, Sellick Davies, was the only opponent to stand against RC Wallhead, the ILP incumbent, who was not endorsed by the Labour Party. Sellick Davies received 10,834 votes, 30.6 per cent, in an 80.8 per cent turn-out; he and Horner received approximately the same percentage of the votes cast in their respective constituencies. Pollitt and Campbell lost their deposits in Stepney and Ogmore respectively. Gallacher's vote in West Fife only increased by just under 800 to 6829. His Conservative opponent had come last in the three-cornered fight in 1929; this time he was standing on a National Government ticket, endorsed by MacDonald. He surged ahead of Gallacher to defeat Adamson.

Andrew Thorpe observed that the Rhondda East result showed that even when assisted by Horner's personal popularity and charisma, the CPGB was unable to break through the barrier of political credibility. His point is borne out by the fact that the CPGB's only parliamentary victories (Gallacher in West Fife in 1935 and 1945; and Piratin in Stepney in 1945) were due to exceptional local circumstances.[333] Horner probably had not expected to win in 1931. After his first, sporting attempt in 1929, it is likely that he scrutinised the results – ward by ward – carefully and had drawn his own conclusions. Nevertheless, he had evidently thrown all his energies into the campaign, anxious to show that he remained a committed communist. There was the additional compensation of standing in tandem with Jack Davies; there would have been significant economies of scale in organising speakers and demonstrators to appear in each constituency at different times of the same day.

Horner had little time to reflect or rest after the general election; Arthur Cook died, aged forty-eight, on 2 November, five days after polling day. Horner was profoundly affected. The two Arthurs had been intimate confidants for ten years; their private friendship had endured through the periods when they were publicly engaged in intense political conflict. Horner's observation in *Incorrigible Rebel* that he and Cook were 'like brothers' and 'remained friends and comrades to the end' reflected his abiding sense of loss some thirty years later.[334] The *Daily Worker* reported on 4 November that Horner was speaking at meetings marking the fourteenth anniversary of the Russian Revolution throughout South Wales. He probably attended Cook's funeral on 5 November, along with men and women from the Rhondda who could afford the journey to London.

After the funeral Horner resumed his routine as an unemployed miner, an official 'non', because he remained a member of the disaffiliated Mardy Lodge, and a leading British communist, albeit on probation as far as the Young Turks on the CPGB Executive were concerned. Along with the anti-Horner 'lefts' in South Wales, they remained hostile to his rehabilitation, and determined to confine him to the role of humble penitent. Two further articles rehearsing Horner's mea culpa appeared in the *Daily Worker* on 6 and 17 November. Rust's decision to publish them was not, however, merely personal vendetta. It was evident that Pollitt and Campbell were planning an all-out offensive against the Young Turks. When Pollitt attended a meeting of the ECCI Presidium at the end of December, he stressed that the CPGB's poor election performance was due principally to 'its isolation from the masses, particularly in the factories and trade unions. Communists had to do more to get involved in the workers' daily struggles, particularly as shop stewards. Crucially, he said it was "extremely wrong" to believe that the reformist unions were "played out" ... it was imperative that the party should work through them ... '

The Presidium endorsed Pollitt's interpretation in a unanimous Resolution, which Pollitt and Campbell used to manoeuvre their own carefully worded resolution through the CPGB Executive.[335] Pollitt summarised it on 20 January 1932 in the *Daily Worker*: '[The Communist] Party cannot be sure of any solid influence amongst the masses unless it sees to it first, that throughout all its mass work the demarcation in principle between its line and the reformist line is exposed in the clearest terms; and secondly, that its mass influence is rooted, above all, in the factories and trade unions.' The critical factor influencing the ECCI to back Pollitt and Campbell was the Young Turks' lack of results.

Rust and his allies refused to admit their failure and follow this more centrist interpretation of Class Against Class simply because the Comintern had approved it. Pollitt and Campbell faced a fierce reaction from the 'lefts' to the sea change they were working to effect. A fierce ideological conflict ensued at party meetings and party publications, which culminated at the Twelfth Party Congress in November 1932. In the early part of 1933, Horner's errors and self-criticisms were frequently cited as examples of 'right legalism'. Jack Jones of Blaenclydach wrote in the *Daily Worker* on 23 February, '[I]t is in Rhondda Fach [Mardy and Ferndale] that strong traditions of "Hornerism" still prevail.' He added that whilst there were party members on the Ferndale Lodge Committee, only 30 to 40 men attended lodge meetings. Rhondda Fach and Rhondda Fawr each had Local Party Committees (LPCs), but the Rhondda Fach LPC was still neglecting its revolutionary mass work and committing the right legalist error of relying on union bureaucracy.[336]

But Horner himself had been detained in Cardiff Gaol on 25 February 1932, and was therefore unable to participate in this intense ideological conflict. The events leading to his imprisonment and his time in gaol are the subject of the next chapter.

Chapter 8

Watershed

If Pollitt and Campbell had tried to arrange a spectacular martyrdom for Horner, they could hardly have bettered the train of events which began on 10 November 1931, when the bailiff arrived at Bill Price's house in North Terrace, Mardy, with a lorry and a court order which the Rhondda Urban District Council had obtained against him for rates arrears. Price was at work, one of the few men in Mardy with a job. He was a fireman at Cilely colliery, a Locket's Merthyr pit fifteen miles away. He had recently paid the arrears, but the machinery of local government ground slowly, and the bailiffs had not yet been informed.

At the time of the bailiff's appearance, there were large numbers of unemployed miners in the centre of the village at the local labour exchange. (It was one of the two days in the week when the unemployed were obliged to appear at the exchange and sign on as fit for work in order to obtain unemployment benefit.) When they saw the bailiffs, someone rushed to the Workmen's Hall, to find Horner, who they expected to be playing billiards in a local handicap contest being held there. Horner was a keen competitor, and was playing against Dai Connolly and Tommy Rowe, both of whom played billiards at just below South Wales champion level. On receiving the news, Horner gathered up the players and spectators and then interrupted the Mardy Council of Action meeting in another part of the Hall. Frankenberg's interview notes, fuller and more candid than *Incorrigible Rebel*, recorded the next scene:

> [E]verybody flocked out to [Price's] house, nr. police station – whole [Council of Action] cttee in house – baby in cot – company's house.

232

Horner acted decisively to contain the volatile situation:

> [E]veryone roaring and tearing – I said be quiet –
> Mr. Bumford and Mr. Jones Bailiff – lorry outside house.
> Sat on edge of table asked Mrs. P[rice]. – there was court
> order and she had complied – and after looking at
> receipts satisfied that she had. Proposed that Bumford
> should come to telephone to talk to [UDC] treasurer. B.
> afraid to go through crowd – Jones came –

Horner evidently accompanied Jones and they probably went to
his own home, since the Horners were one of the few people to
have a telephone in Mardy, and Horner could vouch for Jones'
personal safety. Horner spoke to the Council Treasurer first. After
describing the scene, including the large numbers congregating
around the Prices' house, he suggested a face-saving solution.
If the Treasurer instructed the bailiff and his men to withdraw
their lorry immediately, and return again when Bill Price had
returned home, there would be time to verify Mrs Price's insistence that the payment had been made. The Treasurer agreed;
but Horner was prudent:

> To be doubly sure I handed telephone to Jones to receive
> similar message ... When lorry about to withdraw – a
> posse of Police turned up under Inspector Rees – one
> of persons who I regard as greatest discredit to Police
> ever lived.'

The appearance of Inspector Rees and his men was not unexpected. The Prices lived near the police station, and the
duty constable would have heard the crowd rushing from the
Workmen's Hall to North Terrace. The South Wales constabulary had evidently established a standard procedure for dealing
with the evictions and seizures of moveable property, which had
become a constant accompaniment to life in the Rhondda. The
Mardy Council of Action had also developed an effective standard procedure for these emergencies, which included, when necessary, stones being thrown to force the bailiffs to retreat before
they could discharge their duties. Horner executed one of the
standard manoeuvres when, en route to North Terrace, he had

'given instruction to Charley Jones to fix a man at each wheel of [the bailiff's] lorry with a knife to puncture tyres if they tried to withdraw lorry [loaded with furniture] – That was never in the evidence.'

On 10 November, after the treasurer had stayed the bailiff's hand, neither stones nor tyre slashing proved necessary, and the potentially explosive situation ended peacefully, in large part due to Horner's intervention. When Horner and Jones arrived back at the Prices' house, they found Rees and his men in attendance. Arthur greeted Rees with, 'Too late, inspector, Too late.' He then 'Held meeting of Mardy people.' According to *Incorrigible Rebel*, this took place in the Workmen's Hall. Horner was evidently anxious to bring the crowd in off the street to avoid giving Rees any pretext to intervene. Once the Prices' possessions were safe, neither he nor the Council of Action were interested in challenging the forces of law and order. After the meeting was over, Horner finished his allotted quota of games in the billiards competition. Against most people's expectations, he won. Rowe had allowed Arthur a very generous handicap (100 start in half an hour), and just failed to catch him at the end. Ebullient euphoria probably pervaded the Hall that evening in celebration of Horner's double victory.[337]

Horner left Mardy by car soon after, on the first leg of a journey to Moscow to help the other MIC leaders prepare for the MIC Annual Conference in mid-December. He planned to stay until January, and return via Berlin, where he would transact more MIC business. The winter fixture of an MIC conference and post-conference activities in Moscow, Berlin, and/or Essen had been part of Horner's routine since 1929, although he and Ethel would have regretted his being away over Christmas and New Year.[338]

Horner's engagements diary had a number of Berlin addresses, most of which puzzled MI6, when they received the photograph copy from the Harwich constabulary who had arrested him on his entering Britain.[339] This may be because he was engaged on serious coalmining trade union business, outside the normal purview of MI6 operatives. Annual wages and hours agreements were pending throughout Europe, including British district coalfields, and the MIC intended to form an effective mineworkers' international cartel. Because coal was still an essential energy source for industry, their plan was not wholly utopian. The MIC cartel was potentially as powerful as OPEC (the Organisation of Petroleum Exporting Countries), and could have forced coalowners to increase international coal prices to much higher levels, and then pass the increase on to miners in higher wages and shorter hours. OPEC implemented this strategy successfully in 1973 to 1974 when its members raised their prices precipitately in unison, and compelled the hitherto all-powerful international oil companies to increase their ex-refinery prices accordingly.

Horner arrived in Berlin safely, but he failed to keep any of his appointments. He left after finding a recent British newspaper, probably the *Daily Herald* or *Reynolds' News,* at the Comintern WEB offices. He read an announcement of a memorial meeting for his close friend and manager of the Porth Co-operative Society, David Evans, at the Porth Empire Cinema on Sunday evening, 3 January 1932. Evans had died unexpectedly, and news of his death had not reached Horner in Moscow.

Horner read other newspaper reports that the Glamorgan constabulary had summonsed three women and thirty-two men, including himself, to appear at Porth Magistrates' Court by the end of January to answer charges of having committed civil offences ranging from unlawful assembly to incitement to riot on 10 November 1931 in Mardy. The report noted that Horner was alleged to be missing. (Ethel and the girls may have gone to stay with friends or family over the holiday period, and no one in Mardy had felt either obliged or inclined to disclose Horner's whereabouts to the police.)

Evidently, after consultations with Inspector Rees and the Home Office, Lionel Lindsay, the Glamorgan Chief Constable had decided to prosecute the Mardy 'rioters' in early December, despite a palpable lack of evidence. Lindsay evidently believed that the Mardy Council of Action were a dangerous force, and was unwilling to allow them to operate unhindered, even though on this occasion they had kept within the law. Horner, reading the news in the atmosphere of late Weimar Berlin, was surprised, but probably not shocked. Along with other communists who regularly spent time in Germany, he must have reflected that a comparable polarisation of British politics was gathering momentum.

Horner recalled that he had immediately decided to leave Berlin and return to Britain, in order to speak at Evans' memorial. He also had no intention of allowing the British press to speculate about him having absconded to avoid arrest. He caught the night train from Berlin on Tuesday 29 December, and arrived in Harwich the next morning. Along with other veteran communists, he knew that the party leadership's activities attracted regular Special Branch surveillance. Nevertheless, he was apparently surprised to be arrested the moment he stepped onto British soil. The Police Sergeant at the Port of Harwich reported:

> HORNER was stopped by P.C. Pocock, and I spoke to him informing him that I was a Police officer, and also that I was going to detain him for an offence committed in South Wales. HORNER replied 'Good God! What, for that? Send a message to the Superintendent in Porth and tell him I am coming. He can meet me at the station'. I told him that was impossible, and he then asked to see my warrant card, as he said 'You probably remember the Fascists took Pollitt for a ride at Liverpool and I don't want that to happen to me here'. I produced my warrant card. I then sent a telephone message to Acting Superintendent Special Branch, and later conveyed HORNER to Harwich Police Station, where he is being detained pending the arrival of an escort from Glamorganshire County Constabulary, Pontypridd.[340]

Horner was kept waiting in the Harwich police station for the whole of Wednesday. Press reports stated that the Welsh police escort was required to prevent Horner disappearing. It is more likely that Lindsay and Rees felt obliged to provide a show of force appropriate to Horner's status as a dangerous revolutionary. He had been allowed to ring Paynter from Harwich. Horner's MI5 file contains a copy of the telegram sent by Paynter to the Party Secretariat on Thursday 31 December. 'Comrade HORNER wishes me to inform you that it is indeed to hold a European Miners Conference sometime in February and that 12 delegates are to go over from this country. Campaign to be commenced immediately. Comrade Horner is tonight in Pontypridd

Police Station.' Paynter saw Horner in the Pontypridd Police
Station, where he was apparently detained on New Year's Day.
He appeared before the magistrates in Pontypridd on Saturday
2 January, to answer the charge, and was then released. The
Pontypridd police evidently had no desire to prevent him
from speaking at David Evans' Memorial Meeting in Porth on
Sunday.

The trial of the Mardy thirty-four commenced on 18 February
1932 and lasted three days. (The police had dropped the charges
against a Salvation Army member, Trevor Davies, at the arraign-
ment.) Horner recalled: 'Every day buses used to come from
Mardy to take us to Cardiff Assize Court and each day there were
tremendous demonstrations in the Mardy streets as we left.'[341]
Because the events outside the Prices' house on 10 November
had been neither riotous nor violent, bringing the prosecutions
misfired. News of the summonses themselves had produced
disgust and disbelief in the coalfield. The Mardy Council of
Action had been re-invented yet again as the Mardy Defence
Committee to raise money to defray the defendants' expenses.
Although most of the accused men were not members of the
official Mardy Lodge, the SWMF probably provided discreet
financial assistance to enable good South Walian barristers to
represent them.

Horner conducted his own defence. There were two barristers; one appeared for the Council of Action members who
had been inside the Prices' house and the other for the people
caught up in the general melée outside. Both gave Horner prec-
edence, so that he made the first speech in the defence case
and the first speech in the final summing up. He had prepared
his defence with characteristic meticulousness, and challenged
the prosecution case in virtuoso fashion. He had obviously been
attentive to trial procedure and barristers' conventions during
his past appearances in various courts. For example, in response
to the police evidence that Tommy Rowe had been about to
throw a stone, Horner asked the police witness to identify Rowe,
who was sitting in the front row in the dock. He was unable to
do so. Horner told Frankenberg that Lord Justice Branson, who
was hearing the case, intervened during the proceedings 'to say
that he was sure Arthur had had legal experience, it was the only
explanation possible for his ability in cross examination.'

The case excited great interest. Francis and Smith observed:

> The bulk of the evidence (provided by the Glamorgan Constabulary) was of a political character which provoked the *Manchester Guardian* to demand an enquiry because politics was allegedly used to sway the judgement ... [Chief Constable] Lindsay stated that it was important to provide the political background of the defendants because 'definite proof was difficult to obtain' ... Horner ... was described as assuming the role of 'dictator at Mardy'. It was implied that he was a paid Russian agent and that during his absence Mardy was normal.

After lengthy deliberation, the jury found twenty-nine men and women, including Horner, guilty of unlawful assembly. A juryman later told Horner they had not realised one could get up to two years for this. They had declined to find the accused guilty of the more serious charge of incitement to riot; but they had evidently been afraid to reject the judge's instructions completely, and had believed that the lesser offence would not attract long sentences. The prisoners were removed to the cells for the night, returning the next day to the cages under Cardiff Court to await Branson's sentences. Horner received the stiffest sentence, fifteen months hard labour. The South Wales DPC and the Mardy Defence Committee organised a demonstration outside the court, to protest against the verdicts. Horner was convinced that Branson had meted out longer sentences because of it: 'Gang sang Red Flag and the International and AH asked them to shut up but they wouldn't. Judge very annoyed at demo when Arthur went up first. "I am going to send you to prison for a long, long time, short sentences evidently do not appeal to you." ... Five others received nine months ... The others received three, and some one month.'[342] The twenty-nine began serving their time in Cardiff Gaol on 25 February.

The harsh sentences meted out to the six 'ringleaders', most of whom were members of the disaffiliated Mardy Lodge Committee, wholly misfired. They had been intended to isolate them further from 'law-abiding' SWMF office-holders. However, already angered by the prosecutions themselves, the Executive and Federation Lodge Committees recoiled at this further example of class justice in South Wales. The judge's homily that he was sentencing Horner to a protracted term of hard labour to teach him a lesson was especially offensive. Even though they were no longer Federation members and officially 'nons', the SWMF organised a campaign for the men's early release. It had a palpable impact. Watts Morgan and two other SWMF MPs, Dai Grenfell and George Hall, had seen the Home Secretary, Sir Herbert Samuel, on their behalf, and all six were granted three months remission of their sentences.[343] Horner was released on 10 December, after serving only nine and a half months.

Horner recalled: 'I realise that it marked a turning point in my career. Once you make up your mind to it, prison is a very good place to think ... I set to work to analyse the period since I left jail thirteen years before after my hunger strike ... '.[344] Aged thirty-eight, he had a lot to think about, having been in the forefront of British trade union life and the international communist movement for nearly a decade.[345] Having made up his mind, he embarked on a course of study and reflection with single-minded determination. He emerged from his confinement armed with a new, systematic approach to economic conflict, which guided his conduct of union affairs until his retirement as NUM general secretary in 1959. He set himself an ambitious individual training regime, treating the development of mental stamina and intellectual strength with the same rigour he had applied to physical training for boxing and football. 'During my first time in jail [1918 to 1919] I got hold of an arithmetic book, and in the period when I was only allowed to read the Bible I discovered that it was a source of beautiful literature. In Cardiff jail I had another month on the Bible and nothing else, but after that we were allowed one library book a week ... Later on ... I was able to have lessons from Marx House.'[346]

For the first six months Horner was set to work as a cleaner, a bath attendant and in the kitchens. He can have had little time for rigorous study. But the arrival of a new Prison Governor, Captain Roberts, transformed his prison existence. Roberts had been governor at Dartmoor Gaol, and was transferred after a mutiny there, precipitated in part because of the friction caused by his decision to implement a more humane, liberal regime. The experience reinforced his commitment to prison reform. He appreciated Horner's character, and granted him the privilege of becoming prison librarian, leaving him free from manual labour. He also became secretary of the prison education programme.

Horner remembered that '[h]e had in fact not had too bad a time ... and spent his time between smoking and reading. Roberts ... used to say that the other lags went into the library to smoke as the extra smell did not notice there. The worse [sic] thing about prison was the attitude of irresponsibility that one developed there because you knew that whatever happened you had to stay ... He once knocked out a warder by mistake when skylarking and was very frightened of a charge but the other screws hushed it up.'[347] Arthur was conscientious in discharging his librarian's duties. He had the run of 6000 books, and took great care in choosing reading material to suit the tastes of individual prisoners.

He recalled that the Marx House syllabus he had followed included 'the first volume of Marx's *Capital* and I also read some philosophy. I used to take a chapter of Marx and summarize it on my slate. Then I would wipe the slate and start on something else. Finally I made a curriculum and adhered to it very strictly indeed. It was amazing how it made the time pass.'[348] Readers who have encountered Volume I of *Capital* at a comparatively early age may recall their own mounting excitement and awe at recognising, one by one, the features of their own everyday lives. The underlying connections and tensions of a capitalist economy are suddenly illuminated by the dual nature of all commodities. The reader muses again and again on the conflicting facets of use-value and exchange-value and finds countless examples from their own experience which verify Marx's points. The other inspiration is the succinct, vivid account of the response of British factory operatives to their increasing rate of exploitation by self-organisation. Far from being martyrology, Volume I tells a story as gripping as the ripping yarns Horner devoured in cowboy magazines. The formation of trade unions, the organisation of Short Time Committees, and their ad hoc alliances with sympathetic Tory activists was a complex story which Marx relished telling. Horner probably also found the tone of Volume I vastly appealing. It is upbeat, brimming with confidence and also, paradoxically, gradualist.

Horner found a book by another famous Prussian, Karl von Clausewitz, in the library. Clausewitz had witnessed the wars arising from the French Revolution as an army officer, taking part in the Waterloo campaign in 1815 as Prussian chief of staff. His analysis of those wars and the reasons for Prussia's initial defeat by Napoleon, *Vom Kriege* (*On War*), published posthumously in 1832, became a staple of European army officers' and politicians' reading, including socialists. Described by Michael Howard as an autodidact, who 'devoured literature on any available topic, not only military affairs but philosophy, politics, art and education', Clausewitz had been imbued with 'an ambition for military glory ... that gave a peculiar intensity to his analyses of the qualities demanded of a commander in the field, of the intense moral pressures that commanders must learn to withstand and of the bloody drama of battle'.[349]

Frankenberg's notes state: 'Studied Clausewitz in prison – "War in arms is logical continuation of the trade struggle between nations". Used his tactics often since.' The militarism which formed the book's background was attractive to Horner. He was no pacifist, and had enthusiastically emulated the militarist discourse used by veterans of new unionism such as Tom Mann and Ablett. Clausewitz's famous aphorism was that war was the continuation of political conflict between nations. It is not surprising that Horner elided trade unions and politics. Lenin, HN Brailsford, and his mentors at the Aberystwyth Restaurant had all agreed that the underlying cause of World War I was imperialist rivalries over capitalist trade. *Incorrigible Rebel* recorded three examples of Clausewitz's impact on Horner. First: 'I read it [*On War*] with very great interest ... Clausewitz taught that if you enter into active struggle you can succeed only if you adopt the principle of inflicting the greatest degree of damage on your opponents, with the least possible hurt to your own forces ... Sometimes it would be necessary to fight a defensive battle ... But when it came to fighting back we had to be sure that if we attacked we were in a position to win.' The second reference was in his description of a dispute that he had conducted as Federation agent in the Anthracite, culminating in a substantial wage increase without a strike – 'my first application of the Clausewitz principle ... '.

241

His final reference to Clausewitz was in his recounting of his defence of the agreement he concluded as SWMF President with the Bedwas colliery owners to end the war of attrition the Federation had been waging against the SWMIU: "'The fact is, that scientifically applied class struggle has given us Bedwas without any undue loss of expenditure or manpower." Then I added the phrase which I had learned from Clausewitz. "In the Bedwas Agreement we have gone a long way towards the objective of maximum results, with the least damage to our own forces.'"[350]

Horner encountered Clausewitz at a point when he was susceptible to new ideas. He recognised that the approach of his militant mentors, fighting every industrial conflict at maximum strength to inflict maximum damage, had not yielded the results he had expected. During the British mining conflicts of the 1920s, inspired by the Russian revolution, he had refined this strategy into a total war doctrine which stressed the importance of vigilant organisation and total mobilisation. He argued persuasively that the unions' defeats, including the 1926 Miners' Lock-Out, were due to their failure to marshal sufficient force with sufficient energy and commitment. Intellectual honesty had compelled him to acknowledge that this approach had produced a succession of failures and defeats. He knew a re-think was required, and prison gave him the time and freedom to do so.

Having conducted rigorous, private self-criticism, and concluded his self-prescribed course of study, he emerged as a scientific Clausewitzian. The consequent emotional relief and intellectual satisfaction were immense. He contemplated his imminent release with an elation he found difficult to contain. He believed that his new approach would make a decisive difference to the future fortunes of the SWMF and MFGB. He was also impatient to resume communist activity.

Horner knew from visitors that the Twelfth Party Congress in mid-November was expected to be a watershed. The news he received, however, hardly lived up to his high expectations, fuelled by the feeling of having been intellectually reborn. He wrote Ethel on 2 December: 'Now Eth old girl I've been very sorry that I said I might go to the Conference [the MIC Annual Conference] on December 12th. Since you were here it seems outrageous for me to leave for Germany the day after my release. So don't think about it any more unless of course it is a definite Party decision, and if this is so write to Harry to explain that it would be against the grain for me to go away so soon ... The news on Saturday [about the Twelfth Congress] was not very good, particularly about Wally [not being re-elected to the Executive]. The political vendetta is apparently being deepened and extended regardless of the meritorious actions of the individuals attacked ... You say Harry Pollitt is coming down to see me upon my release. I shall be very glad to have a heart to heart talk about a number of questions ... Cheer up, the trouble is all over, bar shouting. Don't forget about Gwen's as proposed.'[351]

Ethel was probably delighted that Arthur would not have to rush off to Essen. Apart from having him home for the holidays, she could look forward to handing back all the political responsibilities she had exercised on his behalf during his absence. She was a competent committee person and an indefatigable organiser, but she had never enjoyed public speaking. During his imprisonment, she had only reluctantly deputised for him at the public meetings and social occasions mounted by the Mardy Defence Committee. She could expect some respite from the day-to-day problems of keeping three growing children. She had received constant support from friends and comrades, but their material resources were frequently more meagre than her own. The relief available from the Public Assistance Committee, the local authority quango which had replaced the Poor Law Board of Guardians in 1929, provided families with a bare subsistence existence. Vol and Joan had vivid memories of the unrelieved poverty they had shared with the rest of Mardy. Ethel received some assistance from Arthur's younger brother, Albert, and probably also from their father. Pollitt organised a weekly subvention from King Street, and it is unlikely that he would have arranged a mere token payment.[352]

Horner's release from gaol coincided with the elections being held at Mardy for a new checkweighman to service the newly re-opened pits, and he wanted the job. Locket's Merthyr had gone into voluntary liquidation in 1932, and the colliery had been bought by Bwllfa & Cwmaman Collieries Ltd., with plans to re-open the pits on a limited basis in 1933; they were expected to employ 600 to 700 men. The British economy was showing the first tangible signs of a slow recovery from the 1931 slump. Although competition from low-cost Polish and American coal was keeping South Wales coal out of most of its old, staple export markets, South Wales coal companies were making serious attempts to penetrate the British domestic market, and making steady inroads into an area hitherto dominated by Midlands coal companies.

Horner's ambition to win his old job back was plausible. The statute law pertaining to checkweighmen did not specify that the workmen's committee organising the election had to be an official trade union committee. Horner believed that his previous record on the job and personal popularity would enable him to win, even though he had forfeited his SWMF membership. He wrote to Ethel on 2 December:

> Urge the boys to do everything possible about the job. Personal approach, put out how we will all fight for the right of each man to return to his working place ... Don't forget the extra hundredweight ... which meant hundreds of pounds in the workmen's pockets [payment for small coal which Horner had won previously] etc. Ability to deal with Compensation and Wages Disputes etc ... Tell Charlie [Jones] to keep at it, everything may depend on the next few days. Efforts, not only for me and the job, but from the viewpoint of unity, organisational and otherwise in Mardy.

Horner no doubt believed that his election as checkweighman would provide the occasion to finesse the merger of the disaffiliated Mardy Lodge with the official one.

Charlie Jones duly finessed the nomination. He was still on friendly terms with the secretary of the official lodge, Bob Thomas. They had actually been two of the four signatories on Horner's nomination papers for checkweighman in 1919, and they went forward to nominate him for the same post. They also embarked on a vigorous canvas of the official lodge members on Horner's behalf. (It is unlikely that any of the members of the disaffiliated lodge would have been taken on by the new owners.) The new Mardy coalowners, however, had other ideas.

They had no intention of allowing a return to the favourable customs and practices over which the old Lodge leaders had presided. Horner was released shortly before the election.

Horner was the last of the Mardy 'ringleaders' to be freed, and his return was the occasion for exuberant public celebration. The prison authorities decided to free him on the night before his scheduled departure in order to pre-empt the demonstrations they suspected were being organised. But Horner outflanked their manoeuvre by staying overnight in Cardiff with communist friends, and taking the train home on the day scheduled for his release. Frankenberg's notes recorded his public appearances en route.

> Next morning Arthur returned to the Rhondda, he left the train at Tylorstown to attend a welcome home meeting in Ferndale Hall. There was a March from Tylorstown to Ferndale and when they arrived there was already a big meeting in progress. George Maslin, then a communist councillor, was speaking. He was very sincere but inclined to be a revivalist in style and he went on at some length about Arthur's alleged suffering in prison. Arthur then spoke and pointed out that he was 2 stone heavier than when he went in whereas most of his audience were 2 stone lighter as far as he could see.[353]

Pollitt arrived in Mardy, as promised, to talk about the Twelfth Party Congress. Frankenberg noted Horner's memory of the Congress result. 'In future the organised working class in work were not to be treated as a labour aristocracy but had to be regarded as a decisive element.' Pollitt had praised rank-and-file movements, citing the AEU Members' Rights Movement and the London Busmen's Rank-and-File Movement as examples of RILU's prescribed Revolutionary Trade Union Opposition. Both movements were operating wholly within their respective 'reformist' unions, and they had mobilised rank-and-file trade unionists without committing either left sectarian or right legalist ideological errors. He notably failed to mention the Minority Movement in any shape or form. The Young Turks continued to predominate inside the Great Ormond Street *apparat*, however, and evidently intended to use it as a last redoubt to re-launch revolutionary voluntarism. They maintained their extreme left interpretation of RTUO, and denounced right trade union legalism as the main enemy of communists and militants.[354]

Armed with Pollitt's imprimatur about a return to activity inside the SWMF, Horner waged his usual vigorous campaign in the contest for checkweighman. He came top of the list in the first ballot. Although he had fierce local enemies and detractors, most of the miners who remained in Mardy were his contemporaries or even older. They had families who were reluctant to uproot, and many were unable to sell the houses bought in past prosperity. Horner was one of them. He had stood up for them and won great victories in that palmy past. Their self-image was that they were their own men, and it did not include deferring to the rumours and predictions that Horner's election was bound to produce terrible consequences.

But the Mardy pits were closed again after Horner's victory.[355] On receiving the news of his election, Bwllfa & Cwmaman Collieries simply switched production to other pits they owned in Aberdare and Cwmaman, where they believed the checkweighmen would be less obstructive. Horner had to live with the consequences of his pyrrhic victory. Most of the men who had voted for him had lost the possibility of working for the first time since 1926. Some of them and their families blamed him for their ill fortune and lost any sense of loyalty towards him. Others who had remained unemployed without prospect of re-starting at Mardy would have sympathised with these men's frustrated hopes.

Nevertheless, the pits' failure to re-open did not precipitate a civil war in Mardy. Horner remained at the heart of Mardy life. The disaffiliated Federation lodge had kept its lien over the Workmen's Hall. Horner remained its chairman and was a constant inhabitant of its billiards and reading rooms. The official SWMF lodge felt constrained to meet elsewhere. (Francis and Smith hint that it may have been in the Conservative Club.) Nevertheless, *all* the men in Mardy socialised in the Hall. In the billiards room, Horner was one of the boys. His evident bona fides and bonhomie were strong deterrents to the escalation of grudges and vendettas.

Horner's enforced political idleness was due to his lack of an industrial base. Nominally still employed by the MIC, he made no move to assimilate back into the Miners' Minority Movement or the NMM London office. He returned to trade union activity by launching the South Wales Miners' Rank-and-File Movement. He resurrected the South Wales Miners' Unofficial Reform Committee, of which he had been chairman at its last appearance in 1923. Readers will recall that the SWURC had been conveniently merged into the Miners' Minority Movement. But Horner did not allow this formal nicety to stand in his way. He gathered up the communist and left allies who were still active inside the Federation or willing to resume trade union 'mass work'. They convened as the SWURC to transform the old movement once again, this time into the South Wales Miners' Rank-and-File Movement, re-dedicating themselves and the new movement to the Unofficial Reform Committee's (and MMM's) original aim of modernising the SWMF and the MFGB. Since the extreme left activists in the South Wales party were preserving the MMM as a revolutionary union in embryo, even though it had atrophied into a pale shadow of its former self, there were now two rival left groupings in the coalfield.

The Rhondda East MP Dai Watts Morgan died in February 1933. The by-election was scheduled for 28 March 1933, and the general expectation was that Horner would stand again for the CPGB. The question of his Labour opponent was more problematic. The Labour leadership in London wanted the seat for Arthur Henderson, whose absence from the House of Commons was damaging the credibility of the depleted Parliamentary Labour Party. But they withdrew Henderson's claim when the SWMF Executive put WH Mainwaring forward. (In addition to asserting their claim to determine the nomination, the Federation Executive may have feared that Horner would be able to discredit Henderson as an uninvited carpetbagger.) In contrast to 1931, there was a Liberal candidate, who followed the party's policy of supporting the National Government. But local and national interest remained focused on the contest between Mainwaring and Horner.

The parties commenced a three-and-a-half week campaign in early March. The Horner side mounted an exemplary campaign. Pollitt wrote 'Our comrades, badly fed and badly clothed, work with an enthusiasm that puts other districts to shame.'[356] The by-election afforded excellent opportunities for public exposure and the chance to put the communist case to a far wider spectrum of the population. It also provided a practical reason for the disputatious South Wales party to unite, at least temporarily. Despite Horner's self-criticism, rehabilitation and prison sentence, the internal fissures which had opened up during the Hornerism conflict had not yet closed. Nevertheless, South Wales was one of the districts selected by the Executive in January 1933 for 'concentration' – Comintern jargon for intensive recruiting and party activity.

On 26 February Pollitt told the South Wales DPC that Idris Cox would arrive 'within the next few days to take charge of the Election campaign in East Rhondda'.[357] Cox was established in Lancashire as the District Organiser; his temporary secondment to South Wales was probably arranged because the Party Centre were confident that he would enforce party unity around Horner's candidacy. They also knew that he was a capable administrator, who would mount an efficient campaign. He brought Pat Devine down with him from Manchester to augment the number of speakers. Pollitt lavished time and energy on the campaign. Tom Mann also arrived, no doubt pleased to be assisting Horner and addressing enthusiastic South Walian audiences.

Cox was able to sub-divide his organisational responsibilities. In addition to the Mardy Distress Committee, there was a central committee and four area committees, enabling detailed preparation and efficient execution of activities. Horner's election conference was attended by 46 delegates from 28 organisations. There were four mass meetings held, presumably one in each area. The appeal to voters was designed to encourage tactical voting. Because this was a by-election, the people of Rhondda East had the opportunity to teach the Labour Party a lesson. Thus, the front page of the *Horner Election Special* asked:

> What would the return of Mr. Mainwaring ... mean for the working class? It would mean that things would remain as they are ... Nothing would change except that one Labour MP would take the place of another. What would the return of Arthur Horner mean for the workers. It would mean one Communist MP to put forward the demands of the workers and challenge the whole capitalist class. If Mainwaring is returned, the capital-

ists will smile and carry on with further attacks on the workers. But the return of Arthur Horner will change the whole situation. It will be a signal of warning for the capitalist class. It will show the determination of the working class to change things.

The message was a firm indication that the CPGB leadership were well attuned to the realities of British electoral politics. Rather than proclaiming the ideological verities of the Third International, an attitude to which the party's 1931 campaign had been prone, Horner's propaganda refrained from attacking Labour frontally. Horner utilised his public appearances to accuse Mainwaring of neglecting his duties as Rhondda No. 1 District Agent. He probably also revelled in the knowledge that Mainwaring's lacklustre speaking style made him a particularly unappealing opponent in a close-fought by-election. The Labour *apparat* deployed overwhelming forces in the constituency to counter Horner's popular appeal and ensure that Labour loyalists did not stray away from the fold to cast a tactical vote. Labour held 51 meetings, using Herbert Morrison, Arthur Greenwood, and three neighbouring mining MPs, Dai Grenfell, Ted Williams and Will John. Both Morrell and Harris and the new MFGB general secretary, Ebby Edwards, issued appeals for Mainwaring. Horner recalled his resentment at the intervention of the South Walian MPs, SWMF officers, and Ebby Edwards, 'many of them personal friends of mine who had been with me for many years in the struggle'.[358]

Mainwaring himself fought a defensive and negative campaign. The Mainwaring *Election Special* described Horner as 'a wrecking candidate' with 'tactics which would lead the workers to disaster', and claimed that it was Mainwaring who had convinced the new coal company to re-open the Mardy pits. He declined to answer a question put to him at a meeting about whether he still agreed with the *Miners' Next Step*. He drew attention to the communists' recent volte-face at the Twelfth Party Congress in relation to their 'New Line', and cited the internal party row about Hornerism as evidence of the CPGB's duplicity.

The *Horner Election Special* replied with a hard-hitting story, probably written by Campbell.

The Labour Party has made a remarkable discovery. It has found out that Arthur Horner some time ago had a difference of opinion upon the methods of the Communist Party to organise the struggle of the workers against the attacks of the employers and the treacherous policy of the reactionary union officials. How strange! ... Arthur Horner was allowed to criticise his own Party, and continues to have the honour of being the standard-bearer of the Communist Party for the House of Commons.

True, Arthur Horner criticised the policy of the Communist party in the strike of the South Wales miners in January, 1931 ... After thorough discussion of every point of criticism, Arthur Horner agreed that the Policy of his Party ... was correct and that he had been mistaken. But his criticism on many points revealed important weaknesses in the carrying out of Communist Party policy ... The Communist Party is so strong and well disciplined that it is not afraid to discuss differences openly before the workers.

The final paragraph highlighted the party's turn back to trade union work. 'Only militant criticism and reconstruction can make the Miners' Federation once again the power that it was and still can be. Today it is bankrupt under the leadership of those who co-operate with colliery managers ... Tomorrow it will become an effective instrument in the workers' struggle ... by the removal of those autocrats who have captured power and used this power against the militants.'

Chris Williams considered that Mainwaring's 'identity as essentially a Mid-Rhondda man, when only part of Mid-Rhondda came into the constituency, may ... have been a handicap, and it seems likely that Horner pulled a great deal of his support from the Upper Rhondda Fach [Mardy, Ferndale, Tylorstown].'[359] Mainwaring was returned on a slightly higher turn-out, 74.9 per cent, than 1931. His majority had declined by nearly 8000 votes compared to Watts Morgan in 1931; most of these votes went to the Liberal candidate. Although Horner came second, his total only increased by 869 votes.[360]

It is unlikely that Horner expected to win the seat with the Liberals standing. Since it was his third contest in Rhondda East,

*James Jobson Horner
and Emily Lewis Horner
in their garden at Clare
Street, Merthyr, ca 1945*

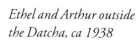

*Ethel and Arthur outside
the Datcha, ca 1938*

OUR THOUGHTS THIS XMAS

May the spirit and achievements of our
March prevail and hasten the day when
the working class in Britain shall march
victoriously to the conquest of power

Men will then truly say:

"A MERRY XMAS"

Xmas Greetings to the Old Comrades
of the Miners' March

From the Marchers' Central Council:

Wal Hannington   Dai L. Davis
Tom Thomas   Emrys Llewellyn
Arthur Horner   Jack Jones
Jack Thomas   C. Ashleigh (Press)

From the N.U.W.C.M.:

J. W. Holt   Charlie Jones

To Arthur & Ethel from
Wally

*Christmas card sent
to the Horners from
Wally Hannington in
1929. In the front
row of the march,
from left to right, are
Hannington, Tom
Thomas and Horner.*

Wally. Tom. Arthur

AJ Cook addressing miners lodges in Durham during the 1926 Lockout

Executive Committee Anthracite District of SWMF, December 1933.
Back row: D.J. Evans, Gomer Evans, D.R. Owen, Jim Griffiths,
R. Lewis, D.J. Jones. Front row: Arthur Horner, Wm Davies,
Evan (Ianto) Evans, JNO James

Horner playing snooker in the Working Men's Hall, Mardy, ca 1933

*Mid-Rhondda demonstration against the new unemployment
regulations, 1934*

he had had ample opportunity to analyse the constituency's pse-phological profile. Nevertheless, he had used the by-election campaign to political and personal advantage. Because of the intense interest the contest aroused, most active Federation members would have observed the CPGB's decisive turn away from attacking 'reformist' unions and renewed encouragement of militant activity inside them. Horner had used the opportunity to concentrate on union issues. He declared unswerving loyalty to the Federation, but hostility towards its 'autocrats'. This emphasis was underpinned by strong support from Pollitt and Campbell. For them, and for Horner, the campaign had been a great success. It re-established the South Wales communist party's credibility with non-communist union activists who had been repelled by the *Daily Worker*'s and MMM's condemnation of themselves and the SWMF as social fascists.

As a result of his experience in the campaign, Cox was alarmed by the state of the party. He told Pollitt that 'With regard to the position in S. Wales, ... something drastic would have to be done to improve things.' It is likely that many anti-Horner veterans and younger party members were channelling their frustration and disappointment at Horner's defeat into political criticism. The Party Centre evidently agreed. On 6 April after 'a very detailed discussion of the Party's situation in 'South Wales' at the Politburo meeting, '[i]t was finally decided to send comrade Cox to S. Wales'. On 7 April Pollitt gave this news to a meeting of the DPC. Cox replaced Charlie Stead as South Wales Organiser. In July Lionel Lindsay reported that Cox had rented a house in Pontyclun, in the Ely valley, and travelled daily to the party offices in Tonypandy.[361]

After the campaign Horner re-channelled his energies into building up the South Wales Miners' Rank and File Movement His aim was to counter the influence of the loosely organised centre bloc on the SWMF Executive and in the lodges, which had coalesced after 1926. Following Tom Richards' death in November 1931, Oliver Harris had been elected to succeed him as general secretary. In the aftermath of the Lock-Out, Harris had moved, along many other activists, away from unalloyed militancy to a more cautious, circumspect position. He had defeated SO Davies, the left candidate, by a narrow margin on the final ballot in February 1932. The centre bloc's intervention had also secured the election of Richards' protégé, Jim Griffiths, as Vice-President in June 1932. An energetic, purposeful operator, his victory had sealed the Federation's retreat from the consistently militant stance it had adopted from its inception in 1898. Harris limited his activities as general secretary to administrative and organisational tasks, and left the political and strategic direction of the union to Morrell and Griffiths.[362] They continued Richards' moderate tactics, taking care to marginalise the militants, whenever possible, in the Federation's policy making.

We have already observed that after the 1926 Lock-Out, the SWMF Executive, with the full support of the MMM, had tried the traditional methods of enforcing solidarity amongst the large numbers of men who had become 'nons', members of neither the SWMF nor the SWMIU. Recruitment campaigns were organised with rousing revivalist meetings at which speakers appealed to their listeners' self-respect and honour. Their culmination was the application of moral coercion. A show-cards day was announced for a particular date, well in advance, when Lodge officials would stand at the colliery entrance and ask each miner entering the gates to show their Federation membership card, marked by the Lodge secretary to certify that the bearer was up-to-date with his weekly union subscription. Men who had left or fallen out of compliance were expected to come back into the fold to avoid being publicly shamed. The ritual had been effective in economically favourable conditions. But the collective mood in the coalfield was different from what it had been in the epic days of the Federation's youth at the turn of the century. Moreover, a critical mass of men had lost faith in the Federation. They no longer believed that it could win concessions from the owners or curb managers' arbitrary behaviour. Neither official membership drives nor the MMM's Save the Union campaigns made any permanent impact on the haemorrhage of working miners.

By 1929 the contraction in employment in the coalfield, combined with the failure of Federation lodges to retain all the miners who were working, meant that the Federation faced bankruptcy. Its overblown district bureaucracy had to be decisively pruned in line with its diminished membership. Federation militants had been arguing for greater centralisation, complemented by greater rank-and-file control, since 1910. In 1929 it was Richards and Morell who were determined to press ahead, and convinced the Executive to appoint an Organisation Sub-Committee. After three years deliberation it produced a scheme, which was put before a delegate conference in November 1932. In the absence of support from the left, it was narrowly rejected on a card vote of 48,750 to 40,700. Another subcommittee, jointly composed of Executive members and conference delegates, was appointed to prepare a modified draft.

Horner was released from prison whilst the joint subcommittee was sitting. He told Frankenberg that he had 'a lot to do with framing of new constitution'. His estimation of his own role is highly plausible. He was consulted by his close party colleague, Ianto Evans, a prominent SWMF activist in the Anthracite, who was probably serving on the subcommittee. Four years older than Arthur, Ianto had lived in a village near Tredegar when the two men became foundation party members in 1921. We have observed them both at the Fourth RILU Congress in April 1928, arguing against the rigidities of the New Line. Ianto had moved to the Anthracite in 1924. Probably victimised and unemployed for much of the period after 1927, he had started back to work in 1929 at Cross Hands colliery in the Upper Gwendraeth Valley, and soon became Lodge Chairman. They had little help from the South Wales party, however. Drawing on his experiences of the Rhondda East by-election, Pollitt told an Executive meeting in June that the South Wales district was 'a graveyard'.[363] Many leading comrades had left the coalfield for work in England. Few new recruits had been attracted by the Young Turks' messianic message.

When the second subcommittee's scheme was put before a reconvened delegate conference in March 1933, delegates again failed to ratify it. Horner and the rank-and-file movement evidently intervened to persuade left-wing lodges to change their votes. Despite its undoubted imperfections, they argued that the twice-amended scheme had to go through to enable the Federation to survive. With the exception of revolutionary militants, communist and non-party Federation activists responded to this initiative. In June a delegate conference approved the scheme by a majority of 2 to 1 on a card vote.

Ness Edwards' description of the new scheme bore the marks of someone who had participated in its protracted gestation. The new Executive:

> ... was to consist of rank and file members ... , on the basis of one representative for each 6,000 members. Funds previously kept in districts were to be remitted to the Central Office. All officials [including district agents] were to be servants of the organization as a whole, and were to be paid from Central Funds. Central Departments for Compensation, Finance, and organization were to be set going, and apart from the autonomous powers of lodges, the direction and administration of the affairs of the organization became the tasks of the new Executive ... The [nineteen] old autonomous districts were abolished and eight Area Councils, for reporting purposes only, replaced them. With much 'creaking at the joints' the old form of organization disappeared.[364]

However, until 1 January 1934, the Area Councils operated in tandem with the old district structure and its complement of full-time agents.

Once the scheme had been accepted, the urgent priority for both the Federation and the rank-and-file movement was to defeat the right breakaway, the SWMIU. By 1933 it was well-established in three or four colliery strongholds, where the coalowners had de-recognised the Federation. Together with its larger Nottinghamshire counterpart, the NMIU, the SWMIU constituted a major obstacle to the MFGB achieving the restoration of national wages and conditions. The credibility of the SWMIU had been significantly strengthened by the existence of the NMIU. Although organisationally separate, and registered separately, the South Walian union drew moral and probably financial support from Spencer's union. A former Labour MP and official of the NMA, George Spencer was neither interloper, gold digger nor right-wing evangeliser. The SWMIU general secretary, William Gregory was all of these. He viewed himself as the saviour of British workmen, and believed the SWMIU would be his stepping stone to fame and fortune. His brash charisma helped to keep the SWMIU in the news, and provided a credible front for his self-important claims.

Horner gained up-to-date intelligence and first-hand experience of the NMIU in August 1933, whilst helping Harry Pollitt who was standing in the Clay Cross, Derbyshire by-election. Horner's high profile was a major asset in this predominantly mining constituency. The vacancy was caused by the death of the Labour MP since 1922, Charles Duncan, general secretary of the Workers' Union before its merger with the TGWU in 1929. An intense conflict ensued in the Labour Party about his successor. The Derbyshire Miners Association nominated their left-wing veteran vice-president, Samuel Sales. Bevin vigorously asserted the TGWU's claim. The candidacy was finally secured by the central Labour Party machine for Arthur Henderson. He faced Pollitt and a National Conservative, John Moores, the football pools magnate.

Herbert Howarth, drafted in to help from nearby Sheffield, recalled being shocked at Horner's shabby appearance. 'He had the ass out of his trousers.' Basil Barker, a Chesterfield engineer who was also mobilised for Pollitt, remembered:

> And he were unemployed, out of work, and you know, really – something about him were very unsettling ... Pollitt said, "I want you to go and see Sammy Sales ... Anyway, we went and of course Sammy made a fuss. Went and fetched some bottles of beer ... And then we'd got to get back ... from Sammy Sales which is about half way between Clay Cross and Chesterfield. And Arthur actually got Sammy to give us t'bus fare back – we hadn't got t'bus fare between us – we'd walked it there.[365]

There was a 71.2 per cent turnout at the by-election on 1 September. Pollitt lost his deposit, receiving 3434 votes to Moores' 6293 and Henderson's 21,931 The CPGB had been able to do little more than show its face. However, it is unlikely that either Pollitt or Horner had higher expectations.

Communists active in the Nottinghamshire party were probably given their fares by the party to travel the short distance into Derbyshire to help Pollitt. They came with news about the current state of the NMIU and the low morale amongst NMA loyalists. They would have been keen to renew their friend-ships with Horner, who had not been to the coalfield for some years. He returned to South Wales with discouraging news of the NMIU's good health and secure strategic position. He is likely to have expended time and energy reflecting on his findings before drawing some provisional conclusions.

It was clear that the SWMF was faced a similar situation to the NMA. Nevertheless, there were important differences, both positive and negative from the Federation's vantage-point. The Nottinghamshire coalowners had de-recognised the NMA, and granted sole recognition to the NMIU in 1926. Miners who remained loyal to the NMA gained no material advantage from paying their union subscriptions, neither collective representa-tion nor on-the-job protection. They received only modest social insurance benefits and the moral satisfaction of remaining true to their belief in trade unions which were truly independent of the owners. In contrast, the South Wales coalowners associa-tion adopted a public position of watchful neutrality towards the conflict between the SWMF and the SWMIU. Privately, they encouraged Gregory to undertake recruitment drives, and offered covert financial assistance.

The President of the South Wales coalowners, Evan Williams, was able to follow the Nottinghamshire coalfield vicissitudes closely, from his position as MAGB president. Habitually cau-tious, he was unwilling to take the radical step of de-recognising the SWMF, despite being urged to do so by more volatile col-leagues. Spencer used the threat of an NMA revival to extract regular financial concessions from the Nottinghamshire owners. The South Wales coalowners avoided this pitfall by only recog-nising the SWMIU in its few pit strongholds whilst continuing to recognise the SWMF for district negotiations. They were able to divide and rule with their competing unions. It was problematic for the Federation to mobilise an all-out district strike, because of the likelihood that the SWMIU pits and significant numbers of non-members in others would enable the owners to maintain production.

Horner could now recognise what had been clear to Tom Richards at the end of 1926. The root of the problem was the changed attitude of the coalowners' association to the union. The South Wales owners had no incentive to return to the *status quo ante*. Before Evan Williams would abandon the association's benevolent neutrality towards the SWMIU, the Federation had to show a changed attitude towards economic conflict. The SWMF had to demonstrate a commitment to orderly collective bargaining, and abandon its pre-1914 approach of relying on 100 per cent militant conflict to achieve their aims. By contrast with the Federation, the Durham Miners' Association had swiftly persuaded the Durham coalowners in 1927 to refuse recognition to their local 'non-pol' union, even though the breakaway was gaining members and a high public profile. The owners believed in the DMA's sober moderation, and valued the orderly collective bargaining which had evolved in the coalfield after epic battles in the 1860s. The coalowners' association combined with the DMA to freeze the breakaway out, taking civil court action to enforce their collective agreements.

Horner could also see, however, that the moderation being promoted so assiduously by the SWMF centre bloc was insufficient in the Federation's current dire circumstances. The DMA had gone to the owners with its members' loyalty substantially intact. There had been little loss of membership or collective discipline. In South Wales, the Federation had to regroup its forces for an offensive against the SWMIU. It was apparent that Gregory would not surrender his status and standard of living without a fight. A means would have to be found to pressurise a critical mass of miners who had become habitual 'nons' to make a fresh commitment to the Federation. Horner concluded that a protracted war of attrition would have to be fought to dislodge the SWMIU, and it would have to be fought on Clausewitzian principles rather than the total war approach.

Horner threw all his energies into propagating his new strategy through the only avenue open to him, the rank-and-file movement. The first issue of its fortnightly paper, the *South Wales Miner*, appeared on 26 June 1933, two weeks after the re-organisation scheme had been approved. Horner's recollection, that he was responsible for most of the intellectual and manual labour involved in its production, is plausible. 'I would type out the articles, count the words, because we couldn't afford to pay for any more printing than we had to; then, when the paper arrived, I used to parcel it up, take it to the stations to be sent to the lodges ... '. He was helped by Jack Jones, from Clydach

Vale in mid-Rhondda. A Labour College graduate, he was four years younger than Horner, whom he had probably known since the early 1920s. Victimised in 1927, he had remained unemployed and, like Arthur, was apparently keen to re-enter union activity.[366]

The statutory publisher's address on the *South Wales Miner* was Horner's, 93 Edward Street, Mardy. This expedient avoided acknowledging any overt connection with either the CPGB or the SWMF. A list of the editorial board and their union positions appeared in the second issue, in response to requests from readers for the movement's supporters to declare themselves. There were four members: Horner, described as 'Chairman, Mardy Old Lodge'; two others from the Rhondda Fach, David James Davies, Chairman of Ferndale Lodge, and Will Parfitt, disputes agent and checkweighman, Tylorstown; and H Lewis, member of the Cambrian Lodge Committee. Evidently, only Horner's veteran allies from the Rhondda No. 1 District felt sufficiently secure to associate themselves publicly with the new movement. (Jack Jones may have been omitted from the list because he was hoping to get work in the Anthracite and therefore needed a low profile.)

Horner recalled the *South Wales Miner*'s circulation as being 3000. '[I]t was read by nearly all the active trade unionists ... and I think it had a lot to do with my victory when I came to stand for the Presidency'.[367] This conclusion is not unreasonable. Because the MFGB and the SWMF had discontinued their journals due to straitened finances, it was the only reliable source of information about mining trade union matters at a time when there were significant changes and developments. The SWMF's new structure involved elections for the new executive positions, enabling greater opportunities for rank-and-file activists to influence union affairs and Lodge Committee men to advance themselves. Morrell was due to retire as Federation President in April 1934, and it was widely expected that Griffiths would win the election to succeed him. Arthur Jenkins, Ruskin-educated and Monmouthshire County Councillor, was the favourite to succeed him as Vice-President. These imminent changes engendered renewed interest in union affairs amongst ordinary members, aspiring office-seekers, and above all those interested in politics on both left and right.

Horner had abundant time to lavish on writing the *South Wales Miner*, and he had something new to say to Federation activists. Producing the rank-and-file paper enabled him to develop his ideas into accessible, persuasive prose. The editorial line was that the Federation could be revitalised by involving the rank-and-file membership. It could become a *real* union again by mobilising strong support from below to successfully challenge the coalowners and the rival SWMIU. Armed with Clausewitz, Horner could also provide a coherent answer to the centre bloc's insistence that any offensive strategy involving industrial conflict would risk the destruction of the Federation's depleted forces.

Soon after his return from Clay Cross in September 1933, Horner spoke at a meeting of the rank-and-file movement in the Anthracite District, at Pontyates in the Gwendraeth Valley. It had probably been organised to promote the rank-and-file movement's candidates in the first elections for the newly re-organised Federation Executive. But another Federation election was also likely. One of the Anthracite agents, William Jones, was seriously ill. Under the re-organisation plan, Federation districts would remain in existence until 1934. If Jones were to die within the next few months, a successor would need to be chosen.

Horner recalled in the third interview with Frankenberg that during a break in the conference, he was standing by the bridge over the Gwendraeth River, and some delegates asked him to stand for the agent's position should the opportunity arise. His initial response was disbelief. He was neither Welsh-speaking, a requirement for full-time officials in the Anthracite, nor a current SWMF member. However, his erstwhile supporters cited a precedent in relation to Federation membership. Whilst working for the Labour Party in the early 1920s, Jim Griffiths had allowed his SWMF membership to lapse. He had nevertheless been allowed to stand in 1925 for the Anthracite agent's position in 1925 and been elected.

When the Executive election results were announced in mid-September, the case for Horner standing for agent was significantly strengthened. In the new Area No. 1, combining the Anthracite and Western Districts, rank-and-file movement candidates, Ianto Evans and Gomer Evans, had won two of the three contested seats. Gomer Evans was a left-wing Labour activist and unapologetic ally of the Anthracite's pragmatic communists. He had attended the Central Labour College in 1923 to 1925, and lectured for the NCLC on his return. In 1933, he was checkweighman and lodge secretary at Trimsaran colliery in the Lower Gwendraeth Valley and a Carmarthenshire County Councillor.

Horner's chances had been further improved by the fact that a leading right-wing Federation activist from Cross Hands, who was keenly interested in the agent's position, was also a monoglot English-speaker. Carmarthenshire County Councillor Edgar Lewis had been actively canvassing in the district for the Welsh language requirement to be waived. After William Jones' death, Horner's supporters made their move. At an Area No. 1 conference, Gomer Evans proposed that there should be no bar to either Horner or Lewis standing.[368] Ianto Evans was in the chair; he ruled that conference delegates could vote freely, i.e. without being mandated by their lodges, a process which would have entailed at least a week's adjournment – sufficient time for a backlash to build up amongst conservatives from left and right. Since both Lewis and Horner camps were anxious to commence their campaigns, Gomer's motion was passed immediately.

Horner was now compelled to consider seriously his position. Although his emotional and political ties with Mardy were profound, Rhondda No.1 District party and union comrades wanted him to stand. He believed that his future lay inside the Federation, because he was the only activist capable of rescuing the union from obscurity and impotence. His acquisition of a Clausewitzian strategy had reinforced his commitment to this mission, to which he had felt called since the early 1920s. The prospect of receiving a secure living wage would also have been a great incentive. The party Secretariat were publicly encouraging communists to stand for full-time union positions, and Pollitt probably added his personal reinforcement to the official view.

However, even if he decided to stand, his victory was far from certain. The odds remained stacked against the leading Communist English-speaking outsider from Little Moscow. Having weighed up these considerations, Horner agreed to stand. When the election campaign commenced in mid-October, he was geared up to win. The electorate comprised 16,500 to 17,000 SWMF members. Horner faced fourteen candidates. Of these, Horner and Alderman JD Brazell from Ystalyfera, in the Swansea Valley and adjacent Western District, were the only candidates from outside the Anthracite. Apart from Edgar Lewis, the others were standing with no expectations of winning; they were either favourite sons who accepted their lodge's nominations as a badge of honour or young men with ambition, who viewed the election as an opportunity to become known in the district. Nevertheless, their numbers made the contest difficult to predict. SWMF elections were conducted on the exhaustive vote system. If no candidate received an absolute majority of votes over the combined total of the other candidates, those with the lowest number of votes were progressively eliminated. With fifteen candidates, three ballots would probably be required.

Horner decamped in the Anthracite for the duration. He told Frankenberg that the fight 'was as intense as any parliamentary election'. In *Incorrigible Rebel* he recalled: 'My supporters and I used to distribute leaflets at the pit-heads from the first morning shift to the last shift at night.'[369] He stayed for a while with a comrade in the pit village of Pontyberem in the mid-Gwendraeth Valley, whilst using Edgar and Dolly Bassett's house in Ammanford as his campaign headquarters. In the later stages, he moved in with the Bassetts. Edgar Bassett was a pillar of the community, managing the large Ammanford Co-operative Society, with excellent business and social connections throughout the Anthracite. Like David Evans in Porth, his communist party membership was kept discreetly quiet. But his left-wing opinions were hardly clandestine. Arthur's status as his house guest was a positive asset in the campaign. Ammanford was a large, prosperous town, some four miles east of the Gwendraeth Valley, where printing facilities and meeting rooms could be easily obtained using Bassett's influence. An ironic twist was Bassett's long-standing close friendship with Jim Griffiths, originating in their both being keen ILP members and pacifists during World War I.[370]

Horner's supporters concentrated on his proven ability to extract concessions from the owners, arguing that he was simply the best man for the job. They paid special attention to the many miners who were working and lodging in the Anthracite whilst their families and permanent homes remained in the East Glamorgan and Monmouthshire coalfields. Horner's inability to speak Welsh was the subject of much partisan correspondence

261

in the *South Wales Voice*, a weekly paper published in Ystalyfera. Founded at the turn of the twentieth century as *Llais Llafur* (Voice of Labour), it had initially been a Welsh language paper. By 1933 it was published largely in English. The *Voice* covered the election in detail. On 28 October it reported, 'a rush for ballot papers' and there were signs of a record vote:

> ... though only a few of those running for the post have published election matter. There was, however, much speculation as to the candidates polling the highest number of votes. It is safe to presume that [a candidate from] the Gwendraeth Valley will be represented in the final election, which is to prove one of the keenest contests in the anthracite district in recent years.

The interest aroused in the contest caused literally scores of public meetings to be convened by various groups throughout the Anthracite District. Horner's reputation as a magnetic speaker meant that meetings which included him attracted larger audiences, and they were often held in cinemas to accommodate the crowds. None of the other candidates could match his command of language, his understanding of coalfield issues and emotional fervour. (The *Voice*, Horner's most vociferous detractor, nevertheless acknowledged: 'His speeches are marked with great lucidity and clarity of expression, and are delivered with great force and vehemence.'[371])

There was a 90 per cent turn-out in the first ballot. The two outsiders, Horner and Brazell, came first and second, followed by Edgar Lewis and DB Lewis, from Cross Hands. The *Voice* report carried a sizeable photograph of Brazell, accompanied by the headline, 'BALLOT FOR MINERS' AGENT. Ald. J.D. Brazell in Second Round.' Four paragraphs singing his praises followed, including an oblique apologia for his lacklustre oratory, ending with the assertion, 'there can be no doubt that if elected, Ald. Brazell will more than justify the appointment.'[372] In the second and third ballots Horner's opponents sought to discredit him by raising Rhondda canards. The *Voice* stories carried insinuations and assertions against the man from Mardy, which were magnified and embroidered in readers' letters and editorials. Horner's rampant, unchecked militancy was blamed for the Mardy pit closures. His loyalty to the disaffiliated Mardy Lodge and consequent ineligibility for Federation membership were condemned as beyond the pale. The Horner campaign vigorously countered these allegations at public meetings and in leaflets. His supporters wrote rebuttal letters to the *Voice*, some of which were published.

There was an even higher turn-out for the second ballot, on 7 to 8 November, precipitating allegations about election malpractice in the *Voice*'s letters column. The result was a sensation. Although the order of the candidates remained unchanged, Horner pulled decisively ahead of Brazell, by a margin of nearly 3500 votes. Reporting the result, the *Voice* put on a brave face. 'It is interesting to note that although the votes cast for Mr. Horner in the second ballot were over 40 per cent. above those in favour of Mr. Brazell, signs are not wanting to show that in the final contest the latter has exceedingly good chances of topping the poll. Both unsuccessful candidates [Edgar Lewis and DB Lewis] are enthusiastic supporters of Mr. Brazell.'[373]

A four page newspaper, *Horner Special in Answer to the Lies and Slander of the Press and Opponents*, appeared late in the campaign. Published by the Anthracite Militant Miners Committee, it included a prominent article by Sam Davies, the Siloam Chapel deacon and Communist, described as Secretary of the Mardy Federation Lodge, without reference to its disaffiliated status. He replied to a letter from 'Pauper', an unemployed miner from Mardy, which had appeared in the *Voice* on 11 November 'Pauper' had charged:

> First, I wish to say we had had reason in Mardy to agree that these people [Communists] are only in the organisation [SWMF] for personal gain. Now that the town is derelict, most of these leaders have deserted the place ... We are now the paupers of the coalfield ... Many of us blame the Communists for the state of affairs in the town. Mr. D.L. Davies, who was Mr. Horner's right hand man, was chairman of the lodge and local institute, a councillor and checkweigher, three nice little jobs when Mardy was prosperous ... [He] is now a capitalist! He owns a dairy business and milk round in London. Mr. Charles Williams, another Communist, and who

was local secretary is now working with R.O.P. [Russian Oil Products], and so is Mr. Reg. Simmons ... If any of your readers doubt what I have written, let them come to Mardy and see for themselves. They will see 1,200 people drawing the dole, with about 800 depending on the Public Assistance Committees. They will see the kiddies going to school, with their toes out through their boots, and their clothes in rags. The Communists will say that all this is due to depression in trade, but it is due to their activities.

Sam Davies replied:

It is alleged that Arthur Horner is in the movement for personal gain ... [H]e is now dependent upon unemployment benefit. We challenge all comers to show another person who has sacrificed as much as Arthur Horner for the principles he believes in. He is now contesting for the position of miners' agent only by the consent of the Mardy workmen, who think it is a crime he should be shut out of Fed. activity in this period of grave crisis for the miners ... The Mardy workmen (in whose name I write) declare that if you elect Arthur Horner ... you will render a great service to yourselves and to the miners of the whole coalfield.

The Horner campaign organised a meeting at Gwaun-cae-Gurwen, on Sunday evening, 12 November. It was the third meeting the Horner campaign had organised for this large group of collieries employing over 2000 men, and was extensively reported by the *Voice*. Sam Davies was on the platform in the 'crowded out' hall. He praised Horner: 'almost all the reforms gained by the workmen must be attributed to his strenuous agitation and indomitable courage'. Having explained that he himself had worked at Mardy for 45 years, 'he, the speaker, alleged that the ruin of Mardy Colliery was definitely attributable to mismanagement.'

Horner spoke for over an hour, and:

dealt with international and mining problems, attribut-
ing the existing crises to the failure of capitalism to function progressively. Towards the conclusion, he appealed
for a renewal of confidence to place him first in the final
ballot. He promised them no miracles. Some people
thought he was a wild man, but his policy in industrial
strife was first to knock at the front door and if the door
was not opened, to smash it up.[374]

In its 18 November issue the *Voice* announced a final meeting
featuring Brazell and Horner on Sunday evening 19 November
at Gwaun-cae-Gurwen Welfare Hall, organised at the request
of three Federation lodges. 'It is anticipated that there will be
a crowded house, representative of all quarters of the upper
regions of the Amman and Swansea Valleys. In no previous election for a Miners' Agent ... has excitement and speculation run
so high as to the winner.'[375] Horner and Brazell spoke again at
a later meeting that evening in Ystradgynlais. These may have
been the first occasions when audiences could compare the two
men side-by-side.
   Horner's performance may have swayed a critical number of
undecided voters. Horner's majority over Brazell in the third
ballot was nearly three thousand, only slightly lower than his
lead in the second ballot on a marginally lower turn-out. Miners
who had voted for Edgar Lewis and DB Lewis in previous ballots
had cast their votes roughly evenly between Horner and Brazell.
The result was officially declared on Saturday 25 November at
a meeting of district officers in the Mackworth Hotel, Swansea.
Horner's dramatic victory had immediate repercussions. The
Voice reported that rumours were circulating that Edgar Lewis
would seek an injunction preventing Horner from taking office
because of his membership in the disaffiliated Mardy Lodge.[376]
   From the outset of the campaign, Horner and his supporters
had speculated that if he won, the Federation Executive would
set the election result aside on the same pretext. They had
accordingly taken precautions during the third ballot. Horner
told Frankenberg that 'Anthracite held firm' behind him. Ianto
Evans had apparently approached other Anthracite District
officers, who agreed that if Horner were elected, he should
be given a chance to prove his loyalty to the Federation. On 2

December the *Voice* reported that John James, Agent and District Secretary, had sent Horner a telegram on 24 November about the Mackworth Hotel meeting. 'Mr. Horner attended the district meeting by invitation, and he was welcomed as the elected agent for the Gwendraeth Valley by each of the district officials. It was decided that he should commence duties immediately.' The article noted that the Federation Executive had decided to accept the election result, even though the rules clearly precluded Horner, a non-member, from taking office. Whilst Edgar Lewis might take out an injunction, '[i]t is more than likely that the position will be accepted, and that no action will be taken.'

The other Anthracite agents closed ranks very publicly behind Horner. When Horner and Brazell had spoken at Ystradgynlais, the issue of Mardy Lodge's expulsion from the Federation had so inflamed emotions that a further meeting had been arranged for Sunday evening 26 November to clear the air. To accommodate the anticipated numbers, it was held at the Astoria Cinema, Ystalyfera. Griffiths was booked to give the Federation Executive's version of events, with Horner and Brazell supplying rejoinders. After Horner's victory, Brazell declined to attend. The *Voice* report of the meeting noted that Griffiths and Horner 'were given a good hearing, the large audience sitting patiently for nearly three hours', and that '[b]oth speakers appealed for unity in the ranks'.

Griffiths confined himself to a full narrative of events, taking care to acknowledge Horner's absence at the critical SWMF delegate conference which had heard Mardy Lodge's appeal against its expulsion in January 1930. He also reminded his audience of the disruptive behaviour of Mardy's supporters on that day. 'Some of the delegates even stood on chairs, waved their hats, and shouted.' Horner agreed with this 'recital of events'. But he reminded the audience of the incident during the 1926 Lock-Out when the Rhondda Labour Party had split over whether to support a scheme for feeding miners' children. This oblique reference to the faults of the official Labour Party in the Rhondda (failure to affiliate to it had been a prima facie cause of Mardy Lodge's expulsion) was evidently intended to plant the suggestion in the audience's mind that the lodge had been justified in defying the official Labour machine. Horner, however, declined to press this point home. He concluded with diplomatic emollience. 'Whatever Mardy had done had been done with one objective, to maintain a decent standard for their fellow-workers. The Lodge and members were ready to join and desirous of rejoining the Federation, because they believed that in unity alone could great things be achieved. His aim was to secure solidarity, as there was no hope for success unless everyone was solid for the principles of the Federation.'

Once it was apparent that the Federation would accept the election result, the *Voice* was also emollient. Its first editorial after Horner's victory declared: 'During the campaign we opposed Mr. Horner as vigorously as possible, and we do not regret it ... If Mr. Horner takes advantage of his position to conduct Communist propaganda in the coalfield, we shall again oppose him; if, on the other hand, he is loyal to the body he now serves, he will receive the support of all right thinking men and women. There is more than a possibility that the Communists will know Mr. Horner no more, for his recent associations with them have not been happy.'[377]

On 30 December, the *Voice* reported a dinner that had been held on 23 December to celebrate the Anthracite District's history, on the eve of its disappearance on 1 January 1934. There were 120 members present, including twenty former district chairmen. As agent, Horner was one of the guests. But he was also accorded the notable honour of being one of the speakers, evidence not only of Ianto Evans' use of his chairman's prerogative, but also that the other agents were keen to test Horner's mettle as a loyal servant of the Federation.

The remaining members of the disaffiliated Mardy Lodge discreetly disbanded it in February 1934, and re-joined the SWMF as unemployed members, as they were entitled to do under the Federation's new rules.[378] They and Horner had evidently decided that disbanding before his election would give a dangerous hostage to anti-communist fortunes. But after his victory, they could take this step back into the fold with honour. Now that coalfield unity on the left had been re-established, the Federation and Horner could concentrate on attacking the breakaway union, the SWMIU.

Chapter 9

The Datcha in the Anthracite

The scab union

Horner commenced his new job as Federation Agent for the Gwendraeth Valley on Monday 27 November 1933, two days after the election result had been declared. Having re-thought his approach to the economic struggle, he was not unprepared. In the year since his release from Cardiff gaol, he had had ample opportunity to experiment with different ways of explaining his Clausewitzian principles. He evolved metaphors and examples to make his case, as he had done in Churches of Christ pulpits and at the Unofficial Reform Committee meetings. On 28 December he attended the Special MFGB Delegate Conference, and intervened in the high profile debate on the Executive's proposals for a wages strategy. He and Bevan spoke against the proposals on behalf of the SWMF delegation.[379] They both argued that the MFGB should take the offensive and press for substantial improvements in wages and conditions.

Horner quickly mastered the complex detail of the collieries on his new patch. He probably enjoyed discovering the variation in collective bargaining arrangements and learning the complicated web of local custom and practice. He lodged in Pontyberem whilst searching for a comfortable house with sufficient accommodation for his family and his official duties. Federation Agents were expected to live in the part of the coalfield for which they were responsible. Their home was also their office, where lodge officials and members could call to discuss problems, formulate grievances and fill in the paperwork for industrial injury and industrial disease cases, which were a major part of a Federation agent's job.[380]

At the end of January 1934 Horner rented a bungalow in Upper Tumble on the edge of the upper Gwendraeth Fawr valley, nine miles north of Llanelli on the A476. Ethel and the children moved in mid-February. Their new home stood on a substantial piece of land in beautiful, open countryside. The setting evidently reminded Arthur of the dacha they had shared in Russia. He christened it 'The Datcha'. The address was recognised by the postman and the GPO clerks who forwarded Arthur's mail to MI5. The rural location did not motivate Arthur to learn to drive. Instead, Tom Evans, a Federation activist in the Labour Party who lived nearby, became a fast friend and used his motor car to ferry Arthur about on union business. The Horners had only moved about twenty-five miles, but the psychological distance between Upper Tumble and Mardy was immense. Everyone thrived in the new space. The Datcha became the setting for house parties, with Arthur's and Ethel's friends and family coming to stay. Ethel took advantage of the roomy house to entertain comrades from Mardy whom she judged to be in need of respite care. Charlie and Hannah Jones were frequent guests; since Charlie was unemployed, they regularly stopped for days on end. It is not clear how, or even whether, Arthur and Ethel disposed of 93 Edward Street, Mardy. But back in regular employment on a reasonable wage, Arthur resumed repaying his father the £200 he had used to buy the house. Given the demands of a growing family, the process was protracted. Having experienced the dilemma of negative equity, Arthur vowed never to buy property again.[381] Horner was also conscious of a political debt, to his editorial assistant on *South Wales Miner*, Jack Jones of Blaenclydach. Horner and Ianto Evans are likely to have been instrumental in arranging Jack Jones' election as checkweighman at Cross Hands, a large colliery on Horner's patch, in mid-July 1934.

Horner settled comfortably into a new routine. His habitual amiability eased his way into an office where the clerks and shorthand typists may have been apprehensive about meeting the Dictator of Mardy. He established stable working relations with the other three agents, including Jim Griffiths. Along with them, he spent some time every week at the Area No.1 office in Swansea discharging administrative duties.[382] They also travelled to Cardiff regularly to attend meetings at the Federation head office and confer with Oliver Harris and the head of the Compensation Department, Evan Williams.

Operating in the hothouses of the CPGB and NMM head offices had given Horner a strong aversion to working in atmospheres of intense personal and political conflict. He thrived amongst the mundane comings and goings of the busy Federation offices, where the culture revolved around providing efficient administration. The Federation's links with New Unionism meant that, compared to older district coalfield unions, SWMF officers operated in a comparatively egalitarian style. Having been habitually frustrated by the thankless labour of typing the *South Wales Miner* and agitational leaflets with two fingers, Horner appreciated the services of the clerks and shorthand-typists in the Swansea office, and the labour-saving luxuries of being able to dictate correspondence and delegate his filing.

Horner's return to union activity coincided with a generational change in the MFGB leadership. Non-communists in Horner's age cohort were succeeding to high union office. Ebby Edwards, aged forty-eight, had defeated Joseph Jones and WH Mainwaring to become MFGB Secretary in succession to Cook in February 1932. Joseph Jones, aged forty-two, was subsequently elected MFGB Vice-President at the MFGB Annual Conference in July. When Peter Lee, the incumbent MFGB President, died in 1933, aged sixty-nine, Jones won the election to succeed him. Will Lawther, aged forty-five, was elected Vice-President in Jones' place in 1934. Of the three national officers, Joseph Jones was the most right-wing. He and Lawther were both immensely intellectually capable and personally ambitious. They also possessed the overweening self-confidence necessary to lead a large national union.

Parallel changes were taking place in the MFGB's affiliated district unions. Jim Bowman, aged thirty-seven, succeeded the long-serving William Straker as general secretary of the Northumberland miners in January 1935. In South Wales, we have already observed that Oliver Harris, in his fifties, had succeeded Tom Richards as general secretary in November 1931. Enoch Morrell had retired as SWMF President in March 1934. At the union's Annual Conference in April, the election to replace him was won, as widely predicted, by Jim Griffiths, aged forty-four. Arthur Jenkins, aged forty-seven, was the front runner to take his place as Vice-President. Arthur Horner, who had just turned forty, was again eligible as an SWMF member to stand against him, and did so. On a card vote, he received 40,100 votes to Jenkins' 42,050.[383] The close result showed that Horner's victory in the Anthracite was not an aberration. In Durham, the deaths of two DMA leaders in 1934 to 1935 created vacancies for full-time agents. In July 1936, after an unprecedented three ballots of the membership, one of the positions was won by an outsider, Sam Watson, aged thirty-eight. Like Bowman, he had a left-wing, and even Marxist, reputation.

This new cohort were determined to make their mark on the MFGB's fortunes. Even though they occupied different positions on the political spectrum, they had nevertheless drawn similar conclusions from the 1920s coal wars. They were united in advocating progressive, forward-looking policies, which they believed would enable the MFGB to win a national wages agreement and restore miners' wages to their pre-war levels. They all recognised that Smith's and Cook's reliance on a total war strategy had failed. Although they had all reflected about how to conduct the campaign differently this time round, Horner had gone the furthest in evolving a coherent strategy. Joseph Jones had been refining tactics for applying pressure on the government. At his first MFGB Annual Conference as president in July 1934, he piloted a resolution through that called on the Executive to take immediate steps to achieve a National Wages Agreement, with wages at 20 per cent above their present average rate, and the restoration of a seven-hour working day with no compulsory overtime.

The MFGB Executive and most delegates recognised that the union was in no position to achieve these ambitious demands. The national coalowners' association, the MAGB, was still dominated by Evan Williams. He was adamantly opposed to a return to national bargaining, and had no intention of conceding to a seven-hour day. Moreover, the MFGB could not credibly threaten to unleash an effective national strike. The Nottinghamshire owners' refusal to recognise the NMA and the high degree of non-unionism in South Wales meant that even if all affiliated district unions came out, coal would still be produced in significant quantities. The new leadership cohort were not discouraged, however. The 1934 conference resolution was their first

271

move in a long game to build political momentum and muster public support.

Because the British economy was showing the first signs of recovering from the shocks of 1929 to 1931, the domestic market for coal was expanding. Coalowners in the exporting districts had already contracted their undertakings, dismissed significant numbers of workers and tried to gain entry into the domestic market for their reduced output. The contraction in miners' numbers and improved prospects for coal made a significant increase in wages for those miners who remained a practical demand; but the MFGB Executive did not expect the MAGB to concede a national increase except under duress. In order to bounce the National Government into pressurising the coalowners, they needed to build a plausible united, national force which could present a credible threat to national coal production.

Horner's re-entry into the SWMF occurred on this terrain. In January 1934 he attended an SWMF delegate conference for the first time since 1929, and took the lead in opposing the Executive's proposals for a modest revision of the Schiller Award. He remembered arguing for the more ambitious demands which the rank-and-file movement and the *South Wales Miner* were promoting. He had proposed a Miners' Charter accompanied by a campaign that would culminate in handing in notices for a coalfield strike. Horner recalled:

> The clash [between Horner and the SWMF Executive] was whether we should threaten strike action or attempt to negotiate. I believed in negotiation but I also believed in making it clear that we would use our strength if we had to. I intervened ... after a defeatist speech by a delegate ... who said that the industry was in such a bad way and that the coal owners were suffering so much loss that it was impossible for the miners to get anything at all ... [He] wanted us to wait another three years on the old plea that we might get a Labour Government. I took the floor and I said that the coal owners had brought the industry to ruin and that was no reason why the miners should continue on starvation wages ... Jim Griffiths ... replied to me and said that in main he agreed with all I had said, but he thought it would be better to

272

go to the coal owners first with demands more in accord
with the economic situation of the industry; he agreed
that the miners would have to fight for their demands
but he thought it would be unwise at that stage ... [384]

When the delegate conference opted for the Executive proposals, Horner loyally accepted the decision, although he continued
to urge more militant action after Griffiths' election as President
in April 1934.

Although Horner reduced his time commitment to the
South Wales Miners' Rank and File Movement and the *South
Wales Miner*, he maintained his political leadership of the activists involved. Most of the writing and production of the *South
Wales Miner* still took place at the communist party offices in
Tonypandy. Cox recalled that he, Jack Jones and Lewis Jones
had taken responsibility for production. Paynter continued his
own participation. It is likely that Horner relied on Paynter to
ensure that editorial policy continued to stress the importance
of working loyally inside the Federation. Horner also widened
the movement's catchment area to include his new home patch.
Although the unofficial newspaper was being read by Federation
lodges throughout the coalfield, activity around the rank-and-
file movement was largely confined to the Rhondda, where veteran activists (communist and non-communist) from different
lodges were in the habit of meeting together in a mutually convenient place to discuss union issues. On 19 September 1934,
the *Daily Worker* reported that the Rank-and-File Movement had
held a conference at Ammanford, chaired by Jack Jones, with
delegates from eleven lodges, probably all from the Anthracite.
The conference elected an additional sub-editorial board for
the *South Wales Miner* from amongst its number. Horner may
have anticipated that it would provide a useful counter-weight
to revolutionary militants in the Rhondda, who were holding
fast to their principled belief in total industrial war, as the only
effective means of winning workers' demands.[385]

Early in January 1934, Horner executed the first moves in
a campaign to uproot the SWMIU at the Emlyn colliery, near
Penygroes, in the Upper Gwendraeth Valley, the only colliery in
the Anthracite where the scab union was recognised. The Emlyn
No. 1 Slant had opened in 1904; when the No. 2 Slant had

begun raising coal in 1926, it was an ideal opportunity for the SWMIU to recruit the new employees. Management had recognised the SWMIU in the No. 2 Slant, and Federation membership had fallen away in the No. 1 Slant. A membership drive in 1931 to revive the SWMF in the No. 1 Slant and establish a base at the No. 2 Slant had been unsuccessful.

Horner may have discussed possible strategies for dislodging the SWMIU at Emlyn with Ianto Evans and Gomer Evans before his election as agent. Although the colliery was not on his patch, Horner's arrival in the Anthracite raised local Federation loyalists' expectations. As newly elected members of the Federation Executive, they apparently interceded with SO Davies, the new full-time head of the union's Organisation Department, to depute Horner to lead the attack on Emlyn. SO Davies had remained firmly on the left, and remained on cordial terms with Horner. He agreed that Horner should be seconded and obtained the approval of the other agents in Area No. 1. The details of Horner's secondment were easily arranged. Since Gomer Evans was checkweighman at one of the largest collieries on Horner's patch, and an experienced lodge official, he could deputise for him and deal with individual cases and minor problems at other pits.

Horner's plan was to bore from within. To do this, he had to find Federation loyalists who could establish an effective Federation presence underground. Using personal and Federation networks, he succeeded in establishing effective intelligence in the No. 2 Slant. When the Federation cell persuaded a miner to resume his Federation membership, he was encouraged to also maintain his SWMIU membership to avoid suspicion and victimisation. Whilst building up a clandestine Federation majority, Horner provided the public face of the SWMF, addressing 'mass meetings of the men on top of the slant despite being "warned off" by the company'.[386]

By the end of April, he was sufficiently confident to launch an all-out offensive. The Federation members, who now constituted a majority in the slant, declared themselves and voted to dissolve the SWMIU Lodge. In a dazzling coup, the SWMIU lodge chairman turned coat to become chairman of the new Federation Lodge. The scab union checkweighman was sacked by majority vote, and Ianto Evans elected in his stead. But the new lodge had to win recognition from the owners. Ianto's constant presence at the slant head would provide essential stiffening for the men in the next, critical stage, when a counter-offensive from Gregory was anticipated. The SWMIU made no attempt, however, to regain its hold at Emlyn, instead relying on management to resist the Federation.

Horner and the Federation Lodge officials made their move in June, presenting a claim for a return to the customs, wages and conditions enjoyed by Federation members in the rest of the Anthracite. When the owners refused, 900 men came out on strike, supported by a levy from the other Anthracite lodges. SO Davies had been elected Labour MP for Merthyr in a by-election on 5 June, and vacated his Organisation Department post.[387] The Organisation Department was subsequently disbanded by the Executive, presumably as a costly experiment which had produced few results. Horner assumed sole charge of the Emlyn dispute, reporting directly to the SWMF officers and Executive.

After nine weeks out on strike, the Emlyn men returned to work without having obtained either material concessions or recognition for the Federation lodge. Nevertheless, in these adverse circumstances Horner had organised the retreat to keep his forces united and give himself time to organise a superior force capable of inflicting greater damage. On 24 August, the *Daily Worker* reported that the Anthracite Combine Committee delegate conference had voted to give fourteen days notice of a strike to support the Emlyn members' demands. This declaration of serious intent apparently frightened the other Anthracite owners into pressurising their Emlyn counterparts to give way. On 6 September the *Daily Worker* reported that the company had negotiated a settlement with the SWMF. Ianto Evans told the full story on 15 September. The men in both Emlyn slants had threatened to down tools and come out with the rest of the Anthracite. 'No small measure of the credit is due to Comrade Arthur Horner, who while not being an agent in charge of the Emlyn collieries, threw himself wholeheartedly into the struggle and when it was decided to retreat temporarily, no other man could have persuaded the strikers of the advisability of this step and maintain their confidence and keep up their morale.'[388]

The victory was the Federation's first advance since Red Friday in 1925. It had a potent effect on Federation loyalists' expectations. Horner's standing rose, and communists who were active in the Federation benefited from his enhanced status.[389] For the first time since the Lock-Out, it seemed possible to regain the Federation's pre-1926 bargaining position. Griffiths had been elected SWMF President on a platform of continuing the prudent moderation practised by Richards and Morell. He recalled a consultation with the Federation's London solicitor. 'I told him that what we contemplated was to sue the colliery company in the name of the first workman ... to be sacked because he refused to allow deduction from his pay towards the Spencer Union [SWMIU], and seek an injunction ... [He replied], "I agree the contract you have described is wicked, but a lot of things are wicked without being illegal. You will have to find some other remedy ... "'[390]

Griffiths and the more audacious Executive members were anxious to try Horner's method of 'boring within' on other targets. The two collieries where the SWMIU enjoyed sole recognition were about seven miles apart in the Federation Area No.6, which incorporated the old East Glamorgan and the Rhymney Valley districts. Taff-Merthyr was jointly owned by the Ocean and Powell-Duffryn companies. Bedwas was owned by a small independent company, the Bedwas Navigation Colliery Company (1921) Ltd. Also in Area No. 6, the SWMIU and the SWMF were both recognised at the Nine Mile Point colliery, owned by the Ocean company, not far from Risca in the lower Sirhowy Valley.

After Emlyn, the Federation Executive were hopeful that the SWMIU could be routed in its other strongholds, enabling the SWMF to regain its former pole position. Then the 'nons', miners who had dropped out of the union in 1926 to 1927, could be persuaded/pressurised back into the Federation. Lodge officials had been unable to persuade them to re-join, even in the majority of South Wales collieries where the Federation still had sole recognition. Working alongside 'nons' was a constant irritant for SWMF loyalists, who viewed them as free-loaders, taking advantage of the wages and conditions won by the Federation. In collieries with large numbers of 'nons', lodge morale suffered. The Federation's ability to pressurise the coalowners was also weakened.

276

In the summer of 1934, Ness Edwards, agent for Area No. 6, and Billy Crews, recently elected Executive member for the area, established an ad hoc organising committee with the intention of mounting challenges to the SWMIU at Taff-Merthyr and Bedwas. They were assisted by Noah Ablett, still Federation agent at Merthyr, and Glyn Jones, secretary of the nearby Penallta Lodge. They began to tour the Taff Valley, throwing out feelers. 'They discovered that only the unemployed [miners] would talk to them freely ... They [then] produced a leaflet, "A Call for Action", sketching the role the Federation would like to see adopted by the men working in the two collieries ... [It] met with an "unexpectedly cordial" reception from Taff-Merthyr men ... '[391]

The ad hoc organising committee decided to concentrate the Federation's resources on Taff-Merthyr, and leave an assault on Bedwas until a more favourable time. In addition to the miners' positive response to 'A Call for Action', there was a communist enclave in the nearby village of Bedlinog, whose activists could be mobilised to help. Finally, there were the substantial human, moral and financial resources of the Federation's Ocean Combine Committee. The Anthracite Combine Committee's threat of a combine-wide strike had been a major factor in persuading the owners to make concessions at Emlyn. It was fortuitous that the Ocean Combine Committee were currently engaged in an organising campaign to compel 'nons' working at all Ocean collieries to (re)join the Federation.

The Taff-Merthyr Steam Coal Company Limited had begun raising coal in 1926, when the SWMIU had taken advantage of the national Lock-Out to recruit members. In 1929, when there were 1500 men employed, the Taff-Merthyr management responded to the Federation's organising efforts by granting sole recognition to the SWMIU. The colliery was in East Glamorgan, 'in a small valley [the Taff-Bargoed] between the [old SWMF] Dowlais and Taff and Cynon Districts ... between the small villages of Bedlinog to the north-west and Trelewis to the south, with Treharris just beyond'.[392] The villages' growth in the late 1870s had coincided with the opening of two pits, Bedlinog and Nantwen, which had both closed in 1924.

The Federation Executive had appointed paid collectors to position themselves at all collieries with a high SWMIU membership in 1929 to 1930. But although they had made progress at the Ocean's Parc and Dare collieries in Rhondda Fawr, there was no advance at Taff-Merthyr. Nevertheless, SO Davies, at that time agent for Dowlais, had continued the campaign there. His report to the Federation Executive in 1930 was bleak. The men at Taff-Merthyr were 'kept on a Day-to-day Contract – this is a most effective Victimisation weapon ... [H]undreds of men have been victimised because of their resisting the Non. Pol. Union'.[393]

After 1930, the only opposition to the SWMIU at Taff-Merthyr came from the village of Bedlinog, where a militant political culture had flourished since the early 1920s. 'The ... main street and its tributaries ascend, from the village square, a 1-in-3 hill ... [There was a] relatively high proportion of North and mid-Walians ... whose isolation allowed for a strong Welsh-speaking tradition ... '.[394] A left-wing presence had been maintained in this enclave, probably due to the leadership qualities of Edgar Evans, a leading communist, who presided over 'meetings at a brick hut on Bedlinog Square ("the Kremlin") [which] initiated many young, unemployed miners into the YCL and the CP'.[395] Both NUWM and CPGB branches flourished; members probably spent much enforced leisure time debating at Evans' ironmongers shop, also in the Square. When Ness Edwards succeeded SO Davies as agent in 1932, he stopped at the ironmongers shop in Bedlinog to gather the local news after he had conducted union business at neighbouring collieries.

Combine Committees had been formed on an ad hoc basis in the late 1920s in response to the increasing concentration of ownership in the coalfield. During the post-war economic slump, many small coalowners had sold out at knock-down prices to larger companies, known as combines in popular parlance. In 1933 the Federation's re-organisation accorded four combine committees an official place in the union structure, alongside the lodges and Areas. They were the Ocean, the Cory, the Anthracite (coinciding with the Amalgamated Anthracite company), and the Powell Duffryn. The Ocean and the Cory committees had capable, energetic leaderships and wielded significant influence inside the Federation.[396]

The Ocean Combine Committee chairman was Alf Davies, a left Labour activist, who worked at the large Ocean colliery complex at the head of the Garw valley, where pits and villages had a similar political/cultural character to their counterparts in nearby mid-Rhondda. Three years younger than Horner, the two men knew each other from MMM meetings and Federation delegate conferences. They discovered they were kindred spirits, and established a lasting friendship during the Taff-Merthyr fight. Alf's wife, Mary, and their two daughters, Olive and Vera, enjoyed keeping company with Ethel and the two youngest Horner daughters. Vera and Joan became good friends.

Albert Thomas, the Area No.6 agent responsible for the Rhymney Valley, approached Jim Griffiths with a request for Horner's secondment to Taff-Merthyr. Edgar Evans recalled that Thomas 'told the EC that "Horner was the only man who could make a mark in Bedlinog, or impress the essential people there"'.[397] There were strong arguments in his favour. Horner knew the surrounding terrain and its activists, including Edgar Evans. He travelled regularly to Merthyr to see his parents, and the Merthyr and Dowlais NUWM took advantage of his weekend presence to enlist him as a speaker.[398] Griffiths and Horner had worked together in the Swansea office for the previous nine months. Their relationship had apparently moved from being professionally amicable to one of mutual trust. He and Harris evidently arranged for Horner to be 'unofficially' seconded from his agent's duties for six months. It is likely that the other agents in Area No.1, working with Gomer Evans, covered Horner's routine duties. Horner kept in personal contact with the Upper Gwendraeth miners during his visits to the Datcha in Upper Tumble.

Horner had probably been advising Edwards and Crews about tactics since August. On 21 September the Executive placed Edwards and Crews in formal charge of the campaigns against the SWMIU at Taff-Merthyr and Bedwas. It also granted permission to establish an SWMF Unemployed Lodge at Bedlinog. This arrangement had the hallmarks of Horner's acute tactical sense.[399] Although the Bedlinog NUWM maintained its separate existence, it is likely that its members all joined the Federation lodge, and were joined there by other unemployed miners from nearby villages who were drawn into the vigorous activity which now commenced. The unemployed lodge gave the Federation a formal institutional lien over the men who would become the key first wave of skirmishers; it also enabled Horner to invoke union and communist party discipline simultaneously at critical points in the campaign.

Some members of the unemployed lodge immediately started work on the night-shift at Taff-Merthyr. The SWMIU's hold over Taff-Merthyr was maintained by the colliery management's policy of sacking known Federation members. All the men working were expected to join the SWMIU, and subscriptions were deducted at source by the colliery wages clerk. Workers regularly travelled to the pit by coach and train, and consequently the company found the night-shift difficult to fill. Because management were always sparse on a nightshift, it presented the Bedlinog infiltrators with a favourable opportunity to agitate about union issues.[400]

Whilst these preparations were in train, Griffiths had continued to negotiate with the coalowners over the District Agreement. The South Wales coalowners refused to consider any wage increase, leaving the Executive with little choice but to recommend handing in notices for a coalfield strike. The *Daily Worker* and the *South Wales Miner* carried on a brisk agitation for a coalfield strike, arguing that the victory at Emlyn was evidence that a militant approach would succeed. However, a delegate conference on 28 September heard that if the coalfield strike notices were suspended, the owners had agreed to the appointment of an Independent Tribunal to report on the miners' case by 31 October. The Executive recommended acceptance of this offer.

Horner's speech at the delegate conference was uncompromisingly militant. 'The Federation is stronger today organisationally and from every other point of view than it has been at any time during the last ten months ... Now either the conference was bluffing when it made the demands and when it decided to give notice, or it was sincere ... We are set out for wages not for arbitration ... '[401] Horner's private opinion was different, and he was trying to persuade Pollitt and Allison to trim the CPGB's national line in line with his own views. After the MFGB Annual Conference in July had adopted its ambitious resolution for a National Wages Agreement, he was convinced that the Federation should subordinate its pursuit of a District Agreement to the campaign for a national agreement.

Nevertheless, as the acknowledged leader of the SWMF left wing, and a communist party member subject to party discipline, he had issued a militant challenge.[402]

Horner was probably not surprised when the delegate conference accepted arbitration by an overwhelming majority on a card vote, 57,650 to 14,600. The *Daily Worker* report on 1 October declared that the 'No' vote was 'not as big as expected from the strong opposition which manifested itself at the conference', and blamed the low numbers on 'the protracted nature of the negotiations, the scaling down of the miners' demands, combined with the subtle propaganda of the reformist officials and capitalist press on the serious state of the industry, loss of orders in the event of a stoppage etc.' The story concluded on an optimistic note. There had been more militant delegates than at any conference since 1926, and at least twenty-five had been ready to speak for a militant policy. The lesson drawn was the importance of the rank-and-file movement and the need to ensure that more militant delegates were chosen at lodge elections in December.

Horner knew that the left-wing advances inside the Federation were due to the increased interest generated by the fight against the SWMIU. By 1 October he was probably in residence above the ironmongers in Bedlinog. On 9 October, the Taff-Merthyr company sacked twelve members of the Federation unemployed lodge, including Dai Gittens. On 12 October, the *Daily Worker* reported that members of the 'non-pols' had smashed up Edgar Evans' shop, assaulted four SWMF members there, and vandalised a loudspeaking van outside it. The SWMF Executive sanctioned official industrial action at Taff-Merthyr on 13 October, enabling the sacked men to draw strike pay. The status of the Bedlinog (unemployed) lodge was changed into the Taff-Merthyr (employed) lodge. The *Daily Worker* had reported on 13 October that 911 men had recently joined the Federation, and total lodge membership was over a thousand, including men from the afternoon shift.[403] A wider offensive was also taking place. On 15 October, the *Daily Worker* reported that the Ocean Combine Committee's recruitment campaign had climaxed in strikes at Treherbert and Fernhill collieries in the Rhondda Fawr. The strike notices, which were handed in a fortnight previously to compel the few 'nons' to join the union, had expired.

Federation members had also come out at Taff-Merthyr. The campaign at Bedlinog, 'in which Communists and Labour Party members participated alike ... [was] inaugurated by the SWMF three months ago with Arthur Horner, the well-known militant miners' leader as the chief speaker.' Horner had not intended the Taff-Merthyr undercover Federation members to show their hand this early in the struggle. The nightshift infiltrators had conducted themselves with an audacious militancy that contrasted with the circumspection exercised by the Federation men at Emlyn. His objective was now to persuade as many working miners as possible to join the strike. Executive members and agents were drafted in to help in the fight. They slept in the spare room above the ironmongers, usually sharing a double bed with colleagues. They were all inspired by Horner, who threw himself into the fray with his habitual total commitment. There were no objections when Horner included Edgar Evans in the councils of war he held with Federation lieutenants around the kitchen table; his local knowledge was critical in planning the next moves. Orders for the following day were prepared in meticulous detail. Their execution required extensive co-ordination from a wide variety of people in various locations.

Horner's role was described in Frankenberg's interview conducted with Ned Gittens, Dai Gittens' older brother. Born in Bedlinog in 1899, Ned started work in the Bedlinog pit in 1913. Having been victimised at Treharris colliery in 1926, he remained unemployed until 1934, when he became the secretary of the Ocean Combine Committee at Alf Davies' suggestion. Frankenberg's notes described the backdrop, and then paraphrased Ned's recollections of the strike at the end of October:

> The scene of these conflicts is a valley running more or less due north to south and lying between the Taff Valley on the one side that leads up to Merthyr Tydfil and the Rhymney Valley on the other. It is not so long as these others; it is a small valley rising up to a height on which stands ... Bedlinog. A couple of miles down ... [t]here are no houses whatever. It is a bare hillside. Then a road ... quite steeply down below the extensive top-hamper of the Taff Merthyr pit, and then the bottom of the Valley with the stream and railway line.

This was the scene of some of the most exciting incidents ... All meetings about that time, the 30th [October] were surrounded by the police, and not only local police, but police from Liverpool and Bristol.

[There was] a mass meeting ... to be held on the verge between the road and the railway above Taff Merthyr pit ... When we went to the meeting we found not only the police but Colonel Lindsay ... and in a very militant mood. Superintendents and inspectors were with him ... Now Arthur Horner had taken the precaution ... to get George Hall MP ... to come to this meeting, and before he arrived the atmosphere was becoming very tense. Of course we had timed it to begin just as the men would be coming off shift ... A superintendent called Goronwy Griffiths walked up and said: 'Mr. Horner, you are taking a liberty', to which Arthur shrugged his shoulders, said 'So what?' and walked away. At this point a great number of police assembled and in a very menacing attitude. George Hall's taxi came up the road ... When he saw the situation, he went white as a sheet. But Arthur said he should have a word with Colonel Lindsay or with the superintendent ... They said: 'We will allow you to hold a meeting, but at the top of the mountain.' ... 'No', said Arthur, 'we will hold the meeting here.' And then there was an argument, and finally the police ... said it would be held on the mountain side of the road where, of course, there is a little bit of pavement and walling which provide a most excellent platform. It was better actually. But naturally Arthur grumbled a good deal and finally, as a compromise, agreed, and then stepped on to this really splendid platform ...

... Now there was an occasion, a meeting, just about then when it was clear the police would not allow a meeting that night. So Arthur came up ... He said: 'Well it isn't absolutely necessary, I can't hold a meeting every day ... I have to go into the Cardiff office, and I will slip away.' Well, that got round to the police in a matter of minutes, if not seconds, and they saw Arthur get into the 'bus going down to Cardiff. But he got out at Treharris, went into the railway station, booked a ticket right through to Dowlais at the very top where the train runs beyond Bedlinog ... When the train got to Taff Merthyr and the other train [with the working miners] got through, there was Arthur leaning out of the train window making a speech and urging them to join the union. They [the police] were wild. They never thought he would do a thing like that – and neither did we. But he was very ingenious as well as very bold.[404]

The Federation Executive financed the 1100 Taff-Merthyr strikers for four weeks.[405] But the company found new men to work the pit alongside those who had not come out; marketable outputs of coal were still being raised. The Ocean and Powell Duffryn Combine Committees demanded a total coalfield war. The Executive agreed. They convened a delegate conference for 7 November and recommended giving one week's notice of a coalfield strike. Delegates voted unanimously to back the Taff-Merthyr men. This show of unity produced an offer from the Taff-Merthyr management to meet the Federation. A delegate conference on 11 November accepted the Executive recommendation to postpone handing in the strike notices whilst negotiations continued by 150 to 35. Most delegates had evidently understood the Executive's recommendation to hand in notices as a bargaining manoeuvre.

On Saturday 17 November another delegate conference approved the Executive recommendation to accept the terms offered by the Taff-Merthyr management and withdraw the coalfield strike notices. The terms were harsh in human terms, although important ground had been conceded. The owners had agreed that a ballot would be held after full working was resumed, giving employees a choice about which union they wanted to represent them at the pit. But they refused to sack the men who had worked during the strike or to take back the strikers. In the run-up to the ballot, propaganda from both unions aimed at Taff-Merthyr miners would be banned. Meanwhile, recognition for the SWMIU would continue.[406] The settlement was also accepted by the Taff-Merthyr Federation lodge, although there was impassioned opposition from many communists/NUWM members. It is notable that no statements from Horner were reported. He evidently took care in communist and union meetings to support the Executive and delegate conference decisions.[407] His arguments were probably decisive in persuading a majority of the Taff-Merthyr lodge members that nothing more could be gained by staying out.

Pollitt and Allison successfully imposed party discipline to ensure that there was no public opposition to the Federation Executive's negotiations before the delegate conference accepted the terms they had negotiated. On 16 November, the *Daily Worker* described the strike as 'a fitting reply to the reformist leaders of the TUC who aim to sabotage such examples of unity'. It is likely that there was a strenuous debate about the terms at the South Wales District Party Congress on 17 to 18 November. It had been scheduled as part of the preparation for the CPGB's Thirteenth Congress in February 1935. But because it coincided with the end of the Taff-Merthyr strike, there was probably a vociferous debate in which many comrades demanded that the rank-and-file movement continue the struggle independently of the Federation. The *Daily Worker* trimmed and temporised in order to avoid going directly against the Comintern's Class Against Class line, which was still formally in place. It reported the SWMF conference vote on Monday 19 November without either comment or giving the voting figures, as it had done for 11 November. However, it noted that the Taff-Merthyr lodge had been persuaded to accept the settlement 'despite intense opposition'.[408]

Horner probably went back to the Anthracite in late November, having spent some two months in Bedlinog. His six months leave of absence had been planned in the expectation that there would be a long period of boring within before open conflict began. Instead, the confrontation at Taff-Merthyr had begun soon after his arrival. The Bedlinog militants, moreover, had been dug-in and determined to carry on the fight until the last ditch. In 1960, *Incorrigible Rebel* recorded his memory of the regret he had felt in 1934. 'Unfortunately events moved too rapidly at that time, with the consequence that a strike was provoked, before enough had been done to win over the large majority of the workmen'.[409] He had drawn deeply on reserves of moral courage and intellectual conviction. He had promised the men another opportunity to fight when the balance of forces was more favourable in good faith. But he had not enjoyed using his personal authority to compel men to cease resistance.

During December, opposition to the Taff-Merthyr settlement gathered momentum inside the South Wales communist party *apparat*. The *Daily Worker* gave the disagreement space. On 19 December, Enoch Collins, a member of the CPGB Executive, wrote a long article complaining about the neglect of 'Independent Party activity', which had allowed the reformists 'to betray the Taff Merthyr workers'. He identified the problem as the South Wales Miners' Rank-and-File Movement; 'two years ago ... one of the best unofficial rank and file movements in being ... [and] now nearly a thing of the past'. He noted that the *South Wales Miner* was being published without any back-up from below; the implication of this criticism was that if the editorial committee had involved party activists, the paper's editorial line would be different.

Collins' complaints were in accord with party policy enunciated the 1932 Twelfth CPGB Congress. However, Pollitt and Campbell had been steering the CPGB for sometime in the direction of the change of line they expected to emerge at the Comintern's Seventh World Congress, which had been planned for September 1934. Pollitt was manoeuvring inside the Comintern to make the new line more flexible, enabling communists to unite with socialists to fight fascism more effectively. The Comintern Congress had been postponed at the last moment, when internal ECCI opposition to the change proved unexpectedly strong.[410] Pollitt and Campbell were forced to temporise on the domestic front, taking care not to offer unqualified support for united front activity or compromise decisions taken by 'reformist unions'. For example, on 26 November, the *Daily Worker* provided a gloss on the acceptance by the Taff-Merthyr lodge of the terms of settlement. 'After many questions were asked, the vote went in favour ... by an overwhelming majority. There was tremendous opposition at first, arising from a demand to clear out the 70 imported blacklegs ... There has been a magnificent struggle and a complete victory could have been won if the colliery notices [for a coalfield strike] had not been withdrawn ... Disappointment with only partial successes must not be allowed to create apathy, and all efforts must be made to build a strong militant lodge of the Federation to fight in the future.'

The delay in changing the Comintern line was problematic for Horner. Since his election as Federation Agent and removal to the Anthracite, he had not attended many DPC meetings, usually giving union business as his reason for absence. But his habitual non-appearance was resented, particularly by DPC members still committed to 'Class Against Class' and building independent leadership. They argued that the DPC had not only the right but the duty to exercise control over Horner's conduct of the economic struggle. The fact that he was a full-time SWMF official did not exempt him from communist discipline. Horner relied on Pollitt to deal with the DPC's complaints against him. Pollitt took his conciliators role extremely seriously, partly because he valued Horner as a gifted working-class leader and was anxious to keep him inside the party. But when Horner consistently ignored the DPC injunction to members to oppose decisions taken by the SWMF Executive, the DPC appealed to Pollitt for redress. He typically intervened to persuade Horner to attend the DPC and account for his actions. Pollitt viewed this as sufficient recompense, and the DPC had little choice but to accept Horner's *ex post facto* apology, along with his justification for adopting a Clausewitzian position. But his appearances at the DPC continued to be erratic, angering party activists who remained convinced that 100 per cent all-out conflict was the only way to achieve success against the coalowners.[411]

The conflict between Horner and the DPC was alleviated after the Thirteenth CPGB Congress in early February 1935. The British congress had been scheduled on the assumption that the Comintern Seventh World Congress would be held in the autumn of 1934. When it was postponed, Pollitt and Campbell were evidently determined to effect at least a partial change in the CPGB's line without the Comintern imprimatur, particularly in regard to trade union work. The Young Turks and other supporters of holding fast to Class Against Class and independent leadership mounted a spirited opposition to Pollitt's and Campbell's arguments for the 'real united front' during the pre-Congress discussion and at the Congress. However, they were decisively defeated.

The Congress resolution on the party and the economic struggle omitted all mention not only of the Revolutionary Trade
Union Opposition, but also of rank-and-file movements as dis-
crete organisations separate from trade unions. Instead it committed members to concentrate on trade union work and take
the lead in: 'activising the branches, district committees and
areas of the various unions'[412] In addition, there were also significant changes in the Executive personnel. Enoch Collins and
Lewis Jones, two members of the South Wales DPC who opposed
Horner's Clausewitzian approach, were dropped. Horner and
Hannington were restored, and joined by Paynter, who was generally regarded as Horner's protégé.[413]

Horner's return to the Executive formally sealed his rehabilitation inside the CPGB. Although he may have attended
the Congress, there was no report or record of his speaking.
He and Pollitt may have agreed that it was expedient to avoid
giving the Young Turks and his South Walian opponents the
opportunity to lay charges of Hornerism from the floor. They
were also anxious to avoid publicity in the *Western Mail* and *Daily
Herald*. Horner was campaigning hard for the post of SWMF
Vice-President, hoping to unseat Arthur Jenkins. The election
would take place at the Federation Annual Conference in March,
giving him and Pollitt reason to downplay his role as a controversial communist.[414]

The editorial line and style of the *South Wales Miner* had
changed on the eve of the Thirteenth Party Congress. In its
5 February 1935 edition, the pseudonymous 'G. Griffiths'
replied to a letter from 'Anthracite Miners' which opposed the
Federation Executive: '[I]n actual fact the Fed. has become a
movement of the rank-and-file fighting for improvements in
wages and working conditions of the miner and politically carrying out the policy of class struggle against the capitalists in
general'. When a lodge 'has been decisively won for the policy
of the Rank and File Movement, and has become the organ of
struggle, the lodge itself is the expression of the Rank and File
Movement'.[415] The logic was clear – the South Wales Miners'
Rank-and-File Movement was increasingly redundant.

When the *South Wales Miner* ceased publication in July 1935,
the formal reason given was lack of finance. Pollitt and Campbell,
however, could have found the money if they had considered it a

political priority. A more plausible explanation is that the rank-and-file paper's closure and the South Wales Miners' Rank-and-File Movement's unannounced disappearance coincided with the Comintern Seventh World Congress, which declared the new line, the formation of United and Popular Fronts to fight fascism. Horner and his allies could now concentrate solely on union activity, and use the Seventh World Congress pronouncements to compel the die-hard partisans of independent leadership to do the same.

The real united front

In May 1934, the government laid its plans for rationalising and centralising the payment of unemployment relief before parliament. An Unemployment Assistance Board would be vested with powers 'to determine the rate of assistance and the conditions to govern its payment'. Local Public Assistance Committees, whose personnel were drawn from local authorities, would be abolished. Centralisation would bring the amount of relief paid under Whitehall control. The UAB was designed to ensure uniformity in the administration of the household means test, leaving no room for local discretion in the depressed areas. In areas of high and persistent unemployment, where local authorities were predominantly Labour, Public Assistance Committees had presided over an equally persistent upward drift in the amount of relief paid to workers who had exhausted their insured unemployment benefit. When the Minister of Labour, Oliver Stanley, informed the House of Commons of the new rates and conditions, Labour MPs, especially from mining constituencies, warned of dire consequences. Griffiths recalled: 'Of the 160,000 unemployed in South Wales at the time, 100,000 of them had exhausted their benefit and were subject to the inquisition and indignity of this household means test.'[416]

The new regulations were scheduled to be introduced in two stages, with the first commencing on Monday 7 January 1935. Even though the government had restored unemployment benefit scales to pre-1931 levels during 1934, the new regulations did indeed unleash 'an unprecedently widespread political protest'.[417] The events began in South Wales. Paynter believed that the ground had been prepared in mid-1934, when Wal

Hannington had been the communist candidate in a by-election in the Merthyr Tydfil constituency. '[The] campaign was fought on the issue of unemployment and the need for new industry, and although Hannington lost his deposit, the campaign of meetings undoubtedly had a tremendous effect. The biggest meetings of the campaign were held by us, with Harry and Marjory (*sic*) Pollitt assisting Hannington, all extremely powerful and attractive speakers.'[418]

On Saturday 12 January, the *Rhondda Leader* reported 'numerous protest meetings being held across the Valleys'.[419] Horner's MI5 file reported that he had addressed a meeting in mid-Rhondda, at Judge's Hall, Trealaw, 'organised by the local C.P.G.B.: about 700 people were present. HORNER spoke at length on the new Unemployment Bill and Regulations: criticised the Cabinet ... In conclusion, he urged all present to join the United Front.'[420]

A demonstration was organised in De Winton Field, Tonypandy on Sunday 20 January. The venue was not only convenient for both Rhondda valleys, it also evoked memories of the 1910 Cambrian Combine strike. There were five speakers' platforms to cater for the 50,000 people who assembled, no doubt encouraged by the bright winter sunshine. Horner, the two Rhondda MPs, Will John and Mainwaring, and Mark Harcombe, SWMF Agent for the Rhondda, spoke on each in turn. It is unlikely that there had been such a large gathering since the last South Walian revival in 1904. Press reports described the dramatic scene. 'People who have lived in the valley all their lives were emphatic that they had never witnessed such a scene of protest and indignation ... not a movement initiated by any particular Party, but a united front of Lodge Officials, Communists, Ministers of Religion and business and professional men, with Members of Parliament, Magistrates and Councillors rubbing shoulders with all sections of the populace'.[421]

The Federation officers speedily positioned themselves at the head of the upsurge, convening an 'All-In' Conference in Cardiff on Saturday 26 January, open to all civic organisations except the CPGB and NUWM; 1600 delegates attended. Horner attended and spoke in support of a motion from the Anthracite area calling for a conference of union executives to consider calling a one-day strike. The *Daily Worker* reported that his speech was 'greeted with a storm of cheering, and it was some time before he could speak'. But the Federation Executive was only willing to sanction political protest; Griffiths did not put the Anthracite motion to the vote, even though the *Manchester Guardian* reporter observed that it would have been carried. Instead, the conference decided to send a deputation to put their case to Stanley.[422]

On Sunday 27 January, two more monster demonstrations were held; 30,000 people marched to Aberdare Park, and 20,000 assembled at Ynysangharad Park, Pontypridd. When the SWMF Cambrian Combine Committee met in the evening, they agreed to allow Lewis Jones to speak, even though he was not a member, and accepted his proposal for a one-day strike. Meanwhile ad hoc united fronts in areas of high unemployment, notably Belfast, Liverpool and Sheffield, were organising highly successful marches and meetings. Their size and serious intent were wholly unexpected by the organisers and the government. Francis and Smith judge the scale of the protest to have been greatest in South Wales, although there has been no systematic research to test their conclusion.[423]

The Cambrian Combine decision in favour of a one-day strike was not reported by the *Daily Worker* until 4 February, and then only in passing, in a summary of the Thirteenth CPGB Congress. The central party leadership was not anxious to promote a strike which might take place without Executive sanction, i.e. unofficially. And they certainly had no intention of calling one under the party's independent leadership. The emphasis at Congress was on party members integrating into union activity.[424]

Oliver Stanley met the South Wales deputation on 1 February. Griffiths and Glamorgan County Councillor, Mrs Rose Davies, 'one of the most respected women in our public life', put their case. Griffiths recalled: 'We decided to place before him a factual account of the effect of the new scales and regulations upon the unemployed and their families. He turned to the officers at his side and asked if they could dispute the accuracy of the facts ... and was told that they could not ... Then turning to me he thanked us for coming to see him and for stating our case so clearly. "I will go into the whole matter immediately," he said with a voice full of emotion, and, brushing his brief aside, walked out of the room.'[425]

On 3 February, there were demonstrations for the third Sunday in succession in South Wales. At least 300,000 people marched and demonstrated. De Winton Field was filled by 60,000 to 70,000 people; large open air meetings were held in Blackwood, Neath, Briton Ferry, Merthyr and Barry. Ernest Bevin spoke to 20,000 people in Pontypool. Although it was evidently decided that it would be prudent for Bevin to speak in Monmouthshire rather than the Rhondda, his presence showed the significance assigned to the South Wales protests by the Labour *apparat*. On Monday 4 February, the NUWM led 1000 women and 2000 men to the Merthyr UAB offices and destroyed their records. 'Prominent in the attack were three leading Communists: J.S. Williams of Dowlais (later an International Brigader), Mrs. Ceridwen Brown of Aberdare (whose son was to serve in Spain), and Griff Jones, an unemployed miner ... (another later to serve with the International Brigades).'[426]

On Tuesday 5 February, Stanley announced to the House of Commons that he was deferring the operation of the new regulations and also granting higher rates of relief. His concessions were apparently accepted as sufficient to redress the widely and deeply felt grievance, and social equilibrium was restored. By the time a revised set of regulations for unemployment benefit was finally announced in July 1936, Horner was President of the SWMF, and he led the union in a vigorous protest against them. However, this time the regulations had been re-formulated to take account of the objections from Labour MPs and the wider movement. Although unemployment remained exceptionally high in the Rhondda and in Durham (the other coalfield adversely affected by the loss of exports) no more than token resistance was offered on this second occasion.[427] The government had clearly learned its lesson.

Not surprisingly, communist and other left-wing activists were invigorated by the upsurge of collective feeling during the four weeks in January 1935 when the regulations had been in force. After their withdrawal, the most enthusiastic rebels looked for ways to prolong the conflict. On 11 February, the *Daily Worker* reported that in South Wales the communist party had organised a march of 7000 people in the Ogmore Valley to protest against the new regulations. Horner spoke to a meeting afterwards about the need to continue the fight.[428] The South Wales DPC also continued to press the Cambrian Combine Committee's case for a one-day protest strike. To keep it alive, the committee had attached additional demands, citing the ongoing negotiations for a new District Agreement between the Federation and the coalowners, as well as various unresolved colliery disputes. In response, the Federation officers mounted a concerted offensive to pre-empt the strike and prevent militants from seizing the initiative. Horner, however, agreed with the Federation officers, and opposed the militants' enthusiasm as unrealistic, and parochial. Although he had been a prominent participant on meeting platforms in January 1935, he is unlikely to have taken a significant role in organising them. The Anthracite remained on the fringes of the protest movement, and he remained focused on union problems.

On 25 February, the *Daily Worker* reported that the one-day coalfield strike had been postponed, and explained the delay by intimidation from the coalowners, adding that the SWMF delegate conference convened to vote on the Cambrian Combine resolution had accepted the Executive's recommendation that miners should not take action on their own, in isolation from the rest of the labour movement. As a result of this decision, the four Cambrian Combine pits where lodges had already voted for a one-day strike decided to postpone their action until 25 March, when they hoped to achieve an all-in South Wales General Strike.[429]

Although the *Daily Worker* carried a page one story by Cox on 26 March under the headline 'Strike Movement Spreads in South Wales', there were no strikes to report. Cox complained that even though strike notices had been served at two pits in the Garw Valley, reactionary miners' officials were trying to prevent strikes taking place. 'There was never a greater opportunity for unity of the employed and unemployed in struggle, and to combine this fight against the pit grievances with the united struggle against the slave Act and the National Government'. But despite the enthusiasm of many party militants and the South Wales DPC, Pollitt and Campbell were firmly committed to working inside official union institutions. They were usually successful in controlling their activists who were keen to lead independent, unofficial action.

In fact, the prospects for an official union offensive had been transformed by the success of the January *démarche*. Encouraged by the government's climb-down, union leaders exhibited self-confidence. On 17 January 1935, the MFGB Executive felt sufficiently confident to convene a national conference on 14 February 'to consider the establishment of a National Agreement'. Joseph Jones and Ebby Edwards had been patiently building trust and cultivating good relations on the Executive, whilst encouraging the younger activists in District Unions to support their forward-looking plans. W Hogg of Northumberland opened the discussion, reminding delegates that 'the outstanding lesson we must have learned is that it is quite impossible for any one district to be fighting a lone battle to regain even a tithe of the reductions in wages that have been sustained over a period of years.' Delegates accepted the Executive's recommendation to approach the coalowners to co-operate in devising a national wages machinery; if the owners refused, the government would be asked to legislate.[430]

George Allison, now the party's Industrial Organiser, convened a meeting of mining comrades at King Street on 13 April, to discuss, 'Our campaign with regard to the MFGB Conference; Improvements of collective leadership of the mining fraction'. The date was chosen at Horner's suggestion to facilitate his attendance. The meeting decided on a plan of action, and Horner subsequently spoke at public meetings organised by the party at Wigan in Lancashire in mid-June and in Nottinghamshire on Sunday 20 June.[431] He probably promoted pragmatic tactics which he judged would be more effective than Allan's more abstract approach. MI5 noted his letter to the South Wales Secretariat about the MFGB campaign 'to raise the demand for "a real national wages agreement containing the 2/- per shift increase"; he thinks the demand should be for "strike action to enforce 2/- ... for all British mineworkers", leaving the question of a formal national agreement to emerge from the struggle to achieve general uniform wage increase. The former line, put forward by W. ALLAN. appears to be leading away from action.'[432]

When the coalowners continued their refusal to even meet the MFGB, the Executive decided to approach the government for assistance. The increasingly frail MacDonald had been a lame duck for some time when Baldwin succeeded him as prime minister on 7 June. Baldwin had been profoundly affected by the rise of European fascism, a movement which he felt was unpredictable, potentially divisive and even revolutionary. Nearly a decade after the traumatic events of his first prime ministership, he recognised that British unions had proved reliably democratic, moderate and loyal to traditions of English voluntarism. He had said as much to Harry Crookshank MP, a close friend of both Eden and Macmillan on the left of the Conservative Party, when he appointed him Minister of Mines in mid-June.[433] Although Baldwin was not statutorily obliged to call a general election until October 1936, it was anticipated that he would opt for an earlier contest. Jones and Edwards calculated that he would be keen to avoid a damaging national mining dispute in the meantime. The aftermath of the 1926 Lock-Out had inflicted serious damage on the Tories' performance in the 1929 general election.

The week before the MFGB Annual Conference, Harry Crookshank had informed the MFGB Executive that the government did not intend to intervene on their behalf with the coalowners. At the conference, Joseph Jones attacked the government's refusal. As Vice-President, Lawther moved a resolution on behalf of the Executive, strongly protesting at the government's inaction. 'We therefore endorse the demand for a flat rate advance of 2s. per day, and [resolve] that following an intensive campaign in support of this claim a Special Conference be convened to decide what action should be taken to enforce the demand.'[434] In a conspicuous display of South Walian support, Jim Griffiths seconded the Executive resolution, followed by Arthur Jenkins. (The SWMF delegation continued to be much attenuated, reflecting the union's straitened finances, which may have been why Horner did not attend.)

On 15 July, during the MFGB Annual Conference, the *Daily Worker* published a petition in support of the Executive's recommendation that District Unions should hand in simultaneous notices ending their respective agreements. The subsequent absence of any collective agreements would increase the pressure on the MAGB to commence national negotiations. The petition had seventeen signatories identified by their coalfields and union positions: eight from Durham, four from Northumberland, three from the County Union in Fife and two from South Wales, Dai Dan Evans and DG Wilkins, respectively described as chairman and Executive Committee member of the Anthracite Combine Committee. Most of the Durham and Northumberland signatories were not CPGB members, evidence of the success of the party's new united front policy. The absence of any signatories from the Rhondda was notable in view of Jack Jones' claim at the CPGB Congress in February.[435]

Delegates at the Annual Conference gave the Executive an unqualified endorsement to pursue the national wages agreement. The 'forward-looking' group on the executive was further strengthened by four new members, who took office after the conference, Bowman from Northumberland, and Watson, Ned Moore and Will Pearson from the DMA. Along with the Federation members Harris and Griffiths they provided unfaltering support for the national officers in the national wages campaign. On 25 July, the Executive formally requested affiliated district unions not to conclude District Agreements with their coalowners' associations, and to collect a levy of 2d. per member to build up a national campaign war chest. The MFGB printed eight million copies of a four page *Miners' Campaign Special*. An MFGB Executive circular explained that the 'primary object of the campaign is to make the citizens of this country conscious of the serious plight of the mineworkers and their families as a result of low wages'.[436]

The CPGB leadership positioned the party four square behind the MFGB Executive's efforts. The Labour Research Department published a well-produced pamphlet, *The Miners' Two Bob* (a 'bob' is a shilling), by Ben Francis, marshalling the facts and figures behind the miners' case. Cox had replaced Jimmy Shields as *Daily Worker* editor after the Comintern Seventh World Congress in August, and he now lavished page one headlines and purple political prose in support of the MFGB campaign.[437] The South Wales DPC acquiesced in King Street's stress on the need to subordinate coalfield issues to the national campaign, and directed party members' activity accordingly. But they were aggrieved at Horner's failure to take responsibility for co-ordinating union activity in the district, as he had been deputed to do.[438] He remained aloof from the DPC, however, evidently fearing that his close involvement in the South Wales party would precipitate another confrontation between himself and Rhondda revolutionary militants. His party activity was mostly conducted at King Street or in West Wales, where he apparently worked amicably with Charlie Stead, the party's sub-district secretary in Swansea.

On 3 September, the *Daily Worker* reported that the SWMF Executive had agreed to support the MFGB demand for a flat-rate two shillings a day increase. 'In the anthracite coalfield most of the lodges are planning meeting for weeks ahead ... The Workmen's Combine Committee in the anthracite is the spearhead of the campaign and is leading the activity of 38 separate lodges.' The absence of activity in the Rhondda was again notable. Evidently, the outlook of Rhondda communists and their allies remained parochial.

The renewed optimism amongst trade union activists was reflected at the pre-TUC conference, which Pollitt and Allison revived after a gap of six years. Nominally organised by *Labour Monthly*, it was well attended by 330 delegates from 142 union branches. Horner introduced the special debate on urgent problems in industry. The Special Branch Report described his giving a 'rigorous and characteristic speech'. The *Daily Worker* noted his statement that the movement needed to return to the pre-1926 struggle against the employing class. 'He then instanced many forms of rationalisation ... all calculated to drive the workers into more intensive labour and into giving of greater production per shift ... He said we must understand that in order that the unions can do their job we have to become union builders, not only criticisers of leaders.'[439]

When the TUC convened in Margate the following week, delegates were welcomed by Bob Smith, a Kent miner and chairman of the Isle of Thanet Trades Council. He used the traditionally ceremonial speech to deliver a scarcely veiled condemnation of the 'Black Circulars', Nos. 16 and 17, issued by the General Council in autumn 1934, which had recommended trades councils and affiliated unions to ban communists and fascists from holding lay and full-time office. Two motions on the agenda condemned them, one from the MFGB, moved by Lawther, and the other from the AEU, moved by its president, Jack Little. Although neither was passed, when Bevin opposed them on behalf of the General Council, he conceded much of the substance of the movers' case. He declared that he would have no truck with unions practising political discrimination. When Citrine read a telegram of fraternal greetings from Russian trade unions, and implied that he would not acknowledge it, the general secretary of the Distributive Workers told delegates that a failure to reply would be a great affront to Russian comrades. Even though Citrine retreated, delegates insisted on taking a vote on the floor of Congress and he suffered the additional affront of being instructed to reply. Ianto Evans, Bevan and Ablett were SWMF delegates; Griffiths and Arthur Jenkins were the principal spokesmen in the debate on unemployment, with Jenkins being particularly eloquent.[440]

Conservative Party managers had advised Baldwin to delay calling a general election until early 1936. But when Mussolini invaded Abyssinia on 3 October 1935, the British public's shocked revulsion convinced Baldwin to opt for an earlier date. On 25 October, after a flurry of well-informed speculation, he dissolved parliament in preparation for a general election on 14 November. By this time both the TUC and the Labour Party, at its conference in the first week of October, had registered strong endorsements of the MFGB's case. On 17 to 18 October, the MFGB Executive had convened a Special Delegate Conference to discuss its recommendation to hold a national strike ballot, whilst promising to try to achieve the 2 shillings increase through meaningful negotiations with the government in the meantime. National officers had hoped to achieve a decisive vote. However, some delegates questioned the propriety of holding a national strike ballot on the eve of a general election. Others gloomily speculated that a strike ballot would produce a repetition of the 1926 events, with a protracted siege and ultimate rout. 'One District leader rather pessimistically put the view that if the ballot were held and it went against a strike ... they would all be in a much worse position. Here a closely argued speech from ... Bowman had a heartening effect.' The Executive recommendation was eventually accepted on a card vote, 320 to 172, evidence of the contentious debate. Opposing votes came from the Midlands Federation, Derbyshire, Leicestershire, South Derbyshire, North Wales and Durham.[441]

Nevertheless, the conference decision to hold a national strike ballot was major national news. The prospect of a coal strike had the desired effect of compelling the government into action. Crookshank had told the Cabinet at the end of September that the miners' case was 'unanswerable'.[442] He now met the MFGB Executive on 21 October to formally hear their case and intention to strike 'unless steps were taken to deal with the claim'. On 24 October, he told parliament 'that the Government had repeatedly pressed on the coal-owners the view that only by a reorganisation of the selling side could a reasonable price be obtained by the sale of coal ... [that] would permit better wages to be paid'. On the same day he also told the MFGB Executive that the government did not intend to take any further action. The decision to dissolve parliament had enabled the cautious Baldwin to postpone difficult decisions. The MFGB Executive decided to hold the national strike ballot on 11 to 13 November, dates 'deliberately chosen by us for the purpose of using the election to further publicise the miners' case.'[443]

International security, the League of Nations and rearmament dominated the general election campaign. But District Union activists were able to use the election as a rallying point to persuade their members to vote 'Yes' in the national strike ballot and then Labour in the general election. There was a 93 per cent turn-out in the national strike ballot; a majority of 14 to 1 voted 'Yes' to the question, 'Are you in favour of authorising the Executive Committee to press the claim for an advance of wages of 2s. per shift for adults over 18 years, and 1s. per shift for youths and boys under 18 years, even to the extent of tendering your notice to enforce the claim if necessary?' South Wales recorded the largest majority, closely followed by Yorkshire and Durham. The MFGB Executive requested a meeting with Baldwin, newly re-appointed prime minister, on 20 November, the day after the public announcement of the strike ballot figures.[444]

Mainwaring was defending his Rhondda East seat in a two-man race for the first time. The DPC and Rhondda communists felt it was a matter of honour to put up a good show against the former left-wing and CPGB militant. Horner had good reason not to stand again; the Party Centre agreed, reasoning that it was more important to safeguard his position as SWMF agent and ambitions to hold higher union office.[445] Pollitt stood in his stead. Pollitt was the party's most high profile candidate. He probably welcomed the opportunity to stand in a constituency where he would get a significant vote, rather than losing his deposit as he had done in Durham and Derbyshire mining constituencies.

As in 1933, Morgan Phillips, veteran SWMF-sponsored MPs, and the South Wales Labour *apparat* assigned the highest priority to routing the communist threat in Rhondda East. Writing in the CPGB *Rhondda East Special*, Paynter complained that Labour workers had been drafted into in Rhondda East from constituencies like Newport, Swansea and Cardiff, which Labour was contesting against National Government candidates. 'In these towns it is the Communists who are assisting Labour to win, and who are being warmly welcomed ... by the members of the Labour Party.' He dismissed Mainwaring's article in the special issue of Labour's *Rhondda Clarion* which had appeared '[u]nder a senseless headline, "Pollitt – ical News" ... a farrago of lies and vacuous nonsense is presented in the guise of political argument.'

Pollitt's campaign invoked Horner whenever possible. Page one of *Rhondda East Special* carried a picture of Horner, not Pollitt, accompanied by a banner headline 'Horner says vote for Pollitt'. Horner's message concentrated on union matters:

> Pollitt's trade union standing and experience of industrial problems, including the mining industry, are second to none ... We are about to enter a National struggle for a wages increase. The return of Pollitt gives every miner and his family the guarantee that our case will be presented with facts, arguments, lucidity, power and feeling ... He will do his best ... to rouse support for a National Agreement, for he knows that we are the only body of organised workers having district settlements that destroy our national unity and power.

Page two featured a picture of Horner, Willie Gallacher, who was the communist candidate in the Scottish mining constituency of West Fife, and Pollitt, standing together outside Pollitt's Committee Rooms, 'Three Communist Leaders'. It was flanked by an article, 'The Miner's Ballot for the Two Bob', by Jack Davies, described as Chairman of the Llwynypia Lodge and the Powell Duffryn Combine Committee. After a rehearsal of the terrible working conditions in mid-Rhondda, he urged support for Pollitt, 'who is a tremendous champion of the miners' cause'. Two slogans in large type concluded, 'On Monday, Tuesday, Wednesday, vote for Action to win the 2/- [in the MFGB strike ballot] ... On Thursday – Vote for Pollitt.'

The back page was dominated by a German photomontage of Dimitrov in a suit, leaning thoughtfully over a lectern; in the corner was superimposed a much smaller back view of Hitler, arms akimbo in uniform with jodhpurs and jackboots with illegible German slogans spewing out of his head. The strap line underneath was, 'Dimitrov told Hitler where to Get Off!! For Unity, Peace, Socialism'. Vigorous campaigning by both parties increased the turn-out by 5 per cent, to 80.8 per cent. There was no significant increase in voters' willingness to vote Communist however. Pollitt won 2400 more votes than Horner in 1933. But Mainwaring attracted most of the Liberal votes; his total increased by nearly 8000.

After the election, there was a predictable move on the SWMF Executive to sack Horner, even though he had only spoken for Pollitt once, at the eve of poll meeting held at the Workmen's Hall, Trealaw. At the meeting, as with his endorsement in *Rhondda East Special*, he concentrated on mining issues, declaring that the miners would not be seduced from the path of struggle to achieve the 2/- increase. Griffiths resisted the anti-Horner manoeuvre. 'I persuaded them not to on the ground that this would have involved the SWMF in fatal internal strife when we were only just beginning to climb out of the slough of despond after 1926'. The knowledge that communist influence was increasing inside SWMF lodges, and his estimation of Horner's usefulness as a union leader, were probably both influential factors in his decision.[446]

Blake judged the general election result 'a notable triumph for Baldwin', even though Labour won over 100 seats from the government, receiving 38 per cent of the vote – comparable to their share in 1929.[447] Labour's creditable performance provided the prime minister with a credible political reason to defuse the miners' dispute. On 28 November, during the debate on the King's Speech, he spoke positively about the merits of the MFGB case with the aid of notes provided by the Department of Mines. Crookshank was despatched on shuttle diplomacy between the

MFGB and MAGB. Although Evan Williams believed the Mines Department's threat to legislate district selling schemes, he still refused to commit the MAGB to making voluntary arrangements. The MFGB also held firm, with no District Union breaking ranks by signing a separate District Agreement. The MFGB Executive intensified national pressure at a Special Conference on 18 December, at which delegates accepted the recommendation to tender strike notices on 13 and 20 to 21 January 1936, by a vote of 478 to 28 for a strike to commence on 27 January.[448]

This result produced behind-the-scenes action from the government. Instead of exerting further direct pressure on the coalowners, Baldwin outflanked them. Large industrial consumers of coal, led by Imperial Chemical Industries, wrote to the Department of Mines expressing their readiness 'to agree to an advance over 1935 prices of one shilling per ton under all the forward contracts ... as a step towards bettering the wages of workers in the coalmining industry'. These apparently voluntary acts precipitated a rush of sympathetic emulation from the British public. The MFGB began receiving letters from smaller firms with similar charitable offers. 'The movement extended to the public utility concerns and to the domestic coal market: soon all the retail merchants and Co-operative Societies were paying and charging more for their coal, "thus enabling members of the public actively to associate themselves with the movement for getting better wages for the miners."'[449]

Having been presented with the financial means to pay better wages, the MAGB could hardly refuse to grant them, although they refused to conclude a national settlement. District coalowners' associations offered increases of differing amounts, from 1 shilling to 5 pence per shift. The official historian of the coal industry concluded that the MFGB 'had secured a significant degree of protection for wages and hours in the face of a deepening slump and had laid the basis for advances in subsequent years'. It was also notable that the MAGB had accepted the principle of national wage determination, by agreeing to participate in a new Joint Standing Consultative Committee on wages and conditions.[450]

An MFGB Delegate Conference on 24 January voted to accept the district increases and the JSCC by 360 to 112. Opposing districts included South Wales and Northumberland, seeking firm assurances that the wage increase would be national and uniform in character. (Joseph Jones refused to accept a motion from Jim Griffiths that the MAGB offer should be put to a district ballot.) The *Daily Worker* conspicuously abstained from challenging the settlement, although some of its reports stressed the intensity of dissatisfaction with the meagre gains, particularly in South Wales.[451] On 25 January a *Daily Worker* story noted Ebby Edwards's fulsome thanks at the December delegate conference for 'the great assistance rendered by the Communist Party in the campaign to rouse public support and sympathy by the distribution of literature etc ... ' An anodyne conclusion followed which displayed the paper's militant bona fides. 'Most delegates were unanimous that this was only the first stage of the fight ... One of the big weaknesses reflected in the campaign was the failure to maintain a high level of agitation and organisation in the coalfield. The main lesson to be learned ... was that negotiations must be accompanied by an active campaign among the rank and file to prepare them for action.' The leader had criticised the TUC General Council for not rendering greater support to the miners. 'No single miner can be satisfied with these terms. But it is the biggest all-round increase achieved by the miners since 1926. It is the first result of national unity of the miners of this country. If this could be achieved by a short national campaign, what could have been achieved with a stronger leadership for the miners and more definite organised support from the trade union movement.'

Horner's public role in the national dispute was minimal. He strictly observed the etiquette of trade union organisational hierarchy, deferring to Griffiths and Jenkins at all union meetings. He did, however, speak at meetings in the English coalfields organised by the CPGB. He is also likely to have used the occasions when he attended MFGB delegate conferences to renew his 1920s contacts in other coalfields with non communist activists, notably Lawther, Edwards and Joe Hall. He probably also met Bowman and Watson for the first time. Despite many activists' frustration, the concessions gained in the national wages campaign had been achieved against the odds, and owed much to the officers' determination and political acumen. The settlement was generally regarded as a victory for the miners.

After January 1936, a more aggressive mood was evident inside all the district unions.

Throughout the national campaign the SWMF Executive had refused to conclude a District Agreement. They had, however, endeavoured to use the coalfield's modest economic recovery to reverse the decline in Federation membership. In July-August 1935, the Cory and Ocean Combine Committees organised a 'Show Cards' offensive against the large numbers of 'nons' working in the pits. When few gains were made, both committees requested the Executive's permission to hand in strike notices to compel the employers to enforce 100 per cent membership. The Executive agreed, and notices were tendered on 16 September. The companies remained intransigent, and on Monday 30 September, over 14,000 SWMF members working in Cory and Ocean pits went on strike in the Garw, Ogmore and Rhondda valleys, as well as Treharris in East Glamorgan and Nine Mile Point in Monmouthshire. The Executive's statement, reported in the *Western Mail*, expressed confidence that the non-unionists would join the SWMF in a few days.

On Thursday 3 October, the *Daily Worker* reported that the strike was still solid at eleven pits, with 9000 men out. The number of 'nons' had been reduced to 30; three pits had won 100 per cent Federation membership; the SWMIU had been expelled from collieries in the Garw Valley. But the strike brought latent antagonisms to the surface:

> In Rhondda only safety men were at work, except in the Dare Colliery, Cwmparc, where the [SW]MIU maintained its hold; at Parc Colliery some fourteen men continued at work. At Nine Mile Point police protected a number who had begun work. Presumably as a tit-for-tat, the Special Purposes Committee of the Coal Owners' Association authorised the Cory and Ocean Combines to keep their collieries idle for up to six days after the dispute had ended.[452]

The SWMF Executive were keen to husband the Federation's meagre financial reserves and check inclinations to wage an open-ended conflict. After a week, the Executive recommended a return to work. Strikers in the Cory collieries returned to work.

Strikers in the Ocean pits went back on 10 October. But the *Daily Worker* reported:

> The feeling of the Nine Mile Point miners is that the question of the continuance at work of the blacklegs imported during the dispute at Nine Mile Point and Taff Merthyr etc. is a coalfield issue and that the coalfield conference on Monday should declare for district action to stop the blacklegs and get 100 per cent trade unionism throughout the coalfield.

On Saturday 12 October a stay-down strike commenced at Nine Mile Point; about seventy-eight men on the day shift in the West Pit stayed down to prevent management giving their underground places to SWMIU members. Enterprising members of the Federation Lodge Committee, inspired by newspaper reports of a pit-bottom occupation by a thousand Hungarian miners in 1934, had conceived the stratagem. They had forewarned the local agent Sid Jones, Harold Finch, who worked in the Area office, and Griffiths; Horner and Alf Davies may also have been told. Many Federation loyalists at Nine Mile Point had moved en bloc from the Rhondda when the colliery had first opened in the early 1920s. Although there was no communist presence, the Rhondda men had maintained exemplary union habits of solidarity and militancy. By Monday 14 October, the stay-down had spread to another pit in the same colliery, Rock Vein; its replication at a third, East Pit, was averted by management's refusal to let any miners underground.

The stay-down 'sparked off a massive wave of pit occupations across the coalfield ... on Wednesday afternoon there had been stay-in [sympathy] strikes at Nantymoel, Blaengarw, Treherbert, Ton Pentre, Treharris and Cwmparc [Parc and Dare collieries] ... There were, according to the Federation, 335 men down in Nine Mile Point pits and at Risca.' Inspired by the stay-downs, 5600 men came out in a sympathy strikes at Tredegar collieries; 4000 men came out in the Garw and Sirhowy Valleys.[453]

On 16 October the Executive recommendation to end the sympathy stay-downs was approved by a delegate conference, but only after 'a three-hour stormy meeting'. On Thursday 17 October, men at North and South Celynen Collieries who had loyally accepted the conference decision to go back to work were confronted by 2000 men and women marching up the Sirhowy Valley; 25,000 men remained out on strike. On Friday 18 October, stay-down strikes continued at Parc and Dare Collieries, at Garw Colliery, Blaengarw and at Fernhill, Treherbert. The *Daily Worker* reported on those pits where men were still staying down, but it noted the return to work of miners at Risca, Tredegar, Treherbert and Glyn-neath without adverse comment.[454] There was no public indication that either the South Wales DPC or the Party Centre supported the escalation of the strikes in defiance of the delegate conference recommendation. Paynter had been acting District Secretary since Cox's departure for London, and he was determined to enforce King Street's policy that party activists should observe official union decisions. There was the additional consideration that a coalfield-wide upheaval in South Wales would disrupt the momentum and legitimacy of the national wages campaign. Many party activists, however, particularly battle-hardened veterans in mid-Rhondda, remained committed revolutionary militants. They regarded Paynter as Horner's creature, and had no scruples about defying official party policy.

The melodrama of miners pledged to stay underground indefinitely, dependent on management's agreement to allow food and drink to be sent down, aroused great popular interest, reinforcing the English media's image of South Wales as an exotic foreign place. The strikes' momentum and intensity surprised colliery managements and the Department of Mines, as well as the Federation officers. Griffiths and other officials who descended the pits to meet the stay-downers recalled their disorientation on walking through the empty roadways and stints to find the cluster of men. The prospect of losing control in the coalfield preoccupied the police and the Cabinet. Griffiths and Jenkins were also haunted by the spectre of anarchy.

In these extraordinary circumstances, the Ocean Coal Company felt compelled to meet most of the Federation demands. On Monday 21 October the *Daily Worker* reported that the Nine Mile Point stay-downers had agreed to ascend after Griffiths, Jenkins and the Lodge Committee had related the company's agreement to withdraw recognition from the SWMIU. (The story also noted that police reinforcements had been drafted in from Birmingham, Liverpool, Bristol and Gloucester.)

Griffiths recalled that it had been a fine morning on 20 October:

> Arthur Jenkins and I made our way to the glen and when we reached the colliery thousands of men, women and children had assembled on the hillside, with hundreds of police to keep them company ... I was greeted [at the pit bottom] by the 'patriarch' who had opened and closed each day with prayer, and in between had transformed the stay-down strikers into a choir ... They listened to me intently as I explained the terms ... and plied me with questions ... It was one of the proudest moments of my life when every lamp was raised [in support of the settlement]. We sang 'Bread of Heaven' ... Then in good order, the older men first, they ascended the shaft to the sunshine and home.[455]

An SWMF delegate conference convened on 21 October to consider the settlement. Cox's *Daily Worker* leader on the same day observed:

> The Delegate Conference last Wednesday [16 October] underestimated the support for the Nine Mile Point miners. It failed to realise the extent of the mass revolt in the coalfield, and the determination to put an end to the blacklegging and company unionism ... The Coalfield Conference today can retrieve the position by taking a decision for immediate coalfield strike action unless there is a written guarantee for the withdrawal of blacklegs and Company Union men from all pits in the coalfield. The South Wales miners are ready. It is now for the Delegate Conference to take the decision and for the Executive Council to lead the revolt until victory is won.

The leader reflected the South Wales DPC's decision to oppose the Griffiths-Jenkins settlement. Horner, Ianto Evans and Paynter disagreed.

Griffiths succeeded in winning support from the delegate conference for a return to work. With Pollitt's support, Paynter used official communist networks to organise a concerted rebellion against the Griffiths-Jenkins settlement. The *Daily Worker* story on 22 October was carefully supportive, quoting Griffiths extensively without comment:

> Before the Conference closed the Chairman made a stirring and inspiring speech in which he pointed out that during the past two years the Executive ... had spent £74,000 upon strikes and disputes ... He appealed to the delegates to maintain the present feeling and fervour ... and to carry this feeling into the pits so that more effective work could be done ...

On 23 October, the *Daily Worker* reported an exchange of letters between King Street and the Federation, which Pollitt had initiated, to make it 'perfectly clear that we have no desire to interfere in any way with the organisation of the campaign or the policy put forward by your organisation. We recognise that this is entirely a matter for the members of the SWMF and the Executive ... '. Harris had acknowledged the letter with punctilious politeness. The DPC's decision to oppose the settlement had evidently become public knowledge, and Pollitt had felt it advisable not only to mend fences, but also to be seen doing so.

The veteran revolutionary militants in the party were unwilling to let matters rest there. Utilising the anger and frustration felt by many activists in Glamorgan and Monmouthshire, they organised a *démarche*. Pollitt and Allison were either powerless or deemed it imprudent to rein them in. On 28 October the *Daily Worker* published a statement from the South Wales DPC. Citing the communist party's 'foremost part' in rooting out the SWMIU, the statement noted that:

> at this stage when thousands of miners were on strike and a storm of indignation raging against company unionism ... the district leadership ... wavered in its policy and was in favour of postponing a coalfield strike ... It is clear that ... [it] was wrongly influenced by its concern for national unity of the miners and the possible con-

sequences of lightning strikes which would deplete the resources of the Federation ... This was a serious error, for united coalfield action would have strengthened the fight for the miners' national demands.

Horner's MI5 file situated the DPC's public self-criticism as part of an all-out offensive. On 31 October, a party member, WE Jones, wrote to the London Secretariat:

> informing them that at the last meeting of the Monmouthshire Sub-District ... the mistakes of the ... District in connection with mining were discussed. Having regard to the higher status of A. HORNER and W. PAYNTER ... it was decided to refer our resolutions to the Central Committee [Executive]:- '(1) that the C.C. shall consider A. HORNER's line in the S. Wales situation as being opportunist and shall take steps to prevent the recurrence. (2) As the line was endorsed and drawn up by the S. Wales District we call for steps as will make such policies impossible in the future.'[456]

Latent hostilities inside the South Wales party had forced their way to the surface under the pressure of the dramatic success of the stay-down strikes. There is insufficient evidence to assess the level of support for each camp. Comrades who opposed defiance of delegate conference decisions and agreed with subordinating South Walian concerns to the national wages campaign included not only Horner, his allies and protégés, but also Len Jeffries, recently released from prison. Opposition to Horner and the new party line was centred around mid-Rhondda, stronghold of the URC and the Cambrian Combine militants. Principled support for militancy was their touchstone because they believed that revolution would inevitably emerge from a militant upsurge of industrial conflict. A serious civil war might have erupted if Baldwin had not dissolved parliament on 25 October. The general election campaign commenced the following week. Billy Griffiths recalled his own partisan feelings to Hywel Francis in 1969. 'Paynter failed as new secretary. Sabotaged a strike against non-unionism ... told all CPers to send all men back to work. (30,000 men out on strike). [Billy Griffiths] had to tell Cambrian

Combine [party members]. Pollitt (there for parliamentary campaign) told them to obey.'[457]

Pollitt's virtually continuous presence during the three week campaign had a soothing effect on troubled inner-party relations. Unlike Horner, he commanded unconditional loyalty and affection from veteran revolutionary militants. His personal friendship with Horner was well-known, but his public approach to economic conflict was sufficiently different to allay any doubts about his revolutionary bona fides. Soon after Pollitt's return to London, however, the DPC wrote to Ianto Evans and Horner, asking for their observations on the stay-down strikes. They were evidently determined to extract an admission from the two men that they had been wrong to support Griffiths' and Jenkins' negotiated settlement of the stay-down strikes. Evans replied that 'in view of events since settlement he is personally more convinced than ever that the correct line was pursued.' The MI5 report observed, 'Writer [Evans] makes one final observation: "These perennial inquests which are held after every event of importance, and endeavours to find scapegoats are doing the Party no good, and some very caustic comments are often made by Non-Party elements nearest us."'

Ianto's frustration with the DPC was echoed by King Street, albeit in a more aesopian fashion. Since the Seventh World Congress, Pollitt's and Campbell's approach to the economic struggle, which I have described as revolutionary pragmatism, balanced unconditional support for all militant action, with an equally unconditional injunction to union loyalism. For much of the time in the daily 'mass work' of communist union activists, it was possible to operate on the basis of giving these two imperatives equal weight. But inevitably, there were situations when party union activists had to choose between the two. On these critical occasions, the Party Centre usually remained publicly silent, anxious not be seen condoning an end to militant action. But Pollitt and Allison intervened privately to ensure that party union activists did not commit themselves to last-ditch opposition to decisions taken by union executives. After a strike had been abandoned, a compromise agreed or retreat effected in good order, the *Daily Worker* and Party Executive might regret the settlement and offer the pious observation that more might have been achieved if union leaders had honoured the rank-and-file's desire to fight to the finish.[458]

The *Daily Worker* announced a District Congress being held in South Wales over the weekend of 17 to 18 November. At the Congress, delegates evidently agreed with the DPC's determination to bring Horner and Ianto Evans to book for their support of the SWMF Executive and their failure to push for a coal-field strike. The next entry in the MI5 narrative reflected the South Wales DPC's determination to bring Horner and Evans to book. 'John JONES, Llanelly (*sic*) writing to Lewis JONES [in the Rhondda] stated: "Arthur is on the mat at Cardiff [DPC meeting] on Tuesday." On 27 November, however, the District Secretariat wrote to Charlie Stead in Swansea advising that the District Conference planned for Sunday 1 December to discuss "mining mistakes" has been cancelled in view of decision of comrades at Party centre, who now consider it advisable to request HORNER to go to London for further discussion ... ' This further discussion did not, however, result in any change in Horner's conduct. By superimposing their authority and moving the issue to London, Pollitt and Allison extricated Horner from a situation which threatened to escalate into another confrontation between himself and revolutionary militants.

King Street's intervention produced a temporary truce. On 29 November, the *Daily Worker* reported that the Taff-Merthyr management were breaking their agreement with the SWMF, concluding:

> The South Wales coalfield will have to resort to a General Strike before Taff-Merthyr miners can hope to gain any-thing from this struggle.' Local party branches continued to send their criticisms of Horner to the DPC in Cardiff. On 9 December C Parry, Unit Leader of Pontardulais, accused Horner of flouting the agreed party line. 'Did Cde. HORNER know of the line of the Party prior to going into Conference [on 21 October] and why did the other Cdes weaken to HORNER in spite of the fact that their's was the Party line.' Mavis Llewellyn, a close friend of Lewis Jones, reported to the DPC on the Maesteg Aggregate which she had attended, along with eleven other comrades. She sent a list of four questions aris-

311

ing from the discussion, including '1. To what extent
did Com. HORNER display legalist tendencies prior to
October? ... 3. Are we justified in saying that our leading
comrades underestimated the mood of the masses? 4.
Do we find that the line of HORNER is winning more
adherents?'

The MI5 file did not record the denouement to this inner party
battle. In the Rhondda many comrades took ideological dis-
putations seriously, as matters involving personal honour and
integrity, to be fought to the bitter end.[459] It is likely, however,
that Horner and his supporters there, notably Paynter, Gwen
Ray Evans and remaining comrades in the Mardy enclave, had
developed a strong aversion to entering into essentially theological arguments. From the Datcha in Upper Tumble, Horner concentrated on his union job, and abstained from participation in
the ongoing conflict about what line the party should take about
coalmining issues. He became even more adept at avoiding DPC
meetings. His supporters may have found it more politic to keep
silent and not argue his case inside branch meetings where they
were in a minority. They relied instead on Life Itself to present
the empirical proof of Horner's arguments. Most party members who were SWMF activists were compelled to trim towards
Horner's position under pressure of events. Their conduct in
the real world, as opposed to ex cathedra disputation in party
branch meetings, showed a willingness to subordinate the principle of fighting industrial conflict to the last ditch to the need
to work inside 'reformist' unions.[460]

From mid-December the escalation of the MFGB national
wages dispute enabled Pollitt and Allison to invoke Life Itself
as a pressing reason for the restoration of party unity. On 18
December, the MFGB delegate conference had voted to tender
strike notices for a national stoppage beginning on 27 January.
MFGB officers and the Executive were anxious to convey a determined, pugnacious public image, signalling their intention to
strike unless the coalowners and the government made concessions. In South Wales, Griffiths and Jenkins used the prospect of
a national strike to rebuild cordial relations with their activists.
In mid-December, the Federation Executive agreed to second
Alf Davies to prepare another offensive at Taff-Merthyr to chal-

312

lenge management's behaviour, in particular their victimisation of SWMF members.

When the prevailing mood inside the SWMF was so martial, it was difficult for Horner's opponents inside the party to press for his public censure for the transgression of 'union legalism'. However, some revolutionary militants were unrepentant. Party discipline did not prevent them from challenging Horner's increasingly public enunciations of his Clausewitzianism principles. The Comintern's new United Front line did not extend to support for the strategic theory of *On War*.

The Federation Executive elections in December 1935 marked a significant advance for left candidates standing on a united front platform. On 1 January 1936, the *Daily Worker* reported victories for four of the nine candidates standing on the united front slate, only one of whom, Ianto Evans, was an incumbent. The new entrants were Dai Dan Evans, Jack Davies and Alf Davies. The story also welcomed the election of two unaligned militants; Will Arthur was elected for Area 2, and Billy Crews re-elected for Area 6. Its leader of 2 January was euphoric. 'The Welsh miners have chosen well ... Not the least factor ... is the election of two new Communist members and the re-election of the only Communist member on the old Executive. But in addition, several of those elected [not on the united front slate] have shown in recent months that they are capable leaders of a body of men always in the vanguard of the workers' struggle for a higher standard of living.' The moral was clear.[461]

Little more than a year after Horner had led the campaign against the SWMIU at Emlyn, further significant advances had been made. Inside the MFGB, SWMF leaders could again participate on terms of equality with the other district unions of comparable size, Yorkshire and Durham. SWMF officers resumed their accustomed influence on the MFGB Executive; SWMF activists self-confidently went back to playing a dominant part in MFGB delegate conferences. In sharp contrast to 1928 to 1931, the South Wales coalowners were making no attempt to impose further wage reductions or lengthening of hours. The softening of their bargaining stance reflected not only the improved economic situation, but also different political conditions.

The palpable improvement in the Federation's fortunes had greatly assisted Griffiths and Jenkins in containing the culture of principled militancy to which many veteran activists still adhered. Nevertheless, as successive delegate conferences had shown, the URC's tradition remained strong in many mid-Rhondda lodges, and its exponents' powerful rhetoric often gained significant support. Horner was certain not only that he could win greater gains for the Federation than Griffiths and Jenkins, but also that he was the genuine heir to the URC legacy. He did not believe that scientific Clausewitzian principles violated his commitment to militant struggle; their application rather enabled maximum advances to be made for the minimum expenditure of force.

During the official and unofficial strikes of 1935, Horner had ample opportunity to observe that Griffiths' and Jenkins' responses were reflexive and ad hoc. By contrast, he was operating with scientific principles which were more effective in gaining results. It is hardly surprising that he was ambitious to replace them. Jenkins had been elected MP for Pontypool at the 1935 general election. His victory presented an opportunity to unseat him as SWMF Vice-President, which Horner was not slow to seize. He and his supporters planned a campaign to change the SWMF rules so that Federation officers who became MPs would have to give up their union position. There were strong precedents reinforcing their arguments. After his post as SWMF general secretary had been made full-time in 1920, Tom Richards had voluntarily resigned as Labour MP for West Monmouth. In 1923 the MFGB Executive had disbarred Frank Hodges from continuing as MFGB general secretary after he had been elected Labour MP for Lichfield. Though neither the Federation President nor Vice-President were full-time positions, Horner and supporters could show that their responsibilities had greatly increased since 1920. Their point that the union should come first for all its officers was popular for Lodge activists, for most of whom Westminster was strange, even hostile terrain.

In February 1936 the death of the Dr JH Williams, Labour MP for Llanelli, made the projected rule change even more prescient. Griffiths had been Labour agent in Llanelli in the early 1920s, and had retained a strong lien on the seat. He yielded to temptation and accepted the constituency party's invitation to stand, even though he knew that the militant left would propose the rule change at the Federation Annual Conference in April which would disqualify MPs from holding SWMF office. His victory at the by-election on 26 March was a foregone conclusion.[462]

On the eve of the by-election, the *Western Mail* bemoaned the union's probable fate: if Jim Griffiths were elected, 'the heir presumptive to the Presidency of the SWMF [would be] none other than the chief Communist agitator of the South Wales coalfield'.[463] The writer did not need to mention Horner by name.

Having single-mindedly pursued their parliamentary ambitions, Griffiths and Jenkins mounted a belated campaign against the rule change on the basis that it would enable Horner to hold office. Their arguments had little resonance. The Federation's self-image as a democratic, rank-and-file union, to which both men also subscribed, continued to have a strong appeal across the political divide. Moreover, moderate and right-wing activists did not consider that Horner was a typical militant. They could see that his personal position often differed from more dogmatic militants. They also appreciated the concessions he was winning for his members in the Anthracite. It is not surprising that the Executive voted to recommend the rule change to Annual Conference on 18 April.

Alf Davies and Will Arthur moved the Executive's recommendation, that the offices of President and Vice-President could not be 'adequately filled by members of parliament'. It was passed on a card vote by 86,450 to 27,000. The elections, due to take place that day, were postponed, and the conference adjourned so that lodges could make new nominations.[464] When the conference re-convened on 23 May, there were five candidates for President. Horner had been nominated by a large number of lodges, including Mardy.[465] He won decisively on the first ballot, receiving 155 votes from the 235 delegates present. The runner-up, Alderman Bill Saddler, Agent for the Western Monmouthshire Area, won 43. Saddler had also been nominated for Vice-President, and won after several ballots had narrowed the field of 20 candidates, with a vote of 143. The runners-up were Alf Davies, with 93 and Ness Edwards with 39. The *Merthyr Express* announced the result with a front page headline: 'COMMUNIST ELECTED MINERS' PRESIDENT. A Native of Merthyr. OVERWHELMING VOTE FOR MR. ARTHUR HORNER.'[466]

Chapter 10

Federation President

The *Manchester Guardian* headline reporting Horner's election was, 'ONCE EXPELLED, NOW PRESIDENT'. The story portrayed a man of the people. 'Six years ago he was expelled from the federation for supporting the communists. Thousands of miners welcomed him at Mardy to-day after his election to the highest honour they could confer upon him.' Horner was quoted in triumphant mode. 'The increase of Communism ... is due to the bankruptcy of the present system ... Communism is growing rapidly in South Wales, but thousands of miners voted for me who are not Communists. They stand for strong, militant trade unionism. This is a demonstration of the spirit of the militancy among the miners and their determination to improve their conditions.' The *Daily Worker's* report said it was a 'sign of the times that the most courageous fighters in the British working class movement have placed their confidence in a prominent Communist fighter to lead the future struggles in the South Wales coalfield'. Its leader concluded that the election was 'the reply to all who oppose the affiliation of the Communist Party to the Labour Party. It is a clear call to the TUC General Council to drop once and for all the policy of class collaboration and industrial peace and the attacks on militants in the trade union movement'.

Horner's victory was a severe political embarrassment for the Labour establishment. In London the TUC and Labour Party *apparats* made dire predictions about Horner's plans for unleashing class war. But Morgan Phillips and Citrine could hardly complain that he had staged a coup to win power. Griffiths and Jenkins had opted for political careers. Comparatively young and ambitious, they had entered parliament with the intention of making their mark, rather than remaining on the back benches amongst the largely silent rank-and-file of trade union sponsored MPs. Griffiths was probably less angry than Jenkins at Horner's succession. Having worked in close proximity to Horner for over two years, he recognised his abilities, and had learned to respect his judgement on union matters. From the House of Commons, he took care to maintain the friendly relations established during Horner's tenure in the Swansea office.[467]

On the ground, there was little evidence of an anti-communist reaction against Horner amongst Federation activists. Most recognised his and other communists' contribution to the advances made since 1934 in the Federation's conflict with the SWMIU. In mid-April 1936, at the SWMF Annual Conference, delegates had voted by a two to one majority to support communist affiliation to the Labour Party. The *Daily Worker* reported that the show of hands in favour was so decisive that opponents had not called for a card vote. The story highlighted Horner's statement that he had the full authority and backing of the communist party leadership to pledge that the CPGB would observe the Labour constitution.[468]

Communists, moreover, were hardly the only political group offering damning analyses of the vagaries of capitalism in South Wales. Whilst British inland coalfields had benefited from the recovery in the domestic economy, the coalfields producing for the export market continued to languish. It was simply not practical politics for any Federation leader to espouse a moderate approach as the answer to their members' bleak situation. The rhetoric of Griffiths and Jenkins at the 1935 TUC had been as passionate as any communist's in insisting that the government take action to redress the situation.

Horner remained unequivocal that his status as a prominent communist had no bearing on his fitness to be head of a union affiliated to the Labour Party. Since the 1920s he had publicly attested his willingness to abide by the Labour Party constitution at SWMF and MFGB conferences, arguing that there was nothing in the Labour canon with which he, as a committed trade unionist and communist, could disagree. He was evidently sincere in this profession. His history as an outspoken opponent of the extreme left variant of Class Against Class reinforced his professions of bona fides towards the Labour constitution, even though his close Labour comrades, including Bevan, found the facility with which he skated over the Comintern's undisputed hegemony over affiliated parties disingenuous. After the Comintern Seventh World Congress, Horner's vision of the labour movement's fundamental unity became more credible. Bevan and other left-wing activists were prepared to work more closely with the CPGB and more prepared to defend Horner's integrity inside the trade union movement.

The office of Federation President was voluntary, and Horner's full-time job continued to be agent for the Gwendraeth valley. But he spent most of his working time at the Federation Central Office in St Andrews Crescent in Cardiff. Custom and practice enabled him to delegate routine administrative and case work to the other Swansea agents and Gomer Evans. Horner settled easily into the new routine, taking a close interest in all departments' day-to-day business, including the compensation department, whose officials dealt with the numerous claims for accidents and industrial disease. (He was meticulous in keeping well-informed of developments in coalmining occupational health.) He found both Harris and Saddler to be supportive co-workers. They were clearly prepared to accept his declarations that the union always came first. Harris had recognised Horner's abilities in the early 1920s, when he himself had been a committed left-wing social-ist. Hostile to the CPGB's and Horner's leftward turn in 1927, Harris had trimmed to Richards and then Griffiths. Saddler, whose base was Newbridge in Monmouthshire, was a keen Bevanite, and had had ample opportunity to observe Horner's leadership qualities in the Taff-Merthyr events.

In the autumn of 1936 the Horners moved fifteen miles south along the A476, to Felinfoel Road on the outskirts of Llanelli. Their detached house had been built in 1928, part of the town's suburbanisation. The move substantially shortened Arthur's journey to Cardiff, and formalised the arrangement whereby Gomer Evans dealt with routine business for collieries in the Gwendraeth Valley. Arthur walked down the long flight of steps in his front garden to board the tram which started its journey half a mile up the road in the village of Felinfoel and terminated at Llanelli railway station. He then caught the main line train via Swansea to Cardiff. He could usually complete the door-to-door journey in under two hours.

Horner named their new house the Datcha again. In 1936 its vantage point on Dimpath Hill looked out over an undulating landscape of fields and scrubland. Because they were much more accessible than at Upper Tumble, Ethel began to entertain friends who came by train and tram, or who owned motor cars, like Alf Davies. Alf regularly arrived at the Datcha with his wife, Mary, and their daughters, Olive and Vera, who were similar in age to Rosa and Joan. International comrades passing through South Wales also found it easy to arrive by train and tram. Ethel also continued to hold open house for Rhondda friends and family. Rosa and Joan enrolled at secondary school in Llanelli. Vol had gone to London in late April 1935, aged seventeen, principally at Arthur's urging. He wanted her to see more of the world, and through Pollitt's good offices arranged a job for her at the Workers' Bookshop in Charing Cross Road. She stayed with Arthur's younger sister, Mabel, until she found lodgings in Bloomsbury. Arthur took care to stay in regular contact, taking her out for meals when he was in London for MFGB or CPGB Executive meetings.[469]

In contrast to their generic anti-communism, neither the government nor the South Wales coalowners displayed any apprehension about doing business with Horner. As a member of the South Wales District Conciliation Board Arbitration Tribunal, Sir David Shackleton had already observed Horner at close quarters. He told the Department of Mines in October, 'The appointment of Mr. Horner as chairman of the SWMF is not as disturbing as was expected by some. A big responsibility sometimes has this effect.'[470] Horner had first crossed verbal swords with Evan Williams, the veteran President of the South Wales coalowners, in 1926. The two men established combative but never hostile relations. They each possessed forensic negotiating abilities, and had a healthy respect for the other's intelligence and negotiating abilities. Horner used his fluent mastery of large amounts of information to dominate meetings and negotiations, regularly embarrassing civil servants and coalowners' representatives by his superior analysis and recall of facts. Federation colleagues appreciated these virtuoso qualities, and increasingly relied on his initiative and judgement.

Perhaps because Evan Williams was preoccupied with the MAGB's increasingly problematic relations with the Baldwin government, Horner conducted most of the Federation's business with the South Wales Coalowners Secretary, Iestyn Williams.

Two years older than Horner, Iestyn Williams was the son of a Cardiff mining engineer. Like Horner, he had not been educated beyond elementary school and had joined the staff of the South Wales coalowners aged twenty-one.[471] He probably knew Horner by reputation only before his election. Soon afterwards, he arranged to meet Horner in the tearoom at Swansea railway station, a venue lacking *gravitas*, probably chosen because it allowed the two men to talk informally without being observed. A shrewd tactical operator, Williams evidently decided to put his relations with Horner on a firm and frank footing from the outset. Horner recalled in *Incorrigible Rebel*:

> Iestyn asked whether I was going to make trouble in the coalfield ... I said, 'If the class war is going to continue as bitterly as it has in the past, there is going to be the greatest trouble.' He said, 'I have come to persuade you that there is no need to destroy the coalfield ... and that within reason the owners are prepared to make concessions.' I told him that the last thing I wanted to do was to destroy the coalfields ... but that if they wanted to fight, I knew more ways of fighting than they had dreamed of. We reached a tentative sort of agreement that they would see what they could do to improve the conditions ... and I on my side would do what I could to see that there were no unnecessary disputes.

By 1960 Horner had told this anecdote many times, but its gist was probably accurate. He went on to explain why he had made the tentative sort of agreement, in phrases which he deployed repeatedly to explain his conduct to assembled union delegates:

> By the time I was elected to the presidency, I had pretty well formulated my philosophy as a trade union leader ... The function of a trade union is to sell a commodity. The function of the employer is to buy that commodity. Whether the employer be the State, a private owner or a co-operative organization, this transaction of buying and selling labour still has to be carried out. Once you accept that view, the rule has to apply in a

capitalist society and, with different factors involved, in a socialist society as well. You have to seek to place the buyer in the position where he cannot buy from anybody except you. This of course is the basis for the drive for one hundred per cent. trade unionism.[472]

Horner's appearance as a delegate, for the first time since 1928, at the MFGB Annual Conference held in Scarborough in July, marked his return to the centre stage of the British trade union movement. Not surprisingly, the corps of labour correspondents assiduously followed his every nuance and gesture, reporting many of them. The conference agenda included pro-united-front motions from South Wales, Durham and Northumberland. Evidently, the prolonged depression in these coal exporting districts was propelling Labour union activists towards more radical positions.

The Labour Party *apparat* were fearful of what might happen at Horner's debut as the South Wales President, and arrangements were set in train to minimise the damage. Joseph Jones' decision to hold the debate on a composite motion in private session was unsuccessfully challenged by Horner and Jack Williams, from the Forest of Dean. The motion committed the MFGB to support the CPGB's affiliation to the Labour Party, provided that the communist party declared its readiness to accept the Labour Party constitution. Horner moved it in a closely argued speech calculated to appeal to delegates and districts who were not left-wing; it was seconded by Ned Moore from Durham. The debate was full of feeling and well-informed. Horner was compelled to indignantly deny that the German communist party's refusal to co-operate with the SPD had significantly contributed to Hitler's success. The motion was carried on a card vote, 283,000 to 238,000; Yorkshire, Lancashire and Scotland were the principal opposing districts.

This important debate and its result were reported by labour correspondents who had congregated outside the conference hall to engage with delegates leaving the session and ply them with drink to find out what had happened. Their stories appeared on 22 July. The *Daily Herald's* headline, 'SMALL MAJORITY FOR ADMISSION TO PARTY' was a model of damage limitation. The right-wing *Morning Post* headline was doom-laden,

'COMMUNISTS WIN CONTROL OF MINERS ... LEADERS ROUTED: BITTER DEBATE'. The story continued the horrific narrative:

> Ten minutes later [after the vote] Mr. Arthur Horner, who eight years ago was forcibly ejected from the Conference Hall at Llandudno, stood at the door to receive the congratulations of fellow Communists ... Mr. John McGurk [of Lancashire] moved an amendment, which would have had the effect of killing the proposal. The amendment was defeated amid a storm of applause ... One after another the delegates rose and startled the officials with violent advocacy of the Communist cause. Passions rose rapidly to blood heat, and invective was hurled across the floor by both sides ...

The *Morning Post* leader on 23 July added:

> in the counsels of Trade Unionism the Miners' Federation occupies the status of *primus inter pares*: its influence is attested by the fact that it contributes no less than one-quarter of the total Socialist membership of the House of Commons. Its edict, therefore, is not to be despised. The upper hierarchy of Socialism is aghast ... We, for our part, find some little difficulty in distinguishing all the infinitely subtle gradations of doctrine which lead from Communism, via Sir Stafford Cripps, to the official policy of the Labour Party.

As further evidence, the leader cited the elation on the left of the Labour Party after the French elections in May 1936 which had resulted in a Popular Front government with a socialist prime minister, Leon Blum, supported by the French Communists, who had won a significant number of seats in the Assembly. There was certainly evidence that left-wing Labour MPs and intellectuals were in favour of replicating the French. Stafford Cripps, Bevan and GDH Cole had publicly supported communist affiliation to the Labour Party; the number of pro-CPGB affiliation motions from union branches and local Labour Party organisations had also increased.[473]

Liberal papers were more sanguine about the possibility of a united front in Britain. On 22 July the *Manchester Guardian* quoted an upbeat Horner, without adding its own adverse comment. 'I am very glad that the South Wales experiment in the united front is being extended nationally. We hope and believe that it will be carried into all spheres of our work and will have the most beneficial results.' In the *News Chronicle* Ian Mackay noted that the MFGB was the second large union to support the 'Left Wing movement in favour of the United Front against War and Fascism', following the AEU. 'It is now clear that the movement for the United Front has been tremendously stimulated by the success of the Popular Front in France and Spain'.

Horner was in no doubt that the Federation's protracted war with the SWMIU was part of the anti-fascist struggle. Speaking to the re-convened SWMF Annual Conference after being elected President, he declared that 'Scab Unionism is fascism in embryo ... One hundred per cent conscious militant Trade Unionism is the most important safeguard against fascism.'[474] He made the continuing fight against the SWMIU his first priority. The front line was Bedwas, the only colliery where the SWMIU was still accorded sole recognition. If the SWMF could compel the Bedwas Navigation Colliery Company (1921) Ltd. to withdraw recognition, the victory would give them a decisive psychological advantage. They could then exert strong pressure on the large number of non-unionists working at neighbouring pits in the Rhymney Valley. Horner told Frankenberg that Federation membership was only 30 per cent in this part of the coalfield. The continuing lack of critical mass in what had previously been a Federation stronghold was a significant weakness in the union's bargaining position and Horner's ability to win wage increases.[475]

During the summer and autumn of 1936 most British political observers were preoccupied by the opening military engagements in the Spanish Civil War. In South Wales, however, Spanish events were eclipsed by the conflict in the Rhymney Valley. In March 1936, after the successful conclusion of the MFGB's national wage campaign, the Federation Executive had sent Horner to reconnoitre the situation at Bedwas. The Executive discussed the situation on 28 April, 2 and 12 May, and decided to proceed at Bedwas using the boring from within strategy.

The terrain they faced was exceptionally difficult. The colliery company had inflicted a humiliating defeat on the SWMF in 1933. At the end of February, the Bedwas Federation lodge had come out on strike in defence of their established customs and practices, which the management had revoked. The colliery company, having withdrawn from the coalowners' association, had been free to de-recognise the SWMF. They also sacked Federation activists, leaving the SWMIU in sole possession of the field.[476] On 6 March the SWMF Executive had recommended to a delegate conference that lodges tender the fortnight's notice required under the district procedure agreement for a coalfield strike in support of Bedwas and to compel the owners to withdraw recognition of the SWMIU. Delegates agreed, and the next stage in Federation procedure was for lodges to vote on whether to accept the conference recommendation.

The majority of Federation lodge meetings voted in favour of striking, but most were sparsely attended. This poor result was due to many lodges' organisational disarray during this period and the absence of an organised left-wing to marshal support. Well aware of the Federation's depleted membership, the coalowners' association did not treat the threat of a coalfield strike seriously: Evan Williams declined to put any pressure on the Bedwas company, who, in any case, were no longer association members. Uncertain that lodges would honour strike notices, and certain that Federation funds were insufficient to sustain a coalfield strike, the Federation Executive had decided on 22 March not to call a coalfield strike, and instructed the Bedwas men to return to work. Horner traced the history of the situation in *The Miners' Monthly*, the new Federation journal edited by Harris. 'The Truth Behind the Bedwas Settlement' was written in the terse narrative of his favourite Western novels:[477]

[E]arly in 1933 Bedwas Lodge – one of the strongest Lodges of the SWMF – was driven off the Colliery it had controlled for many years. The men fought like the heroes they were. The old Executive Council picketed the approaches to the Pit and the outlying stations. Hundreds of pounds were spent. Yet the blacklegs came in under police protection until the Pit was full of them. Two thousand Bedwas men were thrown out. The Coalfield Conference recommended strike notices, but when it was reported that only 40 per cent. had signed, the Executive decided against a coalfield strike. The coalfield continued to work normally, and the Bedwas Lodge became composed of unemployed members. Their leader [Billy Milsom] died – in the main because of the humiliation arising from seeing his men beaten and sacrificed, whilst blacklegs worked in the Pits. From 1933 to the beginning of 1936, there was quiet at Bedwas except for occasional outbreaks by the old leadership of the Bedwas Lodge in their vain efforts to make contact with the men in the Pit. In 1934 Emlyn was won over for the Federation. Victory was achieved at Parc and Dare. Taff Merthyr was seriously weakened in its resistance to the Federation. The men employed in Bedwas remained unaffected by what was happening around them. Bedwas was still 100 per cent. Miners' Industrial Union, and against this there was no evidence of a spontaneous revolt from within. Four to five hundred ex-Bedwas workmen got jobs individually [back in Bedwas] from time to time, and they were chosen carefully by the management. The strikes at Emlyn, Taff Merthyr, Blaenavon, and scores of other places took nearly all the finances of the Federation; but these struggles had dealt a serious blow against the Miners' Industrial Union. In 1936 there were just two Collieries where it still had members – Taff Merthyr, where there were no longer any deductions from wages and where it is claimed nearly 200 are still paying voluntary contributions [to the SWMIU], and Bedwas, where 1,700 men were compelled to allow a deduction from wages amounting to 4d . per man per week. It was obvious that the financial basis of the Miners' Industrial Union was at Bedwas, and that the task of destroying this Union at Bedwas was of urgent importance.

If Griffiths had remained President, the SWMF might not have achieved its objective. Although committed to fighting the

SWMIU to the last ditch, he lacked tactical skills, or the stomach, to lead a serious industrial conflict from the front. Readers interested in military history will recognise Horner's capabilities as being well-suited to generalship. He possessed flexibility, finesse and audacity, qualities which were important for taking decisions under fire and during negotiations. He had a taste for individual and collective combat. His early sporting passion for boxing had developed his fighting instinct, willingness to take risks and sense of timing. His meticulous attention to detail and planning were critical prerequisites for leading large-scale operations. He refined techniques and tactics used at Emlyn and Taff-Merthyr for Bedwas, 'the best planned and directed of all the forays against company unionism'.[478]

Horner commenced the campaign at a favourable moment. The miners' credibility as a fighting force had risen, due to the MFGB Executive presenting the credible threat of a national miners' strike. South Wales coalowners had begun to penetrate the British domestic market for coal and were even finding their export markets improved. Given the proximity of Taff-Merthyr to Bedwas, it was decided to launch a simultaneous offensive to try to rebuild the SWMF's severely eroded position at both pits. The Executive seconded four members to assist Ness Edwards and Billy Crews. Three, Jack Davies, from Llwynypia, DR Davies from Ebbw Vale, and Dai Dan Evans, went to Bedwas. They 'lived in the locality for weeks, adapting their tactics to the circumstances at the pit.' They rose every morning at 5 am and held meetings at the two entrances of the pit. They also organised public meetings in the wider catchment area from which the company now recruited. But Dai Dan Evans remembered that 'the people we would get ... would be the men who were idle there ... we would hold meetings in Caerphilly ... in Llanbradach ... all the way up the Rhymney Valley, and all the way up the Merthyr Valley ... ' The fourth seconded Executive member, Alf Davies, went to Bedlinog, to lay the ground for a fresh assault on Taff-Merthyr.[479]

Underground at Bedwas, a cell of Federation members working under cover were agitating amongst their fellow miners. To minimise victimisation, they were organised in groups of three; they then approached the miners whom the cell had identified as willing to leave the SWMIU in order to sign them up for the Federation at a special reduced subscription. The SWMF central office kept the Pit Committee (*pro tem*) supplied with a steady stream of one page leaflets; these were effective, hard-hitting propaganda and were distributed widely above and below ground to prevent management identifying the Federation members responsible. Horner probably wrote most of them after consulting the cell and seconded Executive members. In July, Leaflet No. 45 declared, 'Your fight for freedom must be timed to begin when the forces of the Coalfield have been prepared to take simultaneous action. We must keep in step with the Coalfield ... With discretion and courage resolve to play the part of men.'

Leo Price, a communist Federation activist who lived in nearby Abertridwr, was conscripted to serve in one of the trio teams. When he started at Bedwas, feelings were running high amongst workers commuting long distances to Bedwas. They reacted against management's close supervision, and the enforced deductions from their wages for SWMIU subscriptions.[480] The Federation's well-organised precautions, and probably also non-Federation miners' well-founded fear of reprisals if they informed, meant that management had a dearth of evidence about suspected Federation men. Increasingly insecure, their attitude to their employees became even more arbitrary.

In mid-July, the Federation cell calculated that they could count on 800 men, about half the workforce. Horner evidently considered that this was a sufficient bridgehead and commenced the second stage of the operation. A coalfield conference was arranged for 12 August. In late July, Leaflet No. 48 was distributed, urging the men to sign Revocation Cards prepared by the Federation to 'Let the men of the Coalfield know that Bedwas is ready'. One side of the card contained an instruction to the management revoking the employee's previous forced consent to having SWMIU subscriptions deducted from their wages; it was followed by spaces for signature, address, lamp number, and occupation, as well as spaces for a witness's signature and address. The other side was addressed to the SWMF central office in Cardiff, with a reply-paid stamp.

The Revocation Cards were posted to miners at home, enabling them to reflect on their contents in privacy. This manoeuvre was possible because the Federation had fortuitously obtained the addresses of all Bedwas employees, probably as a result of a burglary arranged by Ness Edwards to obtain evidence about the company and its dealings with the SWMIU. The number of returns reflected the success of the campaign. Around 1000 employees, out of 1600, signed and posted their cards.[481]

Horner kept the returned cards in the office safe at St Andrews Crescent, and did not refer to them publicly until the delegate conference on 12 August. He signalled his intention then of delivering them to the colliery management, challenging them to carry out the 1000 employees' express wish to cease paying contributions to the SWMIU. Favourably impressed, delegates voted in favour of the Executive's recommendation to issue an ultimatum to the coalowners' association and the Bedwas coal company: if the management sacked any employee who had signed a Revocation Card, then a re-convened delegate conference scheduled for 24 August would tender the required fortnight's notice to the coalowners' association of a coalfield strike to commence on 5 September. The decision was endorsed by lodge meetings the following week. 'The Truth' commented, 'Ninety per cent. of the coalfield did in 1936 what only 40 per cent. was prepared to do in 1933 to help Bedwas.'

The decisive result enabled the union to exert intense indirect pressure on the Bedwas Coal Company via the coalowners' association. Horner did not deliver the Revocation Cards immediately. They still remained locked away in the Federation safe, constituting his principal weapon in the tactical skirmishing which now commenced. He regularly reminded the company, the press and the Department of Mines of the written, legally sound evidence which he possessed. The possibility that he might deliver them continued to act as a powerful incentive to Evan Williams and the coalowners, as well as Crookshank and civil servants at the Department of Mines, to seek a peaceful solution to the conflict. His notoriety as a combative, aggressive personality reinforced the economic reasons for taking a coalfield strike threat seriously.

Horner allowed sufficient time for Federation activists to build up momentum in the coalfield in order to present a credible threat. He knew that the SWMF was incapable of financing a coalfield strike for more than a few days, since it would be paying strike pay to its entire 120,000 members. (The union's funds had been severely depleted during 1935, when members in the Ocean and Cory combines had received strike pay for weeks on end.[482]) But a consummate sense of timing enabled Horner to extract the maximum effect from every move he made on the Federation's behalf, with the minimum of risk. His intention was to break the owners' resolve without calling a coalfield strike.

The Bedwas owners, Sir Samuel and Theodore Instone, were well aware of the Federation's financial straits. Their strong capitalist principles made them determined not to back down in the face of threats from a union led by a communist. They responded with counter-threats, announcing that if Horner delivered the Revocation Cards, they would lock-out every employee who had signed one. As the conflict continued, their zeal in opposing militancy and communism intensified. On 21 August, Samuel Instone published a pamphlet rehearsing the sequence of events at Bedwas since 1926, and invoking the South Wales coalowners' constant refrain in the 1910s and 1920s. The SWMF 'had to be stopped in the name of freedom and "business-sense"', because it was not a normal, moderate British union.[483]

Horner ratcheted up the conflict another notch. On 24 August, the Federation handed in the fortnight's notice required for a full coalfield strike to the South Wales coalowners. On 25 August, the *Financial News* quoted Horner's explanation of why the strike action was necessary. 'The company has issued a statement that if the revocation cards are handed in that action will be treated as tantamount to the men terminating their contract with the company ... This is a fight not against the South Wales coalowners, but against this particular colliery company ... '

Although the *Times* noted the delivery of the strike notice in its understated house style, the reporter's view was clear that the threat was real and extraordinary stakes were now in play.

> On the floor of the Cardiff Coal and Shipping Exchange to-day operators were inclined to await events. Meanwhile the market was bare of important orders for forward loading, while large steam coals were abundant to the point of congestion ... [L]arge buyers of coal are watching the position ... anxiously, and on any definite sign of a stoppage of the coalfield taking place will place contracts with other coal-producing countries. Already

it is stated that German, Polish, Russian, Belgian and Turkish coals have been offered ... on long-period contracts at low figures ... the threat of a strike might mean the loss of important business for six, nine or even 12 months ahead.

The *Daily Herald* reported a meeting between Horner, Harris and Saddler, the three Federation-sponsored Monmouthshire MPs, and the Under-Secretary of the Department of Mines. 'The Ministry [*sic*] of Mines promised yesterday to get in touch with the owners of the Bedwas Colliery with a view to securing a settlement of the dispute ... Before the meeting Mr. Horner said "Our purpose is to secure the intervention of the Mines Department so that workmen employed at the Bedwas Colliery shall be free to join the South Wales Miners' Federation."' The *Financial News* was emollient on the following day, quoting the Department of Mines' statement issued after the meeting, which 'recorded that the deputation ... [emphasised] the general improvement in the relations between the owners and the workmen in the South Wales coalfield'.[484]

The anticipated compromise settlement did not, however, materialise. Sir Samuel Instone and Horner continued their intense political duel throughout the following fortnight, with civil servants and Crookshank at the Department of Mines sidelined and increasingly frustrated. Instone was confident that the SWMF would not embark on a strike, and he urged Crookshank to join him in resisting the SWMF's 'game of bluff'. Crookshank told Baldwin on 27 August that 'to count on this [the strike's being called off] is taking too great a risk since the stoppage might be the final blow to the South Wales coalfield.'[485] The right wing of the Conservative Party and some members in the coalowners' association were keen to let the Instones fight the good fight. But the Tory centre, from Baldwin leftwards to Macmillan and Boothby, decided that the Instones were irresponsible employers, indifferent to the dangers of class conflict.

The fact that Sir Samuel and Theodore Instone were Jewish was probably an important contributory factor in persuading the government of the need to broker a compromise. The Federation Executive had mounted stiff opposition to the anti-semitic sentiments regularly expressed at lodge meetings when the Bedwas dispute was discussed. Horner recalled:

> Nye Bevan and I were going to speak at a mass meeting ... at Cardiff, when some of the miners approached us to know whether they could smash the Jewish shops because ... Sir Samuel Instone was a Jew ... I remembered with a shudder of horror that there had been a precedent to this attitude in about 1911 when the miners smashed Jewish shops at Rhymney, Pontypridd and the Yeomanry was called out against them. I was playing football for Rhymney at that time and I saw these riots going on.

He subsequently told a delegate conference that 'if anybody started anti-Jewish activity on this issue I would resign the presidency ... in protest'.[486] Frankenberg's notes of his third interview with Horner recorded that 'George Hall (now Lord Hall) and Sir William Jenkins [SWMF-sponsored MPs for coalfield constituencies] intervened and Arthur believes persuaded the Jewish Council [Board of Deputies] to put pressure on Sir Samuel'.

On 30 August, with just over a week left before the strike notice expired, Horner and Harris went to the Department of Mines with a finely calculated concession. The Federation would accept the results of a secret ballot of the Bedwas men, supervised by an independent person, to decide which union should represent them. The *Daily Herald's* page one headline on 31 August announced, 'SOUTH WALES MINERS' PEACE GESTURE'. The story noted that Horner had only obtained the SWMF Executive's sanction for the move retrospectively. He was evidently uncertain of winning decisive support for this compromise, which he judged essential, and calculated that presenting a fait accompli was more likely to succeed in persuading members in favour of having a coalfield strike.

Horner had six reliable allies out of the eleven elected Executive members: Crews, Alf Davies, and four communists, Jack Davies, Ianto Evans, Dai Dan Evans and Paynter. (Paynter had been elected in August 1936, when an additional third seat was created for the Rhondda, Area No. 4, as a result of the recovery in union membership.) Horner argued his case for retrospective approval to the full Executive, including the Federation

Agents and sponsored MPs whom he took care to invite to these crisis meetings. He correctly calculated that no member of the Executive would risk throwing the conduct of the dispute into crisis by repudiating the officers' offer.

Immediately after the Executive had endorsed the secret ballot, Horner, Bevan and Ness Edwards met with the Bedwas Federation members to explain why this substantial concession had been made. Horner evidently felt Bevan's contribution would be important in winning what he knew was a difficult argument. The *Manchester Guardian* reported details of this closed meeting and published the full text of the resolution, supplied by Edwards, which had been passed, in which the men pledged themselves to abide by decisions taken by a Federation delegate conference. The resolution was a decisive victory for Horner. Having won the men's support, he could be reasonably confident that he could settle for a compromise without fear of being repudiated from below.

Informed opinion continued to be divided about whether there would be a coalfield strike in South Wales on Monday 7 September. Crookshank kept the Cabinet apprised of the situation, while applying pressure on the Bedwas Coal Company via its bankers, Barclays. (Horner told Frankenberg that 'the other coalowners and financiers to whom Bedwas owed money' threatened to foreclose unless the company settled with the Federation.) On 4 September, Crookshank informed Runciman, his immediate superior as President of the Board of Trade, that a coalfield strike would be 'practically complete throughout the coalfield' and would probably use the 'stay-in' method.[487]

Militants at Fernhill colliery in Treherbert, upper Rhondda Fawr, had already come out on strike on 3 September, evidently in the expectation that other lodges would come out in solidarity, as had occurred in 1935. They were apparently joined by other militant lodges; the Cardiff correspondent of the *Financial News* reported on 4 September that 6000 men were idle in the Upper Rhondda. He continued: 'The Communist element ... is now very strong in the coalfield, and the leaders have lost much of their control over the men ... On the other hand, it is probable that, even if a general strike takes place ... many thousands of men would ignore the notices and continue to work.' The leader, 'Trouble in Wales', observed:

The investor has never found it easy to understand the rights and wrongs of coal disputes ... South Wales has suffered peculiarly from recent international conditions. With its Italian market gone and its French market curtailed, it is now condemned to see its Spanish market disappearing. What there is of prosperity in the area cannot escape grave injury from a coal stoppage at the moment ... [I]f it is true, as has been rumoured, that the South Wales Federation is ready to make concessions but the proprietors of the Bedwas Colliery have refused even to negotiate, it will know where to lay the blame.

It is unlikely that either Horner or his allies on the Executive were consulted by the Fernhill militants about their attempt to precipitate a coalfield strike. The situation remained literally poised on a knife-edge. The Federation officers were in London on 3 September for a three and a half hours' meeting with Crookshank. The *Financial News* reported that when they 'returned to Cardiff for the executive meeting. Mr. Arthur Horner, the president, said "As far as we are concerned the position is unchanged."'[488] His calculated silence about the unofficial strikes was not challenged by the *Financial News* reporter, who was apparently concerned to find reasons for optimism. One unintended consequence of the Rhondda upsurge was that the SWMF officers appeared moderate in a coalfield at flashpoint, and the only reliable channel by which the militants could be contained.

Although the Instones remained intransigent, Horner's calculation that the Conservative government would intervene proved correct. Armed with the prime minister's approval, Crookshank enlisted the assistance of Iestyn Williams. Officially invisible, Iestyn Williams spent the whole of Friday 4 September at the Board of Trade, in a flurry of telephone calls to mobilise a variety of contacts, including larger South Walian coalowners. They induced the Instones to make sufficient concessions to enable the Federation officers to claim victory and call off the coalfield strike. Late on Friday night, Sir Samuel Instone informed Crookshank that he had agreed to meet Horner, Harris and Saddler in following week under the auspices of a neutral chairman chosen by Crookshank, providing the imminent coalfield strike and current unofficial strikes, including stay-in strikes, were called off. He was prepared to discuss arrangements for holding the secret ballot with them. At Instone's insistence, the Department of Mines released a press statement from Crookshank about this dramatic development, saving him from the indignity of publicly announcing his own retreat. Just after 3 am on 5 September, Harris sent telegrams to lodge secretaries informing them that the coalfield strike notice had been withdrawn. Crookshank wrote in his diary in the dawn of 5 September after the settlement had finally been reached: 'I think we are right to have strained every nerve to stop the coalfield strike. Even though it seems loading the dice against the non-political Union which I didn't like doing as the Federation aren't such good people as all that. We may get criticism – but [what] we did was off our own bat.'[489]

On Sunday 6 September the *Observer* reported Crookshank's statement that he had been asked by Instone to say 'that he and his colleagues had made the offer solely to avoid the national calamity of a stoppage in the South Wales coalfield'. Horner was jubilant. Although the Instones had refused to guarantee to re-employ the men they had sacked for supporting the Federation, it is unlikely that he had expected to win this demand, since its concession would have been a significant encroachment on management prerogative.

On Monday 7 September, the *Financial News* front page headline was: 'SOUTH WALES BACK TO COAL PEACE. GREAT BUSINESS RELIEF AT STRIKE CANCELLATION. WAY FREE FOR HELD-UP CONTRACTS TO BE CONCLUDED'. The reporter noted that, unlike the rest of British public opinion, the stock market had been unaffected by the strike threat, 'the feeling having been prevalent here that wiser counsels would prevail'.

> The new spirit of optimism was endorsed by Mr. Arthur Horner ... in a conversation I had with him ... Looking well pleased with the turn of events, he told me that the trouble at Bedwas constituted the only really serious threat of unrest in the coalfield ... 'Several other mat-

ters which are outstanding can, I am sure, be settled amicably'.

The *News Chronicle* concluded:

> Congratulations are due to the Secretary for Mines and to the South Wales Miners' Federation for averting the strike ... Congratulations are also, we suppose, due to Sir Samuel Instone for at length admitting some spark of reasonableness into his attitude ... Until Saturday, then, the position was that this paternalistic employer was compelling his workers to belong to the union of his choice, refusing them the right to express a preference for the Federation ... The Federation has shown exemplary patience in calling off the strike on so slender an assurance that Sir Samuel Instone has really begun to yield to common sense.

Horner's description of the final countdown in 'The Truth' was triumphant:

> The Bedwas owners had declared the Federation was not prepared to fight the issue. Sir Samuel Instone said: 'Call their bluff' ... The Secretary for Mines had in effect been told to mind his own business. The barracks were ready at the pit-head to house scab labour and to feed them ...
>
> The coalfield must fight, even although it had no direct quarrel with the Coalowners' Association. The Coalowners intimated that, if they were dragged into the dispute, they would terminate their agreements with the miners. Despite this, the coalfield stood ready ... There was little money, but as much as there was would go to help the weakest links. Then the message came. The Bedwas Coalowners would meet the Federation if the coalfield notices were withdrawn. The first round went to the Federation. The Executive Council had not been bluffing. It was in deadly earnest, fully convinced of the justice of its cause.

Horner knew that there was substantial opposition to the settlement from many militant activists, including communists. They believed that a coalfield strike would succeed in winning the union's full demands. Pollitt and Allison applied pressure on the South Wales DPC to enforce democratic centralist discipline on party members who were agitating for a repudiation of the compromise settlement. Their willingness to intervene was in sharp contrast to their failure to support Horner in the autumn of 1935 about the unofficial stay-down strikes. They were evidently not prepared for anti-Horner militants to undermine Horner's position as Federation President. They probably also felt more secure in insisting on the observance of a united front position. In the year between the first stay-down strikes and the Battle of Bedwas, the party leadership had been energetically propagating the Seventh World Congress line. They apparently arranged changes in the DPC personnel in an attempt to ensure that the South Wales district party line supported Horner and the Federation Executive.

On 7 September, the *Daily Worker* reported:

> If the feeling of the stay-in strikers [at Fernhill] who obeyed the instructions of union officials to postpone action till after Wednesday's meeting [between the Instones and the Federation] is any indication, there will be overwhelming support for the action of the Miners' Federation officials. There was great enthusiasm when they came out of the pits on Saturday.

On 8 September, the *Daily Worker* reported meetings of the Rhymney Valley SWMF Area Committee and 1200 Bedwas men, at which the settlement had been supported, as a 'tremendous victory'. But the paper's optimistic spin was premature. An unofficial strike broke out at Bedwas in protest at the settlement. Horner staunched it by going to the colliery to meet the men. He not only put a closely argued case, but also made it clear that he would remain at the meeting until the men voted to go back to work.[490]

The first round of talks between the Federation officers and the Instones, joined by the Bedwas manager, Stuart Martin, became problematic after the company's precarious financial position was revealed. Horner, Saddler and Harris recognised that unless a settlement of the union recognition issue was speedily achieved, the colliery would be forced to close. Management's rationalising measures, involving the abolition of hard-won customs and practice, also had to be accepted in order to secure the jobs of the miners who had joined the SWMF. Consequently, when Horner completed the negotiations by mid-September, he agreed that if the Federation was recognised as a result of the secret ballot, there would be no restoration of pre-1933 customs and practice.[491]

Horner's willingness to pledge that the Federation's Bedwas members would not demand the favourable, old working conditions apparently surprised the Instones, who had anticipated that his intransigence would enable them to regain the initiative. They were further surprised when, on 17 September, the Federation Executive accepted the agreement. In early October the Bedwas men also endorsed it at a mass meeting. The Bedwas Coal Company now had no choice but to let the secret ballot of working miners go ahead at the colliery on 28 to 29 October. If the Federation won, the terms of the agreement provided that the re-constituted Bedwas Lodge would include only men currently working at the pit; no unemployed members of the old lodge would be allowed to join.

Horner, Saddler and Harris ensured that the full terms of the agreement were not made public until after the ballot was held. This enabled them and the Executive union to concentrate on winning support for the question on the ballot paper, which union should be recognised. The officers, the agents and the SWMF-sponsored Monmouthshire MPs co-operated in an energetic campaign to explain the ballot's strategic importance to the mining communities in the Rhymney Valley.[492] The South Wales DPC was apparently also extremely vigilant. On 25 September the SWMIU produced a leaflet containing extracts from the negotiations. They revealed that Horner had agreed that neither the men from the old Bedwas lodge nor their customs would be reinstated. Both the SWMF and the South Wales DPC dismissed the revelation as vexatious and irrelevant without, however, denying its accuracy. The campaign produced a decisive result. There was a 91 per cent turn-out: 1177 men voted for the SWMF; 309 for the SWMIU. 'The result of the ballot,' Horner told the *Daily Herald*, 'is just what was anticipated.'[493]

When details of the agreement finally became public, influential communists and other militants declared that the terms were a sell-out. Some went further and declared that Horner's bloodless, compromise victory undermined the Federation's founding principle, class conscious militancy. They had expected him to square up and fight the coalowners, unlike Griffiths. Veterans whose self-image included a view of South Wales as one of the storm centres of the international working-class movement, invoked Horner's insistence that the SWMIU was fascism in embryo, and compared an all-out coalfield strike over Bedwas to the Spanish republican government's struggle against Franco.

Horner led the Executive in a tenacious defence of the Bedwas settlement. He conducted a spirited dialogue with the militants, providing reasoned answers to every twist and turn in their arguments. He recognised the importance of activists' participation in the union; their sacrifices and courage were vital in maintaining the Federation's credibility. The concluding paragraphs of 'The Truth' reflect his empathy with activists' rebellious cast of mind, but also his confidence that he had not betrayed their trust by pursuing a scientific, Clausewitzian strategy:

> In the event of the Company refusing or failing to carry out the letter and spirit of the Agreement, there can and there will probably be many strikes. A strike cannot be an objective, it must be a means to some end. In the Bedwas Agreement we have gone a long way toward the objective of the maximum results, with the least damage to our own forces. The Bedwas Agreement, which has many formulations which we agreed to under duress, is a good Agreement in a number of respects. It places things in proper proportion. It releases energy from care for small things to allow for attention to big fundamental things.
>
> The Bedwas Agreement will be carried out by us. We will see that it is carried out by the Company. It has not endangered coalfield solidarity. It has paved the way, in a period of relative weakness, for the final elimination of Scab Unionism from the South Wales Coalfield.

Let the 'Rights' sneer who failed with men and money to win Bedwas: let the 'Lefts' who secured isolation for themselves and security for Scab Unionism jeer. The fact is, that *scientifically applied class struggle* has given us Bedwas without undue loss of expenditure of man-power.[494]

Having refused to be faced down by the left, Horner maintained the momentum of his own and the Federation's activity. He was confident that the victory over the SWMIU and the Bedwas Coal Company had produced favourable conditions for achieving further advance. His insistence in 'The Truth' on the need to place the Bedwas agreement 'in proper proportion' to enable the release of energy 'for attention to big fundamental things' was an aesopian reference to his Clausewitzian strategy. He began to plan the defeat of Spencer's non-pol union in Nottinghamshire, the NMIU, and also embarked on a final round of negotiations with the South Wales coalowners for a new District Agreement.

The Bedwas dispute was the occasion when Horner stamped his authority on the Federation. He had achieved what most well-informed observers had believed impossible. Without a coalfield strike, he had persuaded Baldwin's Conservative government to intervene on the Federation's behalf against a non-political union. He had also convinced the SWMF Executive and hitherto intransigent militants in the Rhymney Valley to accept the compromise settlement he had negotiated. Having performed this feat, he was henceforth able to rely on support from centre-right members of the Executive. After the ballot, Horner handed over routine business at Bedwas to Bill Saddler, a measure of their growing mutual confidence. Saddler had apparently been Griffiths' and Arthur Jenkins' choice for the presidency, and his developing partnership with Horner was further evidence of Horner's success in the job.

Nevertheless, the Bedwas dispute was probably also the occasion when the breach finally became irreparable between Horner and other leading South Walian communists, including Dai Llewellyn and Billy Griffiths. Horner, his allies and protégés were on one side, defending his Clausewitzian strategy as scientific and successful, in accord with the Popular Front line and the Party Centre's injunction to work loyally inside the trade union movement. On the other side were the pure revolutionary militants, who viewed total industrial war as the fulcrum of trade union activity, and the proven way of precipitating a proletarian revolution. King Street's attempt to enforce party discipline had the unintended consequence of forcing the division to the surface. After October 1936, two opposing camps co-existed inside the South Wales communist party. Probably tacitly encouraged by Pollitt and Campbell, the DPC steered a course of de facto toleration of both. But officially the party centre at King Street ignored the polarisation until coalfield events precipitated overt hostility between the two camps, and decisive intervention from London was required to damp down the conflict. King Street's connivance in the DPC's 'live and let live' approach was possible because many party members, including respected veterans like Lewis Jones, owed allegiance to neither camp; they sometimes supported the revolutionary militants, but then allowed themselves to be convinced by Horner's arguments. Or they held out until the last ditch and then deferred to the DPC's and King Street's injunctions to back Horner.

Horner continued to absent himself from DPC meetings, apparently determined to avoid a situation where, as Federation President, he would be instructed by the CPGB to either change decisions he was taking as union leader or render himself liable to communist democratic centralist discipline. He justified his conduct *ex post facto*, usually to Pollitt, and made perfunctory apologies for his failure to turn up. However, he regularly attended meetings of leading communist miners convened by Allison in London, where he was confident that he would not be instructed to take a particular course of action. He also valued the opportunity to meet comrades from other coalfields in order to hear their news and concert strategy for the MFGB Executive.

The South Wales DPC refused to countenance Horner's non-appearances and regularly appealed to King Street for support. Pollitt and Allison were anxious to maintain Horner's continuing credibility as a good communist, and invariably went through the motions of reminding him of his party obligations. Nevertheless his absences continued, and King Street continued to grant him de facto immunity from party discipline. The DPC had little choice but to accept what was to them an unsatisfactory

state of affairs. There were evidently clear, unspoken boundaries beyond which Pollitt and Allison would not go for fear that
Horner would leave the party. They had to rely on Horner's
voluntary desire to remain a communist to retain his loyalty.

After the Bedwas settlement, Horner was drawn back into
the life of the international communist movement through the
Spanish Civil War. Horner was a member of the MFGB delegation to the MIF Congress, held in Prague in early August 1936.
It was his first journey to Europe since 1932, and gave him the
opportunity to observe conditions in western Germany, just as
his trips to Berlin and Essen in the late 1920s had provided an
insight into the disintegration of the Weimar Republic. It was his
first contact with the MIF since 1926, when he had accompanied
Cook to meetings and acquired detailed knowledge of the personalities and concerns of the social democratic European coalfield unions. The MFGB motion opposing fascism, proposed by
Lawther, was amended to include a reference to Spain. Horner
criticised the motion for being 'too defensive in its composition',
when he spoke in the debate along with delegates from Poland,
Czechoslovakia, Romania and France.[495]

Hostilities in Spain had commenced on 18 July 1936, when
General Francisco Franco mounted a coup d'etat from the
Canary Islands aiming to overthrow the Spanish Popular Front
Government. Perhaps because it was not immediately successful,
the news attracted comparatively little interest in either Britain or
France.[496] Franco was opposed by a substantial number of officers
in the upper echelons of the Spanish Army, who remained loyal
to the legitimate government. But he had made a political ally,
the Falange, a nascent fascist movement with a secular political
base from which he could rally Spanish nationalism. He could
also rely on the Spanish Catholic hierarchy, a vital asset in many
parts of Spain. The nationalists, as Franco and allies described
themselves, soon controlled northern Spain, with the exception
of the mining and industrial region of Asturias. Southern Spain,
from Catalonia to Malaga, remained loyal to the republic. The
area around Madrid formed 'a broad promontory projecting
into nationalist territory, which threatened it from three sides.
A shifting frontier was manned, not very effectively by both
armies ... [D]irect engagements were comparatively few'.[497]

Pollitt had been in Moscow on Comintern business on 18 July; he responded immediately to the coup attempt with arguments about the necessity of supporting the republican government. Back in Britain in early August, Pollitt spoke publicly about the importance of a Spanish republican victory, even though the Comintern Secretariat had yet to pronounce on the situation. He justified his stand under the umbrella of the Seventh World Congress Popular Front line. Horner and Bevan were early passionate supporters of the Republican government. There had been commercial and industrial links between Northern Spain and South Wales since the 1870s, involving the import of Spanish iron ore, the export of Welsh steam coal and the migration of Spanish workers. Maritime connections via the Bristol Channel and the Bay of Biscay made Spain seem much closer to South Walians than the rest of Britain.[498]

During August, European non-fascist governments, including the Soviet Union, had adopted a neutral stance towards the civil war. Stalin had fallen in behind a declaration of non-intervention, promoted by the French prime minister Leon Blum of the Popular Front government and swiftly endorsed by the British Conservative government. By the end of August, Germany, Italy and Portugal had also placed an embargo on the export of arms and munitions to both sides.[499] The reluctance of the socialist Blum and the communist Stalin to adopt a more supportive stance towards the Spanish government was understandable in realpolitik terms. Nevertheless, socialists and communists throughout Europe were disappointed and fearful that Hitler would flout the terms of the non-intervention agreement he had signed.

On 18 September 1936, the Comintern Secretariat met for the first time after its summer recess to discuss Spain, amidst much uncertainty. Dimitrov argued that: 'The state for which the Spanish people were fighting would not be an old-style democratic republic, but a "special state with genuine people's democracy". It would be "not a Soviet state, but an anti-Fascist state, with the participation of the genuinely Left part of the bourgeoisie".'[500] Dimitrov's arguments were endorsed, but not without strong reservations from orthodox old Bolsheviks. When the Latvian veteran Knorin used *Pravda* to attack Dimitrov's arguments, Palmiro Togliatti, the Italian communist leader and one of the Comintern Secretaries, wrote a counter-article, 'attuned to Dimitrov's pragmatism rather than ... ideological purity', which like-minded communists were soon circulating throughout Europe.[501]

Despite Dimitrov's commitment, however, the Comintern Executive were extremely chary of applying this new position. They were worried about their own backs, in the wake of Stalin's first round of show trials centred on Zinoviev, former Comintern General Secretary, and Kamenev. Nevertheless, Dimitrov, Manuilsky and Togliatti persisted, and a discreet, coded debate in the Soviet party press ensued. By mid-October, Stalin had signalled his acceptance of Dimitrov's case, and the flow of covert Soviet military aid, as well as Red Army and Comintern personnel – notably Togliatti – to the republican government began.[502]

Through their regular meetings with European trade unionists in international union federations and also at the International Labour Organisation in Geneva, British trade union leaders across the political spectrum were better informed and more concerned about the march of fascism across Europe than the government and Whitehall. By the time of the TUC, held in Plymouth in early September, a full-scale civil war was under way in Spain. But Bevin's and Citrine's genuine concern about continental fascism did not soften their opposition to a united front in Britain. Moreover, the paragraphs in the General Council's Report which compared 'non-pol' company unions and communist-subsidised unions (the French CGT) were approved, with only a few opposing speeches, including one from Ianto Evans. Although Horner, Harris and Saddler had intended to be there and were registered as delegates, in the end they spent most of the week in Cardiff and London in negotiations about Bedwas.

The MFGB's resolution in favour of the communist party's affiliation to the Labour Party surfaced at the Labour Party Conference in October, when the Labour Party Executive's rejection of the CPGB's application for affiliation was debated. MFGB Vice-President Lawther spoke in support of the motion calling for communist affiliation proposed by the Edinburgh Trades and Labour Council. The MFGB delegation cast its 400,000 block vote in favour.

As a communist, Horner was barred from being a conference delegate; but the MFGB Executive accepted his attendance at the MFGB delegation's pre-conference meeting, which considered the agenda and decided how to cast the block vote. Before the conference, King Street had appealed to party members to gather a million signatures for a petition supporting communist affiliation. But activists apparently viewed the Spanish Civil War as a more compelling issue, and concentrated on organising support for the Spanish republican government.[503] The Transport House *apparat* took its pre-conference preparation more seriously. The Edinburgh Trades and Labour Council motion was overwhelmingly defeated, winning fewer votes than comparable motions at Labour conferences in the 1920s.[504]

The Labour Conference passed a motion on Spain endorsing the government's policy of non-intervention, despite strong opposition from many delegates, including Bevan. But later in the week speeches from the two Spanish fraternal delegates 'profoundly moved the delegates, and simply swept away the pretence that the Non-Intervention Pact was not proved to have been broken'. The PLP leader, Clement Attlee, and his deputy, Arthur Greenwood, were despatched forthwith to interview Baldwin. On their return to conference, Attlee moved a strong resolution qualifying Labour support for non-intervention. It was passed unanimously, having been 'strengthened on Cripps's motion with a phrase placing on record the Conference's view that the Fascist powers had already violated the Pact ... '.[505]

Franco launched his first attack on Madrid at the end of October, forcing the Republican government to flee south to Valencia. An international brigade, made up of German, French and Polish battalions, appeared in Madrid on 6 November, marching 'amid the cheers of the population to take up positions, for the first time, at the front.[506] Before the end of the month, France's offensive against Madrid had stalled.'

The failure of the nationalist forces to take the city acted as a heady tonic to communists and socialists everywhere, including Britain. Certainly, within the MFGB, the NMA members participating in the first skirmishes in an industrial battle with the NMIU at Harworth colliery in Nottinghamshire are likely to have considered their possible arrest and imprisonment as a serious risk, but of a different order of magnitude than that faced by the volunteers in the International Brigade, who were braving death.

The NMA activists' decision to begin preparations for an all-out conflict against the NMIU was probably the result of the SWMF's victory over the SWMIU at Bedwas. SWMF officials and volunteers had played a conspicuous part in stiffening the NMA resistance during the 1926 Lock-Out, and subsequently in attempts to uproot the NMIU, and Horner had remained in contact with communists and NMA loyalists. He spoke at a meeting organised by the CPGB in Nottinghamshire during the national wages dispute in June 1935. Clarrie Mason and Herbert Howarth probably arranged for him to meet communist miners, led by Mick Kane, who lived just across the county line in South Yorkshire.[507] They were keen to apply the boring from within strategy used at Emlyn and Taff-Merthyr against Spencer. Harworth colliery near Mansfield was one of the NMIU's strongholds. By launching a frontal challenge to the NMIU on this terrain, Kane and comrades were hopeful of breaking Spencer's dominance.

Horner is likely to have counselled the need for careful preparation, and his advice was evidently heeded. The communist miners revived contact with NMA loyalists living around Mansfield, most of whom had been unemployed since 1926. They also looked for volunteers from South Derbyshire and South Yorkshire, where they themselves had been working. The willing veterans began looking for work at Harworth in early 1936. The Harworth owners, Barber Walker, had access to the Nottinghamshire coalowners' blacklist. But it appeared that it did not extend to men who had been victimised outside the county. Once Kane and others were established, they patiently cultivated good relations with the small number of NMA members in the un-recognised NMA Lodge. In June 1936, they effected a change in the lodge leadership. Kane was elected chairman on a platform of militant resistance to Spencer. His comrade, Dave Buckley, was elected secretary. Thereafter agitation underground intensified, particularly on the night-shift. There were significant advances amongst the substantial contingent of Durham men, economic migrants from their own coalfield. Many of the Yorkshire miners who commuted by bus, attracted by the wages paid at Harworth, were also won for the NMA.

By August 1936 the Harworth NMA had 640 members on its books, over one third of the miners working underground.[508] The first skirmishes took place in early September. Although Kane tried to avoid a confrontation, his men responded to provocation from Barber-Walker by coming out on strike. At the end of a week, management had sacked 43 men, including most of the NMA branch officers. The NMA Council approached the MFGB Executive for financial assistance. Jones and Edwards met the NMA Council, and on 24 September they recommended to the Executive that the MFGB offer a subsidy to support the victimised men. The rest of the men went back to work, and the rump of NMA lodge activists continued to bore from within.

Horner would have reinforced Jones' and Edwards' view that the Harworth conflict had the potential de-stabilise Spencer. He had taken Griffiths' seat on the Executive, and his dextrous handling of the Bedwas dispute had inclined centre-right MFGB leaders to value his opinion. He also had recent experience in dealing with Spencer, albeit at one remove. The SWMIU had merged with the NMIU during 1935 to form the MIU, and Spencer had become its president. He is likely to have been involved on the periphery of the Bedwas negotiations, giving Horner some opportunity to gauge his current attitude to the MFGB. The Executive decided to take the risk, and offer the requested financial assistance.

In December, the MFGB Executive sanctioned a decisive widening of the conflict. Joseph Jones met members of the NMA Harworth lodge and authorised them to hand in strike notices expiring on 14 December. On 15 December the *Daily Worker* described the scene, under a page one headline:

MINERS PATROL STREETS:
700 miners formed into marching order this afternoon ... On the instructions of a superintendent, police tried to disperse the gathering ... Witnessing this, a number of miners, who had continued working at the pit came forward and handed in notices to join the strikers.

On 30 December Horner moved an SWMF motion at the MFGB Executive which called for a Special Delegate Conference to be convened to consider the dispute. Many Executive members were fearful of taking the first step to what they all realised might precipitate another national conflict. Horner was joined by Joe Hall and Bowman, and along with Jones and Edwards, their arguments persuaded the doubting members to give the SWMF motion unanimous support. The Special Conference met on 20 January 1937, and Horner moved the resolution on the Executive's behalf. It empowered them 'to take a ballot vote of the entire coalfields upon the question of enforcing the principle of the freedom of organisation and Trade Union recognition for those so organised', and requested them 'to approach the [TUC] General Council in order to enlist the support of the whole Trade Union movement for this principle ... '

Horner spoke after Edwards had described the dispute's long gestation and been closely questioned by delegates. It was the first time since 1927 that Horner had occupied centre stage at an MFGB conference. His passionate performance was undiminished, and he reached out to delegates, inciting them to emulate his own commitment to serious collective action. His arguments were now permeated by close Clausewitzian logic. He made it clear that he did not want a national strike, but viewed the threat of one as an essential weapon. He also stressed that the motion did not bind the Executive to hold a strike ballot, leaving the door open for a settlement to be reached at any time.

> Mr. Chairman and comrades: the question which we are discussing ... is one of the most important that has presented itself ... since 1926. Company Unionism, which is really what Spencerism is, was born in 1926 ... We in South Wales have very great sympathy with our Nottinghamshire comrades in the struggle against this conspiracy. We have very good reason to hate it ... We are happy to say that in South Wales we are now almost at the end of the rope, but we shall not be satisfied, and I am sure this Federation will not be satisfied, until this foul thing is swept out of the coalfields altogether.
>
> After all, Notts is a part of this Federation, and if there are any tendencies here this afternoon to treat the

347

difficulty in which they found themselves as one which they themselves must solve, a very serious mistake will be made by all of us. This is a national question. The scene of the battle for all of us happens to be in Notts, but that is a mere accident ...

Notts is an important coalfield situated in the heart of other coalfields belonging to this Federation; 40,000 men are there in slavery, wanting to be free, but kept by economic pressure under the control of the Company Union, which is the instrument of the coalowners of Nottinghamshire ...

If this resolution is carried we want the Delegates here ... to go back to the districts and explain the significance of the fight we are waging, telling the members that what is at stake is not merely the fate of the Nottinghamshire miners, but the fate of all of us. This battle must be fought, and this battle must be won, even if we have to use as a last resort the tremendous weapon of a national strike ... But the Executive is not going to take that ballot until it has taken certain other steps to see if the ballot is absolutely essential, because if the ballot is taken and its results in a decision for strike action, then it must be understood clearly that unless the enemy capitulate, strike action will take place. This is not a bluff. We do not want anybody to vote for it on the assumption that it is a bluff for the consumption of people outside.

The resolution was passed unanimously. However, many delegates explained that they had decided to support it only after Horner had assured the conference that the Executive would exhaust all other avenues for a settlement before resorting to the ultimate weapon of a national strike ballot. It was evident that his protestations of a measured, non-militant approach were important in convincing more moderate delegates and districts. After the conference, Jones and Edwards duly approached the TUC General Council for assistance over Harworth. Bevin was TUC Chairman for the Congress year that ran from the end of the 1936 Congress until the end of the 1937 Congress. He and Citrine were quick to offer the General Council's full support.

The TUC had been committed to defeating Spencer since 1926, and Bevin and Citrine were keen to play a major role in what seemed likely to be the *coup de grace*.[509]

Armed with their backing, the MFGB Executive pursued two parallel lines of action, which often appeared contradictory. First, they campaigned to win a decisive result in the national strike ballot in support of the Harworth strikers. In the week following the Special Conference on 20 January, a special MFGB message was published, displaying the uncompromising rhetoric of a side prepared for conflict: 'The issue is one of fascism versus democracy in trade union affairs. Unless wiser counsels prevail than those now observed by the Notts. owners, the country may once again be plunged into the horrors of a coal war ... '[510] In the following weeks, representatives from other District Unions were despatched to Nottinghamshire. They resumed the public meetings which had been the mainstay of the MFGB's fight-back in the late 1920s. Their presence was evidence that Spencer would have to resist the combined might of all the British coalfield unions.

The second line of action was probably more difficult and certainly more delicate. The Executive aimed to achieve the de-recognition of the NMIU by the Nottinghamshire coalowners by a tactical manoeuvre involving the dissolution of both the NMA and the NMIU, and the creation of a new Nottinghamshire union which would affiliate to the MFGB. The MFGB Executive had to persuade the NMA Executive Council to accept Spencer back into the fold, and work alongside him in a collegial fashion inside a fused union. Then in order to persuade Spencer to merge, they had to push Barber Walker into a compromise settlement of the Harworth strike.

In February 1935, Jones and Edwards had induced the NMA Executive to grant them plenary powers to enter into merger discussions with Spencer. Horner had been an early advocate of fusion. A critical difference between Nottinghamshire and South Wales MIU was that after the 1926 Lock-Out, the South Wales coalowners had continued to recognise the SWMF, whilst the Nottinghamshire coalowners had left the national coalowners' association in order to de-recognise the NMA, and recognise the NMIU. If the Harworth strikers won, Spencer would sustain a substantial loss of credibility. He would, however, continue to enjoy the Nottinghamshire coalowners' support. But many NMA stalwarts, including right-wing Labour loyalists, had sworn undying resistance to the NMIU. They refused to acknowledge the logic of fusion and instead sought revenge and Spencer's unconditional surrender.

Like the other progressive, 'forward looking' members of the MFGB Executive, Horner recognised that Spencer could not be frontally defeated on his home ground, and that the best possible outcome would be some form of merger or fusion between the NMA and the NMIU. After 20 January 1937, unlike previous national disputes, South Walian delegates neither proposed nor seconded resolutions at MFGB delegate conferences convened to consider Harworth. The most likely explanation for this silence is Horner's diplomatic discretion. He made few public statements about the Harworth dispute, and evidently used his considerable presidential prerogative to ensure that the SWMF also kept a low profile. He was already planning his next moves to disband the South Wales MIU, and was intent on enlisting Spencer's help. Despite the setback at Bedwas, the South Wales MIU was clinging onto existence. Its members at Taff-Merthyr were a last redoubt. The 1935 Taff-Merthyr strike settlement had provided for a ballot to be held over recognition (see p. 284) SWMF activists at the colliery were confident of winning it; but Horner was not so sanguine. He calculated that it would be almost impossible to dislodge the MIU, principally because since the settlement management had been covertly favouring the non-pols and increasingly marginalising the Federation lodge.

Jones and Edwards began preliminary meetings with Spencer in mid-February 1937 at the Department of Mines. Crookshank showed himself keen to obtain the best possible terms for the MFGB. Spencer aimed to preserve his own position and put the NMA personnel in a subordinate role. By mid-March, the MFGB officers concluded that they would have to settle on the terms Crookshank had obtained. They were sceptical about achieving a convincing majority in a national strike ballot because, unlike the national wages dispute, miners would not be voting to achieve their own material gain. Harworth strikers' stomach for resistance was also limited.

Behind the scenes, Horner used his influence with Pollitt to facilitate a compromise. The terms for fusion and settling the strike became public knowledge in early March. On 17 March Pollitt and Campbell, after some hesitation, signified the CPGB's opposition to them. But they refrained from attacking either the MFGB officers or the Executive during their ongoing negotiations with Spencer. On 24 March, the MFGB Executive met to consider fusion terms. Letters from Yorkshire, Lancashire and Northumberland were tabled, requesting a Special Delegate Conference to consider and vote on the terms, and also to consider Barber Walker's refusal to take any of the Harworth strikers back. The Executive agreed, and convened the conference for 1 April.

The absence of a similar letter from the SWMF was conspicuous. Horner may have deflected the SWMF Executive from joining the other three districts by reminding them of the delicately poised situation at Bedwas. There were also the negotiations for a new District Agreement in which final terms were in the process of being agreed. Horner may have stressed the need to show the South Wales coalowners that the SWMF was approaching the new agreement in good faith, i.e. with every intention of avoiding industrial disputes. The Federation Executive did, however, decide to submit a resolution to the MFGB Executive calling for a Special Conference of the TUC to consider the situation in Spain, which the MFGB Executive subsequently agreed to forward to the General Council. The Spanish Civil War was reaching its own climacteric, and the South Wales miners' persistence in keeping it at the forefront of British unions' agenda was no mere gesture. The MFGB's position carried real weight, not only inside the trade union movement but also in the formation of 'public opinion'.

On 24 March, a *Daily Worker* story quoted Horner extensively about the situation in Nottinghamshire, without comment '[T]here are several conditions which are unpalatable, and which, in other circumstances, would be held to be unacccpt able. My view of the present situation is that every effort must be made to establish trade unionism in the Notts. coalfield within a reasonable period of time. The continuance of the past ten years in Notts. cannot be thought of ... Subject to a way being found to save the Harworth men from unemployment and victimisation, I am for a merger which ... is necessary for the restoration of unity.' The appearance of Horner's support for the merger

351

terms in the *Daily Worker* signalled the Party Centre's continuing support for him. But the story also highlighted his support
for the position adopted by the other district unions' letters to
the Executive. His public support for the need to protect the
Harworth strikers from victimisation was finely calculated to
protect his left flank. He was not in favour at this stage in the
struggle of leaving the strikers to their own fate.

When the SWMF Executive met on 31 March to decide their
position on Harworth for the MFGB Special Conference on 1
April, Horner made no attempt to deflect members' feelings. It
was resolved that the SWMF delegation 'be instructed to oppose
acceptance of the suggested agreement and support a [national
strike] ballot'. Horner spoke on behalf of South Wales at the conference, and he had a difficult task. During the previous week,
an unofficial dispute had broken out at Bedwas, culminating
in a stay-in strike. Since the Bedwas men were operating a no-
strike procedure agreement, their action was a direct challenge
to the SWMF's authority, and also to the impending new district
agreement. Had the stay-in continued at Bedwas, the coalowners
might have abandoned the final stages of the negotiations for
the district agreement. Horner and Saddler had succeeded in
persuading the Bedwas men to go back to work. The ILP paper,
Forward, had published a long story, with details of the Bedwas
dispute and the no-strike clause in the Bedwas procedure agreement. It had then proceeded to draw unfavourable comparisons
between Bedwas and the situation at Harworth.

Before Horner rose to speak, other prominent delegates,
including Sammy Sales, had accused South Wales and Horner
of rank hypocrisy. How could they support the Harworth men
in good conscience when they had refused to back their own
Bedwas miners for doing the same thing. Horner kept his temper
and refuted their charges in detail, invoking his Clausewitzian
principles:

> In order that there may be no idea of inconsistency con-
> sequent upon the lying, slanderous, and ill-informed
> statement in *Forward* [ILP journal], may I say that so
> far as the Bedwas Agreement is concerned every point
> in that agreement was accepted by the Bedwas men,
> and accepted by a Conference ... [I]t has given a pos-

sibility to South Wales which has not been obtained in the rest of the coalfields and which they would be glad to get ... [T]his week we have been considering wage increases [in the new District Agreement] which would never have been made had Bedwas remained outside the Miners' Federation in South Wales. We cannot consider a wages position nationally with Notts in this situation. We cannot consider that with Notts remaining outside, as Bedwas was for a number of years.

South Wales is definitely opposed to remaining where we are. There are two other courses. One which we have carried a good way on the course of trying to destroy the Industrial Union *with the least possible damage to our own forces*.

The South Wales Executive are of the opinion that we have not reached the best bargaining situation to obtain the most advantageous terms. The South Wales Executive is not opposed to the principles of merging but they are against the merger which is involved in the acceptance of these terms ...

The fight cannot be given up ... We think that a [national strike] ballot must be taken, but before a ballot is taken we believe there must be a campaign not only in the minefields outside Notts but an intensive campaign in Notts itself. We must remove this argument that they will not strike ... We see no reason why we should not include the Notts men out of the position they are in ... We think that joint action at this particular time can be more effective than at any time in our memory. If there is one thing that is feared in this country at the present time, with the preparations which are going on for the Coronation Celebrations, it is a great industrial disturbance which this Federation could be responsible for. We do believe that arising out of our own experience the Government can be helpful. We found that at a critical moment in the Bedwas trouble that the Government could be useful.

During the debate, the change in collective mood was evident. Delegates were angry and determined to use national solidarity to prevent the Harworth strikers' victimisation. Jones adjourned the conference over night to allow the Executive to re-formulate a recommendation to delegates. Sufficient support now existed in key districts, notably Yorkshire, to produce a decisive national ballot result in favour of strike action, which would give the MFGB a stronger hand to play with Crookshank against Barber Walker and Spencer. The following morning, Vice-President Lawther moved a new resolution, seconded by McGurk, calling for a national strike ballot. The voting was 503 to 32, with only four small districts opposing. Executive members made it clear that delegates from all district unions were expected to deliver their vote.

South Wales delegates returned home in the afternoon of Friday 2 April. They attended a recalled Special Delegate Conference of the Federation the next day. A full complement of lodge delegates assembled in Cory Hall, Cardiff, to record their lodge votes on the new District Agreement which Horner had been negotiating for the last five months with Evan Williams and Iestyn Williams. The SWMF Executive had considered it in draft on 23 March, which it had unanimously agreed to recommend to a Special Delegate Conference on 27 March. The conference minutes recorded that 'The President reviewed events that had led up to the New Conciliation Board Agreement ... Protracted negotiations had taken place ... [He] explained in detail the clauses of the Agreement, the grades of workmen and the schedule of rates applicable thereto.' After questions had been put, the conference had adjourned until 3 April for delegates to consult their lodges.

The due democratic process of adjourning in order for lodge votes to be taken was not unusual in the Federation. However, during further discussion at the Federation Executive on 31 March, it emerged that many Executive members were unclear about the agreement's contents, and unable to explain its features at the lodge meetings where votes would be taken. To deal with the lack of clarity, it was resolved to print the shorthand notes of the Executive's discussion of various clauses and supply copies to every Executive member and all agents.

Uncertainty about the agreement was hardly surprising. It marked a radical departure from previous district agreements, and blazed new paths in coalfield industrial relations.

Horner had won substantial improvements in wages, 'in which every individual working in the pits got at least a five per cent. increase ... the first upward trend in the coalfield since 1926'.[511] In return, he had agreed that the Federation would partici- pate in comprehensive re-grading of jobs, which would involve rationalisation and the abolition of many established customs and practices. He had also negotiated a new conciliation agree- ment, similar to the one at Bedwas. It was a no-strike agreement at local level. Disputes which could not be settled by the col- liery lodge committee would progress to the district for ultimate settlement by a joint committee of Federation and coalowners' officers. The Executive could decide to take official strike action, but only after the coalfield joint committee had failed to reach a settlement.

The District Agreement was similar to the industry-wide agreements which Bevin had been negotiating in manufactur- ing, for example flour milling and chemicals. Contractual terms and conditions would be jointly regulated across the coalfield, not subject to individual variation or the economic vicissitudes of particular colliery owners. Horner had turned his accumu- lated experience and observations as checkweighman and agent to good account, and had made practical proposals to stream- line the wages structure and introduce uniform grades across the coalfield, making an offer which Iestyn Williams and Evan Williams could hardly refuse. The *Daily Worker* reported favour- ably on the new agreement on 2 April, pointing out that under its terms no variation in any practice, condition or custom would be made until prior agreement had been reached between the union and the coalowners in the conciliation machinery. Moreover, the union side of Colliery Conciliation Committees would be composed of working miners, i.e. rank-and-file union members.

On 3 April, the recalled delegate conference accepted the agreement on a roll call vote of lodges by a 3 to 1 majority, 62,250 to 23,550. Given the five per cent. improvement in wages, the size of the 'No' vote was notable. It is likely that there was organised opposition, perhaps centred around Ferndale and the Cambrian Combine pits, and including anti-Horner communists, that had canvassed lodge meetings, arguing that the agreement betrayed the Federation's democratic traditions. The re-grading exercise and changes in working practices would entail lodges surrendering their rights and accepting the coalfield-wide agreement with the coalowners' association. Supporters of the agreement could rejoin that lodge independence was not compromised. Lodges would now be under an obligation to settle disagreements with management by negotiation and conciliation rather than industrial action. But this argument had failed to persuade hard-line revolutionary militants.

Horner was probably not surprised by the size of the No vote. He was himself a veteran of a myriad of small disputes and skirmishes, which had been an integral part of South Wales coalmining practice since the Federation's formation. He had not proposed these rationalising changes merely as a bargaining counter to win the wage increase. As a scientific Clausewitzian, he now viewed the use of strikes as a weapon of first rather than last resort as a counter-productive dissipation of the union's forces. He continued to view the new District Agreement as one of his major achievements as a union leader, and was sentimental about the fact that he and Evan Williams had signed it on 5 April, his forty-third birthday.[512]

The lodges which had voted against the new agreement were not, however, ready to accept the majority decision in favour. On 13 April, at the last meeting of the SWMF Executive before the Federation Annual Conference on 15 to 17 April, Horner reported that difficulties might arise in connection with re-grading and the new system of uniform allowances across the whole coalfield. It was agreed that the Agents should report to Central Office on any areas of disagreement. It may have been Pollitt who assigned Cox to write a feature article about the Bedwas Agreement in the *Daily Worker* on 14 April. His robust defence offered oblique support for the District Agreement, although he made no overt mention of it.

> There must ... be some system of negotiation, and particularly in an industry like mining where a hundred and one disputes crop up every day. If strike action is the only answer to every dispute in the South Wales coalfield there would never be any work in the mines. Trotsky's theory of permanent revolution would live again in the theory of 'permanent strike action'!

Despite the noises off, the SWMF Annual Conference was a powerful affirmation of Horner's first year as president. The traditional vote of thanks for his presidential address was carried, and further embellished by being made an acclamation. At its culmination, Horner was re-elected to office unopposed. The MFGB national strike ballot over Harworth coincided with the first two days of the SWMF Annual Conference. After the MFGB delegate conference on 2 April had decided to hold the ballot, intensive propaganda had been conducted by the MFGB Executive, the district unions and the communist party to achieve a decisive 'Yes' result. The SWMF Executive had resolved on 6 April, 'That the Area Officials shall hold such meetings as they think necessary'.[513]

The ballot paper asked members of affiliated District Unions to vote on the question of whether they would tender notice, 'with the object of obtaining recognition of the MFGB in the Nottinghamshire coalfield and to secure adequate assurances to prevent any victimisation of the workmen at Harworth'. Arnot stated that the turn-out was 98.9 per cent, a figure which is either suspect or achieved by colliery managements giving permission to hold the ballot at the pit-head. The result was the decisive majority for which the Executive had hoped, 444,546 to 61,445. In South Wales, despite the fact that the ballot-taking had been complicated by the coincidence of the Federation's Annual Conference, the figures were only slightly less decisive, 81,376 to 7945.[514]

When the MFGB officers now returned to the Department of Mines for a fresh round of talks with Spencer and Barber-Walker, they were not alone. In March, Sir Alfred Faulkner, Permanent Under Secretary at the Department of Mines, sent a diplomatically worded letter to Jones and Edwards suggesting that they field a widely-based committee for further negotiations. He was evidently concerned to include officers from the larger district unions, calculating that their participation was the most reliable way of ensuring consent for a negotiated settlement at an MFGB delegate conference. The Sub-Committee duly appointed on 20 April comprised Horner, Joe Hall, James Gilliland from Durham and Bowman. Bowman's presence from the small Northumberland district was supernumerary. It may have been

Horner who pressed for his inclusion, having observed that Bowman's assessments of situations coincided with his own.

The Harworth strike had continued throughout this critical period. Serious skirmishing had become routine over the four months strike. However, after the national ballot result was made public, both sides redoubled their respective efforts. On Friday 23 April the *Daily Worker* reported that a 'busload of scabs from Dinnington Yorkshire' had behaved provocatively on their journey through the Harworth pithead gates to start the nightshift. The small number of pickets responded by throwing stones, and every window in their bus had been smashed. After the police had called at the welfare club for reinforcements amongst the 'blacklegs', a 'pitched battle ensued, and the police and blacklegs retreated'. Mick Kane, who had already served one gaol sentence, and four other strikers were arrested on Saturday night 24 April, and 'a running battle began ... cars [were] overturned ... Men were bruised, cut and bandaged ... Harworth was now national news. The radio and press gave prominence to it, and in all the coal-fields it became a talking point.'[515]

The MFGB Sub-Committee had been meeting at the Black Boy Hotel in Nottingham on 24 April to hear a report from Faulkner about his meetings with the Nottinghamshire coalowners' association, Barber Walker and Spencer. The meagre concessions he had extracted concerned the merger negotiations between the two unions. The coalowners had not budged. Although the decisive majority in the national strike ballot was a strong incentive for the government to act, none of the Nottinghamshire players were apparently moved. They had all invested too much moral capital in defeating the Harworth strikers. If the strike collapsed, as they believed possible after the events of 23 to 24 April, Spencer could regain his unchallenged hold over the coalfield. They did not believe that the MFGB would call a national strike. Moreover, since the Nottinghamshire coalowners (including Barber Walker) had left the MAGB in 1926, they had nothing to lose by calling the MFGB bluff. In a national strike, Nottinghamshire coal would command a premium price.

On 19 March at the Nottinghamshire coalowners annual dinner, Captain P Muschamp, an influential owner and General Manager of the New Hucknall Collieries Ltd, gave the after-dinner address before an audience including the Deputy Chief

Inspector for Mines. Extensively reported in the *Notts Journal* on 20 March, his speech was a piece of defiant self-congratulation and scarcely disguised paean to fascism.

> This district – the Notts area – can take credit to itself for having smashed the national strike [sic, 1926 Lock-Out], and since then we have carried on very peaceably with the Industrial Union for ten years ... This Industrial Union ... has been the buffer which has prevented national strikes ... [The MFGB] have gone round the corner, and with the assistance of the Mines Department, I am sorry to say, are now trying to get in at the back door. We know – those of us who are in a position to know – how these strikes are initiated. They are initiated definitely by Communists. The working men of England do not want to strike ... I say definitely that if the Government does not deal with the question of the Communists in a more definite way, there will be no peace in this country. We want to adopt the German idea. If the Government is to check future trouble, it must put its foot down and put it down strongly.

The MFGB Sub-Committee recognised that the collapse of the Harworth strike was only a matter of time. They also knew that to call an indefinite national strike, when there was no prospect of the MAGB or the government being able to move the Nottinghamshire players, was a great risk. They adopted the only realistic option, and accepted the concessions Faulkner had gained. Merger negotiations were duly opened. As they proceeded, Horner and Spencer developed a very amicable working relationship. Griffin noted that Spencer admired Horner, and that '[they] ... seem to have got on very well'.[516]

On Friday 30 April, at the MFGB Special Delegate Conference, Jones moved and Lawther seconded the Executive motion embodying the Sub-Committee's recommendation. Delegates rejected it by a sizeable majority, including South Wales, 343 to 192. The MFGB Executive seized the opportunity presented to put pressure on the government. Its recommendation that strike notices be handed in on 7 May to take effect on 22 May was agreed unanimously, and delegates returned home with a solid united front behind the Harworth strikers. On Saturday 1 May, the TGWU Central Bus Committee led all London Transport workers out on indefinite official strike. The *Daily Worker* reported on the CPGB demonstration in London, at which Mick Kane had been one of the featured speakers. He had been freed on bail and was awaiting trial for the events of 24 April.

During the first week of May, it was evident that the London bus strike would be a protracted war of attrition. The government faced the embarrassing prospect that the Coronation of King George VI would take place without buses on 12 May, with a national coalfield strike in the offing for ten days later. Probably prompted by Citrine and Bevin as well as the MFGB-sponsored MPs, Attlee approached Baldwin to ask him to speak in the adjournment debate on 5 May in support of a motion he had put down about Harworth. Baldwin apparently took an impromptu decision, and agreed without consulting the rest of the Cabinet. In the Commons he said:

> I agree ... absolutely with what [Attlee] said about collective bargaining. What is the alternative to collective bargaining? There is none except anarchy ...
>
> I appeal to the handful of men with whom rests peace or war to give the best present to the country that could be given at that moment, to do the one thing which would rejoice the hearts of all the people who love this country, that is, to rend and dissipate this dark cloud which has gathered over us, and show the people of the world that this democracy can still at least practise the arts of peace in a world of strife.

Baldwin's speech was his last in the House of Commons before his retirement as prime minister. Bill Deedes, then parliamentary correspondent for the *Morning Post*, remembered it as a 'complete bombshell'. The Commons emptied immediately afterwards, an occurrence which the inexperienced Deedes had not often witnessed. Emmanuel Shinwell, opposition mining spokesman, had been scheduled to wind up the debate. But he tore up his notes and offered only a cursory response to the sparsely filled chamber.[517]

The prime minister's intervention provided the occasion for Spencer, Barber Walker and the MFGB Executive to begin slow, face-saving retreats from the impasse. When the Executive met on 6 May, the day after the speech, they postponed handing in strike notices for a fortnight, until after the Coronation, so that further negotiations could take place. The MFGB Sub-Committee brought back notably better terms from Spencer for the fused union and a pledge from Barber Walker to take back strikers as employment at Harworth became available.

The terms, particularly the qualified promise to take back strikers, enabled the MFGB to claim a victory. On 25 May the SWMF Executive authorised its delegates to the MFGB Conference to vote in favour of them. On 27 May, the MFGB Delegate Conference accepted them by a majority of 5 to 1. Reporting the result on 28 May, the *Daily Worker* offered only token opposition to the settlement, observing that 'with an increased drive and a more centralised organisation of the Federation [the MFGB] much better terms could have been gained'. They also reported Mick Kane's election to the CPGB Central Committee at the Fourteenth Party Congress, which had been taking place in Battersea. Kane told the Congress on 30 May, 'Today in Harworth the Communist Party and *Daily Worker* are looked on as the leadership of the working class movement.'[518] On 26 June, he was convicted of riot, and sentenced to two years imprisonment with hard labour.

Horner had been critical to the MFGB's success at Harworth and to achieving the merger between the NMA and the NMIU with a minimum of friction. His conduct of the Bedwas dispute had been observed and emulated with only slight modifications by Jones, Edwards and Lawther at the centre, and Mick Kane and the Harworth lodge officials on the ground. His personal interventions had acted as an emollient in the negotiations with Spencer and in persuading NMA left-wingers opposed to fusion to accept the merger. His influence was also vital in ensuring that the communists who formed the backbone of the Harworth strike leadership had agreed to retreat, rather than fighting to the last ditch. At the MFGB Conference in mid-July, Spencer was one of the delegates who voted unanimously for the South Wales resolution calling upon the Home Secretary to remit the punitive gaol sentences which had been meted out to the Harworth strikers. Horner moved the resolution with great passion.

[I]t must be recognised that many of our comrades are at this moment behind prison walls for something they have done for us. Personally I am not very much afraid of prison. I suppose I have experienced that as much as any person in this room, but the worst thing about prison is that you are rendered negative whilst there ... The resolution refers ... to the fact that ... a married woman has been considered worthy of being placed side by side with the men as martyrs of the working class struggle ... I can speak on this matter with some sense of reality as I have a wife who has been put behind prison bars of a similar nature ... It may be suggested that we are wasting time in endeavouring to get these sentences reduced. It is not wasted at all. I have had sentences reduced in consequence of the tremendous amount of pressure on the part of the workers, and I am therefore quite sure ... if this great Federation is determined ... to fight for those who are suffering, for the freedom and liberty to which we are entitled, then it will not be long before these people are amongst us again.[519]

Chapter 11

Two Steps Forward, One Step Back

Horner's conduct of the Battle of Bedwas brought him to national notice. A communist who settled industrial disputes without strikes was a curiosity, attracting an almost prurient attention from the British establishment. The *Spectator* published a profile of Horner in November 1936, five months after Horner had assumed the presidency of the Federation. It was written by H Powys Greenwood, after attending a meeting where Horner was speaking to the Conservative Imperial Policy Group. Greenwood observed that 'a coalowner ... told me that he had done more for industrial peace since his election than any of his Labour predecessors. He has crushed the incipient stay-in strike movement; he settled the Bedwas Colliery trouble ... As he [Horner] said, whatever his political views, his job is to sell labour and to maintain the conditions in which it can be sold.'[520]

Horner had outlined his plans for the coming year in his first presidential address to the Federation Annual Conference:

> It is my ambition ... to see the SWMF taking its rightful place in the front ranks, aiming to build the united Labour movement in this country, increasing our membership ... and exercising our influence to transform the MFGB into a single united force. Given clear minds and boundless courage, we will march forward to put an end to this National Government and bring about the situation in which we can return a fighting Labour Government which carries out a policy in the interests of the working people.[521]

Horner had signed the path breaking District Wages and Conciliation Board Agreement on 5 April 1937. Sixty days later, an MFGB Special Delegate Conference had approved the merger package between the NMA and the NMIU, repairing the breach which had crippled the MFGB's bargaining power since 1926. Horner had played an important part on the Executive Sub-Committee which negotiated the settlement. At the MFGB's Annual Conference in mid-July 1937, his influential role on the MFGB Executive was confirmed. He came a strong second to Lawther in the election for Vice-President, and received a significant vote in the contest to choose nominees for the three seats on the TUC General Council allocated to Group No. 1, the Mining and Quarrying Trades.[522]

In the summer of 1937, Horner received the Executive's permission to take a 'foreign holiday' in Spain, and was absent from union meetings for a fortnight from 10 August, returning on 24 August in time to give the Executive a 'lengthy report of his visit to the Government area in Spain' before the scheduled Delegate Conference.[523] The real reason for his visit would have been discussed at the meeting, although the minutes reflected the need for judicious camouflage. Pollitt had called for British volunteers to the International Brigade in December 1936. Soon after the Party Centre had asked the South Wales DPC to find a capable cadre to act as Commissar to the Clement Attlee Battalion, Paynter had been seconded, and served in Spain from March to October 1937. Horner evidently decided to make the journey after receiving a personal letter from Paynter, which he had written in the expectation that Horner would cite it at the Federation Executive. Substantial extracts subsequently appeared in the June issue of *Miners' Monthly*.

The Party Centre had turned to South Wales in part because so many South Walian miners had enlisted. But they were also concerned by evidence of volunteers' morale under leadership of distinctly variable quality in frequently horrendous conditions. Both the Attlee and the Abraham Lincoln Battalions were being steadily depleted by men deserting. Paynter's brief included investigating and addressing grievances with the Brigade leadership.[524]

Along with an American counterpart, Paynter had 'pressed the Brigade command to set up a centre where those whose morale had fallen could be rehabilitated'.[525] Paynter had probably calculated that Horner would not be intimidated by the Comintern *apparat* in Spain, and that his presence would significantly increase his own chances of achieving practical results with the International Brigade political leadership as well as lifting the troops' morale. Horner recalled:

> My immediate concern was the situation of the British members, indeed of all the foreign members ... These men were being given no leave at all. There were only three possibilities before them: to die, to be captured or to be wounded ... I fought this question with the leadership of the International Brigade. I said ... they should at least be sent to the Mediterranean for a brief period. Finally, they agreed that the men should have some sort of leave, but I doubt if the pledge was ever implemented ...

Togliatti later reported to the Comintern on the conflict precipitated by 'delegates of foreign parties' trying to intervene in the Brigade's affairs.[526]

Horner had been a strongly committed anti-fascist since the late 1920s, probably as a result of his reflections on his regular visits to the Ruhr in 1929 to 1932. In the comparatively free atmosphere of the MIC, he would have participated in the discussions about the implications of fascism for the European proletariat and communist parties with other miners' leaders, including the German Gustav Sobotka, and the Czech Gustav Nosek. Whilst in Spain, Horner was a keen observer of the political undercurrents and tensions on the Republican side. His conclusion, that the POUM 'was acting in a treacherous way against the Spanish people',[527] reflected his own experiences of leading serious industrial conflict. Along with most British left-wingers, he viewed the Republican Government's fight to defeat Franco's forces as critical, not only for the Spanish people but also for the chances of defeating fascism in Germany and Italy. During 1937, growing numbers of political observers agreed. One of them was Stafford Cripps. He conceived the Unity Campaign in

November 1936 in emulation of the Spanish and French united/ popular front governments, apparently without any forethought of the predictable hostility from the Labour Party establishment. In November 1936, Cripps, Bevan and William Mellor had led the Socialist League, a Labour ginger group formed in 1932, in discussions about the Manifesto's content with Pollitt and Dutt. Cripps had over-ridden the communists' objections to including the ILP, whose representatives proved unexpectedly amenable to working alongside the CPGB.[528]

Horner was able to prioritise activities related to the Aid Spain Campaign, organised by the CPGB as a United Front venture. His fellow officers and the Executive Committee were also passionately committed to the Spanish Republican cause. Consequently, he could use the Federation's prestige and power of initiative to maximum advantage. At the TUC in September 1937, Horner spoke on behalf of the MFGB delegation in support of the General Council's resolution, which Citrine had moved, on Spain. His speech applauded the resolution's substance, but damned its bland tone with faint praise; it was devoid of any sense of urgency. He also attacked the General Council's refusal to move beyond the National Council of Labour's position of merely putting pressure on the government to recognise the Republican government's right to buy arms on the open market:

> When I think of the boys I saw who have marched over that frontier, and ... are offering their lives, I look with scorn upon the efforts for which we are responsible in this document this afternoon. I urge this Congress, without the Government, to do something ... I say, with all respect, we have not nearly reached the maximum of our possibilities up to now ... Of course there are differences in the ranks, but those differences are being merged in the one task of winning the war ... .[528]

Horner succeeded in provoking Tom O'Brien, general secretary of the National Association Theatrical and Kine Employees, a Llanelli man who had first worked as a cinema projectionist there. He was also an observant Catholic and politically committed to the Labour centre-right. He accused Horner of appealing 'to our emotions', and then moved onto the more contentious ground of the war itself. Citrine had to intervene to row the debate back to the centre ground, as well as refuting Horner's charge that the TUC's campaigning efforts had been weak.

Later in the week, both Horner and Bevan spoke in their individual capacities against the General Council's support for Labour policy on rearmament. They were able to step outside the collective discipline of MFGB delegates by invoking the precedent which Horner had set at the 1928 TUC in Swansea, when he had persuaded the President, Ben Turner, to let him speak as an individual delegate against the MFGB's agreed line.[530] Horner confined himself to the comparatively safe observation that the MFGB Conference in July had passed a resolution which obliged the union to oppose the General Council position. He ended by stating 'One last point. I want to make it clear that I am no pacifist. If £1,500,000 or even £3,000,000, is necessary to withstand the forces of Fascism, I would be in favour of spending it, but I am not satisfied that it is being used, or will be used, to fight against Fascism. I am sorely afraid that it will be used in order to assist Fascism.'

Bevan's frontal attack on Citrine was more outrageous, finely calculated to cause reverberations inside the Parliamentary Labour Party:

> When you drop a Socialist and working-class interpretation of international affairs you have to use very strange arguments, and having dropped it, Sir Walter is now driven by implication to a defence of the trustworthiness of the 'National' Government ... No, comrades, this is far too serious a matter to be dealt with in the language of courtiers. We ought to have it dealt with in the language of honest to-God trade union delegates, who want to know exactly where they are in the matter.[531]

Lawther rose to administer the inevitable rebuke, in his triple capacities as MFGB Vice-President, General Council member and General Council nominee on the National Council of Labour. Having reminded delegates that *all* mineworkers were bound to observe General Council policy on collective security, he made a characteristically venomous reference to Bevan's and

Stafford Cripp's leading roles in the Unity Campaign which had been launched in the New Year:

> [T]he Movement has now reached a stage when members of the Parliamentary Labour Party, both trade unionists and non-trade unionists, will have to be informed very frankly and fearlessly that the decisions of the Trade Union Movement are the decisions that have got to be accepted ... [U]nfortunately, at the moment there are people dominating the political wing of the Movement who live in an unreal world ... [T]he miners at least accept their share of the responsibility, and once the decision is taken, will see to it that their constituent Members of Parliament will not play ducks and drakes with official policy.[532]

Lawther's insult was not a red herring. New Year was the traditional month for socialist revival campaigns, and the Unity Campaign thirteen-point Manifesto had been duly launched in mid-January 1937 with an ambitious programme of meetings. The national campaign began on 24 January at the Free Trade Hall in Manchester. The South Wales Unity Campaign announced meetings throughout the weekend of 30 to 31 January in Swansea, Cardiff, Llanelli, Merthyr and Newport; its complement of speakers included Bevan, Horner, Cripps, JR Campbell, Pollitt, Fenner Brockway, and Mellor.

Horner's and Bevan's speeches were extensively reported in the *Daily Worker*, which noted capacity crowds in every venue over the weekend. In Cardiff, Horner had emphasised the substantial unity already existing in the region, pointing to the 1936 National Unemployed March to London, 'when all sections of the working class movement in South Wales were organised within the local Councils of Action and represented on the Joint Council of Action for South Wales'. Not since 1926 had there been such enthusiasm, and everyone 'worked together as an active team'. He applauded the Cardiff Trades and Labour Council for standing up to the splitting instructions of the Labour Party leaders in London's Transport House and having the courage to associate with Communists, the Socialist League, the ILP and 'other progressive people in calling the all-in con-

ference for South Wales in aid of the Spanish people'. He felt
sure that the SWMF would support the all-in conference and
would place the needs of the Spanish people above all else, 'as
something more inspiring than the frantic efforts of Transport
House to keep the workers divided when thousands of our best
people are dying on the battlefields of Spain'.[533]

Although South Wales was unusual in producing so many
overflowing, enthusiastic meetings, the Campaign inspired
trade unionists and socialists throughout Britain. The Labour
Party political establishment moved swiftly to make their extreme
displeasure known.[534] Under intense pressure from the Labour
NEC, Cripps and Bevan felt compelled to effect the dissolution
of the Socialist League in mid-May, thus ending their own institutional involvement in the Campaign, which nevertheless continued a truncated existence under the auspices of the CPGB,
the ILP, and an ad hoc Labour Unity Committee, formed in the
wake of the Socialist League's demise. It finally petered out after
the TUC in September.[535]

Ben Pimlott's judgement, that the Campaign was a damp
squib, doomed from the start by deep ideological differences, is
misplaced. Compared to the revival campaigns which socialists
had been organising since the late nineteenth century, the Unity
Campaign was a resounding success. Its message was enthusiastically received by audiences whose interest had been aroused by
the Spanish Civil War. They agreed with the Campaign's message that Hitler's rise to power could have been stopped if communists and social democrats had made common cause.

The Unity Campaign's remarkable success in attracting publicity and public interest thoroughly alarmed the Labour Party
establishment. To counter it, an informal centre-right united
front coalesced, led by Bevin, Citrine and JS Middleton, since
1935 the Labour Party's first full-time, paid secretary. Bevin as
TGWU general secretary had found it politically convenient
to let out office suites in Transport House, the massive headquarters of the TGWU opened in 1932, to the TUC and the
Labour Party at attractive rents. Their physical proximity during
the working day facilitated the three men becoming political
intimates, even though Bevin and Citrine disliked each other
intensely. Their co-ordinated political initiatives were facilitated

by their officials, who intermingled over lunch in nearby cafés, or the Marquis of Granby across the road in Smith Square.[536]

After their success in forcing the Unity Campaign to ground, the Transport House centre-right united front led a concerted war of attrition against the left united front. For most of the next four years, they regarded Cripps, Bevan and their supporters as their principal political opponents. The threat which they perceived was, in large measure, due to the willingness of leaders of the other united front, notably Cripps and Bevan, to meet and discuss politics with British communists, thereby conferring legitimacy on the CPGB's views. The Transport House triumvirate excused the French socialists from criticism for consorting closely with the PCF, recognising that Leon Blum was dependent on communist votes to elect socialists to parliament. Bevin, Citrine and Middleton were confident, however, that British communists' importance was minimal, and were determined to marginalise them.

The standard Transport House rejoinder to the Unity Campaign's arguments included a condemnation of the German communist party's culpability for having consistently refused to cooperate with German social democrats against the Nazis. But the incontestable fact of the KPD's unremitting sectarianism was usually ignored or passed over in silence by most left-wing British socialists. Their picture of the German revolution and the SPD was clouded by the assassination of Luxembourg and Liebknecht, and they viewed both the SPD's achievements and mistakes from a visceral anti-German perspective.

Another Transport House argument was that, unlike their continental sister parties, the Labour Party was the only left party which mattered in Britain. Whilst the veracity of this point was self-evident for parliamentary and local elections in England, it was not wholly convincing in either Scotland or South Wales. When other salient facts, such as participation and leadership in trade unions were considered, the argument became special pleading. Nevertheless, despite the existence of clandestine CPGB members in many English constituency Labour parties and a palpable communist presence inside trade unions and trades councils, there was little evidence that communists' presence substantially affected decisions taken in Westminster or constituency parties. The Transport House triumvirate viewed

Willie Gallacher's election as MP for West Fife in 1935 as a freak occurrence. They believed that it was unlikely to be repeated elsewhere, provided that Middleton and Morgan Phillips, the Labour Party Assistant Secretary, maintained due vigilance, and ensured a high degree of supervision of local parties.[537]

Horner's dazzling performance since becoming SWMF President rendered it increasingly difficult for them to succeed in South Wales. At the SWMF Annual Conference in April 1937, Oliver Harris moved the vote of thanks to Horner for his Presidential address, 'If there is one thing to which I respond more than any other, and I am sure the Executive Council does the same, it is to the [President's] statement welcoming the unity of the Labour movement.'[538] Evidently, after the searing experiences of fighting the 'scab union' with divided forces, many Labour activists, including the SWMF Vice-President Bill Saddler, and Executive members Alf Davies and Will Arthur, were committed to co-operation. They had learned to their cost the adverse consequences brought by a split in the movement. The Conference passed by an overwhelming show of hands the Executive resolution about united front activity, moved by Will Arthur and described by the *Daily Worker* as the 'answer to those who have for months tried to break the United Front movement in South Wales'. Dai Grenfell, Arthur Jenkins and Jim Griffiths all spoke against it. They were countered by speeches from Harris and Saddler.[539]

The fusion of the NMIU and the NMA had left the SWMIU isolated, in a potentially vulnerable position. However, although its only remaining stronghold was Taff-Merthyr, winkling them by means of industrial conflict was probably impossible. After the epic four week strike in autumn 1934, the Federation and the SWMIU had stood at an impasse. Since then, the SWMF presence had diminished significantly as a result of management pressure. Alf Davies had been unable to improve the position during his secondment in 1936. The colliery management connived at reinforcing the SWMIU's hold, even though it had signed the November 1934 compromise agreement which stipulated strictly even-handed treatment of the rival unions.

In the summer of 1937, inspired by events at Harworth, the rump of SWMF loyalists at Taff-Merthyr combined with Bedlinog communists to put pressure on Horner and the Federation

Executive to activate the provision in the 1934 compromise under which the company had agreed to a ballot to enable working miners to decide which union would exclusively represent them. Horner was sceptical about the Federation's chances. Under the 1934 compromise, both unions were barred from conducting propaganda prior to the ballot. In 1937 conditions, this meant that the SWMIU would have a clear advantage. The Harworth ballot had been held at the climax of a strike in which the NMA men and their families had been ready to fight to the last ditch. The Bedwas ballot had been held less than three months after a major coalfield confrontation had compelled the management to make major concessions. At Taff-Merthyr, the ballot would be held in cold blood in unfavourable conditions; working miners could daily observe the Federation's inability to counteract management's partiality for the SWMIU.

Horner considered it improbable that a decisive majority of Taff-Merthyr miners could be persuaded to vote for the SWMF. But his practical alternative was for the Federation forces to resume another well-planned campaign of boring from within. He believed that with patient preparation, it would be possible to rebuild their forces underground. He opposed holding an immediate ballot, both inside the Federation Executive and at the South Wales DPC. Nevertheless, militants inside both institutions grew increasingly impatient, and he recognised the need to trim to the prevailing sanguine mood. The SWMF triggered the ballot provision. But when it was held at the end of September, the SWMIU won by a majority of 5 votes.[540] Horner produced detailed plans for damage limitation on 29 September when the Federation Executive discussed the disappointing result. They accepted his approach; indeed it is likely that no other options were put. The possibility of balloting all Federation members for a coalfield strike was evidently not considered viable even by Horner's most vociferous left opponents.

Horner's way out was a fusion on similar terms to Nottinghamshire. The ballot result was publicly announced on 7 October. On 13 October he attended a meeting between Federation and SWMIU officers. Horner had recruited Iestyn Williams as neutral chairman; George Spencer, in his new capacity as president of an MFGB-affiliated district union, attended as adviser to both sides. Merger was the only item on the agenda.[541]

Two further meetings were held in the following fortnight, in which Gregory continued to insist on more favourable terms than Horner was offering, not surprisingly in view of his victory in the Taff-Merthyr ballot. But Horner refused to make significant concessions, being unwilling to accord Gregory and the SWMIU an equivalent position to Spencer and the NMIU. The negotiations were stalled for three months. Horner kept the Federation's terms for merger on the table for three months, during which time Spencer acted as his confidential emissary, exploring whether and at what price Gregory could be bought. Horner and Spencer worked purposefully together in good faith. Spencer's unconditional return to the MFGB fold in 1937 had been genuine, though he refused to play the penitent. He evidently appreciated the Federation loyalists' view that Gregory and most of his South Walian officials were upstarts and interlopers, and understood Horner's determination to mete out different treatment to the SWMIU than the NMIU had received.

Spencer eventually persuaded Gregory to accept a generous severance package; under its terms he and his staff received a year's salary in return for which they discreetly disappeared. When the merger between the SWMF and the SWMIU was duly concluded, the SWMF fused with a hollow shell. No SWMIU officials moved into the Federation offices to occupy full-time positions. Spencer finessed the redundancy deal as an internal MIU administrative arrangement. The substantial sum required for the pay-off was formally supplied by Spencer from the MIU's funds. Horner supplied Spencer with the money from Federation funds, and the deal was successfully managed in strict privacy. Since the 'redundancy money' depended upon the wall of silence holding, Gregory had no reason to breach it. Horner personally entered the sum in the union's accounts as Taff Merthyr campaigning expenses, without reference to either Saddler or Harris. Although he had no scruples about the pay-off or its concealment from the Federation Executive, he calculated that neither were sufficiently flexible to acquiesce in the stratagem.[542]

There were problems, however, in negotiating the merger arrangements on the ground at Taff-Merthyr. It was not until early February 1938 that Horner was satisfied that no further improvements could be gained from either the SWMIU lodge officials or the colliery company. Not surprisingly, the agreement with management included the same no-strike and arbitration clauses as pertained at Bedwas. Provision was made for the chairman and secretary of the re-formed SWMF lodge to a elected by former SWMIU members, whilst the treasurer would be elected by men who were Federation members before the ballot. The colliery management refused to re-employ Federation members who had been sacked in the 1934 strike and wanted to return to the colliery. The agreement with the SWMF stated 'that it is their [management's] intention in general to take back into employment men previously employed', subject to suitability and managerial discretion. SWMF loyalists, including 1934 martyrs living in Bedlinog, found it difficult to stomach.[543]

Having been endorsed by the Executive, the agreement was scheduled to be put to a meeting of the Taff-Merthyr Federation Lodge on Sunday 6 February at the Bedlinog Workmen's Institute. However, the *Western Mail* reported on 3 February that the Lodge Committee had rejected the agreement; without their endorsement the Federation officers could not be certain of winning a vote of approval at the Lodge meeting. Consequently, a meeting between the Lodge Committee, Horner, Saddler, Harris, and Alf and Jack Davies, the two Executive members most involved, was arranged for 6 February before the Lodge Meeting. The précis by Francis and Smith, and their citations from the typescript report in the SWMF files, show Horner at his most didactic and forthright:

> He went through the clauses in the terms, commenting on each in turn, and at length on the awkward points. Essentially his argument was that the SWMIU was finished and that all that followed from that, good and bad, were minor matters ... In his view, the MIU could have insisted on total control of the lodge [committee], by the terms of the ballot; as it was they had agreed to have a majority of one ... 'Because you start off with one less do you give up the ghost and think you have a lost cause?' ... The EC was unanimous in its recommendation ... 'If you turn it down we report it to the Conference but if Conference accepts it [the Executive recommendation] ... the Conference cannot accept responsibility for

your future. If, on the other hand, Conference turns it down we are still confronted with the possibility of the revival of the MIU and the Company could say that the ballot decided the issue ... Do not think the Conference is willing to come out to fight for Taff-Merthyr in face of the fact that the Taff-Merthyr workmen themselves, by a majority, were in favour of the MIU.'

These arguments and contributions from the others persuaded the Lodge Committee and they agreed to recommend the agreement Horner had negotiated. The Lodge Meeting then voted unanimously in its favour.[544] On 8 February the *Daily Worker* reported: 'Recently there has been a lot of loose reporting in the Daily Herald, alleging that there was a strong body of men opposed to the terms, but the Taff-Merthyr vote has shown how solidly the men are behind the agreement. The procedure now to be followed, reference to lodges, gives every South Wales miner a chance to consider and vote upon the issue.'[545] As at Bedwas and Harworth, once the Taff-Merthyr Lodge had accepted the compromise settlement, approval by a district delegate conference followed, although in each case a minority of activists continued to argue that a total war strategy would have achieved 100 per cent of the union's goals. But the lodges they represented evidently preferred not to be seen opposing the general will, and their votes were cast with the Executive.[546]

Horner was now able to step up the pace in the drive to achieve 100 per cent Federation membership. He described his plans to a Delegate Conference on 24 August 1938:

We are fortunate in that everything before us to-day is a consequence of our increased authority and strength . When examination is made of the conflicts in the South Wales Coalfield over a period of many years, it is found that the large majority of them have arisen from Non-Unionism, Company Unionism, and disputes with Unions competing for members against our Union. In addition, practically all the violent happenings which have brought physical damage to our members, and the imprisonment of hundreds of them, have occurred in Non-Union disputes and not in disputes with the Owners

375

over questions of wages or conditions. Your Executive considers these experiences should be rendered unnecessary in the future. It considers this the time to make the claim that membership of the South Wales Miners' Federation shall be a condition of employment. We have already established a Sub-Committee with the Owners to consider this claim, and [i]f you endorse our action ... we can proceed with our task, in the hope a conclusion being reached in the near future.[547]

The final obstacle to unity was not political but sectional, a craftsmen's union which had been formed in 1921 as a breakaway from the Federation. Its formal title, South Wales and Monmouthshire Colliery Enginemen, Boilermen and Craftsmen's Association, was universally ignored, and it was described by its secretary's name, as the DB Jones' Union. Horner conducted vigorous negotiations with this union, in which his personal charm and genial humour probably played an important part. A merger was agreed in November 1938, with DB Jones being employed as one of the Federation's craftsmen's agents. Meanwhile, the Ocean and Cory combine committees, freed from the threat of the SWMIU, had intensified their drive to recruit the remaining rump of 'nons'. Their vigorous rank-and-file campaign channelled militants' energies into positive avenues. The Executive kept a tight rein on the Combine Committees' 'constant threats of large-scale action'. It only sanctioned a one-day strike at Ocean collieries in July 1938, and a three-day strike in January 1939 by 6000 miners in Cory collieries.[548]

Since its foundation in 1898, the presumption that the Federation spoke for the whole of the South Wales labour movement had been integral to its identity. However, by the 1930s, officials from other unions felt marginalised and pre-empted from making their influence felt on social and economic issues affecting their members, for example the unemployed regulations and the region's economic recovery. This was particularly true for the TGWU, whose officials on the docks in the coastal strip had been invigorated by the merger of their previous parochial unions into Bevin's national colossus. Their self-confidence and awareness of being part of a big national union underlay their resentment at the fact that SWMF officers habitually arrogated to themselves the custom of speaking not only for their own members but for the whole of the South Wales labour movement to government and, through their sponsored MPs, on the floor of the House of Commons. To counter the Federation's influence, South Walian TGWU officials began to combine with the centre-right united front in Transport House in London. They acted in concert to promote individual Labour Party membership and looked for organisational ways to counter the Federation's predominant position.

After Horner's assumption of the Federation presidency, the Transport House united front had pressing reason to challenge SWMF hegemony. Horner was not slow to use his presidential discretion and power of initiative to promote left united front causes. An example was the South Wales Council for Spanish Aid, which was formed at a conference on 15 February 1937 convened by the SWMF and the Cardiff Trades and Labour Council, and attended by 300 delegates, representing over 300,000 members of the Labour Party, trade unions and other groups. Francis notes, 'whilst Spanish Aid Committees now began to be formed, other organisations, such as Trades Councils, political parties, women's guilds, Councils of Action, United Front committees, Left Book Club circles, trade union branches and lodges, also continued to do similar work.'[549]

Duncan Tanner commented, 'For a time the [Labour Party] NEC lost the initiative ... [O]rganizers were concerned that any initiative [on the Means Test and Spain] ... in south Wales would inevitably include the Communists.'[550] Horner was a rising star. He was spending most of his working week in Cardiff and was in great demand for public meetings organised by the Cardiff Trades and Labour Council, Fabian Society branches and other labour movement bodies. The press and public were attracted by Horner, his charm, charisma and virtuoso ability to communicate complex arguments simply and concisely. Leo Abse remembered the hero worship with which the members of the Cardiff Labour League of Youth regarded Horner. He never behaved as a great man and condescended, but treated them as equals. He sometimes came on their charabanc excursions, and also set them jobs to do, notably helping to write his speech for the Annual Eisteddfod.[551]

In his 1936 Budget, the Chancellor of the Exchequer, Neville Chamberlain, created a special Treasury fund for the establishment of industries, the Special Areas Reconstruction Association (SARA). Its chairman, Sir Wyndham Portal, had been appointed by the National Government in 1934 as one of the experts charged with reporting on 'distressed areas', with a brief to examine South Wales. Ted Rowlands observed: 'Portal stands apart from the other investigators ... From his very first days, he signalled his intention not only to report but to pursue his conclusions and recommendations ... He was not averse to applying press and public pressure upon Whitehall.' Portal's 'assiduous and approachable manner impressed South Wales'. In addition to chairing SARA, Portal was chairman of the Nuffield Trust for Special Areas.[552] With these interlocking positions, he controlled considerable capital for reconstruction/relief schemes. Because of his previous connection, he was keen to direct substantial sums to South Wales.

In early 1937 Horner and Harris represented the Federation in discussions with Portal in his capacity as chair of the Nuffield Trust. They proposed a contributory pension scheme to which owners and miners would each contribute 6d per week. At the end of five years, 3000 men over the age of sixty-five could be retired. Portal commented: 'as regards unemployment [the scheme] is a very good one, and also the gesture of creating friendship and solidarity behind the Miners' Federation, should be a very great advantage'. Horner found this 'high level' work absorbing and congenial, having no moral doubts about helping capitalism in South Wales back onto its feet. Portal was no decadent rentier, but rather a capable member of the old capitalist elite, with a radical, maverick side. (Along with William Morris, he had been a generous financial contributor to the New Party.) Horner never suffered from the reverse snobbery cultivated by many working-class activists. He had no prejudice against people outside his class, and took aristocrats, industrialists and priests as they came. He and Portal warmed to one another, enjoying each other's legendary charm and conviviality. They shared a practical, positive outlook and an interest in sport.[553]

The centre-right Labour *apparat* were frustrated by how dextrously Horner used his position to shape the South Walian political agenda. They were infuriated by the frequent occasions on which Horner, the Federation President and prominent communist, spoke practical common sense on public platforms. The problem was that they could not usually find fault with the substance of his message. He was pursuing directions and lines of argument which differed little from those of either Lloyd George or Hilary Marquand, the gifted young economist at the University College of South Wales and Monmouthshire who had researched *South Wales Needs A Plan*, setting out the need to attract new, modern industries to the valleys. Transport House were determined to stymie Horner, but found themselves unable to detract from his success.

With Horner in the lead, the SWMF Executive were determined to defend the Federation's virtually unquestioned authority over local organisation and sponsored MPs in the coalfield constituencies. A particularly effective innovation was his institution of monthly meetings between the sponsored MPs and the Executive, at which a full and frank exchange of views occurred. Horner enjoyed presiding over a lively dialogue ranging over the whole of national and international events, often yielding to the temptation to speak himself. The political composition of the Executive was reflected in the fact that they regularly provided virtually unanimous support for Bevan in his disputes with the PLP and Party NEC. His fellow Monmouthshire MPs sponsored by the SWMF, Arthur Jenkins and Sir Charles Edwards, were implacably hostile; but the meetings made them uncomfortably aware that the Federation was standing behind Bevan.[554] They recognised that the Federation officers and the Executive would strenuously resist what they viewed as unwarranted attempts by Transport House to encroach on their terrain.

The Transport House triumvirate of Bevin, Citrine and Middleton pursued Horner with mendacity, bordering on obsession. And they were also keen to loosen the Federation's hold on the regional labour movement. To this end they deployed the assistant party secretary and ex-SWMF activist, Morgan Phillips, and George Morris, Labour Party divisional organiser in Cardiff. Bevin had an additional goal. He aimed to stamp the TGWU's authority on the South Wales Labour Party, and considered that he and his union should take over the lien to choose and sponsor candidates throughout this contracting coalfield, where he argued the Federation was increasingly irrelevant.

In early 1937, the Transport House united front took the offensive. EP Harries, head of the TUC Organisation Department, provided the TUC General Council with a summary of the origins of the Joint Unemployment Council, a united front organisation which the SWMF had taken the lead in establishing, and which Transport House now proposed to supersede. Horner did not explain that its title had been expediently altered from the South Wales Council of Action, probably in order to pre-empt objections from local Labour Parties who were chary of revolutionary sounding names. But he did point out that: 'For part of the time the Communist Party and the Independent Labour Party were associated with it, but as a result of protests, this association has been discontinued.' Its current joint secretaries were Oliver Harris and EA Robson, Secretary of the Cardiff Trades & Labour Council.

According to Harris:

> The position in South Wales has been causing grave difficulty to the Labour Movement ... in view of the activities of the South Wales Joint Unemployment Council. ... [I]t was thought that probably the Council would go out of existence on the termination of the agitation against the Regulations, but recently it was reported that a decision had been made to extend the terms and activities of the Council; to put it on a permanent basis, and to increase wherever possible the number of local Committees attached to the Council. The Labour Party regarded this as a direct challenge to the Party machinery ...

Accordingly, a proposal was put forward by Transport House to establish a South Wales Regional Council of Labour, as an alternative to the TUC – an alternative that would be less under the control of the united front left. On 22 January 1937 George Morris had convened a conference of union representatives 'to consider the position ... A further conference ... on February 10th appointed a deputation to meet the Joint Unemployment Council and see if it was possible to secure their co-operation'. But the JUC were clear that they 'would be prepared to enter into consultation ... re the setting up of a South Wales Regional

Council of Labour *providing there is no discrimination of delegates from Trade Unions'.*[555] As a result of General Council concerns, the proposal was subsequently revised in favour of a bifurcated Regional Council – one half for delegates from constituency Labour Parties and the other for representatives from trades unions and trades councils.[556]

On 7 April, Harries and George Shepherd, Labour Party National Agent, travelled to Cardiff to present their revised version to the unions and Labour Party officers. Neither the Federation nor the AEU were represented. But a deputation was received from the JUC.

> The deputation pointed out that the ... [JUC] had stepped in to do a job of work which was not being done by anyone else. The work had been very well done, and although they had no objection to extending the scope ... they wanted to make it clear that the South Wales Miners' Federation was not associating themselves with the proposed new body if there was any discrimination against Trade Union representatives. In their own words – and they said this quite plainly – that if Mr. Arthur Horner could not be a member of the new body, the South Wales Miners' Federation would not have anything to do with it.[557]

The lines of conflict were clearly drawn. The Federation would lack any direct representation in the section for constituency parties. In the second section, for trade unions and trades councils, Citrine and Middleton ruled that the TUC's Circular No. 16, which disbarred communists and fascists from membership of trades councils, applied. Local union officials from the NUGMW, AEU and ETU were swift to back the proposed structure. Perennially jealous of the Federation's power, their comparatively weak skills rendered them easy meat for the formidable delegates whom the SWMF routinely fielded in ad hoc committees, at public events and government consultations. George Morris's successor, Cliff Prothero recalled that it was 'in our favour that the Regional Council was housed in Transport House, in Charles Street, Cardiff', and described Bevin as 'a good supporter'.[558]

Horner led the Executive in a spirited resistance to the SWRCL. The Federation Executive told the Labour and TUC *apparats* that the SWMF intended to decide whom to appoint to the trades union and trades council section of the Regional Council of Labour, just as they did with their TUC delegation; in other words SWMF delegates might be members of the CPGB or ILP. Months elapsed during which attempts to find a compromise, notably by Jim Griffiths, failed. Citrine, Middleton and Bevin bided their time, whilst political temperatures and tempers were rising in Cardiff.

On 2 June 1937, Middleton and Citrine received Harris, Horner and Saddler, to discuss the SWRCL, and the fact that two competing conferences on the new unemployment regulations were scheduled in Cardiff later in the month, one organised by the putative SWRCL, the other by the JUC and backed by the SWMF. Middleton and Citrine proposed that *both* conferences be postponed until the impasse was resolved by the National Council of Labour, 'with the view of avoiding any conflict between the two bodies in South Wales, and to secure the fullest co-operation of all sections of the working class movement'.[559]

George Morris duly honoured the compromise and postponed the conference. On 7 June the Federation Executive received representations from the Cardiff Trades and Labour Council, hitherto a staunch supporter of left-united frontism, favouring postponement of the JUC all-in conference. The Executive agreed. Horner chose not to take a stand, and now led an orderly retreat. He was evidently keen to avoid an open breach with the Labour left-wingers inside the Federation and local Labour organisations, who were finally responding to pressure from the Transport House centre-right united front. On 28 June, Saddler gave a long report to an SWMF Delegate Conference about the new unemployment regulations and the proposed Regional Council of Labour. A resolution was passed unanimously expressing profound regret that the SWRCL's constitution precluded the free election of trade union delegates.[560]

Middleton, Citrine and Bevin finally lost patience with the SWMF's persistent delaying tactics. In July Federation officers were informed that the Labour Party had organised an 'all-in' conference on unemployment on 28 August, at which the SWRCL would definitely be established. The Federation Executive decided to pre-empt Transport House, and on Saturday 14 August convened an 'all-in' conference on unemployment, open to communists, ILP members and their party organisations. The occasion was a moral victory for left-united frontism. Since Horner was in Spain, the Executive asked Griffiths to take the chair. Predictably, he did not attend. Bill Saddler presided, and his dual role as Federation Vice-President and Monmouthshire County Council Labour Alderman lent lustre to the proceedings. The business was a model of labour movement propriety, including a motion proposed by Ness Edwards, urging the government to adopt the measures in the National Council of Labour's recent Memorandum urging the promotion of new industries in South Wales.

The Federation Executive used the conference, the last public occasion before the SWMRCL's formation, to put their position on record. The *Daily Worker* reported both Saddler's and Ianto Evans' speeches. Saddler acknowledged the SWMF's intention of participating in the SWRCL. He also added that 'the SWMF would do everything possible to broaden the constitution ... so that all sections of the working class movement could be represented and take their part in the campaign against unemployment'. Ianto Evans 'pointed out that only by united action was it possible to carry out the decisions of the conference. Transport House had broken up the old Joint Council of Action ... The Communists, however, were anxious to maintain unity and ... [for the SWMF] to participate in the Regional Council and would insist upon the right of the trade unions to elect delegates of their own choosing to the Regional Council.'[561]

A *Manchester Guardian* story appeared on 16 August under the headline, 'Labour Differences in South Wales. A New Regional Council'. The reporter had evidently been briefed by the Cardiff Labour *apparat*. No mention was made of the SWMF all-in conference, but a discursive account was provided of the conflict over the SWRCL and the Federation's retreat. 'There was, therefore a danger of a serious split in the Labour movement in South Wales, because a Regional Council without the Miners' Federation would be unthinkable ... Realising the danger, the Miners' Federation has now abandoned its previous position and has decided to co-operate ... Under pressure from Transport House the Cardiff Trades and Labour Council has also regularised its position ... [T]he new body which will be launched on August 28 ... conforms with the orthodoxies of Labour headquarters.'[562]

On 24 August, the SWMF Executive considered the draft rules and constitution of the SWRCL, and put forward amendments to them. They also appointed Will Arthur and Gomer Evans to attend the conference on 28 August. Both were Labour stalwarts (Evans was a Carmarthenshire County Councillor), as well as being high profile Horner supporters. Many SWMF lodges were also represented on the day, enabling the Federation to mount an imposing presence. The *Daily Worker*'s report of the conference noted that all Federation delegates but two (probably Arthur and Evans) had left at an early stage in protest against the chairman's ruling that voting would be by show of hands. By refusing to allow card votes, the Federation delegates' numerical predominance would make no difference to results. All nine SWMF amendments to the constitution, enabling unions to select any of their bona fide members as delegates, had been ruled out of order.[563] After what must have been an impressive display of political pyrotechnics from both the floor and the platform, the South Wales Regional Council of Labour was inaugurated, and Will Arthur and Gomer Evans were duly elected onto the Executive.

Despite the formal victory won by Transport House, the catholic, tolerant culture which had marked the South Wales labour movement since the 1890s proved remarkably durable. The Federation initially treated the SWRCL with marked pusillanimity. On 2 November, the Federation Executive minutes noted that a request from the Regional Council to pay their affiliation fees had been 'considered'. Although it was decided to pay them, it was also agreed that the SWRCL should be asked to raise the 'general principle of protest' against the government's refusal to increase unemployment benefit and allowances in order to compensate for the increased cost-of-living. The Council would also be asked to convene an immediate conference to discuss this issue.[564]

Horner's friendships and alliances with Labour loyalists in the SWMF and the Cardiff labour movement limited the SWRCL's lien.[565] His open-handedness and lack of sectarianism were the paradigm to which left united front Labour activists throughout Britain pointed as evidence of the CPGB's bona fides. A Scottish delegate's observation during the united front debate at the MFGB Annual Conference in July 1937 was typical: 'I see nothing very seriously wrong with him [Horner], he is a decent fellow, he is a capable man ... no one can deny his sincerity when you hear him speak ... '.[566]

Horner was nominated for MFGB Vice-President by the SWMF at the annual conference. He received 39,000 votes, probably from Northumberland, Nottinghamshire and the Forest of Dean, in addition to the Federation's own 85,000.[567] In contrast to 1936, however, the Conference decisively rejected the SWMF's 'united front' motion, which condemned the TUC 'Black Circular' 16 and pledged the MFGB to seek its withdrawal. (It was Circular 16 that justified the prohibition of communist delegates to both sections of the SWRCL.) A Durham motion containing no mention of the circular, calling on the MFGB to promote working-class unity, was more narrowly rejected.[568] At the TUC and the Labour Party Conference MFGB officers confidently wielded their block vote against all manifestations of left united frontism and were conspicuous in support of the Transport House centre-right united front.

Horner was not deterred by these setbacks, however. He continued to cultivate Labour left leaders in the other district unions and to develop his personal political network. The NCL's implacable refusal to challenge the Conservative government's abstentionism in European affairs was causing increasing numbers of Labour loyalists to move towards the CPGB's united front initiatives. They felt they had to do something to stop Franco and Hitler, and, in the absence of Transport House activity, began to co-operate with the CPGB 'fronts' organising aid for the Spanish Republicans and promoting united front/popular front politics inside the Labour Party. They also had few compunctions about supporting workers' delegations to visit the Soviet Union to see the socialist experiment at first hand.[569]

Inside the MFGB, more of the 'forward looking' progressive leaders had moved rightwards on political issues, notably Lawther and Edwards. But those who remained on the left were in wholehearted agreement with SWMF positions, as articulated by Horner and Bevan. Moreover, they were self-consciously aiming to supplant the older generation of Marxists/left-wing-

385

ers, most of whom they considered dogmatic, and also unrealistic with regard to the economic conflict with coalowners. Watson, Bowman and George Jones had been profoundly impressed by Horner's success in the scientific application of Clausewitzian principles in the coalfield economic struggle, and had become his staunch admirers in this respect.

The MFGB national officers, Joseph Jones, Edwards and Lawther, had expediently constructed a Chinese wall between their opposition to left united frontism and their determination to effect a return to national collective bargaining. The left network, with Horner at the centre, reciprocated the national officers' willingness to co-operate, and erected their own Chinese wall between economic and political issues.

The de facto alliance of left and right progressives, which had coalesced in 1934 around the national wages campaign now moved forward on another plank of their ambitious, modernising agenda. Joseph Jones had used his presidential address at the 1937 Annual Conference to make a high profile plea for a united mineworkers' union, as the only realistic means of countering the coalowners' strength and ending district wage bargaining. Edwards offered a rigorous defence of a united union during a lengthy private session. Delegates were considering a motion from Kent directing the Executive to produce 'as soon as practicable a scheme for the formation of one National Association for all mineworkers and upon completion ... the same to be placed before a Special Conference for consideration and endorsement'.

Jones used his chairman's prerogative to declare the motion carried without a show of hands, though he was evidently unwilling to declare it unanimous. As with the beginning of the national wages campaign in 1934, sceptics and parochial conservatives chose to keep a low profile in the face of this vigorous progressive initiative. It was impossible to predict whether the kings and princes of the district union cabbage patches would ultimately move behind unification. Much would depend on the ability of the Reorganisation Subcommittee appointed by the Executive in August to produce a scheme which took adequate account of vested interests.

The Reorganisation Subcommittee predictably included members from the three largest districts, Horner, Watson, and Herbert Smith. The other members were Henry Leese from the Midlands Federation, where favourable collective bargaining conditions would be subsumed in a national union, and J Harrison, from the Northeast craftsmen's union, another important special interest group. The choice of Watson, rather than more senior veterans from Durham, was probably evidence of Horner's influence. He is likely to have calculated that he and Watson together could manage the Sub-committee business purposefully and also outflank Herbert Smith.[570]

The *Manchester Guardian* reporter noted that Horner had 'seemed to make a deep impression' at the MFGB annual conference. In the report on the Lancashire resolution calling for an immediate national wages increase, the *Daily Telegraph* described Horner as 'formerly the extremist leader of the expelled Mardy lodge, and now the comparatively moderate [SWMF] president ... His speech was a model of restraint ... [and] amazed the conference for its moderation'.[571] (The motion was referred to the executive without a vote being taken, an outcome interpreted by the non-communist press as a break with militancy.)

Two days later, delegates supported the Executive resolution committing the union to seeking 'both nationally and internationally, to effect a reduction of the hours of labour in all coal-producing countries'. Edwards made a perfunctory proposing speech; Horner's lengthy seconding speech provided the substantial arguments:

> [T]he Mining Industry of the country has before it two plans ... [E]ither reactionary opposition on the part of the miners to the application of science to the industry [mechanisation], or a progressive constructive method of reducing hours in order to keep pace with that development. There are, in our own ranks, thousands of our people who regard the machine as our enemy ... We could, if they forced us to do it, like the Luddites of long ago, throw our shoes in the machinery, that is sabotage ... I don't think we ought to attempt to sabotage our employment by preventing progress ... that is the path of

> reaction. The answer to this problem ... [is] by reducing
> the working time ... .[572]

A fortnight after the Annual Congress the MFGB Executive accepted an invitation from the Soviet Miners' Union to send a delegation to the USSR in November. (Although an SWMF delegation had visited the Soviet Union in 1936, no one from the MFGB had visited the Soviet Union since 1927, when Arthur Cook had gone, in his personal capacity, to thank the Russian trade union movement for their major financial support in the 1926 Lock-Out.) The geographic and political spread of the seven delegates chosen on 23 September 1937 was finely balanced: on the centre-right, Joseph Jones, Ted Jones from North Wales and James Cook from Fife; on the left, Horner, Bowman, and Joe Hall from Yorkshire. The seventh was Will Lawther, whose political alignment at this juncture resembled that of a chameleon. A General Council member since 1935, he had initially provided public support for the General Council line, making personal attacks on Horner and Bevan at the TUC. However, under pressure of European events and the MFGB Executive's leftwards progress, he had moved back towards his previous left-wing position.[573]

Lawther travelled to Moscow with Horner and Bowman on 2 November, before the rest of the delegation, in order to attend celebrations of the twentieth anniversary of the October Revolution. The delegation remained in the USSR until 17 December, and toured the principal coalmining regions in the Donbas and the Urals. In the Donbas they met the champion coal-hewer Alexei Stakhanov, who had become a Soviet celebrity in August 1935 by over-fulfilling his production quota by 1400 per cent. Unremitting propaganda, comparing this communist achievement favourably with results achieved in capitalist countries, had made Stakhanovism synonymous with super-efficient labour productivity.

Relations inside the delegation were hostile. Joseph Jones had issued a public statement en route from Berlin, that 'if he had to choose between Communism and Nazism, he would choose Nazism because it was more efficient'. Hall reported his remark to Horner, Bowman and Lawther in Moscow. Horner recalled that:

Joseph Jones was determined to see nothing good. When we went into the pit-head baths on one occasion, after we were well away from the mine, he said, 'Did you see the bugs on the wall?' I saw no bugs and the baths looked very clean to me ... At another pit we checked the lamps in the lamp room. We were told that sometimes a miner did not bring his lamp back at the end of a shift, but used it to light his way home. This would have been impossible in a British mine, and certainly this lax-ness on the part of the Russians was not good ... But Joseph Jones drew ... the conclusion that the Russians were working unlimited hours, and that what they told us about the working hours of the miners was all bluff. We had endless quarrels.

Not surprisingly, the delegation were unable to agree an official report. Horner, Bowman and Lawther were on one side, the two Joneses and Cook on the other, 'with Joe Hall in between'.[574] The crux of their disagreement was whether to mention the lapses in health and safety, which they all agreed had occurred, or to confine themselves to the uncritical narrative which was the typical product of official fraternal delegations to foreign trade unions. The internecine conflict continued, and was common knowledge at the TUC in September 1938.[575]

Horner had not visited the Soviet Union since 1931, when the Comintern heard his appeal against expulsion from the CPGB. Returning as a prominent member of an important trade union delegation, his six and a half weeks was profoundly disquieting. In January 1937, a grand show trial of the 'Anti-Soviet Trotskyist Centre' had commenced, culminating in thirteen middle-rank-ing old Bolsheviks being sentenced to death. Soon afterwards, a CPSU(B) Central Committee Plenum 'repeated the claim that Trotskyism menaced socialism, asserted that spies roamed the country and reiterated the doctrine of "sharpening class strug-gle"'. In March, Bukharin and Rykov were incarcerated in the NKVD prison fortress the Lubyanka.[576] Renewed campaigns followed throughout the party *apparat* in the USSR to uncover more scapegoats, counter-revolutionary Trotskyist spies and wreckers. Party members who had spent time abroad were espe-cially vulnerable.

In April, Max Petrovsky, a Ukrainian-Jewish socialist who had been Comintern representative in Britain from 1924 until his return to the USSR in 1929, was arrested, investigated and convicted of counter-revolutionary activity. Petrovsky had worked at the high profile Commissariat for Heavy Industry. The Deputy Commissar, Piatakov, had been one of the defendants at the January show trial. The Commissar, Sergei Orzhonikidze, a long-time ally of Stalin, had mounted a last-ditch defence of Piatakov, and his conviction had driven Orzhonikidze to despair and suicide. After his two superiors' fall, Petrovsky was a predictable next victim. Nevertheless, after receiving the news of his sentence, Pollitt mounted a spirited defence of Petrovsky. He made a written statement to the ECCI stressing 'that Petrovsky had always appeared a loyal Stalinist ... and when they had last met in January, Petrovsky had denounced the Trotskyites' "foul work"'.[577] Horner and Pollitt had known and worked with Petrovsky throughout this period. They also knew Petrovsky's wife, Rose Cohen, whom he had met in London. (Pollitt had fallen in love with her, and proposed marriage.) In Moscow Max Petrovsky and Rose Cohen had cultivated friendly relations with visiting CPGB delegates and the small British community living in the Hotel Lux.[578] The Horners had probably socialised with them in 1930.

Rose Cohen was arrested in August 1937. Pollitt had arrived in Moscow on 13 August and made a serious attempt to clear her name and secure her freedom, pressing Dimitrov and Manuilsky to intercede with Stalin and pass on his testimony of her innocence.[579] Pollitt took this course of action knowing not only that it was likely to fail but also that his attempt would render his own person extremely vulnerable. Bela Kun had already named Pollitt as one of his collaborators in an anti-Comintern conspiracy, and Thorpe considers it possible that Dimitrov was considering Pollitt's imprisonment.[580]

Horner had good reason to be apprehensive for the safety of his friends and comrades in the Miners' International Committee when he arrived in Moscow in October 1937. Knowledge of Cohen's and Petrovsky's imprisonments is likely to have been shared by a small number of veteran party members and veteran Moscow-watchers like the *Daily Telegraph* ex-communist industrial correspondent, Hugh Chevins. At the beginning of 1936 the Profintern *apparat* had been the object of special scrutiny by the NKVD, and many of its workers had been arrested, including Grusha Slutsky. Slutsky was suspect, not only because of his political past as a Left Socialist Revolutionary, but also because he controlled a budget at the MIC, thereby qualifying as a probable swindler of the Soviet people. Horner's MI5 files recorded regular correspondence received from the MIC. The circulars and letters were mostly routine requests for information about miners' conditions and union matters. Nevertheless, many were signed by Slutsky, and often contained additional personal greetings from him to Arthur and his family from Slutsky and his wife.[581]

The Profintern had been disbanded as part of the post-Seventh World Congress popular/united front line in late 1936.[582] Communist activists and communist trade unions were enjoined to seek unity with their socialist and Christian counterparts. As a result, Horner may have met Polish and Czech comrades from the MIC on the fringes of the MIF Congress in May 1936 in France. Although he may have learned about the NKVD probe, he is unlikely to have obtained any definite information about Slutsky.

On his arrival in Moscow, Horner is likely to have been chastened by the changed political atmosphere compared to 1930 to 1931. He could recognise the palpably heightened tension and the barely repressed signs of paranoia amongst many party cadres. But he is unlikely to have confided his observations to anyone in the MFGB delegation. He made strenuous efforts to contact Slutsky and other MIC colleagues. 'I found ... that my old friend Slutsky ... was in prison; when I asked whether I could see him because I had some medicine I had specially bought for him, I was told that I could not, but they would deliver it.'[583] Given his knowledge of Petrovsky's fate, he may have doubted whether Slutsky and other MIC colleagues were still alive.

On his return to Britain in December 1937, Horner told Vol that he was certain of Slutsky's innocence. (She had come back to South Wales in September to enrol in a Gregg's shorthand and typing course in Swansea, to enable her to return to London to obtain a better paid, more interesting job.) Vol had passed through the YCL and become a committed CPGB member. She remembered Slutsky's visits to Mardy, and refused to credit her father's forebodings about his fate. He probably also told Ethel about his failure to find Slutsky, and she too was likely to have refused to suspend belief in the integrity of Soviet justice.[584]

Horner is unlikely to have shared his disquiet about what he had encountered with his closest South Walian confidants. Paynter's commitment to the USSR remained firm, and Alf Davies had no experience of the completely different world of Soviet communism. Publicly, Horner's commitment to the international communist movement was undiminished. Privately, however, his doubts of 1929 returned. Probably fortunately for his psychological equilibrium, Horner had little time to spare to dwell upon his private thoughts. He was wholly preoccupied in the New Year with marshalling the MFGB's left united front in response to the worsening European situation.

Politics polarised in Britain after the resignation of the Foreign Secretary, Anthony Eden, and Lord Cranbourne, Foreign Office under-secretary, on 20 February 1938. Foreign policy was increasingly dominated by the issue of the appeasement of Hitler. In the subsequent Commons debate, twenty-five Tory MPs abstained, a conspicuous display of their opposition to Chamberlain's appeasement policy. In March 1938 Hitler moved German troops into Austria without meeting opposition, and declared the country's annexation, the Anschluss. He also intensified his diplomatic pressure on the Czechoslovak government, alongside scarcely concealed invasion threats, to cede its largely German-speaking province, the Sudetenland, to the Third Reich. In Spain Franco's forces were slowly gaining the upper hand, despite desperate resistance from the Republican army.

Soon after Eden's resignation, the SWMF sent a motion to the MFGB Executive for transmission to the TUC General Council, calling for an all-in Special Conference 'to take such action as may be necessary to prevent this country being subjected to the blackmail of the Dictators as proposed by the present Government'. The General Council declined on 1 April. Faced with this rebuff, the MFGB Executive asked district unions whether the MFGB should convene its own Special Conference on the International Situation. There was apparently a left-right division inside the Executive on the question, which members agreed could only be settled by referring the issue back to district unions. The result was decisive in favour of a conference – 350,000 to 190,000. Durham, Scotland, Northumberland and the Midlands voted with South Wales.

The MFGB delegates conference convened on 28 April. Horner proposed the SWMF motion as an MFGB Executive resolution, and it was seconded by Watson. Horner explained the Executive's intention:

> for the first time to make clear the exact position of the Miners' Federation as an Organisation ... The second purpose is to seek to create a greater co-ordination of workers' forces. We want ... to sabotage by every available means in our power, the help which is being given by our Government to the Fascists ... We ourselves want to mobilise the maximum power we can in an effort to bring greater pressure against the Government ... This Conference to-day is intended to demonstrate the fact that there is a desire in the country for a co-ordinated unified Conference of the Labour Movement which will give greater aid against the enemies of Spain, and do much more damage to the enemies of Spain ... We must not wait until the Fascists have gobbled up Spain.

Watson was passionate:

> It is not chocolates, milk or cigarettes they want, it is machine guns, artillery, aeroplanes and munitions ... We cannot, in my opinion, reverse the policy of this National Government by a mere political agitation day by day. Unless the whole of the political weight of this country is behind any movement we shall be beating the air ... We feel that in calling together the National Executives of several Unions we will be calling together responsible men who have to take responsible decisions ... One cannot afford to ignore the difficulties involved ... One could say that the Miners have tried to salve their consciences. Unless the miners act in conjunction with the Executive Councils [at a Special TUC Conference of Union Executives] then it will have served no useful pur-

pose ... [T]here is still more that our Organisation can do if we were true to our Class, and true to the principles in which we believe.[585]

This dramatic *démarche* had no effect on Citrine and the General Council. No special TUC conference was called and the General Council stayed on the straight and narrow of official Labour Party policy. Joseph Jones, however, judged it expedient to go to Spain in May, accompanying Jack Little of the AEU and WJR Squance of ASLEF, both left-wing socialists from left-wing unions. (Squance was considered a fellow traveller.) Jones was profoundly affected by his journey. He reported to the MFGB Executive on 20 May, and they agreed to contribute a sum equivalent to a levy of 2s. 6d. per member to the Spanish Republican cause. A subcommittee of six to allocate the money was appointed, the three national officers, plus Horner, Watson and Herbert Smith. (Joe Hall took Smith's place after Smith's death in June.)

Along with others on the MFGB Executive, Horner travelled from the 20 May meeting in London to Geneva to attend an ILO meeting on the limitation of working hours. After its conclusion, the MFGB contingent entrained to Luxembourg for the biennial MIF conference. The MFGB sixty-eight strong delegation met with twenty-five delegates from France, twenty-six from Belgium, nine from Czechoslovakia and four from Poland. The conference adopted the resolution on Spain moved by the French MIF President, Alfred Vigne. It re-affirmed the MIF determination to mobilise public opinion against non-intervention and provide the maximum financial support to buy medical supplies, food and other immediate needs for the suffering Spanish people. It was an occasion of heightened emotion in which the hearty bonhomie which accompanied trade union gatherings was tinged with apprehension by the sombre and worsening international background. Evidence that the SWMF delegation enjoyed themselves is found in the postcard they sent Ethel in Horner's handwriting, 'This is to certify that ALH is undergoing great hardship bravely, Signed', followed by the signatures of Gomer Evans, WH Crews, James Evans, M Harcombe, and WJ Williams, alongside 'Liar W.J. Saddler'.[586]

Events in the USSR had been threatening the foundations of European left united-frontism. A spectacularly staged show trial had begun in early March 1938, of twenty-one veteran Bolsheviks, including Bukharin and Rykov. The elite of the European press corps had attended and provided eyewitness reports. Some non-communist observers, including DN Pritt MP and the American ambassador, believed that the confessions of high treason were genuine and that their trial and conviction were conducted according with due process. Most correspondents were deeply sceptical however. In mid-March eighteen of the accused were shot in the Lubyanka prison. Soon after this shocking news, the Foreign Office released the details of Rose Cohen's arrest; the British press carried the first reports in April 1938.

The British party leadership brazened out the awkward and potentially damaging situation. They rehearsed the prosecutor's case in the show trials, and the *Daily Worker* gave prominent place to Pritt's reports. Campbell wrote turgid, Jesuitical editorials, and the CPGB Executive issued statements which justified the trial and the verdicts as being vital to combat the clear and present danger posed by the accused to the Soviet socialist state. After the news of Cohen's arrest was published, the Executive issued no statement, nor did the *Daily Worker* report it. There was only an oblique reference to her imprisonment in an editorial attacking the FO for trying to interfere in an internal USSR affair, since '[t]he individual concerned, it is understood, is married to a Soviet citizen and thereby assumed Soviet citizenship alike in the eyes of Soviet law as of international law'.[587]

Horner acquiesced in the evasions and cover-up. But he was disturbed by the appearance of a new discourse inside the British party, from which debate and the expression of differences were absent. At a CPGB Executive meeting in July 1938, he responded to Pollitt's invitation for open discussion:

> AH says he feels one of the audience at the CC [Central Committee] which is too dominated by party offi-cials ... Says in 1920s there was real discussion, but not now, and that some may be inhibited by stenographer. 'I feel I am doing more service if I have a point to raise, in seeing Pollitt, etc than spending a whole day in this executive. I think we are intimidating many people here. I am not afraid to speak anywhere – but I am full of nerv-ousness speaking here ... It is impossible if everybody

is sincere to have such 100 per cent unanimity every time.'[588]

His public commitment to communism continued undiminished.

At the MFGB Annual Conference, held in the third week of July 1938, at Whitley Bay, the Executive's resolution on Spain was carried unanimously. Moved by Joseph Jones and seconded by Horner, it was a model of left united-frontism, denouncing 'the infamous bargain of the Government with the Italian Dictator, under which ... the withdrawal of foreign forces from Spain is tacitly postponed in the hope that these reactionary forces may win', and calling on the TUC 'to organise immediately the maximum practical assistance for the Spanish people'. George Jones observed that the two speeches were 'the best speeches heard in a Miners' Conference for some time', and they were subsequently issued as a pamphlet.[589]

Conference delegates were polarised, however, on the domestic issue facing them, the Executive subcommittee's scheme for the unification of district unions. The subcommittee had worked hard, sending out a questionnaire to district unions about the welfare and social insurance benefits they offered, which would have to be harmonised in any serious unification. There had also been consultations with district officers and executives. The scheme produced was a more federal structure than the model rules put forward by Horner and the MMM in 1927. He and Watson evidently calculated that concessions would need to be made to the district unions' vested interests.

Joseph Jones' support had been critical in securing conference approval for the Kent resolution to establish the subcommittee in 1937. But he had evidently made no effort to canvass his allies in Yorkshire whilst the subcommittee had deliberated, and conspicuously abstained from taking a stand at the 1938 Annual Conference. (Herbert Smith had been increasingly frail during the year, and had played little part in the committee's proceedings.) Ebby Edwards was committed to unity, but he was increasingly ineffectual on the Executive and at conference. Lawther, who faced a vice-presidential election, prudently refrained from any comment on the scheme either inside

Durham or at the MFGB conference. Horner brought South Wales in behind the scheme. Watson, however, had not committed himself in Durham. Although he and other younger agents were supporters of amalgamation, the old guard, including the veteran general secretary, John Swan, were proud proprietors of the monumental headquarters at Red Hill and zealous defenders of the DMA's elaborate rulebook.

At the conference, the subcommittee scheme was proposed by Watson and seconded by Horner. It was discussed in private sessions, and passions ran high. The positive speeches, notably from George Jones and Bill Saddler, were outweighed by vociferous opposition from Lancashire and Yorkshire delegates. There was no support from DMA delegates. But because opponents did not press their case to the point of moving rejection of the scheme, it was remitted to the Executive for further consideration.

After the conference, neither the Executive nor the subcommittee devoted much attention to the unification scheme. (Watson's term on the Executive had finished, and his successor's commitment to the scheme was unclear.) The principal domestic question preoccupying the Executive was Joseph Jones' future. On 22 June 1938 Harry Crookshank had invited Jones to serve on the Coal Commission, the quango established under the new Coal Mines Act. Its purpose was to formulate proposals for the reorganisation of the industry so as to make it economically viable. Jones had informed the Department of Mines of his acceptance on 1 July. He made no move, however, to inform the MFGB Executive of his decision to surrender his union office. Rumours of his impending departure were circulating in the conference hall and bars at Whitley Bay, and featured in press reports. When challenged about his appointment by a delegate from the floor, Jones declined to make any statement.[590] His silence enabled him to be duly re-elected MFGB President, and also to be re-nominated for one of three seats allotted to Trade Group No. 1, Mining and Quarrying, on the TUC General Council. (During the Congress year September 1937 to September 1938, the seats had been occupied by Edwards, Jones and Lawther.)

The probable reason for Jones' refusal to clarify his future plans was the fate of this General Council seat. If Jones had informed the Executive of his impending resignation before the annual conference, district unions' nominations of him to the General Council for the Congress year 1938 to 1939 would have been withdrawn. After the MFGB Annual Conference, Jones practically withdrew from all union work. He was regularly absent from the MFGB office at Russell Square, and failed to attend MFGB Executive and TUC General Council meetings. Although the *Daily Herald* reported on 1 August that Jones would leave the MFGB on 1 December, he made no statement about his plans to the Executive until its eve-of-TUC meeting on 7 September, and then declined to name a date for his departure. Consequently, the Executive allowed his name to go forward for election to the General Council. He was duly re-elected, along with Edwards and Lawther.[591]

If Jones had revealed his plans to the MFGB Executive before the annual conference in early July, Horner would probably have been nominated for the General Council in his stead. Horner's standing in the MFGB was high and rising. He had opposed Lawther in the Vice-Presidential elections at the conference, and received a significant number of votes.[592] If chosen, Horner would have attracted a great deal of publicity as a high profile left united-front candidate for the General Council.

General Council elections were held at Congress; each affiliated union cast its block vote for candidates in all eighteen trade groups. Horner would have won votes from smaller left-wing unions, notably ASLEF, NUPE, the ETU and NAFTA, as well as the AEU's large block vote. The centre-right united front at Transport House were very anxious to avoid this scenario. To ensure that Horner did not appear on the ballot for General Council, Citrine and Bevin probably encouraged Jones to adopt a protracted exit strategy and then persuaded Edwards to acquiesce in the obfuscation. Edwards' tacit support was necessary to enable Jones to conceal his real intentions inside the MFGB. As Jones' co-equal inside the MFGB, Edwards could have invited the Executive to compel Jones to behave according to accepted standards of professional conduct.

Citrine and Bevin were keen to fill the General Council vacancy resulting from Jones' departure with a TGWU nominee. Although there was a strong personal antipathy between the two men, they were close political allies and relied on one another for support at critical moments. They considered that

the MFGB as a union was unpredictable and liable to communist influence. They were consequently determined to limit its
potential to determine TUC policy.

Bevin was also keen to increase the number of votes on the
General Council which he could directly influence from three to
four.[593] He considered that the TGWU was entitled to a lien on a
Group No.1 seat via the North Wales Quarrymen's Union.[594]

The opening of the TUC on 5 September 1938 was overshadowed
by the European situation, which was worsening daily. In August
Hitler had increased the pressure on the Czechoslovakian government to cede the Sudetenland. Faced with his threats of invasion, the British and French governments, treaty guarantors of
Czech sovereignty, were highly ambivalent – though the French
had been notably more prepared to stand up to Germany.[595]
TUC delegates arrived full of apprehension. In this charged
atmosphere their voting behaviour was difficult for Citrine to
either predict or influence. The Congress President in 1938
was Herbert Elvin of the Clerical Workers, a left-wing leader
of a left-wing union whom Citrine found it difficult to manipu-
late. With Bevin absent, Citrine was compelled to play a more
important part in debates in order to hold the line.[596] Arthur
Deakin, who had risen inside the TGWU to become Assistant
General Secretary, was deputising for Bevin on a major public
occasion for the first time. Compared to Bevin's forceful charisma, Deakin's tight, high-handed manner may have increased
delegates' willingness to vote against the General Council.

Moreover, it was not merely left-wing British socialists
whose anti-fascism was roused by the prospect of the defeat
of Republican Spain and Hitler's invasion of Czechoslovakia.
Probably impressed by Eden's resignation, the statement
adopted by the National Council of Labour and presented to
Congress delegates was forthright: 'Whatever the risks involved,
Great Britain must take its stand against aggression. There is
no longer room for doubt or hesitation.'[597] The MFGB delegation used this opportunity to push Congress decisively leftwards.
With Joseph Jones a lame duck and Herbert Smith dead, no
other miners' leader was willing to counter the pressure from
the left united-front caucus. Horner and Lawther attacked the

General Council's timidity over the past year, and aimed at Citrine in particular. Jack Little then rose to rebut George Hicks, the former left-wing leader of the builders, whose help Citrine had summoned in his defence.

In private session, Congress debated the reference back of the section in the General Council report justifying its refusal of the MFGB request to call a Special Conference of Union Executives on the International Situation. Horner spoke, apparently impromptu, having been provoked by Deakin. 'I did not intend to intervene ... until Mr. Deakin repeated a ... slander against the mineworkers of this country. I do not know what the miners have done to deserve such treatment ... except that they have shown a zeal for causes which the Movement itself accepts as justifiable.' Although the reference back was defeated, a motion to refer back the section of the General Council report on international trade union unity mustered 1.498 million votes, leaving Citrine with an embarrassingly reduced margin of victory.[598]

WJR Squance moved a resolution on arms for Spain in private session. Paynter seconded it, using examples from personal experience, including watching Franco's planes strafe children playing in the sand of the Ebro riverbed at Tortosa. George Woodcock, the recently arrived secretary of the TUC Research Department, told Paynter some forty years later that Citrine had been scheduled to oppose the motion on behalf of the General Council. He decided not to speak at the last moment, evidently reluctant to be seen opposing the groundswell of sympathy for the Republican government. The TGWU and NUGMW delegates also kept their votes in their pockets, rather than be seen to oppose it. Elvin reported the result with some surprise: 'For the resolution 285; against the resolution, none. That means that something like 360 delegates have not voted.'[599]

Bowman, Horner and Lawther travelled to Barcelona after the TUC in order to disperse the £70,000 collected from the MFGB Spanish levy. After completing their business, they 'came back over the Pyrenees by car and the one Jim Bowman and I were travelling in broke down'. They made their way to Paris, where they spent a day waiting for their next connection. Franco's troops had crossed the Ebro river, and 'it was clear that the Spanish people, despite their heroic resistance, were facing defeat'.[600]

German pressure on Czechoslovakia was now at its height. Chamberlain travelled to Germany to meet Hitler a second time on 22 September. The French government had posted notices around 23 September 1938 in towns and cities announcing the call-up of two additional categories of reservists to active service, increasing the number of men in arms to two million. Railway station signs were removed, motor vehicle windows were painted blue, and various other precautions were taken to prepare for war. Horner told Frankenberg his vivid memory. The three men had been 'anxious to get back to England and not be cut off in Spain or France. Watched mobilisation of Paris – over half a million people ... Never witnessed such a distressing mass of people. Sat between Gare de Lyon and Gare du Nord and watched women with paper bags seeing men off. There was no singing or smiling. Only stark despair in faces of the women and children. Crossed ferry next day ... '.[601]

War also seemed imminent in Britain. 'Gas masks were distributed to the public ... Trenches were dug in the London parks, a few anti-aircraft guns were manoeuvred into position ... '. But the fate of Czechoslovakia was sealed on 28 September. Chamberlain was speaking to a specially recalled House of Commons when a telegram was passed to him with:

> the news that Mussolini had persuaded Hitler to consent to a four-power conference at Munich. Almost the entire House rose to their feet and applauded this carefully stage-managed scene. Churchill, Amery, Harold Nicholson and Willie Gallacher ... remained seated. Eden either did the same or walked out 'pale with shame and anger' – the evidence conflicts.[602]

In contrast to their resolution earlier in the month, the Labour front bench did not challenge the prime minister. A contributory factor was the public support for Chamberlain's decision not to go to war for a faraway country. The National Council of Labour were reluctant to stand out against the popular relief that war was not, after all, imminent, even though it was evident that Labour opposition might have been sufficient, along with the dissident Tories around Churchill, to turn both public opinion and the House of Commons against appeasement. Outward calm returned to Britain, and normal routines were resumed. However, most thoughtful observers believed that a European war had only been temporarily postponed.

Over the winter, Horner commuted to the Federation in offices in Cardiff, and dealt with South Wales domestic concerns. He took a close interest in the operation of the new district agreement, which had been in operation for eighteen months. The agreement's success depended on the comprehensive rationalisation of the work process, involving the joint re-grading of jobs and the disappearance of entrenched custom and practice. The majority of lodges had adapted to the new procedures and grades. When colliery management and lodge officials failed to agree on a grade or new working practice, the new agreement provided for the speedy settlement of the matter in dispute. (The previous conciliation scheme had often been protracted when it suited the coalowners not to address the problem.)

The final stage of the new procedure was a monthly one-to-one meeting between the Federation President and the coalowners' representative, who was usually Iestyn Williams. The two men were well-matched opponents. Each defended his corner, relishing the cut and thrust of negotiations, which bore a strong resemblance to sporting encounters. Their sense of fair play underlay the absence of gratuitous point-scoring. Neither forgot that the purpose of their verbal duels was to settle protracted disputes.[603] The majority of these occurred in the Anthracite area, where before the new agreement was signed, some managements had not enforced significant changes to pre-1926 favourable terms and conditions. (The prolonged slump in the export market for South Wales steam coal had compelled most lodges in Monmouthshire and east and central Glamorganshire to accept these changes.)

Horner and the Executive faced down a steady stream of small unofficial disputes in the Anthracite, often stay-in strikes, where lodge officials were apparently willing to flout the new agreement and connive at unofficial strikes. Four of the most strike-prone collieries, Tareni, Brynhenllys, Gelliceidrim and Gwaun-cae-Gurwen, 'remained fractious even after nationalisation'.[604] Horner now viewed unofficial disputes according to his

Clausewitzian principles. He considered them to be a wasteful use of the union's limited capacity to wage industrial conflict. He had set his horizons on transforming the coalminer's job, and believed that if the Federation observed the terms of the new agreement and discouraged gratuitous industrial conflict, they could gain not only better wages but also pithead baths, and an occupational pension scheme.

Horner was also determined to improve the monitoring of industrial diseases associated with mining, and to institute preventive measures to minimise their occurrence, and improved compensation for having contracted them. His experience of handling compensation cases as agent in the Gwendraeth Valley had reinforced his conviction that working in a coal mine was bad for most people's health. As President, he paid special attention to promoting occupational health research. He often used his monthly meetings with Iestyn Williams to canvass the coalowners' support for new working methods, to alleviate, and if possible remove, the hazards encountered underground.

The regular victories which Horner scored in negotiations reinforced his determination to educate the Federation membership in the importance of following Clausewitzian principles. Consequently, he took a pro-active attitude towards infringements of the new agreement. Rather than acquiesce in their continuing occurrence, as 'normal' or 'understandable', he tried to ensure that the agents and lodge officials were vigilant in fulfilling their part of the agreement in good faith. He ensured that unofficial disputes were discussed and condemned by the Executive, and if necessary was prepared to take intractable problems to special delegate conferences.

Horner did not expect either the South Wales DPC or the King Street *apparat* to endorse his reasoned opposition to unofficial strikes. Although Pollitt and Campbell had moved the CPGB away from advocating a total war approach to industrial conflict, the CPGB Executive still routinely espoused rank-and-filism, and only qualified their commitment with appeals to trade union loyalism.[605] Nevertheless, since 1934 Pollitt and Allison had provided effective back-up for Horner when he operated a Clausewitizian strategy. They deflected the DPC's attacks and fudged party discipline to protect him when he staunched 'rank-and-file' industrial conflict. Horner was confident that his immunity from democratic centralism would continue. He knew that Pollitt and Campbell viewed his high-profile union position and effectiveness in public arenas as crucial to the success of their united front strategy.

But Horner had not anticipated the fresh outbreak of political civil war inside the South Wales communist party. This was partly precipitated by the collective stress endured by party local branches where leading members or their sons were fighting in the International Brigade. But Horner's confident repudiations of rank-and-filism in public arenas also contributed. He made no attempt to conciliate the feelings of those revolutionary militant veterans who felt that he was betraying his past. To try to restore members' morale, Glyn Jones, who had become District Party Secretary in 1937, launched a concerted offensive against Horner. He was an SWMF activist from Rhondda Fawr. He had joined the CPGB in 1925, aged twenty, and was probably unemployed after 1926. He attended the Lenin School in 1934 to 1935, where his report noted that he had 'strong tendency to isolate trade union problems'.[606]

Despite the exemplary success of the Aid Spain campaign and the all-in unemployed agitation, the Comintern's and the Party Centre's high expectations for South Wales had remained unfulfilled. On 1 June 1937 the *Daily Worker* reported that South Wales was the only district where CPGB membership was lower than it had been in 1935; there were only 231 members in the Rhondda. Glyn Jones was anxious to prove himself as DPC Secretary. In contrast to his predecessor, Cox, he downplayed united front activity, and concentrated party members' energies on working inside the Federation. He explained the communist party's failure to gain ground in the SWMF by Horner's questionable loyalty. His Moscow training apparently gave him the confidence to press the DPC's long-standing grievances against Horner, and the veteran revolutionary militants in the party offered strong support. Cox's attitude towards Horner had remained ambivalent. Because he himself had evolved no consistent approach to the economic struggle, he had frequently bowed to pressure from his left flank and agreed to issue a DPC statement strongly condemning a Federation Executive decision to which Horner was giving equally strong support, or even – after he had become President – for which he was personally responsible. Subsequently, after receiving countervailing advice from Pollitt and Allison, Cox had trimmed towards Horner and doggedly pushed the DPC back with him.

Glyn Jones' offensive against Horner occurred at a time when the British party was under extreme pressure from Moscow. The ECCI had seriously considered removing Pollitt as CPGB general secretary; they had also considered purging him, i.e. expelling him from the party. The Party Centre had dismissed Lewis Jones, who had been serving as Rhondda Sub-District Secretary, 'towards the end of 1938 on grounds of political confusion and the continuing stagnation of party membership'.[607] Presumably, in response to Glyn Jones' representations, the Party leadership felt they needed to be seen to be addressing the British party's weaknesses. Pollitt and Campbell decided to stage another *démarche* to deal with Horner's lack of communist discipline. On 13 October 1938, Special Branch sent MI5 a note with information they had received on 11 October:

> There is once more considerable friction between the Secretariat of the Communist Party and Arthur Horner ... The former fear they are losing their grip on HORNER, who often acts on his own initiative instead of first consulting the Party. The Secretariat has told him that he must take his instructions on all matters of policy from them. HORNER resents this and has made it clear that, whilst the Party can rely upon him to follow its line, he insists on the right to form his own judgment on questions connected with the conduct of the miners' problems, as he is much better qualified in that respect than are the other Party leaders, who have no personal knowledge of the subject.
>
> ... HORNER has been told that if he fails to abide by the decision of the leaders, he will be expelled from the Party, which would then lend its whole weight in a campaign to oust him from his leadership of the S.W.M.F ... The opinion of more than one member of the Central Committee (expressed in private conversation) is that HORNER may resign from the Communist Party rather than submit to being dictated to, and that

now that he has a good post he is veering towards the Right Wing.[608]

There is no evidence that Pollitt tried to enforce this diktat. He may have been more interested in being seen to reprimand Horner, and for the warning to go on the record as evidence, so that the Comintern and the South Wales DPC could see that Horner was subject to democratic centralist discipline. The Party Centre had administered similar ritual rebukes in 1935 to 1936, when Horner had not supported the DPC's calls for coalfield strikes in support of stay-in strikers or in pursuit of district wage claims, rather than awaiting the result of the national wages campaign. But on this occasion Pollitt, who was skilled in reading Horner's moods, was likely to have detected evidence of Horner's growing doubts about his communism.

Horner's commitment to the international communist movement was probably wavering throughout 1938. On his visit to the USSR at the end of 1937 he had seen that the great purges were accompanied by a much more intense attention to orthodoxy inside the Soviet party than he had experienced in 1930 to 1931. In South Wales he had been unsettled by the DPC's policy of pressurising party members to serve in the International Brigade, and had operated it with misgivings. We have already observed that in Spain Horner had been shocked by the evident lack of concern shown by many of the Brigade's commissars and officers for their men.[609]

In addition, Horner was forging increasingly strong bonds with non-communist, left-wing Labour members of the Executive, notably Watson and Bowman. His cordial alliance with Bevan had become closer, and he had excellent relations with the other left-Labour activists in the Federation, for example Bill Saddler. None of them were willing to give unequivocal support to the USSR, and Horner's rigorous intellectual honesty probably compelled him to acknowledge that they had sufficient reason and evidence to reserve judgement on the Soviet state.

The rebuke administered by the Party Centre in October 1938 achieved the objective of reinforcing Horner's ties to the party without Pollitt having to administer party discipline and risk another potentially damaging eruption of the Hornerism controversy in South Wales. Pollitt was a discerning judge of character, and adept at political manipulation. He understood that Horner's eighteen years of party membership were at the heart of his self-identity. He was also aware that neither Ethel nor Vol showed any inclination to leave the party. If Horner had done so, their probable reaction would have been to condemn him for betraying his bond to the international communist movement. Pollitt could imagine that Horner anticipated that if he left the CPGB, he would face domestic isolation, if not exile from the family home. He also knew that Horner would expect an immediate loss of intimacy with close communist comrades in the Rhondda and London, such as Charlie Jones, Paynter, Hannington and Albert Inkpin.

We can only speculate that these considerations weighed in the balance of Horner's conscience and psyche. But he remained in the party. Rather than face the existential no-man's land which he knew was likely if he left the party, Horner internalised his doubts, at least when he was sober. He continued to operate with a double identity, as a punctilious SWMF President and leading member of the MFGB Executive on the one hand, and an erratic, often perfunctory, member of the CPGB on the other.

The two actual casualties inside the South Wales party were Lewis Jones and Glyn Jones. Lewis Jones died in January 1939 from a heart attack, brought on by his Stakhanovite efforts in organising and addressing public meetings for the Spanish Aid campaign. In August 1939 Glyn Jones was peremptorily removed from his post as District Secretary by the Party Centre, without any prior notice or consultation either with himself or the South Wales DPC. were consulted. King Street apparently wanted to pre-empt any further escalation of the internecine conflict between Horner and the DPC. They drafted Cox back into South Wales to resume his old post. He was 'consequently meeting with opposition by C.C. [DPC] members in Wales and also Glyn JONES.' Cox started at the party office in Cardiff on 10 August, but he 'had to work, with practically no assistance, all day'. Cox was nothing if not determined, however, and he rose to the challenge. After only a few weeks, he had re-imposed King Street's authority. Presumably following instructions from Pollitt, he allowed the SWMF President a slack rein, whilst maintaining a veneer of vigilance for signs of any serious indiscipline from him.[610]

407

Evidence that Horner intended to remain in the communist fold is found in his public appearances towards the end of 1938. Despite his lingering depression about what he had seen and heard in Moscow in 1937, he can hardly have viewed the Labour Party as a welcoming port in a storm; and the USSR's uncompromising opposition to Hitler and Franco reinforced his allegiance to the Comintern. On Wednesday 7 December he spoke at the Memorial Meeting organised by the South Wales Council for Spanish Aid in honour of the thirty-three International Brigade volunteers from South Wales killed in Spain. It was held in Mountain Ash in the Cynon Valley – probably chosen for the hall's large capacity and its central location in the steam coalfield.

Francis estimated that over 7000 people attended the meeting, including many young people from outside the coalfield whose interest had been aroused by the civil war. Alan Bassett recalled sitting in the front row with Joan Horner, and the thrill of being introduced to Paul Robeson by Arthur. Illtyd Harrington recalled the wonderful spectacle of Horner and Robeson embracing on stage – the contrast between the two men's height punctuating their evident affection. Robeson's songs were dramatic and almost unbearably poignant. Horner's closing speech was notable for its passion and lack of sentimentality. 'To die is not remarkable or important, for all must die. The matter we have to concern ourselves is this: What did they die for. In South Wales, we have lived for freedom and we are determined to fight for it ... What we must demonstrate is that we are ready to work tomorrow and the day after against the forces which work to destroy our rights.'[611]

On 17 November 1938 Joseph Jones had finally told the MFGB Executive of his finishing date, 30 November. The Executive appointed Lawther acting President until the union's Annual Conference in July 1939. The vice-president's post which he vacated was not filled. Horner was nominated to take Jones' TUC General Council place. The *Times* report on 18 November was notably vague about Horner's current political status. 'Mr. Arthur Horner ... was chosen to succeed Mr. Jones as the representative of the mineworkers on the General Council ... Mr. Horner is an advanced Left-wing politician and until a few years ago was an active member of the Minority Movement.' Horner may have told labour correspondents that he might be expelled from the party. Or he may have told Lawther, who was keen to stir the pot.

Horner would have known at the Mountain Ash meeting that he was unlikely to gain Jones' seat on the General Council. When it met on 23 November, Bevin attended for the first time since July. Edwards sent his apologies, along with a letter conveying the Executive's choice of Horner to fill the vacancy. Horner's automatic succession was ruled out of order at the meeting, in contrast to the MFGB's successful designation of Herbert Smith to fill Tom Richard's place after Richards' death in 1931. It was agreed that the vacancy would be filled in accordance with Standing Orders. Any union in Group No.1 would be able to place nominations before the next meeting of the Council on 21 December, followed by a formal election.

Edwards sent his apologies again on 21 December. His two expedient absences enabled him to avoid all responsibility for Horner's failure to secure the seat. Four nominations were tabled: Horner; JW Williams, the NWQU secretary; and the two general secretaries from regional coalmining craftsmen's unions who had stood in the elections at the 1938 TUC. JW Williams was elected with 18 votes. Horner received 3 votes, and the craft union candidates 4 and 2.[612] On 13 January 1939, the *Daily Worker* reported a press statement from the MFGB Executive, which was described as a sharp protest. They had nominated him '"on the grounds of Horner's industrial ability and experience". They claim that his defeat was due to political prejudice.'

Chapter 12

Fighting the War on
Two Fronts

The MFGB Executive had little ground for optimism as they considered the prospects for 1939. The uncertainty on the continent made the economic situation uncertain for the export coalfields, and there was scant evidence of domestic expansion. Edwards tabled a gloomy statement at the Executive meeting on 17 December 1938, 'covering the attempts made during the last five years to reorganise the Federation ... [T]he Executive had made recommendations and even Annual Conference endorsed [them in 1937] ... yet no progress was made because each district or area were voluntary free agents ... It was obvious certain general principles should be settled before any detailed scheme was prepared.'[613] Reorganisation was not discussed perhaps because no Executive member believed that either Lawther or Edwards would lead a fresh campaign to persuade the districts of the need for unification. Lawther, as Acting President, faced an election at annual conference in July 1939. He was unlikely to champion reorganisation when he knew there was entrenched opposition from so many district union officials. And Edwards' reluctance to progress even routine union business with due care and attention had increased during the uncertainty over Joseph Jones' departure. The reorganisation subcommittee, which should have been preparing a fresh scheme to accommodate the objections expressed at the annual conference, had not met since it had been re-appointed in August.

The imminent defeat of the Spanish republican government and the prospect of war in central Europe produced a palpable move leftwards on the Executive. Horner's nomination for the General Council seat vacated by Joseph Jones was firm evidence of the new political balance. Another example was the DMA motion about Spain adopted by the Executive on 15 December. Addressed to Chamberlain, its wording stopped just short of insult.[614] Edwards was quick to take account of the change. We have observed that Lawther had already moved back to the left in response to European events. On 25 January 1939 both officers represented the MFGB at an overflow 'Arms for Spain' meeting at the Queen's Hall, near Broadcasting House in London's West End. They shared the platform with Bevan, Victor Gollancz, JB Priestley 'and a host of other considerable personages who had not previously been engaged in united political activity'.[615] The meeting may have been planned to influence the Labour Party NEC meeting taking place that day. It was expected to vote on whether to expel Cripps, whose offence had been the distribution of a Memorandum urging the NEC to participate in a Popular Front open to every opposition grouping. An ad hoc National Petition Committee had been organised to gather support for the memorandum. But the NEC motion was carried to expel Cripps; and it also threatened the other petition signatories, who included Bevan, Watson and Lawther, with the same fate. Lawther and Watson speedily withdrew their signatures, but Bevan stood fast. He could afford to resist because of Horner's unstinting support for him on the Federation Executive.[616] The NEC's pursuit of Bevan significantly strengthened the two men's mutual regard. Horner admired Bevan's courage in continuing to defy Transport House and most of his fellow MPs. Bevan recognised that Horner's personal support was crucial for his own political survival.[617]

On 26 January, Franco's forces moved into Barcelona: 'The indiscriminate massacre of republicans went on for some days ... The remnants of the battered republican army crossed the frontier into France, preceded and followed by a horde of refugees; it stands to the credit of France that these were ... not turned back.'[618] Horner and Lawther would have encountered Spanish refugees in Paris in mid-February when they delivered £20,000 to the French miners' union, part of the MFGB's contribution to building a home for Spanish miners' orphans in southern France.[619]

The German Army marched into Prague on 15 March, 'one of those rare days which can be described as a turning point in history'. The Reich made Bohemia and Moravia protector-

411

ates, and launched Slovakia as a client state. In consequence, the Chamberlain government executed a volte-face. In concert with France, invitations were issued to Russia, Poland, Romania, Yugoslavia, Greece and Turkey to conclude an alliance to repel aggression in eastern Europe. Only Poland accepted. 'On 31 March Chamberlain announced that along with France the British government would, if Poland were attacked, "feel bound at once to lend the Polish government all support in their power".'[620] British involvement in another European war now seemed inevitable. The domestic political conflict between the centre-right united front of Transport House and supporters of left united-frontism intensified against this grim background. Many hitherto loyal Labour Party members expressed solidarity with Cripps and Bevan, and declared that they would also risk expulsion in defence of a Popular Front and alliance with the Soviet Union.

The Conservative government began serious preparations for another war. In April 1939 they appointed regional commissioners for civil defence. Wyndham Portal was the obvious choice for Wales. He took his duties seriously, and spent much time consulting widely in South Wales. Iestyn Williams and Horner probably began preliminary discussions with him about how to deal with the collieries in the event of an invasion. Horner's attention to detail and interest in military matters were positive assets in the preparation of the contingency plans being drawn up by the regional military and civilian defence authorities in the event of an invasion.[621]

At the Labour Party Conference at the end of May, Bevin caused surprise when he argued that war with Germany could still be averted by an ambitious system of global governance, providing for a fair and assured distribution of scarce raw materials to the industrial powers.[622] He adopted a socialist view, that a European war would be primarily about the issue of which empire controlled supplies of coal, oil and minerals. The MFGB continued to take a strong anti-fascist position.

After the Labour Party NEC had expelled Bevan on 31 March, the SWMF let it be known that they would continue to sponsor him as an MP. Lawther, Bowman and Ness Edwards, who had been elected to the MFGB Executive in 1938, informed the NEC that the MFGB expected to support Bevan as an independent

Labour candidate at the next election. Not surprisingly, the NEC capitulated to this pressure and re-admitted Bevan to the party in November 1939.[623]

Delegates at the Federation's Annual Conference in April had overwhelmingly re-elected Horner President. They also accepted the Executive's recommendation that Horner should be relieved of his Agent's duties 'in view of his being fully occupied with disputes etc. throughout the coalfield'. The decision regularised the situation which had faced both Griffiths and Horner.[624] On 17 April the *Daily Worker* reported '[r]ound after round of applause' after his presidential address, as well as Saddler's formal response: 'Although Arthur does not grow in stature, his constant growth in stature as an advocate for the miners and as a negotiator is a constant source of wonderment.'

The climax of the conference was a political skirmish between left and right. Two left motions were debated at the final session. One rejected the strongly pro-fascist policy of the National Government, and demanded that the labour movement should initiate the broadest Popular Front as a means to secure its defeat. The second expressed regret at the expulsion of Cripps 'and other parties', and recommended 'that they be given an opportunity to state their case to the Labour Party Conference, and that their reinstatement be arranged forthwith'. Four sponsored MPs, Sir Charles Edwards, Arthur Jenkins, Griffiths and Grenfell, spoke against the second motion, and made Bevan their primary target. Horner gave Bevan a full right of reply, and the *Times* reported that he received 'an enthusiastic hearing'. The first motion was passed by a majority of three to one, and the second almost unanimously. The *Times* noted 'only half a dozen dissentients'.[625]

Bevan called an impromptu press conference after the debate. Flushed with victory, he told reporters that:

> the rank and file of the Labour movement is overwhelmingly in favour of the Popular Front, but the machine of the party is able to give the impression that the movement is opposed to it. But that is only because the machine does not provide effective expression of rank-and-file opinion. If the opportunity, which was accorded to this conference, to listen to an exhaustive statement of

both sides ... were also accorded to the rest of the Labour movement, I am satisfied that the decision would be similar.[626]

The MFGB's fortieth anniversary was marked in July at the Annual Conference, held in Swansea. The Federation Executive were well aware of the honour conferred on the district by the choice of a South Walian venue. It was an acknowledgement of the SWMF's prominence, as a current and pioneer foundation member.[627] Oliver Harris discharged most of the introductory rituals on the opening day, and also the lion's share of hospitality duties. Horner and the SWMF Executive were probably keen that the general secretary's contribution to the movement should be publicly recognised and praised on his home ground before he retired in 1941. Federation delegates probably felt suitably proud that English and Scottish delegates could see for themselves the return of the SWMF to rude good health.

The mood of the conference remained distinctly muted in the shadow of impending war. Delegates were in no mood to embark on any ambitious project. The resolution on reorganisation, proposed by the Executive subcommittee, was referred back 'after considerable discussion' to districts for further discussion. As Acting President, Lawther had been notably unenthusiastic about pressing forward. After his election during annual conference, he had continued to exhibit a marked reluctance to provide the lead in potentially divisive questions such as reorganisation.[628] The elections for officers and delegates confirmed the existence of a tactical Northeast/South Wales bloc. In a significant departure from previous years, the SWMF did not nominate Horner for either President or Vice-President. Their large number of votes were cast for Lawther and Bowman.

Lawther's margin of victory was close. He defeated Henry Hicken from Derbyshire by only 46 votes on the second ballot. Although Hicken was more consistently left-wing than Lawther, he was supported by more moderate districts for geographic reasons. The other Midlands affiliates, Yorkshire and Scotland all voted for him. District unions whose members were primarily producing for the domestic market distrusted officials from the main exporting coalfield unions, and habitually doubted their bona fides in representing the interests of all British miners.

Bowman, standing for the first time to fill the vice-presidential vacancy caused by Lawther's elevation, won the election on the first ballot. The other candidates, from Lancashire, the Midlands and Scotland, failed to gain votes from outside their own districts. The decisive result was evidence of Bowman's personal magnetism, and the fact that he came from a small coalfield towards which there was less antagonism felt by other districts than towards Durham. But had Horner chosen to stand, he would have run Bowman very close, and might even have defeated him. Horner was once more elected as the other candidate for the TUC General Council, alongside Edwards and Lawther. The MFGB Vice-President had frequently been chosen for the third place and, Bowman – anticipating his victory in the Vice-Presidential election – could have exercised a lien on the General Council place. The fact that he refrained was evidence of a de facto tactical alliance, although an understanding may have been explicitly concluded between the two men.

On 21 August, the Soviet foreign minister, Molotov, and his German counterpart, von Ribbentrop, sealed a Non-Aggression Pact between their two countries. In the Commons debate on 24 August, Bevan refused to condemn the pact, and berated the government for not pursuing a military agreement with Russia.[629] But most MPs and activists from across the political spectrum viewed it as an abject surrender to fascism by the USSR. The CPGB leadership strenuously denied this accusation, arguing that Stalin had been compelled to act when the French and British governments refused to ally with the USSR against Hitler. The SWMF Executive agreed. Telegrams were despatched to Chamberlain and Arthur Greenwood, Labour deputy leader in the House of Commons, stating that 'South Wales Miners Executive Committee convinced that Anglo-Russian Pact more urgent than ever in view of German-Russian Pact.'[630]

The TUC was due to convene in the Yorkshire seaside town of Bridlington on Monday 4 September. It was likely that an intense debate about Horner's suitability to serve on the General Council, as an outstanding leader but also a leading communist, would have taken place in the hotel bars and at union socials. But the German army invaded Poland at 4.45 am on Friday 1 September. 'The Polish government at once invoked the British alliance. There was a chilly response and a pause.' On Saturday 2

415

September at an emergency session of the House of Commons, '[p]arliament forced a reluctant government into war.' Many TUC delegates, including Horner, Bevan, Jim Griffiths and Ness Edwards, had travelled to Bridlington on 2 September. Chamberlain's ultimatum to Hitler expired on Sunday 3 September at 11 am. On Monday, after hurried consultations, Congress proceedings were reduced to two days, including the General Council elections. Although Horner did not defeat the NWQU incumbent, RW Williams, he gained 650,000 votes in addition to the MFGB's 584,442. These probably came from the AEU and smaller left-wing unions, such as the ETU, ASLEF, NAFTA and Sheet Metal Workers.[631] Congress delegates returned home on Tuesday evening to deal with the myriad problems which they anticipated would arise, and which many knew of from personal experience of 1914, in putting their industries onto a war footing. Horner was preoccupied by Vol's return from France, where she had been on holiday the previous fortnight. She had begun making her way to northern France after hearing news of the German invasion of Poland; and she succeeded in crossing the Channel on Sunday. Arthur and Ethel had been 'going crazy with worry'.[632]

The German invasion of Poland had strengthened Pollitt's and Campbell's conviction that democracy could only be safeguarded by an alliance of progressive political forces. Despite the logic of the Molotov-Ribbentrop Pact, they continued to promote united-frontism. On 2 September the *Daily Worker* page one headline, 'Nazis Plunge World Into War ... The mad dogs of Europe – Hitler and his Nazi Government – have set out on their last bloody adventure', was followed by an Executive statement, probably written by Campbell.

> The essence of the present situation is that the people now have to wage a struggle on two fronts. First to secure the military victory over Fascism; and second, in order to achieve this, the political victory over Chamberlain and the enemies of democracy in this country. These two aims are inseparable, and the harder the efforts to win one, the more sustained must be the activity to win the other.

The theme was skilfully developed in the *Daily Worker* over the next few weeks. Individual union leaders, including Bevin and Jack Tanner, recently elected AEU President, adopted permutations of the 'war on two fronts' position. The TUC General Council adopted a position of careful support for the war. They were determined not to declare a domestic industrial truce without cast-iron guarantees that workers would be amply compensated for the increased effort and relaxation of customs and practice which they were likely to be asked to make in the wartime emergency.[633] The Federation's support for the war effort was more positive. Although British battleships now used oil instead of steam coal from South Wales, it was clear that adequate coal supplies would be critically important to the war effort. Horner re-affirmed the importance of observing the 1937 district agreement. He and his Executive remained wholly committed not only to fighting fascism, but also to defusing any industrial conflict. Not surprisingly, however, memories of the SWMF's militancy in 1915 had re-surfaced amongst civil servants in the Department of Mines.

The SWMF Executive had discussed defence precautions in collieries on 29 August, perhaps as a result of the ongoing discussions which Portal had been having with Iestyn Williams and Horner. On 12 September, Horner reported a meeting *Daily Worker* with the SWMCA to discuss Air Raid Precautions to the Executive, which made suggestions for a further meeting.[634] Portal also met representatives from the SWRCL Industrial Section. He was evidently aware that local protocol required him to maintain formal relations with both the Federation and the SWRCL, even though there was a Federation representative on the Industrial Section. The Industrial Section told EP Harries, head of the TUC Organisation Department, that 'as a result he [Portal] has agreed to attend their meetings when they wish him to do so. If and when central government breaks down they will constitute the Industrial Advisory Committee to the Regional Commissioner.' Harries sent a memo to Citrine on 9 October: 'I am wondering whether it would be a good thing to ask the General Council to agree to recommend the extension of this idea.'[635] But consultations between the TUC and the government were proceeding so slowly that Harries' suggestion was not implemented nationally until early June 1941.

On 14 September, Pollitt suppressed a Soviet press telegram, received by the *Daily Worker* which described the war as 'an imperialist and predatory war for new redivision of the world ... a robber war kindled from all sides by the hands of two imperialist groups of powers'. He and Campbell were determined to maintain their qualified support for the war, and they were evidently doubtful of being able to win an argument inside the party Executive if the official Soviet view was known. On 24 September, when the CPGB Executive met for the first time since the war, Dutt and Rust attacked their arguments that the party's domestic political position would be fatally undermined by refusing to back a war on fascism. Horner and Paynter had attended; most speakers, including Horner, Cox and Kerrigan, had supported Pollitt and Campbell. In view of the impasse, the meeting was adjourned until the next day.

At the morning session on 25 September, Dave Springhall, the party's representative at the Comintern who had returned from Moscow the previous evening, described discussions with Dimitrov and Marty about the ECCI's directive on the war. Everyone accepted that the CPGB's position had to be adjusted. There was sharp disagreement, however, about its extent. The Politburo met during the lunch break, but were unable to resolve the deadlock. Dutt and Rust insisted that the party condemn the British and French governments' motives for declaring war as imperialist, from which it followed that there was no basis for supporting the war against Hitler. Pollitt and Campbell insisted that with some minor tweaking, the existing 'war on two fronts' position would pass muster at the Comintern.[636]

The afternoon session was short, because the Politburo was still split. Pollitt announced that the meeting would stand adjourned whilst the Politburo agreed the new party line. He said that 'Comrade Cox should explain the situation to Comrades Horner and Paynter who had to leave and the indispensable necessity of these comrades being present [whenever the meeting reconvened].'[637] When the CPGB Executive reconvened on 2 October, it was clear that Dutt and Rust had prevailed inside the Politburo. The resolution put forward condemned the war, without qualification, as an inter-imperialist conflict. After a highly charged, acrimonious debate, the resolution was passed, with

418

Pollitt, Campbell and Gallacher dissenting. Horner and Paynter were both absent, probably on union business. Horner's recollection and Vol's memory of their conversations in September-October 1939 were the same. Had he attended the meeting, he would have voted according to his anti-fascist principles.[638]

Contrary to his injunction on 25 September that they should attend, Pollitt had probably acquiesced when he knew that Horner and Paynter would be absent. He would have calculated that Horner, at least, would have voted against the resolution. After dissenting on 2 October, Pollitt and Campbell had performed the requisite act of contrition, and publicly repented their opposition to the new party line. If Horner had undertaken a similar public repentance, Pollitt recognised that Horner's dismissal as SWMF President would have been the most likely result. But Pollitt probably also recognised that if Horner had attended and voted 'No', he would have refused to retract his opposition. At this juncture, he would have been determined to remain true to his own conscience and also to retain his union office. Another likely consequence of his recusance would have been a recurrence of internal party conflict along the same political fault-lines as the Hornerism controversy in 1931.

The public presentation of the new line proceeded circuitously. Dutt, who had now replaced Pollitt as party general secretary, and Rust, who replaced Campbell as *Daily Worker* editor, required no significant changes in party activists' mass work inside trade unions and workplaces. They evidently concluded that a rigorous execution of the new line would prove counterproductive for the party's standing inside the working class. Palliatives were provided, such as Campbell's gloss on the new line in *Daily Worker* stories, which enabled party members to finesse their position as sincere anti-fascists. The Comintern acquiesced in their highly ambiguous interpretation of their new line. The ECCI were either indifferent, and/or aware that enforcing an absolute imperialist war line would leave the CPGB isolated from the labour movement.[639] The British party's degree of separation from the prevailing orthodoxy was evidently not a pressing concern for Dimitrov or indeed Stalin.

Gallacher spoke the new line punctiliously in the House of Commons, though he was quick to take advantage of its blurred edges by concentrating on economic and trade union issues.

Horner offered no public statement about his own position. Since his previous enthusiasm for fighting fascism was well-known, his silence was conspicuous. Dutt made no attempt to compel Horner to publicly register his support for the new line. As on most domestic issues, Dutt took advice from Pollitt, and usually followed his recommendations.

Cox had re-imposed some order inside the party since his return to South Wales as district secretary in August. But he was evidently concerned about the effect of the change of line. Although he switched to support Dutt on 2 October, he had pointedly observed, 'I have more faith in Comrade Pollitt as a political leader than either Comrades Dutt or Springhall, and without Comrade Pollitt in the leadership we should be working under a serious handicap.'[640] He was evidently fearful of another outbreak of internecine conflict. As in other districts, the South Wales District Committee had obediently followed the Executive and voted 14 to 0 to support the new anti-war line. The result reported in the *Daily Worker* was that one abstention had also been registered, which is likely to have been Horner's. On 13 October the *Daily Worker* stated that reports of a split in South Wales were without foundation.

With Joseph Jones' departure, Horner had now assumed the leading progressive role on the MFGB Executive. His tactical virtuosity and clear view of the MFGB's strategic priorities were important in enabling the Executive to fight the war on the domestic front and seize the opportunities presented by the wartime emergency. Nevertheless, the MFGB faced formidable obstacles before the goals of higher wages and national collective bargaining could be won. The new Secretary at the Department of Mines, Geoffrey Lloyd MP, was pursuing two goals, with the MAGB's approval, which the MFGB considered contradictory: ensuring adequate supplies of coal and discouraging wage increases which would fuel wartime inflation.[641]

The Department of Mines decided to use the Joint Standing Consultative Committee, which had been established in 1936 as part of the settlement of the national wages dispute, to deal with wages questions during the wartime emergency. The MAGB had not hitherto allowed the JSCC to function as a genuine national forum, but Lloyd now exerted pressure on them to take it more seriously. Horner had deputised for Oliver Harris on the JSCC since his serious illness in mid-September 1939, and although Harris had recovered sufficiently to begin attending MFGB Executive meetings from mid-October, it is notable that Horner continued to attend the JSCC in his stead. At the earliest opportunity, in August 1940 at its first meeting after Annual Conference, the MFGB Executive appointed Horner to the JSCC in his own right.

At the JSCC on 28 September the MFGB tabled a claim for a national flat-rate wage increase of one shilling per shift, to compensate for the increased cost of living. On 19 October the MAGB offered sixpence to be paid for three months, from the beginning of the war until 31 December, but increased their offer to eightpence under pressure from the union's negotiators. The government were not prepared to face up to the need to put the economy on a total war emergency footing, and introduce comprehensive control measures similar to those used in World War I. Consequently, the MAGB could rely on getting away with this strictly ad hoc response.

The MAGB's national offer had to be ratified district by district in the MFGB. When Horner argued in favour of accepting the eightpence offer at the SWMF Executive on 20 October, they unanimously agreed that it was reasonable, and was at least a first step in moving the coalowners towards national wage bargaining. A Federation delegate conference accepted the Executive's recommendation by 125 to 95 on Saturday 21 October. However, lodge votes taken on Sunday and throughout the following week overturned the recommendation by a decisive majority.

The result was probably not unexpected by Horner. He recognised that there were disparate political and parochial interests arrayed against it. There was strong dissatisfaction with a flat-rate increase per shift from hewers, who stood to gain more from a percentage increase, which would maintain the monetary differential between themselves and the lower paid labourers and surface workers. Then there was the CPGB, where Dutt and Rust were promoting opposition to the offer on the militant principle that coalowners should be compelled to pay more. Following the Party Centre's instructions, Cox and the DPC had directed party members in the SWMF to oppose the offer and argue for a national strike ballot.

421

Inside the Federation, there was strong pressure to revert to district negotiations; militants as well as usually moderate opportunists were convinced that South Wales could win more at district level. Communists and ILP activists conducted a vigorous agitation against the agreement, invoking memories of the spectacularly successful strike in South Wales in July 1915, and pointing to the comparably advantageous position which the coalfield now occupied.[642]

Horner did not inform the South Wales DPC (nor evidently did they ask him) whether or not he would accept the party line and oppose the MFGB Executive's recommendation to accept the offer. A letter from Cox to the Party Centre, written on 24 October, set out the case against him, and complained that other party members were following his lead:

> [There is] a serious situation with regard to the attitude of Comrade Horner and the Party members of the EC of the SWMF ... Although those comrades knew that the decision of the Secretariat was to press for a bigger [national] increase, all ... spoke for acceptance, with the result that the EC were unanimous in recommending the acceptance ... [R]eports are coming from all parts that the Lodges are refusing to accept the offer ... [T]here is strong indignation against our leading members in the SWMF for their attitude ... Comrade Horner is in a furious temper arising from the instruction of the Secretariat to reject the terms (although he was present at a discussion last week where the view of the Secretariat was made clear). He refused to attend a meeting of the [District Party] EC members today to discuss the matter, and up to the moment refuses to talk the matter over with Comrade Cox. We understand that Comrade Horner wants to have a discussion at the Centre, and we fully agree with this for it is extremely urgent that we should know where we stand on this matter. But first of all, it is important for the Centre to have a talk with Comrade Horner BEFORE the MFGB conference on Friday.[643]

But Horner and the SWMF Executive had no intention of defying the lodge vote. They had faced up to its consequences on

24 October, when sufficient numbers of lodge voting returns had been available for rejection to be clear. Horner immediately commenced discussions with the South Wales coalowners on a district wage increase. SWMF delegates to the MFGB delegate conference on 27 October voted against the national agreement. At the conference Horner convinced SWMF delegates to allow him to speak in favour of the offer. He argued that as a member of the JSCC, he was bound by collective responsibility.

Lawther called him immediately after Bowman's speech on behalf of the MFGB Executive. Horner mounted a robust defence, 'in full appreciation that the district of which I am President has turned down the offer by nine votes to one: that does not make me feel that what we have done is a mistake':

> I believe in national control of the wages policy ... I do not even believe that the exigencies of war should produce a position where export districts such as I come from might entitle us for a period, to wages far in excess even of inland districts ... Why don't the Owners want national control? Because relatively they are weaker ... [I]f we can establish national control for the period of the war we have gained a stronger position for the miners of this country ... [W]e should be much more effective in exercising pressure against the Government as a unified Mineworkers' Federation ... than as 20 separate districts grumbling about the dissatisfaction of the men ...

After a heated debate the MFGB Executive's recommendation was carried on a card vote by 342,000 to 253,000; Yorkshire, South Wales, Scotland and the Forest of Dean were the opposing districts.[644] The MFGB had avoided a potentially serious internal division, an outcome which Horner's tactical acumen had played an important part in ensuring. Although some SWMF lodges objected to his support for the national offer, the Federation Executive refused to censure him. Moreover, in November they decided to publish the verbatim report of his MFGB conference speech, to enable members to read his argument for themselves.

Despite Cox's persistent lobbying, Dutt declined to prosecute the case against Horner and extract the party's pound of flesh.

Cox accepted Horner's immunity, even though hard-line party veterans were arguing that unless he was called to account he would repeat his Hornerism deviation. Cox worked hard to implement the party's revised line, arguing for the MFGB Executive to seek an improved national agreement. In mid-November, the DPC held a conference for communist miners which adopted a national programme, including shorter Saturday shifts, a demand which the SWMF had been vigorously pursuing before the war. Fifty thousand copies of the programme were printed and distributed in South Wales. Its introduction explained that 'despite differences on the wage offer ... the Communist Party is without exception united around the programme'. An air-brushed version of recent events was presented without overt reference to Horner. Party members on the SWMF Executive who had voted to accept the coalowners' offer in defiance of opposition from the CPGB and SWMF lodges were exonerated as having acted in good faith.[645] Nevertheless, revolutionary militants who had persuaded their lodges to vote against the offer continued to feel aggrieved.

In November 1939 the Red Army invaded Finland to pre-empt any other state using Finnish territory as a base from which to attack the Soviet Union. The small Finnish Army mounted a stubborn defence and held down a much larger, better equipped Soviet force until March 1940. (Significant numbers of Finnish communists ignored party discipline and participated in civil defence and as army reservists and volunteers.) The Finns' gallant stand in the Winter War evoked a strong response in Britain, which the centre-right Labour leadership used to further domestic political ends. However, in mid-December, when the MFGB Executive considered a DMA motion condemning Soviet aggression in Finland, it was only narrowly passed by 13 to 12. The *Daily Worker* reported an unusual departure from customary procedure: Durham, Yorkshire and South Wales had not voted as blocs; their delegates' votes had been split. South Walians had voted 2 to 1 against the resolution; although not named, Horner would have been the dissentient.[646]

By November the CPGB leadership had formulated its revised line for mass work. *Daily Worker* conferences took place in key cities, which presented the party's anti-war line in a palpably diluted form since its formulation in October. (The Winter

War was an additional complication in presenting French and British action as imperialist.) The conferences emphasised the domestic class war, evidently to persuade left-Labour supporters to continue united front activity. In South Wales the conferences exacerbated internal party differences. On 4 December, the *Daily Worker* stories on the three South Wales conferences noted three different messages. In Cardiff, Cox told an audience of 78 that if there were differences about the international dimensions of the war, there could be no differences about the war which the capitalist class was conducting against British workers. In Pontypridd, Horner addressed 65 people; he failed to say anything about the imperialist war, strictly adhering to the war-on-two-fronts position. In Bridgend, Len Jeffries made a scarcely veiled attack on Horner. He told an unreported number of listeners that anyone who supported the war was an enemy of the working class, even though they might be an official working-class leader.

The differences in the South Wales party spilled over into the Federation, where the national press had been reporting rumours of an intensifying conflict between pro- and anti-war positions since early December. The Party Centre and Cox were probably subjected to increasing pressure from members who wanted to propose an anti-imperialist war position to an SWMF delegate conference. But Pollitt and Allison knew that a principled anti-imperialist war motion was certain be defeated, and that other party members were likely to oppose it, exposing the CPGB's internal divisions to public scrutiny. They would have advised Dutt that the motion's defeat and the spectacle of internecine party strife would significantly diminish the CPGB's influence in the Federation, and might even precipitate Horner's resignation from the party.

Differences about the war were also opening up inside the union itself. A succession of protracted meetings took place between the Federation Executive and the sponsored MPs in an endeavour to reach a unified position. SO Davies and Bevan, flanked by Saddler and Will Arthur, may have sided with Horner, Alf Davies and Ianto Evans against Arthur Jenkins and other MPs in pressing a 'war on two fronts' position. The Executive finally decided on 30 December to hold a Special Conference 'to discuss policy of the Federation towards the present war'.[647]

Pro- and anti-war supporters were both determined on a trial of strength. Hard-line opponents of the war inside the CPGB coalesced with activists from the ILP and nascent Trotskyist movement to press their case.[648]

The Federation Conference was scheduled for 17 February 1940. The Executive and sponsored MPs met on 6 and 10 February to decide on the procedure to be followed. On 10 February Horner used his chairman's casting vote to decide that the pro- and anti-war resolutions would be put without an Executive recommendation about which lodges should support. After the Federation's position had been decided by due process, members of the Executive would be bound to support it.[649]

Horner continued to maintain a low political profile. On 3 February, an article by him appeared in the *Daily Worker*, which did not endorse an anti-imperialist war position. His public appearances were outside South Wales; he spoke at a Russia Today Society Conference in Newcastle-on-Tyne in January, and on 25 February at a *Labour Monthly* Conference in London on Labour and the War. Whilst he declined from taking a full-blown anti-war position, he also refrained from describing the British war effort as anti-fascist. He was apparently willing to trim towards the party line.[650]

The Federation conference on 17 February was held in private session. The two opposing motions were proposed by Executive members. The closely reasoned pro-war motion was moved by Will Arthur and seconded by Ted Williams on behalf of the Federation MPs, with the exception of SO Davies, who made a separate speech explaining his reasons for principled abstention. Its prose bore Bevan's stamp, and differed only marginally from the Federation's current war-on-two-fronts position. 'This Conference is opposed to Fascism in all its forms. Long ago we took the lead in demanding that the British Government should adopt a policy of resistance to any further aggression by Fascist Germany ... [W]e stand firm to our decision, and will support the war so long as it is fought against Fascist aggression and for the achievement of permanent peace ... We welcome the refusal of Labour to join the Government. We expect this political independence to be exerted with the utmost vigour lest the war be deflected from its declared purpose of defeating Fascism.' It called on the Labour Party 'to end the bye-election truce in order to intensify the struggle of the workers on the Home Front'.

DR Llewellyn, communist International Brigade veteran, moved the anti-war resolution on behalf of Blaengarw lodge; it was formally seconded. The wording was evidently calculated to appeal to the Labour left. It is likely that Cox had helped to draft it. After condemning the war as 'being waged for imperialist aims and not for the defence of democracy against fascism', it called upon 'the Labour Movement to exert its energies to stop the war and establish peace and as a first step to end political truce'.[651]

Delegates accepted the Executive's recommendation that the normal procedure be followed. The conference stood adjourned for a fortnight whilst a lodge vote was held. The reconvened conference was held on 2 March. Horner used his chairman's prerogative to keep silent about which motion he supported, and neither side challenged his ruling. He took the vote after peremptory discussion, and again his chairman's discretion was not questioned from the floor. The Executive's priority was evidently to prevent the ventilation of high emotion and vituperative challenges from one side about the other's bona fides. The pro-war-on-two-fronts motion was carried on a roll-call vote by 1940 to 607 votes, representing a lodge vote of 97,000 to 30,350.[652]

The Executive's success in minimising the conflict and the clear defeat of the anti-war motion reinforced the Federation's self-image as a strong, united union. Horner's personal position was also strengthened. He could conscientiously accept the motion which conference had endorsed, in the knowledge that the party leadership were not likely to discipline him. The substantial minority of lodges which had supported the anti-war resolution provided firm evidence that there was a continuing need for Horner's emollient skills and communist credentials.[653]

In mid-March the SWMF Executive decided to support a National Council of Labour appeal to contribute to a fund for the relief of the Finnish people. Horner, the consummate strategist, had interpreted Stalin's decision to invade Finland as defensive, an essential operation to secure the USSR's western flank against Hitler. He delegated the responsibility for personally signing the appeal cheque to Saddler, the Vice-President, who had no scruples about acting in Horner's stead. The Federation Executive and most non-communist activists tolerated his conscientious objection. Frankenberg's notes of his interview with Horner recorded, 'Arthur remembers saying at the time, "There are certain things you cannot ask a man to do. One of them is to ask a man to hold office at the price of sincere conviction. That I will not do."' At a subsequent delegate conference, a lodge motion was put demanding Horner's removal for declining to sign the cheque. The delegate proposing the resolution 'apologised for the attitude of his Lodge in bringing the matter forward and someone immediately moved next business'.[654]

Horner's position inside the South Wales district party had been bolstered at the end of 1939, when Alf Davies resigned from the Labour Party and joined the CPGB. Davies' new political alignment was an important addition to the communist party's influence inside the SWMF, since he had been elected Agent for Area No. 3 in July 1939.[655] As a consistent ally of Horner, he also provided valuable support in the conflict with the revolutionary militants inside the South Wales party.

Davies' agent's duties meant that he was a regular caller at the Federation Offices in Cardiff. He and Arthur probably relished the occasions when he stayed to lunch, which was supplied by Mrs Evans, the caretaker, for everyone in the office. Other circumstances reinforced the close relations between the two men. Paynter, who had probably been Horner's confidant about Federation affairs, had recently been elected Agent for Area 4, an area not noted for its support for communist politics. In the summer of 1940 he moved from the lower to the upper Rhymney Valley, to a geographically remote mining village. The new location was convenient for his agent's work, and simplified his domestic arrangements. (His wife had died in May, soon after giving birth to twin boys.)

At the beginning of 1940 the MFGB Executive had submitted a claim for an additional wage rise, since they 'would under no circumstances agree to any policy which meant that our members' hard-earned pre-war standard of living should be reduced during the war'. The MAGB's negative response was supported by the government. The Treasury was keen to avoid making even a de facto provision for automatic upward adjustments in wages to compensate for the higher cost-of-living. The MFGB Executive took the offensive, threatening to hold a national strike ballot, and demanding an agreed formula to provide for wages to automatically increase in line with further increases in the cost-of-living. The MAGB conceded the case after some hard bargaining; they evidently considered the strike ballot threat to be very credible.

The MFGB Executive recommended the owners' final offer of an additional 5d per shift for the first quarter of 1940, and there-after '[t]hat 0.70d. per shift be the variation in the flat rate war additions ... corresponding to a variation of one point in the cost of living index number, subject to three-monthly reviews, and that there should be no change in the flat rates unless the index figure varies by not less than 5 points.' The national delegate conference on 25 January 1940 accepted the offer by a large majority, which included the SWMF, on a card vote of 524,000 to 70,000. However, when the conference decision went to dis-trict unions for ratification, the South Wales lodge vote rejected the national offer; the aggregated national vote for acceptance declined to 421,721.[656]

The SWMF lodges' rejection was partly due to the energetic activity of party activists inside the SWMF, encouraged by the DPC and the Party Centre. A Special Branch report on 25 January noted Horner's 'horror' at a party circular urging rejection of the offer, and the party leadership's anger at Horner's failure to consult them. 'There was considerable risk that Arthur Horner would resign from the Party on this issue but ultimately he was persuaded not to although the position is still very strained.'[657] On 26 January the *Daily Worker* described the agreement as the worst since 1926: 'no plea of national unity can wipe out this shameful act [the MFGB conference acceptance of the offer]'. It predicted that Scotland and South Wales were practically certain to reject the offer. If the MFGB refused to hold a national strike ballot, each district would have to 'consider what action they can take in unity with the miners in other coalfields ... '.

Even though the new national agreement provided compen-sation for cost-of-living increases, district union executives in Yorkshire, Scotland and South Wales opened separate negotia-tions with their district coalowners to further improve their mem-bers' wages. The strong demand for coal considerably enhanced their bargaining position. Horner and the Federation Executive had initially opposed such parochial behaviour as undermining the MFGB's national integrity. But after the second rejection by South Walian lodges of a national officer, they prudently opened district negotiations for a substantial district wage rise. (Other district unions' abstention was probably due to their executives' unwillingness to risk overt conflict in wartime.)

Chastened by the three districts going it alone, the MFGB Executive had re-opened national negotiations during February. A marginally improved agreement was finally ratified by the MFGB Executive on 20 March, but the *Daily Worker* reported on 19 March that Scotland and Yorkshire would hold strike ballots about the agreement. Although the ballots did not take place, as Horner had grimly predicted, the three districts' separate negotiations enabled the MAGB to dilute their commitment to a national wages machinery. The first clause of the national agreement provided for the continuation of district wage arrangements; the only increases subject to national negotiation were those 'necessary to take account of the special conditions arising out of the war, and particularly the increased cost of living'.[658]

Led by Horner, the Federation Executive was continuing to take the wartime emergency seriously. They concluded an agreement with the SWMCA to enable disputes to be settled speedily outside the formal conciliation procedure. The Ministry of Labour Regional Industrial Relations Officer (RIRO) noted on 9 March that he had attended 'a recent social gathering in Cardiff' where Horner and Iestyn Williams were present. Williams had praised 'mutual compromise' as 'the key-note of the success achieved in industrial negotiation in the South Wales coalfield over recent years ... Mr. Horner commented on the conduct of negotiations which "had been played according to the rules" and the whole secret of success, he said, was that the agreements were strictly kept.' From the RIRO's subsequent weekly reports it is evident that Horner and Williams arranged mutually acceptable settlements in many trouble spots at their weekly informal meetings.[659]

Despite the apparent willingness of most working miners to take the war effort seriously, a powerful undercurrent of opportunism continued to motivate many Federation lodge activists. On 19 April 1940 the Executive recommended the coalowners' proposal to delegates at a Special Conference, to minimise the disruption to production by postponing the traditional May Day Monday holiday for a fortnight and taking the Tuesday after Whit Monday off. The proposal was narrowly accepted on a card vote by 70,950 to 59,200.[660]

Inside the South Wales party, anti-Horner feeling was increasing. The failure of the anti-war resolution and the postponement of the May Day holiday provided evidence for veterans who suspected Horner of Hornerist recidivism. The Party Centre and Cox explained the anti-war motion's defeat by reminding members that they had not taken their duty to do daily mass work seriously.[661] They remained notably reticent about condemning Horner's conduct either publicly or apparently inside the party. Campbell and Pollitt were drafted into South Wales to re-establish a veneer of internal unity. Campbell was writing for the *Daily Worker*, and probably attended DPC meetings with Pollitt.[662]

Horner explained his complicated personal position in his Presidential Address at the Federation's Annual Conference in April. Its content was sufficiently anti-war to satisfy Dutt and Rust, but provided insufficient evidence for Arthur Jenkins and Sir Charles Edwards to accuse him of flouting the Federation's official war-on-two-fronts position.

> So long as I am President ... I will operate majority decisions. When I cannot carry out the wishes of the majority ... I will do the only honourable thing, that is, offer my resignation. It would, however, be dishonest and out of harmony with my whole record in this coalfield if I did not take this opportunity to publicly inform you and the members generally that I did not and do not now agree with the majority in this matter.'
>
> ... I am honestly of the opinion that in the near future the majority will accept the view that the best interests of the workers of this and all other countries can only be served by bringing an end to the war and the system which has caused it.

Conference delegates re-elected Horner President 'almost unanimously'.[663] Nevertheless, he continued to be under attack from militant opportunists for his stance on the national agreement, as well as experiencing political opposition from the zealots in the pro- and anti-war camps. Most members of the SWMF Executive, however, remained confident that he would continue to be an outstanding president. He had made few enemies and many friends in the course of the recent coalfield conflicts, and his personal networks of Federation activists and lodge officials extended across the coalfield. Amongst Federation sponsored MPs, he enjoyed unstinting support from Ted Williams and SO Davies, and virtually unconditional loyalty from Bevan.

Vol was married in early summer. She and her husband, John Tofts, were thrown together in September 1939, when the Head Office of the Legal & General Assurance, where they both worked, was evacuated to a public school with extensive grounds and gardens, St Monica's Girls' School in Kingswood, Surrey. (Because John worked in another department, their paths had never crossed in London.) Emergency conditions, balmy autumn weather and the absence of landladies facilitated intimacy. Mutual attraction was heightened by the discovery that they were both communists. Vol took John home to the Datcha for Christmas 1939 to meet her family. He recalled their warm welcome and the general merriment that followed. When he was called up to the Royal Army Medical Corps in March 1940, they decided to get married. John made the necessary arrangements at the Shoreditch registry office, and was given three days leave. The ceremony took place on a Friday, evidently without a Horner family representative present. The newly-weds met Arthur at Paddington station – he had probably been attending an MFGB meeting – and went back to the Datcha with him. On Saturday, Arthur took them to visit his parents in Merthyr. Emily approved of John as a tidy boy, and told Vol, 'he'll do'.[664] Vol and John returned to their respective postings on Sunday.

The South Wales coalfield was working at maximum intensity at this point, in order to meet the increased French demand for British coal. As part of the government's response to the wartime emergency, Geoffrey Lloyd had established the Coal Production Council. Not surprisingly, it strongly resembled the World War I joint consultative machinery. The current President of the Board of Trade, Andrew Duncan, had been Coal Controller in the coalition government in 1919 to 1922, and many senior civil servants had served in the Department of Mines in 1914 to 1918.[665]

The CPC was a tripartite body, with three MAGB representatives, the three MFGB national officers and the permanent secretaries of the Ministries of Transport and Shipping and the Department of Mines. Duncan appointed Wyndham Portal Chairman. (Portal had resigned as Regional Commissioner for Wales in early December 1939, on the grounds that he was unable to spend sufficient time in Wales during the wartime emergency.) The first CPC meeting was on 5 April 1940, after which Portal 'toured the coal-fields that month and encouraged the setting up of the [district and pit production] committees'. Coal Production Advisers were appointed in June to liaise between the CPC and the principal coalfields. They 'were extremely useful in seeing that advice was drawn up in London with reference to the varying needs of the districts, that it was communicated to the districts ... and as far as possible carried out.'[666] It is unlikely to have escaped the notice of either the coalowners or the MFGB that the network of advisers and their links with district coalfields could form the bare bones of a national production directorate if the government found itself again compelled to take charge of coal production. In contrast to other coalfields, Portal had refrained from appointing a Coal Production Adviser in South Wales, perhaps because he had intended to fulfil the role himself. He would also have recognised the acute sensitivity of Evan Williams to any potential challenge to the coalowners' prerogative.

The MFGB representatives did not, however, play a significant part in the CPC's proceedings. Ebby Edwards had been badly affected by the increase in union business as a result of the war. The problems over negotiating the second national agreement had precipitated a serious loss of morale. His commitment to the MFGB and his attention to the job of general secretary palpably diminished. Edwards had, in fact, allowed the efficient administration at the MFGB central office to decline since 1937, when Bryn Roberts had poached the capable chief clerk, Fred Hill, to help him in his new job as NUPE general secretary. Hill had started with the MFGB and Frank Hodges in 1919, when the office in 50 Russell Square had first been opened. Edwards had relied on Hill to manage the voluminous filing system, which held records of the MFGB's communications with the MAGB and the Department of Mines, as well as the byzantine correspondence with the district unions. Sid Ford, who had worked under Hill as a clerk since 1925, refused to apply for the vacancy caused by Hill's departure, because of his personal animus towards Edwards. Edwards had hired Joe Elliott as a willing but not very capable replacement. Ford had volunteered for the army in September 1939, partly for patriotic reasons, but also to compound Edwards' and Elliott's difficulties.[667] When Don Loney, Ford's own junior since 1938, was called up, the standards of administration had evidently deteriorated still further.

As president, Lawther should have intervened to reverse the decline at head office. But he had neither the stamina, inclination, or personal skills to function as a de facto general secretary in the face of Edwards' inertia and depression. Bowman, young, keen and capable, was evidently reluctant to step into the breach. Horner and Watson, both of whom could have provided the necessary emollience and energy to resolve the situation, were both sidelined. Watson occupied a junior position in the DMA hierarchy. Horner was excluded from Edwards' and Lawther's confidence for political reasons. The TUC General Council were currently promoting a vigorous anti-communist offensive, which the MFGB general secretary and president were assiduously suporting.[668]

The phoney war ended abruptly when the German army's Blitzkrieg invasion resulted in the collapse of the Netherlands' resistance on 14 May, and Belgium's unconditional surrender a fortnight later. The evacuation of the Allied, mostly British, troops from Dunkirk took place between 26 May and 4 June 1940. The German army entered Paris on 14 June, and granted requests for an armistice from Marshal Petain on 22 June. Chamberlain had resigned as prime minister in early May, and had been replaced by Churchill at the head of a coalition government that included the Labour parliamentary leadership. (The Parliamentary Labour Party remained in official opposition.) Attlee and Morrison were joined by Ernest Bevin, who was found a Commons seat, as members of an inner war cabinet. Chamberlain had belatedly presided over preparations for putting Britain on a total war footing during the Blitzkrieg.

Under Churchill, the coalition government proceeded with renewed determination to complete them. The dramatic worsening of Britain's prospects in the war produced a tangible change in the public mood. Apprehension that an invasion was imminent became widespread, followed by a collective willingness to take the war effort more seriously. People who had been indifferent or even sceptical now began to work virtually unlimited overtime and to participate wholeheartedly in production campaigns and civil defence preparations.

The SWMF Rules Revision Conference took place on 29 May. The RIRO's report on 1 June noted that delegates had 'pledged themselves to do everything possible to help in the present national situation. Mr. Arthur Horner ... is reported to have said "Whatever opinion I may have of the government, past or present, all are agreed that the maximum must be done to assist in the production of coal and to raise that production to meet the needs of the Country in its present dangerous situation."' The *Daily Worker* report on 31 May stated that Horner had been strongly opposed to the government's proposed emergency powers legislation; but a retraction and statement from Horner appeared the following day. 'In fact, the greater part of my speech was concerned to make clear the measures the SWMF intends to use in order to maintain and improve the output of coal while at the same time doing everything possible to ensure the continuation of all safety provisions and protecting the wages and working conditions of the members.'[669]

The advent of the coalition government dramatically changed the domestic political terrain. But the changed political circumstances apparently made little difference to Horner's conduct as a union leader. He continued to fight the war-on-two fronts. He took the lead inside the MFGB to seize the opportunity presented by Bevin's Essential Work Order (EWO) to promote the progressives' agenda for the industry. His ability to combine the pursuit of long-term goals with sufficient attention to the detail of the day-to-day problems enabled the MFGB Executive to win repeated concessions. He was, however, also affected by the concerns of the CPGB leadership, who believed that they would share the fate of the PCF, and be banned by the government. The possibility was considered by the Cabinet, but probably also widely discussed inside Labour Party and union networks. Many centre-right Labour activists and MPs were actively canvassing for the CPGB to be banned. The CPGB leadership made detailed preparations for maintaining an underground leadership and clandestine organisation. Party mythology, still current in the 1960s, recounted that the party records were sent from King Street to caves somewhere in South Wales.

In these very different circumstances, there was a reaction against him when a postal ballot of lodges rejected the Rules Revision Conference recommendation to make the Federation president a full-time position. The Executive extemporised, and agreed that he should continue on a full-time basis until the next Annual Conference, whilst Gomer Evans continued to deputise as agent.[670] Horner probably saw the negative vote as evidence that his opponents had organised efficiently against him. Left and communist-influenced lodges wanted to signal their unwillingness to abandon rank-and-file principles as well as their dissatisfaction with Horner's refusal to support militancy in these favourable circumstances. Centre-right Labour loyalist lodges had evidently decided not to allow Horner to take a permanent place at the top of the Federation pyramid.

Certain of loyal support from Harris and Saddler, and reinforced by Alf Davies' companionship, Horner managed his personal position adroitly. Nevertheless, now that a genuine total war effort had begun, the contradiction between his personal anti-fascism and the CPGB's anti-war position became more acute. On 28 May a note on Horner's MI5 file stated: 'The Ministry of Labour considers that, in the event of prominent members of the C.P. being detained under the Defence Regulations, that HORNER should not be taken, as this would cause serious trouble in the S. Wales coalfields.'[671] Horner's MI5 file later recorded: 'in a letter dated 6.8.40, [it is stated] that HORNER ... though publicly disapproving of the war, had privately recommended the miners to join the Home Guard, and had done nothing to retard the war effort. Source was an unknown Assistant Editor ... who claimed to know South Wales, inside out.'[672]

As a result of the French armistice, there was now a severe contraction in demand for South Wales coal. Having lost its main export outlet, the coalfield suffered a dramatic slump. Younger miners began to leave the pits to join the armed forces; older men found work in war factories. (The exodus of miners from the South Wales pits was replicated in the other coalfields, but the government made no attempt to stem the tide.) Despite this depletion, the SWMF and SWMCA co-operated throughout the autumn to keep the pits operating at maximum strength in expectation of the anticipated shortage of coal. But another pressing problem soon appeared: 'It was with much concern that the Mines Department in September 1940 watched the German air raids begin to break up the distribution of coal supplies in the big coal-consuming area between the Thames and the Bristol Channel. The great change came with the intense raiding which started early in that month.'[673]

Duncan was moved from the Board of Trade in early October 1940 to become Minister of Supply. Portal moved with him as an additional parliamentary secretary with responsibility for control of all raw materials. Churchill appointed one of his younger intimates, Oliver Lyttelton, to succeed Duncan. Lyttelton discharged his brief competently, with the exception of coal, where he lacked Duncan's experience. The new Secretary of Mines, Dai Grenfell, was left by Lyttelton very much to his own devices. During the nine months he remained at the Board of Trade, Lyttelton's apparent indifference towards the coal situation and failure to deal with Grenfell's evident weakness had far-reaching negative consequences.[674]

In addition to co-operating in the war effort, the SWMF continued to pursue its pro-war-on-two-fronts policy. With the Federation Executive's continuing support, Bevan played a leading role on the opposition benches. The war cabinet was steering an omnibus of legislation through the House of Commons which would finally put the economy on a total war footing. This included the Essential Work Order, which tied employees in 'controlled' war industries to their workplaces, and Order 1305, which made strikes illegal.[675] Horner moved an SWMF pro-war-on-two-fronts motion at the MFGB Annual Conference in mid-July 1940. When Lawther asked Horner from the chair to withdraw the motion, he refused. Edwards spoke against it on the Executive's behalf, but he was notably diplomatic and refrained from any personal attack on Horner. The motion was supported by the district votes of the SWMF, Scotland, Cumberland and the Forest of Dean.[676] Horner was probably also supported by

Scotland, Cumberland and Northumberland in the elections for
the three General Council seats; he came fourth, having been
overtaken by Bowman.[677]

Edwards re-emphasised unity in the traditional farewell
speech on the last day of conference:

> I think the delegates in the situation we are passing
> through at the moment have proved themselves pos-
> sessed of the highest degree of toleration. Anyone who
> attended Conferences during the last war – and there
> are many I see in the Conference who did – will remem-
> ber that a good deal of bitter animosity was displayed. In
> this Conference we have had none ... In fact the feeling
> when you met delegates outside this hall was all appre-
> ciative of how the exchange of points of view helped
> every one in their areas ... After Arthur had delivered
> that fine speech yesterday, an ordinary delegate later
> said to me, 'Arthur's a fine chap; I like Arthur; he's a
> wonderful fellow when you are dealing with industrial
> problems, but you know, when he talks about Russia he
> is just like a cross-eyed Salvation Army lass singing in
> the market place – "Looking This Way."' Arthur is not
> here, but he would have appreciated the joke, I know,
> because I want to say this, and say it in his absence, he is
> as good an Executive man as we have – a very thorough
> and honest worker.[678]

In early September 1940 Arthur and Ethel rented a cottage on
Waingron Road in Ely, a suburb about two miles west of Cardiff
city centre, with good connections on the suburban railway line
to the centre. Their decision to move had not been easy. They
moved in spite of the uncertainty about his tenure as president,
probably because of the wartime dislocation of passenger railway travel. Arthur's daily commute from Llanelli had become
increasingly onerous and uncertain. This was also the case for
Rosa, who had probably returned to South Wales at the outbreak of the war, and was now working in Cardiff. With afternoon meetings and public political meetings in the evening,
Arthur had been regularly staying the night in a Cardiff hotel.
The family had been happy at the Datcha, and Joan now had to

change secondary schools. But Rosa and Arthur could now be reasonably confident of getting home after work. Alf Davies had bought a new car on becoming agent, and with his petrol allowance as a union official, he was able to regularly give Horner a lift home. His membership of the CPGB earned him and his family an even more cordial welcome from Ethel.

The Battle of Britain was fought in the skies of London and the South Coast between July and mid-September 1940. Its purpose was to wear the British down prior to an amphibious invasion, Operation Sealion. The outlook for Britain's survival was bleak, and many people felt a great need to talk about events and the outlook for the future.

In the midst of the destruction and sacrifices of the war, it was not surprising that a collective desire arose to believe that a truly different new world must emerge from the ruins. This millenarian response was tapped fortuitously and unintentionally by the CPGB.

At the end of July 1940, the party leadership had embarked on a routine initiative, designed to muster support for left-wing resolutions and speakers at the TUC in October. The *Daily Worker* reported workplace meetings where DN Pritt MP had urged shop stewards to support a People's Vigilance Campaign.[679] Pritt had cited some already existing local vigilance committees, which had been formed in emulation of the World War I vigilance committees to safeguard workers' wages and conditions. The party leadership was wholly unprepared for the upsurge of interest which then followed, outside the circle of the usual left-wing activists. Pollitt spoke to 15,000 people in Hyde Park about vigilance committees, and the Home Office reports judged it to be the biggest public meeting since the outbreak of war.

The party leadership worked with Pritt to form a national People's Vigilance Committee, which campaigned for Peace and a new People's Government. Its programme was not unrealistic. Ruling out an immediate, unilateral exit from the war, it called for a negotiated peace in the interests of the people of all Europe. Many activists found this position compatible, even complementary, with their pro-war-war-on-two-fronts position. Union branches and local Labour Party bodies began to promote the movement enthusiastically. The Committee issued a

'Call for a People's Convention' the week before the TUC convened on 7 October. A flurry of activity ensued, with local and regional conferences and conventions.

Horner was not only the most high profile trade union signatory of the call. Since he was in full agreement with the programme, he was also genuinely enthusiastic. In South Wales the movement was a useful channel for the party DPC to direct the energies of anti-war communists, deflecting them from their previous priority of fanning economic conflict. A South Wales conference in support of the Convention programme was convened on the Sunday before the TUC, with delegates attending from 231 organisations, representing 220,000 people.[680] After the TUC, the People's Vigilance Committee announced a National People's Convention to be held in Manchester on Sunday, 12 January 1941. *Labour Monthly* published 500 names in November 1940 of people in favour of the Convention. There were 58 signatories from Wales, of whom 19 held SWMF positions; many also held office in Labour Party constituency organisations.[681]

The coalition government and the Labour *apparat* and were greatly exercised by the campaign's success. Transport House made strenuous efforts to damp down the groundswell of enthusiasm for its 'defeatist' programme. However, there were few resources at Citrine's, Middleton's and Deakin's disposal. With the Labour Party and TUC central bureaucracies focused on the war effort, constituency and trades council organisation had been neglected. Local activists had often lost touch with the centre, and had become accustomed to fending for themselves. In mid-November 1940, the Labour Party circularised internal party organisations, and the National Council of Labour wrote to unions, warning against official bodies having any association with the People's Vigilance Committee's invitation to appoint delegates to a People's Convention. They cautioned that the campaign was led by expelled members of the Labour Party, with the full backing of the Communist Party. 'The seriousness of the times demands that note should be taken of this latest attempt of the Communist Party to rise above its normal futility'.[682]

The SWMF Executive had initially agreed to support the People's Convention by 13 to 3 votes. But on 10 December the Executive considered the National Council of Labour's circular.

Another vote, 10 to 8 in favour, showed that many delegates had changed their minds. On 4 January 1941, the RIRO reported a 'very stormy' meeting between the SWMF Executive and its sponsored MPs during which the Executive had stood its ground.[683] Four Federation delegates were appointed on 10 December: Horner, Ernie Watkins, EA Bennett and DR Davies from Ebbw Vale. German bombers determined that the Convention was not held in Manchester, but London. Bomber fleets had been attacking British cities by night from mid-September 1940, and the centre of Manchester was so damaged in the week before the Convention was due to be held that the organisers moved the venue to central London.

Despite the best efforts of Transport House, the convention was a resounding success. The *Daily Worker* reported that there had been 1900 voting delegates. Queues of people wanting to listen to the proceedings assembled outside the three halls of the Convention, the Great Hall of the Royal Hotel, Holborn Hall and Holborn small hall.[684] Mass Observation volunteers who attended reported that a majority of delegates came from the organised working class, 'from all over the country and from many sources untapped in ordinary conferences and leftwing meetings', their 'pre-eminent concern being the world to be created after the war, and social conditions to be aspired to at that time'.[685] Horner served on the Standing Orders Committee, with Rust and two engineering delegates, one from Napier's aero-engine factory at Acton Vale in West London and the other from Metropolitan Vickers at Trafford Park, Manchester. At the conclusion of the Convention, the Standing Orders Committee, having received nominations, recommended 26 people to serve on a permanent National Committee. They included Horner, Dutt, Gallacher, Krishna Menon, the Dean of Canterbury, JBS Haldane and Will Pearson from the Scottish miners.[686]

Horner's membership of the Standing Orders Committee may have been arranged to keep him out of the limelight, thereby avoiding repercussions from the anti-Convention members of the Executive and the National Council of Labour. Nevertheless, his presence on the committee provided gravitas, prestige and pragmatism. The official report of the Convention did not report him as having spoken, and did not include his picture. By contrast, two retired national union leaders, Harry Adams and

Jack Squance, veteran allies in many CPGB initiatives, figured prominently. A speech from Paynter was reported:

> [W]e are proud to be able to say that the South Wales Miners' Federation, through its Executive Council, despite organised pressure from the Trades Union Congress General Council and the National Executive Council [of the MFGB], will take the initiative in developing the campaign in South Wales, deriving much inspiration from the experiences and discussion at this Convention.[687]

The Blitz had initially been directed at city centres. From mid-November 1940 the night bomber attacks were also directed against strategic targets, particularly ports and industry. Docks and factories in Cardiff came under severe attack in early January 1941. The Horners' house in Ely was destroyed in the week before the People's Convention, as a result of the common practice of pilots who had failed to drop all their payload on intended targets discharging the remainder randomly. On the evening of the raid Alf Davies had given Horner a lift home from the Federation office, and the two men were playing a game of darts in the kitchen. Rosa was still at work and Joan was in Llanelli staying with friends, having taken advantage of the school holidays. Ethel had gone to Newport to help her youngest sister Lizzie with the birth of her baby. Arthur's youngest sister Mabel was keeping house in her absence, and was extremely distressed by the Luftwaffe raid. The family story is that just after Arthur said, 'Don't worry Mabe, there's a one in a million chance that we'll be hit', a high explosive bomb, designed to cause maximum damage, exploded in front of the house, demolishing it and Alf's car.

Joan remembered, 'My father spent some of the night shovelling soil onto a burning gas fire.' When Rosa was able to make her way home in the early hours of the next morning, she found the house in ruins and could see no one there 'until my father, who had gone back into the house to find something warm to put on, suddenly emerged from the debris'.[688] On 8 January 1941, Horner's MI5 file noted that he had removed to the Rhondda Urban District. The Horners had gone to Ynyshir, where Arthur's and Ethel's former landlady, who had become a firm friend, opened her house to the family. Ynyshir was well away from night bombing targets, and Arthur and Rosa could commute to Cardiff by train without much difficulty.

Being bombed out was an experience which millions like the Horners were enduring at this time. The fortunate who survived without serious injury usually experienced extreme elation and relief. But days or sometimes weeks and months later, post-traumatic stress disorder, fatigue and feelings of insecurity were typical responses. Horner apparently suffered neither. Neither SWMF nor MFGB Executive minutes recorded him as missing meetings due to incapacity or domestic circumstances. He apparently took the bombing, his lucky escape and dislocation in his stride. Like other men and women of action, he was evidently mentally prepared and ready to take any eventuality on the chin.[689] On 1 February, even though there was still a danger of Luftwaffe raids, the Horners rented a furnished house in Whitchurch, a suburban village northwest of central Cardiff, and Joan started school there.

Horner's principal concern at this time was to deal with the looming crisis of coal production, whilst also ensuring that the MFGB continued to maximise the opportunity presented by the emergency to gain concessions. Nevertheless, he found it increasingly difficult to cope with the frequently contradictory demands coming from the other parts of his existence. Ethel and Vol remained passionately committed to the party anti-war line. His responsibilities as a high profile member of the CPGB, and member of the party Executive and DPC, were increasingly irksome. He managed the balancing act by not discussing his preoccupations as a union leader either at home or at any party meetings. He began to drink alcohol more heavily to anaesthetise himself against the stress of leading an increasingly divided life. Alf Davies' company probably made it easier for him to drink more than he usually consumed at home, since he could justify his indulgence to Ethel by his keeping Alf company and having a good crack.[690]

The government and the Labour establishment were fearful that the communist party would exploit the unexpected success of the People's Convention movement and build a genuine mass movement which could undermine the war effort.

Ironically, the CPGB leadership had no intention of developing the Convention's evident potential. Dutt was the only member of the Politburo who favoured exploring its subversive possibilities. In a minority of one, he watched as the party leadership, through conscious neglect and lack of attention, allowed the Convention's momentum to dissipate.[691]

But neither the government nor Transport House were prepared to believe that the CPGB leadership would put the war effort before the formal party line. On 17 January 1941 Morrison used his powers as Home Secretary to ban the *Daily Worker*, the only national daily newspaper which had reported the movement's progress and the Convention's proceedings. Also on 17 January the SWMF Executive considered a letter from Edwards on behalf of the MFGB Executive, despatched after the Executive had considered a letter from the Labour NEC expressing serious concern at the SWMF's support for the People's Vigilance Committee. The MFGB Executive had endorsed the NEC's view, which deemed 'the People's Vigilance Committee ... to be an Organisation ancillary and subsidiary to the Communist Party'. Edwards' letter requested the SWMF to 'adhere to the Constitution of the Labour Party' and dissociate themselves from the Vigilance Committee.[692]

Horner led an expeditious retreat to this polite threat. The SWMF Executive speedily and unanimously agreed to cease all support for the Committee. The RIRO reported that their decision 'has occasioned general surprise'. On 23 February, his MI5 file noted that Horner had told the communist District Party Congress in Cardiff that 'the S.W.M.F. had dissociated itself from the People's Convention'. This unambiguous statement at an official party meeting was evidence that the SWMF volte-face had been accepted by the CPGB leadership. The South Wales Labour Party, however, wanted to extract their pound of flesh. An ad hoc coalition of the Regional Council of Labour and SWMF centre-right activists conspired to unseat communist lodge officials. Horner's MI5 file noted: 'It is believed to be the intention of the Labour Party in South Wales to remove all Communists out of the Miners' Federation'. The RIRO reported that there had been a clean sweep in the Treharris Lodge, near Merthyr, expulsions in the Llanelli Labour Party, and in addition 'a very prominent member of the Monmouthshire County

Council, Alderman and Agent', probably DR Davies, had been successfully targeted.[693]

There was also a vendetta pursued from Transport House in London. On 5 March Ebby Edwards notified the MFGB Executive of further correspondence from the Labour Party complaining about the SWMF. Edwards had replied: 'that the SWMF had stated they were not identified with the aforementioned [People's Vigilance] Movement, but evidently the [Labour] Party was desirous of seeking a more specific assurance from the SWMF ... To this he had replied that he did not see what more specific assurance could be obtained than the one already given'.

The MFGB Executive endorsed Edwards' curt reply and resolved to take no further action. The Executive's refusal to call the Federation to book was not merely due to their desire maintain unity. There was growing anger in the district unions about the lack of commitment from the Labour NEC and Labour members of the coalition government to the MFGB's agenda for ensuring adequate supplies of coal. The MFGB and its sponsored MPs were arguing that the government should enforce joint MAGB-MFGB control of the industry through the vehicle of a National Board serviced by the Department of Mines. But the war cabinet had no intention of making such a comprehensive commitment in any war industry. It viewed its own role as ensuring an adequate supply of labour, leaving production problems on the ground to be tackled jointly by employers, managers and trades union representatives.

The Essential Works Order was the keystone of this strategy. It enabled the Minister of Labour to schedule an industry, for example aircraft production, because it was essential to the war effort. The establishments in a scheduled industry became 'controlled'. Workers received a guaranteed weekly wage, whose minimum conformed to the agreed trade union (or Wages Board) rate for the job. Their conditions also had to conform with those negotiated by the appropriate unions, for example for overtime and piecework rates. Women doing jobs which were normally filled by men were awarded equal pay. Workers employed in scheduled undertakings were compelled to remain in their jobs unless their employer was willing to release them to work in another scheduled undertaking.

The EWO required the registration of all men and women able to work by age cohort. Registration established their liability to be reasonably directed, i.e. compelled, by the Ministry of Labour to essential war work. Order 1305 made it illegal to strike without first reporting the dispute to Ministry of Labour officials and giving them a chance to settle the conflict. The CPGB leadership labelled these measures as proto-fascist, and an unwarranted infringement on British democratic rights. Bevin was attacked with particular venom. ILP activists and youthful Trotskyists also opposed the EWO's restrictions.

Bevin used his EWO powers to schedule aircraft and engineering firms producing war materiel on 5 March 1941. But as a veteran of the 1926 General Council, he was well aware that tying coalminers to their jobs would be fraught with difficulty. He waited until the Department of Mines could assure him that the MAGB and the MFGB were ready to accept being scheduled and controlled. The process began on 6 March, at a meeting of the JSCC. Edwards, Lawther and Bowman opposed any extension of the working day. They had also opposed the principle of compulsory retention of coalminers by their employers, or ex-miners' compulsory return to the industry, unless satisfactory wage standards could be negotiated and some effective measure of control of the industry be extended to include the workmen's representatives. Their attitude was subsequently endorsed by the Executive. The MFGB officers had invoked the Labour Party 1936 policy statement to justify their demand for joint national control of the industry, including a national wages machinery. The MAGB were equally adamant that they should retain sole control, and refused to contemplate national wages.[694]

The practical political reality was that scheduling coalmining under the EWO required the government to accept responsibility for facilitating serious negotiations between the MAGB and the MFGB. Bevin and the Department of Mines mandarins were well aware that this would mean subsidising coalmining wages. They knew that the coalminers in many districts were not being paid a living wage because significant numbers of coalowners were not behaving as efficient employers with an interest in the industry's future, but rather relying on intense exploitation and low wages to make their profits. The district unions' Executives, including the Federation, signalled their unwillingness to concede the extension of the EWO to coalmining without gaining major concessions first.

The mining workforce were beginning to show serious signs of strain. Not only was the pace of work intensifying, but workers in other war industries, including miners' wives and daughters, were earning better wages for shorter hours. The South Wales RIRO's reports for mid-March 1941 reflected rank-and-file discontent. On 15 March he noted that there had been more strikes in the previous week than any week since September 1939. On 22 March he observed 'a growing tendency on the part of workmen to resort to tactics contrary to the declared policy of their leaders'. He also reported on the SWMF's Annual Conference. Horner had been the only nominee for the new post of full-time president, the first time in the Federation's history that there had been only one candidate.[695]

Although a plethora of conflicting motions were considered by the conference, none from either left or right extreme were passed. (Some had attacked the Executive for rescinding support for the People's Convention, whilst others demanded Horner's resignation.) Having led the Federation's tactical withdrawal of support for the People's Convention, Horner felt sufficiently confident to proclaim his own support for its programme in his Presidential Address:

> Neither the People's Convention, nor myself, stand for Peace at any price, or for Peace as a result of capitulation before Hitler's power ... The Peace I want is ... a Peace that will end divisions in society and between nations ... In these dark hours, I once again proudly proclaim my faith in my own class – the working class in its strength and in its power and my belief that the working peoples of all lands now involved in this war will yet find the ways and means of taking their destinies into their own hands.[696]

Meanwhile, the coal supply situation was reaching crisis point. Because a cold winter had been followed by 'an unusually cold spring', domestic coal consumption had remained high. Coal production had failed 'to reach the weekly figure of 4,500,000 tons required'.[697] The result was acute coal shortages, and many

447

people who were regularly short of coal for heating their houses, or faced with electricity cuts, blamed the miners for lack of effort and absenteeism. But the shortfalls were not wholly, or even mainly, due to miners' lack of effort. Too many coalowners' response to the decline in demand for British coal had been to economise on the maintenance of existing capital equipment, and to cut back on investment in new labour-saving, more efficient machinery for cutting and transporting coal. Many pits were being run down, without any provision for continuing production once their ageing equipment and winding engine gear could no longer be repaired. With British industry working at full strength to meet the war emergency, it was literally impossible for more coal to be mined to meet the increased demand.[698]

Veteran observers, such as Ernest Gowers and Lord Hyndley, were well aware that it would not be possible to expand coal production sufficiently to meet the growing demand from industry, whilst continuing to supply coal for domestic consumption at its peacetime levels. But in March 1941 they occupied positions on the periphery of the Department of Mines. Their political masters, Grenfell and Lyttelton, were apparently unwilling to face this grim reality.[699] In the short run, without new capital investment, there were only two options to meet the shortfall: (i) increase the number of coalminers; and (ii) increase the number of hours which coalminers worked. The first was difficult, if not impossible, because of the armed forces' demand for labour. The second was impossible without the MFGB's co-operation, which would not be forthcoming unless major concessions were made on wages and conditions.

Bevin was not the only member of the war cabinet who anticipated recurring coal shortages, but he was the only one willing to grasp the nettle. Although Churchill had scant regard for the coalowners, he anticipated the unrest on Tory backbenches and local Conservative associations which would follow if the government made concessions to the MFGB in the teeth of MAGB opposition. Attlee and Morrison feared the MFGB's reversion to its old militant habits, and were as reluctant as Churchill to risk class conflict in the middle of the war.

The Cabinet finally faced up to the 'coal problem' in late March, when responsibility for reaching an agreement between the MFGB and MAGB was transferred from the Department of Mines to the Lord President of the Council, Sir John Anderson. The official justification for the move was the inter-departmental nature of the problem. Anderson's qualifications were impressive – a lack of party political allegiance, his extra-departmental position in government and his long experience of civil service committees. A more efficient solution would have been to put the Ministry of Labour in charge. But relations between the Department of Mines and Ministry of Labour had long been difficult. By convention, the Ministry of Labour had no remit to deal with industrial conflict in coalmining. Even though they frequently questioned the judgement of Department of Mines civil servants, Ministry of Labour officials were required to observe the boundaries of demarcation.[700]

Anderson moved the EWO discussions from the JSCC to the Coal Production Council, perhaps hoping that the change of forum would facilitate a fresh start. He was in the chair at the CPC meeting on 27 March, with Grenfell in attendance. Union and coalowners' representatives from each District Production Committee had been invited, a device which enabled both Horner and Watson to play active parts.

Having recently been declared the SWMF's first full-time president by acclamation, Horner felt confident of his own position. His easy familiarity with Evan Williams, and the fact that Williams regarded him as a man of his word, enabled him to play a leading role, with Watson seconding his initiatives. It was the first time that the MFGB side had been serious about achieving a positive outcome. Lawther had declined to engage in earnest with negotiations that would inevitably involve acceptance of the EWO's restrictions on freedom to leave one pit and work at another. Edwards and Bowman had also failed to go beyond ritual exchanges of view. The Northumberland Executive was resolutely against the EWO and a national wages machinery, and they were evidently afraid to move too far away from the majority district view.

Horner agreed with Evan Williams that the application of the EWO to coalmining was problematic, observing that 'it was a dangerous policy and might defeat the purpose it was intended to serve'. He cited the example of miners in South Wales who could only get to work by paying expensive bus fares, because the bus operators offering cheap fares had all been commandeered by the government: 'This was indicative of an attitude of mind. Either mining was all important or it was secondary, that issue must be settled. If it was feasible for Sir Evan Williams to talk of consultation then it was time to talk of an organised national control for the industry.' He demanded, 'like some other industries, a guaranteed weekly wage which would be independent of the busy and the slack period.' Watson reaffirmed 'that national control was needed over both owners and men'.[701]

Once it was clear that the impasse had been surmounted, Anderson left the detailed negotiations to the Department of Mines and Bevin's senior civil servants, with Horner and Watson pushing the MFGB towards an agreement. Although the MFGB negotiators did not achieve a joint National Board to control the industry, they gained two significant concessions: a guaranteed national weekly wage, 'for the first time since the war of 1914–18 ... whether short-time was being worked or not'; and the transfer of the coalowners' prerogative to deal with persistent absentees to Pit and District Production Committees.[702] Horner won an additional concession for South Wales; the guaranteed weekly wage for South Wales miners would continue to be based on a five day week, rather than the six days worked in other coalfields.

On 15 May an MFGB Special Delegate Conference approved the Executive's recommendation to accept the arrangements for applying the EWO, whilst instructing their negotiating committee to seek further minor improvements. SWMF delegates voted against acceptance, along with Northumberland, Cumberland, Scotland and Kent. When Horner and Watson were explaining detailed points of settlement, they acknowledged the depth of feeling amongst delegates at the prospect of miners being tied to their pits. Horner even remarked on the similarity between Bevin's powers under the EWO and those exercised by the Labour Minister in a fascist state, an observation with which Watson declined to take issue. (Bevin finally applied the EWO to coalmining on 9 June.)

Horner had invoked his collective responsibility as an MFGB Executive member at the conference when a delegate accused him of flouting the Federation mandate to oppose the agreement on the EWO. He was, however, unable to use the same justification to explain why he had flouted democratic centralist party discipline, since the Party Centre were formally opposing Bevin's measures. Horner's MI5 file summarised a letter from Fred Thomas, a veteran communist and also vice-chairman of SWMF Caerau lodge to the Party Centre, reporting on Horner's conduct at the SWMF delegate conference which had considered the EWO settlement. His position had been contradictory, 'not only as a Communist to whom the South Wales miners are looking to help them but also as a member of the E.C. of the M.F.G.B ... [B]ut in this case he seemed to behave in a manner up till now always condemned by the Party. That is, not allowing the ordinary rank and file a chance to state their wishes but forcing a course of action on them in a bureaucratic way.' Thomas wrote that Horner had told him that '[he] was afraid of a split with the M.F.G.B. if the agreement should be turned down'. Another letter to the Party Centre noted that Horner's conduct was the only subject discussed at a meeting of the District Mining Bureau in Llanelli. There was 'not sufficient scope given in the [SWMF] Conference to testing the issues and ... no vote taken [on] the Removal of the Essential Works Order and A National Ballot. Walt FERRIS blamed Arthur HORNER but IANTO [Evans] after blaming HORNER at first, later strongly defended him.'[703]

The Party Centre's response was muted. If they had held Horner to account for supporting the EWO, it was likely that he would threaten to leave the party – an outcome they were not prepared to countenance. Nor were they willing to encourage party trade union activists to embark on a serious campaign to oppose the EWO. Dutt rang Cox on 10 June to explain that the Centre had discussed the mining position. Having exonerated Horner, he temporised: 'we do need a statement that expresses our whole position on the issues that have now arisen and we would like you to draft it for World News and Views next week. COX said he would do it today.'[704]

Horner had attended the CPC on 27 May and 18 June, even though, apart from the national officers, he had been the only member of the MFGB Executive present.[705] On 22 June the German invasion of the Soviet Union prompted Churchill's immediate proposal to Stalin for a military alliance against their joint enemy. The communist party's response to Soviet entry was as instantaneous as Churchill's. The CPGB declared that the war could only be won through the efforts of the British working class. Pollitt was re-installed as general secretary, and he and Campbell were brought back onto the Politburo.

> Pollitt threw himself immediately into a campaign to increase war production. He reminded the large working class audiences ... he was addressing more or less continuously that they had to make sacrifices because ... they ... were providing the vital ingredients for victory. 'The Tories must be made to realise that we are not living in 1935, when the last General Election took place ... but [now] when the working class is the main force upon which both production and manpower for the army, navy and airforce depend, and upon whose fighting power, resilience and leadership the fate of Britain depends.'[706]

Horner no longer had to cope with the contradiction of being a communist who formally opposed the war whilst at the same time playing a leading role in the war effort as Federation president. Had Hitler delayed the invasion of the Soviet Union, Horner would probably have been compelled to choose between his union position and party allegiance. The anti-Horner group in the South Wales party would have eventually forced the issue and made it impossible for the Party Centre to excuse his conduct.

Horner had been maintaining his habitual bonhomie by consuming increasing amounts of alcohol. This method of dealing with a threat to psychological well-being was not unusual at the time. Horner, however, found it difficult to control his intake. In early May 1941, his MI5 file noted a report from 'our representative in South Wales by a local business man who has influential contacts in the coal trade'. Having accurately summarised Horner's current predicament, it concluded, 'In recent months, he has shown a tendency towards liquor, especially in the evenings, and looks like becoming a hard drinker. During these periods he is extremely talkative.'[707]

Ethel and Pollitt had both recognised and regretted his lack of control, and had become concerned with the political problems caused by his loosened tongue. Ethel probably developed a variety of manoeuvres to ensure he returned home early in the evening, enabling her to regulate his consumption. In September 1941, the Horners moved to the Gables, a comfortable, detached house in Porthamal Gardens, Rhiwbina Garden Village, a recent, well-designed suburb of Cardiff, which the SWMF Executive had purchased for them.[708] Its exterior was painted white stucco. Since it was a president's residence, family and friends renamed it the White House. The new sobriquet was widely adopted, and postmen delivered letters for the Horners at the White House.

In the wake of Soviet entry into the war, Churchill embarked on another round of government changes. Duncan returned to the Board of Trade on 29 June 1941, and immediately turned his attention to the coal problem. The consequences of Lyttelton's neglect and Grenfell's weakness had still not been addressed by the war cabinet.[709] Duncan dealt with Grenfell by manoeuvring around him. Grenfell had declined to chair the Coal Production Council, which met increasingly infrequently, delegating the job to his Permanent Under Secretary, Sir Alfred Hurst.[710] Duncan now exercised his prerogative to chair the Council, and then convened its meetings with renewed frequency. Presiding over the CPC gave Duncan the power of initiative and also direct access to the MAGB and MFGB. He worked hard to demonstrate the government's changed attitude towards coal questions. As a result of Grenfell's evident indifference, CPC meetings had been sparsely attended by both owners and the union. On 27 August, for example, there was no MFGB representative present.

Horner appeared at the CPC on 17 September, 1 and 8 October; on each occasion he was the only MFGB representative present. His presence was unexplained in the minutes, although he attended regularly thereafter. Iestyn Williams may have taken the initiative in urging Hyndley to speak to Duncan about Horner's ability to turn the situation round. One of the official reasons for the non-attendance of MFGB national officers was the removal of the MFGB's office to Durham in the summer of 1941. Lawther, Bowman and Edwards came to London intermittently and with difficulty, facing a long and frequently disrupted rail journey. By contrast, Horner's train journey was shorter, and less likely to be held up by the priority given to freight carriage.[711] (Monthly Executive meetings continued to be held in

London at 50 Russell Square until the offices were directly hit in an air raid in 1944.)

On 3 December, the first meeting after Lawther's return from the USA, where he had been TUC delegate to the American Federation of Labour convention, the CPC 'unanimously agreed that Mr. Arthur Horner should be invited to be a member'. Horner duly accepted on 8 December, and on 17 December attended in his own right.[712] Duncan had probably been persuaded by civil servants to take the lead in inviting Horner to join the Council. Having had the opportunity to observe him at close quarters, and probably also after sounding out Evan Williams, he agreed that Horner's special personal qualities were indispensable at this critical juncture.

The three MFGB officers were evidently also keen to include Horner, because they finessed his co-option with great care at the MFGB Executive. On 19 December, Edwards told the Executive that Horner had been invited onto the Council by Duncan and asked them to confirm his appointment. In order to disguise the fact that Horner was the crucial addition to the CPC, the Executive requested the CPC to further expand its representation from major coalfields, and nominated John Barbour from the NUSMW and Ernest Jones from the YMA as additional members. The Department of Mines concurred, and re-fashioned the CPC as a comprehensive national forum. Its membership having been expanded to include one union officer and a coalowner from every large coalfield, the new model CPC met on 21 January 1942.[713]

Chapter 13

Winning the War
and Saving the
Socialist Motherland

The four years from the Soviet Union's entry into the war until VE-Day were unique in Horner's life. His conduct as a leading member of the MFGB Executive was critical in determining the course of world history. Horner had now assumed pole position on the MFGB Executive. When the national officers were asked to respond to reports of coal shortages, he was frequently deputed to speak in their stead. The Allied war effort in western Europe depended on a reliable and sufficient supply of British coal. And when in early 1944, miners' unofficial strikes disrupted coal production to such an extent that the war cabinet was afraid that the Allied landing in Normandy would have to be postponed, it was Horner's management of negotiations with the government that defused the crisis. By June 1945, Horner had become a well-known public figure.

But Horner was more than a good communicator. Neither Lawther nor Edwards had developed the facility of thinking strategically. For different reasons, they lacked the will and tenacity to promote the union's agenda through the gruelling rounds of meetings that were the decisive terrain on which concessions were won and compromises agreed. Horner could step into the breach and use the strategic, political and interpersonal skills needed to take the lead. Bowman recognised Horner's outstanding abilities, and co-operated closely with him. The two of them concentrated their own and the union's energies on four areas, which often overlapped: (i) the need to ensure coal production continued at sufficient levels to meet domestic and wartime needs; (ii) the need to minimise industrial conflict; (iii) the need to win significant wage increases for mineworkers; and (iv) the need to use their favourable bargaining position to win national wage bargaining and coal nationalisation. Thus, for example, in the previous chapter we observed Horner making the argument about the connection between the low level of mining wages and the disappointingly low levels of coal production.

Citrine was quick to emulate Churchill with regard to treating the USSR as Britain's gallant allies. He led the General Council in cultivating close fraternal relations with Soviet trade unions, apparently with the intention of stealing a march on the CPGB and left-leaning unions. He also abandoned the tactic he had adopted since October 1939 of treating Horner with open contempt, stopping just short of personal insult.[714] In May 1943, he arranged Horner's co-option onto the TUC Workmen's Compensation Committee, where membership was usually limited to General Council members. This was an arduous job, requiring thorough knowledge of existing compensation law. The committee's urgent task was detailed scrutiny and negotiation on the government's proposed legislation to amend the 1925 Workmen's Compensation Act. It was vital for the MFGB's own political agenda that the miners' interests were fully represented, and Edwards may have insisted that Horner was the best person for the job.[715]

In April 1943 the Labour NEC Coal and Power Sub-Committee was expanded to include MFGB nominees, including Horner. Watson, who had joined the Labour NEC in 1940 on behalf of the MFGB, chaired the committee. It may have been his idea to co-opt MFGB representatives. The meetings gave Horner the opportunity to re-establish cordial relations with veterans of the Labour left, notably Shinwell. Prior to Horner's arrival, Lawther's bluster and habitual gratuitous insults to colleagues had isolated the MFGB. Lawther now stepped back during the proceedings, evidently calculating that Horner's mastery of detail made him the more appropriate person to make the running. Horner quickly became a leading member, earning the admiration of the TUC and Labour junior bureaucrats for his fluent command of the industry's structure.[716]

Horner had also joined the other Federation officers on the regional Invasion Committee, which had been formally constituted in the summer of 1941. But because of the continuing antagonism between the Federation and the Regional Council of Labour, Colonel Sir Gerald Bruce, Portal's successor, found it expedient to meet the TUC's representatives and the SWMF separately. On 9 September 1941, for example, Bruce filed a report of his meeting with Horner and Iestyn Williams to discuss using miners to assist the military in the event of an invasion. Horner recalled, 'We drew up plans for miners to get hold of the power which was to be kept in every pit, in order to blow up the mines if the Germans got there. We were ready to form guerrilla bands in our mountains, and to fight against Nazi tanks with picks and shovels. I used to lecture them about my experiences in Ireland.'[717] Soviet entry into the war also legitimated Horner's de facto participation in the Whitehall war machine.

The government had by now acknowledged that the solution to the coal problem depended on solving the Grenfell problem. Grenfell had made no attempt to persuade the MAGB and MFGB to agree on changes in working practices and conditions. Consequently, unlike their counterparts in charge of shipbuilding, aircraft and engineering, civil servants in the Department of Mines were unable to promote practical measures to increase labour productivity, working hours and management efficiency. But as a long-serving SWMF sponsored MP, Grenfell was considered to be virtually immovable as Secretary for Mines, except by force majeure.

Icy weather in the winter of 1941 to 1942 had further compounded the coal supply problem. The month of February was the most severe for many years. It may have been the inclement weather that finally precipitated the high level decision to replace Duncan with a leading Labour MP who could execute the requisite forensic manoeuvre. On 22 February Hugh Dalton, somewhat reluctantly, became President of the Board of Trade.[718] His diary was soon complaining about the coal industry's byzantine complexities, whilst awarding Duncan full marks for his handling of the difficult situation. After Dalton chaired the CPC on 11 March, his diary described Grenfell as 'my Calvary', and continued: 'The miners' leaders unload great quantities of complaints and Horner makes by far the most effective speech, summing up a series of practical proposals to increase output.'[719]

On 24 April, after a meeting of the war cabinet Coal Subcommittee attended by the MFGB Executive, Dalton observed that Horner 'is much the nimblest'.[720] (The subcommittee was the cabinet's tardy recognition that the coal problem was serious.) Generally positive about Bowman, Dalton recorded few impressions of Edwards, probably because he played such a minor part in meetings. His consistently negative views of Lawther were influenced by his experience as a Durham MP of Lawther's arrogance and unreliability.[721]

Supple described the spring of 1942 as 'the definitive wartime crisis of the coal industry and its management'.[722] Dalton continued the course which Duncan had plotted, but increased the momentum, pressing the war cabinet to accept more drastic, radical intervention by government. He made his own dispositions after consulting his protégés, Hugh Gaitskell, Harold Wilson, John Fulton and Douglas Jay, bright young academics who were serving as seconded civil servants. Having interrogated Department of Mines civil servants, listened to the MAGB and the MFGB, and perused the statistics, they gave Dalton detailed advice and, often conflicting, policy suggestions. After appreciating these virtuosi sparring with one another, Dalton drew his own conclusions. He was simultaneously engaged in a long game to remove Grenfell.[723]

In the House of Commons, Dalton's principal opponents were the group of thirty sponsored coalmining MPs. Since the advent of the coalition government, they had played a spoiling role in Commons debates about coal. For example, after the MFGB Executive had agreed the compromise settlement under which the EWO would apply to mining, most of the sponsored MPs continued to argue for the MFGB's maximum demands. They were also prepared to go to the last ditch for Grenfell.

On 28 April 1942, Horner broadcast a talk on the BBC Home Service radio station, 'Coal Production and the Struggle of the United Nations', during prime evening time, 9.30 to 9.45 pm. The choice of Horner was probably based on the Ministry of Information's judgement that he was the most effective communicator in the MFGB leadership. The talk was vintage Horner; its emotional rhetoric was accompanied by closely reasoned argument. His brief was evidently to prepare the ground for the major concessions which the Coal White Paper would offer the miners. He spoke on the miners' behalf, interpreting their behaviour for the millions of listeners in middle England. His aim was to counter the widespread public belief that coalmining was the one essential industry where working practices and conditions had not been substantially modified to meet the wartime emergency.

He dealt only obliquely with questions of absenteeism and low production, whilst arguing that the coal shortage would only be alleviated by paying miners a great deal more money. The miners were not trying to hold other citizens to ransom, unlike some capitalist war-time profiteers. His peroration was also directed at miners themselves. But its earnest, concentrated passion would have suitably impressed the non-mining audience.

> The general public must give due credit to the miners for the manner in which they have performed their exceedingly difficult task ... Miners resent criticism from ill-informed persons who could not do the miners' job and who would not tolerate the conditions of life which obtain in the mining villages.
>
> The mass of miners are very highly patriotic; they love their country and desire to make it a better place to live in ... They love freedom and ... they are convinced and loyal fighters in the struggle against these dark Forces [fascism and nazi-ism] ...
>
> They remember the lavish promises during the last war, and the terrible experiences which were forced upon them in the years following the war ...
>
> The problem set before the mining industry is, to overcome and cancel out these war difficulties by better organisation and a stronger will to produce ... [The] intelligent and efficient organisation of production is not the responsibility of the mineworkers alone. Those responsible for the direction and supervision, must co-operate with the mineworkers so that the ideas of the men might be given prompt attention and opportunity be provided to test out these ideas in practical day to day work at the colliery ...
>
> That there is a small minority who fail to realise the seriousness of the present situation, is undeniable, and

459

I am sure that mineworkers everywhere will deal with those elements who are refusing to carry their fair share of the burden of coal-production ...

At this time when the Soviet Union is engaged in a life and death struggle with the Axis Powers, when we ourselves are calling upon our Government to undertake measures which will ease the pressure upon our gallant allies, when our own countrymen are facing death daily, we cannot expect to remain immune from the stress of war ...

I want consumers to realise that it is not possible for the industry, to produce coal in sufficient quantities to permit the same free use of it as in Peace times.

The maximum economy must be practised, and supplies cannot be made available for luxury purposes, when every ton is needed by vital industries and the domestic consumer ...

If miners are expected to carry on their work under conditions of unusual risk of life and limb, due to wartime conditions, then compensation should be provided which will enable the victims and their dependants to live above destitution level.

I mention these things because they are burned into the heart and mind of every mineworker, and so as to re-assure them that whilst they are asked to give of their best in this period of grave national emergency, we shall claim the recognition for present sacrifices from the community in whose interests the sacrifices are now being made ...

Let every miner be inspired with the thought that the coal he produces will fire the furnaces of the armies of freedom in which mankind's most hated enemy, Fascism, will be destroyed for ever.

For if Coal is the bread of industry, we need to remember in these fateful moments of world history that bread means life.[724]

Dalton combined with Bevin, who was thoroughly conversant with working conditions and industrial relations in coalmining, to push through a comprehensive policy change on coal, which was signalled in a government White Paper. It was the product of weeks of intense political discussion in Cabinet, and close-fought disputes about the shape of future government involvement in the wartime coal industry. Both men were acutely aware that the industry was functioning on borrowed time.[725] Supple noted that '[b]y May the situation appeared to be getting out of hand ...'. In illustration, he cited Dalton's diary entries recording Watson's observation that in Durham the coalfield was 'seething with unrest ...'. In the third week of May the number of man-days lost through industrial action were eight times the pre-war average.[726]

The MFGB Executive responded to the upsurge in militancy by pressing for higher wages. On 20 May 1942, Dalton noted in his diary: 'Ebby Edwards gets me in a corner and speaks ill of his colleagues. He says that he has never known wage discussions conducted so badly as this time through the press by Lawther ... He says that the miners' organisation is in a very bad state. There is certainly a great lack of mental grip as well as of good comradeship among the miners' leaders.' Dalton noted approvingly the comment from Gordon Macdonald, Lancashire mining MP, that Lawther 'always led from behind; you never know where he is.'[727]

Against this troubled background, Dalton pressed ahead with the White Paper. His diary described a meeting between Anderson and the miners' leaders to discuss it, probably convened under the auspices of the Lord President to sidestep Grenfell:

> They [MFGB leadership] have not really thought out their proposals ... Horner then says that he wishes to put some questions to JA [Anderson] ... They have to contend with psychological difficulties. He has never been received so coldly at meetings in S. Wales as during the past few weeks. The men must feel that they are not working for the profit of the owners. Asked whether EPT [Extra Profits Tax] does not give them this assurance, he replies that the men just 'won't believe it at all'.[728]

The White Paper was published on 3 June. As a socialist member for a constituency with many mining votes in a mining county,

Dalton was pleased by what he and Bevin had managed to achieve. Its compromise terms balanced the conflicting demands of the erstwhile radical re-organisers in the Department of Mines, the conservative MAGB and the MFGB, whose Executive were still formally committed to the maximalist demands of the 1936 Labour policy document.[729] A new Ministry of Fuel, Power and Light would assume responsibility for the strategic operation and overall decision-making about coal production and distribution, and electricity generation and distribution. The day-to-day running of collieries remained the coalowners' prerogative. But the MFGB had won a far-reaching reform of collective bargaining. In the teeth of fierce opposition from the MAGB, Dalton and Bevin had convinced the Cabinet to underwrite the expense of a comprehensive national wages system. After the meeting of the Coal Sub-Committee of the National Council of Labour on 4 June, Dalton noted that 'AH [Horner] says their decision must depend on whether the choice is between this and something better or this and nothing at all'.[730]

An MFGB Special Delegate Conference was scheduled for 11 June to vote on the Executive's recommendation to accept the White Paper. The White Paper would be debated and voted on by parliament on 10 to 11 June, where the government's majority virtually assured its acceptance.[731] Anticipating that the MFGB Executive would need tangible evidence of the government's bona fides about wages in order to win delegates' approval, Dalton and Bevin exercised their joint departmental authority on Friday 5 June to appoint an independent Board of Investigation, chaired by Lord Greene, Master of the Rolls. Its brief was to report on miners' wages and future arrangements for national collective bargaining.[732]

The Board of Investigation was routinely described as the Greene Committee. Its first meeting took place on Tuesday 9 June, giving the MFGB Executive spokesmen firm evidence that the process of levelling up miners' wages had already begun. The Committee opened its proceedings with evidence from Edwards. He began apologetically: 'we are here as a result of a telephone message only – we have prepared a case'.[733] Nevertheless, a bulky, mimeographed document was duly distributed to the committee and MAGB representatives. The national officers had travelled back to the Northeast on Friday evening, apparently leaving

Horner in charge of preparing the evidence. The only employee working at 50 Russell Square was Joe Elliott, who was evidently acting more as a caretaker, doing little more than keeping the accounts in order. Horner turned to the coalmining experts at the Labour Research Department, Billy Williams and Margot Heinemann. They worked with Horner and Elliott to prepare the evidence at the LRD offices, located conveniently near Russell Square. Horner praised Elliott for being 'at our service throughout every minute of the time we were working'.[734]

Working with Horner over this hectic three days was not Heinemann's first encounter with Horner. She had met him at LRD Executive meetings, and at communist party functions. But it was her first opportunity to observe him at close quarters, engaged in serious union work. She recalled 'his tremendous grasp of where he wanted to go and also how far he calculated he could take the Board towards the miners' aims'. The MFGB evidence, accompanied by a raft of statistics, set out a case: firstly, that the miners had to take home enough pay for their families to live on; and secondly, that they had to justify miners' wages moving back towards the top of the manual workers' league table. By late Monday night the evidence had been written and typed onto mimeograph stencils. The LRD chairman, Henry Parsons, and another staff member, Noreen Branson, stayed to help Heinemann and Williams duplicate and collate it.[735] The MAGB was unable to respond in kind. Evan Williams could only speak ex tempore; his lack of statistical evidence was a serious handicap to the coalowners' case.

Despite the Greene Committee's deliberations, the MFGB national officers and Horner were apprehensive about how delegates would react to the White Paper on 11 June. On 10 June, Dalton's diary entry noted that he had been hauled out of the House at 2.30 pm by Willie Hall, Labour MP for Colne Valley, saying: 'Lawther must see me on a most urgent matter and that a "major crisis" has arisen at the ... [MFBB] Executive Meeting this morning ... I find W.L., J.B., and A.H. in the Whips' Room. They want to know whether the Govt. has really decided in favour of a National Wages Board ... I read them the relevant passage from the White Paper and also from the Minute of appointment of the Board of Investigation. Reassured, they depart.'[736]

At midnight on 10 June, the Ministry of Fuel, Power and Light commenced existence. The new ministry absorbed the Department of Mines, whose *apparat* was transferred wholesale from the Board of Trade. Churchill's appointment, as Minister of Fuel, Power and Light, of Lloyd George's son, Major Gwilym Lloyd George, the long-serving Liberal MP for Pembrokeshire, was tactically astute. Although he lacked direct coalmining connections, he was nevertheless known to both the SWMF and the South Wales coalowners. An additional effect of these institutional changes was that Grenfell's job disappeared. He was not sacked, merely made redundant. The Ministry's MFGB connection was provided by the appointment of Tom Smith, a Yorkshire miners' MP, as parliamentary secretary. Smith had been privately critical of Grenfell's performance, and had been one of the few mining MPs to even obliquely question his performance during parliamentary debates on coal.[737]

At the delegate conference on 11 June Horner introduced the Executive's recommendation to accept the White Paper. His discursive speech was a dazzling display of propaganda. His purpose was to deflect the anticipated criticism from many left-wing delegates, including Tom Stephenson, MP for Cumberland, who complained that Dalton should have gone further and nationalised the industry. Whilst acknowledging that there were opportunities to win further improvements, Horner argued that the White Paper was a giant step towards the miners' goals:

> I have heard it said here this morning that it is possible that whatever is conceded and whatever plan might be produced the men won't work. Well, unfortunately, if the men in this industry won't work, this country will be defeated in a short time ... And our men will work. (*Hear, hear.*) The Russians are working, and British prisoners are working in the German mines ... We are not considering this question in a vacuum ...
>
> The Government's scheme for production is in our opinion most unsatisfactory ... we think that the Government is placing itself in an untenable position ... In our view events will demonstrate that by experience the Government will be compelled to resort to further measures, and Sir John Anderson in the discus-

sion yesterday indicated that they might be compelled, and if necessary will, resort to further measures ... We prefer Government control over the owners even though the industry rests in the hands of the owners, in preference to the archaic and impossible situation that obtains in the mining industry.

After the speech, Lawther commented from the chair, 'You will agree with me that nobody here now can say that he does not understand what we are seeking, nor what the White Paper contains, after that very plain and lucid statement from Arthur Horner ... .'[738]

The Delegate Conference approved the White Paper by a show of hands. Lawther apparently judged it impolitic to call for a unanimous vote. However, unlike previous wartime conferences, no district union or individual delegate called for a card vote. It is likely that a card vote would have revealed that delegates from some districts, for example Cumberland, had been mandated to oppose the Executive. A show of hands enabled the MFGB to display a united front, whilst the dissidents, who were opposed to any outcome except nationalisation, remained anonymous.

On 20 June, the Greene Committee's Interim Report was presented to Bevin and Major Lloyd George. Its recommendations for an immediate substantial wage increase and a guaranteed minimum weekly wage marked the first tangible step towards a national wages structure. Bevin was adamant, and the rest of the government agreed, that it was essential to distance the Ministry of Fuel, Power and Light from the collective bargaining process. The MAGB and the MFGB had to accept responsibility for industrial relations. When the Committee reconvened in early July to consider the structure of conciliation and negotiation machinery, Lord Greene's introductory remarks included a favourable reference to South Wales having 'very elaborate agreements and rather elaborate machinery if I remember rightly, for settling disputes'. Edwards had rejoined tartly, 'in fact, I think there is better machinery elsewhere than in Wales'. Nevertheless, when it reported in March 1943, the committee recommended a comprehensive national conciliation machinery which strongly resembled the South Wales arrangements negotiated by Horner and Iestyn Williams in 1937.[739]

As the state machinery for dual control of coalmining evolved, the MFGB required well-briefed representatives. Whilst the owners retained their formal prerogative over day-to-day production, in practice their authority was diluted by the Ministry's control of production decisions, and insistence that MFGB representatives should play a full consultative role at all levels in the production process. Neither Edwards nor Lawther were prepared to apply themselves to these new tasks. Horner and Bowman therefore stepped in to restore the order and momentum of MFGB business. As a result of their application, the MFGB London office maintained an operational capability, although the servicing of officers and district unions was often haphazard. They were assisted by Edwards' son, Denis, who had been employed as a clerk.

When Joe Elliott died unexpectedly at the MFGB Annual Conference in July 1942, Edwards voiced his despair at the final days proceedings. 'My position is rather an unfortunate one as General Secretary from the point of view of the Staff ... Anyone who runs a Trade Union office knows the loss of a man [Fred Hill] who has been 18 years in the office ... Now we are left with only one employee [Denis Edwards] in one of the most critical and important stages in the history of this Federation. It is very difficult ... to do justice to the membership. I feel really depressed.' In August, Edwards applied for Sid Ford's release from the army on the grounds that MFGB administration was vital for the war effort. The government accepted that unions needed to maintain a functional bureaucracy, and Ford returned to Russell Square in September. He resumed his vendetta against Ebby Edwards, whilst working amicably and efficiently with Horner and Bowman. Horner spent two or three days a week in London, deputising for Edwards in the MFGB office, and attending meetings at the Ministry headquarters in Millbank. Bowman probably came to London as often as trains and district union business allowed.[740]

In June 1942 Bowman replaced Ebby Edwards as secretary of the strategically important and time-consuming Executive Re-organisation Subcommittee. The rump of the progressive group on the Executive hoped to use the Greene Committee's

466

recommendation for a National Negotiating Committee and a National Reference Tribunal to put the question of one united mineworkers' union back on the MFGB's agenda. They succeeded in this at the MFGB Annual Conference in July when they obtained a resolution of intent to proceed with a scheme for one national mineworkers' union; it was passed with only two opposing votes.[741]

Horner liaised closely with Pollitt and Allison when he was in London. The CPGB leadership were waging a high profile campaign for a Second Front in western Europe to relieve the pressure on the USSR. Horner and Bevan were prominent in promoting its aim, arguing the need for equality of sacrifice. Pollitt was spending one weekend a month in South Wales at this time, nursing the parliamentary constituency of Rhondda East, where he hoped to defeat Mainwaring at the next general election. He often stayed with Arthur and Ethel.[742] The visits enabled him to observe and influence the South Wales communist party at close quarters. The Party Centre continued to view the internal situation in South Wales as volatile and potentially explosive. Although Cox was energetically promoting the campaign to maximise coal production, it was evident that many young mining activists and various revolutionary militants would not be so easily reconciled.

On the home front, Horner prioritised the Battle of Coal Production. At the TUC in September, he developed the theme of his April broadcast, incorporating the General Council into his vision of how the mineworkers were helping to win the war:

> In the mining industry, largely due to the support which they [the MFGB] had received from the General Council through the National Council of Labour, they had now arranged to establish what he considered to be the most advanced form of joint control that had ever existed in this country. They were aware that as a consequence ... they had undertaken responsibilities as well as having received the opportunity to have a say in production ... He was hoping that as a consequence ... workers would demonstrate that they had a capacity for initiating methods which would increase production, but which did not necessarily mean harder or longer work ... He

believed that there was, in the experience of workers of
this country, the possibility of unleashing an initiative
which had never yet been known in all our industrial
history. The story of Stakhanovism was not the story of
harder work; it was the story of greater inventiveness,
greater initiative, and the exercise of enthusiasm in the
task in hand.[743]

Horner's optimism proved misplaced. Output per manshift,
the standard measure of miners' productivity, failed to increase.
Nevertheless, between June 1942 and October 1943 there were
no coal shortages, probably due to the combination of an unusually mild winter, vigorous BBC propaganda about the need
for fuel economy, and more efficient coal distribution.[744] The
sixteen months were a comparative respite for the MFGB and
the new Ministry.

Horner's domestic life was especially full. For a short time,
the whole family were re-united at Rhiwbina, and a grandchild
arrived. John Tofts had been told in the autumn of 1941 that
he was being posted outside Britain, and Vol asked Arthur if she
could come back home. She had decided to become pregnant,
and wanted a safe, secure place to give birth. Vol's and John's
son, Julian, was born on 17 April 1942. On 28 December 1942,
Rosa married Cliff Marshall at the Cardiff Registry Office. John
Tofts remembered that Arthur had found some excellent green
bean chutney to serve with fish for their wedding feast. Cliff was
serving in the RAF, and Rosa moved to a village near where he
was stationed. She 'camp followed' him loyally wherever he was
transferred, until he was posted overseas in 1945.[745]

During the portion of the week that he was in Cardiff, Horner
participated in the city's political socialising, and evidently revelled in having the opportunity. Lorraine Griffiths first met
Arthur and Aneurin Bevan at the Grand Hotel. Her husband,
John, worked for the BBC and:

> we went out to meet Vic Jones who worked on the *News
> Chronicle* ... [H]e said, 'I'm meeting a couple of interest-
> ing people tonight, would you like to come along?' ... And
> so we went ... and there was Aneurin Bevan and Arthur
> Horner ... and I must say I was charmed by both of them.

> They were ... very very natural and asked for your opin-
> ion ... I think they had been friendly then ... And what I
> remember was that, you couldn't stop laughing because
> Aneurin Bevan said to Arthur 'what's the party line on
> that Arthur?' with his stammer you know ... and he said
> 'what do you mean what's the party line?' and he said
> 'oh come on' and Arthur said 'oh all right' he said 'I'm
> a bugger for a line' ...

When he discovered that the Griffiths lived near him in
Rhiwbina, Horner insisted that they come home with him and
meet Ethel. Having given them a cordial welcome, she produced
a meal. 'And of course John sat down and made himself at home
straight away ... we just sat down and from then on we were great
friends.'[746] The house was big enough for the Horners' close
friends from Mardy, Charlie and Hannah Jones, who had been
regular house-guests in Upper Tumble and Felinfoel. As at the
two Datchas, the White House required Charlie's manual skills
to get it into shape. And Wal Hannington, who had been elected
to one of the new AEU National Organisers' posts in 1942, took
care to arrange his duties to include South Wales so that he could
stay with Arthur and Ethel. Having had few occasions to socialise for some years, Arthur and Wal were delighted to be able to
spend leisure time together.

Pollitt's weekend visits were also occasions of great conviviality.
Alf Davies, in particular, often came to see him. It is also possible
that Pollitt and Hannington effected a mutual reconciliation in
the emollient atmosphere of Ethel's kitchen.[747] Arthur and Ethel
both cherished their friendship with Pollitt; it stretched back
over twenty years, punctuated by emotional debts and shared
memories of surviving Hornerism. Pollitt appreciated Ethel's
hospitable working-class household, maintained with pride
but without social pretension. He also observed her efforts to
manage Arthur's drinking, and probably made it clear to her
that he was a reliable ally in this struggle.

When he worked at the Federation office in Cardiff, Horner
liked to enjoyed himself. He had inherited an efficient, well-
administered organisation, which Tom Richards and Oliver
Harris had maintained in robust running order. Horner was also
a highly efficient administrator, but in addition he made the

office a more lively, sympathetic place to work. He continued his predecessors' professional approach to union business, but set a new example of egalitarian camaraderie and informal manners. He improved human relations by introducing welfare and fringe benefits for all staff, including travel allowances, a war bonus for under 21 year olds, and a pension scheme.

Under this new regime, Federation employees became accustomed to abandoning hierarchy in the lunch hour. Most of the young women who worked in the office lived in Cardiff and went home. But Sybil Griffiths, the newly arrived shorthand-typist and telephonist who lived in Newbridge in Monmouthshire, accompanied the older women, Elsie Lewis and Molly Hughes, Arthur's secretary, down to the Federation basement for lunch. They joined Horner, Saddler, Harold Finch, Joe Hughes, Haydn Lewis and any agents who had business in Cardiff. Ianto Evans was another regular visitor, and often drove Horner to any appointments. They all enjoyed the cooked meal provided by the caretaker, who was a relative of Tom Richards. Afterwards everyone played sevens, a highly competitive card game with arcane rules; chicanery, bluffing, and high spirited banter prevailed. Sybil remembered:

> Of course, Arthur Horner was the biggest cheat. He was terrible. And Bill Saddler used to say, 'Arthur it's two o'clock'. Arthur [said], 'Oh come on, one more game.' Bill Saddler replied, 'Arthur don't lead these people astray.' He used to love his cards.[748]

Sybil Griffiths had started work at the Federation office in November 1942, aged eighteen. She travelled to Cardiff on a double-decker bus, where she frequently encountered Bill Saddler, who travelled the same route. She recalled that Horner's war bonus and travel allowance had added £1.17s.6d. to her weekly wage and reinforced her loyalty to the SWMF. She remembered Horner's working style as efficient, but informal. 'It wasn't an office, it was one big family ... It was a treat to go to work because everybody was so friendly ... Mr. Horner was a bundle of a man, little, and always smiling. He was full of nonsense. He was a kind man.'[749]

470

Because he was spending so much time in London, Horner delegated much routine business to Saddler and later to Dai Dan Evans, who was appointed Chief Clerk on 1 January 1943. Although Dai Dan later acquired a reputation for dour sobriety, Sybil Griffiths remembered him at this time as being a prolific joker, fitting in with the prevailing conviviality.

One routine duty which Horner tried not to delegate was his weekly discussion with Iestyn Williams. The two met over lunch, and usually hammered out agreements in the disputes that colliery managements and lodge committees had passed up to them for settlement. Although they were local, they often involved points of principle for both sides, i.e. surrender of management prerogative and/or long-standing workplace custom and practice, making them potentially capable of sparking off a district or even coalfield strike. Sharing responsibility for their resolution in the wartime emergency deepened their mutual regard. Sybil Griffiths remembered that Arthur routinely arrived back at the office 'half cut', because Iestyn would 'fill him with whiskeys'. Mrs Evans, the caretaker, always had a plate of sandwiches ready and Molly Hughes always waited for him, even though he did not always return to the office.

Horner took care to maintain a strict Chinese wall between his party and his union obligations. He would not receive any party functionary in the Federation office, and he instructed Sybil Griffiths not to put telephone calls about CPGB business through to him. As Chief Clerk, one of Dai Dan Evans's duties was apparently to act as a reliable conduit between Horner and Cox. His go-between role was facilitated when the South Wales district party offices were at No. 9 St Andrews Crescent, near the Federation moved to No. 22. Lorraine Griffiths recalled, 'There used to be jokes that there was an underground passage, to connect the two, and it was Arthur that started all that. He used to play on people's nonsense ... people would say they're just doing what the Party tells them to do over there.'[750]

The Party Centre and Cox were certainly keen to exploit Horner's status as an important wartime union leader. Horner remained preoccupied with MFGB affairs, however, and apparently indifferent to the manoeuvres which Pollitt and Allison devised for promoting the party line in the trade union world. For example, his MI5 file noted a conversation at King Street

471

between Pollitt and Dutt at the end of the September 1942 TUC. Pollitt said that this Congress:

> had been the first time when the Party had been in the position of the decisive factor. Speaking in the names of the [miners'] UNIONS, HORNER had apparently made one speech of five minutes, which was reported in the Press and on the B.B.C. and POLLITT said he had worked very hard on this other speech, which he gave HORNER on Tuesday night and had stopped and argued with him on the subject. The speech was attacking the A.F. of L., demanding the reopening of negotiations with the C.I.O ... and it explained that the Trades Unions in the Soviet Union were bona fide Trades Unions ... and it had proposed that the Congress should send an address of greetings to the Trades Unions of the entire world, of the United Nations against the Fascist countries, and to those enslaved by Fascism ... HORNER had gone [to see Lloyd George] and given POLLITT'S notes to (ALLAN) ... [who] had made the speech very well and impressively but it obviously did not carry as much weight as if HORNER had done it.

Pollitt had berated Horner for leaving Congress, telling him 'that he had no business to take on other commitments and that he was to tell LLOYD GEORGE that the Congress was as important for getting coal production as anything else. This had apparently left HORNER unimpressed and POLLITT was furious as he said that the speech he had taken so much trouble with would have put the Party "on top of the world".'[751]

Horner's MI5 file noted that in May 1943, Pollitt had asked to see Horner at King Street. Horner arrived at 17.37 as agreed. The following dialogue was recorded:

> H[arry] ... What about signing the pledge?
> A[rthur] What about it?
> H ... you'll take no notice, but it's best to be careful ... (I'll have to have a talk to you?) For the last three weeks JACK TANNER and other draughtsmen, sent word to me, but I have always warned you about the treacherous charac-

ters of those b. you are knocking around with BOWMAN and LAWTHER ...

HARRY went on to say it was 'everywhere about the blinking booze', that he had let the Party and himself down. ARTHUR (HORNER) said HARRY drank twice as much as he (ARTHUR) did, and they had an argument over this. HARRY gave ARTHUR a good talking to – said he felt ashamed of him, etc., ... The argument developed – but it was not very clear ... The latter tried to defend himself by saying that the T.U. fellows never saw him, and that he never made a fool of himself; he had never drunk in Cardiff 'during the day at all'. But HARRY had talked to 'the lads' there, and they were very worried.

About 18.10. ARTHUR left.[752]

Pollitt and Allison were determined to seize the opportunities presented by increased interest in British communism as a result of the Anglo-Soviet alliance. The MFGB and the AEU remained the CPGB's most influential trade union supporters. Jack Tanner, AEU President since 1939, had been a consistent, often outspoken, supporter of communist causes. An AEU motion urging the withdrawal of the 'Black' Circular No. 16 had been narrowly defeated at the 1942 Congress. By the following Congress, Allison and Pollitt had organised such formidable support for the Circular's withdrawal that Citrine decided to pre-empt another debate. On the first day, without prior warning, he announced that the General Council had decided to withdraw the Circular.[753] This meant that the General Council could no longer exclude communists. Thus when the TGWU nominated the communist busman, Bert Papworth, for the General Council at the 1944 TUC, he was duly elected without any objections from the TUC *apparat*.[754]

The party leadership were also hoping to advance on the political front. Pollitt had sent Middleton a fresh application for affiliation to the Labour Party in December 1942. He omitted any reference to the CPGB's obligations as an affiliate of the Communist International, but pledged that the British communist party was prepared to abide by Labour Party conference decisions and observe its constitution. Watson may have consulted Horner before proposing to the Labour NEC on 27 January 1943 'that the Communist Party be asked whether if they became affiliated, they would still consider themselves bound by the instructions of the Communist International'. Having rejected Watson's motion, the NEC voted by 15 to 4 to turn down the CPGB's application.[755]

The Comintern was officially dissolved on 8 June 1943, enabling the party leadership and individual communists to argue in formal good faith that they no longer had any ties with Moscow. The MFGB tabled a motion at the Labour Conference in mid-June 1943 supporting the CPGB's application, 'provided the Communist Party agrees to accept and abide by the constitution of the Labour Party'.[756] Lawther proposed the motion eloquently, refuting the NEC's contention that the Labour Party would be broken by the CPGB's affiliation:

> That is not the experience ... of the Mineworkers' Federation in meeting with members of the Communist Party as trade unionists. I have been present during the last twelve months in deputations to Mr. Morrison ... along with our colleague Arthur Horner, and I have heard nothing but compliments paid to Arthur Horner as a member of the Mineworkers' Federation for the way in which he deals with practical issues. And yet we are told that if he comes inside the political party there will be an upset of arrangements. I want to suggest to you that that is sheer begging the question that is involved.

Supported by the AEU and NUPE, where Bryn Roberts probably cast the block vote, the motion was rejected by a 3 to 1 majority.[757] Although the defeat was disappointing for King Street, the substantial number of votes cast for the MFGB motion embarrassed and alarmed the Transport House *apparat*.

The palpable increase in communist influence inside the trade union movement precipitated counter-offensives from Transport House. In March 1943, centre-right loyalists in South Wales announced the formation of a Labour Industrial Group to act inside the SWMF to oppose 'the undue influence of the Communist Party in the coalfield'. Assisted by Transport House in Cardiff and some Federation MPs, they had limited support on the Federation Executive. But they continued to make their presence felt, and were evidently determined to take every opportunity to attack Horner.[758] Horner responded in a *Daily Worker* article:

> During my seven years of office as President, there have been many difficult situations where we have had to make decisions which were unpopular, but on every such occasion these decisions were, to all intents and purposes, unanimous. The Labour and Communist members on the Executive ... have contributed fully towards the ultimate decisions and there has been complete unity ... The C.P. has never approached a majority and there are at least twice as many Labour members as Communists on the Executive.[759]

Confident of firm support from the SWMF Executive and many sponsored MPs, Horner was not slow to settle scores. In 1943, the SWMF's traditional programme of May Day meetings included communist speakers in virtually every venue. (Because of the war, the forty-six meetings were held on Sunday 2 May.) The Federation Finance and Organisation Committee even had the audacity to book Pollitt and Ernest Brown to speak in the Rhondda alongside Mainwaring, Alf Davies, Sydney Jones and Alderman John Evans. Isabel Brown spoke in the Anthracite; Palme Dutt spoke in the Rhymney Valley, flanked by Bevan, Horner and Paynter; Rust and Saddler occupied the same platform in Monmouth.[760] It is likely that when many of the speakers reminded their audience that such an all-in platform had not been seen since 1926, they received an appreciative response. Some of those attending were politically literate activists, for whom the spectacle had great emotional resonance, if not a unanimously positive response.

The TUC General Council's unqualified acceptance of Horner as a trade union leader was confirmed in September 1943, when he was elected, along with John Brown of the Iron and Steel Confederation, as TUC fraternal delegate to the 1944 AFL Convention. His overwhelming victory over two other candidates would have been impossible without Citrine's and Deakin's tacit support. Facing a left-wing groundswell inside the

475

TGWU, Deakin evidently found it expedient to cast the TGWU's votes for Horner.[761]

Meeting after the 1943 TUC, the General Council selected Ebby Edwards as its chairman and Congress President for the twelve months to September 1944, when he would preside over the TUC throughout Congress week. Although serving as TUC President was viewed as a union leader's crowning glory, it was not merely honorific. The office-holder chaired both the General Council and its 'inner cabinet', the Finance and General Purposes Committee. An ambitious President, who shared Citrine's priorities, was able to launch significant initiatives, as Bevin had done in 1937.

Edwards was the first miners' TUC President since 1910. Being chosen by his fellow General Council members was evidence not only of his personal standing, but also of Citrine's preference. Citrine may have been keen to bind the MFGB Executive more closely into General Council decisions. The MFGB Executive had been applying intense pressure on the General Council to provide unqualified support in their negotiations with the government, and Citrine was concerned to moderate what he regarded as the MFGB Executive's implacable determination to use the war as a means to redress the balance of class power in coalmining.

We have already observed Edwards' demoralisation and progressive withdrawal from the routine business of the MFGB Executive; becoming TUC President now presented Edwards with an acceptable reason to disengage further. At its first meeting after he became President, the MFGB Executive agreed, presumably at his request, that Denis Edwards should be seconded to assist his father on TUC business. On 21 October 1943, Edwards informed the Executive he was still having difficulty fulfilling MFGB obligations, and requested 'some scope in connection with this matter'. The minutes record that he was assured by them that the fullest possible assistance would be rendered.[762] Both he and the Executive were evidently clear that he would cease from now on to have any formal role in the administration of MFGB business.

Edwards' formal withdrawal had a minimal practical impact on the Russell Square regime. The de facto arrangement, whereby Horner and Bowman had driven the MFGB's business in Whitehall, arranged the Executive's agenda, and tended its subcommittees, simply became more transparent. Lawther continued to avoid any detailed administration. Horner and Bowman probably briefed him 'just in time' before meetings. Because he was a quick study, Lawther would intervene at some point in the proceedings to maintain his premier status, usually supporting the points the other two had been making. As the Coal Problem worsened, the three men remained headline news. Industrial and Labour correspondents christened them the Three Musketeers, an apt sobriquet, given their contrasting characters and physical demeanours. They were presented as paladins, like their French namesakes, courageously shouldering the responsibility for alleviating the coal shortage. *Pathé News* and photographers followed them in and out of the Ministry of Fuel and Power, where they executed Horner's stratagems to extract concessions in return for co-operating in coal production drives. At this juncture, the three men probably spent more time in one another's company than with their wives and families. Their strong personal bond was reinforced by Horner's habitual cheerfulness and the other two men's appreciation of his abilities. Although Horner's equals in intelligence, neither Bowman nor Lawther could match his ability to tailor tactical moves in accordance with a long-term aim. Nor could they emulate his virtuosity in the hand-to-hand combat during negotiations.

Anglo-American planning and preparations for the invasion of France proceeded throughout the autumn of 1943. The presumption was that there would be a sufficient, reliable supply of British coal available to meet the requirements of industry during the build-up of production of war materiel. However, as we have already noted, miners' productivity had not increased. Supply and demand for coal remained in precarious balance. The Coal Problem precipitated a succession of political crises, played out in parliamentary debates, arguments in the war cabinet and an apparently endless round of negotiations between the MFGB, the MAGB and Gwilym Lloyd George and Bevin.

The government's aims were threefold: firstly, to ensure that there was sufficient coal mined to meet domestic and industrial demand; secondly, to show the public and the House of Commons that the Ministry of Fuel and Power was acting effectively in difficult circumstances; and thirdly, to keep the peace between the MFGB and the MAGB. Horner understood these desiderata better than most of the other players. He ensured that the MFGB remained proactive, and that the MFGB Executive always had a response to the increasingly shrill accusations that the miners were unpatriotic slackers, indifferent to the fate of the soldiers and sailors who were sacrificing their lives for their country. The coalowners' political ineptitude, and Churchill's reluctance to be drawn into a confrontation with the miners, increased the attraction of Horner's coherent suggestions for solving the Coal Problem.

Horner's regular visits to King Street kept Pollitt and Campbell up-to-date with the MFGB view of the coal supply situation. And Pollitt had also remained in regular contact with Cripps, who had joined the war cabinet in February 1942. They knew that a crisis of coal supply in 1943 was likely, even if winter temperatures were normal.[763] Pollitt and Campbell were keen to ensure that a public case was made deflecting any blame for the coal shortage away from the miners. Consequently, the Party Centre planned a series of *démarches* in which the union and its activists were seen to be encouraging and promoting miners to prioritise production, despite the continuing obstacles presented by the coalowners' negative attitude and the government's refusal to move away from dual control. Pollitt began attending meetings of the CPGB National Mining Bureau, and probably presiding over them, a role usually taken by Allison. Its work was praised by the Executive as a model to be emulated by the other industrial bureaus. Rather than merely discussing internal union affairs, the bureaus needed to 'work out positive lines of policy ... so as to meet the general needs of the people; they would deal with wages and conditions ... only in relation to a general scheme for improving production and services, and not as isolated trade union issues': 'Under Comrade Pollitt's guidance ... [the Mining Bureau] has been developing this approach ... [But even here] a certain widening is possible and desirable.'[764]

Pollitt and Campbell refined propaganda which emphasised the miners' contribution to the war effort, but also sought to inspire them to even greater efforts, at the same time as motivating the rest of the working class to demonstrate solidarity by emulating the anticipated productionism. It was government's duty to ensure that miners' grievances about management's arbitrary behaviour and obstructive attitude towards increasing production were summarily dealt with by the Ministry's District Production Managers. It was miners' duty to ensure that their knowledge and determination to win the war were utilised in Pit Production Committees and Production Drives. This line received unconditional support from most leading party mining activists, including Abe Moffat and Willie Allan. The impact of Soviet entry on this veteran cohort had been profound. They gave no quarter to party members and militants who argued that domestic class war came before the defence of the Socialist Motherland.

In July 1943 Bevin had warned the House of Commons that he might find it necessary to direct a proportion of the young men who were being called up into the armed forces into coalmining. In one of the regular debates on 'Coalmining Situation', held on 12 to 13 October 1943, Lloyd George was uncharacteristically forthright in citing coalminers' conduct as a reason for the coal shortage. 'There was unrest and a deterioration in discipline. There were many stoppages of a trivial kind ... [and] the lack of confidence which the men showed in their own leaders and the frequent disregard of the advice of trade union officials by their members.'

Churchill spoke on the second day of the debate on behalf of the war cabinet, in response to repeated challenges from mining MPs, including Bevan, to abandon the system of dual control in favour of nationalisation. Whilst expressing profound sympathy and boundless admiration for the miners, he declined to infringe the coalowners' prerogative:

> We must also be careful that a pretext is not made of war needs to introduce far-reaching social or political changes by a side wind ... It [nationalisation] would raise a lot of argument, a lot of difference of opinion ... and unless it could be proved to the conviction of the House and of the country, and to the satisfaction of the responsible Ministers, that that was the only way in which we could win the war, we should not be justified in embarking upon it without a General Election.[765]

It is not necessary to follow the parliamentary debates and Cabinet agonisings about the Coal Problem. We should, however, note Horner's offensive to deflect attempts by the backbench Conservatives, the MAGB and the press to place the blame for coal shortages on the miners. He gained emotional and political sustenance for this from close co-operation with the CPGB leadership, who were anxious to play their part in winning the battle for coal. Campbell was probably the only one who appreciated the intellectual logic of Horner's Clausewitzian approach. The others acquiesced, because their principal priority at this conjuncture was to ensure the opening of the Second Front. Horner's strategy provided them with a positive alternative to rank-and-file militancy.

On Saturday 16 October 1943, the Party Centre convened a Coal Conference. An internal Circular from Pollitt explained that it had been attended by 'Party District Secretaries, the members of the Mining Bureau and certain specially invited comrades who have an expert knowledge of the Mining industry [probably Heinemann and Billy Williams]'. They discussed 'how best our Party could help to convince the mass of the people of the seriousness of the Coal situation' and also help the MFGB 'in fighting for the policy they consider can solve the existing crisis'.

An ambitious campaign was mapped out:

> In the principal cities, our Party should organise special mass demonstrations, at which we can explain the situation ... the urgent need for making every kind of economy fuel consumption ... To bring pressure to bear on all Local Authorities, with a view to their calling Towns Meetings, issuing publicity material, that can help fuel economies in every possible way ...

Pollitt concluded:

> We assure you that if this practical line of campaign is worked out throughout the country, the crisis in Coal can be solved ... with the keynote of 'Britain's Responsibility to the Miners and the Responsibility of the Miners to Britain'. It is our responsibility to show how by a united

effort of the whole of the working class behind the miners, a speedy victory [in the coal crisis] can be gained ... The debate in parliament ... has solved nothing, and we shall see how in the next few weeks the Coal situation again comes very sharply into the political picture.[766]

Pollitt's internal Circular was adapted and published in the re-emergent *Daily Worker* as a CPGB Executive Committee Statement.[767] He anticipated that the Statement would be 'accepted by the South Wales [Miners' Federation] Executive, put by HORNER to the M.F.G.B. and [then become] ... the MFGB's programme of demands.' King Street expected that the MFGB and SWMF 'would launch the campaign, and appeal to other working-class organisations, and the Communist Party would be foremost in backing up the campaign'.[768] These ambitious plans were stillborn. For the MFGB to have embarked on such a radical campaign, much higher levels of personal and political commitment would have been required from all district unions.

But the party published a pamphlet by Horner, *Coal and the Nation. A Square Deal for Miners*, under its own imprint in late October. The evidence of its communist provenance appeared in very small italics on the inside front cover. Horner addressed readers as a leading MFGB activist, and there was no direct reference either to the CPGB or his membership of the CPGB Executive in the text. Whilst criticising the government for minimising the gravity of the coal crisis, Horner argued that it was a profound mistake for miners to be diverted by political conflict about the industry's ownership. Even though Churchill had been wrong not to nationalise the industry, miners still had to concentrate on producing more coal:

> I have often heard coal called 'Black Diamonds'. Well, to-day every piece of coal is more precious than diamonds, and should be treated with greater care. That is why you ought to add your voice to those others who are demanding the rationing of fuel ...
>
> If you are a Labour man or woman, call upon the local Labour Movement to rouse the people in their locality to a sense of realism and responsibility ...

> The nation needs coal and it needs the miners, but it has got to be prepared to treat us as one of the most important sections of the working population and to provide wages and working conditions and all the facilities that modern civilisation has in its power to give these workers, who are the salt of the earth ...

He declared that:

> every responsible miner, whether in the rank and file or the leadership has deplored and tried to prevent [strikes]. But they are small compared to what one would expect, in view of the record of the industry in its treatment of the men. It is the same spirit which causes miners to rescue a comrade who is buried under a fall; as that which actuates him to support a comrade in conflict with the employer, right or wrong ... [769]

Party networks were mobilised to ensure that Horner's pamphlet was distributed widely, particularly to miners' lodges. In South Wales, some communist activists 'said that it was the best pamphlet that had ever been published'. Nevertheless, Horner came under pressure from the Labour Industrial Group for writing a pamphlet under the CPGB's imprimatur.[770]

The MFGB Executive continued to insist that miners' wages should be further increased. On 28 October 1943 the MFGB Negotiating Committee met Gwilym Lloyd George, seeking assurances that the government would increase coal prices if necessary, i.e. in the event of a significant increase in the national minimum wage rates awarded by the National Reference Tribunal, the successor to the Greene Committee. They also wanted a guarantee that miners' increased war wages would continue into the peace and reconstruction. Lloyd George refused to promise either. Nevertheless, the Executive proceeded with their submission to the Tribunal. Their justification was that miners' wages had remained stationary since the Greene Committee Award in June 1942, whilst other workers' wages had continued to increase, 'with the result that the position of the miners in the list of industries had fallen back from 29th place to 40th or 41st place'.[771]

In December 1943, Bevin finally exercised his powers under the EWO to direct men between the ages of eighteen and twenty-five into coalmining. On 5 January 1944 the National Reference Tribunal commenced hearing the MFGB's case for a substantial increase in national wage rates. Horner and Joe Hall acted as Assessors to the Tribunal, flanked by Evan Williams and WA Lee for the MAGB.[772] As an Assessor, Horner apparently observed the conventional Chinese Wall, and took no part in the preparation of the MFGB case. Yvonne Kapp, who worked at the LRD, told Billy Williams that Ebby Edwards had delegated its preparation to Sid Ford, and that neither Bowman nor Lawther had assisted him. The result was partial and unconvincing.[773]

The national officers may have been lulled into complacency because '[e]veryone knew in the winter of 1943–44 that a new coal-mining wages award was coming'.[774] Nevertheless, the Tribunal chairman, Lord Porter, required empirical evidence before he could justify awarding the miners a sizeable increase. Horner helpfully presented the essential figures using Margot Heinemann's small book, *Profits in the Coal Industry*, published by LRD. Despite Lee's protest at the introduction of new evidence, Porter asked Horner to see them. 'He looked at the table and said "This is very interesting, alright Mr. HORNER I know what the point is now."'[775]

The Porter Tribunal's decision was published on 22 January 1944. Within its remit, i.e. to recommend wage increases to compensate for wartime conditions, the award made sense. The weekly minimum wage was increased to £5 for underground workers and £4 10s for surface workers. Although both amounts were £1 short of the MFGB's demand, they were nevertheless substantial. Nevertheless, the Porter award 'produced the severest crisis of industrial relations of the war'.[776] To explain this paradox, it is necessary to examine the wages structure of the industry in some detail.

The Porter award provided flat rate increases to the weekly minimum wage. Its unintended consequence was to significantly reduce the traditional differential between the higher earning hewers at the coalface and the lower paid surface workers and underground hauliers and labourers. However, because piece-rates for hewers in the coastal coalfields were significantly lower than in the inland coalfields, differentials in the coastal coalfields were less affected by the Porter Award.[777] Not surprisingly, the first unofficial strikes against the Award began in inland coalfields, Lancashire, Staffordshire and Yorkshire, only days after its publication.[778] The outbreak was contained after an MFGB Special Delegate Conference accepted the Executive motion, noting that the Award 'had created serious anomalies' and instructing the Executive to 'consider the whole question of the wage structure of the industry and enter into immediate discussions with a view to an early revision of the same.' It was summarily moved by Edwards and seconded at some length by Horner.

Horner argued that the Porter Award put the miners in 'a position more favourable than any we have ever had before. We were discussing with Major Gwilym Lloyd George the week before last the possibilities of a reconstruction of the wages system in the mining industry as a post-war problem. The Tribunal's decision has made it an immediate war problem; it has done more – it has enabled us to discuss this revision on an irreducible minimum of £5.'

He cited the unofficial strikes, threats of others in some coalfields, and 'suggestions and ... proposals before the day is out that the British mining industry should be brought to a stoppage. He responded from the front:

> We are not bucking the fight with any of our members who would advocate such a policy. We believe that we can convince the great majority of the members gathered here, and the miners in the coalfield ... [that further strikes would mean we] should be taking responsibility for prolonging this war ... with the position that all the factories would have to stop if we stopped, we could not without a better case than we have got ... having been given the greatest opportunity in our history ... fling back the challenge to the Government that we would endanger the Forces in order to [win further improvements] ...

He ended with a pledge:

> All our plans are aimed not merely at getting a wage increase to-day, and something else tomorrow ... our

whole strategy is aimed to raise the status of the miner to a position that he never previously held, to place him in his rightful position as the most important man in this country, entitled to the best treatment from the country.[779]

Horner's speech convinced Spencer to change the Nottinghamshire vote. He announced his intention to vote for the Executive resolution, because he could now see there was no practical alternative. But Ted Hall, the Lancashire miners' secretary, was implacable, and called for a general coalfield strike. After Bowman summed up, the Executive resolution was passed, with Lancashire the only dissenting district.[780]

The MFGB Executive put their case for a post-Porter top-up at the newly created Joint National Negotiating Committee on 3 February. The MAGB agreed that the anomalies resulting from the Award should be addressed, and that negotiations to restore the narrowed differentials should proceed at district level. This outcome was apparently reached without serious disagreement, an indication that pre-negotiations had probably taken place, possibly between Horner and Iestyn Williams in Cardiff.

However, also on 3 February, the Ministry's Controller-General of Coal, Hubert Houldsworth, informed the two parties that there would be no blank cheque from the government to guarantee district advances. Lloyd George confirmed this caveat on 4 February. The war cabinet had only agreed to underwrite the Porter Award. The government evidently had no intention of being bounced into paying for its aftermath, either through sanctioning increased coal prices or through providing further direct subsidies to the industry. The MFGB Executive were clear that industrial unrest would continue until the differentials had been restored. The MAGB were adamant that their members could not afford to fund adjustments to district wages systems necessitated by a short-sighted decision from the National Reference Tribunal.[781]

At this point, an intense political conflict broke out between the industry and the government. If coal prices increased, engineering and aircraft companies would be able to demand higher prices from the government for their war materiel, because the coal to power their boilers cost more. Engineering and aircraft workers' unions would be able to justify demands for increased wages to fund the increased cost of domestic coal, electricity and town gas. Veteran politicians, and particularly Churchill, were determined to avoid being condemned for capitulating to blackmail from the MFGB. Even though the MAGB were equally complicit, they feared that the *Daily Mail* and *Daily Telegraph* would place sole responsibility on the miners. Consequently, the war cabinet remained resolute. Bevin was probably the only member who recognised that there was likely to be further trouble.

On 8 February Houldsworth was informed by telephone that the SWMCA and the SWMF had reached a district agreement to correct the Porter anomalies, on the presumption that the Government would foot the bill. Both parties denied having been told on 4 February that Lloyd George had confirmed Houldsworth's refusal to fund any increases. It was difficult for the government to accuse them of lying, since Lloyd George had evidently not believed it was necessary to write formally to the district coalowners and unions. He had evidently telephoned the MAGB, and 'in the case of the mineworkers it was communicated, not given by the Minister personally to their representatives'. Court's judgement was that the South Walians behaved disingenuously. 'The Minister's refusal to commit himself on the financial point may have appeared to them ambiguous ... But if this was their doubt, then district negotiations should have been held up until the principle had been thoroughly thrashed out.'[782]

The close relations between Horner and Iestyn and Evan Williams underpinned their joint willingness to take the calculated risk that the war cabinet would capitulate. It is unlikely that any other district coalfield union would have taken this step into the unknown; coalowners in other district had much less financial reason to do so. The three men were willing to force the government's hand in order to pre-empt widespread industrial unrest. Once district negotiations had reached official agreement on restoring differentials, unofficial action would quickly cease and production could continue unimpeded.

On 11 February Lloyd George met the Lord President's Committee to discuss the acute coal problem which the South Walians had precipitated. A press release was issued denying that the government had incurred any responsibility for post-Porter increases, apart from ironing out very minor anomalies. The war cabinet confirmed this position on 12 February. Court observed, 'There are traces of confusion in the policy of the Ministry [of Fuel and Power] ... There was a failure to keep pace with events.' Negotiations in the other districts gained momentum:

> The new piece-rates negotiated in South Wales were understood to raise the rates by fifteen per cent. This was too much for the better-paid [inland] regions, such as Nottinghamshire, Derbyshire and Yorkshire. So far, they had been disposed to accept the award as it stood. Now they declared that they were not willing to see a change in piece-rates elsewhere without enjoying some increase in their own district. The second week in February saw the industry carrying through on a district basis ... a general raising of wage rates throughout the industry, intended to preserve the old relations between grades of workers and rates of pay ... [783]

By refusing to pay the increases unless the government agreed to compensate them, the owners were colluding with district unions. When the two parties realised that the war cabinet were standing firm, they knew that a second wave of unofficial strikes was inevitable. These would coincide with a period when war factories were operating at maximum intensity to produce sufficient supplies for the Allied landing in France. There were strikes on 24 February in Durham, on 6 March in South Wales, and in Scotland on 8 March. The biggest outbreak was in South Wales; 100,000 miners were affected, and 550,000 working days were lost. In Durham 7400 men came out, and 15,000 in Scotland.[784]

At this point, Bevin persuaded the Cabinet to empower Gwilym Lloyd George to start discussions with the JNNC on a complete overhaul of the industry's wages system. He explained that once the government recognised the need to fund the increases required to address the post-Porter anomalies, they also had to accept responsibility for re-structuring the industry's national negotiating machinery. Unless the government acted to impose swingeing structural changes on the industry's wage structure, problems of anomalies and district differentials would continue to recur. As the expert, it is not surprising that Bevin 'not only carried the Cabinet with him but, working closely with Lloyd George ... played the leading role in the negotiations'. Together they met the JNNC on 8 March.[785]

Not surprisingly, Bevin and Lloyd George found an open door in their discussions with the MFGB and the MAGB. The principal obstacle remained the war cabinet. Horner travelled up to London on 14 March 'so that he, the Controller, HOLDSWORTH [sic], and GWILYM could have a heart-to-heart talk':

> At this meeting, it had been decided that the increase of the piece-workers wages should date from the previous Monday [8 March]. HORNER seemed to think that this decision was of great importance, and said what he now had to do was get sufficient pressure from South Wales to get Mr. EBBY EDWARDS to ask the Minister [Lloyd George] for an answer, and he now knew what the answer would be. He hoped that by the following Thursday, a pronouncement would be made to the whole country that the wages structure might take a little time to adjust, but it would date from the Monday before. HORNER said what a big thing it all was and there was no other industry where wages had been doubled during the war, and there was now a guarantee of those wages for the next four and a half years ... GWILYM couldn't make it more because that would have upset the agricultural workers, whose guarantee was just a month or two short of that.[786]

News of the government's concessions facilitated a full return to work in South Wales by 18 March, and in Scotland by 20 March. On 16 March, however, a third strike wave commenced in Yorkshire and continued until 11 April. It was the most serious, involving 120,000 miners; one million working days were lost.[787]

Although most of the unofficial stoppages were short, their effect on production was highly disruptive.[788] Bevin told the MFGB Executive:

[A]greements had been entered into with the Allies, definite dates had been fixed and the ability to carry out the obligations with the Allies were being jeopardised by the strikes. The South Wales strikes had not had decisive results, because by one means or another the works had been kept going. But the Yorkshire stoppage on top of South Wales had caused a very serious position. In Sheffield and Coventry, more than 100 vital works had stopped production, and they had to bring coal from the North, not to work the factories, but in order to keep the ovens warm. BEVIN had indicated that they were manufacturing at Sheffield a certain armament which was considered to be an essential condition to the launching of military undertakings.[789]

The strikes were a severe test of nerve for the MFGB Executive and the war cabinet. The principal protagonists, Horner and Bevin, were playing for extremely high stakes, the successful completion of preparations for the D-Day landings. They needed an agreement which was acceptable to the government and would get the miners back to work. Horner calculated that Bevin shared the progressive MFGB leaders' belief that a radical reform of the industry's wage structure was the way to ensure maximum production. He recalled Bevin saying: 'they were at the parting of the ways when they could break all this machinery or develop it.'[790] Not surprisingly, the coalowners were hostile to such far-reaching rationalisation, recognising that it brought the likelihood of permanent national wages machinery nearer. Bevin 'ignored' the MAGB throughout the negotiations, however, 'concentrating his attention on the miners' representatives'.[791]

Further meetings between the MFGB Negotiating Committee, Bevin and Lloyd George followed on 23 and 24 March. Horner told Pollitt:

BEVIN had pointed out that he could be put on the spot and told [by the War Cabinet] that either he must agree to the measures to enforce continued production or else he would have to resign. He had told them that before he would undertake the role of Noski (Phonetic) [Gustav Noske, SPD Minister of Defence in the 1919 provisional

489

German Republican Government], he would resign, and he had pointed out that the people who would succeed him and GWILYM would not be as favourable to the miners as they had been.'[792]

Noske had ordered the summary military repression of revolutionary soldiers' and sailors' soviets and works councils in January 1919. This profoundly shocking event was seared in the memory of young British socialists at the time, including Bevin and the MFGB Negotiating Committee. Bevin clearly intended them to interpret the reference as meaning that if the MFGB did not hammer out an agreement with him and get their members back to work, he would leave the summary military repression to Winston Churchill!

Horner and Bevin displayed characteristic virtuosity from opposite sides of the bargaining table, probing each other's positions to identify their respective sticking points and establish where there was room for manoeuvre. Watson's report to the MFGB delegate conference on 12 April captured the heat of the moment:

He [Bevin] said he had not time to go into the details of this Agreement, but he was quite willing to leave that to the Minister and to the Negotiating Committee ... providing that when the final settlement was reached then it was a settlement final and binding upon the Districts. Arthur Horner then said to Bevin, 'Are you prepared to consider a wider interpretation of the words "skilled workmen"?' He said, 'Now Horner, don't you try a fast one on me the way you did with your local Owners, which would have cost us 20 million pounds' ... Bevin then used the words, 'I am prepared to take a gamble' ... The figure of a million pounds was mentioned, the figure of a million-and-a-half was mentioned, and he even went so far as to mention a million-and-threequarters.[793]

Horner was equally graphic to Pollitt:

ARTHUR said that he was not frightened of BEVIN withdrawing the Porter award or the security plan [guaranteeing miners' wartime wage levels to 1948], because the Government couldn't afford the result that would cause. All the way through, it seemed to ARTHUR that they were saying that they must have a measure of stability before they started on this big job [the invasion of France]. They were going to have to throw an unknown number of men into battle, dependent upon support from the rear, and they were not prepared to do it, unless they were assured beforehand that there would be that support.

The Porter Award strikes confronted communist and left-wing miners throughout Britain with a clear existential choice. If they accepted the need to maintain coal supplies in order to fulfil the Allies' undertakings to open the Second Front, it was logical to argue against militants who proposed strike action at lodge meetings and vote against strike resolutions. The Party Centre faced an uphill struggle to keep their mining members united. On 2 February 1944, Pollitt introduced an emergency item on the coal situation at the Executive Committee. He tabled 'a number of proposals agreed to at a meeting of Party mining comrades', and endorsed by the Politburo. These proposed a proactive role for the party in support of the MFGB Executive: 'To appoint a Party Commission to work out guiding lines for the CP on wages policy ... To carry out a campaign explaining the positive gains under the Porter Award, and for the real functioning of Pit Production Committees, and a drive for increased Coal Production ... '.

Unusually, the proposals were not unanimously approved. Cox insisted on recording his opposition, and the Executive agreed to circulate his views. His intransigence was partially due to the strong pressure being applied on him by the South Wales DPC. Horner had been sending apologies for non-attendance at DPC meetings again, evidently preferring to evade rather than inflame old antagonisms. On 19 March at the request of the Politburo, Horner introduced the discussion on coal at an Executive meeting. Cox's opposition to accepting the Porter Award subject to negotiated improvements was even further entrenched. The Executive endorsed the Politburo's position and agreed that Horner and Pollitt would produce a pamphlet immediately, presumably along the lines of *Coal and the Nation*. Events overtook the pamphlet's production. Although the Politburo continued to follow Campbell's lead in standing behind Horner, some were uneasy about being seen to oppose the unofficial strikes. At the Politburo meeting on 30 March, a majority regretted Horner's isolation from the South Walian party leadership and from those rank-and-file miners who were on strike:

> PETER [Kerrigan] said that the thing he was really worried about was the position in the Executive of the S.W.M.F., because it was becoming an impossible position when HORNER started denouncing the Communist Party [South Wales DPC] ... PETER asked what the reaction of the Labour party was going to be to the fact that HORNER was fighting (?) the workers on the one hand, and the [communist] Party on the other. He thought that this would all come up again later on, when the Labour people and the Communists would not be united and 'MR. HORNER' would be used as an example. HARRY said he had given him a good talking-to the night before, and he didn't know what more he could do ... HARRY spoke of the D.P.C. meeting where all the comrades were against ARTHUR and were 'ready to jump.' He could not do anything then. They were all after him. PETER said gloomily, well, they would have a nice problem on their hands if the M.F.G.B. [Delegate Conference] agreed to accept the [MFGB Executive's] decision [to agree the new national wages structure]. JOHNNY [Campbell] spoke of the situation that would arise in Scotland and S. Wales and said the comrades there would have to face it.[794]

A contributory factor in the Politburo's disquiet was their failure to comprehend the complexities of the miners' wages system. On 14 March: 'HORNER asked HARRY if he understood the allowances and the wage formula. HARRY didn't understand any of it. So HORNER sighed heavily, and said, "Oh dear, dear, this is terrible. I don't know how to make you understand." He then gave HARRY a lesson on the intricacies of a piece-workers wages.' On 30 March, Pollitt complained: 'He's [Horner] the only bloody man that I can understand when he puts a case and he knows that.'[795]

The continuing strikes assisted Bevin in inducing Churchill and the war cabinet to agree a package, that represented an 'extensive compromise with the miners' position'.[796] Horner and the MFGB Executive then had to face down left-wing militants in all districts, who were hostile to giving any ground to government ministers, and unwilling to betray the unofficial strikers in Yorkshire. Joe Hall and other YMA officials were notably reluctant to support the MFGB Executive. Horner's and Campbell's sang froid was vindicated when a combination of public pressure and news of the government concessions precipitated the collapse of the unofficial strikes in Yorkshire.

By 11 April, when the National Mining Bureau met, production had resumed virtually everywhere. Pollitt's relief was palpable:

> HARRY said that he wouldn't have believed it if anyone had told him a short time ago that the Miners could hold up the Second Front, but in view of what was happening on the Eastern Front, with the possibility of shortening this war by months and after what they had been told by a responsible Cabinet Minister, he had been shaken in relation to all that ... ARTHUR pointed out that the M.F.G.B. had issued no statement except the resolution of the [Executive] meeting, which he had drafted ... [H]e had gone to the meeting prepared to fight BEVIN to the last, if he used threats, but no threats had ever been made ... He said that he also was shaken if, after all the speeches that the Party had made about the Second Front, they might be the people who gave the alibi. Nobody could justify what had happened in Yorkshire. This brought forth some argument, and several critical remarks about JOE HALL.[797]

On 12 to 13 April, an MFGB Special Delegate Conference gave the Executive a mandate to accept the agreement subject to further improvements being secured. Scotland, Lancashire and

Kent opposed the Executive's recommendation on a card vote. When Lawther asked delegates 'to give us a unanimous vote', even these die-hard districts fell into line.[798] The agreement between the government and the MFGB was signed on 20 April by Bevin, Lloyd George and the MFGB national officers. Lasting four years, it committed 'the government to maintain control of the coal industry after the end of the war'.[799] District wage rates were replaced by 'a national minimum wage, consolidating the wartime advances ... fixed at a higher rate than in any other industry, while piece workers were to be given proportionate increases'.

This time, as Horner had promised and Bevin had gambled, the coal problem dissipated. As the Cabinet minutes recorded on 3 May, after the settlement had been considered, 'The moment seems propitious, therefore, for the removal of coalmining from the limelight.'[800] During the first four months of 1944, two million tons of coal were lost owing to unofficial disputes; another half a million tons were held up through transport difficulties. 'After the strikes, however, the increased effort of the miners to make up their loss of earnings resulted in an unexpected increase of output.'[801] Those who had been on strike were keen to make up the money they had lost; the majority who had remained at work were keen to reap the fruits of the higher wage rates. Strikers and non-strikers were also conscious that they had a critical part to play in the war effort.

From May 1944, young miners were amongst the highest paid youth workers in any industry. In 1938 adult miners had been virtually the lowest paid manual workers, eighty-first in the earnings league table. After the Greene award in 1942, their position in the league table moved up to twenty-third. After the 20 April agreement, they were very nearly at the top of the list, overtaken only by skilled trades in the munitions industries, where large amounts of overtime were worked. 'Given their successful resistance to the working of any overtime, the miners had indeed done best of all out of wartime labour scarcities and sensitivities.'[802]

Horner and his supporters in the SWMF, both communist and Labour, had led the campaign to get the strikers back to work. Paynter remembered that in the Rhymney Valley, where he was agent, 'I was able to get the lodge committees and mass meetings to ... continue working ... but other pits were out, with the result that for a whole week the position was one of complete chaos with some men on strike and others working, some men going in and coming out like a concertina.'[803] As a result of Horner's success, the mining MPs found it expedient to dilute their opposition to him. Although seasoned anti-Horner right-wingers inside the Federation, such as Edgar Lewis, were keen to carry on the fight, strong pressure was evidently applied from Transport House in Cardiff and the MPs. When Lewis stood against Horner for the Presidency at the SWMF Annual Conference in April 1944, he received only four votes. The men who had been on strike had apparently not taken offence at his implacable opposition to their unofficial action; they were probably also impressed by the size of the wage increase he had obtained from Bevin.

Veteran activists recognised that Horner's conduct in February-March 1944 was similar to the course he had pursued since 1934. Principled militants who believed he had taken the wrong path then were not surprised by his attitude to the disputes in 1944. Other militants, whom Horner had convinced in 1934 to 1939 by force of consistent, sustained argument and notable practical success, continued to support him. This continuity may have been the reason underlying Vol's memory of her father being hardly disturbed or disorientated by the 1944 strikes. He had indeed been there before. He knew what to do, and why he was doing it. In 1944, however, he probably felt vindicated by the support he received from hitherto doubting communist and left-wing activists who were swayed by the additional consideration that the Soviet Socialist Motherland was at risk.

Horner remained vigilant throughout the strikes in guarding his right flank. He probably discouraged opposition in March 1944, when Cliff Prothero, on behalf of the Regional Council of Labour, attended the SWMF Finance and Organisation Committee to discuss the forthcoming May Day meetings. Prothero offered as speakers all the South Wales mining MPs, except Griffiths, George Hall and Grenfell, who had meetings elsewhere, and promised to obtain additional speakers of national stature from London. His suggestions were adopted; and, although further arrangements were left to lodge committees, the outcome was that no CPGB speakers were officially invited onto Federation platforms – except where left-leaning committees took the initiative.[804]

The CPGB's support for Horner's line precipitated the exit from the party of the leading anti-Horner mining activists, including DR Llewellyn. Although few in number, they remained implacable revolutionary militants. They had joined in with the ILP, Trotskyists, and the right-wing Industry for Labour group to lead the final strikes, which were, however, smaller and more sporadic than those in Yorkshire. Most of the strikers had been neither revolutionary nor unpatriotic, but merely parochial. Horner vividly recalled the situation to Pollitt on 14 March:

> He said the whole thing had been an 'awful bloody business', but there were 60,000 going back next day. Monmouthshire were holding a big meeting which would probably result in a return to work, and then apart from a patch in ABERDARE valley, it was finished ... FERNDALE Lodge where the [centre-right Labour] industrial group fought the Party like hell, wouldn't even let JACK BAKER speak; Blackwood, Markham and Tredegar had held three meetings where the voting had resulted in a tie each time; some places were unanimous and in others they wouldn't even let the men vote. It had been the most unreasoned thing and it had come to almost Fascist tactics in some place. Some committee men in some places had been beaten up in the black-out. All the miners' wives and daughters were working and they [striking miners] were glad of a chance to dig their gardens and stop at home. HORNER was full of indignation and spoke of the delegates apologising for their men. He went through the various districts and said that it was not so bad in the Rhondda, but in Aberdare there were so many I.L.P. men. HORNER told HARRY that it had all been boiling up for a long time, and he said that they howled down anyone who mentioned the war. He said that the men had been so stupid and when he had told them that they were risking British lives, they had just said that it was a bloody lie. ARTHUR showed him an extract from a West of England paper headed 'Dogs, get back to Work'. ARTHUR said that

that was why he had agreed to write an article in the *Daily Express*.[805]

The D-Day landings commenced on 6 June 1944, fifty-five days after the last unofficial strikes had ended in Yorkshire. After a week's intense combat it was clear that the meticulously planned amphibious invasion had been successful. The Second Front had finally been opened, and the Allies' victory over fascism was now only a matter of time. There was no respite for the Three Musketeers, however. Bowman and Horner were preoccupied with the preparations for the twice-postponed MFGB Special Delegate Conference, which would consider and vote on the Model Rules for a unified miners' union. (The rules had been tabled but not debated at the 1943 Annual Conference.)

Horner had time to ponder the new world emerging from the ashes during his weekly train journeys between South Wales and London, and also in the evenings at the Hotel Russell in London. Much of his reflection would have been in the company of intimates, either with Bowman and Lawther or with Pollitt and Allison. Sometimes, through Pollitt's and Allison's careful conniving, these two networks coincided, and Labour correspondents were also present. There was much pause for thought about the era opening before them.

Horner's sense of time passing would have been intensified by the deaths of three close comrades-in-arms: Tom Mann in March 1941; Oliver Harris in January 1944; and Albert Inkpin in April 1944. Horner spoke at Mann's funeral, along with Ben Tillett, Krishna Menon and Gallacher. He probably spoke at Harris' funeral. He was one of the pall-bearers at Inkpin's funeral, along with Gallacher, and Tom Bell.[806] Plans for the belated birth of the new united mineworkers' union in August 1944 and the prospect of speaking at the AFL Convention in New Orleans in December 1944 would have provided a welcome injection of excitement. Horner had new continents to see and old friends in the CPUSA to look forward to seeing.

Notes

Abbreviations

The following abbreviations have been used for frequently cited sources:

CWM   *Colliery Workers' Magazine*
DE   *Daily Express*
DG   *Doncaster Gazette*
DH   *Daily Herald*
DT   *Daily Telegraph*
DW   *Daily Worker*
FBI file   Arthur Horner's FBI file obtained by Professor Michael Casey.
FBI report Report on Arthur Horner's visit to Colombia, passed from MI6 to MI5, dated 18 January 1945, PF 601.V.2, NA Kew.
GAR   Glamorgan Assizes Report on Arthur Lewis Horner, compiled by Ferndale Police office, 9 February 1932.
ICR   *Incorrigible Rebel* by Arthur Horner
LM   *Labour Monthly*
MAF   *Miners' Against Fascism* by Hywel Francis
MG   *Manchester Guardian*
MGen   *My Generation* by Will Paynter
MRC   Modern Records Centre, Warwick University
NA   The National Archive, Kew
PHMM   People's History Museum, Manchester
SMT   Serving My Time
ST   *Sheffield Telegraph*
SWCC(SU)   South Wales Coalfield Collection, Swansea University

SWM	*South Wales Miner*
SWML	South Wales Miners' Library, Swansea University
SWV	*South Wales Voice*
WL	*Workers' Life*
WM	*Western Mail*

Note on pre-1969 sterling

Conversion from
pre-1969 sterling to post-1969 sterling

s.	=	shilling(s)
d.	=	pence
£1	=	20s.
1s.	=	12d. (5p.)
10s.	=	50p.
1d.	=	0.417p.

Footnotes

Chapter 1. Introduction

1   Barry Supple, *The History of the British Coal Industry, Volume 4, 1913–1946: The Political Economy of Decline*, Clarendon Press, Oxford, 1987, Table 1.1, pp. 8–9; William Ashworth, with the assistance of Mark Pegg, *The History of the British Coal Industry, Volume 5, 1946–1982: The Nationalized Industry*, Clarendon Press, Oxford, 1987, Table AI, pp. 672–3.

2   Harold Hutchinson, 25 June 1958. He was writing on the eve of the NUM's Annual Conference, which would be Horner's last as general secretary.

3   Horner's height and appearance are detailed in his MI5 file, PF601/V1, NA Kew.

4   JRL Anderson, *MG*, 9 December 1960.

5   Hugh Clegg described the post-war cohort of union leaders as 'below the standard of its predecessors who had led the unions before the war and ... through the war years.' *A History of British Trade Unions since 1889, Vol. III, 1934–1951*, Clarendon Press, Oxford, 1994, p. 319.

6   Giles Romilly, 'Gentle Revolutionary: A Portrait of Arthur Horner', *The Changing Nation*, A Contact Book, Contract Publications Limited, London, 1947, pp. 36–50. This number was the seventh in the series of Contact Books, whose editor was AG Weidenfeld. The Board of Editorial Associates included JD Bernal, Richard Crossman MP, Kingsley Martin, Harold Nicholson, Stephen Spender and Solly Zuckerman.

7   VL Allen, *Trade Union Leadership, Based on a study of Arthur Deakin*, Longmans, 1957. Frankenberg recalled that James Klugmann and Jock Kane had both expressed approval of his undertaking the biography. Klugmann was engaged in the research for the first volume of the CPGB's official history. Jock Kane was a veteran communist activist in the Yorkshire Area NUM. N Fishman, interview with R Frankenberg. Deakin's mother was a domestic servant, and he was illegitimate. When they moved from Warwickshire to Dowlais in 1901, Deakin's mother married soon after,

and may have left Arthur Deakin in the care of the Harding family. Horner's elder sister Annie married Joe Harding, probably around 1910. Joe's father ran a boot mender's shop in Dowlais, and it is possible that Arthur Deakin and his mother first met the Hardings at the shop. Arthur Deakin had spent much time in a cobbler's shop during his first ten years, which may have been where his father worked. The Harding family treated Arthur Deakin like an adopted son, and he lived them for some time. During Joe's courtship of Annie, Arthur Deakin may have accompanied him on visits to 76 Clare Street to see Annie, where he became friendly with Arthur Horner. The two Arthurs may also have met at meetings at which Keir Hardie spoke and they both attended. Deakin visited Annie and Joe Harding in Merthyr when he visited Wales as a TGWU national official. (They lived in Christopher Terrace in Merthyr, 300 to 400 metres from Clare Street; in 1948, after Horner's mother had died, they moved to 76 Clare Street.) The two Arthurs may have met when they were both back in Merthyr on the same weekend. *ICR*, pp. 183–4; letter from Hubert Harding to N Fishman, 29 July 1999. He recalled that in 1948 'Arthur Horner and Arthur Deakin were very much in the news, I remember my father [Joe Harding] saying, one is my brother in law, and the other was my brother when we were very young, he did explain but my memory is a blank on that.' Deakin's entry in the *Dictionary of Labour Biography*, eds. J Bellamy and J Saville, Macmillan, 1974, Vol. II.

8 I worked as a secretary to the NUM research officer between the winter of 1969 and the spring of 1972. Hywel was working in the Organisation Department of the TUC during the 1972 NUM strike. We first came into contact when he rang the NUM office to offer to accommodate miners who were picketing London power stations. Since I was arranging accommodation on behalf of the pickets, he spoke to me.

9 'The Role of Industrial Correspondents', *British Trade Unions and Industrial Politics, Vol. I, The Post-War Compromise, 1945–64*, eds. A Campbell, N Fishman and J McIlroy, Ashgate 1999, p. 26.

10 Vol recalled being in pubs and bars with Horner when he happily made social conversation about football and rugby. She had marvelled at his peerless recall of past and current football and rugby fixtures, their heroes, victories and disappointments. Horner was fond of recalling that he had been a good enough amateur boxer as a lad to fight professional opponents who went on to be famous in the hard world outside the Merthyr gymnasium where he had sparred and worked out. He was one of the sponsors of the NCB Amateur Boxing Association, and regularly attended the National Finals of the Mineworkers Championship. Squaring up with mock intent was an habitual form of his greeting boys and young men. Harry Pollitt's son, Brian, recalled a party at his house when Arthur inadvertently made his nose bleed with a vigorous punch, producing a loud rebuke from Ethel.

11 Letter dated 22 November 1960 in John Tofts' collection of Arthur Horner papers.

Chapter 2. Growing Up

12 Arthur Horner, *Incorrigible Rebel*, MacGibbon & Kee, 1960, p. 11.

13 In his autobiography, Horner says that his father had walked from Northumberland aged sixteen in search of work, reflecting probably a family elision of memory, (*ICR*, p. 11). Mary Jane was born in Alnwick, Northumberland, and it may be that William, born in Derbyshire, had met her whilst working in Northumberland and that the family migrated to Wales by foot from there. From the Census returns, James appears to have been an only child, born when his mother was 42 and his father 44.

14 David Egan, 'Noah Ablett 1883–1935', *Llafur*, Vol. 4 No. 3, 1986, p. 20. Frank Hodges settled and worked in Abertillery, Monmouthshire.

15 Census Returns for 1891. They originated from Manchester, Yorkshire, Westbury in Wiltshire and Breconshire.

16 *ICR*, p. 11. Arthur's youngest daughter Joan remembered 'that Gran Horner was referred to as serving from the front window of the house in Clare Street Merthyr, It being the

first co-op shop.... [S]he was quite a lady.' (E-mail from Joan Horner Morris to N Fishman, 10 July 2000). The Dowlais Co-operative Society was the first co-operative society to have been founded in the Merthyr-Dowlais community. I am grateful to Alun Burge for this information. When Arthur and his younger sister Millie enrolled in the Caedraw Infant School, their address was listed as 2 Co-operative Cottages. I am grateful to Carolyn Jacob, Librarian at the Merthyr Record Office, for this information.

17 *ICR*, p. 54. 'I remember', transcript of Horner interview by John Griffiths on BBC Home Service, n.d., ca. 1960, Horner papers, SWCC(SU): NNA/PP/46/48, p. 2.

18 Horner's nephew, Hubert Harding, recalled his mother' Annie Horner Harding, telling these stories about the young Arthur. (Letter from H Harding to N Fishman, 29 July 1999. Horner's niece-in-law, Mrs Marjorie Harding recalled the same stories which she had heard from her mother-in-law. Interview with Mrs Harding by H Francis and N Fishman, Merthyr, 15 June 1998.) Horner's various diaries examined by Customs and Excise and the Constabulary in the 1930s contained the addresses of some of the siblings. His 1948 diary also noted, in addition to Frank's and Albert's addresses, his siblings' birth dates. Horner's youngest daughter, Joan, remembered Millie's resentment of Arthur (E-mail from Joan Morris to N Fishman, 7 August 2001). The youngest surviving child, Frank, was not enumerated in the 1911 Census.

19 *ICR*, pp. 11–13. Horner told Ronnie Frankenberg that he remembered his maternal grandfather and uncles paying their SWMF subscriptions.

20 'Report supplied to Glamorgan Assizes, compiled by Ferndale Police Office', dated 9 February 1932, signed by Wm E Rees, Inspector, and JL Rees, Superintendent., (hereafter *GAR*), Horner papers from R Frankenberg. In the 1911 Census Arthur Horner was enumerated as a lodger at Rhiew House, Woodlands, near Queens Road, Lower Merthyr Tydfil, the house of William Henry Miles, aged 30, the manager of a drapery. Horner's occupation is described as commercial traveller. Horner was their only

lodger, and I think it is likely that the Miles family were members of the Churches of Christ.

21 'I remember', Transcript, p. 1.

22 Kenneth O Morgan, 'The Merthyr of Keir Hardie', Glanmor Williams, ed., *Merthyr Politics: The Making of a Working-Class Tradition*, University of Wales Press, 1966, p. 63.

23 Quoted in Morgan, 'The Merthyr of Keir Hardie', p. 67.

24 Morgan, 'The Merthyr of Keir Hardie', p. 72. Tom Mann was the candidate favoured by Aberdare Trades Council. In the Aberdare part of the double constituency 40 per cent of the electorate were coalminers. As a ratepayer, James Horner could vote in both local and parliamentary elections.

25 *ICR*, p. 15.

26 KO Morgan, *Rebirth of a Nation, Wales 1880–1980*, Oxford University Press, 1988, p. 80.

27 See, for example, *ICR*, pp. 13–14. I am grateful to Chris Hill for his recollection of baptisms at the Newport Baptist Chapel in the 1950s and 60s. He remembered that his chapel and others he attended in South Wales had a cast iron tub which was stored permanently under the altar. It was brought out for confirmations, when children were judged to have reached maturity and be able to make an adult commitment to the church.

28 AF Adams, *A Brief Survey of the History of Churches of Christ in South Wales, 1870–1939*, Brecon, 1939, pp. 2–3. See also Michael W Casey and Peter Ackers, 'The Enigma of the young Arthur Horner: From Churches of Christ preacher to Communist militant (1894–1920)', *Labour History Review*, Vol. 66 No. 1, Spring 2001, pp. 3–23. In 1900, the first year in which there figures were recorded for Merthyr, there were 76 members of the Churches of Christ in Merthyr (p. 23). Casey and Ackers state that James and Emily were members of the Churches of Christ. The evidence they cite is Will Paynter's entry for Horner in the *Dictionary of National Biography* written soon after his death. Paynter had not met Horner until 1929 and had no occasion to observe Horner's parents' habits of religious observance. In 2004, neither of their surviving grandchildren, Joan Morris and Hubert Harding, could recall any memories of their grand-

parents' religious observance. Horner made no recorded reference to their religiosity.

29 Churches of Christ *Yearbook*, 1913, p. 118. The Churches of Christ Divisional Committee Book noted that Horner was employed as a shop assistant in the Nicholls' grocery business after attending the Plymouth Street Sunday School (Cited in AF Adams, *Brief Survey*, p. 10).

30 The *Birmingham Morning Post* contains detailed reports of the Avery's strike and suffragist activity. Horner speaks in his autobiography (p. 14) about hearing Horatio Bottomley, who is recorded elsewhere as having spoken in the Birmingham Town Hall in December 1913.

31 *ICR*, p. 14.

32 *ICR*, p. 16.

33 Quoted in 'The Enigma', Casey and Ackers, p. 11.

34 Egan, 'Noah Ablett', *Llafur*, p. 28.

35 David Egan, 'The Unofficial Reform Committee and the Miners' Next Step', *Llafur*, Vol. 2 No. 3, 1978, pp. 66–7. for new unionism, see HA Clegg, Alan Fox and AF Thompson, *A History of British Trade Unions since 1889. Vol. I, 1889–1910*, Clarendon Press, Oxford, 1964, ch. 2.

36 Quoted in Egan, 'Noah Ablett', p. 26.

37 Tonypandy had been the URC's meeting point in the lead-up to the Cambrian Combine Strike in 1910. Once the practice of meeting in the Aberystwyth Restaurant was established, SWMF activists were reluctant to abandon it. Readers perusing a South Wales map will observe that Porth and Pontypridd are both larger than Tonypandy, and more accessible for people who did not live in the Rhondda Fawr valley. The SWMF Rhondda District Office was in Porth, as was one of the largest co-operative department stores in East Glamorgan. But having an accustomed meeting place had the advantage that curious, random attendees knew where to find Sunday afternoon socialist and unofficial trade union activity. The restaurant had the additional advantage of not being a public house for teetotal participants, who probably comprised a substantial minority of those attending at this time. The Restaurant proprietors may have been sympathetic to the cause.

38 Merthyr brethren had helped to 'plant' the Churches there in 1900, purchasing a vacant chapel, Calfaria, in 1904 to house the growing congregation. In 1910, their own Hope Chapel, on Bridge Street, was opened. In 1915, 'the Church was set in order by the appointment of Elders and Deacons' (Davies, p. 4). Information about Millie Horner from Joan Morris and Hubert Harding.

39 Chris Williams, 'Democratic Rhondda: Politics and Society, 1885–1951', University of Wales PhD 1996, ch. 5, fn. 17.

40 Horner interview with Frankenberg. 24 July 1957. Alun Burge's notes record a letter from TJ Watkins in the *South Wales Daily News* on 13 April 1918, stating that the URC had been revived in Pontypridd at a meeting on 17 June 1917, with Noah Tromans in the chair and Bill Mainwaring as Secretary. The URC organisation was apparently dispersed and informal at this point.

41 *ICR*, p. 22. The autobiography recalled their meeting as taking place in a Merthyr grocer's shop. The GAR recorded his employment with Evan Evans in Aberfan. The Merricks were enumerated at 66 Aberfan Road, Aberfan in the 1901 Census, and at 17 Oakfield Street, Aberfan in the 1911 Census. Aberfan was designated as a village in the County Borough of Merthyr Tydfil. Joseph Merrick, born in 1860, was ten years older than his wife, Martha Harris Merrick. Ethel's younger sisters were Mabel Ellen, born in 1899, and Martha Lizzie, born in 1902. In the 1911 Census, Joseph Merrick's occupation was described as Pitman, Colliery Surface. In 1901, his occupation was general stationer.

42 The details of Joseph Merrick's naval enlistment are found in ADM 188/110, NA Kew. For the *Camperdown's* collision with the *Victory*, see Andrew Gordon, *The Rules of the Game, Jutland and the British Naval Command*, John Murray, 1996, chs. 10–14. Horner's recitation of Merrick's naval career is in *ICR*, pp. 23. The details were probably gleaned from Ethel's stories and general Merrick family conversation. Horner stated that Merrick, along with ten others, received a medal from the King. However, no state medals were awarded to those who survived the collision. The Royal Humane Society, a charity, awarded five bronze medals for life saving in the incident in August 1893. Two were to offic-

ers, one to a cadet, one to a Petty Officer and one to a 'boy 1ˢᵗ class' (Royal Humane Society, file LMA/4517/A/06/038, London Metropolitan Archives). Merrick may have known the Petty Officer and accompanied him to receive the medal. I am grateful to Andrew Davies, Curator of Manuscripts, National Maritime Museum, Greenwich, for information about state medal-giving and also for suggesting that I research Royal Humane Society records.

43 *ICR*, pp. 22–3. Horner described E Roderick Jones as Ethel's uncle. The marriage certificate recorded Ethel's residence at time of marriage as Wuislay House, Taffs Well, Jones' home perhaps. Arthur's residence was listed as 2 Cross Street, Ynyshir. The late Joseph Merrick's occupation was listed as Retired Seaman. Witnesses to the marriage were Ethel's mother, M Dane, stepfather, George Edward Dane, Tom Knight, a friend of the couple's from Barry, whom they probably knew from the Rhondda Socialist Society and/or ILP, and Joseph Arthur Jones, who may have been Ethel's cousin.

44 Paul Davies, *A.J. Cook*, Manchester University Press, 1987, p. 13. Charlie Gibbons was another of Ablett's protégés, moving from the Bertie colliery, part of the Lewis Merthyr group of collieries, to Mardy with Ablett in 1910, and then being put forward by Ablett for an SWMF scholarship to the Central Labour College in September 1911 (Robert Pitt, 'Educator and Agitator: Charlie Gibbons 1888–1967', *Llafur*, Vol. 5 No. 2, p. 73).

45 Horner recalled 'he was really angry and hardly spoke to me for six months'. *ICR*, p. 22.

46 AF Adams, *A Brief Survey*, p. 10, and Casey and Ackers, pp. 12–14. Horner's articles appeared on 11 and 25 September 1915. The first, subtitled 'Has Christianity Failed?', concluded, 'Christianity as a system, through its followers, should have made more difference than she has yet done towards preventing and discountenancing any connection with the war. This lack of success ... is due not to the inadaptability of the religion of Christ, but must be charged to the unfaithful individual's failure to abide by that which in times of trouble they professed to adhere to.' The second, subtitled 'Has Socialism failed in relation

to peace?' argued that Socialism had not failed because it had not yet had a trial. 'For such a trial we appeal, not for our own sakes, but for the sake of the dying, suffering heart-broken men and women who totter on the brink of the grave, this state being traceable to the systems now in power.' Horner told Frankenberg about these articles, but recalled having written them in 1914. He had written an earlier article in the *Pioneer* on 28 August 1928, entitled 'Upside Down', which had begun, 'Upside down, how true It Is, of every sphere of life, in practically every country in the world, and especially in this England of ours to-day. Oh! what a huge joke, yet withal what a terrible tragedy, that Britain, the land of solid and clear-minded inhabitants, should have lost in her time of trial her equilibrium.' His concluding paragraph was: 'Socialists and Christians, remember the old professions and stand firm for *Liberty, Equality and Fraternity*, through the Idea of the Brotherhood of Man and the Fatherhood of God.' I am grateful to Chris Williams for the *Pioneer* references.

47 Casey and Ackers, *The Enigma*, p. 13, citing *Bible Advocate*, 26 May 1916.
48 The two oldest Horner daughters had enjoyed sampling the wide variety of Sunday school classes on offer in Mardy. Vol Tofts recalled their parents had encouraged them to make these experiments. Interview with Vol Tofts, South Wales Miners Library.
49 *ICR*, p. 15.

Chapter 3. The Young Man

50 'Almost every leading miners' agent took part in the recruiting campaign, not merely moderates ... but even militants such as [C.B.] Stanton and [George] Barker.' Kenneth O Morgan, *Wales in British Politics, 1868–1922*, University of Wales Press, Cardiff, 1963, p. 276.
51 For British miners and conscription, see Supple, *Coal 1913–1946*, pp. 92–8.
52 *ICR*, pp. 42, 44; 'I Remember'. It may have been Cook's participation in the Baptists which caused Horner to elide his membership of the Churches of Christ into being a

Baptist in his self-descriptions. One can imagine the two Arthurs describing themselves to others in the 1920s as having had similar early life stories, including both being Baptists.

53 P Davies, *Cook*, pp. 7–8.

54 The letters preserved in the Horner papers from Cook to Horner contain frequent references to Ethel and the Horner's children which go beyond courteous, mannerly greetings. Cook evidently developed close ties with the Horner family. He and his wife were childless, and he may have embraced the Horner daughters as a surrogate family.

55 *ICR*, pp. 23–4; Report to Glamorgan Assizes. Charlie Jones remembered that the assault had been on a banksman, the row may thus have been about working conditions. Jones interview with R Frankenberg, 11 October 1957. Horner's correspondence arranging meetings for the RSS is in the Horner papers, SWCC(SU).

56 *ICR*, p. 24; Notes of Interview with R Frankenberg, 24 July 1957. In the Frankenberg interviews and *ICR*, Horner conflated Cook's pivotal role as Lewis-Merthyr lodges chairman in 1917 with his similar role as SWMF Agent for the Rhondda No. 1 District in 1920.

57 For wartime engineering and coalmining industrial relations: GDH Cole, *Trade Unionism and Munitions*, Clarendon Press, Oxford, 1923, chs. IX, X, XI and XIII; HA Clegg, *A History of British Trade Unions Since 1889 Volume II, 1911–1933*, Clarendon Press, Oxford, 1987, ch. 5; Supple, *Coal 1913–1946*, pp. 62–9, 79–85, 99–110.

58 David Egan, 'The Swansea Conference of the British Council of Soldiers' and Workers' Delegates, July 1917', *Llafur*, Vol. 1 No. 4, 1975, p. 173.

59 Egan, 'Swansea Conference', p. 168.

60 Interview with R Frankenberg, 24 July 1957. On 31 August 1917, the Mardy Lodge minutes noted a report from committee member, Dai Lloyd Davies: he and Henry Jones had spoken with 'Horner, Ynyshir', who told them that Tom Mann would be visiting South Wales again soon. There is also a letter from Horner to Tom Mann in the Horner papers (SWCC), dated 13 August 1917, about his visit.

61 P Davies, *Cook*, pp. 29–30.

62 Alun Burge's notes from the *WM*, 30 March 1918. Burge also noted URC agitation reported in *Merthyr Pioneer*, 29 December 1917; *South Wales Daily News*, 25 March, 3 and 8 April 1918; and *WM*, 3 April 1918. For Cook's wartime activities, see p. Davies, ch. 2, pp. 21–47, and Deian Hopkin, 'A.J. Cook in 1916–18', *Llafur*, Vol. 2, No. 3, summer 1978, pp. 81–8.

63 Egan, 'Swansea Conference', p. 179. No district in The Federation voted for strike action; votes were closest in the Western (anthracite), Aberdare and Merthyr districts, not Rhondda No.1. For the conscription issue in the MFGB, see Supple, *Coal 1913–1946*, pp. 93–5.

64 The tram up the Rhondda Fach valley had not been extended as far as Mardy until 1912. It was not until 1920 that there was a road route via bus. Hywel Francis and David Smith, *The Fed, A History of the South Wales Miners in the Twentieth Century*, Lawrence & Wishart, 1980, p. 159. Their description of Mardy and the Rhondda is lapidary, pp. 154–61. We have used the spelling Mardy, not Maerdy, in these volumes because this was the term used by Horner and his contemporaries.

65 Charlie Jones first appears in the Lodge committee minutes as a member on 4 April 1917. He was on the night-shift repairing: 'There was a very big haulier came by pushing a tram with a little fellow who looked familiar ... He [Charlie] went to give them a hand and noticed [the little fellow had] two fingers missing, this identified Arthur as the man who had sat in front of him at a meeting. When the big fellow had gone off to fetch something, Charlie asked Arthur his name – Arthur Jones. I used to know you as Arthur Horner. Damn – found out on the first night. But Charlie reassured him that his secret was safe.' Interview with Charlie Jones by R Frankenberg at Mardy Institute, 11 October 1957.

66 Frankenberg interview with C Jones. Transcript of discussion between Harold Jones, Neil Fisher and Alun Burge, Part 2, 12 June 1982, held by Alun Burge. Sam Fisher signed the URC Circular convening a conference in Cardiff on conscription. Burge notes, *WM*, 30 March 1918.

67 Francis and Smith, *The Fed*, p. 23. The ITGWU was founded
in 1912 by Connolly and James Larkin. It was part of the
surge of 'new unions', which had begun in 1889 with the
London Dock Strike, of which the SWMF was also a part.
See *Vol I*, n. 35. In November 1913 Larkin told a rally outside the union headquarters in Liberty Hall that 'trade
unionists, and especially members of the ITGWU, were
going to be given a military training ... He called upon
all the other trade unions to encourage their members to
join "this new army of the people" so that Labour might
no longer be defenceless.' White succeeded in producing
a credible core of men who were 'disciplined and armed,
not yet with rifles and revolvers but with stout hurley
sticks ... ' (Andrew Boyd, 'Jack White, First Commander
Irish Citizens' Army', Donaldson Archives, Belfast, 2001,
pp. 18–19). The industrial conflict ended in early 1914,
without either side having scored a decisive victory. White
was relieved of his command and most of the Army drifted
away. Nevertheless, Connolly and Larkin were keen to preserve its shell. Sean O'Casey drafted its first constitution in
March 1914, and at Larkin's suggestion included the provision that every applicant should be a trade union member.
Uniforms were dark-green with broad slouched hats of the
same colour, procured and paid for by the Army members
in weekly instalment. In April, the distinctive Starry Plough
banner was carried by the Army for the first time at the
head of a demonstration, after the Dublin Trades Council
had officially approved the insignia. See Donal Nevin, 'The
Irish Citizens' Army, 1913–1916', ch. 36, *James Larkin. Lion
of the Fold*, ed. D Nevin, Gill & Macmillan, Dublin, 1999,
pp. 257–65.

68 *ICR*, pp. 28–30. Notes of interview with R Frankenberg.

69 *ICR*, p. 31. For Voltairine de Cleyre see Paul Avrich, *An
American Anarchist: the life of Voltairine de Cleyre*, Princeton
University Press, Princeton NJ, USA, 1978.

70 Interview with WJ and Mrs Davies (*née* Phippen) by Hywel
Francis, 14 October 1974, Transcript, South Wales Miners'
Library, Swansea University.

71 Letter dated 3 September 1918. No. A1 in Horner Papers, SWCC(SU).
72 Interview with WJ Davies by David Egan, 3 November 1972. Transcript, SWML(SU).
73 *ICR*, pp. 32–4; Horner interview, R Frankenberg. Arthur remembered Emily's profound shock at seeing him in prison. The only words he remembered her speaking during the visit were, 'My God, fancy seeing you here.'
74 British miners' unions fought tenaciously to win government legislation in 1860 guaranteeing their right to elect a checkweighman. Though receiving his pay packet from the colliery company, the checkweighman was chosen by and answerable to the miners in the colliery he served. The colliery company deducted a contribution from their colliers' wages to pay his wages. Recognising that the checkweighman was of critical importance in enforcing union membership and solidarity, coalowners, particularly in Scotland, flouted the 1860 law, necessitating the passage of a supplementary act in 1886 by a supportive Liberal government under Gladstone. MFGB leaders, most of whom had begun their union careers as checkweighmen, recognised that this institution was the key to the mining unions' growing strength. They met further evasions and challenges from the coalowners with determined political lobbying. In 1912 Asquith's Liberal government passed additional legislation safeguarding checkweighmen's rights. See N Fishman, unpublished paper, 'Union-state-employer relations in Britain and Germany. A comparison using checkweighmen and their absence, 1844–1926', given to Sixth European Social Science History Conference 2006.
75 Frankenberg interviews with C Jones and Horner.
76 The Mardy Lodge Minute book is in the SWCC(SU). Minutes for 29 April to 14 May are on p. 61. Frankenberg interview with C Jones. The Rhondda No.1 District Committee minutes of 12 May 1919 noted: 'Letter received [probably from Mardy Lodge] asking Council to take steps to secure the release of Mr. A. Horner who was now in prison as a conscientious objector and who had been appointed checkweigher at the Mardy Colliery. Resolved: That the Officials

[Brace and Richards as President and Secretary] see the Home Office and the Welsh Office on this matter.' SWCC: MNA/NUM/K10a 1919 in SWCC(SU).

77 *ICR*, pp. 35–7. Under legislation enacted to deal with hunger striking suffragettes, 'the Cat and Mouse Act', the government acquired powers to temporarily release a hunger striking prisoner, but re-incarcerate them after they had recovered their health. In practice, suffragettes who were freed were not re-arrested if they refrained from further militant protests.

78 Francis and Smith, *The Fed*, pp. 154–6. There is a map of collieries in the Rhondda in ED Lewis, 'The Coal Industry', in KS Hopkins, ed., *Rhondda Past and Future*, Rhondda Borough Council, Ferndale, 1975, p. 35.

79 *ICR*, p. 49.

80 For Cook's election see P Davies, *Cook*, pp. 37–9; and R Page Arnot, *South Wales Miners, Glowyr de Cymru, A History of the South Wales Miners' Federation (1914–1926)*, Cymric Federation Press, Cardiff, 1975, pp. 181–2. The strike, which commenced on 23 February 1920, is reported in *Workers' Dreadnought* (information from Alun Burge's notes). It is also remembered in Charlie Jones' interview with Frankenberg. The strike aimed at achieving reinstatement for Horner and another SWMF activist, Romaine Pritchard, who worked at Parc and Dare. Jones remembered that Pritchard's case had not been a very popular cause, however. Another attempt to oust Horner was recorded in the minutes of the Rhondda No.1 District Committee on 25 August 1919. The meeting was chaired by Dai Lloyd Davies. A deputation had been received from Mardy Lodge 're Summons issued against one of the Checkweighers. Resolved, "That the Delegates representing the Rhondda No.1 District, attending the Special Conference of the S.W.M.F. To-Morrow, 26ᵗʰ August, 1919, shall among themselves constitute a Joint Deputation, with Officials from the Mardy Lodge, to interview the Central Officials, with a view of withdrawal of the Summons issued by the Colliery Company for the Removal of Mr. A.L. Horner, Checkweigher. Meanwhile, an Adjournment of the hearing (returnable 27ᵗʰ August, 1919) to be applied for, fail-

ing a satisfactory arrangement, a Special District Meeting shall be convened to consider its attitude to be taken in the matter.'" MNA/NUM/K10a 1919 in SWCC(SU).

81 Information from Joan Morris. Amongst the postcards in the Horner papers is a picture of Rosa Luxemburg. Postmarked 1 January 1920, it conveyed New Year's Greetings, and was sent by Tom and Bella Anderson, Crosshill Glasgow. Tom Anderson may have been imprisoned with Arthur in Wormwood Scrubs, since the postcard is the only evidence of an acquaintance. Arthur and Ethel evidently kept the card as a memento of the Andersons and Luxemburg. They may have decided to name their second daughter after receiving it, at a time when they would have known that Ethel was pregnant. Horner papers, SWCC(SU).

82 P Davies, *Cook*, p. 35. Burge's notes citing *The Merthyr Pioneer*, 22 February 1919, and *Workers' Dreadnought*, 26 July 1919.

83 Andrew Thorpe, *The British Communist Party and Moscow 1920–43*, Manchester University Press, Manchester, 2000, p. 9; James Klugmann, *History of the Communist Party of Great Britain, Volume 1, 1919–1924*, Lawrence & Wishart, 1968, pp. 31–6; LJ Macfarlane, *The British Communist Party, Its origin and development until 1929*, MacGibbon and Kee, 1966, pp. 23–4 and 47–51. Macfarlane notes that in June 1919, the SWSS joined the Socialist Labour Party and Workers' Socialist Federation in calling for a 24-hour strike against intervention in Soviet Russia and Soviet Hungary. The WSF paper *Workers' Dreadnought* reported on 9 August that thousands of South Wales miners had answered the appeal.

84 For example, Mardy Lodge minutes on 21 June 1922 noted Horner's detailed explanation of the new national wages agreement and 'handling claims, rates of wages for colliers in headings, compo [compensation] cases won in the Court of the Referees, war wage on overtime work'. He also turned his attention to the restrictive practices in the Health Insurance panel in Mardy. Having failed to dislodge the corrupt, incompetent doctor employed by the company, he organised a counter scheme with Lodge members paying fourpence a week. 'It was a tremendous

achievement, because men were able to go for medical advice without the consciousness that they were confiding in an agent of the company ... There was a similar scheme in Tredegar, where Aneurin Bevan was active at that time.' *ICR*, pp. 61–2.

85 Hewlett was allied with Arthur MacManus and Tom Bell, prominent Clydeside shop stewards who had split the SLP by endorsing Lenin's arguments accepting the importance of parliamentary politics and fighting elections. Klugmann, *Vol. I*, ch. 1; Thorpe, *British CP & Moscow*, chs. 1–2; Macfarlane, *British CP until 1929*, chs. I and II.

86 Quoted in Klugmann, *Vol. I*, p. 42.

87 At the TUC in Portsmouth in September 1920, Arthur MacManus approached Cook, Horner and Ted Williams, an ILP member, to ask them to join the Unity Convention's communist party. Horner recalled that Cook and Williams had refused, but he had said yes, presumably because he had assumed that he was already a member by virtue of his RSS affiliation. Horner was not a delegate at the 1920 TUC. He had evidently travelled to Portsmouth with Cook and Williams, who were delegates, to observe a Congress meeting for the first time. All three men had been in London the previous week when they had been SWMF delegates to the national MFGB conference on 2 September, the eve of Congress. They probably proceeded to Portsmouth from London. Frankenberg Interview with Horner.

88 Newbold's memoirs noted: 'Arthur Horner had a moral force and a compact physical energy that combined with bulldog courage to make me spend two nights in 1921 demolishing his every objection to enlisting in the Communist Party of Great Britain.' I am grateful to Kevin Morgan for this reference. It is likely that Newbold misremembered the year and that his encounter with Horner occurred after the September 1920 meeting. Horner recalled, 'I joined the Party as a member of the Mardy Group of the Rhondda Socialist Society which affiliated as an organization and sent a delegate to the inaugural conference. Ethel joined in the same way and we both took out individual cards as well.' *ICR*, p. 50.

89 For the CP of South Wales and the West of England, see
    p. Davies, *Cook*, p. 43. The BSP was the largest and best
    organised of the groups which constituted the CPGB.
    Foundation groups and their members conducted their
    political activities little differently after joining a com-
    munist party affiliated to the Comintern. Their separate
    organisational forms and behaviours remained more or
    less intact until 1923–4, when the Comintern started its
    drive to bolshevise affiliates and transform them into repli-
    cas of the formidably efficient, effective organisation which
    communist theology maintained the pre-1917 bolshevik
    wing of the Russian social democrats had been.
90 For the sparse, intermittent nature of Labour Party organ-
    isation in South Wales see Duncan Tanner, 'The Pattern
    of Labour Politics, 1918–1939', D Tanner, C Williams and
    D Hopkin, eds., *The Labour Party in Wales 1900–2000*,
    University of Wales Press, Cardiff, 2000. Tom Bell noted
    that 'the [communist] party at this time was extremely feeble
    in South Wales, as in some other sections of the country'.
    British Communist Party. A Short History. Lawrence & Wishart,
    1937, p. 77. Klugmann concurred in this judgement. *Vol. I*,
    p. 330. Horner interview with R Frankenberg.

Chapter 4. The Coal Wars: Skirmishes and Manoeuvres

91 Supple, *Coal 1913–1946*, pp. 134–5.
92 Clegg, *Vol. II*, pp. 298–9. He noted: 'According to the
    owners, they varied from slight advances on current wages
    for some pieceworkers in Yorkshire to cuts of 30 per cent in
    Durham and 40 per cent in South Wales.' Supple observed
    that in February 1921 almost 90 per cent of South Wales'
    coal was produced at a loss (pp. 158–9).
93 MFGB Delegate Conference, 17 March 1921, quoted in
    Clegg, *Vol. II*, p. 299.
94 Quoted in Clegg, *Vol. II*, p. 299. The course of events is
    vividly encapsulated by Jack Lawson, a close observer, in
    The Man in the Cap, The Life of Herbert Smith, Methuen &
    Co., London, 1941, chs. 29–31.

95   Clegg, *Vol. II*, pp. 300, 302. The Citrine quotation is from his autobiography, *Men and Work*, Hutchinson & Co., London, 1964, p. 131.

96   Supple, *Coal 1913–1946*, pp. 161–2. There were three improvements over the owners' original offer: the government subsidy, a 20 per cent increase in the minimum wage, and a guaranteed subsistence wage for low-paid men. The new contracts' main features remained intact until World War II. 'The "basis" rates were determined locally, and ranged from agreements concerning the rate for piece-work in a particular pit or even seam, to district-wide rates for whole categories of daywage workers. Percentage additions were determined for the district as a whole.' Although the percentage additions depended upon the profitability of each district, the agreement provided for a minimum. 'Low-paid men were to be paid locally determined subsistence allowances if necessary. In each district a joint audit would ascertain the industry's "proceeds" ... The net proceeds of the ascertainment, if any, would then be divided between wages and profits in the ratio 83:17.' A National Board was established to administer the system. Its membership was appointed equally by the MAGB and MFGB, presided over by a neutral Chairman.

97   Frankenberg notes of Rhondda Lodge minutes, p. 30.

98   *GAR*. Frankenberg's interview with Charlie Jones, and *ICR*, pp. 54–5, corroborate the GAR outline of events.

99   *ICR*, pp. 55–7; P Davies, *Cook*, p. 57; Horner interview with R Frankenberg. In *ICR*, Horner stated that forty men were arraigned from Mardy. The GAR gives the numbers from Mardy in addition to Horner as twelve. Horner may have elided the Mardy men with the total number of Federation men in court that day. Francis and Smith cite *The South Wales News* for 5 May 1921 for their statement that Horner's and Dai Lloyd Davies' sentences were three months (*The Fed*, p. 160). I have found no evidence to corroborate this.

100   The 1834 Poor Law distinguished between indoor relief, awarded when the applicant was not only indigent but also homeless, and when s/he would be sent to the local Work House, and outdoor relief given to the claimants who were merely indigent. Outdoor relief was awarded either in

money or food tokens redeemable at local shops to relieve families' distress during periods of unemployment.

101 *ICR*, pp. 57–8. Horner decided, after reading law textbooks, that the Guardians were not entitled to reclaim outdoor relief money. The Federation agreed to fight a case up to the Court of Appeal, and the judges agreed with Horner. Nevertheless: 'I found, years later, when I became an agent for the anthracite pits, that the employers were still deducting money from the pay packets for repayment to the Guardians. I stopped that, but we failed to get a refund.'

102 *ICR*, p. 60.

103 *Colliery Workers' Magazine*, published by South Wales Miners' Federation, January 1923, pp. 12–13, SWML(SU); P Davies, *Cook*, p. 62. It is possible at this time that only the most modern of the four Mardy pits, Nos. 3 and 4, were being worked, and that Horner and Dai Lloyd Davies apparently took it in turns to work as checkweighman for them. Wilson was probably the Industrial Workers of the World activist from America (IWW activists were universally known as Wobblies) whom Edgar Evans remembered hearing in Mardy at a communist party meeting. Edgar Evans Interview with R Frankenberg, 21 July 1962; R Frankenberg interview with Horner.

104 A national conference of shop stewards, convened in Manchester in August 1917, founded the SSWCM with the aim of achieving workers' control and the ultimate 'triumph of the workers' (quoted in Macfarlane, *CPGB to 1929*, p. 39). Though the SSWCM failed to establish an effective national existence, *ad hoc* committees of engineering union activists led strikes in Sheffield, Coventry and West London, which spread from factory to factory.

105 *ICR*, p. 66. Horner misremembered the date of the conference as being 1920. Roderick Martin, *Communism and the British Trade Unions 1924–1933. A study of the National Minority Movement*, Clarendon, Oxford, 1969, p. 33. Macfarlane cites minutes of a meeting on 23 February 1921 between the CPGB Executive and the National Administrative Committee of the SSWCM, *CPGB to 1929*, pp. 110–112.

106 P Davies, *Cook*, pp. 62–3; Martin, *Study of NMM*, pp. 32–3; Macfarlane, *CPGB to 1929*, p. 129. Klugmann, states that the MMM founding conference in Cardiff took place in August 1923, *Vol. I*, p. 279.

107 Report in Sam Watson Papers, Durham Record Office, box 41, NMM file. Horner's resolution was seconded by J Adams from the Woolwich Trades Council. The TUC convened in a different city in Britain each year.

108 Martin, *Study of NMM*, p. 53. Loeber was a member of the National Union of Railwaymen. Booth was a Central Labour College graduate active in the Nottinghamshire Miners' Association. He dropped out of Minority Movement activity quickly, however, reacting against the palpable CPGB influence. Alan R Griffin, *The Miners of Nottinghamshire 1914–1944*, Allen and Unwin, 1962, pp. 39, 143.

109 Clegg, *Vol. II*, pp. 380–1.

110 Macfarlane, *CPGB to 1929*, p. 130; P Davies, *Cook*, p. 60.

111 *ICR*, p. 65; Mardy Lodge minutes, 13 June 1923. The Lodge minutes recorded Horner in the chair at a Lodge meeting on 5 June; his next appearance at a Lodge meeting was 31 August. Horner went with high expectations. In his autobiography Horner recalled talking with Mann in 1921 about his visit to Russia to attend the RILU and Comintern Congresses, conveniently held in tandem. Mann told him that the largest delegation had been the Germans, 'where we had high hopes of success for the working-class forces'. *ICR*, p. 64. Pollitt recalled the moment during the final sessions of the Comintern Congress, when he and Mann had passed Lenin in the corridor. 'Tom Mann stepped forward, Lenin's face lit up as he told Tom how he had followed his revolutionary activities all over the world.' Harry Pollitt, *Serving My Time*, Lawrence & Wishart, 1940, p. 139.

112 Special Branch and customs provided MI5 with detailed information about leading communists' movements abroad. But Horner's MI5 files for this period were part of a large number which were destroyed by fire in 1940 in the blitz. Therefore his precise date of departure and the means by which he travelled to Moscow in 1923 remain unknown. The only relevant entry on his MI5 file noted on 8 September 1923 that he had recently returned from

Russia. Horner and Watkins were the only miners in the British delegation. Will Hewlett and two Scottish miners, Davey Proudfoot and James Stewart, had attended the first RILU Congress. Hewlett had been tragically killed in a train crash whilst touring Russia afterwards. It is likely that the leading communist miners from Scotland were preoccupied at this time by internal union politics; the formation of the Mineworkers' Reform Union of Fife, Kinross and Clackmannan by militants was proceeding at this time.

113 Klugmann, *Vol. I*, p. 212. Pollitt had been elected onto the Executive at the CPGB's Fifth Party Congress in October 1922. Along with R Palme Dutt, he had played a leading role in the bolshevisation drive inside the CPGB.

114 Horner told Frankenberg that he had 'spent a lot of time' with Haywood and Browder.

115 'Wal Hannington's Autobiography', n.d. bound typescript, pp. 161–2, J Tofts collection of Horner papers.

116 *ICR*, p. 65. '[Back in Moscow] Arthur brought greetings of British working class at a demonstration in the Bolshoi theatre, at which Trotsky and others also spoke.' Frankenberg notes of second interview. The Russian term, Donbas, is used to describe the coalfield on the Donets river in the Ukraine. (It is sometimes spelled Donbass.) Part of the French term for coalfield, *bassin houiller*, became incorporated in Russian word to describe a coalfield. One of the meanings of the French *bassin* is geological, describing a river basin.

117 Dai Lloyd Davies sent the Horners two postcards from Berlin in mid-August, reflecting communists' optimism about the imminent collapse of Weimar. 'Under the circumstances things are not bad with us. The Communists are playing hell with the authorities ... the only factor in the way of their immediate triumph is the existence of a strong Facisti Movement here ... ' Postcards dated 13 and 16 August 1923, in Horner Papers, SWCC(SU).

118 Hannington typescript, pp. 163–4; *ICR*, pp. 65–6; Wal Hannington, *Never On Our Knees*, Lawrence & Wishart, 1967, pp. 164–9. In Hamburg, 'I [Hannington] could exchange one dollar in a bank and draw enough German marks to provide all my needs for several days.' p. 171.

119 Frankenberg notes of second interview. *Worker's Weekly* on Saturday 8 September 1923 advertised an Unofficial Conference in Ferndale Workers' Hall on 9 September where Horner would report on his visit to Russia.

120 Clegg *Vol. II*, pp. 393–4. Horner's resolution was seconded by Charlie Hoyle, a foundation communist AEU activist.

121 *CWM*, pp. 250–253.

122 Arnot *SWM II*, p. 232. Arnot noted that the MFGB had adopted the transferable vote 'not only as providing several advantages over a system of second and third ballots but as the most democratic method for a big electorate: and, on request, the Proportional Representation Society took charge.' In 1919 there were eight nominees, each major coalfield putting forward its favourite son. Hodges led at the first count, and kept his lead throughout, winning on the fifth count by 141,813 votes to 94,239 for J Robson from Durham. For the importance of the SWMF vote in Hodges' election, Clegg, *Vol. II*, p. 277.

123 Ablett had probably been most URC activists' choice. He was beaten into second place by Hodges, however. George Barker, a veteran from Abertillery, and two Rhondda men, William John and Mardy Jones, took vital votes away from him.

124 *ICR*, p. 43; Arnot *SWM II*, p. 232; SWMF Executive Minutes 1924, p. 138. Horner omitted all mention of Mainwaring's candidacy in *ICR* and the Frankenberg interviews, perhaps because Mainwaring had been quickly eliminated from the Mardy comrades' calculations. He may also have been reluctant to relate the subsequent conflict he had with the CPGB Executive about not supporting Mainwaring. Cook's biographer cites Ablett's alcoholism as a contributory factor affecting Horner's decision, as well as Cook's more attractive public persona and greater support for the Minority Movement. P Davies, *Cook*, pp. 65–6. 'The final figures were: AJ Cook 50,123; WH Mainwaring 49,617; majority 506.' When Ablett was eliminated, three times as many of his transferred votes went to Cook than Mainwaring. Arnot *SWM II*, p. 231.

125 Arnot *SWM II*, pp. 231–2. Robin Page Arnot was a founder member of the CPGB, and remained a central figure in the

leadership until the late 1930s. Elected to the Executive at the Sixth Party Congress in 1924, he served until 1938. Born in Greenock in 1890, he was the son of a journalist. Having joined the Fabian Society whilst a student at Glasgow University, he embraced guild socialism and joined the National Guilds League, formed in 1915. He worked with GDH Cole and other guildspeople at the Fabian Research Department in London until 1916, when he was conscripted. Refusing to serve, he was imprisoned until 1918. He then resumed work at the renamed Labour Research Department as secretary. The question of when Cook left the party continues to be contentious, partly because he appears as an informant in intelligence reports passed to the Home Office and thence to the Cabinet. (See for example, Macfarlane, *CPGB to 1929*, pp. 130–1 and P Davies, *Cook*, pp. 56, 58, 60–3.) I am grateful to Kevin Morgan for the following information, from a letter from J Walton Newbold to Ramsay MacDonald on 2 June 1926. Newbold told MacDonald that it was Borodin who had decided that South Wales communists should support Cook. 'Cook was chosen because he was *not* in the Party but [also] because, like Maxton would lean to Gallacher but far more so, he would always "blab" everything to Horner and Pollitt.' NA, PREM 30/69 1171. It is plausible that Horner discussed the merits of the five South Walian candidates with Borodin and Pollitt before the URC Conference.

126 Horner and Hannington were both elected onto the CPGB Executive in their own right at the Sixth Congress, having previously been co-opted Executive members by virtue of their Politburo positions. Thorpe, *British CP & Moscow*, p. 68; Macfarlane, *CPGB to 1929*, pp. 88, 114, 135. *Workers' Weekly* reported on 23 May 1924 that Horner had been elected onto the CPGB Executive at the Congress. Although Macfarlane stated that Horner had been co-opted onto the CPGB Politburo in 1923, Klugmann (citing the CPGB Executive Report) omits Horner as a co-optee. He also observed that the Politburo's 'exact status, authority and role' were a 'problem' at this juncture (*Vol. I*, p. 328).

127 R Page Arnot, *The Miners: Volume II, Years of Struggle. A History of the Miners' Federation of Great Britain (from 1910*

onwards), Allen & Unwin, 1953, p. 350. At the last count, Cook won by 'a comparatively narrow 217,000 votes to 202,000.' P. Davies, *Cook*, pp. 66–67; WG Quine, 'AJ Cook, Miners' Leader in the General Strike', Manchester University MA, 1964, fn. 50 quoting *Daily Herald* , 19 April 1924.

128 R Page Arnot, *Vol II*, p. 351. Macfarlane, *CPGB to 1929*, pp. 158–9.

129 The letterhead listed Scottish district secretaries as Alec Kirk of Stonyburn, West Lothian, and W Allen (*sic*) of Blantyre, Lanarkshire. The South Wales secretary was Tom Thomas from Ynyshir.

130 Macfarlane, *CPGB to 1929*, pp. 129–30; Martin, *Study of NMM*, p. 32; N Fishman, 'The British Communist Party and the Trade Unions, 1933–45: the Dilemmas of Revolutionary Pragmatism', University of London PhD, 1991, ch. 7.

131 *ICR*, p. 72.

132 In March and April 1922, the Mardy Lodge had complained about Cook's general attitude and inefficiency as agent for Rhondda District No.1. A subcommittee, including Horner, investigated and proposed that the Lodge move his resignation at the next District meeting. Cook visited the Lodge and agreed not to write or give out interviews in the press, admitting that 'he had made mistakes and would in future be more careful in his actions and deliberations' (Lodge minutes 19 March, 21 April). Though political hostility may have been subsumed into this administrative complaint, Cook's erratic attention to detail was universally acknowledged.

133 *CWM*, December 1924, pp. 294–5. Harris came from the Blackwood Lodge, in western Monmouthshire. He was elected as treasurer of the SWMF, a lay position, in December 1921, after three ballots from a large field of candidates. Earlier in the year, he had been appointed secretary of the newly created statistical department. The department was integral to the Executive's ambition to make their union not only efficient, but also able to compete with the coalowners in gathering information for collective bargaining at lodge, district and coalfield levels.

When the SWMF decided to publish *Colliery Workers' Magazine* in 1921, Harris was a logical choice for editor. He produced a lively journal with a balanced mixture of factual, political and news articles. He published adverts informing readers that birth control information was available from the Marie Stopes clinic, and reports on the labour movement's attitude to contraception. Articles appeared by Elizabeth Andrews, Labour Party's women's organiser for South Wales, about the importance of women's activities in the life of The Federation. Arthur Jenkins and WH Mainwaring regularly translated articles from French and German trade union publications. Comparisons with the journals of Northumberland and Durham justify the SWMF's self-image as the most modern coalfield union.

134 Ianto Evans recalled Richards 'after a conference when they were having a meal at The Continentale ... telling Arthur Horner "not to make such a fuss about Communism".' R Frankenberg interview with Ianto Evans, 21 July 1962; *ICR*, p. 100.

135 Supple, *Coal 1913–1946*, pp. 193–4. The Keynes quote is from his collected works, Volume IX, pp. 222–3.

136 Arnot noted: 'Within the MFGB Executive Cook found that he had the aid of the representatives of South Wales other than Tom Richards. Tom did not actively oppose but took a kindly neutral position and a pleasure that one of the boys from the Rhondda was playing such an active part in all these contests. But Cook had a firm backing through the election in the spring of 1924 not only of ... Morrell but of Noah Ablett ... and S.O. Davies ... Vice-President [of the SWMF] since 1924 ... [A]lso he had the constant support of Jack Williams, formerly of the Garw Valley, who had been chosen to be the Secretary of the Forest of Dean Miners' Association.' *SWM II*, p. 244.

137 Clegg, *Vol. II*, pp. 308–10. In its first year of existence, 1921, the TUC General Council members for Group No. 1 were Smillie and Hugh Murnin from the MFGB and RT Jones, general secretary of the North Wales Quarrymen's Union. Smillie and Jones continued to serve on the General Council; Smillie until 1926 and Jones until his retirement in 1932. Murnin was replaced by Herbert Smith in 1922;

When the NWQU merged with the TGWU in 1922, the terms specified that the NWQU would retain its separate identity for affiliation to the TUC and its entitlement to stand candidates for the General Council.

138 Clegg, *Vol. II*, pp. 390–4. Quotations are from the 1925 TUC Report. Horner did not attend the 1925 TUC as a delegate, though he was probably present as an observer.

139 The result of the delegates' vote by show of hands was 112–100 against accepting the terms. The card vote confirmed the result: 87,600 to 61,150 (*CWM*, June 1924, p. 142). The subsequent delegates' vote recorded 112–92 in favour of the Executive's recommendation to keep the agreement; but this result was reversed on a card vote by 70,200 to 61,450 in favour of Horner's and Jones' resolution. Ablett had opposed Horner saying 'no one would attempt to defend the terms offered ... but they must face the fact that the previous terms were only rejected by a [small] majority ... ' (*CWM*, March 1925, p. 54).

140 *CWM*, March 1925, p. 54 and pp. 62–3. The report of the district meeting, written by Mainwaring, concluded, 'It is regrettable that, as is usual, in discussing matters of principle, mere personal affairs were dragged in, and but succeed in generating feeling and clouding real issues.' *CWM*, April 1925, p. 81.

141 *CWM*, October 1925, p. 230.

142 James Klugmann, *History of the Communist Party of Great Britain. Volume Two: The General Strike 1925–1926*, Lawrence & Wishart, 1969, pp. 94–5; *ICR*, p. 71. Horner's leave of absence was not recorded in the Lodge minutes, presumably because the committee was exercising discretion with regard to the job to which Horner was going.

143 See entry for Hardy by Kevin Morgan and Andrew Flinn in K Gildart, D Howell and N Kirk, eds., *Dictionary of Labour Biography*, Vol. XI, Palgrave, 2003.

144 Klugmann, *Vol. II*, pp. 67–83.

Chapter 5. The Coal Wars: Battle, Siege, Rout, Retreat

145 Third interview, Frankenberg's Notes. Even with the loss of members, the Rhondda No. 1 District remained the largest district in the SWMF with 40,000 members. SWMF Executive Committee minutes, 6 and 27 February 1926, pp. 147, 149.

146 SWMF Executive minutes, 16 March and 22 April 1926, pp. 166, 193. See also the Review of 1925 which appeared in the January 1926 *CWM*.

147 MFGB Conference Report, 12.3.1926, pp. 15–22. The bonus turn was 'six for five', the concession won in 1915 under which hourly paid workers were paid an extra shift for completing a five day week. Tom Cape MP from Cumberland was another prominent delegate who referred to Horner's speech.

148 The SWMF affiliated to the MFGB on 148,400 members; the DMA and YMA affiliated on 120,000 and 150,000 respectively.

149 Smaller districts fielded larger numbers, presumably in a desire to make their voices heard. Lancashire and Cheshire, affiliated on 75,000 members, fielded 10 delegates; the Midlands, affiliated on 60,000, had a complement of 11. Scotland with 80,000 had 16 delegates; and Northumberland and Nottinghamshire each had 7 delegates, with 37,836 and 25,000 members respectively.

150 MFGB Conference Report, p. 24. On 16 August, another Scottish delegate, J MacNulty, spoke in similar terms to Doonan: 'It seems as though no-one was anxious to carry on the fight except South Wales.' Report, p. 47.

151 Sam Watson papers, box 41. The DMA kept the letter sent by Nat Watkins to its Secretary on 11 March inviting their Executive 'to send a delegate either with the power to represent your organisation and participate in the work of the Conference, or in the capacity of a fraternal delegate with a watching brief'.

152 Marx Memorial Library, YA11, Minority Movement pamphlets. The conference was described as a Special National Conference of Action. Its report was published with a strapline, 'Solidarity Spells Success'. There were 883 delegates,

representing 957,000 workers, including fifty-two trades councils. Macfarlane, *CPGB to 1929*, p. 161; See *ICR*, pp. 73–4.

153 Mardy Lodge minutes. He had first been nominated for the MFGB Executive in 1921, securing one of the Lodge's nominations thereafter. He had never previously been nominated for SWMF President, being nominated for Vice-President in 1922 and 1924. Horner chaired Lodge meetings on 2, 5, 10, 19 February; 10, 19 March. On 5 February he was chosen as Lodge delegate to the International Class War Prisoners' Aid Society conference held on 6 February to discuss the imprisonment of the Anthracite miners and communist leaders. On 10 March, he was appointed delegate to the Rhondda Borough Labour Party conference; on 13 April he reported on the East Glamorgan Labour Party conference which he had attended. Information from Joan Morris. Ethel's second pregnancy had been difficult, and she had developed erypselas after Rosa's birth.

154 R Frankenberg, notes from second interview with Horner; *ICR*, p. 66; information from Joan Morris. Kevin Morgan suggested that I should ask Joan Morris whether her parents had seen Saint Joan.

155 Letter in Modern Records Centre, TUC deposit, 272.61(1).

156 C.B. may be Claude Berridge, a London AEU communist activist who was a leading member of the Willesden Council of Action in 1926. Cook made a similar observation in his pamphlet, *The 9 Days*.

157 Mardy Lodge Minutes; Clegg, *Vol. II*, p. 400, quoting TUC General Council 'Report on Mining Dispute National Strike' to the postponed conference of union executives scheduled for 25 June 1926 and 'Supplementary Report', both presented to conference of union executives held on 20 January 1927.

158 Clegg, *Vol. II*, pp. 402–3; Alan Bullock, *The Life and Times of Ernest Bevin, Vol. I. Trade Union Leader 1881–1940*, Heinemann, 1960, pp. 297–8, 311–2.

159 Clegg, *Vol. II*, 409–10, quoting 'Report on Mining Dispute National Strike'; Mardy Lodge minutes; R Frankenberg notes from second interview with Horner.

160 Clegg, *Vol. II*, pp. 408–9 quoting Charles Dukes, Lancashire District Secretary of the NUGMW; Bullock, *Bevin Vol. I*, pp. 323–4.

161 Clegg, *Vol. II*, pp. 412–4.

162 Supple, *Coal 1913–1946*, pp. 245–6.

163 Arnot, *Vol. II*, p. 471. In Yorkshire, Herbert Smith's implacable oppositionism undoubtedly influenced the vote.

164 Lodge committees met first to discuss the proposals and consider the recommendations made by the Executives of the District Unions affiliated to the MFGB. The decision-making process conventionally involved lodge committees meeting first to consider the MFGB delegate conference's recommendation and the District Executive's recommendation, which might differ from the national delegate conference. The lodge committee would then make up its collective mind and put its own recommendation to a lodge meeting (along with an account of the national and district recommendations). Most lodge meetings conducted votes on a show of hands. Even though a lodge might have voted against the national conference's recommendations by a narrow majority, the total number of its memberships' votes would be aggregated and cast against the proposals. Each affiliated District Union's vote was determined on the basis of aggregated lodge results. Thus, all of Durham's and Northumberland's votes were cast in favour of the proposals, even though many Durham and Northumbrian miners had voted against them. Equally, the votes in favour of the proposals in Yorkshire and South Wales did not 'count' because they were aggregated into those districts' vote against the proposals.

165 Clegg states inaccurately that only Nottinghamshire and Derbyshire had not had notice of wage reductions. *Vol. II*, pp. 414–6.

166 This important precedent would have been a common collective memory for most veteran members of the MFGB Executive and in the district union leadership. Younger activists would have known about the dispute and its settlement by repute, as part of the dense union culture into which they were socialised by attending lodge committee

meetings and socialising afterwards. For the dispute and Smillie's role see Clegg *Vol. II*, pp. 43–51.

167 MFGB Conference Report 15–16 August 1926, pp. 35–41.

168 MFGB Conference Report 15–16 August, pp. 45–7.

169 Pollitt, *SMT*, p. 254. Macfarlane cites *Workers' Weekly* of 29 October reporting that Nat Watkins and Pollitt 'helped to bring back on strike some thousands of miners at Coalville, Leicester'. *CPGB to 1929*, p. 174.

170 Horner's address is listed in the TUC Report for 1926 as 50 Russell Square, the MFGB head office.

171 TUC Report 1926. The telegram report is on p. 463. Horner's and Wilkinson's questioning of Section D of the General Council Report on unemployment occurs on pp. 312–3. Horner, Elsbury and Tanner questioned the paragraph of the Council's report on action taken to implement the 1925 motion on promoting amalgamations, p. 326. Horner challenged the Council's report on trades councils' conduct of the General Strike, pp. 344–5. The section of the General Report on abandoning the General Strike, comments by Horner, Wilkinson, Elsbury and Tanner, pp. 369–70. When Horner and Elsbury intervened on the paragraph dealing with international trade union unity, Horner's lengthy speech was again tolerated by Pugh. pp. 435–6.

172 TUC Report 1926, pp. 488–9.

173 *CWM*, October 1926. Churchill had spent the summer months, when Baldwin was recuperating from nervous exhaustion in the South of France, in consultations with Cook, Smith and Evan Williams of the MAGB, in an attempt to effect a settlement. Although he despaired of Smith's negotiating skills and mistrusted Cook, Churchill exerted himself energetically. His radical streak and Liberal past inclined him towards a strategy of exerting strong pressure on Williams. Baldwin, however, was unwilling to be seen to push the owners.

174 Clegg, *Vol. II*, p. 416.

175 MFGB Conference Report 29 September 1926, pp. 32–3.

176 Clegg, *Vol. II*, p. 415.

177 Arnot, *Vol. II*, pp. 494–5; Alan R Griffin, *The Miners of Nottinghamshire 1914–1944*, Allen & Unwin, 1962,

pp. 186–9. Griffin cites the speech made in Spencer's support at the conference by CA Pugh, a Digby Lodge official and also a communist. (Miners returning to work at Digby colliery had asked Spencer to negotiate terms and conditions on their behalf.) When Varley rose to identify Pugh as a communist, Horner responded, 'I was never more ashamed in my life. He will be dealt with. I want to know whether the ILP will deal with Mr. Spencer ... '

178 Horner's name did not appear on the MFGB delegation list in the conference report. He may have agreed to attend at the last minute, because of Cook's absence abroad. Cook could easily have arranged for Horner to be accredited at the last minute.

179 Cutting from unidentified newspaper in Sam Watson papers, 1DMA248, 'cuttings from coal strike 1925–6'. It is likely that the paper was local, perhaps the *Newcastle Chronicle*. The official conference report omitted this exchange.

180 '1926 Labour Party Conference Report', pp. 196–8, 201.

181 'Diary of the British Coal Trade Lock-Out', *CWM*, December 1926, p. 265, Arnot *Vol. II*, p. 497.

182 Macfarlane, *CPGB to 1929*, pp. 173–4. He cites the Report of the 1927 CPGB Congress, which observed that staff from the party centre were drafted into the coalfield, leaving only a small bureau in London. Twenty-nine speakers were mobilised and 220,000 copies of four leaflets issued in a concentrated fortnight's campaign.

183 Griffin, *Miners of Nottinghamshire*, p. 194. Spencer's use of the term, council of action, was an accurate reflection of the terminology being adopted by many Executive members, including Cook and probably even Smith. It had been the widely accepted description of the Hands Off Russia Committee in 1920. Its resonances included not only the February 1917 Russian Revolution, but also the November 1918 German Revolution. SWMF Lodges had frequently used 'Council of Action' to describe their own ad hoc united front committees during the 1921 Lock-Out.

184 MFGB Conference Report, 13 November 1926, pp. 24–7.

185 Macfarlane, *CPGB to 1929*, p. 174. The results of the vote are in Arnot, *Vol. II*, p. 505. Richards' speech is in the MFGB conference report, pp. 34–6. The Delegate Conference card vote is recorded in the conference report, p. 103.

186 Arnot, *Vol. II*, p. 504, Clegg, *Vol. II*, p. 418, Francis and Smith, *The Fed*, fn. 59, p. 110.

187 Arnot *Vol. II*, pp. 505–6; *CWM* 'Diary of the Coal Trade Lock-Out.

188 Francis and Smith provide evidence to show that Tom Richards knew about the return to work and had sanctioned it. See *The Fed*, fn. 5, p. 237.

189 Thorpe, *British CP & Moscow*, p. 96.

190 Supple, *Coal 1913–1946*, pp. 253–5; Clegg, *Vol. II*, pp. 418–9.

191 Report of CPGB Ninth Party Congress, 7–8 October 1927, p. 38.

Chapter 6. Regrouping

192 *ICR*, p. 95; Frankenberg, notes of second interview. Horner said in *ICR* that unemployment benefit had been stopped for three weeks.

193 Francis and Smith, *The Fed*, pp. 162, 164.

194 PFI 601, V.2, NA Kew.

195 MI5 file, PF 601 V.1, fact sheet. Supple, *Coal 1913–1946*, Table 10.2, pp. 446–7. In 1927, the average cash earnings for South Wales miners were £3.12.0. In 1928, these declined to £2.17.0., and remained at that level until 1931, when they declined further to £2.14.0. There were persistent rumours circulating in Mardy about Horner and other party members were in regular receipt of money from the communist party. Vol and Joan both said that Horner had received no subventions from the CPGB (Francis interview with Vol Tofts; information from Joan Morris).

196 R Frankenberg, notes of second interview with Horner. On 11 February, the *Mineworker* reported the failure of management's fresh attempt to 'be rid of the checkweigher, the well-known figure in the Miners' Federation, and President of the National Miners' Minority Movement, Arthur Horner'. The company had exercised its statutory

right to hold a fresh ballot for checkweighman, and only men currently employed were eligible to vote. Horner won a resounding victory, 153–18. Horner's support came from men who had taken the places of Lodge loyalists.

197 The SWMF Executive minutes of 21 February 1927 noted the manoeuvres.

198 Macfarlane, *CPGB to 1929*, pp. 173–4; CPGB Report of 8th Party Congress, 16–17 October 1926, p. 12.

199 Martin, *Study of NMM*, pp. 93–97; Noreen Branson, *History of the Communist Party of Great Britain 1927–1941*, Lawrence & Wishart, 1985, pp. 6–11.

200 Peter Kingsford, *The Hunger Marchers in Britain 1920–1940*, Lawrence & Wishart, 1982, pp. 40–2. In 1922 the Rhondda men marched sixteen miles to Cardiff to rendezvous with the other Glamorgan contingents. They then proceeded through Newport and picked up the Monmouthshire marchers on the way.

201 HO144/12143, Folder 516773/3, NA Kew. Kingsford lists two additional members of the Organising Committee: John Hughes, Agent for Llwynypia and Noah Rees, Agent for Clydach Vale (p.82). His source is the MFGB paper, edited by John Strachey, the *Miner*.

202 Arthur Horner papers. MNA/PP/46/8–11, SWCC(SU). The minimal punctuation in the original reproduced here is interesting re. Cook's writing skills. Horner consistently wrote with good grammar and punctuation.

203 *Sunday Worker*, 9 October 1927. The headline continued: 'Determined "Reds" from mines, mills and workshops at Communist Conference. Peace Talk Useless. Bosses preparing War at Home and Abroad.' The report described Horner as 'Miners' Federation Executive'.

204 HO144/12143, Folder 5167773/3, NA Kew. The *Mineworker*'s page one headline on 4 November proclaimed, 'Miners' March Not "official". Despite Cruel Sabotage Efforts Will still be Made.' On 23 September, its report had noted that the Rhondda NUWCM was sending a deputation to meet the Rhondda No. 1 District to stress the importance of the march, and the need for the fullest official co-operation with it.

205 HO144/12143, Folder 5167773/3, NA Kew. The London Trades Council voted to support the march on 14 October, passing a motion from Hannington and H Flower. Their decision was reversed by the Trades Council Executive on 7 November after a three hour debate on a card vote of 153–77.

206 NA Kew, HO144/12143, Folder 5167773/3.

207 P Davies, *Cook*, pp. 142–3. Report of Mann's visit in the *Mineworker*, 25 November 1927.

208 R Frankenberg notes of second interview with Horner. Horner wrote an analytic and warm appreciation of Hannington's leadership in a review of Hannington's book, *Mr. Chairman!* in *LM*, July 1950, pp. 331–2.

209 *DH*, 21 November 1927. The Mons Star medal's official name was the 1914 Star. It was awarded to all members of the armed forces who had served in France and Belgium between 5 August 1914 and midnight of 22–23 November 1914. A bar inscribed '5 Aug to 22 Nov 1914' was added underneath for all those who had served under fire.

210 NA Kew, HO144/12143, Folder 5167773/3. The Home Office file noted that Home Office guidance had been conveyed to Boards of Guardians to ensure that the marchers were not given workhouse accommodation. Horner noted that the marchers had been accommodated in workhouses in Maidenhead, Hungerford and Slough, *ICR*, p. 102.

211 *DH* 25 November 1927; NA Kew, HO144/12143, Folder 5167773/3. Saklatvala was a member of the CPGB and a legitimate Labour MP. He had been adopted by the Battersea North constituency Labour Party as their candidate in 1922, when there were no bans or proscriptions against Communists. He had lost the seat in the 1923 general election by 186 votes, but regained it in the 1924 general election with a majority of 542. By the time of the 1929 general election, Communists were unable to stand as Labour candidates and Saklatvala came a poor third after Labour and the Tories, when standing as an outright Communist.

212 Hannington, *Never On Our Knees*, ch.16. Archival research is needed to confirm Hannington's assertion. It does not, however, seem implausible.

213 Horner recalled 'I realized that a new process had to begin ... based on progressive rebuilding ... and defined aims and objectives. This found expression in the publication of a pamphlet, *British Mineworkers' Union*, which Nat Watkins ... and I drafted for the Minority Movement after consultation with miners in all the coalfields.' *ICR*, p. 92.

214 SWMF Executive minutes, 12 March, 27 May, 19 July. The meeting on 19 July noted that whilst the count for the third place had not yet been completed, it was probable that Horner would be elected. His victory was therefore declared so that he could attend the MFGB conference the following week and take his seat.

215 MFGB Annual Conference Report, 1927, pp. 193–4; 134–141.

216 Conference Report, pp. 95–112. Speakers included J Tinker MP from Lancashire, Mardy Jones MP, J Swann, J Sullivan MP, Duncan Graham MP, and Vernon Hartshorn MP, all of whom remarked that they had not intended to speak, but felt compelled to rebut Horner.

217 CPGB Report of Ninth Party Congress, p. 38.

218 Labour Party Conference Report 1927, pp. 196, 220, 266.

219 27 July 1928. On 22 June, the advert. for *Mond Moonshine* in the *Worker* reported that the first 25,000 copies had sold out and described it as 'the pamphlet that stirred the entire labour movement'.

220 Clegg, *Vol. II*, p. 464–71. Branson, *1927–1941*, pp. 32–3. P Davies, *Cook*, pp. 49–51. Thorpe deals with the Cook-Maxton manifesto and the campaign around it on pp. 129–31. Although brokered by the CPGB leadership, the party played no public official role in its dissemination. Branson explained, 'by the time it appeared, the new line had been introduced. This impelled Party headquarters to issue a statement which, while welcoming the Manifesto, nevertheless criticised it as 'weak and sentimental''.

221 M. Worley, 'Courting Disaster? The Comintern in the Third Period', M Worley ed., *In Search of Revolution, International Communist Parties in the Third Period*, IB Tauris, 2004, p. 7.

222 The *Worker* was sanguine, to the point of vanity, about the impact of the British delegation. On 30 March, it reported that the British delegation was entirely composed of men

and women direct from the working class struggle. 'In view of its importance the British situation will receive special attention ... This is as it should be, because the Minority Movement is one of its most active sections, and the British situation of course is of paramount importance not only to British workers, but to workers in the countries oppressed by British imperialism. Reporting back in the *Worker* on 13 April, Gossip noted, 'The British delegates – and the British Minority Movement in particular – came out on top, and in my humble opinion, our own NMM deserved the commendations showered upon it.'

223 The *Worker*, 27 April. Having chaired the Mardy lodge meeting on 22 February, Horner did not do so again until 4–5 May. This was his longest absence since 1923, when he had been in the USSR. Charlie Williams had reported on the RILU Congress to the Lodge on 27 April.

224 Branson, *1927–1941*, quoting Klugmann's notes of the Central Committee.

225 Thorpe, p. 132; Branson *1927–1941*, n. 2, p. 30.

226 Early Lenin School students from South Wales included Bill Williams and Bert Williams from Abertillery, Fred Jenkins, Charlie Stead and Max Goldberg.

227 Matthew Worley, *Class Against Class. The Communist Party in Britain between the Wars*, IB Tauris, 2002, p. 183. Fishman, *British CP and TUs*, chs. 2–3.

228 Roderick Martin, *Communism & the British Trade Unions 1924–1933, A study of the National Minority Movement*, Oxford University Press, 1969, chs. IV and V. Copies of NMM circulars are in the Sam Watson papers, Durham County Record Office. Right-wing DMA lodge officials had received them, and regularly sent them to Richardson.

229 SWMF Executive minutes, 17 May 1927, pp. 7–8. If the cards had not been initialled for two months, the member must be struck off. Lodge books would be subject to inspection.

230 South Wales still fielded the largest conference delegation; Yorkshire and Durham each had eight delegates; Lancashire twelve and Scotland thirteen. AJ Cook submitted the list of nominees for the MFGB Executive from each district along with their nominations for the two elective

national officer posts to the MFGB Executive on 1 June. The Executive nominations were, of course, based on the old distribution of seats. Most districts had renominated Richards for Vice-President; the only other nominees were Horner, who received one nomination from the NMA, and SO Davies nominated by Derbyshire. Horner's version of events is found in *ICR*, pp. 99–100 and the R Frankenberg's notes of the second interview.

231   R Frankenberg, notes of second interview with Horner; report in the *Worker* 27 July 1928. The report stated that this was not the first time Smith had provoked Horner. 'He rose from his chair at the Executive meeting the previous week, not so much to attack as for Horner to attack him, but was restrained by members of the Executive Committee.' See also *ICR*, p. 99, where Horner estimated Smith's weight at sixteen stones. The accounts in *ICR* and the *Worker* are more partisan than Frankenberg's notes, and imply that Smith would have proceeded to hit Horner if Watkins and Horner had not drawn back from the fray.

232   Horner made a reference to the incident at the Fifth NUM Annual Conference in Llandudno in July 1950.

233   Report in the *Worker*, 27 July 1928. The *Worker* now incorporated the *Mineworker*, which consisted of two pages of MMM news. The publication of the *Mineworker* had antedated the *Worker*'s appearance. Its disappearance as a separate paper was probably due to a combination of the need for financial stringency and the decline in ordinary miners' interest in the MMM. Jack Williams was born in 1888 at Kenfig Hill, between Bridgend and Port Talbot. He began work in the International Colliery at the head of the Garw Valley. By 1924, he was General Secretary of the Forest of Dean miners, whilst remaining a militant left-winger in the early SWMF mode. He served on the MFGB Executive in 1924 and 1928. The district unions voting for the resolution were probably South Wales, Lancashire and other smaller districts, for example Cumberland. Cook's article appeared in the *Worker* on 17 August 1928.

234   1928 TUC Report, pp. 74–5, pp. 359–60. R Frankenberg, notes of second interview with Horner. Turner had been

socialised into the strong democratic, civil libertarian traditions of Lancastrian socialism and was evidently swayed by Horner's arguments about the movement's traditional respect for liberty and freedom. Turner's ruling was treated as a precedent, which successive TUC Presidents evidently deemed it impolitic to violate. Left-wing delegates regularly invoked it to justify speaking against the decisions of their delegations. Horner recalled this episode with apparent pride. He regularly reminded youthful Congress delegates that his 1928 achievement was responsible for their freedom to speak as individuals.

235 The figures are in Clegg, *Vol. II*, p. 446.

236 See A Flinn, 'William Rust: The Comintern's Blue-Eyed Boy?' in J McIlroy, K Morgan and A Campbell, eds., *Party People, Communist Lives, Explorations in Biography*, Lawrence & Wishart, 2001.

237 *WL*, 4 January 1929. The strapline was 'The Miners' Voice Calls for One National Union'. The left-hand display box at the top of the page was 'A New Year Resolution'. The corresponding right-hand box was 'One Miners' Union and an end to 1928 conditions'. The headline for Horner's article was '1929. What will it bring the miners? The begging bowl or One Miners' Union?'. There was a sketch of his head alongside the by-line.

238 *WL*, 25 January 1929; M Worley, *Class Against Class*, p. 139. Other members were Bell, Gallacher, Stewart, Rothstein, Murphy, Aitken Ferguson and Inkpin.

239 *WL*, 18 and 25 January 1929. Horner spoke with Ernest Brown on 20 January. The Profile contained several inaccuracies, including that he had lived in the Rhondda all his life. Its description of his union activities began that he had been everything from doorkeeper to chairman. 'Even now he is the elected member to both [SWMF and MFGB Executives], but the reduction in membership of The Federation caused the reduction to be made in the number of Executive members.'

240 Nina Fishman, *The British Communist Party and the Trade Unions, 1933–45*, Scolar Press, 1995, p. 33; Branson, *1927–41*, pp. 33–6.

241 Macfarlane, *CPGB to 1929*, p. 269. At the party Executive meeting which had taken the decision, Pollitt had emphasised that there should not be new unions until they had been 'forced upon us'. Horner observed that Scotland 'cannot be treated as a thing apart from the MFGB ... We should not ... take any step in Scotland that might ease our position there but damn us in every other part of the country. The smaller struggle must submit to the larger. We should not have talked about setting up new organisations, but only of capturing the old and keeping the old even if the reformists set up new ones.' Pollitt Papers, CPGB Archive, PHMM. Thanks to Kevin Morgan for this reference.

242 For example, during the 1929 general election, Horner and Pollitt exchanged meetings in Rhondda East and Seaham, where Pollitt was opposing MacDonald. Pollitt commented: 'I believe that the only national speaker who helped me ... was Arthur Horner. I needed that opportunity in Rhondda very badly. For no matter what I did in Seaham Harbour it was impossible to arouse any enthusiasm for our policy. To get into Judges Hall in Tonypandy and feel the place rock with applause was like wine after the stormy silence at my meetings in Seaham Harbour.' Harry Pollitt papers, early draft of *Serving My Time*. I owe this reference to Kevin Morgan.

243 CI archives, Moscow, 495/100/497, Politburo meeting, 8 June 1928. I owe this reference to Kevin Morgan.

244 There were 44,834 votes cast in Rhondda East, a turn-out of 84.7 per cent. The result was: Morgan 19,010 (50.2 %); Chalke 10,269 (27.0 %); Horner 5789 (15.2%); JF Powell, 2901 (7.6 %). The other three constituencies were: Battersea North, where the communist S Saklatvala came third with 6554 votes (18.6%) after the Labour and Tory candidates (see n. 211); Greenock, where the Liberals continued their ascendancy, Labour coming second, and the communist Alec Geddes third, gaining 7005 votes (20.4 %). Geddes had stood in the seat in every election since 1922, coming second in 1922, 1923, and 1924. The 1929 election was the first time he had stood on behalf of the CPGB. In 1922 he was the candidate of the local unemployed movement; in 1923 he stood as a communist endorsed by the local

Labour Party; in 1924 he stood as the Trades Council candidate, and beat the Labour candidate into third place. Thorpe reckons that Geddes' vote cost Labour this seat in successive elections (p. 141); Fife West, where Willie Gallacher stood for the first time and gained 6040 votes (20.5 per cent), beating the Conservative into third place. Will Paynter, *MGen*, Allen & Unwin, 1972, p. 34.

245 Mardy Lodge minutes; *WL* 20 September 1929. The conference was 14–16 September. NUWM headed paper used for correspondence in 1930 listed Horner as Vice-President.

246 MI5 file PF 601, V.1. The file noted that he had been present in Berlin for the discussions between Petrovsky and members of the CPGB Politburo, which took place immediately after the general election. He was absent from Britain between 5–9 June, leaving for Berlin via Harwich, where he would have caught the ferry and proceeded by train.

247 Worley, 'Courting Disaster?', *In Search of Revolution*, p. 9; Flinn, 'William Rust', *Party People*, p. 87.

248 Thorpe, pp. 130–1. The only other proponent of obeying the Labour constitution was Bill Loeber, veteran NUR activist and carriage cleaner from Hornsey. Horner held this position consistently, declaring that as an individual communist he would have no problems in conscientiously observing the Labour Party's constitution and rules, in 1938, 1943 and 1946, when questions around the CPGB's position towards Labour and its affiliation to the Labour Party were debated at Labour Party Conference.

249 *WL*, 11 January 1929.

250 Information from MI5 file PFI V1, 44A, from Police Officer who arrested Horner in Harwich on 8 December 1931.

251 John Mahon, *Harry Pollitt, A Biography*, Lawrence & Wishart, 1976, p. 171; Martin, *Study of NMM*, p. 124. Martin acknowledged help from Renshaw and JT Murphy, mentioning interviews with Renshaw in particular, (p. vi).

252 Worley, *Class Against Class*, pp. 139–41; Thorpe, *British CP & Moscow*, pp. 141–4.

253 Branson, *1927–1941*, p. 48.

254 Branson, *1927–1941*, p. 46–7; Thorpe, *British CP & Moscow*, pp. 142–4.

255 Branson, *1927–1941*, pp. 48–51.

256 Thorpe, *British CP & Moscow*, p. 157.
257 Central Committee Meeting, 15 March 1931, C12, CPGB Archive, PHMM.

Chapter 7. Trials of Will and Conscience

258 MI5 file PF601, V.1.
259 Horner had attended the Fourth RILU Congress in Moscow in March 1928. Horner's MI5 file recorded his visit to Berlin in March 1927, 'where he obtained "the doings" [money and/or policies for the MMM]'. He was in Berlin on 25–28 January 1929 for 'the annual conference of Revolutionary Miners, convened by the Miners' International Propaganda and Action Committee [MIC]', which he described in *WL* on 8 February. He was in Germany again on 9–13 September 1929.
260 Michael Foot, *Aneurin Bevan A Biography, Vol. 1 1897–1945*, MacGibbon & Kee, 1962, n. 2, p. 125; he noted that Bevan's diary of the trip was 'stuffed with pig-iron statistics'; Michael Newman, *John Strachey*, Manchester University Press, 1989, pp. 32–3.
261 Report of Ninth CPGB Congress. The 'Brief Summary of District Organisation Reports' to the 1926 Congress stated that South Wales membership had approximately doubled, to slightly over 1500, with local organisations increasing by 16 to 41. Having had few women members, there were now 250. Trade union fractions were functioning well, 'especially' in SWMF lodges.
262 Worley, *Class Against Class*, n. 47, p. 264.
263 The importance of party members undertaking self-criticism had been stressed by Stalin at the Fifteenth Congress of the Russian Communist Party in 1927. Prior to 1926–7, there was insufficient membership in South Wales to warrant the formation of membership groups in most mining villages. The Executive's report to the 1925 Seventh Congress enumerated only 5 local party committees and 19 group leaders committees in South Wales. The increased membership gave rise to serious attempts to institute a more regular organisational structure. Thus, when the twenty-three years old Will Paynter joined the party in 1929, 'It

was not long before I was made secretary of the small Porth branch, given two paper rounds covering a very wide area, one to deliver the *Workers Life* on Fridays and the other the *Sunday Worker* on Sundays.' *MGen*, p. 34.

264 Thorpe, *British CP & Moscow*, p. 157; Lewis Jones, *We Live.* pp. 192–5, Lawrence & Wishart, 1988. The novel was published posthumously in 1939, and the introduction states that it was considerably edited by Mavis Llewellyn, who was Jones's close friend and companion. She was a keen communist, as were her father and uncle. Her editing may have magnified Jones' uncertainty about Horner's conduct and attitudes. As a member of the South Wales DPC in the mid-1930s, she continued to oppose Horner and demand that he accept party discipline.

265 Letter from Horner to RILU Executive, Moscow, 29 November 1929, Photostat obtained by H Francis at Comintern archive, May, 1984. Horner's signature appears to be hand-written; Duplicated letter of 7 January 1930 in Jack Tanner Papers, Nuffield College, Oxford, Box 1, folder 1.2. Dates of Horner's travel, MI5 file, PF501, V.1, NA, Kew.

266 Worley, *Class Against Class*, pp. 236–7; Thorpe, p. 157.

267 CPGB Archive, PHMM, Minutes, CI2 Central Committee (CC), 15 March 1931.

268 SWMF Executive Minutes, SWCC(SU).

269 *ICR*, p. 109; Frankenberg notes, third interview.

270 H Francis interview with Vol Tofts, information from Joan Morris.

271 SWMF Executive minutes, SWCC(SU).

272 MI5 file, PF601. NA, Kew. *ICR*, p. 109. The telegram would not have been an official SWMF notification. It was probably sent by SO Davies.

273 Quoted in Worley, *Class Against Class*, n. 72, p. 38. On 1 February, the *DW* reported that a leader from the Central Organisation Department, Rust perhaps, had spoken at an extended District Party meeting in South Wales. 'The discussion showed that there was agreement in "principle", but many practical difficulties were raised [about building factory pit cells and strengthening party organisation for the main task of waging mass struggles against the Labour

government]. It was clear that some comrades were more concerned with the difficulties than with the measures to be adopted to surmount these difficulties. This form of opposition to the formation of pit cells arises mainly from lack of political understanding ... Contradictory as it may seem, the militant tradition of the SWMF, now a fully-fledged Mondist union is an important factor in preventing clarity among Party members on this question.'

274 *ICR*, p. 109.

275 Frankenberg notes, third interview. Horner told Frankenberg that before he left for Russia he had counselled the Mardy Lodge to continue to pay their subscriptions into a separate fund as evidence of their sincere desire to return to the SWMF fold. In *ICR*, Horner omitted any mention of the role of the MMM and Dai Lloyd Davies in determining the Lodge's refusal to compromise. Information about Dai Lloyd's emotional reaction from Frankenberg interview with Charlie Jones. The Allan/Laughlin version is given in the NMM pamphlet, *Why Mardy was Expelled! A Lucid Account of the Struggles between the South Wales Miners and the SWMF Bureaucrats*, with a Foreword by Allan.

276 Worley, *Class Against Class*, p. 247. Allison, acting MMM chairman had observed, 'if we cannot form a pit committee in South Wales, how can we form a union?'

277 Thorpe, *British CP & Moscow*, pp. 162–163 (italics mine). Tom Bell had continued as the British ECCI representative until November 1929. In December he was replaced by a Liverpool ETU activist, Alec Hermon, who never managed to master the intricacies of Comintern politics. Campbell, a self-taught fluent Russian speaker, was despatched to 'assist' him in January 1930. Campbell displayed such political dexterity that his position as British representative was formalised by June.

278 MI5 file, PF601, NA, Kew. They were seen off by well-wishers from the family, Hannington and Ernie Cant. Cant was one of the twelve party members convicted and imprisoned in 1925. He was originally a miner, Horner probably came to know him well during the Save the Union campaign in Nottinghamshire. He was a keen Horner sup-

porter who had recently been demoted from Nottingham CPGB organiser to Sheffield sub-district organiser.

279 Joan remembered that she baulked at being put to bed by anyone but Arthur. He arrived to sit with her every evening and held her hand until she fell asleep. She and Ethel also became friendly with an American child in the Hotel Lux, Bobby. Joan recalled, 'I think my mother might have taken us to the park where Bobby accosted every Russian soldier he came across' (Information from Joan Morris).

280 *ICR*, p. 112.

281 I am grateful to Reiner Tosstorff for information about Slutsky. MI5 file, PFI 601, V1, NA, Kew. Horner made the arrangement by telephone, and presumably chose Tilmanstone colliery because the Russians were coming by boat across the Channel. His contact in the Kent Miners' Association might have been Will Lawther's younger brother, Ernie, or Bob Ellis, who may have already moved from the Rhondda to the Kent coalfield.

282 Thorpe, *British CP & Moscow*, pp. 165–7.

283 Thorpe, *British CP & Moscow*, pp. 167–8, 170; Francis notes of Comintern archive 1984; JK folder 14, CPGB archive, PHMM. Herbert Howarth, a young Sheffield engineer at the Lenin School, attended Commission meetings presumably for their learning value. He remembered a battle between the ECCI representatives and the British Politburo about trade unions. He recalled Pollitt, Horner and Campbell attending, and also that Kuusinen 'didn't half hand some bloody stick out. I was wondering what was going on.' Interview with Nina Fishman, 1990.

284 Thorpe, *British CP & Moscow*, pp. 168–71.

285 Francis notes of Comintern archive 1984; JK folder 14, CPGB archive, PHMM; Thorpe, p. 170.

286 MI5 file, PF601, NA Kew; transcript of Frank Williams interview SWML; Thorpe, *British CP & Moscow*, p. 175.

287 Supple, *Coal 1913–1946*, p. 334–5.

288 MI5 file, PF 601, V.1, NA, Kew.

289 Transcript of Executive meeting 30 May to 1 June 1931, JK folder 14, CPGB archive, PHMM.

290 P Davies, *Cook*, pp. 109, 176–8.

291 P Davies, *Cook*, p. 183. Horner had assisted Cook on international negotiations in 1926. He recalled that he had 'accompanied Arthur Cook on several occasions when we met the Russian trade union leaders' (*ICR*, p. 93).

292 MI5 file, PFI 601 V.1, NA Kew.

293 Francis and Smith, p. 175; Supple, *Coal 1913–46*, p. 336; Ness Edwards, *History of the South Wales Miners' Federation*, Vol. I, Lawrence & Wishart, 1938, pp. 145–7.

294 Francis and Smith, p. 176. Francis and Smith refer to this first dispute as a strike. Ness Edwards makes it clear that it was, in fact, a lock-out.

295 MI5 file PF601 V.1, NA Kew.

296 Francis and Smith, p. 176. They noted, 'The EC declared themselves satisfied for, in difficult circumstances, the "intentions of the Owners had been thwarted, and the Organisation was maintained unbroken even in parts that were known to be fragile".'

297 Rothstein told the CPGB Secretariat in a letter on 8 May that on 21 January Horner had also sent a letter to the AAS, which may have been addressed to Arnot. This is likely to have had similar contents, and was presumably sent in the expectation that the AAS personnel would provide him with ideological support. 'Letter of Horner to RILU (International Miners – via AR) Jan 21 1931', in JK folder 14, 756 – Misc 1931 – chiefly Horner', CPGB archive, PHMM. Events in the coalfields in February and March had been equally bleak for expectant militants. Laughlin had been active, but unable to record positive results. See *DW*, 17, 21, 23, 28 February 1931.

298 JK folder, 14, typescript, Horner's statement to Executive 30 May to 1 June 1931, pp. 97–100, CPGB archive, PHMM; Worley, *Class Against Class*, n. 102, p. 267.

299 JK folder 14, PB meeting, 23 January 1931, p. 5, CPGB Archive, PHMM.

300 Thorpe, *British CP & Moscow*, pp. 175–6.

301 *ICR*, pp. 107–108. Citrine recalled the afternoon in *Men and Work: an autobiography*, Hutchinson, 1964, p. 210. He and Horner both misdated it, as did I in 'Horner and Hornerism' (p. 137), *Party People*, eds. J McIlroy, K Morgan and A Campbell. Citrine's conversation with Mikhail

Tomsky, President of the All-Russian Central Council of Trade Unions, had probably taken place in 1925, when Citrine and George Hicks had visited Moscow as Tomsky's guest (*Men and Work*, chap. 6).

302 Horner had been MMM president since the post was created. However, the post was elective, and a formal contest took place during the Industrial Section meetings at the NMM annual conference at the end of August. Horner had been duly re-elected in August 1930. On his return to Britain, having been fully rehabilitated by the Special Commission, he had resumed his leading role in the MMM.

303 The MI5 file noted that Sobotka had written to Horner with news of a meeting in Berlin on 13–14 February 'to consider his quarrel with the Central Committee'. PF601 V.1, NA, Kew.

304 Horner's MI5 file quoted a letter written by Horner stating that he had had a '30/- food ticket from the Guardians'. PF601 V.1, NA Kew.

305 Thorpe, *British CP & Moscow*, pp. 176–177.

306 Francis and Smith, pp. 176–177.

307 For strikes, see *DW*, 4–7, 9–12, 14, 16–20, 24 March 1931.

308 Thorpe, *British CP & Moscow*, p. 177.

309 PF601 V.1, NA Kew. Emphasis is Horner's.

310 Francis and Smith, pp. 176–7. The Award was accepted with the caveat that the Government be approached to enact an amendment to the Minimum Wage Act of 1912, to ensure that the wage awarded by Schiller would be the same in real terms as the 1914 level.

311 JK folder 14, PB of 9 April 1931, pp. 15, 190, CPGB archive, PHMM; Thorpe, *British CP & Moscow*, p. 177.

312 *DW*, 9,10 April 1931. Paynter recalled 'I found myself supporting his [Horner's] stand. The issue became the subject of widespread discussion with the Party ... I felt there was a tendency to pillory Horner and that the facts were more than a little distorted and I stated this. The experience left me a little sour for a time' (*MGen*, p. 49).

313 The Plenum took place from 26 March to 11 April. EH Carr, *The Twilight of the Comintern 1930–1935*, Macmillan, 1982, p. 211; Thorpe, *British CP & Moscow*, p. 177.

314 Francis, photostat from Comintern Archive, May 1984.
315 R Skidelsky, *Oswald Mosley*, Macmillan, 1975, p. 255. Towards the end of April Cook was incapacitated and unable to work. He would have listened to Strachey in a debilitated and psychologically uncertain state.
316 The Executive was due to meet on 30 May. Francis, photostat from Comintern Archive, May 1984. Horner's penury was reflected in Pollitt's final sentence: 'Let us know at once whether the above time and date will be suitable to you, and we will then wire you the fare. All the best, Yours fraternally, Harry Pollitt.'
317 JK folder 14, pp. 16–24, 86–132, PHMM. Rust's attack on Horner is on pp. 111–2.
318 *ICR*, p. 111.
319 MI5 file PF601 V.1, NA Kew; Thorpe, *British CP & Moscow*, p. 178. The account in *ICR* is inaccurate in many details, and Horner told Frankenberg very little about the Hornerism conflict. The ECCI letter was copied by the Special Branch officer who searched Horner on his arrival back from Berlin on 30 December 1931. It was amongst his effects, along with a carbon copy of the Comintern 'Resolution on the question of Comrade Horner'. Horner may have felt vulnerable to political attack from hostile party comrades. The two documents on his person would have been his defence, providing firm evidence that he had completed the requisite self-criticism and the ECCI had exonerated him of ideological error. Otto Kuusinen was a long-serving member of the Comintern Presidium. For more on this EH Carr, *The Twilight of the Comintern 1930-1935*, Macmillan, 1982, p. 5.
320 JK folder 14, pp. 16–24, 86–132, PHMM. Thorpe cited the letter which Horner sent to the CPGB Secretariat on 5 June, which stated that 'he could not make the unequivocal statement it [CPGB Executive] wanted, but that he now welcomed the chance to go to Moscow to discuss the matter with a view to reaching "a final conclusion".'
321 Thorpe, *British CP & Moscow*, p. 178, quoting Politburo minutes, 25 June 1931.

322 R Page Arnot, *A History of the Miners' Federation of Great Britain, Vol. III (from 1930 onwards), The Miners in Crisis and War*, Allen & Unwin, 1961, pp. 55–7; Supple, *Coal 1913–1946*, pp. 336–7.

323 Thorpe, *British CP & Moscow*, pp. 178–9. Rust also sent Arnot a copy of a letter from Garfield Williams, keen supporter of the new line and prominent in South Wales MMM, with further evidence of Horner's 'deviations'. N Fishman, 'Horner and Hornerism', *Party People*, n. 66, p. 142. I differ from Thorpe's assessment of Arnot's role.

324 H Francis, 'Notes of discussion about Hornerism in CPGB Historians' Group 1985'.

325 *ICR*, p. 111. Horner recalled that he had gone swimming at the Dynamo Club between hearings. Arnot had 'put the case against me in a very kindly and objective way. I put my case in reply ... We would meet for two or three days and then adjourn while the translations were considered.'

326 JK folder 14, Politburo meeting of 17 September, p. 25, 153–5, CPGB Archive, PHMM.

327 Central Committee meeting of 19–20 September, pp. 25–28, 282–8 JK folder 14, CPGB Archive, PHMM. The MI5 file PF601 V.1, NA, Kew, noted Horner's return from Russia on 19 September.

328 MI5 file PF601 V.1, NA Kew.

329 On 6 November, the *DW* noted that the communist party had gained 206 recruits in South Wales as a result of the election campaign, all of whom came from Rhondda East: 47 from Mardy, 40 from Tylorstown, 20 from Ferndale and 8 from Ynyshir. On 4 November, the *DW* had lamented the fact that only a small number of employed miners had joined the party as a result of the campaign.

330 In 1930 the national Miners' Relief Committee Under Auspices of Workers' International Relief was still sending out correspondence with its letterhead listing: National Executive. Arthur Horner, SWMF; S O Davies, Vice-President, SWMF; Philip Hodge; Willie Allan, Secretary Lanarkshire Miners' Union; J Stephenson, DMA; H Hicken Derbyshire Miners' Association; Isaac Burns, YMA,; George Wood, Lancs. and Cheshire Miners' Association; Mrs AJ Cook;

Mrs Helen Crawfurd, Hon. Sec. Workers International Relief; JV Leckie, Secretary.

331 Branson, *1927–1941*, p. 88. Thorpe, *British CP & Moscow*, p. 181. I have used Thorpe's figure of 7.5 per cent rather than Branson's 7.3 per cent. Pollitt was contesting Stepney Whitechapel and St George's for the second time, and again lost his deposit. His vote increased from 2106 in the 1930 by-election to 2658. The New Party candidate received 154 votes.

332 Davies was well known in the Rhondda. He worked at Llwynypia, and was a 'foundation member' of the SWMF. The *DW* noted that he had led picket lines in the 1910–11 Cambrian Combine strike and that he had been chairman of the Llwynypia lodge since 1925. He was also one of the veterans sent to Nottinghamshire in 1926 by the SWMF Executive to help the NMA combat Spencer and staunch the return to work.

333 Letter from Andrew Thorpe to N Fishman, 3 December 2004. '[It] seems to me that there was a strong anti-Labour feeling in 1931 and Labour shipped votes in every direction. *Even the CP* could get *something* from this, especially where it was the only alternative to vote for.' See also Andrew Thorpe, *The British General Election of 1931*, Oxford University Press, 1991.

334 ICR, pp. 106–7. Horner's comment that 'when we quarrelled we quarrelled like brothers and our quarrels were very bitter indeed' was a reflection on both men's volatility and strong emotions.

335 Thorpe, *British CP & Moscow*, pp. 183–4; Fishman, *British CP and TUs*, chs. 2 and 3.

336 See also *DW*, 14–16, 23, 26 January 1932; and Idris Cox in *DW*, 15 February 1932.

Chapter 8. Watershed

337 Frankenberg notes of third Horner interview. *ICR*, pp. 113–5. Francis and Smith, pp. 180–3, using an interview with Trevor Davies in 1973, transcript in SWML, describe the Council of Action as 'virtually an anti-bailiff committee' with the same personnel as the Mardy Distress

Committee. The *ICR* account describes Horner as having been engaged in an election committee meeting. We have already observed that the Distress Committee functioned as Horner's election committee in 1931. It was evidently an all-purpose agitational institution, whose name changed according to the circumstance, but whose roots and networks probably stretched back to the 1921 Lock-Out.

338 Horner told Frankenberg that he left for Russia on 10 November (R Frankenberg notes of third Horner interview). This coincides with the sequence of events recorded in *ICR*. His MI5 file, NA Kew, PF601.V.1 records his date of leaving Britain as 24 November. He may have left Mardy on 10 November to visit MMM activists in English and Scottish coalfields to gather support for the MIC conference in the intervening fortnight.

339 R Frankenberg, Notes of third Horner interview. MI5 file PF601 V.1, NA Kew.

340 MI5 file PF601 V.1, NA Kew. Pollitt had been abducted by a group describing itself as 'British Fascisti' whilst travelling to Liverpool in March 1925. See Mahon, *Pollitt*, pp. 116–7.

341 *ICR*, pp. 115–6.

342 Francis and Smith, pp. 180–182, R Frankenberg notes of third Interview with Horner.

343 Francis and Smith, p. 182.

344 *ICR*, p. 124.

345 Horner celebrated his thirty-eighth birthday in prison. Encouraged by ICWPA, comrades and well-wishers sent birthday cards to him in Cardiff Gaol. Some, including Jack Tanner's, are in the Horner papers, SWCC(SU).

346 *ICR*, p. 122. Frankenberg's notes recorded a more human account of Horner's time in prison than the pious narrative in *Incorrigible Rebel*. It is unclear whether it was Schaffer or Horner who sanitised the narrative.

347 Frankenberg notes of third interview with Horner.

348 *ICR*, p. 122.

349 Michael Howard, *Clausewitz*, Oxford University Press, 1983, pp. 5–6.

350 *ICR*, pp. 125–6, 141, 152. The second *ICR* reference refers to a protracted dispute over the payment for small coal in

the Anthracite which Horner conducted through litigation. It was not finally settled in the miners' favour until after Cripps had argued the case in the House of Lords. The quotation in the final *ICR* reference is from the Federation journal, *The Miners' Monthly*, December 1936. Goodman recalled that Horner regularly acknowledged his debt to Clausewitz.

351 Arthur Horner papers, MNA/PP/46/1–5. The reference to Gwen's is probably a party planned to celebrate his release at Gwen Ray Evans' house in Pontypridd.

352 MI5 file PF601. V.1, NA, Kew. There is a copy letter from Arthur's younger brother Albert to Ethel, dated 29 February 1932, enclosing a five shillings Postal Order which he promises to send every week, 'from the boys where I am working'. It is signed 'Your affectionate brother Albert'. It is not clear whether the postal order in fact continued. The notes on file state that Horner's wage ceased in February 1932. 'For a few weeks after his imprisonment his wife did not receive any money from the Communist Party, but Harry POLLITT informed her that this was due to a mistake which would be rectified.' It is possible that Horner's income from the MIC, which would have been paid via King Street, was stopped from Moscow, and that Pollitt found money for Ethel from his own budget.

353 Len Jeffries and other Cardiff comrades had also suspected the authorities' likely moves. They had accordingly organised 'a reception in a little cafe near the prison just off the Newport Road' in case Arthur was released early. R Frankenberg, notes of third interview with Horner.

354 For the Twelfth Party Congress, Pollitt's manoeuvres, and rank-and-file movements, see Fishman, *British CP and TUs*, pp. 40–57 and ch. 6.

355 Frankenberg interview with Charlie Jones. Francis and Smith, pp. 189–190.

356 Letter quoted in Mahon, pp. 179–80.

357 KV2/1769, NA Kew. Letter from Pollitt to the South Wales DPC and letter from Cox to Garfield Williams on 11 March 1933 are noted in the Narrative at the beginning of each personal file. Denominated Minute Sheet, it provided a

chronicle of dates, followed by the number and title of each piece in the file.

358 *ICR*, p. 128. Horner recalled the content of his *Election Special* and commented that 'Naturally in the campaign – and I did not blame him – he [Mainwaring] made use of my quarrel with the Communist Party ... ' The number of Labour's public meetings and their speakers are from Chris Williams PhD, ch. 7.

359 Chris Williams PhD, ch. 7, fn. 46. The quotation from Mainwaring's *Election Special* is from Williams, ch. 7, fn. 45.

360 The by-election result was Mainwaring 14,127; Horner 11,228; WD Thomas (Liberal) 7851.

361 KV2/1769, NA Kew. Narrative and piece 65b summarising letter from Secretariat to Trevor Robinson, full-time party official in Bolton. Cox's official title was 'South Wales Organiser and representative from Party Centre'. Letter from Lindsay to Vernon Kells, 18 July 1933. Pontyclun was about eight miles south of Tonypandy.

362 Ness Edwards, *History of the South Wales Miners' Federation Volume I*, Lawrence & Wishart, 1938, p. 152. The final ballot result for general secretary was Harris 35,000, SO Davies 32,040. Edwards observed that the ballot 'was conducted in an indecent display of personalities and personal advertisement'.

363 Quoted in Thorpe, *British CP & Moscow*, p. 204.

364 Edwards, *History of SWMF Vol. I*, pp. 154–5. For the reorganisation scheme see Francis and Smith, pp. 183–6.

365 Taped discussion between Basil Barker and Herbert Howarth, transcribed by Bill Moore, ca. 1980. It was not surprising that comrades from South Yorkshire and Derbyshire, where unemployment was also a problem, were shocked at Horner's poverty. In the Rhondda, the margins of subsistence had slipped very low indeed.

366 *ICR*, pp. 132–3. Frankenberg notes of third interview.

367 *ICR*, p. 133.

368 Frankenberg Notes. Horner recalled the gist of Gomer's speech, 'If there are going to be no bans, let there be no bloody bans at all'.

369 *ICR*, p. 129.

370 Edgar had gone to work for a co-op in Basingstoke, probably to avoid the draft. Whilst there he met his own future wife, Dolly, and Winnie Rutley who he introduced to Griffiths. Winnie and Jim were also married in 1918. Interview with Alan Bassett by Nina Fishman; James Griffiths, *Pages from Memory*, JM Dent, 1969, p. 23.

371 2 December 1933. The *Voice* found it expedient on this occasion to describe Horner more extensively and positively than it had done throughout the campaign. Thus, 'He has been one of the advanced members of The Federation for many years, and was closely associated with the late Mr. A.J. Cook ... Even his bitterest political opponent, and he has as many as any man in Welsh politics, pay [*sic*] tribute to his ability as a speaker and as an organiser.'

372 *SWV*, 4 November 1933, published full results. The top four candidates received: Horner 3057, Brazell 2038, E Lewis 1821, DB Lewis 1722.

373 *SWV*, 11 November 1933. The second ballot result was Horner 7725, Brazell 4381, E Lewis 3323, DB Lewis 2410.

374 *SWV*, 18 November 1933. Sam Davies' article in the *Horner Special* appeared as a letter in the same issue of the *Voice* along with a letter from Evan John Samuel, an Executive member of the Rhondda No. 1 District opposing Horner. Samuel pleaded, 'I make an earnest appeal to the anthracite miners to fully realise what is at stake in the final ballot ... *The future of the Anthracite District is at stake, so return Brazell, and uphold the traditions of your district in the mind of the Rhondda miners.*'

375 *SWV*, 18 November 1933.

376 *SWV*, 2 December 1933. The third ballot vote was Horner 10,130, Brazell 7,186.

377 *SWV*, 2 December 1933.

378 Francis and Smith, p. 191.

Chapter 9. The Datcha in the Anthracite

379 Arnot, *Vol. III*, pp. 122–6. Ebby Edwards refuted them at length in his winding-up speech for the Executive.

380 Claims for compensation for industrial injury and industrial disease required detailed care and attention to ensure that the colliery company accepted liability and also that the claimant received the maximum amount from the company.

381 Information from Joan Morris. Upper Tumble was the colloquial name for the group of houses on the northern outskirts of the village of Tumble. The standard English spelling is 'dacha'; I have used Horner's spelling 'Datcha' to refer to his house's name.

382 The number of agents had been reduced in the other seven areas. The Garw, Rhondda, Aberdare and Tredegar areas each had two agents; the Rhymney and East Glamorgan areas each had three; and the Afan Valley one.

383 *DW*, 14 April 1934.

384 *ICR*, p. 132. Horner probably recalled the occasion so clearly because it was his first appearance at a union conference in four years. See also Francis and Smith, pp. 198–200.

385 Horner probably travelled to the party office in Tonypandy for editorial meetings of SWM, then published monthly. Idris Cox, 'Story of a Welsh Rebel', unpublished typescript, p. 57, SWCC (SU); Paynter, *MGen*, p. 101.

386 Francis and Smith, p. 201.

387 SO Davies was returned with a majority of 8000 votes over the Liberal candidate in an 81.8 per cent turn-out; the ILP and CPGB candidates lost their deposits. Hannington was the high-profile communist candidate, well-known and regarded in Merthyr for his extensive NUWM activity in the area. Despite the party's energetic campaign of public meetings, addressed by Harry and Marjorie Pollitt, Mrs Elsie Despard, and Tom Mann, Davies swept all before him. Rhondda party members were also drafted in, including George Maslin, Jack Davies, Fred Llewelyn and Lewis Jones. Phil Abrahams and Enoch Collins from the DPC also participated. Horner was signed up for three of the main meetings at 7 pm. In the Square in Treharris with George Harris and in the Town Hall Square with Marjorie Pollitt, Tom Mann and Nicholas (Glas). And in Aberfan in The Park, with Cox and Jack Davies. Horner and Tom Mann were the only peripatetic speakers and were proba-

bly conveyed to successive engagements by car (Duplicated schedule of meetings, deposited in Merthyr Tydfil Central Reference Library, by Ion Williams).

388 Francis and Smith quote a letter which made the same judgement of Horner's role from EG Cox, secretary of the Emlyn Lodge, to CJ Prosser, secretary of the Gwendraeth Valley SWMF Group. fn. 109, p. 210.

389 Paynter, *MGen*, p. 101.

390 Griffiths, *Pages from Memory*, pp. 35–6.

391 Francis and Smith, p. 216, quoting Ness Edwards' unpublished *History of the SWMF, Vol. II*. Ness Edwards became full-time Secretary of the large Penallta Lodge in the Rhymney Valley in 1927, succeeding Bryn Roberts. He had become Agent in 1932.

392 Francis and Smith, pp. 91–2, 211–2, 93.

393 Francis and Smith, pp. 215, 93. The collectors were paid 10s. per week and a commission of 6s.8d. in the pound for subscriptions collected.

394 Francis and Smith, pp. 211, 215. 'During the coalfield strike of January 1931, Taff-Merthyr, with a work-force of 1,600 men produced 2,000 tons daily ... '

395 Francis and Smith, p. 216. They add: 'There was no Labour Party as such in Bedlinog; even the Chamber of Commerce had, for a time, a CP majority. Edgar Evans joined the CPGB in 1926, and served on the DPC from 1933.

396 Francis and Smith, pp. 275–7; Chris Williams, *Capitalism, Community and Conflict. The South Wales Coalfield 1878–1947*, University of Wales Press, 1998, pp. 4–5. The Chairman of the Cory Combine Committee was Archie James, a party activist who worked at Tydraw Colliery in the Upper Rhondda Fawr. The Anthracite Combine was the most geographically concentrated. Powell Duffryn and the Ocean owned pits throughout the steam coalfield, stretching from western Monmouthshire to west Glamorgan. The Committees were intended to be merely advisory. In practice, there were regular tensions between the committees and the Executive, notably when the Executive was requested to sanction a committee's decision to take official strike action. Official strikes in a combine committee involved thousands of men and the Executive therefore

incurred a heavy financial responsibility for strike pay. The Combine Committee officers claimed to be nearer to the rank-and-file and therefore more capable of taking decisions which were really democratic.

397 Francis and Smith, fn. 30, p. 239; and transcript of interview with Edgar Evans on 14 July 1973, pp. 36–7. The 'essential people' may have been a euphemism for either SWMIU members or leading militants.

398 The Merthyr and Dowlais NUWM was well organised. Illtyd Harrington's father, who was a party member and NUWM activist in Merthyr, was friendly with Horner. Illtyd had a vivid memory of his childhood excitement and sense of importance when he marched with his father and Arthur. Interview with N Fishman.

399 Wayne David, *Remaining True: A Biography of Ness Edwards*, Caerphilly Local History Society, 2006, p. 14; Francis and Smith, p. 217. It is likely that Horner had been advising the Ocean Combine Committee on their campaign earlier in the summer.

400 We have observed Horner's success as an agitator on the nightshift at Ynyshir in 1915. See pp. 53–54. The paucity of management on nightshifts facilitated union activity on hostile terrain. Engineering union activists at Ford's Dagenham used the night-shift as their first redoubt in the 1930s, as did Trevor Robinson, a Sheffield toolmaker. See Fishman, *British CP and TUs*, p. 58; and N Fishman interview with Trevor Robinson, 11 April 1979.

401 *DW*, 29 September 1934.

402 MI5 evidence here.

403 David, *Ness Edwards*, pp. 14–5. 'At a mass meeting on a steep mountainside above the colliery over 200 joined The Federation and in the villages it was a similar story, with 200 men in Bedlinog alone paying their dues. "But the Federation campaigners", wrote Ness, "had underestimated the length to which the Company Union would go".'

404 Frankenberg's notes of interview, 19.10.1961, undertaken in connection with Arnot's history of the SWMF. RF file, 'Welsh Mining History'.

405 David, *Ness Edwards*, p. 15. David states that there were 1500 employed. Francis and Smith cite an SWMF estimate of the numbers of strikers as 1400 on 7 November, p. 227.

406 Francis and Smith devote a chapter to 'Taff-Merthyr: the Crucible', pp. 211–243.

407 In interviews during the 1970s, Edgar Evans recalled the high emotion and anger in meetings of the village party branch and the NUWM, but made no mention of Horner's position. He was apparently determined not to unlock what he thought was still a Pandora's box for Horner's reputation in South Wales (Transcripts in SWML).

408 *DW*, 15–16 October; 7–8, 13, 17, 19, 26, 29 November; 4, 19 December 1934. The South Wales District Party Congress was chaired by Charlie Stead, party organiser for the Swansea sub-district. He and Horner were probably allies.

409 *ICR*, p. 135. Francis and Smith cite this passage with approval on p. 231.

410 Thorpe, pp. 208–219.

411 For example, Pollitt wrote to Rust in Moscow: 'We had Cox up yesterday to discuss mining. Horner sent us a wire saying that he had missed the train. For your information you must realise that we have not got, and it will get more difficult, an easy time trying to get Arthur and [Ianto] Evans to work closely with the Party leadership in Wales. They have always good excuses you understand of why trade union engagements prevent them attending Party meetings. At the District Congress Horner proposed that he should not go on the DPC because he would not be able to attend so often. He even went to the Panels Commission on this, but was defeated.' I am grateful to Kevin Morgan for this reference, 27 January 1934. No. 42, Moscow Archives. The MI5 file contains other examples of Horner's avoidance of party meetings.

412 Fishman, *British CP and TUs*, pp. 74–75.

413 Hannington had been dropped from the Executive at the Twelfth Party Congress in 1932. His return was evidence of his political rehabilitation.

414 PF601/VI, F.I. Report. 142, 18.3.35, NA Kew. 'Visited Party Headquarters with Comrade Bob ELLIS. It is reported

that Horner expected to be the next Vice-President of the S.W.M.F.' Ellis had been a member of the MMM in Mardy between 1921–24. In 1935 he was a member of Kent Miners' Association.

415 *SWM*, 6 February 1935, Paynter, *MGen*, p. 101. The argument that unions which had a democratic structure were genuine rank-and-file movements was also used by Joe Scott and Claude Berridge in relation to the Aircraft Shop Stewards' National Council. Fishman, *British CP and TUs*, pp. 129–135.

416 Griffiths, *Pages from Memory*, pp. 42–3.

417 Peter Clarke, *Hope and Glory, Britain 1900–1990*, Penguin Books, 1997, p. 180; Chris Williams, 'Labour and the Challenge of Local Government, 1919–39, in Duncan Tanner, Chris Williams and Deian Hopkin (eds), *The Labour Party in Wales, 1900–2000*, University of Wales Press, Cardiff, 2000, pp. 154–7; Stephanie Ward, '"Sit Down to Starve or Stand up to Live": Community, Protest and the Means Test in the Rhondda Valleys, 1931, 1939' *Llafur*, Vol. 9, No. 2, 2005, pp. 27–32. Ward noted: 'Rumours about the implications of means testing were prevalent in the weeks leading up (*sic*) its introduction. There was almost a sense of paranoia ... One of the most prominent fears was that relieving officers would force the unemployed to sell their homes and furniture' (p. 28).

418 Paynter, *MGen*, p. 98. He stated that twenty-four ministers from Merthyr signed a letter to the government protesting about the new scales.

419 Ward, 'Sit Down', p. 39.

420 MI5 file, PF601/VI, NA Kew. The date of the Trealaw meeting in January was obliterated by burns.

421 Francis and Smith, p. 256. The quote is from the *WM*, 21 January 1935. Other reports are cited from the *Rhondda Leader* and the *Rhondda Fach Gazette*, 26 January 1935.

422 *DW*, 28 January 1935. The *DW* report on 29 January cited the *MG* reporter's belief that the motion would have been carried.

423 Francis and Smith, pp. 253–8. On 31 January 1935, a Special Meeting of the NCL was convened to receive Griffiths, Arthur Jenkins and Harris representing the South Wales

Deputation. '[E]ach in turn described the prevailing conditions ... which had led to the Cardiff Conference being the most representative ... that had ever been held and indicated that had the Delegations been extended to Churches, Chapels, Chambers of Trade and other Organisations, the Conference would have been very considerably larger ... Demonstrations that were being held in the valleys and other centres were larger and more spontaneous than they had ever previous witnessed.' 'National Council of Labour minutes', TUC files, MRC Warwick.

424 For the Thirteenth Party Congress, see Fishman, *British CP and TUs*, pp. 73–6; and Thorpe pp. 216–8.

425 Griffiths, *Pages from Memory*, p. 43. The Special Meeting of the NCL deemed it expedient to be publicly associated with the deputation. At the end of the 31 January meeting, it was resolved that all NCL members 'who could make it convenient' should meet the deputation at the Ministry of Labour after their interview with Stanley and then proceed to the House of Commons, where Lansbury, the current PLP leader, 'would introduce the Deputation and Mr. Citrine speak in association with it on behalf of the National Council'. A motion from Bevin was then carried that 'official approaches should be made to the B.B.C. with a view to a representative of the South Wales Deputation being afforded an opportunity of broadcasting upon the circumstances that had led to them coming to London.' 'National Council of Labour minutes', TUC files, MRC Warwick. The Press Statement issued by the NCL on 1 February outlined plans for a full-blown nationwide campaign. Citrine, Bevin and Middleton had evidently decided to take the offensive.

426 Francis and Smith, p. 260.

427 Ward, 'Sit Down', pp. 42–3.

428 A précis of the *DW* report is in the MI5 file, PF601/VI.

429 The story noted that coalowners 'had convened meetings of the men down the pit and each man and boy employed had to declare whether he was going to work on Monday.' Paynter offered a sanitised version in *MGen*, p. 101.

430 R Page Arnot, *Vol. III*, p. 147.

431 For Allison's work and Horner's visits to Party Headquarters, see MI5 file, PF601/VI, 'F.I. Report 142, 18.3.35', 'Horner to 16 King St. 6.4.35, 'Secretariat CPGB to Horner 9.4.35.', NA Kew. Party organiser Clarence Mason's letter to Horner asked whether he 'might like to stay with his brother who apparently lives not far from Kirkby'. Albert had recently started work with the Russian Oil Products depot in Colwick, a job which he probably obtained through Arthur speaking to Jock Wilson, now in charge of ROP. Mason probably knew Albert reasonably well, since he had arrived in Nottinghamshire in 1931, and was either a communist party or close fellow traveller. MI5 file, PF501/VI, NA Kew. For Horner in Lancashire, see *DW* 15 June 1935.

432 Letter from Horner to Cox, postmarked Llannelly (*sic*), perhaps after a West Wales DPC. MI5 file, PF501/VI, NA Kew. Willie Allan was now working in Northumberland at Cambois Colliery, and active in the Northumberland Miners' Association. Horner also opposed the tactic, canvassed by party activists at the MFGB Conference, of each district giving notice to end its agreement. 'HORNER's opinion is that they should not contest the S. Wales owners' application (to S.W.M.F. for a decrease in wages and for the re-application of the Schiller conditions ...) to Arbitration Board but should report to M.F.G.B., "in order to strike on October 1ˢᵗ if wages are reduced".'

433 Crookshank recorded in his diary: 'It was SB [Stanley Baldwin] said a Brigadier's job: brought one into contact with men: it would do me good to be in touch with Labour problems: I was on good terms with Labour MPs: I must beware of being too clever ... Saturday 15 June 1935. During the following week, Crookshank took his first parliamentary questions from Labour Mining MPs. He observed: 'all kind: many came to shake hands and all said they would help with information.' On 19 June, he wrote: 'I told SB about the miner MPs and he was very pleased' (p. 62).

434 Arnot, *Vol. III*, pp. 149–50. The Federation only sent 12 delegates to the Annual Conference, comparable to Yorkshire's 12, Durham's 14 and the Midlands' 11. Horner was again absent.

435 Jack Jones had told the Thirteenth CPGB Congress that out of eighteen SWMF lodges in the Rhondda, the CPGB either had a majority or a decisive influence on twelve. *DW* 5 February 1935.

436 Arnot, *Vol. III*, p. 153.

437 Branson's description of Cox as the *DW* editor who succeeded Shields was based on information from Cox, (1927–41, p. 57). I have been unable to corroborate it. Cox worked on the *DW* editorial staff for varying periods between 1935 and 1939, but it is not clear in what capacity. On 28 June 1938, his MI5 file noted that he was a member of the *DW* editorial board; on 15 September the file noted that he was assisting Springhall on the *DW* editorial board. On 19 October, a Special Branch report noted that he was 'signing as "News Editor"' of the *DW*; but on 3 April a Special Branch report noted that Fred Pateman 'now appears to be the *News Editor ... assisted by COX*.' KV2/1769, NA Kew. In his unpublished memoirs, Cox states that he returned to South Wales in August 1936 and remained there until the summer of 1937 when he returned to London to assist Dutt in his new role as *DW* editor (pp. 65–9).

438 The compiler of Horner's MI5 file commented after logging a letter of 24 July 1935 from the DPC, 'Still apparently a member of S. Wales D.P.C. of C.P.G.B.'. On 2 July the DPC wrote to him, 'saying that at their meeting on Saturday strong criticism was expressed at the failure to hold regular meetings on the Trade Union Commission [which he had evidently been assigned to convene]. Members ... felt that there is a serious tendency on HORNER's part to neglect this matter.'

439 MI5 file, PF601/VI, NA Kew. *DW*, 26 August 1935. The conference was held on Saturday 24 August.

440 For Griffiths' and Jenkins' speeches, see TUC *Congress Report*, 1935, pp. 291, 344. For the Black Circulars, see N Fishman, *British CP and TUs*, pp. 85–6. On 21 January 1935, the Finance & General Purposes Committee of the General Council was furnished with a summary of replies received from unions in response to Circular No.17 which recommended that trade unions should change their rules to prevent communists and fascists holding office. The

TGWU was one of the nine unions not in agreement with General Council policy. 'General Council minutes' TUC files, MRC, Warwick.

441 Arnot, *Vol. III*, pp. 155–6.
442 Supple, *Coal 1913–1946*, p. 340, quoting CAB 24/257/19–26 (27 September 1935).
443 Arnot, *Vol. III*, pp. 156–7 and pp. 164–5 quoting MFGB Executive.
444 *DW*, 21, 22 November 1935, Arnot *Vol. III*, pp. 166–7.
445 I am grateful to Alan Campbell for this information. The ECCI had pressed the case for Horner's standing in the election with the CPGB leadership.
446 Griffiths, *Pages from Memory*, p. 141, *DW* 8 and 12 November 1935. Francis and Smith, p. 308. Paynter wrote in *Rhondda Election Special* that six lodges were supporting communist candidates for the SWMF Executive.
447 Robert Blake, *The Decline of Power 1915–1964*, Paladin History of England, Paladin, 1986, p. 192. He noted that it was the first general election since 1880 to be fought on foreign policy; Baldwin sought 'a mandate for rearmament in the interests of Britain, world peace and collective security'. 'To repeat the results of 1931 would have been inconceivable. To lose as little as he [Baldwin] did – less than 100 seats – was a remarkable success in the light of recent by-elections.' Clarke, however, viewed the result as highly favourable to Labour, *Hope and Glory*, p. 179.
448 For the Mines Department and Baldwin's attitude, see POWE 20/39, NA Kew. The Mines Department regularly sent the King lengthy memoranda, furnished with statistics and facts, on the miners' national wages dispute, apparently in response to his desire to be kept fully informed. Arnot *Vol. III*, pp. 170–1.
449 Arnot *Vol. III*, pp. 171–2, quoting MFGB Executive.
450 Supple, *Coal 1913–46*, p. 338.
451 *DW*, 27, 28, 30 January; 3, 13 February 1936.
452 Francis and Smith, pp. 277–8.
453 Francis and Smith, pp. 282–3. The epic is narrated on pp. 277–293.
454 Francis and Smith, pp. 285–6. The *DW* on 17 October noted that the conference had lasted four hours. The Parc

and Dare stay-downers were pursuing their own grievances, *DW*, 18 October 1935.

455 Griffiths, *Pages from Memory*, pp. 37–8.
456 MI5 file PF601/VI, NA Kew.
457 H Francis, notes of interview with Billy Griffiths, 3 October 1969, in H Francis' possession, p. 3b.
458 Fishman, *British CP and TUs*, ch. 6 and pp. 216–21. MI5 files, PF601/VI, NA Kew.
459 Francis and Smith, pp. 291–2. To evoke the atmosphere they quote Lewis Jones' novel, *We Live*.
460 Fishman, *British CP and TUs*, pp. 8–16, 74. Life Itself was an integral part of communists' and the Comintern's world-view. It was a 'potent ideological balm' (p. 16), invoked when events necessitated party members in leading a retreat or countenancing a compromise. It enabled party members to absolve themselves from the charge of betraying the revolution. A revolutionary situation could not be willed by party members, but would only occur when the material circumstances, i.e. *Life Itself*, combined to produce one. For example, on 28 November 1934, a *DW* article observed: 'Not by raising the question of Soviet power as an issue for the united front, not by putting forward ultimate aims, but taking the questions that are uppermost in their [the masses'] mind as a starting point. This is building the united front. Life itself is going to force this question of Soviet power to the front ... '.
461 The one incumbent was Ianto Evans, re-elected for the Anthracite; he was joined by Dai Dan Evans there. Jack Davies had been elected for Area 4, the Rhondda, and Alf Davies for Area 3, the Garw. On 3 December, the *DW* reported Jack Davies's return, unopposed for the first time in a decade, as lodge chairman for Llwynypia, and noted that he had been joined by a number of militants on the lodge committee. The Seventh World Congress line also enabled the communists in Fife to disband the United Mineworkers of Scotland with political honour. Because they remained unemployed and most of the officials in the Scottish district unions were hostile, they were unable to rejoin the official Scottish mining unions. Eventually, sympathetic union officials arranged for their return to mining

NOTES

work and their quiet entry back into the district unions. In the case of the more prominent leaders, however, this did not occur until the onset of World War II.

462 His memoirs are disingenuous (J Griffiths, *Pages from Memory*, p. 44). They contain an oblique reference to a possible rule change and the positive memory that he expected to continue as President. However, the potential rule change was common knowledge amongst the South Walian political establishment. After Griffiths' election, the SWMF complement of MPs increased from 12 to 13, and remained the largest in the MFGB. There were seven YMA sponsored MPs; five from the DMA; the Lancashire and Scottish miners' unions each had four. Northumberland, Derbyshire, and Cumberland miners' associations each sponsored one mining MP. For trade union sponsored MPs see David Howell, "Shut Your Gob!": the Trade Unions and the Labour Party', in Campbell, Fishman & McIlroy, *The Post-War Compromise, 1945–64*, pp. 117–44.

463 Francis and Smith, p. 310. *WM* 25 March 1936. On 31 March, The Federation Executive voted by 8 to 6 to recommend the proposed rule change to the Annual Conference. Francis and Smith, n. 11, p. 345. They cite the *WM*, which noted that there had been absentees, which, it implied, had affected the result. This is interesting evidence of the inability of Griffiths and Jenkins to rally moderate and right-wing opinion against Horner.

464 *DW* and *MG*, 20 April 1936. The *Times* for 20 April observed, 'Although the decision was stated to have been carried by a "substantial majority", there were many who deplored the loss it involved to the organization of two of its ablest officials ... In some quarters the decision is interpreted as an adroit Communist manoeuvre to obtain control of The Federation ... '

465 *ICR*, p. 147. The *DW* reported the Mardy nomination on 25 May 1936, using the euphemistic phrase that the two Mardy lodges had recently been re-united.

466 *DW*, 25 May 1936; *Merthyr Express*, 30 May 1936. In the presidential contest, the other three candidates, Will Betty, Iorrie Thomas and John Evans, received 11, 10 and 8 votes respectively. In the vice-presidential election, the remain-

563

ing three candidates on the last ballot received 30,16 and 13 votes.

Chapter 10. Federation President

467 J Griffiths letter from John Tofts collection.

468 The *DW* reported that the resolution had been moved by Ted Withers of Caerphilly, one of the non-party candidates on the United Front slate for the SWMF Executive. The choice of a non-communist, non-Rhondda, non-Anthracite delegate, was evidently calculated to gain support from Monmouthshire.

469 PF V1. 14 June 1935, NA Kew; Information from Joan Morris; H Francis interview with Vol Tofts, SWML. Joan Morris remembered that the landlord had wanted Horner to buy the bungalow at Upper Tumble, an offer which he flatly refused. Horner's aversion to mortgages apparently precipitated the decision to move, and initially Arthur and Ethel took a house on a short-term basis. The Horners moved first to a small terraced house at 11 Felinfoel Road, on the outskirts of Llanelli, and then on 7 December 1936 to 182 Felinfoel Road. Information about 182 Felinfoel Road from its present owner, Mr M Fisher, 27 December 2008.

470 Shackleton to WG Nott-Bower, Mines Department, 7 October 1936. POWE 20/40, NA Kew. Shackleton was a Lancashire textile union leader, who had served on the TUC parliamentary committee from 1904–10. He became a civil servant in 1910, Permanent Secretary to the Ministry of Labour in 1916–21 and Chief Labour Adviser in 1921–5.

471 Evan Williams was born in 1871, the son of a small colliery owner in the Anthracite. After graduating from Cambridge, he worked for his father's company, and was elected chairman of the South Wales coalowners' association in 1913. He was elected President of the MAGB in 1919 and remained in that post until 1944. Iestyn Williams was born in Cardiff in 1892. After joining the staff of the association in 1913, he became chief assistant to the secretary, Finlay A Gibson, in 1922, Assistant Secretary in 1924, and Joint Secretary in 1936 (*The Dictionary of Welsh Biography 1941–1970*, London

2001). Although nominally Joint Secretary, Iestyn Williams probably took the lead in industrial relations matters for the Association. Gibson was now on the MAGB Executive, and served on various technical committees concerned with shipping, coke ovens and by-products, as well as participating in the National Confederation of Employers' Organisations and The Federation of British Industries. He had joined the Association in 1891, and had risen to become Secretary in 1915.

472 *ICR*, pp. 147–8.

473 Branson, *1927–1941*, p. 152. Horner argued for a 'People's Front' in a CPGB pamphlet, *Towards a Popular Front*, published after the MFGB conference. He made a closely reasoned, forceful case with a view to influencing the vote at the Labour Party conference.

474 Francis and Smith, p. 322, quoting *DW*, 25 May 1936.

475 Frankenberg notes of third interview with Horner.

476 Francis and Smith, pp. 312–20. The Bedwas SWMF lodge voted to follow the Executive's instruction by the slender majority of 19. The two Bedwas pits were sunk in 1911 and 1913, and had attracted workers from the upper Monmouthshire valleys, cradles of the new unionism from which The Federation had sprung at the end of the nineteenth century. The new owners, Bedwas Navigation Colliery Company (1921) Ltd., a subsidiary of S Instone Ltd. Shipping Agents, had invested in conveyors, pneumatic picks and coal-cutters (Chris Williams, *Capitalism, Community and Conflict* p. 36). However, the colliery did not return a profit until after the dispute in 1933. In 1928 Barclays Bank threatened to call in the huge overdraft which kept the colliery float. A protracted war of attrition ensued between the company and the confident Federation lodge, which had maintained 100 per cent membership and an unbroken record of winning disputes to keep its pre-war customs and price-lists. The full-time lodge committee Secretary, Billy Milsom, 'a fearless uncompromising character', was aptly characterised by the oxymoron conservative militant. He prove[d] an obdurate opponent for both management and SWMF officials'. In addition, two committed communist MMM activists, Billy Nind and

Garfield Williams, 'produced a pit paper, *The Bedwas Rebel*, which attacked the old Lodge Committee whenever they detected signs of conciliation' (Francis and Smith p. 313). In November 1930 management had given notice of a wholesale change in working practices; but the lodge had successfully resisted. A succession of lock-outs, uneasy truces and unofficial strikes followed, but failed to produce a decisive result. The strike at the end of February 1933 had been precipitated by management bringing in 'some men to work on a conveyor in place of the old workmen (55 per cent were ... unemployed ... Over 1,000 men came out, but the "strangers", already sixty in number continued in work ... The company kept the colliery open by employing new labour from ... Merthyr and the Upper Rhymney Valley.' (Francis and Smith, pp. 317–18).

477 *The Miners' Monthly*, December 1936. *MM* began publication at the end of 1934, probably as a riposte to the *SWM*. It was probably distributed at lodge meetings. Harris, as editor, was probably pleased to resume regular written communication with the membership. Horner's December 1936 article is henceforth referred to as 'The Truth'.

478 Francis and Smith, p. 322.

479 Francis and Smith, pp. 322–3. Quotation from interview with Dai Dan Evans 1973, transcript in SWML.

480 Interview with Leo Price, 21 November 1971, transcript in SWML. Price had persuaded Dowlais men 'after three secret meetings not to start a "stay-down" over a minimum wage dispute.' Francis and Smith, n. 52, p. 347.

481 Francis and Smith, pp. 324–8.

482 See pp. 304–5. The SWMF Annual Conference was reported by the *Morning Post* under the headline, '£51,000 STRIKES BILL. S. WALES MINERS' DISASTROUS YEAR.' The story noted the Executive report that after spending £115,612, 'expenditure of the central fund exceeded the income by £24,795, and the value of the fund had dropped ... to £53,328 at the end of the year.' 17 April 1936.

483 The pamphlet was entitled *The Bedwas Colliery – the Truth*, quoted by Francis and Smith, p. 329. Horner's May 1936 article *The Truth behind the Bedwas Settlement* may have been

an allusion to Instone's pamphlet. Samuel Instone was
chairman of the Bedwas Navigation Colliery Company
(1921) Ltd. Samuel was also the chairman of Samuel Instone
and Company Ltd., colliery owners and coal exporters, the
chairman of Askern Coal and Iron Company Ltd. Askern
was a colliery in Barnsley. His brother Theodore was a
director of the Bedwas company and managing director of
Askern (information about the Instones from *Colliery Year
Book and Coal Trades Diary 1928*).

484 *Times, DH,* 25 August 1936, *Financial News,* 26 August
1936.

485 Note from Crookshank to Baldwin (27 August 1936, PREM
1/201, NA, Kew), quoted by Francis and Smith, p. 331.

486 *ICR,* p. 152. Leo Abse, an adolescent in Cardiff at the time,
had vivid memories both of the miners' anti-semitism and
Horner's forthright opposition to it. Interview with Leo
Abse by Nina Fishman, March 2004. Horner remembered
that at elementary school: 'There was a Jewish boy called
Abe Prague, and his mother and father used to dress him
in an Eton suit and, because he was different from the
other boys, he used to get bullied quite a lot, but I very
soon let people know if anyone wanted to touch Abe they
would have to fight Fatty Horner as well. I had a number
of fights ... ' (*ICR,* p. 12). See 'The Valleys Communities',
A Glaser and URQ Henriques, in Ursula RQ Henriques,
editor, *The Jews of South Wales, Historical Studies,* University
of Wales Press, 1993. There was a substantial Jewish community in Merthyr; the first synagogue was built in 1848.
'In the first decade of the twentieth century there were
synagogues in Merthyr, Tredegar, Pontypridd, Brynmawr,
Aberdare, Ebbw Vale, Aberavon, Ystalyfera and Llanelli'
(p. 55).

487 Francis and Smith, n. 69, p. 348.

488 *Financial News* 4 September 1936. Fernhill was part of
Paynter's SWMF Executive constituency. He recalled that
he 'took it upon myself ... to enquire of the [Fernhill lodge]
secretary ... whether the executive committee could be of
assistance. I was told that assistance was not required ... '
(*MGen,* p. 114). Paynter's attempt was probably made early
on. The strike continued until 9 September when an SWMF

Executive delegation persuaded the men to ascend. It had become 'the longest stay-down strike in this country ... 60 men had been underground for 292 hours.' (*Colliery Year Book and Coal Trades Directory 1937*, p. 751). There was an unofficial strike at the Rock pit in Bedwas colliery. On the morning of 3 September 80 men on the night shift 'barricaded themselves in a side way or return air-way and refused to ascend the pit ... From what I could gather from the excited groups of miners outside the colliery premises the men – or a section of them – resent the intention of the management to provide sleeping accommodation for those who may desire to work after the coalfield notices expire on Saturday.' *Times*, 4 September 1936.

489 Crookshank diaries, Bodleian Library, Oxford, p. 135. Crookshank had reported on the situation to the Cabinet on 2 September. On 4 September Sir Horace Wilson told Crookshank that 'the PM quite agreed with what was going on, but oddly enough didn't care to be told specifically the result'. The Mines Department had not approached Iestyn Williams in his official capacity. On 3 September, Crookshank wrote that he 'rang up Noah Lewis to say I thought some representative owner should be in London tomorrow. Things very black. I see no way of avoiding the strike.' On 4 September, Crookshank met Iestyn Williams, 'he being the emissary that Mark Lewis raked up from the owners', at the Board of Trade, because Williams refused to come to the Department of Mines office. After he and Crookshank had agreed, based on the evening papers and Williams' latest intelligence from Cardiff 'that orders had been given for the men to come out', Williams 'got busy with triangular telephoning to Instone [in London], Cardiff and we thought to Hann and others he got out the formula to which Instone agreed. (Faulkner and I went for sandwiches to a dive opposite the House of Commons) ... Sir Alfred Faulkner was the Permanent Under Secretary for Mines in the Mine Department of the Board of Trade. Hann was a prominent South Wales coalowner. Noah and Mark Lewis may have been prominent Conservative supporters. Crookshank telephoned Instone at 10.30 pm. and confirmed the deal which Iestyn Williams had brokered.

'And after that we sent the telegram off to [Oliver] Harris plus a personal message to each of the three MPs [William Jenkins, Sir Charles Edwards and George Hall, who accompanied Horner and Harris to meet Crookshank on 3 September] that something was on its way ... ' pp. 133–4.

490 The Fernhill stay-down strike, however, did not end until 9 September, 'after 60 men had been underground for 292 hours. They had alleged that 12 of them had not been paid the minimum wage. A deputation of the South Wales Miners' Federation Executive Committee descended the mine and persuaded the strikers to come up.' (*Colliery Year Book and Coal Trades Directory 1937*, p. 751).

491 See n. 476.

492 Francis and Smith, pp. 335–338. On 25 September, the SWMIU produced a leaflet containing extracts from the negotiations revealing that Horner had agreed that neither the men from the old Bedwas lodge nor their customs would be reinstated. The revelation was apparently dismissed by both the SWMF and the South Wales communist party as vexatious and irrelevant.

493 The voting result is from the *DW*, 30 October 1936. *DH*, 30 October 1936.

494 My emphasis. The Federation Executive were keen to keep the article in print, probably calculating that lodge officials would need to refer to it in the coming months.

495 Arnot, *Vol. III*, pp. 246–7.

496 EH Carr, *The Comintern and the Spanish Civil War*, Macmillan, 1984, p. 12. The government, led by left republicans, socialists and radicals, had taken office in February with the support of the small group of sixteen communist deputies out of the 278 members of the Cortes. Franco's Manifesto of Las Palmas was broadcast at dawn on 18 July.

497 Carr, *Comintern & Spanish Civil War*, p. 11.

498 Francis and Smith, pp. 11–13; Hywel Francis, *Miners Against Fascism, Wales and the Spanish Civil War*, Lawrence & Wishart, 1984, pp. 34–6. By 1911 there were 264 Spaniards living in the county borough of Merthyr Tydfil.

499 Carr, *Comintern & Spanish Civil War*, pp. 11, 15.

500 Thorpe, *British CP & Moscow*, pp. 230–1. Thorpe notes a letter from Pollitt to Dimitrov on 12 August 'that he had

"absolute[ly] reliable information" from British government sources that the Spanish government would win.' On
26 August, he wrote Dimitrov that 'he tried to persuade
Thorez [PCF general secretary] to launch a stronger critique
of the Blum government's support for non-intervention.'
Carr, *Comintern & Spanish Civil War*, p. 13, pp. 20–1.

501 Carr pp. 21–2. See also Aldo Agosti, *Palmiro Togliatti*, IB
Tauris, 2008, pp. 117–21. Agosti concludes that it became
'a semi-official expression of the communist position' and
that 'it was a significant development'. 'Togliatti stressed
again that the fight of the Spanish people had the charac-
teristics of a "national revolutionary war" ... ' (p.121).

502 Scholars who are hardly pro-Comintern have concluded
from recent research in the Comintern archives: '"In the
end, the documents suggest that the Soviets achieved so
much in Spain not because of their overwhelming effort,
but rather because they were more competent and united
than their hapless opponents", i.e. their opponents in the
Republican governments.' Raymond Carr, 'Spain and the
Communists', *New York Review of Books*, Vol. L No. 6, 10
April 2003, p. 62 quoting R Radosh, MR Habeck and G
Sevostianov, eds., *Spain Betrayed: the Soviet Union in the
Spanish Civil War*, Yale University Press.

503 Thorpe notes, 'It had been hoped to deliver a million-sig-
nature petition to the Labour conference ... However, the
CP's efforts regarding Spain meant that less time could
be devoted to this ... The campaign faltered, and the petition had ultimately to be abandoned.' *British CP & Moscow*,
p. 231.

504 Thorpe, *British CP & Moscow*, p. 232. Branson records
the figures as 1.728m. against the Edinburgh motion and
592,000 for (*1927–41*, p. 155). The motion was moved by
AH Paton on behalf of the Edinburgh Trades and Labour
Council and seconded by Councillor JA Da Palma on
behalf of the West Fulham Divisional Labour Party. An
AEU motion in support of the united front in Britain was
defeated by 1.805m. to 435,000 (Labour Party Conference
Report, 1937).

505 GDH Cole, *History of the Labour Party from 1914*, Routledge
& Kegan Paul, 1948, p. 328.

506 Carr, *Comintern & Spanish Civil War*, p. 27.
507 Mick Kane started his working life in collieries in the Lothians and Stirlingshire. His younger brother Jock, a Lenin School graduate, was secretary of the Sheffield communist party. Both brothers had worked at Harworth, along with other militants, in the late 1920s. See Fishman, *British CP and TUs*, p. 172.
508 The section on the Harworth dispute draws substantially on the chapter, 'The Battle of Harworth' in Fishman, *British CP and TUs*, pp. 164–199. The change in the political composition of Harworth branch officers is found in AR Griffin, *Mining in the East Midlands 1550–1947*, Frank Cass 1971, p. 309.
509 The TUC's voluminous file on Harworth at the Modern Records Centre includes accounts of Citrine's interview with Sir Horace Wilson, Permanent Under Secretary at the Ministry of Labour, and Harry Crookshank's audience with the new King George VI, when he is likely to have enlisted his support in moving Barber Walker management away from their un-English intransigence. There is also a lengthy paper trail reporting on Horner's involvement in the dispute. Vincent Tewson, the TUC assistant general secretary whom Citrine had posted to Nottinghamshire, kept a weather eye open for Horner. He reported on the few occasions when Horner appeared as a private individual, probably in response to requests from Allison or Mick Kane to provide on-the-spot advice and speak at communist meetings. Tewson's surveillance revealed nothing sinister.
510 Quoted in the *DW*, 26 January 1937.
511 *ICR*, pp. 154–5.
512 *ICR*, p. 155. Iestyn Williams and Horner probably colluded to arrange this date, to give Horner an additional anniversary to celebrate on 5 April.
513 The SWMF Executive also decided on 6 April to send Jack Davies and Will Arthur to assist at meetings in the Nottinghamshire coalfield.
514 Arnot, *Vol. III*, pp. 220–1.
515 Lord Taylor of Mansfield, *Uphill All the Way*, Sidgwick & Jackson, 1972, pp. 75–6. Bernard Taylor was an NMA official whom the NMA Executive had seconded to Harworth.

He became Labour MP for Mansfield in 1941. He asked Gwyn Williams, a lifelong Labour loyalist and then President of the NUM South Wales Area, to read the manuscript of *Uphill All the Way*. Williams did so and suggested that he had failed to acknowledge the contribution played by the CPGB, notably Horner and Mick Kane. Interview with Gwyn Williams by H Francis and N Fishman, 1999.

516   AR Griffin, *Mining in the East Midlands*, p. 313 and note 54, p. 318.

517   Baldwin's speech quoted in Arnot, *Vol. III*, pp. 230–1. N Fishman interview with W Deedes, 10 October 2001.

518   *DW*, 31 May 1937.

519   At the TUC in September, the General Council report noted that the Council had also decided to appeal to the Home Secretary. Eight of the Harworth prisoners' sentences were remitted by the Home Secretary in October. There were remittances for three of the remaining four still in gaol in January 1938. Kane was finally released at the end of August 1938, having served just over a year of his two year sentence. Arnot, *Vol. III*, pp. 239–40.

Chapter 11. Two Steps Forward, One Step Back

520   H Powys Greenwood, 'Can South Wales be Saved?'. The *Spectator* article was published in two parts, on 13 and 27 November 1936. The quotation is from Part II, p. 938. Greenwood observed that Horner 'was almost the only plain Mister' at the meeting (Part I, p. 843).

521   The speech was published in full in the *DW* on 16 April 1937.

522   In the Vice-Presidential election, Lawther received 374 votes, Horner 124 and McGurk 45. In the election for nominations for the General Council, the MFGB officers each received 413 votes, Horner 85 and McGurk 45.

523   There is no evidence for Francis's statement that the visit took place in July. *MAF*, p. 139. Horner's account states that he was sent to Spain by the SWMF Executive 'as an expression of the solidarity of the South Wales Miners with the Spanish people, and also to inquire about the well-being of the Welsh miners serving with the International

Brigade'. *ICR*, p. 157. However, the Executive minutes do not record any formal decision relating to Horner's visit to Spain except their approval of his absence after he had reported his intention of going.

524 'There were altogether 170 volunteers from Wales, and 116 of them came from the mining industry, around 25 per cent. of them union officials at pit level ... the average age was over thirty and 18 per cent. of the Welsh volunteers were married. The South Wales miners provided the largest regional occupational group in the whole Battalion.' *MGen*, p. 78. Paynter's Aesopian description is that his job was 'to look after the battalion's interests at the International Brigade's headquarters, and to deal with individual and other problems'. *MGen*, p. 65. As a serving member of the SWMF Executive, his absence should have been sanctioned by them before his departure. Because of the problematic legal status of members of the International Brigade, however, he wrote to the Executive from Spain informing them that he had joined the Brigade. His letter was received by them on 22 April, when the minutes recorded appreciation of his action. Paynter wrote that he 'went ... with the endorsement of the South Wales Miners' Executive ... I had with me a letter signed by Oliver Harris ... making official my trade union credentials, and this gave me some additional standing in the various negotiations in which from time to time I was involved.' *MGen*, p. 73. I think Harris's letter is likely to have been written after the 22 April. See *MAF*, pp. 168–70. For the Attlee Battalion see Branson, *1927–41*, pp. 229–32. She states that '2,200 volunteers went from Britain to fight against Franco during the two and a half years of the war', and that 526 were killed (pp. 231–2).

525 Paynter, *MGen*, p. 71. See also Francis, *MAF*, pp. 230–2, and Fred Copeman, *Reason in Revolt*, Blandford Press, 1948, pp. 136–140. Copeman omits any mention of Paynter.

526 *ICR*, p. 158; Togliatti report cited in Carr, *Comintern & Spanish Civil War*, p. 58. Horner remarked that Paynter 'was a bit shocked to find I had interfered in military matters when I talked about this leave problem'.

527 *ICR*, p. 158.

528 Thorpe, *British CP & Moscow*, pp. 234–5; Morgan, *Pollitt*, pp. 91–2. For the Socialist League, see Foot, Bevan *Vol. I*, pp. 153–7. Mellor was a Guild Socialist and ex-foundation CPGB member. He was the first editor of *Tribune*.

529 *Congress Report*, p. 272. The differences to which Horner referred were the internecine political battles between the coalition government, including the PCE, and the POUM.

530 For the 1928 TUC, see pp. 171–2 and n. 234.

531 The speeches are on pp. 410–7 of the 1937 TUC *Report*. Clegg has an account of the TUC and subsequent Labour Conference debates as well as the PLP debate in July, when both YMA and SWMF sponsored MPs voted against the Labour Party's official position. *Vol. III*, pp. 134–5. Bevan may have attended the TUC at Horner's urging.

532 *Congress Report*, p. 418. Joseph Jones had made a similar declaration at the MFGB Conference in July.

533 *DW*, Monday 1 February 1937. Although Bevan was at both Swansea and Cardiff, the *DW* reported his Swansea speech. It is likely that he rushed to be present at the tail-end of the Cardiff meeting in order not to disappoint the audience. The audience at the Brangwyn Hall in Swansea had been 1200. The Regal Cinema, Llanelli, which seated 2000, had been almost full and people were still coming in as the meeting started. The queue had formed nearly half an hour before the doors opened. On 26 January, the *DW* announced meetings at the Miners' Hall, Merthyr and the Oddfellows Hall, Dowlais. On 3 February, the *DW* announced that George Strauss MP had signed the Unity Manifesto. This story was accompanied by a picture of the platform speakers at the King's Theatre Cardiff, showing CA Smith from the ILP, Bevan, Horner, and the chairman, 'Mr. Finch', whom Hywel Francis suggests was Len Finch, Harold Finch's brother. Both were SWMF members, and Harold Finch became Compensation Secretary for the SWMF and later an NUM sponsored MP. On 4 February, a picture of Horner was published on page 2 wielding a billiard cue with the caption reading, 'Arthur Horner, President of the SWMF, enjoying a game of billiards shortly after he had opened the new Bedlinog Workmen's Hall'.

534 Ben Pimlott, *Labour and the Left in the 1930s*, Allen & Unwin, 1986, pp. 101–5, deals with the byzantine twists and turns inside the Labour Party establishment.

535 For evidence of continuing Campaign activity in South Wales, see *DW*, 1, 2, 12, 26 February, 14 April 1937. The CPGB Central Committee Report to the 1937 Party Congress lists the SWMF as having endorsed the Unity Campaign, along with ASLEF, NUDAW, and the shop assistants' union, even though there are no references in the SWMF Executive minutes to such a decision. The justification for the statement appears to have been the resolution on working-class unity passed at the SWMF Annual Conference. The *DW* reported on 19 April that Horner had 'made it clear that the acceptance of the resolution also means support for the Unity Campaign of the Socialist League, the ILP and the Communist Party'. On 13 February, Horner was advertised as being amongst the speakers at a high profile meeting of the Campaign to be held on 25 February at Friends House, London. This meeting was apparently disbanded, perhaps in an attempt not to present London's Transport House with a major irritant at the moment when Cripps's expulsion from the Labour Party was being actively canvassed by many outraged loyalists.

536 The TUC and Labour Party also shared some staff and library facilities. Herbert Tracey worked for both the TUC and Labour Party doing publicity. They also shared information; clerical and administrative staff provided back-up for both organisations, underlining the coincidence of concern of interest of the two institutions.

537 For the unusual circumstances of Gallacher's election, see N Fishman, 'The *British CP and TUs*', 1991 PhD, pp. 311–25.

538 *DW*, 14 April 1937; Smith and Francis, pp. 310–1. For CPGB affiliation to the Labour Party, see *Vol. I*, pp. 343–4.

539 *DW*, 19 April 1937. The resolution supported equal rights for all trade unionists paying the political levy. It was an ingenious attempt to circumvent the Labour Party rule that once Conference had rejected a proposition, it could not be tabled at subsequent conferences for three years. The

intention of the resolution was to rescind the party's ban on communists being elected as trade union representatives to ward and constituency party organisations and trade union delegates to party conferences. On 5 March 1937, the *DW* reported that Horner had been elected as an SWMF delegate to the 1936 Labour Party conference. 'His nomination was endorsed by the MFGB. But he was refused ... '.

540 The vote was 453–448. SWMF Executive Committee meeting minutes, 29 September 1937. Francis and Smith deal with Taff-Merthyr events in 1937 in detail, pp. 379–382. (They misdate the ballot.)

541 SWMF Executive minutes for 29 September note that the situation in consequence of the ballot result was considered. It was reported that a meeting between representatives of The Federation and the Taff-Merthyr Industrial Union Committee had been arranged for the following Wednesday morning 'with view of continuing discussions which had taken place before the ballot'. Federation officials were authorised to attend.

542 Francis and Smith, p. 383 and n. 26, p. 420.

543 Quoted in Francis and Smith, p. 384.

544 Francis and Smith, pp. 386–8.

545 The *DW* article reported the terms: there would be nineteen members of the lodge committee, ten from the SWMIU and nine from The Federation. The lodge chairman and secretary would attend the SWMF Executive. SWMIU members would be accepted into The Federation without paying an entrance fee. After the fusion of the two unions, a new agreement would be negotiated with the owners. The communication reporting the terms had been signed jointly by Gregory, Harris and the Secretary of the coalowners' association (Iestyn Williams). The article concluded, 'So, after years of effort, the South Wales miners have succeeded under Communist leadership in ridding themselves of the menace of the Industrial Union'.

546 Francis and Smith, n. 21, p. 420.

547 'Summary of President's Speech to Conference held on August 24th, 1938', SWMF.

548 Francis and Smith, p. 389.

549 Francis, *MAF*, pp. 118–9.

550 Duncan Tanner, 'The Pattern of Labour Politics, 1918–
1939', in D Tanner, C Williams and D Hopkin, eds., *The
Labour Party in Wales 1900–2000*, University of Wales Press,
Cardiff, 2000, *p.* 129. Tanner noted that in Pontypool,
Cardiff and Swansea, the communist party and Socialist
League 'had permeated the [Labour] constituency par-
ties ... There was even more conflict in Pontypridd.'

551 Interview with Leo Abse by Nina Fishman, 2004.

552 Ted Rowlands MP, *'Something Must be Done'. South Wales
v Whitehall 1921–1951*, ttc Books, Merthyr Tydfil, 2000,
pp. 45–9, 124. The Special Areas Amendment Act 1937
reinforced and augmented these arrangements. J Davies,
A History of Wales, Penguin 1993, pp. 585–6. Portal's entry
is in the *Dictionary of National Biography supplement, 1941–
1950*, pp. 685–6. It cites Attlee's warm praise for Portal.

553 *ICR*, p. 155. Horner stated that he became a member of
'a special committee', without providing its title. He may
have been referring to the South Wales Board of SARA
or the South Wales Development Council. The archives of
the Nuffield Trust for Special Areas record Portal's visit
to South Wales in January 1937. On 11 January, he met
AT James, the Chair of the South Wales Board of SARA,
the Mayor and Town Clerk of Merthyr and George Hall
MP. On the 12 January he met Captain Crawshay, the
Government Commissioner for South Wales, George
Williams, Chairman of the Development Council, Hilary
Marquand, Professor of Economics at University College of
South Wales and Monmouthshire, and finally the editor of
the *WM*. Amongst other things, they discussed Marquand's
'survey' which was shortly to be published as *South Wales
Needs a Plan*. On 13 January, Portal met Ministry of Labour
officials, the Lord Mayor of Cardiff, and Arthur Jenkins
MP. In the afternoon, he 'interviewed Mr. Horner and Mr
Oliver Harris who came to see me'. Box 12B of Nuffield
Trust for Special Areas, Nuffield College, Oxford.

554 Paynter described the Executive meetings with the MPs,
MGen, pp. 116–7. Sir Charles Edwards was a Labour whip;
he had been MP for Bedwellty since 1918 and member
of the SWMF Executive since 1922. Born in 1867 in
Radnorshire, he started work underground aged fourteen.

He had been a checkweighman and then agent for Risca in Monmouthshire. He had also served on the Risca Urban District Council and the Monmouthsire County Council.

555 Trades Councils Joint Consultative Committee 5/2, 20 April 1937, 45a–45c, MRC, Warwick. The TUC deputation consisted of Robson, in his Cardiff Trades Council capacity and JUC joint secretary, a member of The Federation Executive and 'another miner'. See Cliff Prothero, *Recount*, GW & A Hesketh, Ormskirk, 1982, p. 40, for an account of Morris's initiative. The Joint Unemployed Council was formed in 1935 on the initiative of The Federation and the Cardiff Trades and Labour Council as an ad hoc mobilising group for the protests against the new unemployed assistance regulations. In the autumn of 1936, the SWMF Executive had sanctioned its representatives on the JUC to approach other affiliated unions and trades councils to discuss a more permanent organisation. This development was probably an example of Horner using his presidential discretion and initiative. Prothero describes the JUC as a 'Council of Action' and states that it included '[constituency] Labour Parties who were not in full support of the Labour Party'. (p. 54)

556 Prothero stated that he had been 'consulted concerning the need for its formation and I took part in drafting its rules and standing orders' (*Recount*, p. 54). He described the Council as 'unique because it was the only one of its kind in Britain, it was political and industrial. Its dual functions were recognised by both the National Executive Committee of the Labour Party and the General Council of the Trades Union Congress' (*Recount*, p. 53). This is inaccurate. Labour Party NEC Organisation Sub-Committee minutes on 16 February and 16 May 1938 refer to regional councils. On 16 February the Lancashire and Cheshire Regional Council constitution and establishment were discussed. On 16 May, a memo from the subcommittee addressed regional organisation and regional councils. I am grateful to Andrew Flinn for this information. Andrew Thorpe kindly informed me that South Wales and Lancashire and Cheshire were the only two regional councils which had been established before the war.

557 Trades Councils Joint Consultative Committee 5/2, 20 April and 21 June 1937, TUC files, MRC, Warwick. The deputation again consisted of EA Robson, an SWMF Executive member, and 'another Miner'.

558 *Recount*, p. 54. Prothero recalled the Regional Council's beginnings 'in the midst of much trouble ... The Communists were very active in the trade union movement'. Bevin had assiduously cultivated the TGWU's patronage in the Labour Party throughout Britain. But even he had only mixed success in constituencies where coalmining unions had traditionally exercised a lien. When Citrine and the head of the TUC Organisation Department, EP Harries, were seeking capable union officials to serve on the South Wales Invasion Committee in 1940, Harries wrote memos to Citrine expressing his concern about the calibre of these unions' officials. The SWMF Executive Minutes (9, 13, 20, February; 31 March; 6, 13 April; 11, 25 May; 1, 5, 28 June; 3, 27 July; 24, 31 August) chronicle the manoeuvres which Harris and Saddler conducted with sponsored MPs, Phillips and Citrine.

559 SWMF Executive Minutes, 5 June 1937.

560 The resolution authorised the Executive to make further efforts to change the attitude of the TUC and Labour Party. On 3 July, another meeting between The Federation Executive and sponsored MPs took place, with Arthur Jenkins, William John and George Hall joining those present at the June meeting. No consensus was reached.

561 *DW*, 16 August 1937. The report noted the SWMF's repeated efforts to build unity in South Wales.

562 *MG*, 16 August 1937. The correspondent wrote that the JUC had 'succeeded in arousing public opinion to a remarkable degree' After a period of inactivity, it had become 'the backbone of the organisation which made possible the unemployed march of last winter', after which 'proposals were made to put the council upon a permanent footing and to extend its scope ... to enable it to deal with the general economic position in South Wales and to set up permanent local committees.' Given 'the composition of the executive committee of the Miners' Federation, the official Labour movement felt that these local committees would, in fact,

become "United Front" bodies, and would nullify the decisions of the Labour Party Conference ... ' Preparations to establish the Regional Council were expedited, 'and within a few weeks the proposal ... was announced'.

563 SWMF Executive Minutes, 27 July and 24 August 1937. *DW*, 30 August 1937. SWMF amendments increasing union representation and changing the voting procedure were referred to the incoming Executive. The report noted the chairman's statement that the Executive had already met and decided to organise demonstrations on unemployment. After its next meeting on Thursday, they would give a lead. 'The most significant feature of this conference was the demand for immediate rank and file action, and strong condemnation and criticism of official lethargy.'

564 SWMF Executive Minutes, 2 November 1937.

565 For Tanner's conclusion, that the 'left was marginalized', see *Pattern of Labour Politics*, p. 133.

566 MFGB Conference Report, p. 121, the delegate was A Clarke.

567 The attribution of Horner's vote to particular districts is my own calculation. I think it unlikely that the DMA delegates would have considered casting their votes in support of anyone other than their own nominee. Bowman's influence probably pushed Northumberland in support of Horner, but their vote also reflected the continuing antagonism between the two districts. Spencer's apparent willingness to vote for Horner is notable.

568 The SWMF motion stated 'that the Conference, believing that working class unity was the only guarantee for the advance of the Labour Movement, declared that an essential step towards this goal was the granting of equal rights within the Labour Party to all Trades Unionists paying the political levy.' It was rejected on a card vote, 413,000 to 130,000. District unions supporting it were the Forest of Dean, Kent, Northumberland and South Derbyshire. The DMA resolution was defeated on a card vote, 284,000 to 259,000. In addition to the 130,000 votes cast for the SWMF motion and DMA's own 113,000 votes, the motion won the Nottinghamshire and Cumberland votes. MFGB

Conference Report, 1937, pp. 115–116, 122. *Morning Post*, 3 August 1937.

569 Evidence of caucus activities is in the Sam Watson papers, Box 37B, County Archives, Durham. For example, the box contains a duplicated letter dated August 1938 from the Hon. Sec. of the Committee for Peace and Friendship with the USSR urging recipients to consider going to the USSR in November to celebrate the Soviet Union's twenty-first anniversary. Signatories appeared in the following order: Horner, Frank Collindridge of the YMA, Bowman, Joe Hall of the YMA, J Kaylor, AEU Executive, and others from smaller unions, including JW Ball, vice-president of the ETU. There is also a note from Thomas Pigford, editor of the DMA's *Durham Miners' Monthly Journal*, to Watson, dated 17 July 1938. 'I met Horner yesterday at the "*Daily Worker*" outing and he told the comrades "G Harvey" had made an attack upon the official (national) element, and to make things look bad Bowman and Golightly were there from Northumberland.' Horner and Watson would have viewed Harvey's attack on the MFGB national officers as gratuitous and inflammatory, encouraging a reopening of damaging political divisions in the district unions.

570 The question of reorganising the MFGB was discussed in the Executive Report, where it was explained that the Harworth dispute had made unification more urgent (p. 201). The goal of one united union was tabled in a resolution from the KMA, perhaps prompted by Horner and Lawther. As a new, small district union, the KMA had no vested interests, and had not yet attracted animosity from other districts. Ex-SWMF members were leading KMA activists; Lawther's younger brother Ernie was its Financial Secretary. The resolution which was passed contained the KMA motion's substance, but charged the subcommittee with producing a detailed scheme for consideration. It may have been carried without vocal opposition because the debate occurred late in conference week. Few delegates, particularly the ageing veterans, were sufficiently energetic to resist the officers' determination to get the motion through on the nod.

571 *MG*, 23 July 1937; *DT*, 21 July 1937. Its headline was 'Miners Take the Long View. Reduction of Hours and Improved Unemployment Benefit. Preparing for Future Difficulties.' The *News Chronicle* conference report of 21 July appeared under the headline, 'Miners Vote for Peace Policy'. It described about the decision 'not to proceed with a new wage demand but to leave the matter in the hands of the executive ... [T]he decision, which was taken without even a vote, represents the change that has come over the scene since the joint consultative committee of miners and coalowners was set up a year or so ago. This means a long period of peace and stability in the coalfields.'

572 1937 MFGB Conference Report, pp. 98–100.

573 See *Recount* pp. 33–5 for the SWMF delegation, which included Prothero and Will Arthur.

574 *ICR*, p. 160. Horner added: 'We also learned from Joe Hall that, as far as Joseph Jones was concerned, he regarded me and Lawther as a lost cause, because of our sympathy with the Russians. He was not so sure about Jim Bowman, whom he regarded as weak-willed, when on the contrary, he is the most strong-willed man I have ever known'.

575 Jones may have been briefed by Citrine and Hugh Chevins about questions to ask and what to look for in order to penetrate the façade of workplace well-being, efficient management and high health and safety standards. A right-wing delegate from another union sneeringly referred to the absence of a report at the 1938 TUC.

576 Chris Ward, *Stalin's Russia*, Oxford University Press, 1999, pp. 114–7. The first show trial of sixteen veteran old Bolsheviks, including Kamenev and Zinoviev, was staged in August 1936. This 'Trotskyite-Zinovievite Counter-Revolutionary Bloc' were accused of carrying out terrorist activities, including the murder of Kirov. They were convicted and then shot on 24 August. Before the executions, their interrogators extracted confessions which 'implied that Bukharin, Rykov and Tomskii [Tomsky] had sympathised with their actions'. Tomsky committed suicide on 22 August, apparently to avoid the same fate, although there was no further round-up of 'counter-revolutionaries' at that point.

577 Thorpe, *British CP & Moscow*, p. 238. Thorpe noted that Pollitt 'made himself vulnerable by stating not only that Petrovsky had "led the fight" to change the CPGB leadership in 1929, but that he had also been "specially interested" in getting Pollitt appointed as party secretary.'

578 On arrival in Moscow Cohen had become foreign editor of the English language *Moscow Daily News*. For details of Cohen, see Kevin Morgan, Gidon Cohen and Andrew Flinn, *Communists and British Society 1920–1991*, Rivers Oram Press, 2007, pp. 78, 154, 163, 164, 215; Francis Beckett, *The Enemy Within*, John Murray, 1995, pp. 70–1.

579 Thorpe, *British CP & Moscow*, pp. 237–240.

580 Thorpe, *British CP & Moscow*, p. 239. Beckett noted that Gallacher pleaded with Dimitrov for Cohen 'and other foreigners who had disappeared ... Years later he told his friend and literary executor Phil Stein that Dimitrov looked at him gravely for a few moments and then said: "Comrade Gallacher, it is best that you do not pursue these matters."' p. 72.

581 See PF 601/V1. On 27 February 1934, Horner received a letter: '"George" (SLUTSKY) writing from Moscow requests HORNER to supply him with material – clippings from papers etc. – especially dealing "with the safety regulations in the mining industry in Great Britain." Suggests the interchange of correspondence between the anthracite workers in this country and those in Moscow. Writer apparently anticipates that HORNER – his wife and children – will be visiting Moscow in the future, as he recently wrote to "Luba" to that effect.' In April 1934 the MIC sent Horner a Circular 'dealing with May 1st Demonstrations ... The 8th May must be specially utilised in favour of the reinforcement of "our" struggle for the creation of the real unity front committees in the pits. Deals also with the campaign for the release of THALMANN (*sic*) and the miners delegation to the Soviet Union.'

582 Reiner Tosstorff, *Profintern. Die Rote Gewerkschaftsinternationale 1920–1937*, Schoningh, Paderborn Germany, 2004, pp. 705–7. Although the Profintern itself was not formally disbanded until the end of 1937, its demise had been planned since 1936. The gap between intention and

execution was apparently due to the other more pressing business which the Comintern functionaries had to discharge. The Comintern leadership effectively managed their sister organ's disappearance and the absorption of some of its surviving people, including Lozovsky, into other party institutions.

583 *ICR*, pp. 214–5. The date of the MFGB visit to the USSR is inaccurately given here.

584 Information about Horner's response to Slutsky from H Francis, interview with Vol Horner, transcript in SWML. Information about Vol's secretarial course from Joan Morris. On completing her course satisfactorily, Vol returned to London where Arthur used his influence to secure her a place at the Legal and General Assurance Co. Legal and General were one of the leading firms providing industrial pensions. H Francis, interview with Vol Horner, transcript in SWML. Apparently, Vol's job at the Workers' Bookshop in London was taken by Rosa. Horner's MI5 file noted that both Rosa and her uncle, probably Frank Horner, were working there (PF V1, 17 September 1937, NA Kew).

585 MFGB Executive Report 1937. The speeches are in the MFGB Special Conference Report, pp. 15–8.

586 Arnot, *Vol. III*, p. 269. Ebby Edwards, as general secretary of the MIF, opened the Spanish discussion. Postcard in Horner papers, dated 27 May 1938 from Hotel Alfa. The address is: 'Mrs. Ethel Horner, The Datcha, Duplath Hill, Llanelly'.

587 Quoted by Beckett, *Enemy Within*, p. 72.

588 CC 1–2.7.1938. CPGB Archive, PHMM. I am indebted to Kevin Morgan for this reference.

589 The resolution and debate are in the 1938 MFGB Conference Report, pp. 104–118.

590 The rumours are in the conference reports of the *Manchester Guardian* 23 July 1938 and *Daily Telegraph* 20 July 1938. The MFGB Executive minutes preceding the conference contain no reference to Jones' new appointment.

591 MFGB Executive Report 1938 and TUC General Council minutes 1938.

592 Horner and Lawther were the only two candidates. Horner's vote of 140,000 probably came from the SWMF affili-

ated on 100,000 members; Nottinghamshire with 30,000 members; the Forest of Dean, Cumberland and Bristol. Northumberland may have abstained to leave them free to nominate Bowman in an interim election which they calculated might take place if the Executive decided to fill the anticipated vacancy before the 1939 annual conference.

593 Custom and practice determined that TGWU nominees filled two seats in their own trade group; since 1935, the veteran TGWU women's officer, Flo Hancock had occupied the General Council seat reserved for women.

594 Two vacancies in the General Council Group No. 1 seats were created at the end of 1931, following the deaths of AJ Cook and Tom Richards. They were filled by the MFGB's nominees Ebby Edwards and Herbert Smith, evidently by agreement with the General Council. At the 1932 TUC, the MFGB nominated J McGurk in Smith's place; he was elected along with Edwards who was re-elected. At the 1933 Congress, when RT Jones retired, Edwards was re-elected, and the MFGB nominee Peter Lee was the second MFGB candidate elected for Group No. 1. At the 1934 Congress Joseph Jones was the second MFGB candidate elected to the General Council along with Edwards. When Lawther was also elected to the General Council in 1935, the three Group No. 1 places were all filled by the MFGB. For RT Jones, see n. 137.

595 Blake credits their stand with stiffening the British government's resolve, and also forcing Hitler to slightly moderate his demands (*Decline of Power*, pp. 215–6).

596 Bevin had sailed from Southampton on 7 July 1938 on an extended ocean voyage and tour which the TGWU Executive hoped would cure the persistent nervous stress he had been suffering.

597 Clegg, *Vol. III*, p. 139, quoting 1938 *Congress Report*, pp. 474–5.

598 1938 TUC *Congress Report*, p. 15, p. 409. Deakin had become a full-time organiser for the Dock, Whart, Riverside and General Workers' Union in 1919 whilst living in Shotton. He became assistant district secretary for the North Wales area of the TGWU when it was formed in 1922. He moved to London in June 1932 as national secre-

tary of the General Workers' Trade Group. He and Horner are likely to have met each other at the TUC in 1936 and 1937. They remained on warm, friendly terms.

599 Citrine subsequently consulted with Lawther, Horner and JR Campbell about appropriate action to follow up the resolution. *MGen*, pp. 75–6; and 1938 TUC Report, p. 23. Citrine recorded his expurgated version of the incident in his memoirs. *Men and Work*, pp. 359–360.

600 *ICR*, p. 160. Frankenberg interview with Horner.

601 I am grateful to Robert Boyce for information about French mobilisation; Frankenberg interview with Horner.

602 Blake, *Decline of Power*, pp. 215–216.

603 Interview with Sybil Griffiths by Hywel Francis and Nina Fishman. The memos from Iestyn Williams in the National Coal Board papers also testify to the durability and amiability of the relationship.

604 Anthony-Jones, PhD, pp. 82–6. Between 1927–39, there were 350 collieries open in South Wales for varying periods. Of these, 148 had strikes, of which 60 per cent were concentrated in 60 collieries; 86 per cent of the man-shifts lost through strikes occurred in 77 collieries. The Anthracite Area had one sixth of the collieries and approximately one sixth of the labour force. Six out of the seven collieries which had more than 20 strikes were in the Anthracite, which also had one half of the strikes which resulted in a complete stoppage and one third of the strikes resulting in a partial stoppage. Anthony-Jones noted: 'The spate of unconnected "stay-in" strikes after 1936 ... cut across the new policy of conciliation in the coalfield and The Federation then did all in its power to discourage such demonstrations.'

605 For the evolution of CPGB strategy towards the economic struggle, see Fishman, *British CP and TUs*, chs. 4–7.

606 Quoted in J McIlroy, 'Welsh Communists at the Lenin School Between the Wars', *Llafur*, Vol. 8, No. 4, 2003, pp. 51–75.

607 Morgan, Flinn & Cohen, *Communists and British Society*, p. 110. The circumstances of Lewis Jones' removal remain unclear. He relied on the CPGB for his means of support, and his dismissal catapulted him into a downward spiral of

poverty. For the Comintern's concern with the CPGB and Pollitt, see Thorpe, *British CP & Moscow*, pp. 239–40, 243–5. Further evidence of problems in South Wales is found in Cox's MI5 file on 5 August 1938 when it was noted that Cox was 'Present at a meeting of the Secretariat ... when he reported on his recent visit to South Wales, and made urgent representations with regard to the financial position there.' KV 2/1769, NA Kew.

608 PF 601 V.2, 130A, NA, Kew. Fred Copeman, who was a member of the CPGB Executive at this time, recalled that in 1938: 'The Executive meetings themselves became quite fiery, and quite often Arthur Horner, Tom Mann and I would be opposing a resolution of the Political Bureau.' *Reason in Revolt*, Blandford Press, 1948, p. 154.

609 For Horner's defiance of the CPGB's support for the Federation's pursuit of a separate district wages agreement and the extension of stay-down strikes, see pp. 280, 304-5, 309–11. For Spain, see Francis *MAF*, pp. 172–3, and p. 365. Dai Francis remembered that 'Paynter had apparently told him that Horner was not needed in Spain as he was too "soft-hearted". What was needed was "strong will" and "courage".' (*MAF*, p. 172, quoting interview with D Francis, 21 June 1976, SWML.

610 The conventional wisdom amongst Lewis Jones' South Wales contemporaries was that he had died of overwork as a result of a punishing round of public meetings. See H Francis notes from additional interview with Billy Griffiths, 16 October 1969, p. 1. I am grateful to Hywel Francis for a copy of his notes. Description of Cox's first day in Cardiff office is from KV2/1769, NA Kew, narrative. In his unpublished memoirs Cox stated that Glyn Jones had relied a great deal on Lewis Jones, and that after Lewis Jones' death there had been a drop-off in communist activity. His memoirs obfuscate the circumstances which led to his taking over as district secretary. He did state, however, that when he arrived, Glyn Jones had already gone to Bristol to work in an aircraft factory (p. 69).

611 Francis, *MAF*, pp. 249–50. Horner's speech quoted from *Aberdare Leader*, 17 December 1938. Francis observes that besides the Welsh miners there were 'Italians, Jews, English

and a hundred from Cardiff's West Indian community. Pride of place was given to the relatives of those who had been killed, to the olive-skinned, clench-fisted Basque children, the thirty Welsh International Brigaders ... and the EC of the SWMF to whom tribute was paid for the help they had given the Republic.' He states that Robeson not only sang but made his own speech and recited. The meeting was organised by the South Wales Council for Spanish Aid. Interviews with A Bassett and I Harrington by N Fishman.

612 The other nominees were John T Lindley, of the Lancashire and Cheshire Colliery Tradesmen, and R Shirkie, of the Scottish Colliery Tradesmen. Lawther, Squance and Kaylor from the AEU probably voted for Horner. The minutes for 21 December noted an unsuccessful attempt was made to disqualify Horner from standing because he was a communist. Tewson, deputising for Citrine, probably invoked Circular No. 16: 'attention was drawn to the difficulties that would be created in representation on various bodies if a Communist were a member of the General Council. Other members took the view that unless it was provided in the Standing Orders, an objection could not be taken to a nominee who would not conform with the policy adopted for the Trades Councils.' General Council minutes, MRC, Warwick.

Chapter 12. Fighting the War on Two Fronts

613 MFGB Report, p. 428.
614 Arnot, *Vol. III*, pp. 272–3. Its final sentences illustrate the tone: 'Viewed in the light of recent events every step of your Government seems to be to give way step by step to the bellicose blatant proposals of the fascist Dictators. To grant belligerent rights to Franco would be ... an outrage of British traditions, a calumny on those members of our race who have in the past fought and died for liberty and freedom.'
615 Foot, *Vol. I*, p. 288.
616 SO Davies was another signatory.
617 Michael Foot recalled Bevan making an oblique reference to Horner's support at this time after his 1957 Labour

Party Conference speech repudiating unilateralism. He had turned on CND supporters, including Foot, and said, 'I'd rather have Arthur Horner on my side than the whole lot of you'. Interview with N Fishman, 25 August 1995.

618 Carr, *Comintern and Spanish Civil War*, p. 74. The Spanish government did not formally abandon its struggle for some weeks. Recriminations and political differences reemerged, and ministers disagreed about whether to continue the fight to the last man.

619 Arnot, *Vol. III*, p. 273.

620 Blake, *Decline of Power*, pp. 220–1.

621 *ICR*, p. 163. Horner recalled, 'I was able to make clear even in this period that I was ready to defend my country.' *Incorrigible Rebel* conflated his discussions with Portal and Iestyn Williams in 1939 and his later participation in the Regional Invasion Committees formed after Soviet entry into the war. See n. 717.

622 Bullock, *Vol. I*, pp. 632–4.

623 *ICR*, p. 64. Along with the other five MPs or candidates who had been expelled in March, he 'accepted the party's decision on the Popular Front and wound up the Petition ... [but] still insisted, however, on their unfettered freedom to 'impress upon the Party the necessity for making effective the opposition to the National Government, and to oppose every tendency to co-operate with that Government which we regard as the gravest menace to the working classes of Great Britain'." Campbell, *Bevan*, p. 84.

624 SWMF Executive minutes, 3 January, 14, 21 March 1939. Harris had drafted the statement for Conference's approval. The Executive declined to suggest a permanent alteration to SWMF rules to make the presidency a permanent full-time post, probably motivated by prudence and politics. They may have anticipated arguments from Horner's opponents that having a full-time president would betray the rank-and-file principles underlying the 1933 rules.

625 *DH, MG, The Times*, 17 April 1939. *The Times* and the *Manchester Guardian* reported that the session had lasted between three and four hours. The decision not to name Bevan in the motion was probably designed to de-personalise it. Foot states that most delegates arrived with lodge

ARTHUR HORNER: A POLITICAL BIOGRAPHY

mandates to vote *against* the motion regretting the expulsions; however, having listened to the debate, they voted for it. *Vol. I*, p. 296.

626 *MG*, 17 April 1939.

627 District unions took turns to host the annual conference, and the host district took pride in showing off local beauty spots on the conference delegates' free afternoon. It also provided generous hospitality. The SWMF had not played host to a conference in the post-1926 period. The SWMF's claim to being a foundation member of the MFGB was based on fact that the Monmouthshire and South Wales Miners' Association was represented at its founding conference, which was held in Newport.

628 The debate is reported in *Miners' Monthly*, July 1939. Lawther's position on unity was complicated by the DMA's strong opposition to the reorganisation plans.

629 Foot, *Vol. I*, pp. 297–8.

630 SWMF Executive Minutes, 22 August 1939.

631 Blake, Decline of Power, p. 225. The voting for the Group No.1 General Council seats was: Lawther 4.276 m., Ebby Edwards 4.208m., RW Williams, 3.118 m., Horner, 1.128 m., JT Lindley, 195,000. The AEU was affiliated to Congress on 333,619 members.

632 Vol Tofts interview with N Fishman. Horner had been scheduled to travel with Watson, Joe Hall and the national officers to the French Pyrenees for the opening of the MIF home for Spanish mining refugees on 20 September.

633 Clegg *Vol. III*, pp. 165–77; Bullock, *Bevin, Vol. I*, pp. 641–8; Fishman, *British CP and TUs*, pp. 261–9.

634 SWMF Executive minutes 29 August noted a letter from the MFGB about ARP, which included a list of South Wales collieries specified for special protection measures under the Civil Defence Act. It was decided to hold a meeting of Miners' Agents and Mines Inspectors to consider what steps should be taken. This prompt, meticulous response to a routine letter is evidence of Horner's commitment. His report to the Executive on 12 September shows his continuing focus on assisting the war effort. It was agreed that Horner should take the necessary steps for Air Raid Shelter at central office and that Agents and Executive members

should do the same for Area Offices. On 19 September it was reported that the SWMCA had appointed three representatives to act as a Technical Committee to consider ARP questions. The Executive appointed Saddler and their two full-time Workmen's Inspectors to act with the SWMCA.

635 Memo from Harries to Citrine, 9 October 1939, TUC Files, 905.32. Modern Records Centre, Warwick.

636 Monty Johnstone, 'Introduction', *About Turn*, edited by F King and G Matthews, Lawrence & Wishart, 1990, pp. 22–8, 34–5. The minutes of the 24 September meeting are summarised in the 'Introduction'. Johnstone observed, 'J.R. Campbell, in a tough and closely argued speech, contended that the two main positions in the discussion were represented by those, like Pollitt and himself, who saw fascism making the second world war fundamentally different from the first, and "those who are returning to the position of the Trotskyists in their criticism of the ... Seventh World Congress, namely that fascism makes no difference ..."' (p. 26).

637 *About Turn*, p. 64. Minutes of Resumed Session of CPGB Central Committee. There is no accurate list of the Politburo's membership. I am grateful to Gidon Cohen for providing the information enabling me to compile a list of its probable members in September to October 1939: Ted Bramley, Emile Burns, J R Campbell, R Palme Dutt, William Gallacher, Harry Pollitt, Bill Rust, Dave Springhall.

638 The verbatim record of the 2–3 October meeting (pp. 67–298), includes the vote taken on 3 October. Gallacher was persuaded by Pollitt to formally change his vote to 'Yes', (p. 299). See also Thorpe, pp. 257–9. Thorpe conflates the votes of Central Committee members and the five non-Central Committee members who were attending the meeting. For Horner's anti-fascism see *ICR*, pp. 161–2; R Frankenberg's notes from fourth Interview with Horner; H Francis interview with Vol Tofts.

639 See Fishman, *British CP and TUs*, pp. 251–61; Ted Bramley, pp. 86–7, in *1939. The Communist Party and the War*, edited by J Attfield and S Williams, Lawrence & Wishart, 1984, His description of his own reasoning about the change of line and account of the Central Committee meetings and

London District's activities is particularly illuminating, pp. 81–93.

640 *About Turn*, p. 248.

641 Court, pp. 231–2; Supple, *Coal 1913–1946*, pp. 498–9. Lloyd replaced Crookshank in April 1939. Born in 1902, Lloyd and RA Butler had formed a lasting friendship as undergraduates at Cambridge. After graduating Lloyd had served an electoral apprenticeship, standing in Southwark in 1924 and then for Birmingham Ladywood in 1929. Until being elected for Birmingham Ladywood at the 1931 general election, he served as secretary to Samuel Hoare, and from 1929 to Stanley Baldwin. He served as Under-Secretary at the Home Office from November 1935. Anthony Howard, *RAB, The Life of R.A. Butler*, Papermac, 1988, pp. 43, 47.

642 During the phoney war, South Wales coalowners were exporting increased amounts of coal to underpin the French war effort and domestic consumption. Moreover, exports from Durham and Northumberland were disrupted, due to enemy activity in the North Sea and war precautions, enabling South Wales coalowners to take over some of their traditional export markets. For reports of opposition to the agreement see *DW*, 21, 28 October, 3, 11, 14 November 1939.

643 NA, Horner file, PF601/V2, NA, Kew. Two photographic negative copies of the letter are in the file along with a letter dated 28 October 1939 from MI5 to FW Leggett, Permanent Secretary at the Ministry of Labour, in which the MI5 officer rehearsed the contents of Cox's letter. A letter from Horner to Pollitt dated 2 November 1939 provides further evidence of Horner's isolation from the DPC. He wrote on SWMF notepaper with sympathy and condolences on the death of Pollitt's mother, announced nearly a week earlier in the *DW*. 'I had not noticed the news of her death until today ... In the present circumstances I have not had many conversations with the Comrades which perhaps explains my lack of information.' Pollitt papers, HPP 42/12, CPGB Archive, PHMM. I am grateful to Kevin Morgan for this reference.

644 SWMF Executive minutes, 20, 21, 24 October 1939. Arnot is predictably circumspect about this episode, *Vol. III*, pp. 289–90. Although dissatisfaction was later expressed from the lodges, the Executive refused to censure Horner's conduct. In support of their decision, they decided in November 1939 to publish the verbatim report of Horner's speech, evidently in the belief that his arguments would convince rank-and-file doubters.

645 *DW*, 28 November 1939. The *DW* of 14 November reported that 50 miners, one from each pit where the party was represented, had attended.

646 *DW*, 16 December 1939.

647 A Special Executive Meeting on 2 December was attended by a virtually full complement of MPs, George Hall, William John, Grenfell, Mainwaring, Ted Williams, Bevan, SO Davies, Griffiths, Arthur Jenkins, Ness Edwards and Sir Charles Edwards. (Ness Edwards had won a by-election on 4 July 1939 to become MP for Caerphilly.) The Executive minutes noted on 5 December: 'Attention drawn to grotesquely inaccurate report of the meeting held with MPs on the previous Saturday which appeared in the *News Chronicle*. Resolved: that protest and ask for withdrawal and apology.' On 12 December, the Executive received a letter of apology, and decided not to take the matter further. Another Special Meeting was held with MPs on 16 December 1939; nearly a full complement attended. The Minutes record a long discussion on the international situation and the prosecution of the war.

648 When the *DW* reported on 27 January 1940 that 38 lodges had passed resolutions calling for a special coalfield conference to discuss the war, the story noted that most of them had been opposed to the war. See N Fishman, *British CP and TUs*, n. 36, p. 281.

649 Francis and Smith, p. 400, citing *WM*, 24 February 1940. MPs present at the Executive meeting on 6 February were Mainwaring, George Hall, Bevan, Ted Williams, SO Davies, Arthur Jenkins and Ness Edwards. On 10 February, those present were Williams, Bevan, Ness Edwards, Arthur Jenkins and SO Davies.

650 *DW*, 6 January 26, 27 February 1940. MI5 file PF601/V2, p. 2 of chronology, NA Kew. The conference took place at the Holborn Hall in London. 878 delegates attended, including 259 delegates from trade union institutions. Horner made the first speech of the afternoon on 'War Economy and the Workers' Struggle'; he was followed by WJR Squance. His speech was report in *LM*, March 1940, pp. 143–4. He was advertised in the programme as President of the SWMF. He concluded: 'It is impossible for anyone to logically argue: I am in favour of carrying on the war, I want war with Finland, I want planes and guns and ammunition and men to go, and then argue I do not want a reduction in the standards of the people living in England. It is not logical, it is not sense.' The nearest he came to making an anti-war statement was: 'The top [union leaders] do not believe in using the trade unions for the purposes for which they were set up. They believe in carrying on the war of victory, whatever the costs, and we are not prepared to pay the cost, and therefore we must stop the war.'

651 SWMF Executive Minutes, report of Special Conference, 17 February 1940. The resolutions are also reported in *DW*, 4 March 1940. Bevan's position was conspicuously lacking in sentimental patriotism. He ensured that *Tribune* followed an unqualified war-on-two-fronts line. After his readmission into the Labour Party in December 1939, the paper argued for a stronger attack on the Chamberlain government. Bevan condemned the Russian invasion of Finland, whilst also attacking British politicians' manipulation of the public's sympathy for the Finns: 'the course of "all aid to Finland" which the Government appeared to accept, which Labour backed and which so few voices were raised to oppose, was fraught with incalculable dangers.' (Foot, paraphrasing and quoting from *Tribune*, Bevan. *Vol. I*, pp. 311–2).

652 Fishman, *British CP and TUs*, p. 269; Francis and Smith, p. 400. The *WM* concluded that lodges in the Monmouthshire, Rhondda and Aberdare valleys had voted for the pro-war-on-two-fronts resolution. All the unemployed lodges and some of the western valleys, notably Dulais, had supported

the anti-war resolution, whilst the rest of the Anthracite and the Garw valley were evenly divided. (Cited in SR Broomfield, 'South Wales in the Second World War: The Coal Industry and Its Community', University of Wales PhD, 1979, p. 579).

653 The *DW* did not carry any coverage of the conference or the resolutions to be discussed either in the weeks preceding the 17 February, or the fortnight during which the conference stood adjourned. It is likely that Dutt and Rust took advice from Pollitt and decided not to increase the pressure on Horner.

654 Frankenberg notes of fourth Horner interview, 2 August 1957. Horner's recollection was a *précis* of his Presidential Address at The Federation's Annual Conference in April 1940. See p. 431. The SWMF Executive minutes for 12 March 1940 record that after a full discussion it was resolved to make a grant, but do not specify the amount. On 19 March, the derisory figure of £5 was inserted in ink and the figure initialled by Horner. However, also on 19 March, Tal Mainwaring's motion to increase the grant to £100 was taken and agreed. This substantial sum probably precipitated Horner's refusal to sign the cheque.

655 There is insufficient evidence to judge whether Alf Davies had been a clandestine CPGB member whilst in the Labour Party during the United Front period. Two other agents were elected: Dai Dan Evans and Edgar Lewis for Area No. 1.

656 MFGB Executive statement to Secretary for Mines, 28 December 1939; and Conference Report, quoted by Arnot, *Vol. III*, pp. 293–4.

657 HO 45/25549, NA, Kew. I am grateful to Kevin Morgan for this reference. Scotland, Kent, Cumberland and the Forest of Dean delegates voted against the offer at the delegate conference; the Forest of Dean lodges had subsequently voted to accept the offer, whilst the SWMF lodges had voted against. In contrast to the 1939 increase, which the MFGB Executive had sought without prior reference to a delegate conference and affiliated districts, this second increase had been authorised by a delegate conference, and therefore

required approval as per the rulebook, i.e. ratification in district ballots. Arnot, *Vol. III*, pp. 293–6.

658 Quoted in Arnot, *Vol. III*, p. 295.

659 LAB 10/366, NA Kew. The RIRO report for 8 June 1940 is also relevant. Regional Industrial Relations Officers reported directly to the Ministry of Labour in Whitehall. They were responsible for conciliation and dealing with industrial disputes.

660 SWMF Executive Minutes, 1940. The SWMF Monday May Day holiday was the last vestige of Mabon's Day, an agreement he had negotiated whereby South Wales miners took the first Monday in every month as a holiday.

661 Horner's MI5 file contains a note of a letter sent from Jack Jones, of Cross Hands, to the DPC in Cardiff stating that 'the whispering campaign against Arthur (HORNER) is very strong'. The Scottish district union, the NUSMW, had passed a stronger war-on-two-fronts resolution, *DW*, 4 May 1940. For the party leadership's injunction about the need for mass work, see Idris Cox, 'South Wales Miners and the War', *Party Organiser*, May 1940, pp. 8–9.

662 Horner's MI5 file contains a note: 'KERRIGAN wrote to POLLITT, who is now at the S. Wales DPC ... ' dated 24 April 1940. PF601/V2, NA Kew. Campbell was reporting in South Wales for the *DW* during March.

663 *DW*, 26 April 1940.

664 John had appeared before a military tribunal and refused to serve in any active combat duty. Interview with John Tofts by N Fishman. Shoreditch was his family home.

665 Duncan replaced Stanley on 5 January 1940. The fact that he was not a Tory was undoubtedly helpful in his relations with the MFGB. The government also benefited from his experience of solving similar problems in the previous war. He was returned as a National candidate for the City of London on 5 February 1940. (He had contested two general elections unsuccessfully, as a National (Lloyd George) Liberal in Glasgow Cathcart in 1922 and as a Liberal in Dundee in 1924.

666 Court, pp. 130–1. Correspondence between Geoffrey Lloyd and Ebby Edwards about the CPC is contained in

the MFGB Executive Report for 1940. For Portal's resignation, see *DT* and *DE*, 9 December 1939.

667 Don Loney, interview with H Francis, June 1997. David Branton, interview with N Fishman, 6 September 1995. Branton recalled stories of rivalry between Ford and Hill. Loney remembered that Bowman had recounted the friction between Hill and Edwards.

668 For example, Horner's MI5 file contains a note sent to Johnny Gollan, who was on the Northeast DPC, by a party member in Durham, reporting on a speech by Lawther at a conference on 20 April 1940. 'He claimed that HORNER spoke one way at C.P. meetings and another at M.F.G.B. meetings. He said that HORNER, at the last meeting of the M.F.G.B. Executive Committee, spoke strongly in favour of co-operation with the Government in trying to produce more coal.' PF601/V2, chronology p. 3, NA Kew.

669 NA, LAB 10/366. *DW* 31 May, 1 June 1940. He also explained that it was not communist party policy to participate in the sabotage of output 'under the present serious conditions'.

670 SWMF Executive Minutes, 25 June 1940.

671 PF601/V2, NA Kew.

672 PF601/V2, Chronology, p. 6, NA Kew. Second note dated 19 October 1940.

673 Court, p. 91. For Lyttleton's tenure at the Board of Trade, see Simon Ball, *The Guardsmen, Harold Macmillan, Three Friends, and the World They Made*, Harper Collins, 2004, ch. 6. As in Lyttelton's published memoirs, Ball makes no mention of Lyttelton's responsibilities for coalmining.

674 Court notes that the CPC did not meet for two months, from 20 November 1939 until 29 January 1941, and that there was another gap from 29 January until 12 March 1941. pp. 137–8.

675 See, for example, Alan Bullock, *The Life & Times of Ernest Bevin, Vol. II, Minister of Labour 1940–1945*, Allen & Unwin, 1967, pp. 233–4. For the Essential Works Order see pp. 57–9. For Order 1305 see N Fishman, '"A Vital Element in British Industrial Relations": A Reassessment of Order 1305, 1940–51', *Historical Studies in Industrial Relations*, No. 8, Autumn 1999, pp. 43–86.

676 ILP influence was particularly strong in the small Cumberland coalfield; it had also remained influential in some lodges in Ayr and the Lothians. Horner acknowledged that the South Wales sponsored MPs had not endorsed the SWMF motion on the war, although they had attended the Executive meeting which discussed it. The motion was put forward as the Federation's considered position. It was seconded by Jack Williams of the Forest of Dean. The conference passed a motion from Durham which endorsed the position taken at the TUC Special Conference of Union Executives held after the coalition government had taken office. Many non-communist veteran delegates expressed disgust at the YMA resolution giving Churchill unqualified support. It was subsequently withdrawn.

677 Horner received 187,000 votes: 100,000 from the SWMF; probably 51,000 from the NUSMW, Northumberland's 30,000 and Cumberland's 8100. Lawther received 414,000 votes, exceeded by Bowman's 509,000.

678 MFGB Annual Conference Report, pp. 152–3.

679 See Fishman, *British CP and TUs*, pp. 271–5; and Nita Bowes, 'The People's Convention', University of Warwick MA, 1976. Pritt had been expelled from the Labour Party in 1940 because of his refusal to support the Labour NEC's opposition to the Russian invasion of Finland. He sat as an independent Labour MP. Vigilance committees had been formed by socialists and trade unionists during the 1914–18 war, to ensure that war workers were not exploited by profiteering employers and union conditions observed. They included both pro- and anti-war activists.

680 It is unlikely that Horner attended, in view of his obligations to attend the normal pre-TUC MFGB Executive meeting. *DW*, 28 September, 7 October 1940; Francis and Smith, p. 401.

681 *LM*, November 1940, pp. 601–6. Numbers from Wales were disproportionately higher in relation to population than all other regions except London. There were very few names from Scotland and Northern England. The Report of the Convention, *The People Speak*, listed 2234 delegates by district. London was disproportionately represented with 1099, followed by Lancashire and Cheshire with 290,

Scotland with 117, South Wales with 100, the North-East Coast with 98 and Sheffield, including Nottinghamshire and Derby, with 95.

682 Letter reprinted in MFGB Executive Minutes, 21 November 1940.

683 LAB10/367, NA Kew.

684 Horner's MI5 file noted that on 7 January, 'C.C. Cardiff's informant had the following message to deliver to Len JEFFRIES:- "London telephoned this message 'Idris, Mavis [Llewellyn], Arthur and Bill [Paynter] to be at Prospect Bookshop London at 9 o'clock Friday Morning. I have seen Arthur HORNER but don't know what to do about the others....'" This presumably is the meeting of the Central Executive Committee. PF601/V2, NA Kew.

685 Bowes, pp. 99–100, quoting Mass Observation. The Convention was actually held in London, because the Manchester venue had been badly bombed the previous week.

686 *DW* 13,14 January 1941; *The People Speak.* Hugh Scanlon spoke on behalf of Metropolitan Vickers, 'the largest engineering factory in Manchester' and the Lancashire and Cheshire Convention Committee.

687 There were comparatively few delegates from coalmining trade unions: 31, compared to 87 from engineering and metal trade unions, and 471 from factories and building sites. *The People Speak.* Paynter is identified in the report as being from the SWMF. One of the other delegates may have been unable to attend. The only other miners' speaker at the Convention was John Sutherland, from the Fife and Kinross Miners. Councillor Frank Davies from Ammanford spoke. He was in the Labour Party; the report did not note that he was chairman of the SWMF Saron Lodge.

688 Information from Joan Morris to N Fishman, March 2000.

689 There is no reference to the bombing in *ICR*. The one reference in his MI5 file, from CC Monmouthshire, is dated 19 January. 'HORNER was unable to speak at a meeting held at Abersychan, owing to being injured in a recent severe Air Raid on Cardiff, when an H.E. bomb exploded on the lawn in front of his house.' PF601/V2, NA Kew. It is

likely that he used the bombing as a good excuse to have an evening at home.

690 Ethel and Harry had probably already been managing, or trying to manage, Horner's alcohol consumption.

691 Fishman, *British CP and TUs*, pp. 274–5; James Hinton, 'Killing the People's Convention: a letter from Palme Dutt to Harry Pollitt', *Bulletin of the Society for the Study of Labour History*, No. 39, 1979.

692 MFGB Executive Minutes, 17 January 1941. Harris and Saddler were present at the MFGB meeting. Horner was reported absent on district business, which he may have arranged in order to avoid any confrontations.

693 PF601/V2, chronology p. 7, 19 February 1941; LAB10/367, 25 January, 1,15 and 22 February 1941, NA Kew.

694 MFGB Executive Minutes, 2 April 1941.

695 LAB 10/367, NA Kew.

696 SWMF Annual Conference Report, pp. 10–1.

697 Court, p. 139.

698 The amount of coal mined in a coal year – 1 May to 30 April – declined continuously during the war. The steepest decline was between 1939–40 and 1940–41, from 228.4 m. to 212.8 m. tons. Between 1942–3 and 1932–4, production declined from 201.6m. to 188.9 m. tons. By 1944–5, when Great Britain consumed 184.6 m. tons, only 182.5 m. tons were produced. Supple, *Coal 1913–1946*, p. 543.

699 Sir Ernest Gowers had been Permanent Under Secretary at the Department of Mines in the 1920s. He was appointed full-time Chairman of the Coal Mines Reorganisation Commission in 1930, a post he continued to hold throughout the war. Hyndley's 'intimate knowledge of the coal trade and his mature executive flair had given him an important place behind the scenes for many years. He stood high in the coal merchanting and producing world', having been managing director of Powell Duffryn. He had been the government's Commercial Adviser on coal since 1918 (Court, p. 205). Hyndley had been head of the British side of the joint Anglo-French Coal Requirements Committee, which commenced proceedings when the French Mission arrived in London on 3 September 1939 (Court, pp. 72–3).

700 Anderson had been elected in 1938 as a National candidate to one of the Scottish University seats. He had previously been a high ranking civil servant.

701 POWE 16/68, POWE 16/54, NA Kew.

702 Court, p. 140. The responsibility for dealing with persistent absenteeism was vested in Pit and District Production Committees. However, this was soon recognised to be largely unworkable. On 9 December 1940, the responsibility was transferred to the Ministry of Labour National Service Officer, a notable victory for Bevin.

703 PF601/V2, NA Kew. Walt Ferris was a younger CPGB miner in the Dulais Valley, active in the SWMF.

704 Idris Cox personal file, KV2/1769, NA Kew.

705 The minutes do not elucidate in what capacity he attended. The legerdemain for his presence may have been Bowman's absence. Court, p. 164, POWE 16/54, NA, Kew. Court notes approvingly Horner's explanation of the causes for low output at the face. 'He thought the discontent was due to the wide difference between earnings in coalmining and the munitions industries. The miner needed to be convinced not only that his work was important, but also that he was getting a square deal economically.'

706 Fishman, *British CP and TUs*, p. 276, quoting Pollitt at 16th CPGB Congress, October 1943.

707 PF 601/V2, 136a, NA Kew. The report was a Memorandum to Roger Hollis from another section of MI5, which he directed to be placed on Horner's personal file.

708 On 29 September 1941, the Finance Committee of The Federation Executive decided – in view of the decision that The Federation President must reside in Cardiff, whomever that might be, and in view of the fact that the President would be appointed for three years and subject to re-election – to recommend that the house which was now available be purchased and let to the present President at a rental of 30s. per week (SWMF Executive minutes).

709 The war cabinet had to face the fact that the fears voiced by Duncan in May 1941 had proved accurate: '[T]he protracted negotiations in regard to the EWO, wages and other matters have already taken up much of the limited

time available for building up coal stocks.' Unless there was a rapid improvement in output it would be 'impossible to escape dire necessity of choosing between definite hardship to civilian population and curtailment of fuel supplies for war purposes next winter'. MFGB Circular on the EWO, 9 June 1941. The circular was careful to observe that Duncan had pointed this remark to the coalowners and not the MFGB. Hyndley may have been keeping Duncan and Portal apprised of the situation, both of whom had access to the war cabinet (Portal via Attlee). They may have agreed that Duncan's return was the most expedient option to deal with the worsening coal situation. Lyttelton became Churchill's political spokesman in the Middle East. Randolph Churchill, on the army general staff in Cairo, had suggested the idea of having a political commissar to mind the general staff to his father (Ball, *The Guardsmen*, p. 234). The prime minister's choice may have been partly motivated by a desire to save Lyttelton's face.

710 POWE 16/56, NA, Kew. Hurst's initials were CS.

711 Edwards reported the problems caused by bombs in the area of Russell Square to the Executive on 16 October 1940. On 21 November, he reported that a house had been purchased in Durham and that the necessary work was in hand to make it suitable for office accommodation at the earliest possible date. The MFGB Executive Report for 1941, dated 31 May, listed two office addresses, 50 Russell Square and 6 Victoria Terrace, Durham.

712 POWE 16/54 and 16/56, NA, Kew.

713 MFGB Executive minutes, 19 December 1941; POWE 16/56, NA, Kew.

Chapter 13. Winning the War and Saving the Socialist Motherland

714 See, for example, TUC Report 1940, pp. 83–5, 281–3.

715 Protracted, complex negotiations were taking place with the government over new legislation to amend the 1925 Workmen's Compensation Act and the miners had particular grievances. The MFGB was insistent that wartime conditions and intensification of labour were bound to produce

more accidents at work, for which miners currently were inadequately compensated. The committee would normally have consisted only of General Council members.

716 MFGB Executive minutes, 14 August and 24 September 1942. Watson had replaced the veteran DMA general secretary, John Swan, on the Labour NEC. He chaired the first meeting of the Labour NEC Sub-Committee on Coal and Power on 21 October 1941. Jim Griffiths, Morgan Phillips, Shinwell, Tom Williamson of the NUGMW, Tom Smith MP, EW Bussey, ETU general secretary, and Lawther attended. On 7 April 1943, the subcommittee included MFGB members, Horner, Sid Ford, George Jones and Joe Hall. On 4 May 1945 the subcommittee was transmogrified into the Joint Committee on the nationalisation of the coal-mining industry, and further enlarged. The TUC General Council, Labour Party NEC and NUM Executive were all represented.

717 Bruce was the joint commissioner for Region 8, which encompassed all of Wales; he had responsibility for South Wales and shared responsibility with the other joint commissioner for North Wales (*ICR*, p. 163). Horner does not date this reminiscence. It is possible, but I think unlikely, that he lectured Iestyn Williams and Portal about explosives in the first months of the war.

718 Duncan was moved back to the Ministry of Supply and an interregnum of 18 days ensued. Colonel J Llewellin filled the post whilst Dalton agonised and tried to negotiate his terms. Pimlott's explanation that the move was part of a more general re-shuffle is not wholly convincing. Churchill had a personal antipathy to Dalton and his agreement on the appointment is likely, I think, to have been the result of Bevin's and Attlee's intervention (Ben Pimlott, ed., *The Second World War Diary of Hugh Dalton, 1940–45*, Jonathan Cape, 1986, p. 372). Dalton, a leading member of the Labour NEC, was an economist. He had been MP for Bishop Auckland, County Durham in 1929–31, and been re-elected for the constituency in 1935.

719 *WWII Diary of Dalton*, p. 392.

720 Entries for 24 April 1942, Dalton diary, LSE Archive. Further favourable mention of Horner is found in entries for 29 April and 20 May 1942.

721 See the entry for 25 March, Dalton diary, LSE Archive, and *WWII Diary of Dalton*, p. 402.

722 Supple, *Coal 1913–1946*, p. 519.

723 For Dalton's moves against Grenfell, see *WWII Diary of Dalton*, pp. 422–3, 431–3 and 453–6.

724 Arthur Horner file, 1938–62 BBC Archives, Caversham. On 1 May, R Fry from the BBC sent a letter to the Department of Mines from Samuel Instone demanding the right of reply. Fry told the Department 'that on 29 April I was rung up by Major Desmond Morton who said there was some disquiet in high circles over the fact of Horner broadcasting – there was no exception taken to his script. I explained the circumstances.' Fry explained that Morton seemed satisfied when he was told that Horner's talk had been arranged with the approval of the Ministry of Information.

725 The published extracts omit the passages which describe Bevin's pivotal role. *WWII Diary of Dalton*, pp. 392–3, 400–1, 438–40. Entries for 12 ,20 March; 3,23, 24 April; 18, 19, 20 May 1942, Dalton diaries, LSE archive.

726 Supple *Coal 1913–1946*, p. 526. The Watson quote is from Dalton's diary for 15 May 1942. Supple inaccurately described Watson as 'President of the local union'.

727 20 May 1942, Dalton Diary, LSE Archive.

728 Entry for 27 May 1942, *WWII Diary of Dalton*, p. 446. See also 6 May 1942, p. 425.

729 There is a useful description of the arrangements in Court, pp. 201–211. For the radical reorganisers in the Department of Mines, see Supple, pp. 520–521.

730 Entry for 4 June 1942, Dalton Diary, LSE Archive. Pimlott's extract for this date does not include this passage. On 5 June, the MFGB Executive thanked Ebby Edwards and Horner for the part they had played in formulating amendments to the White Paper. Arnot, *Vol. III*, p. 340.

731 The only division was forced by Jimmy Maxton, on an amendment condemning the arrangements as too favourable to the owners. It attracted 8 votes. Court, pp. 176–7.

732 Horner made favourable reference to the Board at the MFGB Special Conference (MFGB 1942 Executive Report, p. 451). Greene was joined by Sir John Forster, a barrister who had often acted as arbitrator in inter-war coalfield disputes, Dr AD McNair, Vice-Chancellor of Liverpool University, Colonel Ernest Briggs of Lever Brothers, and George Chester, TUC General Council member and general secretary of the Boot and Shoe Operatives' union.

733 POWE 20/62, NA Kew, shorthand transcript of Board of Investigation.

734 MFGB Annual Conference, 20–22 July 1942. Edwards' forword to the published version stated that 'appreciation of the assistance rendered' to himself by Mr W Williams of LRD and Arthur Horner 'must be recorded'. Williams had been secretary of LRD since 1929. Born in 1900, he had worked in Monmouthshire pits, joined the ILP and then the CPGB in 1922. He had attended the Central Labour College in 1923–25 and was in the first cohort at the Lenin School in Moscow, 1926–28 (McIlroy, 'Welsh Communists at the Lenin School', pp. 64–5). Margot Heinemann, a Cambridge graduate who joined the CPGB in 1934, was described as Organising Secretary on the LRD letterhead.

735 Notes of H Francis interview with M Heinemann 1983, SWML. Information from N Branson, 2000.

736 Entry for 10 June, Dalton diary, LSE Archive.

737 Pimlott, *WWII Diary of Dalton*, p. 453.

738 MFGB Executive Report 1942, pp. 253–4, 260.

739 NA, POWE 20/62. p. 83 of shorthand transcript. When it reported in March 1943 the Greene Committee recommended a comprehensive national conciliation machinery which strongly resembled the South Wales example. The machinery consisted of 'a Joint National Negotiating Committee (with equal numbers of owners' and miners' representatives) and a National Reference Tribunal (with three members with no connection with the industry) to settle disputes referred to it.' Supple commented, '22 years after the great controversy of 1921 the miners had at last achieved their long-desired aim of a national wages system.' (p. 571).

740 MFGB Executive Report 1942, pp. 479–80: Executive minutes, 14 August and 24 September 1942.
741 MFGB Executive minutes, 23 June 1942, cited in Arnot, *Vol. IV*, p. 77; MFGB Executive Report 1942, pp. 479–80.
742 Mahon, *Pollitt*, pp. 306–7.
743 1942 TUC *Congress Report*, pp. 174–5. Due to paper shortages, the 1942 TUC Report contained summaries of speeches and not verbatim reports.
744 Court, p. 216. The propaganda aimed at involving the domestic consumer in the Battle for Fuel. Court observes: 'But perhaps the subject was chiefly brought home to the ears of the ordinary wireless listener by the efforts of Mr. Freddie Grisewood' – a silver-tongued BBC announcer.
745 Information from John Tofts, who had probably been in Cardiff on Christmas leave, and Joan Morris.
746 Interview with Lorraine Griffiths by N Fishman and H Francis, 18 June 1998. This meeting probably took place in the spring of 1941.
747 Political differences with Pollitt and Campbell in the aftermath of the Seventh World Congress had resulted in Hannington's exile from the inner circle of CPGB working-class activists. Although Horner had apparently not shared in the distrust of Hannington's political motives for insisting on the survival of the NUWM, he had lost personal contact with Hannington due to his own workload and preoccupation with employed coalmining problems. In the White House's convivial atmosphere, a reconciliation was apparently effected between Pollitt and Hannington, perhaps deliberately by Horner. Interview with Vol Horner. Information on Hannington's differences with the Party Centre from Monty Johnstone to Nina Fishman.
748 Sybil Griffiths interview with Nina Fishman and Hywel Francis, 18 July 1996. 'She [Mrs Evans] used to cook beautiful food for us. Fish and mashed potatoes, cooked lunch, sausage and mash, home made apple tart. Archie James wasn't used to playing cards. Arthur used to say, "Archie come on mun."'
749 Sybil Griffiths interview. Her general description of the office was: ground floor, Executive Council chamber and the front office; ground floor back, Inspectors; first floor,

the General Secretary, the President, the Chief Clerk, Tom Bateman, the secretaries, Elsie Lewis and Molly Hughes, the Finance Officer and Assistant Finance Officer, and the Committee Room; second floor, cloak room, Compensation Secretary, Assistant Compensation Secretary, four typists.

750 Lorraine Griffiths interview.

751 PF 601/V2,139B, Extract dated 11 September 1942, NA Kew. There were two US trade union centres. The AFL was the older, and more conservative. Members of the CPUSA had been important participants in the CIO.

752 PF601/V2. 139E, 12 May 1943, NA Kew. Pollitt was himself a formidable drinker, but generally controlled his consumption to ensure his continuing ability to function. He was evidently concerned about the overwhelming evidence that Horner was becoming a binge drinker. Because his father had been a habitual binge drinker, he knew how this pattern of drinking had affected his mother and family. Pollitt describes his father's behaviour with circumspection in his autobiography but the contours of alcoholism are clear enough. *Serving My Time*, pp. 19–21.

753 Branson, *1941–1951*, p. 37.

754 The withdrawal of Circular 16 also removed any possible objections to Horner's election to the General Council.

755 Branson, *1941–1951*, p. 17. Watson's motion was supported by Shinwell, and defeated by 16–2. Laski then moved that CPGB representatives be invited to meet the NEC to discuss the application. His motion was supported by Barbara Ayrton Gould, from the constituency section, and defeated by 15–4.

756 Labour Party Conference Report, 1943, p. 161.

757 Conference report, p. 161. The vote was 1.951 m. to 712,000. In addition to the AEU and NUPE, the MFGB motion was also supported by ASLEF, the Pottery Workers and 'half a dozen smaller unions'. Branson, *1941–51*, p. 23. Thorpe provides a concise narrative of the politics involved on the Labour side and the role played by the Comintern's dissolution during the course of the application's consideration. *British CP & Moscow*, pp. 268–70.

758 Pollitt referred to the Labour Industrial Group at the Politburo on 25 November 1943, PF601/V2. 139.O, NA Kew.

759 PF601/V2, chronology 11 March 1943, citing *DW* story 10 March 1943, which quoted *DH* about Labour Industrial Group, NA Kew. The *DW* had been allowed to resume publication in August 1942.

760 SWMF Executive Minutes, 25 March 1943. Alf Davies presided over the Committee in Horner's absence.

761 The election result was, TW Agar (AEU) 807,000; HP Bolton 1.489 m., J Brown 4.933 m., AL Horner 4.176 m, TUC Report 1943.

762 MFGB Executive Minutes, 21 October 1943.

763 Peter Clarke, *The Cripps Version*, Allen Lane, 2002, p. 183. Pollitt's reliable information about the British war plans and the ability of the war economy to meet their demands probably came from Cripps and Horner, who reported Bevin's frank remarks in meetings with the MFGB negotiators. On 21 April 1943, Isabel Brown reported to the Women's Bureau on Horner's discussion on coal at the Central Committee. 'He had said there was not sufficient coal in the country either for people's immediate needs or for the Second Front ... He had, also, said that the reason for the fall in production was due to the attitude of the miners, they were very independent, there was no real discipline, a great deal of irresponsibility among the younger miners and this was coupled with the fact that the average age of the miners was five years higher than before the war ... HORNER, had, also said that there was defeatism on the part of management and difficulties about materials and spare parts but he had expressed the opinion that the main cause for the fall in production was the attitude of the men and the management, both of whom, appeared to feel that they were far away from the war.' PF601/V2, 196D, NA Kew.

764 CPGB Executive Minutes, 'Suggestions for Re-organising Work at the Centre', September 1943, pp. 4–5, CPGB Archive, PHMM. The paper also suggested that the bureaus be renamed consultative committees as part of the post-

Comintern rebranding. They were eventually baptised Advisory Committees.

765 Court, p. 246–8, 303–4. The Churchill quotation is found in House of Commons debates, 13 October 1943, col. 921. Supple comments on the debate's political significance, pp. 552–5.

766 CPGB EC files, Circular dated 18 October 1943, pp. 1–3. CPGB Archive, PHMM. The day after the parliamentary debate, the Executive issued a statement stressing that 'the unrest in the whole of the coalfields and the bitterness shown by the miners is in no small measure due to the traditional policy still being carried out by the National Coal Owners Association.' Documents for Seventeenth Congress of CPGB, p. 31.

767 Since it had resumed publication in August 1942, the *DW* had been enthusiastically promoted by party members. The paper could claim 'plausibly' that only paper rationing 'stood between ... [it] and a genuinely mass circulation'. Kevin Morgan, 'The Communist Party and the *Daily Worker* 1930–56', G Andrews, N Fishman, K Morgan (eds), *Opening the Books, Essays on the Social and Cultural History of British Communism*, Pluto Press, 1995, p. 151.

768 PF601/V2, 139.O, NA Kew.

769 'Coal and the Nation. A Square Deal for Miners.' pp. 22–4. Horner's emphasis.

770 PF601/V2, 139.O, NA Kew. Pollitt regretfully informed the Politburo that 'having got half way with their [coal campaign] plan they were now at a deadlock.'

771 Court, p. 252; Arnot, *Vol. III*, p. 394.

772 Following the procedures laid down for Industrial Courts, the Tribunal called on Assessors for the MFGB and the MAGB to assist them.

773 Supple commented that the Tribunal felt the miners' claim was 'inadequately presented and unjustified', and was 'clearly not persuaded' by the MFGB's arguments, *Coal 1913–1946*, pp. 573–4. Kapp's telephone conversation with Williams is in Horner's MI5 file, PF601/V2, narrative, 14 January 1944, NA Kew.

774 Court, p. 253.

775 PF601/V2, narrative, 14 January 1944, NA Kew. Cited by
     Billy Williams in telephone conversation to Yvonne Kapp.
     MFGB Executive Report 1944 contains the text of the
     Tribunal's proceedings. For Horner see p. 19, pp. 27–29
     and pp. 35–46. Heinemann's 'book' on coalowners' profits
     may have been an advance or proof copy of *Britain's Coal, A
     Study of the Mining Crisis*, prepared by Margot Heinemann
     for the Labour Research Department, and published by
     Gollancz in 1944. It had a foreword by Lawther and was
     dedicated 'To H for whom nothing was too much trouble'.
     H was probably Horner; in her 'Author's Note' she states
     that a 'special debt' is due 'to Arthur Horner ... without
     whose steady assistance I should never have got started at
     all.'
776 Supple, *Coal 1913–1946*, p. 171. For the Award and its con-
     sequences, see Court pp. 254–7.
777 Court's analysis of the effect of the Award is the most
     detailed, pp. 254–8. There was an easy way to restore the
     differential between hewers and other workers, by consoli-
     dating the Porter award increases into the *district* basic wage
     rate. Piece-rates formed a significant proportion of hewers'
     earnings and were reckoned as a percentage of the *district*
     basic wage rate. Overtime rates for all workers were also a
     percentage of district basic wage rates. But the terms of the
     Porter Tribunal's remit specifically excluded the increases
     from being incorporated into the district basic wage rates,
     precisely to avoid such knock-on financial obligations for
     coalowners, and their consequent demand that coal prices
     be increased to enable them to pay.
778 Arnot, *Vol. III*, p. 396. Some of the strikes lasted up to a
     fortnight. Between 24 January and 14 February there were
     19,000 miners on strike in Lancashire; 17,000 on strike in
     Staffordshire; and 15,500 on strike in Yorkshire.
779 MFGB Executive Report 1944, pp. 161–2.
780 MFGB Executive Report 1944, p. 184.
781 The *DW* leader of 31 January observed, 'We do not believe
     that it was intention of the Wages Tribunal in raising the
     minimum wage to deprive men doing skilled and respon-
     sible work of a wage above the minimum. That, however,
     is the unexpected and unjust consequence of the award

which must be eliminated by speedy negotiations ... ' See 31 January, 1, 3, 5, 9 February for reports of strikes.

782 Court, pp. 256–7. The SWMF Cardiff office had evidently been informed by a civil servant on Lloyd George's behalf.

783 Court, p. 257.

784 Arnot, *Vol. III*, p. 396. Arnot does not provide disaggregated figures for the number of working days lost in Durham and Scotland.

785 Bullock, *Bevin Vol. II*, p. 299.

786 PF601/V2, 140.W, NA Kew. Horner's visit to Pollitt at King Street. Horner had arrived 'very exhausted and breathless and HARRY hurried away to get him some tea'. Horner had described his meeting with Houldsworth and Lloyd George 'very confidentially'.

787 Arnot, *Vol. III*, p. 396.

788 Court, p. 261.

789 PF601/V2, 140.Y, National Mining Bureau meeting, 11 April 1944, NA Kew. Those present included Pollitt, Heinemann, Moffat, Allison and Horner.

790 PF601/V2. 140.Y, NA Kew.

791 Bullock, *Bevin*, p. 299. He quotes a personal note from Lloyd George to Bevin of 6 April, thanking him 'for all your help and support during the last few days'. n. 1.

792 PF601/V2, 140.Y, National Mining Bureau, 11 April 1944, NA Kew. See also PF601/V2, 140W, Horner's comments to Pollitt at King Street, 14 March 1944, NA Kew.

793 Special Delegate Conference 12 April 1944, MFGB Executive Report 1944, p. 279. Horner's recollection of how he had bested Bevin in an earlier negotiation about the attendance bonus provides a picture of the personal chemistry between the two men. *ICR*, pp. 164–5.

794 PF601/V2, 140X, Politburo Meeting, 30 March 1944, NA Kew. The MI5 operative's question mark after 'fighting the workers' was evidently inserted because he could not conceive that Horner could be accused of fighting the workers.

795 PF601/V2, 140.W. PF601/V2, 140X, Politburo Meeting, 30 March 1944, NA Kew.

796 Supple, *Coal 1913–14*, p. 575.

797 PF601/V2.140Y. National Mining Bureau meeting, 11 April
     1944, NA Kew.
798 MFGB Executive Report 1944, pp. 510–512. The final
     speech before the vote was taken came from CR Gill from
     Bristol. It encapsulated the Executive's case. 'What is the
     alternative position? ... I know there is unrest ... What is
     happening, my friends, is that we are missing what we have
     got for what has not been achieved for everybody. I am
     saying that I think it is a poor psychology ... which says,
     "So long as everybody is in the gutter, all right." When
     you lift the "bottom dog" it is not fair that the other chap
     should not appreciate what you have done ... I am asking
     this Conference, as a representative of one of the small
     Districts, to give the Executive Committee the mandate
     they want ... Supposing we don't, what is happening? There
     is no Agreement signed. Every District has to go and make
     the best it can on its own. I don't want to be left in that posi-
     tion again. We are thankful for the unity that has existed to
     bring about a National minimum.'
799 Court, pp. 260–261.
800 Quoted by Supple, *Coal 1913–1946*, p. 576.
801 Court, pp. 370–1. Court noted that the consumption
     side of the budget showed 'the most striking results'. He
     cites the 'abnormally mild weather in January, ... a reduc-
     tion of 100,000 tons in the requirements of the Service
     Departments ... and ... a saving in the export programme
     made possible by assistance from South Africa and the
     United States ... '.
802 Supple, *Coal 1913–1946*, pp. 569–70.
803 Paynter, *MGen*, p. 123. See also Francis and Smith, p. 412.
804 SWMF Executive Minutes, 22 March 1944. James Evans
     chaired the meeting.
805 PF601/V2. 140W, NA Kew. 'Horner arrived at 19.14 and
     the two men [Horner and Pollitt] left King Street after
     Horner had found a Hotel room at 20.28.'
806 Arrangements for Inkpin's funeral were finalised at the
     Politburo on 30 March 1944. PF601 V.2, 140.X, NA Kew.
     The identity of the fourth pallbearer is unknown. It may
     have been Pollitt.